Law, Lawyering and Legal Education

Once a highly cosmopolitan profession, law was largely domesticated by the demands of the Westphalian state. But as the walls between sovereign states are lowered, law is globalizing in a way that is likely to change law, lawyering and legal education as much over the next 30 years – when the students entering law schools today reach the peak of their profession – as it has over the last 300.

This book provides a sustained investigation of the theoretical and practical aspects of legal practice and education, synthesizing and developing nearly 30 years of Professor Sampford's critical thought, analysis and academic leadership. The book features two major areas of investigation. First, it explains the significance of the 'critical', 'theoretical' and 'ethical' dimensions of legal education and legal practice in making more effective practitioners – placing ethics and values at the heart of the profession. Second, it explores the old/new challenges and opportunities for ethical lawyers. Challenges include those for lawyers working in large organizations dealing with issues from international tax minimization to advising governments bent on war. Opportunities range from the capacity to give client's ethical advice to playing a key role in the emergence of an international rule of law as they had to the 'domestic' rule of law.

The book should stimulate great interest and occasional passion for legal practitioners, students, teachers and researchers of law, lawyering, legal practice and legal institutions. Its interdisciplinary approaches should be of interest to those with interests in education theory, international relations, political science and government, professional ethics, sociology, public policy and governance studies.

Charles Sampford is the Foundation Dean of Law at Griffith University, Australia (a law school which achieved a top 50 world ranking within 20 years), who has led a range of national and global research centres and currently directs the multi-university Institute of Ethics, Governance and Law.

Hugh Breakey is a Research Fellow at Griffith University's Institute for Ethics, Governance and Law, Australia, and President of the Australian Association for Professional and Applied Ethics.

Routledge/Challenges of Globalization

Edited by Charles Sampford
and
Carmel Connors
Griffith University, Australia

This series seeks to make systematic contributions to international debates over two intimately related issues:

- The values that should inform the governance of modern states and the globalizing world in which they are increasingly enmeshed, in particular whether the liberal democratic values that sought to civilize the sovereign state need to be reconceived as global values.
- The institutions that are needed to realize those values, be they local, national, regional, international, transnational or global.

5 Global Democracy and its Difficulties
Edited by Anthony J. Langlois and Karol Edward Sołtan

6 New Visions for Market Governance
Crisis and renewal
Edited by Kate MacDonald, Shelley Marshall and Sanjay Pinto

7 Shifting Global Powers and International Law
Challenges and opportunities
Edited by Rowena Maguire, Bridget Lewis and Charles Sampford

8 Institutional Supports for the International Rule of Law
Edited by Charles Sampford and Ramesh Thakur

9 Access to International Justice
Edited by Patrick Keyzer, Vesselin Popovski and Charles Sampford

10 Strengthening the Rule of Law through the UN Security Council
Edited by Jeremy Farrall and Hilary Charlesworth

11 Law, Lawyering and Legal Education
Building an ethical profession in a globalizing world
Charles Sampford and Hugh Breakey

12 Norm Antipreneurs and the Politics of Resistance to Global Normative Change
Edited by Alan Bloomfield and Shirley V. Scott

As one of the leading philosophers and innovators of multi-disciplinary study of law and ethics, Dean Sampford illuminates the important struggles to make legal education responsive to the contexts and institutions in which law is made, theorized about, and practiced. This volume of new and updated essays evidencing a life-time of thought on legal education and legal ethics intelligently examines our past, and provocatively and importantly suggests the path for our future.

Carrie Menkel-Meadow, *Chancellor's Professor of Law and Political Science, University of California and A.B. Chettle Professor of Law, Dispute Resolution and Civil Procedure, Georgetown University Law Center, USA*

The book is an outstanding contribution towards understanding the critical issues of globalisation of legal education and legal profession. It systematically discusses the importance of ethics and justice at the intersection of legal education and legal profession. The book will be of great interest to law students, lawyers, academics and judges around the world for it provides new insights for understanding the role of legal education in protecting the rule of law and promoting access to justice.

C. Raj Kumar, *Founding Vice Chancellor of O.P. Jindal Global University and Founding Dean of Jindal Global Law School, India*

Few scholars are as well placed as Dr Sampford to dissect and diagnose the legal academy and the legal profession. A Dean of Law who founded a revolutionary law school, an erudite inter-disciplinary scholar, and a public intellectual of international import, this collection of essays brings Dr Sampford's global, theoretical and practical wisdom to illuminate issues of import to lawyers and law professors in many countries.

Donna Greschner, *of the California Bar, University of Victoria, Canada and former Dean of Law*

Legal education is undergoing a worldwide identity crisis. Legal theorists are at pains to find the common elements that bring societies together in a global yet deeply divided world. In this marvellous and forward-looking work, Charles Sampford and Hugh Breakey, peep into the future of a more humane and anthropocentric approach to law and the rule of law, which though not absolute in themselves, are central to the lawyer's professional ethics and their understanding of the universality of their mission as agents of change.

Luis G. Franceschi, *Dean at Strathmore University Law School, Nairobi, Kenya*

This stimulating collection of essays starts with the place of jurisprudence and legal ethics in lawyering and legal education and ends with some of the challenges lawyers face in a period of accelerated globalisation. As a well-travelled Founding Dean of an innovative law school and director of transnational interdisciplinary research institutes, Sampford is unusually well-equipped to give a distinctively Australian perspective on these issues with clarity and panache.

William Twining, *former Dean of Law at Warwick University, Quain Professor of Law at University College, London and founding editor of the* Law in Context

Theorists have long overlooked legal education and legal practice as areas of interest. This book draws on extensive experience to provide a sustained and illuminating framework to consider the relationship between the way we educate lawyers and the way that they end up practising law. It is a valuable guide to ethical lawyering in many different contexts, from the local to the international.

Professor Hilary Charlesworth, *Centre for International Governance and Justice, Australian National University*

Law, Lawyering and Legal Education

Building an ethical profession in a globalizing world

Charles Sampford
and Hugh Breakey

Routledge
Taylor & Francis Group
LONDON AND NEW YORK

First published 2017
by Routledge
2 Park Square, Milton Park, Abingdon, Oxon OX14 4RN

and by Routledge
711 Third Avenue, New York, NY 10017

First issued in paperback 2018

Routledge is an imprint of the Taylor & Francis Group, an informa business

British Library Cataloguing-in-Publication Data
A catalogue record for this book is available from the British Library

Library of Congress Cataloging in Publication Data
Names: Sampford, C. J. G. (Charles J. G.), author. | Breakey, Hugh, author.
Title: Law, lawyering and legal education : building an ethical profession in a globalizing world / Charles Sampford and Hugh Breakey.
Description: Abingdon, Oxon ; New York, NY : Routledge, 2017. | Series: Routledge/challenges of globalisation ; 11 | Includes bibliographical references and index.
Identifiers: LCCN 2016015427| ISBN 9781138793347 (hardback) | ISBN 9781315761268 (ebook)
Subjects: LCSH: Law–Study and teaching. | Legal ethics. | Practice of law.
Classification: LCC K100 .S258 2017 | DDC 340.071–dc23
LC record available at https://lccn.loc.gov/2016015427

ISBN 13: 978-1-138-59777-8 (pbk)
ISBN 13: 978-1-138-79334-7 (hbk)

Typeset in Times New Roman
by Wearset Ltd, Boldon, Tyne and Wear

Contents

Contributors

Principal author

Charles Sampford graduated from Melbourne University at the top of his class in each of politics, philosophy and law before combining those disciplines in his Oxford DPhil. He was invited to return to Melbourne University in 1983 as a Lecturer and then Senior Lecturer before moving to the Philosophy Department in 1990 to establish the Centre for Philosophy and Public Issues where he was Acting, then Deputy Director and Principal Research Fellow. However, his earlier writings on reforming the Law Curriculum in response to the Pearce Report led to his invitation to come to Queensland as Foundation Dean of Law at Griffith University, starting in March 1991. The Griffith curriculum, which combined theoretical, contextual and skills in mutually reinforcing ways, was hailed by Sir Ninian Stephen as a 'revolution in legal education' that was widely praised and much copied. In the 2010 Excellence in Research Australia (ERA), Griffith secured a '4' in Law in the ERA, despite the law school being half the age of those at other universities securing that score. He established the *Griffith Law Review*, which was the newest A* law journal. In May 2013, the QS World Universities Rankings placed Griffith 43rd in the world, despite being less than half the age of the next youngest law school in the top 50. In research leadership, Professor Samford led the 1998 bid for the Key Centre for Ethics, Law, Justice and Governance (the only Australian centre in law or governance to receive centre funding from the Australian Research Council) and was its Foundation Director for six years. In September 2004, he became the Convenor of the Australian Research Council (ARC)-funded Governance Research Network (the only ARC network in law or governance). At the same time, the Key Centre became the headquarters for the Institute for Ethics, Governance and Law, a strategic research centre established with the initiative of the United Nations University that came to include Queensland University of Technology (QUT), The Australian National University (ANU), OP Jindal Global University and the Center for Asian Integrity. Professor Sampford became its Director. Foreign fellowships include the Visiting Senior Research Fellow at St John's College Oxford (1997) and a Senior Fulbright Award to Harvard University (2000). He has written over 130 articles and chapters and has completed 30 books and edited collections. He has also won over A$15 m dollars in grants, consultancies and awards for research work he has led. In June 2008, his work on corruption and integrity systems was recognized by the ARC, who invited the 20 researchers they thought had most clearly 'made a difference' to the Graeme Clarke Outcomes Forum held at Parliament House, Canberra. Charles was one of only four researchers invited from the humanities and social sciences. Charles is also a Barrister.

Editor and author

Hugh Breakey is a Research Fellow at Griffith University's Institute for Ethics, Governance and Law, Australia. Currently Chief Investigator in two federally funded projects, and research fellow on a third, Hugh's work spans the philosophical sub-disciplines of political theory, normative ethics, applied philosophy and legal theory. The author of *Intellectual Liberty: Natural Rights and Intellectual Property* (Ashgate), and the co-author (alongside Charles Sampford and Ramesh Thakur) of *Enhancing Protection Capacity: Policy Guide to the Responsibility to Protect and the Protection of Civilians in Armed Conflicts*, Hugh's work explores ethical issues emerging in myriad practical fields, including peacekeeping, safety industries, institutional governance and personal integrity, climate change, sustainable tourism, professionalism, private property and intellectual property, medicine, and international law and human rights. As well as writing for newspapers, online encyclopaedias, academic-journalistic outlets, non-government organisation (NGO) websites and high-impact policy guides, Hugh has published in an extensive array of international journals, including *The Philosophical Quarterly, The Modern Law Review and Political Studies*. While at present a full-time researcher, Hugh has taught philosophy and ethics at Queensland's three largest universities. Since 2013, Hugh has served as President of the Australian Association for Professional and Applied Ethics.

Original contributors (co-authors of original pieces)

Sophie Blencowe holds a BA (Hons) and LLB (Hons) from the University of Melbourne and received the 1992 Jessie Mary Vasey Prize for her honours thesis in women's history. She also holds the 1992 Dwight's Prize for Final Examination in Arts, School of History, and the 1993 Sir George Turner Exhibition for Constitutional and Administrative Law. She has worked as a Research Assistant at the Key Centre for Ethics, Law, Justice and Governance from 1994 to 2004 and did primary legal research for Professor Sampford, co-editing three books with him and several articles and essays.

Christine Parker was a dual university medallist in Law and Sociology from the University of Queensland and joined Griffith Law School as Professor Sampford's research assistant in 1993, during which time she co-authored a number of papers and articles with Professor Sampford (including the one included in this book and her first essay on legal ethics). She won a scholarship to the Australian National University, where she completed her PhD, and then worked at the University of New South Wales, the Australian National University and Monash University before taking her current chair at Melbourne. Professor Parker has written, researched and consulted widely on how and why businesses comply with legal, social and environmental responsibilities, what difference regulatory enforcement makes, and how businesses can work with lawyers and compliance professionals to build internal corporate social responsibility systems that work. Her work has been published in academic journals and used in policymaking and enforcement strategy. Her books include *The Open Corporation* (2002) on corporate social responsibility, business compliance systems and democratic accountability of companies; and *Explaining Compliance* (2011, with Vibeke Nielsen), an edited collection of the leading practice- and policy-oriented empirical research on how and why businesses do and do not comply with the law.

David Wood is Principal Fellow in the Melbourne Law School, where he taught courses in jurisprudence, legal philosophy, and criminal law and justice. He is the author of 'Judicial Ethics: A Discussion Paper' (Australian Institute of Judicial Administration, 1996), co-editor of *Essays on Philosophy in Australia* (Kluwer, I992), a co-author of *Just Criminal Law* (Federation Press, Sydney, 2006). He has published on punishment and sentencing, judicial ethics, business ethics, constitutional law and theory, and legal education in numerous essay collections, and in such journals as *Archiv fuer Rechts und Sozialphilosophie, Australian Journal of Corporate Law, Australasian Journal of Philosophy, Criminal Law and Philosophy, Criminal Law Journal, Criminal Law Review, Ethics, Federal Law Review, Journal of Business Ethics, Journal of Judicial Administration, Melbourne University Law Review, Oxford Journal of Legal Studies, Philosophy Compass, Scandinavian Studies in Law, University of New South Wales Law Journal, University of Western Australia Law Review* and *Utilitas.* He co-authored a number of publications with Professor Sampford, starting when they were both lecturers in the Melbourne Law School.

List of cases

Acknowledgements

Charles Sampford and Hugh Breakey would like to acknowledge the invaluable assistance of Carmel Connors, Melea Lewis and Spencer Wright.

The below-noted chapters are republished (with some modifications) from the following journals and previous publications. We would like to thank the publishers for their permissions to use these, and the co-authors for allowing their work to be republished.

Chapter 2: Charles Sampford. 'Law, Ethics and Institutional Reform: Finding Philosophy, Displacing Ideology', *Griffith Law Review* 3 (1994): 2–38.

Chapter 3: This article was first published by Thomson Reuters in the *Australian Law Journal* and should be cited as: Charles Sampford and David Wood, 'Theoretical Dimensions of Legal Education – a Response to the Pearce Report', *Australian Law Journal* 62 (1988): 32–53. For all subscription inquiries please phone, from Australia: 1300 304 195, from overseas: +61 2 8587 7980 or online at www.thomsonreuters.com.au/catalogue. The official PDF version of this article can also be purchased separately from Thomson Reuters.

Chapter 5: Charles Sampford, 'Pearce Revisited [Review of McInnis, Craig and Marginson, Simon. Australian Law Schools after the 1987 Pearce Report (1994)]', *Australian Universities' Review* 38, no. 1 (1995): 70–74.

Chapter 6: Charles Sampford, 'Reflections on a Respectable Revolution', *Griffith Law Review* 11 (2002): 252–262.

Chapter 9: Charles Sampford, 'What's a Lawyer Doing in a Nice Place Like This? Lawyers and Ethical Life', *Legal Ethics* 1 (1998): 35–50, available at www.tandfonline.com.

Chapter 10: Charles Sampford and Sophie Blencowe, 'Educating Lawyers to Be Ethical Advisers', in *The Ethical Challenge to Legal Education and Conduct*, edited by Kim Economides, 315–340. UK: Hart Publishing 1998. (Used by permission of Bloomsbury Publishing Plc.)

Chapter 14: Charles Sampford, 'Get New Lawyers!' *Legal Ethics* 6, no. 1 (2003): 85–105, available at www.tandfonline.com.

Chapter 15: Charles Sampford, 'More and More Lawyers but Still No Judges', *Legal Ethics* 8 (2008): 16–22, available at www.tandfonline.com.

Abbreviations

ABA	Australian Bar Association
ACLEC	Advisory Committee for Legal Education and Conduct
ADFA	Australia Defence Force Academy
AFP	Australian Federal Police
AFR	Australian Financial Review
AG	Attorney General
ALEC	Australia Legal Education Council
ALTA	Australian Law Teachers Association
ANU	The Australian National University
ANZUS	Australia, New Zealand, United States
AO	Order of Australia
ARC	Australian Research Council
ASIO	Australian Security Intelligence Organisation
BBC	British Broadcasting Corporation
BCC	Brisbane City Council
BHP	BHP Billiton
CAE	Centre of Advanced Education
CALD	Council of Australian Law Deans
CASS	Chinese Academy of the Social Sciences
CDOs	Collateralized Debt Obligations
CDS	Credit Default Swaps
CEO	Chief Executive Officer
CLE	Centre for Legal Education
CJ	Chief Justice
CMC	Crime and Misconduct Commission
COLE	Council of Legal Education
Comcar	Commonwealth Cars
CTEC	Commonwealth Tertiary Education Commission
Cth	Commonwealth
DEET	Department of Education, Employment and Training
DJ's	David Jones
DPP	Director of Public Prosecutions
EFTSU	effective full time student unit

EU	European Union
FA–18	Combat jet aircraft
FLPs	fundamental legislative principles
FOI	Freedom of Information
G20	Group of 20 (also known as the G-20) is an international forum for the governments and central bank governors from 20 major economies
GFC	Global Financial Crisis
HES	Higher education system
IAEA	International Atomic Energy Agency
IBA	International Bar Association
ICC	International Criminal Court
ICCPR	International Covenant on Civil and Political Rights
ICESCR	International Covenant on Economic, Social and Cultural Rights
ICJ	International Court of Justice
ICRC	International Committee of the Red Cross
IEGL	Institute for Ethics, Governance and Law
IMF	International Monetary Fund
IP	intellectual property
ISDS	Investor-State Dispute Settlement
IVR	World Congress on Legal and Social Philosophy
JAG	Judge Advocate General
JD	Juris Doctor
KC	King's Counsel
KCELJAG	Key Centre for Ethics, Law, Justice and Governance
KLO	Kosovar Liberation Army
LLB	Bachelor of Laws
LLM	Master of Laws
MAI	Multilateral Agreement on Investment
MD	Managing Director
MOOCs	mass open on-line courses
MOU	Memorandum of Understanding
MP	Member of Parliament
NATO	North Atlantic Treaty Organization
NGOs	Non-government organisations
NILEPA	National Institute for Law, Ethics and Public Affairs
NSWIT	New South Wales Institute of Technology
NTU	Northern Territory University
NYU	New York University
OECD	Organisation for Economic Co-operation and Development
PICT	Project on International Courts and Tribunals
PLT	practical legal training
PM	Prime Minister
PMCs	private military companies
PR	Public Relations

QC	Queen's Counsel
QIT	Queensland Institute of Technology
QUT	Queensland University of Technology
R2P	Responsibility to Protect
RMIT	Royal Melbourne Institute of Technology
SCR	Security Council Resolution
UCL	University College London
UK	United Kingdom
UN	United Nations
UNCITRAL	United Nations Commission on International Trader Law
UNE	University of New England
UNMOVIC	United Nations Monitoring, Verification and Inspection Commission
UNSC	United Nations Security Council
UNSW	University of New South Wales
UNU	United Nations University
USA	United States of America
UWA	University of Western Australia
VC	Vice Chancellor
WTC	World Trade Center
WTO	World Trade Organization

1 Dancing around the vortex

A personal introduction

Charles Sampford

> There are more things in heaven and earth, Horatio, than are dreamt of in your philosophy.
>
> Shakespeare, Hamlet (Act 1, Scene 5)

This book retrieves and builds upon some of my essays addressing issues about the changing face of law, lawyering and legal education over the last 30 years. Those issues were, of course, canvassed by others in their own way during this period. But, each of us comes to them through a unique set of experiences in a distinct set of institutions whose members made assumptions about those institutions. My experiences, not least in my interactions with those institutions and assumptions,[1] provided important insights and influenced the way I addressed those issues. Like all such experiences, they can provide insights that others miss. As well as providing an introduction to the contents of this collection, this chapter provides a narrative of my journey through those experiences and assumptions. In so doing, I hope to explain some of the insights generated and present a case-study about how legal academia shifted over time, and one person's role in that shift: helping instigate it even as I was living within the constraints of a dynamic environment.

Dancing around the 'vortex'

Like most Australian law students in the 1970s, I combined the study of law with another degree – in my case a Bachelor of Arts (BA) in philosophy and political science at the University of Melbourne. It was possible to compress two four-year degrees into six by doing the first two years of the Bachelor of Laws (LLB) at the same time as a four-year BA Honours. By the end of my first year in 1972, I had decided that my interests lay at the 'vortex' where law, philosophy, politics and economics met. Furthermore, after two hours in Oxford with two Doctor of Philosophy (DPhil) students just after my first-year results came in, I had decided there was no better place to dive into that vortex than via a DPhil at that university.

Ever since then, I have been fascinated by that vortex – the issues it suggests, the perspectives and insights on long-standing debates that it provides, and the means by which those perspectives may be, at least partially, integrated. Initially, the vortex influenced my approach to the subjects I studied and my thesis. It influenced my interest in and the positions I took in the work covered in this book, mentioned in the retrieved essays and other areas of my work outside this book. Of greatest relevance here are questions about:

- The nature of law, legal practice and legal education and what constitutes 'good' versions of each (all chapters);
- The 'critical and theoretical' dimensions of legal education (Chapters 2 to 5);
- The questions that should be on the agenda of law schools (Chapters 3, 6 and 8), and the encouragement of lifelong professional engagement with those questions (Chapter 3);
- The role of other disciplines in the teaching of law and the practice of lawyers (Chapters 2 and 4);
- The ethical role of lawyers – including role morality, professionalism, ethical pluralism, the relationship with clients and what it is to be an 'ethical lawyer' (Chapters 9, 10 and 11);
- The sustainability of good lawyering (Chapter 7);
- The cosmopolitan past and global future of lawyering (Chapter 17);
- The role of other disciplines in legal and governance research (Chapters 2 and 9);
- The similarities between ethical and common law reasoning, and the contributions the latter can make to the former – the common law of the mind (Chapter 2);
- The role of ethics and integrity in governance research (Chapters 2 and 11).

The means for bringing those disciplines together *in teaching law* is very much the subject of Chapters 2 and 3. The means for doing so *in research* informs all my work and is touched on in Chapter 2 – in which I reiterate my formula for interdisciplinary approaches to dealing with institutional governance problems: ethical standard-setting, legal regulation and institutional reform – with the latter including political[2] and economic elements.[3] In this process, ethics can play a coordinating role – which is why I call this approach 'values-based governance'. However, I came to realize that although this vortex is a meeting point for disciplines that have taken on lives of their own, those disciplines have emerged from what was once a common intellectual space that engaged thinkers on human affairs right up to the age of Adam Smith and Jeremy Bentham. Indeed, such scholars would not have recognized the separate existence of those disciplines and would have been puzzled by attempts to study them separately.[4] However, one of the problems with disciplinary specialization in governance research is that each of these disciplines have developed strongly theorized but limited conceptions of institutions, their problems, and suggested solutions to those problems. When lawyers look at institutions, they see formal norms (networks of contracts of institutions). If there is a problem, it is that the rules are not well-written, and the solution is to write new ones or rewrite old ones. When ethicists look at institutions, they see informal norms and values. If there is a problem, it is that the values have not been thought through, not articulated or not built into the people, processes and practices of the organization – and their solution is to do so. Many political scientists are impatient with norms and see institutions in terms of power – with defects lying in the poor power structures, which they can address. Economists look at incentives and disincentives, seeing institutional problems as the result of perverse incentives with the solution in aligning incentives and disincentives with the behaviour to be encouraged and discouraged respectively.[5] These different perspectives each give vital but partial insights to institutional problems. However, it is rare that any one discipline on its own can adequately address the governance problems of today. I have also come to realize that professions can play a critical role in governance reform as they are formally dedicated to improved behaviour rather than minimum compliance.[6]

Ultimately, it turned out that the disciplines that provided such a stimulating vortex are, in fact, the disciplines that are necessary to understand governance issues. I later came to dub them the 'governance disciplines' – recognizing that governance required all of those disciplines working together.

In this connection, it is worth noting the difference between 'transdisciplinary' and 'interdisciplinarity'. Interdisciplinarity assumes that the disciplines remain separate but are used simultaneously to address issues and/or solve problems. This can go beyond addressing the issue that generated the interdisciplinary response and may help us understand more about the disciplines and their interconnections, making it easier to deploy those disciplines in the future. However, the disciplines remain distinct and intact. An advocate of interdisciplinarity might suggest that it is better to allow existing disciplines to develop autonomously, addressing internal synergies and conflicts so that they are in better shape for the next interdisciplinary exercise. I am not criticizing interdisciplinarity and have happily accepted and used the description – while finding 'transdisciplinarity' a better term.

Transdisciplinarity seeks to transcend the existing disciplines, embracing parts of existing disciplines to address issues and to reorder ideas. This might be imagined as starting with different disciplines and bringing them together. This is certainly what I try to do at various times in this book – though I emphasize that transdisciplinarity does not create a new unity but rediscovers an old one. To some extent, I am working towards a kind of reintegrative disciplinarity. As the following chapter will indicate, I tend to focus on practical problems that need more than one of the disciplines to address them. Indeed, addressing most real problems of governance and law does generally require more than one discipline. One of the reasons for bringing together in workshops what I call 'reflective practitioners' and 'engaged academics' (a methodology discussed in Chapter 2) is that focusing on the problem, rather than the discipline, provides an opening for the various disciplines to make their contributions in response to the problem. This process encourages contributors to think about the problem rather than the discipline-specific ways those different perspectives address a problem. Most of the problems of modern governance – and certainly the 'wicked' problems – are no more open to solution by one discipline than they would have been under Smith and Bentham. (I note that there is a possible corollary, or at least generalization, that the problems that need only one discipline to address are generally problems created within the discipline.)

This approach might mean that the practical problems indicate the necessary unity of the disciplines – a unity that is exposed gradually as each new problem is addressed. In this way, the problems and solutions shine light on different areas of a common discipline that is gradually seen as a whole. On the other hand, it might not turn out quite as well-ordered as this implies. Any transdisciplinary wholes may be as limited as the disciplines they transcend. If I were a Hegelian, I might even propose a dialectic process. But I am not a Hegelian. Indeed, I took time out (in the 1994 essay reprinted here as Chapter 2) to deride Fukuyama's astonishing embrace of a form of Hegelianism beloved of Marx in the year that communism collapsed. Marx thought that communism would be the end of history: Fukuyama thought that a particular form of neoliberal capitalism in which most issues were resolved through the operation of markets rather than democratic institutions was the end of history. I had always thought that Marx's claim was foolish and Fukuyama's more so, given that the latter was in a position to learn from the exposed foolishness of the former.[7]

The fact that these thoughts were delivered in my inaugural lecture as Foundation Dean and Professor of Law might indicate that it was obvious that my dancing around the vortex was bound to take place within a law school. However, the fact that my interest in the vortex developed out of ideas I first penned in a philosophy department in 1990,[8] indicates that the question of where to dance was a significant one.

The search for a suitable dance floor: law thrice denied

While I was sure that I wanted to learn the complex steps of my 'vortex dance' through an Oxford DPhil, I very much doubted that I could find space for this dance in law schools. Indeed, I did not see much point completing my law degree. While the Melbourne Law School (and others like it) were happy for its students to amuse themselves with other disciplines in other degrees, it was on the clear understanding that they did not bring any of that with them back into law lecture theatres. One of the most explicit statements of this was by Professor Colin Howard who taught Advanced Constitutional Law. He reportedly started his first class with a statement that the subject was about law (not politics) and any students who attempted to include politics in their exam answers would fail. Other lecturers had seen far too much of *The Paper Chase*, a movie and TV series set in Harvard. Each episode started with the formidable Professor Kingsfield stating that he took young minds that were full of 'mush' and sent them out thinking like lawyers. He did this by what was called the 'Socratic method', in which he interrogated students until they came up with the right answers.[9] No doubt the ideas Kingsfield's students gleaned from their undergraduate degrees were rigorously extirpated. There were a number of would-be antipodean 'Kingsfields' who sought to terrorize Australian law students and ensure that the 'right answer' was not seen to include the 'mush' that they were simultaneously learning from the eminent philosophers and political scientists teaching in other rooms.[10]

Of course, there was one subject in the law degree that did consider what other disciplines might say about law – jurisprudence. It might be seen as the remnant of the common intellectual space that preceded the separation of disciplines referred to above. In this one subject was corralled all the insights about law that had been developed by philosophers, political scientists, sociologists (and, in other universities, economists and anthropologists) – and by law professors who rubbed shoulders with them. But very few lecturers either sought to apply such insights in the 'substantive' subjects or welcomed attempts by students to do so.[11] The other place where those disciplines could be mixed with law was in 'Legal Studies Departments' in other universities, which were derided for doing so. The admixture was seen as the reason why such universities could not confer degrees that entitled graduates to practice.

Despite this lack of interdisciplinary teaching, the burden of completing three more law subjects in three years was trivial and did not slow my progress in the other disciplines that mattered to me and in which I was encouraged to synthesize. However, as I was getting ready to apply to Oxford in 1975, one of my mentors[12] gave me some unexpected advice that ended my first attempt not to be a lawyer. He urged me to finish my law degree before I went to Oxford. As he had finished his law degree after he returned from Oxford while a senior lecturer in philosophy and was going off to his first chair, his advice surprised me. His reasons were simple. First, he said that law was easy compared to philosophy because it was much less rigorous – something that did not make it more attractive to me. Second, he said that I could do in law anything that I wanted to do in philosophy: the only difference was that I would do it more quickly and that I, and the work, would get more recognition. I was not convinced, but I went back to law and studied as many law subjects in one year as the previous four. After that experience, I did not think I could take so heavy a dose of the kind of law taught in Australian law schools. When the Head of School at the Latrobe University Legal Studies Department heard that I was looking for a full-time job while I took my LLB in smaller doses, he offered me a two-year job teaching law and criminology. By this time, a small number of law lecturers were more open to the insights of other disciplines. These included the above-mentioned Professor Howard. Having been constitutional advisor to the Whitlam Labor government, he now started his first class in Advanced Constitutional Law with a warning that an understanding of politics was absolutely essential to understanding constitutional law. His new-found interdisciplinarity was atypical of Australian law schools. But, he was Melbourne's Dean, so I felt there was hope for the future.

In Oxford, interdisciplinarity was not controversial and I had plenty of opportunity to explore the 'vortex' in my Law DPhil.[13] I was still ambivalent about teaching in a traditional law school and I planned to apply for a lectureship in philosophy. My reference request to Prof Howard was not acknowledged – though he insouciantly wrote to me two weeks later saying that he had persuaded the Vice Chancellor to create a lectureship for me and inquired when I would like to start. It would have been ungracious to refuse; thus ending my second attempt not to be a lawyer. I returned to Melbourne University in February 1983.

I was pleasantly surprised at the warm welcome I received from my former teachers who were now my colleagues. I could teach the two subjects I wanted from the then curriculum, exploring elements of the vortex in doing so. Constitutional and Administrative Law allowed me to further explore links between law, politics and, through conventions, applied ethics. Jurisprudence is the subject that has always invited interdisciplinary reflection. Additionally, I was invited to create a new elective in which only the course code number was prescribed. (I chose 'Law and Society'). Research support was very generous as was the support for my efforts to build links with other academic departments. Prof Howard, the Dean who had appointed me, had also appointed three others with a strong interest in jurisprudence as well as one legal historian – counteracting a curriculum review that had dropped legal history and downgraded jurisprudence from a core to an elective subject.[14] Even the traditionalists duchessed me, but in a manner that both marginalized my interdisciplinary aspirations and reminded me of my place. A long-standing law professor told me that I had to appreciate that the law school was delicately placed between the academy and the profession. My work was a valuable contribution at the extreme academic end, which was valued by the university. But this could never be the core of the law school, as the profession demanded that the bulk of the degree be confined to 'black letter law'. The limited but prestigious role they described for me was not an unattractive prospect and I was prepared to accept it until the president of the bar used his rights of audience and debate to address the law faculty board. He excoriated the law school for dropping jurisprudence from the core curriculum. He insisted that jurisprudence was the most practical subject he had studied. While the others taught him what the law was, jurisprudence helped him understand the 'structure and functions of law' and hence the directions in which the law might develop.

This completely undermined the narrative with which I had been duchessed. Not only was the interdisciplinary work of those like me valued at the academic end: it was also the part most valued by the most senior members of the profession. This led me to talk to several senior members of the judiciary and profession, whereupon I found that such views were widely held. This gave me the confidence to ask myself, somewhat heretically, if the kind of work that I was doing was what academia and the profession wanted, what were the black letter lawyers doing? Rather than meeting the demands of the profession and linking it to the academy, they were serving neither. I mischievously started to ask if they were not perhaps off on a 'frolic of their own'.[15]

I was not hostile to 'doctrinal' or 'black letter law'. In fact, I was truly fascinated by it and enjoyed diving into the doctrinal debates generated by very able minds.[16] I understood its traditions and the role that it played in legal institutions and the effects of this activity rippled through other institutions and the lives of individuals. Law could not be understood without understanding what lawyers did with legal texts in courts of law and in giving formal and informal advice. But that would not, in itself, allow us to understand the role of those texts in daily practice and what 'lawyers did with texts' affected and was affected by those institutions and individuals. This is where other disciplines were essential – not just for academics but for practitioners as well. What I found refreshing was how clearly this resonated with the best judges and practitioners. Indeed, their observations on the institutions within which, and with which, they dealt were consistently fascinating (not least when those observations could not be easily typecast within the bounds of other disciplines).

The fact that the techniques for interpreting legal texts and applying them to litigated disputes could not provide determinate answers was not fatal to the importance of those techniques – indeed, this fact is central to the development of legal institutions that provide authoritative answers where reason cannot be perfect. Accordingly, I did not agree with critical legal scholars that the law was 'just politics'. It was, to modify Clausewitz, 'politics (policy) carried on by other means'.[17] The 'by other means' is critical. Apart from cases where enemy generals or presiding judges can be bribed, winning cases and battles involves the application of resources to legal argument and military action respectively. To understand which legal and military campaigns are started and won, lost, or degenerate into attrition you need to understand the relevant craft and the larger issues that drive them.

Chapter 2 (Law, Ethics and Institutional Reform: Finding Philosophy, Displacing Ideology) constitutes the first attempt I made to bring these ideas together and outline the relationship between the law and other disciplines, the role of theory and applied philosophy, and the dangers of ideological excess. That I did so in my professorial lecture as a Foundation Dean of Law was something I never would have predicted, and it occurred only after my third attempt not to become a lawyer.

Pearce and the 'critical and theoretical dimensions of legal education'

After returning from my first sabbatical in late 1986, I was expected to give a staff seminar arising from the work I had done. The obvious thing to do was to avoid distractions and talk about the monograph for which I had just won a Blackwell's contract[18] – which would help me win promotion to senior lecturer the following year. But a major review of legal education, chaired by Professor Dennis Pearce,[19] had just been published. The report's first finding was that Australian law schools lacked a 'critical and theoretical dimension' and its first recommendation was that Australian law schools address that deficiency. The only thing that seemed to be lacking was an explanation of what the 'critical and theoretical dimensions' might be and how to incorporate them into legal curricula. I offered to write a paper that sought to address both issues from the perspective of a legal theorist. The deputy dean liked the idea and made it the topic for the once-a-term joint Melbourne-Monash staff seminar in mid-1987.[20] It was received well and I published it in what was then a humble journal that was coming out the next month; it went the 1980s version of viral by being faxed and copied in a number of law schools. It was soon republished with a few amendments and the assistance of a colleague in the *Australian Law Journal* (and reproduced here as Chapter 3, ' "Theoretical Dimensions" of Legal Education').[21] The essay argued that law schools had been asking the wrong questions – what should be included in jurisprudence, when should it be taught, and should it be compulsory? The right question was how we could incorporate the kind of questioning that was associated with jurisprudence into the law school as a whole.

Various universities started to implement my suggestions and I was invited to speak at the closing plenary of the annual Australian Law Teachers Association in 1988. I was asked to write an article for the newly minted *Legal Education Review* on how to incorporate critical and theoretical dimensions into teaching mainstream law subjects.[22] Back at Melbourne University, I was made a member of the curriculum review committee. I put out some comprehensive proposals that I was sure would be supported by most of the faculty.[23] But, on the committee, the professor who had told me my place was implacably opposed. He donned his strongest Kingsfield demeanour, misrepresented the proposal as one of making jurisprudence compulsory and demanded to know what I would do if faced with a lecture theatre of 200 students of whom only 20 wanted to be there. My response was simple. First, we had nearly 140 enrolments in elective jurisprudence courses. Second, we were not proposing large-class teaching. And third, if I thought it was a critical part of the law school, I would no more drop it than contract law (in which he had briefly lectured me 14 years earlier). His further objection was that the profession would be opposed. I could not believe my luck that he had either forgotten or ignored the bar president's excoriating speech. I proposed that the two professional representatives on the committee be invited to give the profession's view at the next meeting. As I expected, they fully supported the proposals (though I took no chances, ringing the president of the bar and a couple of supportive judges to sound out the views of the professional representatives). I also secured the support of an absolute majority of faculty staff and external representatives. But protagonist professor and the new dean (the first not to be elected in decades) were not supportive. After two bruising faculty board meetings at which the professional representatives fought hard to block attempts to water down the proposals, a version of the proposals was passed. As Justice R.E. McGarvie (later Victorian Governor) walked up to congratulate me on what he called the most significant reforms in 20 years he saw my long face and deduced that I saw the glass half-empty. He assured me that students and professionals would love the kind of course I was proposing. The only opposition would come from 'those most conservative lawyers of all – law lecturers who did not want to change their lecture notes!'

I was given no role in the implementation of the reforms and my proposal for a Law and Ethics Research Centre was rejected out of hand – on the remarkably un-prescient basis that there was no money in it. I remember taking private offence on two grounds – normatively, on the basis that one should not judge research by its ability to bring in money; empirically, on the basis that he was dead wrong. I organized a secondment to the philosophy department to set up the Centre for Philosophy and Public Issues with the active participation of very senior lawyers, such as former Governor-General Sir Ninian Stephen. I was Acting (then Deputy) Director, where I was responsible for planning and securing funding[24] and promoted to Principal Research Fellow – the full-time research equivalent of a Reader/Associate Professor. I have to admit that the dean's words stung me to prove him wrong in as substantial a manner as possible. My belief in the practical value of theoretically informed research led me to request such a centre as my 'bride price' at Griffith University and the A$18m we raised demonstrated once and for all that there is 'money in it'. I mention such successes, not merely out of pride for these achievements, but to indicate what is possible, in the hope that others will continue to follow suit.

At the time, I saw this as my third and probably final attempt to dance away from legal academia – or at least move to an area of the dance floor where lawyers were not just dancing with fellow lawyers.[25]

Australian law schools after Pearce – a case study in educating critical, theoretical and ethical lawyers?

After I had been at the Centre less than a year, two universities approached me to be their Foundation Dean of Law and put into practice the ideas I had set out in the *Australian Law Journal* article. Not only were they inviting me to dance, they wanted to move me to the centre of the dance floor; they were asking me to build the dance hall and choreograph the steps. This was somewhat ironic. The *Pearce Report* had recommended against new law schools and its proposals had been for the reform of existing law school curricula – as had my proposals. However, the Dawkins expansion of higher education[26] had changed all that by allowing universities to largely control the courses they taught, 'solving' the relatively limited numbers of university places by renaming Colleges of Advanced Education (CAEs) (what the British called 'polytechnics') as universities; and taking away research money from existing universities and putting it to open competition through the Australian Research Council (ARC). I have to say that I was not a fan of the Dawkins reforms. I suggested that CAEs thought they were becoming universities but that it was more likely that universities would become CAEs! However, I also suggested that: 'in the midst of chaos lies opportunity'. Indeed, there were two opportunities. The first was that the ARC provided the opportunity for a small number of academics to secure much higher levels of funding than hitherto sought – in our case through interdisciplinary teams of researchers. These teams were not only necessary to deal with the kinds of governance issues we wanted to study but could be easily understood by a largely science-based funding body. The other was the opportunity to start a law school from scratch. At this point, I remembered R.E. McGarvie's words and saw the logic – no law school, so no lecturers, so no problem (at least not the one created by conservative law lecturers!). I accepted Griffith University's offer (especially when I discovered that the suggestion had been by Pearce and endorsed by Sir Zelman Cowen, the Vice Chancellor's advisor on legal education). The two opportunities were mutually reinforcing – an interdisciplinary law school was the perfect home for the team-based interdisciplinary research centres we aimed to establish. The first of these centres was the National Institute for Law, Ethics and Public Affairs (NILEPA), established at Griffith to build on the work I had been doing in Melbourne.[27] NILEPA formed the core of the Key Centre for Ethics, Law, Justice and Governance (KCELJAG) – the only ARC-funded centre in law or governance, which in turn formed the basis for the ARC Governance Network and then the UNU-affiliated Institute for Ethics, Governance and Law (IEGL). These research centres, and the performance funding that came with them, made it possible to establish an extremely strong research culture at the same time as developing a radical new curriculum. Research success and a strong research culture attracted some very good academics and the research informed the courses taught.

The next few years were hectic as we built a highly innovative law school with a very strong research base, a radical new curriculum (which Sir Ninian Stephen, former High Court Justice and Governor General called 'revolutionary')[28] – yet one that had extremely strong support from the profession and the state and federal judiciaries. Three of the pieces I wrote in this period are included in the second section of the book. The first (Chapter 5 'Revisiting Pearce') is a review of the McGinnis and Marginson report into legal education after Pearce. I agreed that legal education had changed fundamentally after Pearce – though more through Dawkins than Pearce, not least because Pearce's audience (the Commonwealth Tertiary Education Commission) was abolished by Dawkins. The second (Chapter 6) is an article published in a special edition of the *Griffith Law Review* to celebrate the Law School's first decade. As well as outlining our 'respectable revolution', it also looked forward to the issues of the globalizing of law and legal education. That article was built on a piece Professor Peter Birks, Chair of the Society of Public Teachers of Law encouraged me to write for that society's journal.[29] The third (Chapter 7), deals with one of the complaints about the new law schools – that we were flooding the market with too many law graduates. With the assistance of my then research assistant (now a senior professor herself), I analyzed the 'panic over numbers'. We concluded (a) that most of the extra students were entering existing law schools rather than new ones; (b) there was a significant 'catch up' after a decade of zero growth enforced at the behest of the law societies; (c) law, especially when combined with another degree, was now seen as providing wider career choices. The concern we had was about quality. In the previous round of expansion, new law schools were at least as well funded as existing ones.[30] Many of the newer law schools were very poorly funded indeed. A postscript updates the numbers to show that little has changed. The section is preceded by Chapter 4, which reflects on the promises and perils of philosophy in legal education and ends with a reflection on developments in legal education in the last 25 years (Chapter 8) – appropriately bookending this section with theory and practice.

Legal ethics: opportunities and challenges in education and practice

If jurisprudence was marginalized in traditional law schools, this was even truer for legal ethics. Legal ethics was traditionally included in post-degree/pre-admission training, taught by practitioners and rarely marked beyond a pass. Even Oxford, arguably the world capital of jurisprudence, did not do a lot on legal ethics. While the UNSW had incorporated legal ethics in a first-year course, it was not otherwise built into the curriculum. In my ALJ article, ethical questions were included among the questions on the agenda of the law school. Senior members of the profession took ethics very seriously – they earned quite enough money as highly principled lawyers so there was no temptation to seek more by being unethical. They strongly supported its inclusion within the mainstream curriculum at Griffith. At the same time, the Queensland Law Society was very supportive of legal ethics research and partnered with us in a major legal ethics project.[31] When I consulted the profession about a mooted Griffith Master of Laws (LLM), I was intrigued by the suggestion that we should educate lawyers to be ethical advisors. This initially appeared counterintuitive – or at least contrary to the popular images of lawyers. But it got me thinking. When Richard Hart, senior Oxford University Press (OUP) commissioning editor for both law and philosophy set up his eponymous publishing house, it had a strong emphasis on legal ethics. I was invited to write the very first article in the new Hart-published journal *Legal Ethics*. I took the opportunity to canvass the relationship between law, jurisprudence and ethics (in 'What's a lawyer doing in a nice place like this?' published here as Chapter 9). In an essay in a Hart-published book on *The Ethical Challenges of Legal Education*, I filled out my response to Elizabeth Nosworthy ('Educating lawyers to be ethical advisers' reprinted here as Chapter 10).

One of the concerns lawyers in the early 1990s expressed was the potential difficulties faced by lawyers employed by government agencies. Law societies were keen to have them as members but were concerned that they could not be bound by legal ethics because of the demands of their employers. Similar, and generally stronger, concerns were expressed about lawyers employed by corporations. As law firms corporatized, such concerns went to the heart of the profession. I was asked to deliver a keynote address on 'Ethics navigation for government lawyers' at the Legal Officers Conference in 2011. This keynote forms the basis for Chapter 11 ('The ethics of employed lawyers'), which considers ethical issues for employed lawyers. I argue that good public sector ethics and corporate ethics mutually reinforce legal ethics. Accordingly, if you want to hire a lawyer to do what lawyers do and respect their code of ethics, you have made a very good hire. If you hire a lawyer to do what lawyers should not do, then I hope that it is the worst, and last, hire you make.

This section ends with two reflections. The first, 'Educating ethical lawyers' (Chapter 12) reflects on the purposes of legal ethics and professionalism, issues of content and teaching methods. The second, 'New challenges to ethical practice', examines some of the ethical challenges facing teaching methods and the ethical competences. At the same time, the categories of ethical challenges generated by law and lawyering are not fixed. Chapter 13 ('New challenges') follows these essays with brief commentaries on some new ethical issues. The first ethical issue is the role of lawyers in what the OECD and G20 calls 'Base Erosion and Profit Shifting'. This reprises a long-standing question about the legitimacy of what I have called 'the hunt for the unintended consequence'[32] that excuses clients from paying tax. I raised this in my first major essay on legal ethics,[33] suggesting that the tolerance of such behaviour and the continuation of the legal privileges of the profession would be put at risk unless, 'as the activities, structures and profile of the legal profession change, it must continually reconsider the justification for its existence, ever aware that changes in society, the law, and other legal institutions may justify a different kind of profession'.[34] While the focus then was on domestic taxation, the opportunities for eliminating tax are much greater within the international system. The second issue considers the ethics of confidential settlements where defendants are prepared to pay more to suppress information that would be damaging to the defendant either through the loss of office by governments or through multiple lawsuits from other victims. Chapter 13 then deals with various ways of arguing cases (especially criminal cases) in public, before reflecting on the potential abuse of privilege in making criminal accusations in civil pleadings.

Legal ethics and legal professionalism in a globalizing world

When I was studying law and started teaching it, the primary issues dealt with in law schools (and politics departments) were 'domestic' in the sense of confined to the sovereign state in whose jurisdiction the law school lay. There were always one or two who taught international law in elective subjects, but most of their colleagues doubted that this was 'real law'. While some liked to quote Professor Ian Brownlie's quip that 'anyone who doubted that international law existed should look at my Rolls parked outside', Australian international lawyers drove more modest cars and the majority of Australian law schools did not have a chair in international law. There was more interest in comparative law of current sovereign states or the different kind of comparison made in legal and constitutional history. Legal history looked at the development of English law, generally starting with the assumption that eleventh-century English kings had absolute power, which was gradually constrained through the accretion of laws, conventions and legal institutions. Political philosophy was not so limited, but was still largely concerned with issues within states rather than between states. This was reinforced by public law, which was much more concerned with the relationships between sovereign states and sub-national entities than the relationships between sovereign states and international institutions. In jurisdictions where international law only had domestic force when enacted by domestic legislation, there was an excuse for ignoring international law altogether. Black letter lawyers with no interest in parliamentary debates found it even easier to dismiss the text of international treaties and *travaux preparatoires*.

These tendencies were reinforced by the dominant strands in jurisprudence, which concentrated the nature of law within sovereign states and addressed its questions about that law. The long continental tradition of international lawyers being legal philosophers might have mitigated against this. But the most noted jurisprude/international lawyer, Hans Kelsen, took his legal system international. He saw legal systems within states as part of a larger international legal system that authorized state sovereigns based on their having 'by and large effective control' of territory – making his imagined international legal system far too akin to national legal systems.[35]

As previously indicated, legal ethics was generally not even taught in law schools and it was generally based on the ethical rules set by the relevant bar associations and/or law societies – all of which were confined to a single national or sub-national jurisdiction.

The Griffith curriculum did take international law much more seriously and included an introduction to international law within a large compulsory public law subject in second year (Constitutional and Administrative Law). Students were also required to do an elective in international law, law of another jurisdiction, or legal history – though this was as much to understand the variability of laws and to disabuse them of any easy assumptions that the law they were taught was inevitable – following a 'Whig theory of legal history' in which the application of reason produced continuous improvement in law.

The inclusion of international law into our core public law subject (Constitutional and Administrative Law)[36] was very deliberate. As always, the interest was not in law by itself but law as part of the 'vortex'. I agreed with Professor Howard Mark II (see above) that constitutional law could not be understood without politics. And, I think he came to agree that it was not possible without understanding political philosophy – or economics, which drove much of the litigation and without which the matters were unlikely to be litigated to an authoritative legal result. Finally, it was very hard to properly understand constitutional conventions without ethics and what makes ethics stick (in fact, a mixture of law, politics and the right incentives and disincentives).

Public international law fitted into this subject in a number of important ways. First, international law was a creature of sovereign states and sovereign states were creatures of international law, in a symbiotic way that I did not understand until I read Spruyt's *The Sovereign State and its Competitors*[37] (which also had the huge virtue of indicating the contingency of the way the system developed and the alternative possibilities for global 'order'). Second, the similarities of names are not accidental and, by the end of the decade, I was arguing that the principles in public law and public international law would cross-fertilize and tend to converge.[38] Third, public law dealt with multi-level structures and the problems and opportunities of that multi-level government – though, as in so many other areas, it was important not to learn too much, because the United Nations is not going to be the 'sovereign state writ large' – even as a loose European Union (EU)-type model.[39]

My initial interest in an area of international law came in considering how democracies could deal with coups d'état – something I dubbed a 'disease of the modern state'.[40] As always, understanding the question and structuring an answer requires a combination of ethics, law, state structures (including both the armed forces and the unarmed institutions of the state) and incentives (not least the probability of failure). I argued that the strategy I advocated would deter and defeat pretty well all coups d'états staged by rational generals/colonels/flight lieutenants/master sergeants – leaving only the irrational ones who are generally easier to defeat!

While I did not put the central task of deterring and defeating coups on international law, I did detect a remarkable irony and increasing disconnect. The original basis for sovereign legitimacy in domestic and international law had been the effective control of territory – what Kelsen called a legal system that was 'by and large effective' – and what I referred to more bluntly (and I would argue accurately) as 'the prior successful use of force'. However, with the democratic revolutions starting in the eighteenth century, this was no longer an acceptable basis for domestic sovereign legitimacy. Instead of the prior successful use of force, the new test was popular acquiescence moving to the active choice of the citizens. This was initially something of a protection for democratic revolutions but, as more and more states became democratic, the disconnect between the bases of sovereign legitimacy in domestic and international law became more pronounced. In the first of my papers, I made the incredibly rash prediction (scoffed at by international lawyers) that, within 50 years of that date (that is, 2038), it would be as outrageous in international law and relations to confer legitimacy on a regime established by a coup as it would be for a democratic polity within their own borders. When I repeated this 2038 'prediction' 11 years later in my closing plenary at the World Congress on Legal and Social Philosophy (IVR) many queried why I thought it would take so long.[41] I replied that history is a long game without a single direction with many detours and reversals. In any case, it was not really a prediction but a call to arms because such changes do not just happen but have to be striven for. I hold to my hope and my prediction that the disconnect will be resolved in favour of democracy – not least because I hope to last until then and enjoy a febrile dance on the graves and cells of failed coup leaders.

In so doing, I dismissed the idea that states could recognize other states but not governments. States hosting embassies and high commissions must decide whose credentials to accept; the United Nations has to decide who takes the seat in the UN General Assembly; and bankers have to decide who can borrow on sovereign credit. I also suggested that globalization was turning on its head the principle that the international community recognizes states that were by and large successful. States could not succeed *until* they are recognized.

Coups stimulated me to think about international law and governance and its vortex where international law, international ethics and theory, international economics, and a range of institutions met. During the 1990s, a stream of money, ideas, people and diseases started flowing over and threatening national borders; it seemed clear that sovereign states were 'not the only game in town' and we had to understand that law and governance were becoming much more complex multi-level phenomena. On an increasing number of matters, the relevant law (and the institutions for determining law) was not confined to the law recognized by the sovereign state in which the issue arose – or indeed, the international law that the sovereign was prepared to accept. Instead, it was necessary to look at laws passed at international, regional, national and sub-national levels. However, as I had always argued, understanding the nature of emerging global problems and opportunities required a mixture of governance disciplines interacting at the vortex. The vortex was suddenly becoming more complicated. Not only were there multiple governance disciplines necessary, but they needed to be applied to a range of governance levels – international, regional, national and sub-national – and cross-cut by corporations, professions and NGOs. Some of the most intractable global governance problems involve weaknesses in governance at one level being exacerbated by weaknesses at other levels.

These issues were at the heart of KCELJAG established in early 1999 and were at the centre of the above-mentioned World Congress plenary. The plenary set out a narrative that I have found very fruitful in guiding the thinking and research in my programs at KCELJAG and in IEGL. It drew an analogy to the development of modern states after Westphalia. Strong modern states emerged in the seventeenth century. They were highly authoritarian, which Hobbes argued was necessary to prevent a war of all against all.[42] Philosophers of the 'North Atlantic' enlightenment[43] proposed to civilize the sovereign state with values such as the rule of law, democracy, human rights, liberty, equality and citizenship that were backed by institutional reforms found in presidential and parliamentary democracies. Globalization had weakened the institutions of the strong sovereign state and enhanced a range of other institutions including global corporations and international bodies (see Chapter 17). For me, the three key questions for a new 'global' enlightenment reflect those of its predecessor: 'what values should inform the emerging global order and what institutions would realize those values?' What were the global equivalents of liberty, equality, fraternity/citizenship, democracy, human rights and the rule of law with which enlightenment philosophes sought to civilize the authoritarian states of their time? And, what mix of international, regional, national, sub-national, corporate and civil society institutions would deliver those global values?

The big issue at the time was NATO's bombing of Serbia in retaliation for its actions in Kosovo. 'Liberal interventionists' claimed at the time that it was not a precedent and later, with the Goldstone Report, that it was 'illegal but legitimate'.[44] I sympathized with the dilemmas of well-intentioned democrats dealing with ill-intentioned criminal demagogues.

I painted a path to a future where sovereignty became a collective right of a people – not a right of those who maintained effective control of them – and that state authorities were only recognized internationally as representing those to whom they were accountable domestically. However, I argued that that path involved the evolution of international law (and the international rule of law) rather than trashing it: and that those who sought to enforce international law must abide by it. I argued that states engaging in 'humanitarian intervention' should receive and publish independent legal advice and accept the compulsory jurisdiction of the International Court of Justice (ICJ) for that use of force, even if for no other matter. If the intervening states were correct in their claims to legality, this would lead to the confirmation of those claims and the development of international law. I argued that abiding by international law was not only in line with the principles of NATO members but also in their interests (citing the need for genuine cooperation by other countries to enforce other international agreements concerning the protection of copyright and the prevention of terrorism).[45]

I argued that international law should eventually change from recognizing the prior successful use of force to recognizing governments from only representing those to whom they are responsible. But, the way to develop international law was not to trash it in the meantime. In this, I put a lot of store in the integrity of legal advice on which governments acted, suggesting an advisory opinion from the highest court where this was permissible, the Attorney General acting as an independent law officer, or a non-partisan group of ex-judges.

One week after my address, I returned to Canberra for the first conference organized by KCELJAG ('From Civil Strife to Civil Society')[46] – Kosovo was naturally of interest. At one of the sessions, a very nice young British Judge Advocate General (JAG) officer outlined the official line on the legality of the Kosovo War. He was more or less laughed off the stage. He was clearly shaken by the experience. I have never seen myself as a 'father confessor' but he appeared to do so. He told me that he had been asked to draft the legal advice to NATO on the legality of the war. He told me that he had done what any good lawyer would do – look to find a legal basis for the action his 'client' wanted to take. But he said that he honestly could not find one and, as any good lawyer should, he told his client that. He wryly commented that he must have been wrong, as a much more senior lawyer said that it was legal.

This experience raised some very important questions of legal ethics. The first was whether he had seriously breached lawyer–client confidentiality – an issue that troubled me for years. The second was what the ethical responsibilities of lawyers in such positions should be. Where so much store was placed on the claimed legality of the action and where an admission of its illegality would almost certainly mean that the war would not be fought, lawyers who give governments the advice they want to hear rather than the advice they need to hear bear a heavy responsibility for the deaths that occur. Of course, lawyers may legitimately differ. However, in domestic law, the existence of a court of compulsory jurisdiction must always be in the lawyer's mind, constraining the advice that is given: clients who like the advice they hear but find it comprehensively trashed by the judge who hears the case are not likely to be thankful for the advice they received! I was keen to write a paper on this issue, but I did not feel I could do so given the source of my information.

Luckily, James Rubin, Madeleine Albright's press secretary at the time, put the issue in the public domain in a *Financial Times* piece of bragging triumphalism[47] (explaining how he avoided having the Serbians agree and the Kosovo Liberation Army (KLA) refuse to sign an agreement by putting in proposals that he knew the KLA wanted and the Serbs could not possibly accept). He claimed Secretary Albright had been seeking the commitment of Robin Cook, the British Foreign Secretary. Cook explained that his lawyers had told him it was illegal. Albright's reported response was to 'Get More Lawyers'. This made it easy to write about the ethical issues for lawyers advising on the legality of wars (Kosovo and Iraq) without mentioning the 'first lawyer'. It also provided the title. I coyly wrote: 'I have good reason to believe that Rubin is correct to assert that the initial legal advice was unequivocally negative.'[48] The article (reprinted here in Chapter 14) was published in the lead up to the Iraq War, where the legal arguments for the war were even more out of the mainstream. When I followed this up with an article about the Iraq War, I called it 'More and more lawyers: still not judges' (Chapter 15). In this book, I return to the basic question of what lawyers should do. The conclusion has allowed me to reveal the original inspiration for these articles by using the 'Delinquent Client Rule' in which lawyers who are advised that their client intends to engage in a future criminal act are not bound by lawyer–client confidentiality. The title of this essay is: 'Goldsmith's Delinquent Client' (Chapter 16).[49]

As I was no longer running a law school (and, as director of a nationally funded research centre, not formally part of the law faculty), I did not initially think much about how all these developments affected law schools. However, during a visit to the Chinese Academy of the Social Sciences (CASS) to speak and sign a Memorandum of Understanding (MOU) in 1999, the head of law at CASS said that they were planning to open a law school and wondered what my advice would be. After thinking a little, I said that it would teach 'Global Law' – in the form outlined above. I expanded on this topic by an invitation to deliver a keynote at the Association of South East Asian Higher Education Institutions in 2002 and included some of my thoughts to this end in the essay on our respectable revolution (Chapter 6), in which I took the opportunity to look forward as well as back. I used to start with the teaching of law in Bologna in the eleventh century, about the first recorded law lecturer (a monk called Pepo lecturing in Bologna in 1076 AD), and trace developments since then. I now returned to Pepo, emphasizing that his students could go to any court in Europe (at a time when the two meanings of the word 'court' had not been distinguished) to practice. The rise of strong sovereign states turned a cosmopolitan form of law into domesticated law because the only law recognized in any jurisdiction was that accepted by the sovereign. Globalization was reversing this with fundamental changes in law, lawyering and legal education – a topic that provides the focus of the book's final two chapters (Chapters 17 and 18).

Notes

1 I remember Dr Ian Hardingham, a Reader who, on my first day as a staff member at Melbourne's Faculty of Law, offered to explain the 'lore of the faculty'.
2 The reform of decision-making processes to make it easy to do the right thing, hard to do the wrong thing, and easier to catch those who do.
3 Aligning positive and negative incentives with ethical and unethical behaviour.
4 See Charles Sampford, 'Adam Smith's Dinner', in *The Future of Financial Regulation*, ed. Iain G. MacNeil and Justin O'Brien (Oxford: Hart, 2010).
5 Ibid.
6 Charles Sampford, 'Professions without Borders: Global Ethics and the International Rule of Law and Professional Ethics', in *International Rule of Law and Professional Ethics*, ed. Vesselin Popovski (Aldershot: Ashgate, 2014).
7 As Chapter 2 relates, I found more analogies between 'vulgar Marxism' and the form of market triumphalism of the time, which I dubbed 'vulgar capitalism'. But I was not surprised at how popular Fukyama's ideas were: they were music to the ears of those who played the tunes the powerful liked to hear.
8 Charles Sampford, 'Dworkin's Claim to a Socialist Inheritance', *Bulletin of the Australian Society of Legal philosophy,* 16, no. 56 (1991).
9 For discussion and literature on this method, see Chapter 12, Sect. 3.1.
10 I well recall during my first year when one of them sought to embarrass me because of my disinterest in reading some of the class materials. With the repartee of an intervarsity debater and the cruelty that young men exercise against elders whose claims to be their betters are not accepted, I responded: '*mea culpa, mea maxima culpa.* I did not do my reading. But I still thought your lecture was worth attending. Correct me if I am wrong'. He was stunned. He left at the end of the year and I am glad to say he pursued a much happier career as a solicitor in a large public institution – heading off most of the remorse I might have otherwise felt.
11 In that first year, I addressed the set topic in the form of a judgment in the case 'Layman v Lawyer' and began my practice of starting each examination paper with a high minded quote by Sir Edward Coke that 'reason is the life of the law; nay, the common law itself is nothing else but reason', followed by: 'This paper is dedicated to the refutation of that claim.' See, Edwardo Coke, *The First Part of the Institutes of the Laws of England: Commentary Upon Littleton*, 19 Corrected ed., 2 vols., vol. 1 (London: Clarke, Saunders, Bunning, Maxwell, Sweet, Butterworth, Stevens and Sons, Pheney and Richards, 1832), Section 138 at 97. I should hasten to add that I have developed a long-time interest in Coke and his confrontation with James I – not just for his cheeky *Case of Prohibitions*, but for the historical circumstances that allowed him to get away with his actions in that case. His actions helped England on the path to a proto-democracy rather than the absolutist path that an observer of Tudor politics and Stuart ambitions might have predicted.
12 Prof Lachlan Chipman with whom I had developed a strong friendship despite (or possibly because) we were politically so different.
13 I started in October 1979 having spent another six months teaching at Latrobe full-time as well as being Director of Legal Studies at Ormond College, Melbourne and doing work on university policy and governance for Professor Howard, the Melbourne Law Dean.
14 They went on to impressive careers – but not at Melbourne University. Denis Galligan (an Oxford Fellow who was appointed to a tenurable senior lectureship but, when refused a promotion to Reader, went to a chair of the then Deanship at Southampton and then to Oxford as Director of the Centre for Socio-Legal Studies); Joe Santamaria (an Oxford MPhil appointed to a tenurable lectureship who found the law school uncongenial and went to the bar) and Dr Wojciech Sadurski (a legal philosopher from Poland stranded in Australia by the crackdown on Solidarity who was given a

three-year lectureship which was not renewed – leading him to leave for Sydney and eventual promotion to chair). The Legal Historian, Julie Dodds-Streeton was appointed to a contract lectureship and, although eventually promoted to a senior lecturer, left the law school for the bar and reached the Victorian Court of Appeal before switching to the Federal Court.

15 The term used in Tort Law to describe employee behaviour that has so little to do with their jobs that the employer would not ordinarily be liable for it.

16 While Chipman was right that law was neither as rigorous nor as difficult as philosophy, the reason was that it had to provide answers in disputes rather than wait an infinite time for the perfection of reason. Indeed, the authority of courts to cut short such debates was a critical feature of effective legal institutions.

17 Carl von Clausewitz, *On War [Vom Kriege]*, trans. J.J. Graham, Revised ed., 3 vols., vol. 1 (London: Kegan Paul, Trench, Trubner & C., 1918), at 48.

18 Published in the first months of 1989: Charles Sampford, *The Disorder of Law* (Oxford: Basil Blackwell, 1989).

19 Dennis Charles Pearce, Enid Mona Campbell and Don E. Harding, *Australian Law Schools: A Discipline Assessment for the Commonwealth Tertiary Education Commission (the Pearce Report)* (Canberra: Australian Government Publishing Service, 1987).

20 It was initially to be delivered on 30 April but had to be postponed due to the birth of my second child, Joanna, now a lawyer herself – following degrees in law, philosophy and international relations.

21 Charles Sampford and David Wood, '"Theoretical Dimensions" of Legal Education– a Response to the Pearce Report', *Australian Law Journal* (1988).

22 Charles Sampford, 'Law, Institutions and the Public–Private Divide (Keynote Address)', in *Australasian Law Teachers Association Conference, Brisbane* (Brisbane, 1990).

23 Set out in 'Rethinking the Core Curriculum', *Adelaide Law Review* (1989).

24 I admit that I was determined to prove just how wrong the claim that there was no money in it was.

25 Though the risk was still there. After just six years as a legal academic, I had been approached to see if I was interested in a chair in a law school in another state. I consulted my friend and mentor William Twining who told me that I did not want that because I would be made dean. While having no ambitions to a deanship at that time, I asked why that would be so bad. He told me that being dean in an existing law school was just 'housekeeping'. Like all housework, it is important, necessary and undervalued. However, he did tell me that being a Foundation Dean was very different. So right he was.

26 The Hon J.S. Dawkins, MP, *Higher Education: A Policy Statement* (Canberra: Australian Government Publishing Service, 1988).

27 NILEPA was provided with A$150,000 seed funding as part of my 'bride price' (the more substantial one being 25 per cent more funding per student than the next best-funded law school (UNSW)).

28 Sir Ninian Stephen, 'Once and Future Law Schools', *Griffith Law Review* 1 (1992). See Chapter 6.

29 Charles Sampford, 'Starting a Law School from Scratch: The Griffith Experience', *Reporter of the Society of Public Law School Teachers* (1995).

30 The older law schools had been extremely cheap in the 1950s because most of the teaching had been done by part-time practitioners lecturing to very large classes. This made staffing ridiculously cheap. As law schools started to employ more full-time staff (and engage in serious research), they had to fight for every extra member of staff, which was resisted by other faculties. The University of Melbourne had a notoriously difficult time, made worse by the fact that the Faculty of Medicine had made a large number of consultants at teaching hospitals into professors and was able to dominate the professorial

board. The *Pearce Report* noted that Melbourne had the best research record of any Australian law school, that we had just about the worst staff-student ratio and noted limitations of the teaching. I have never forgotten when the Vice Chancellor, a former dean of medicine, came to the faculty and treated the *Pearce Report* as a criticism of the law school rather than of the university and made the false claim that our research record was poor. Law schools in new universities found it easy to argue that they should be funded as well as an arts faculty and should have a good library as well. More generally, universities could choose to put their resources into law (like UNSW and Monash) or philosophy and politics (like Latrobe).

31 An ARC 'Collaborative Research Grant' (now called 'Linkage Grants').

32 Charles Sampford, *Retrospectivity and the Rule of Law* (Oxford: Oxford University Press, 2006).

33 Charles Sampford and Christine Parker, 'Legal Regulation, Ethical Standard-Setting, and Institutional Design', in *Legal Ethics and Legal Practice Contemporary Issues*, ed. Stephen Parker and Charles Sampford. (Oxford: Clarendon, 1995).

34 Ibid. 21.

35 Hans Kelsen, *General Theory of Law and State*, trans. A. Wedberg (Cambridge. Mass.: Cambridge University Press, 1945).

36 I had taught Melbourne's version of this subject. It included a dose of Whiggish legal history involving English constitutional creation myth – that the king was once all powerful and constitutional history involved the reduction of those powers. In fact, feudal monarchs had relatively limited and contingent power – as dependent on their warlords for support as a modern Australian leader is dependent on the factions in his (or, in one case, her) party. However, it did start with my favourite case (*The Case of Prohibitions*), in which Coke just survived the wrath of a king he had just told could not be a judge by cleverly conceding that the king had perfect reason, but that to be an English judge you had to understand the far-from-perfect reason of the common law. I have since written about the 'Coke moment' and the near-run thing it was – as well as a 'Coming Coke moment' in international law in Charles Sampford, 'The "Coming Coke" Moment', in *UN Security Council as Global Legislator*, ed. Vesselin Popovski (London: Routledge, 2014).

37 Hendrik Spruyt, *The Sovereign State and its Competitors* (Princeton, N.J.: Princeton University Press, 1996).

38 Charles Sampford, 'Sovereignty and Intervention', in *Human Rights in Theory and Practice*, ed. T. Campbell and B.M. Leiser (London: Ashgate, 2001).

39 My view has always been that the EU is essentially a federation that is doing things in a different order (they had their civil wars first and their currency later), but is somewhere between the levels of United States federal unity in 1850 and 1870. It is not the model for a new international order, but that does not mean it should not be recognized and praised for the great good that it has done for Europe.

40 The pathology arises because of the creation of standing armies and the elimination of alternative sources of military power as well as the ending of 'legitimacy' in the traditional sense based on descent (or at least argued descent) from the relevant royal family.

41 Charles Sampford, 'Challenges to the Concepts of "Sovereignty" and "Intervention" (Closing Keynote)', in *World Congress on Philosophy of Law and Social Philosophy* (World Trade Centre, New York, 1999).

42 Thomas Hobbes, *Hobbes, Thomas*, trans. J.C.A. Gaskin, 6 ed. (Oxford: Oxford University Press, 1998).

43 So called because of its French, Scottish and American roots and because it was initially only seen as applying to Europe and North America.

44 See discussion in Charles Sampford, 'Legality and Legitimacy: A Dozen Years after Goldstone', in *Responsibility to Protect and Sovereignty*, ed. Charles Sampford and Ramesh Thakur (Farnham: Ashgate, 2013).

45 I claim no prescience in giving this example in a conference held at the World Trade Centre – I was staying in the WTC hotel that had been bombed by bin Laden six years earlier.

46 The key papers formed the basis for a book of essays by that name. See, William Maley, Charles Sampford and Ramesh Thakur, eds, *From Civil Strife to Civil Society: Civil and Military Responsibilities in Disrupted States* (Tokyo: UNU Press, 2003).

47 James Rubin, 'Countdown to a Very Personal War', *Financial Times*, 30 September 2000. The title suggests the hubris (wars are personal when you or someone you care about is a casualty); the content is worse. Rubin took great pride in avoiding what he saw as a catastrophe: that Serbia would sign the Rambouillet accords and the Kosovo Liberation Army would not. He did this by inserting conditions the KLA wanted and to which no sovereign state would agree. As I had already pointed out in my IVR keynote in New York, these clauses were not only completely unreasonable but were not included in the agreements that ended the war – leading to the conclusion that NATO went to war for something they did not and could not achieve. See Sampford, 'Challenges to the Concepts of "Sovereignty" and "Intervention" (Closing Keynote)', later published as Charles Sampford, 'Challenges to the Concepts of "Sovereignty" and "Intervention"', in *Human Rights in Philosophy and Practice*, ed. T. Campbell and B.M. Leiser (Aldershot: Ashgate, 2001).

48 In other discussions with former State Department officials, I discovered that the State Department legal advisors had come up with similar arguments to the Lt Colonel I had met. I should note that Albright remained troubled by the questions of legality and asked at least twice whether she was a war criminal (I was, on each occasion, a member of the group asked). See Charles Sampford, 'Legality and Legitimacy: A Dozen Years after Goldstone', in *Responsibility to Protect and Sovereignty*, ed. Charles Sampford and Ramesh Thakur (Surrey: Ashgate, 2013).

49 These broader interests did not extinguish my interest in coups with a number of articles and a monograph in progress. After strategizing the judicial reversal of the 2000 Fijian coup, I was contacted by a senior advisor to Madeleine Albright, Mort Halperin, who hated coups as much as I did and believed something could be done about it. I was invited to join a task force on Threats to Democracy (essentially by coups and what Mort Halperin called 'auto coups', where a legitimately elected head of government takes over the powers of other institutions). The task force met in various formats during 2001–2002. It was co-chaired by Albright and Bronislaw Geremek. They happily adopted all my suggestions apart from my proposed opening line: 'Democracy can never be given. It must be taken. But once taken other democracies have a perfect right to help a people who have claimed their sovereignty for themselves.' See, Charles Sampford and Margaret Palmer, 'The Theory of Collective Response', in *Protecting Democracy: International Responses*, ed. Morton H. Halperin and Mirna Galic (Lanham, MD: Lexington Books, 2005): Ch. 4.

Part I

Legal education, theory and ethics

2 Law, ethics and institutional reform

Finding philosophy, displacing ideology

Charles Sampford

Introduction

This chapter began as my inaugural lecture as Foundational Dean of Griffith Law School. Before starting to write it, I asked some colleagues what an inaugural lecture should be. One described it as an opportunity to give your considered view of your discipline and where it should be going. Another told me that it was a time when the university invites you to 'profess' – 'it has anointed you as a professor and presents you to the world in the expectation that you will have something useful to say'.

I must say I treated all this with a fairly robust scepticism. I am not, by nature, a hierarch and I am wary of the tendency to listen with greater intent to professors than others. I was very conscious of the fact that I would be asked to speak in public many times a year when I have, at most, a day or two to prepare. I compare this with my position some years earlier when I would have been asked to speak in public two or three times a year, and enjoy around 100 days to prepare.

But I had not changed. The fact that I was a professor merely carried with it the ever-present possibility that I might be wrong for the simple reason that I had less time to contemplate my errors. In my defence, it might be suggested that I could have relied on accumulated wisdom. However, the gradual accretion of considered thoughts is just as likely to lead to intellectual ossification and dogmatic reassertion.

It might be suggested that one continually questions one's own ideas and is continually dissatisfied with their content and expression. All that is true, but I must admit that the longer one goes on subjecting one's ideas to self-criticism and challenge, the less likely those challenges are to succeed – a reason, I suspect, why we remain so ready to subject them to those challenges. Indeed, the elevation to a chair always carries with it the attendant danger of complacency and smugness. Philosophers are under a particular professional disability in this regard. As the stock in trade is argument, there is a professional tendency to stick to positions once taken and to respond to attacks with new sets of arguments. To some extent, it is true that being a philosopher means never having to admit you are wrong!

Having said all that, I took this opportunity to 'profess', not because this moment stood as a key point at which those long-encrusted thoughts would magically transform themselves into wisdom, but because it was a convenient point in an academic life to reflect on what brought me to think as I do and to see where those thoughts are taking me or, to put it another way, to provide a statement of where my thinking has taken me, how I got there, and why.

This makes this chapter something of a personal intellectual journey. It is a thought path along which I have travelled – sometimes running with expectation and assurance, sometimes walking gingerly, and sometimes getting nowhere. Here, I will take you along that thought path – without dwelling on the stumbles, the wrong turns, the dead ends and the occasional lay-bys.

This is, inevitably, a personal journey because knowledge is always perceived from the point of view of a participant. Knowledge is what is known, and knowing is an active pursuit of an individual with a history.

I will explain how I came to believe in the value of applying philosophy to public affairs in general and law in particular. I will indicate some of the areas in which applied philosophy might make a contribution and discuss a few examples of those. In so doing, I will suggest a role for philosophy in assisting the process of reforming Australian institutions – by coordinating legal regulation, ethical standard-setting and institutional design. In particular, I will look at the role of applied philosophy in attempting to resolve what I consider the biggest question currently facing the West. In so doing, I will look at the potential danger of applying philosophy to public affairs – its ready degradation into simplistic ideologies.

1 Learning to apply philosophy

The vortex between law, ethics and politics

Like many of the most fruitful journeys, it was never planned to happen the way it did and I would have been astonished to be told at the beginning that it would end up here.

I was drawn to the kind of applied jurisprudence that lies at the vortex where law, philosophy and politics meet – thinking, writing and teaching about that vortex and this lecture consists of some of the reflections on that process to which I have been drawn.

'Grand theory' – the disorder of law

After completing degrees in politics, philosophy and law, my postgraduate study was concerned with what is generally called 'grand theory' – questions about the nature of law and, in my case, whether law could be better understood as some kind of system or as a disordered set of rules, principles, institutions and persons.[1]

I looked at the various theories of law. Most of them attempted to portray law as a system of rules, principles or institutions. Legal positivists saw law as a system of rules.[2] Legal rules were seen as ordered by a strict and determinate hierarchy of the sources of authority of those rules. Others, like Ronald Dworkin, saw law as a system of consistent and coherent principles ordered according to their meaning so that there was always one right answer to any legal question.[3] Most of the more 'sociological' theories are essentially 'functionalist'. They saw law as a system of institutions like courts, legislatures and correctional agencies. Each member of such institutions performs a role that enables the institution to perform its allotted 'function' within the legal system.[4]

In turn, this meant that the legal system could fulfil its functions within the larger social system (for example, reducing conflict).

It was here that I gained my first insight into jurisprudence and legal theory and one of the most common problems with grand theories. Each of the theories encapsulated one or more important insights about law. It was that insight, the apparent kernel of truth[5] that explained their ongoing appeal. But it was also upon that insight that the entire theory was constructed. Unfortunately, as I discovered with these and so many other theories, that insight is rarely strong enough to bear the weight of the theory that is built upon it. An idea that provides an important insight into one part of the law and answers some questions about it, does not ring true when applied to the rest of the law, or answer a range of other questions.

Consider positivist theories of the legal system.[6] Rules play an important part in the thinking of lawyers and the source from which they appear to come are important. Furthermore, there is generally a clear pecking order among the most commonly used sources (constitution, legislatures, subordinate legislatures, common law etc.). However, the hierarchies are not always clear, and inconvenient rules from higher authorities are subject to being distinguished or interpreted. The hierarchy of sources and the rules that lawyers derive from them are an important part of the law but are insufficient to comprehend it.[7]

Turning to the insights that lie behind Dworkin's system, judges do attempt to make rules consistent and coherent. However, they do not have to do so. It is common for them to bide their time, waiting for some more cases before overturning an inconsistent judgment.

Much the same is true of the insights of functionalist theories. It is true that legal institutions do many of the things that are identified as functions. But they also do the opposite. They can create conflict as well as resolve it; they can reinforce communal norms as well as challenge and upset such norms. Indeed, I argued that it was at least as helpful to see law as unsystematic in the ways claimed by the systems theorists, as it was to say that it was systematic.

The second insight I had was the inadequate way that institutions were treated in contemporary legal and political philosophy. Functionalist theory from both the right and the left treated them as groups of people whose actions were coordinated to achieve designated functions. The only difference was the description of the functions that each was supposed to perform and the non-native judgements that were applied to those functions. In fact, institutions are far more complex organisms made up of people with their own values, goals and agendas, which are, at best, only congruent and at worst in open conflict. Accordingly, institutions frequently achieve the goals set for them and their opposite.

My third insight is a corollary of the second. It is remarkable how often the left and right can make different versions of the same mistake. Although left and right may occasionally appear to be locked into an ideological debate to the death, to carry on a debate requires more shared assumptions than might be appreciated

The thesis was developed and later published under the title *The Disorder of Law*[8] and I was well pleased with its reception among legal philosophers. This is not to say that I won many converts. Most of the existing theorists clung, like true philosophers, to their pre-existing theories. In attacking each one, I naturally had the others on side. But when I came to the conclusion that the errors they were making were common errors – that is, the assumption that law was a systematic phenomenon – I had the level of agreement to be expected.

One thing, however, surprised, intrigued and rather delighted me. When I outlined the theory to members of the profession, they almost always endorsed it whole-heartedly. Their experience had far more resonance with my theory of a disordered set of rules, principles and institutions rather than with an ordered one. As a consequence, solicitors did not see themselves as plugging into a system of rules, principles or institutions to give their clients definitive guidance on the precise meaning and effect of the law. They related better to the role that my theory identified for them – as assisting clients to steer a course that was well clear of areas of uncertainty, away from the institutions of law. As I used to put it, the good solicitor does not so much advise the precise course for the client to steer between Scylla and Charybdis. The best advice is normally to 'sail around Sicily'.[9] It may cost more initially, it may take longer, but clients have a better chance of reaching their destination unbloodied by a costly brush with a legal institution.

When the client is already involved in a dispute or seeks advantage in sailing close to the precise limits of the law, the lawyer will do their best to navigate the course that is most likely to succeed – but with a list of caveats as long as the faces of those who have ignored such caveats and lost. The reason for those caveats is that legal advice does not involve the application of science to a system of rules, principles and institutions. Instead, it requires a keen knowledge of the dynamics of institutions (dynamics that provide opportunities and dangers for clients) and the vagaries of rules and principles (vagaries that produce a storehouse of debating points for either side).

From pure to applied legal philosophy

This endorsement by working professionals gave me great confidence in the general theory I had developed. However, I must say that I did not relish the idea of spending the next 20 years splitting hairs in academic journals on the fine points of general theory. I was far keener to apply the techniques and insights of legal, ethical and political philosophy to some of the challenging issues of the time. By the time I had finished my general theory book *The Disorder of Law* in 1988, there was no shortage of such issues.

One obvious issue, that I had wanted to tackle ever since 1982, was the use of retrospective legislation. This had become topical when the Fraser government moved to recoup the tax avoided in the so-called 'bottom of the harbour' schemes.[10] Legal philosophy even made it into Hansard when one senator distinguished himself by quoting from Lon Fuller's *Morality of Law*.[11] Fuller tells a parable of a king who attempts to make all rules retrospectively and consequently fails to make law. The senator naturally failed to notice a number of the subtleties of Fuller's argument – notably that it was only if *most* of the legislation was retrospective that it would not be law. More importantly he, or his research assistant, failed to pick up on the fact that a few pages after the quoted passage, Fuller insists that none of his arguments against retrospectivity apply to *tax* legislation. Fuller argues that a law that imposes tax on past financial gains (which were tax-free at the time they accrued) is not retroactive because tax laws always operate prospectively; that is, they tell the taxpayer how much tax to pay in the future, albeit that the amount may have been calculated by reference to past transactions.[12] Fuller's simple reason is that taxation laws never tell us what we should have done yesterday. They only ever tell us what tax to pay tomorrow. Despite this rather inauspicious effort by the senator, the potential contribution of legal and ethical philosophy to issues such as this was clear. An examination of the statute books shows a great deal of retrospective rule-making, most of it completely uncontroversial. Judicial development and clarification of the law is always and inevitably retrospective. Rather than condemning retrospective law-making outright, it was worthwhile to ask: What are the objections to retrospective rule-making? What are the justifications? And when must retrospective rule-making be condemned and when can it be justified or even commended?[13] This raises further questions about how the rule of law should be characterized in a legal world that admits of retrospective rule-making.

Many other questions suggested themselves during the 1980s and early 1990s. I list several that have fascinated me, and on which I have worked in the last five years:

- The growing international emphasis on human rights, and Gareth Evans' attempt to introduce a Bill of Rights into Australia, raised questions about the nature of rights, conflicting rights claims and the best measures for their protection.[14]
- The tenth anniversary of Whitlam's sacking raised questions about the alleged contradiction between federalism and responsible government in the Australian Constitution.[15]
- The attempts during the 1980s to codify the conventions of the Australian Constitution raised issues about the nature of constitutional conventions and the best way to make them effective.[16]
- Questions about the legitimate role of the High Court and the nature of judicial interpretation were raised by the controversies surrounding the High Court – including the taxation decisions of the 1970s, their reversal in the 1980s, the

fresh start with Section 92,[17] and the clean slate given to the federal parliament to legislate into domestic law any treaties entered in good faith.

- Coups in Fiji, Thailand, Africa, the Caribbean and the Spanish-speaking countries raised questions about the nature and justification of coups d'état and whether states could be better protected from them.[18]
- The disasters of the 1980s raised questions about the conduct of some businessmen, auditors and – yes, it must be said – some of their legal advisers. How could such conduct be improved and what is the relationship between the duty to one's client and/or shareholders and more general duties?[19]
- Closer to home were questions of legal education raised by the *Pearce Report*.[20] The report had argued that Australian legal education did not pay sufficient attention to the 'critical and theoretical' dimensions of legal education. What were those dimensions and how could they be incorporated into the legal curriculum? More generally, what were the purposes of legal education and how could they be best fulfilled?[21]
- As Australia moves to the second century of federalism, we need to ask the questions we should have asked ourselves at federation. What are the values that should underlie the Constitution?
- More particularly, how do we deal with the manifest injustices we perpetrated upon the original inhabitants of this country?
- How do, and how should, judges decide controversial cases?[22]

The relevance of legal and ethical philosophy to these issues was obvious and I joined or started debates on them even before I had finished my book on general theory. The range and scope of these issues also meant that it was clear that they could not be tackled by one person alone, so a lot of my energies went into helping to establish institutions in which they could be pursued – the Centre for Philosophy and Public Issues at Melbourne; the National Institute for Law, Ethics and Public Affairs; and, of course, the Griffith Law School itself.

However, the way in which legal and ethical philosophy could assist was not immediately clear. One could write articles in academic journals, but it was not obvious how, if at all, this could have a positive effect on the issues that concerned us and those who could make a difference to the problems covered.

One traditional model was rejected out of hand. Philosophers could not expect to descend from their ivory towers and tell politicians, businessmen, even law deans, how to behave and what to do. Plato had suggested that his ideal Republic would be ruled by philosopher kings. This has always had a totally understandable attraction to philosophers. However, its attractiveness to others is unsurprisingly limited – with only rule-by-econometricians being guaranteed a lower popularity.

Nor was it sufficient to take the theories that were the result of philosophical speculation and debate and apply them directly to modern day problems and deduce the correct answer. The theories that philosophers construct are generated from the consideration of simple examples. In philosophy lectures, the standard example of a physical object was a chair; the standard example of a mental event was a pain. I sometimes wondered if the pain was the feeling they had when contemplating the chair they did not have (but that would have spoiled the chair example because it would not have been a physical object). There is good reason for the use of these simple examples. It is far easier to tease out difficult principles when considering simpler cases. But when it comes to applying those principles to the more complex problems that real people face every day, these theories cannot be applied by a simple process of logical deduction. Applying a general principle to a specific fact situation is a creative act – something that legal philosophers come to realize when looking at legal decision-making. Methodologically, applied philosophy is somewhat akin to common-law reasoning. You apply a general principle to the problem at hand. In attempting to apply the principle, greater specificity will be required and different interpretations may lead to different results. Furthermore, the application of the general principles to difficult practical problems may reveal difficulties with the general principle that were not obvious when it was constructed out of a consideration of pains and chairs.

It is for this reason that I have sometimes referred to applied philosophy as the 'common law of the mind'. And it is one of the reasons why lawyers are becoming increasingly important parts of applied philosophy units. Not only is legal regulation a part of the solution to many problems of applied philosophy (most notably in bioethics): the *methodology* is similar to that of legal reasoning.

There is a very important consequence of adopting this methodology for applied philosophy, and it constitutes the next lesson I learned: Applied philosophy does not merely require applied philosophers who are willing to apply their theories to the practical problems with which we are confronted, it also requires the participation of what I call 'reflective practitioners' – people who are used to the complex problems of everyday life, who are keen to reflect upon them and to consider the insights of the philosophers who have had the luxury of quietly considering the issues in general terms.

Thus, if you are to investigate problems of business ethics, it is not sufficient to have some able philosophers who want to 'road-test' their theories in the complex problems of modern business. It is necessary to add business executives, lawyers, criminologists and management theorists. If you are going to investigate problems of protecting societies from coups d'état, you not only need legal and political philosophers but politicians, political scientists, judges, a head of state, and senior members of the military. If you are going to investigate the way that justices of the High Court reason, you not only need theorists of legal reasoning but political scientists, judges and barristers.

What is needed is a dynamic interchange between the engaged academic and the reflective practitioner. Each brings different knowledge, experiences and perspectives to the discussion of the same problem. If each can see that problem from the perspective of the other, each can learn a great deal.

Of course, realizing the need for such interchange does not solve the question of how to achieve it meaningfully. Many philosophers are sceptical of whether businessmen have any ethics and are the first ones to trot out the tired old jokes about business ethics. And many businessmen are even more sceptical of the contribution that can be made by academics. Bringing together such different groups of people is often attempted. Grasping others' perspectives is the difficult part. It would not be too great a generalization to say that if you get them together without alcohol, they all go away angry with the others for not appreciating their point of view. On the other hand, if you do give them plenty of alcohol, they are no more enlightened about the others' point of view but go away thinking that they are all jolly good chaps just the same. Either way nothing is achieved.

Here, I learnt much from Tony Coady from the Melbourne Centre for Philosophy and Public Issues. On his visits to the Maryland Center for Philosophy and Public Affairs, Professor Coady learnt much of how they attempt to address the same problem in workshops. To assist practitioners and academics from a variety of disciplines to understand each other's point of view requires a process. First, all papers are circulated in advance, then commentaries on those papers by those from a different discipline are circulated. At the workshop, papers are not read but discussion is led by the commentator with the intention of identifying issues for debate within the group. After such exchanges, the papers become essays in a book that is informed by genuine interdisciplinary debate.

These kinds of workshops can provide key points of reference in applied philosophy projects. The applied philosophers can road-test their theories and the reflective practitioners can start putting into practice some of the things they have learnt. In some cases, they provide contacts with the relevant business or profession so that a centre or institute like ours can begin direct remedial work with willing patients.

What applied philosophy can do – questions not answers

One thing workshops like these, and applied philosophy in general, does not purport to do is to provide definitive, clear-cut answers. The role of applied philosophy, like philosophy in general, is to help us sort out the questions, define alternatives and then assist us to think through to our own conclusions.

If you get the impression that philosophers seem to be professionally more interested in asking questions than answering them, there is more than a grain of truth in this. This is partly in deference to philosophical tradition. I have never forgotten the time a professor opined to the class that the real test of a philosopher at the end of a four-year degree was not that he could furnish four good answers but that he could pose four good questions. A cynic in the class called Sampford suggested that this was a matter of philosophical job protection. A philosopher who *answers* a philosophical question puts philosophers out of work whereas a philosopher who *poses* a question provides new work for his fellows for years, even centuries. Accordingly, the philosophers who are praised by their colleagues are those who pose juicy questions – and anyone who purports to find an answer is immediately pounced upon by colleagues.

However, my reasons for emphasizing the questions are not because of concerns for the employment of fellow philosophers[23] or even for the employment of our philosophically literate law graduates. I would argue that the most important part of applied philosophy in general, and ethics in particular, lies in asking ourselves basic questions about what we are doing, giving honest answers, and in trying to live by those answers. We must ask the right questions and rid ourselves of misleading assumptions. We must critically assess our proposed answers, ensuring that the answer we propose really does constitute a reply to the question we posed and, if not, find out to what sort of a question the suggested solution would answer. Finally, and perhaps most importantly, applied philosophy can rid us of the unfounded arguments with which some would seek to close off debate on the issues.

This is not to say that we should not ourselves reach conclusions, argue vigorously and act upon those conclusions. But the greatest service that an applied philosopher can perform is to help others identify the key questions and help them work through their own answers.

I will now work through some of the examples cited above.

2 Some examples of applied philosophy

The critical and theoretical dimensions of legal education

My response to the Pearce committee's call for legal education to include 'a critical and theoretical dimension' is set down in Chapter 3. However, there are two points that I wish to emphasize as to how such theoretical work can be included while avoiding the collapse into ideology.

The first point is the idea of exposing students to a range of critical questions about the nature of law and their practice within it and to answers offered by current legal theory. Not every teacher will be a supporter of every theory. The way I suggest that they deal with theories to which they are particularly unsympathetic is to ask themselves this question: what was the key insight into the nature of human beings, social relations, or the laws that govern them that has led so many to adopt it?

This is not a matter of '200 million Leninists can't be wrong'. They were wrong, terribly wrong, at large. But they were right about some things and it is what they were right about that explained their appeal. It might appear that this idea could be expressed by the old cliché of not throwing the baby out with the bathwater. However, we might have little time for the baby. It may have grown into a monster that needs to be destroyed. Even so, we should appreciate that there was an important insight, an apparent kernel of truth, in the rejected theory that could well form a part of the student's own emerging theory.

The second point is that we want students tentatively to choose and cautiously to review the answers that most appeal to them. We should expect them to come out with a range of views. I would regard it as a failure if they all came out thinking like me or, if it were possible, thinking like us.

Business and professional ethics

In each area of ethics that I have discussed – business, legal and public sector – I have asked a number of questions and suggested broadly similar answers.

Although the first thing we do when we are confronted by substandard conduct is to reach for the statute book; this is rarely sufficient by itself. If we just make rules, we quickly find that law by itself cannot produce behavioural change.

By the same token, purely ethical standards only restrict the conduct of lawyers who are already ethical. They impose no effective constraints on the unethical lawyers who are at the root of the problem. Thus, it is commonly argued, ethical standard-setting and legal regulation must be mutually supportive.

However, even the best combination of laws and ethical standards will be defeated by an institutional environment that is not conducive to legal and ethical compliance. To take a legal example, even the best codes and the strongest support for a high ethical culture would be undermined by a reporting system in which fees and billable hours were the sole criterion of advancement and partners did not want to know how they were achieved.

It is for these reasons that I argue that the solution to maintaining and improving the conduct of lawyers lies in a combination of legal regulation, ethical standard-setting, and institutional design.

The key question is how the three can indeed be coordinated. For me, there is a clear answer to this question in all the areas I have looked at. That answer lies in looking at what we might call the *public institutional justification* of the relevant institution or professional activity.[24] This justification provides a positive guide as to what the institution should aim for and achieve, rather than merely advising as to what it should avoid. This justification has three applications. First, the justifying values provide the basis and purpose for the legislation and regulations that govern that institution's creation, existence and conduct. In so doing, it provides a basis for the purposive interpretation of that regulation – that is, the enforceable codes. Second, those values provide the positive guide that should be at the centre of ethics. They set out the positive standards that lawyers should follow and by which they should judge themselves and be judged by their peers. Finally, these values set out a basis for evaluating the structure of the institution – in that they set standards for the criticism and reform of legal and social institutions.

This approach does not give a neat and instant answer – a key part of the process requires that the institution or profession under consideration reconsiders the justification for its existence as a prelude to considering whether it must reform the laws, ethics and institutional arrangements that govern it.

Mabo and claims to compensation

The *Mabo* case[25] determined that there was a long-embedded mistake in Australian law – the assumption that Australia was 'terra nullius' before the arrival of the British, with the long-assumed consequence that indigenous peoples had no title to land. While not giving back anything that had been taken away, the case did determine that that which had not been stolen still belonged to those who continued to exercise rights over it. The way we have responded, and continue to respond to this issue, constitutes some of the most fertile ground for questions about the way we Australians have treated our native population to date, and the way we should treat them in future. For an applied philosopher, there are some weighty issues: What are the principles that can be used when a people have been so cheated and systematically discriminated against? These are not principles of *distributive justice*, principles about how society's goods are divided. They are principles of *corrective justice* – largely uncharted philosophical territory.

Judicial decision-making

This leads us on to another issue that has been raised by *Mabo* and a number of other high-profile cases. The question is often put in terms of whether judges make law or apply law. However, this is clearly the wrong question. The real issue is how can seven judges read the same material, listen to the same arguments, sit in the same courtroom and come to as many as seven different judgments – *and feel compelled to do so.*

This is one of the longest-standing questions in jurisprudence. There are many answers with which we must grapple. But there are two answers that are just not in the running:

- that there is only one right answer and most or all of the judges are wrong; *or*
- that they just make it up as they go along.

3 The big question for Western liberal democracies – where do we go from here?

The largest question applied philosophy will have to tackle is one that faces Western liberal democracies in the wake of the end of the Cold War: Where do we go from here? Or, more to the point: If the West triumphed in the Cold War, why doesn't it feel like we won? The collapse of the Leninist oligarchies in Eastern Europe gave great joy to all lovers of liberty and democracy. But victory has not been sweet for the victors in the Cold War and even less so for those who have been supposedly liberated.

There are two different ways of seeing the clash of ideals that characterized the Cold War. One way is to emphasize the values that Europe discovered in the eighteenth century and were championed by Adam Smith and John Stuart Mill. The whole tide of socialism is seen as a terrible mistake that is now over and we can return to the verities of the eighteenth century, brought up to date by the econometric work of the 1980s.

Naturally enough, my analysis is rather different. The eighteenth century produced some powerful ideas – emphasizing, celebrating and justifying the role of the individual in law, politics and economics. From them, we have received our ideals of human rights, democracy and the potential of markets – ideals we retain to this day and ideals that are worth fighting and dying for (although I am glad that, as an applied philosopher, this view is unlikely to be put to the test for me personally). In economics, they emphasized the potential of markets to increase human wellbeing by allowing individuals to trade to their own advantage. In law, they gave us the idea of the Rule of Law in which laws would be predictable and allow law-abiding individual citizens to know the legal space in which they could play out the game of life. In politics, the stirring words of the American Declaration of Independence still ring clear: 'We hold these truths to be self-evident, that all men are created equal, that they are endowed by their Creator with certain unalienable rights, that among these are Life, Liberty and the pursuit of Happiness'.[26] (They sure don't write preambles like that anymore!) Most important of all, these Enlightenment philosophers gave us the idea that the ultimate justification of society was what it did for the individuals who were part of it.

However, these eighteenth century liberal ideals were subject to sustained attack from several quarters because of the limitations of those ideals. First, markets work well to allocate efficiently where there are large numbers of more or less equal players. However, they can work very inefficiently and with the most profound injustice where the key players are few and the power of the players is disproportionate. Second, individuals may be the point of, the justification for, the *raison d'être*, of human society. But society cannot be described or understood merely in terms of individuals. Western society is a society of organizations. Despite all the rhetoric, we live our lives largely in (and, to a significant extent, through) the organizations where we grow up, work, play and procreate. Organizations dominate virtually every area of social life and simultaneously sustain and infuriate us by providing the best and the worst experiences of our daily lives. The problems and opportunities of modern Western life are provided by organizations. Modern life as we know it is only possible with organizations. There is no point in idealizing about a society of individuals. We must reform our organizations and make them work. Our goal must be to avoid the harm while seizing the benefits that only organizations can provide – of making organizations operate to enhance rather than reduce the life of the individuals they are supposed to serve. This is true of the organizations of government, business, religion and family. Ignoring the existence of organizations can be profoundly unjust – as when some pretend that individuals and organizations can be equal in bargaining power.

Third, concepts of individual rights were framed by eighteenth-century gentlemen like Rousseau, Franklin, Hamilton and Paine. They saw the greatest threat to life, liberty and the pursuit of happiness as coming from the state. For articulate men with more than adequate means, that was the only threat. Accordingly, they conceived of human rights in terms of protection from the interference of the state in the actions of men. Over the past 200 years, political experience has pointed to the different threats to the ability of men and women to fulfil their goals. Such threats could come from other individuals and especially combinations of individuals in corporations, trusts and unions. And, the greatest threat of all lay in an insufficiency of resources to pursue those goals. Such threats were not felt by the proponents of the original rights bills who already had the material resources to pursue their life goals and who had little experience of large-scale non-state organizations. However, appreciation of these threats led men to claim rights to be free from these threats. There remained the traditional view of rights – of space in which to play the game of life. These were usually called 'freedoms', 'liberties' and 'negative rights'. In addition to these traditional rights, there were claims to protection from the stronger players, especially when they played in teams. And finally, there were rights to the equipment, the resources with which to play that game. Under a variety of names – 'economic', 'socio-economic', 'welfare rights' – the importance of these last rights became more widely appreciated. In fact, many saw them as more fundamental than the traditional, essentially negative, rights.

In most Western countries, more liberal and humane capitalism emerged to deal with the objections to, and problems generated by, less complicated forms of earlier capitalism. It had different names – 'liberalism' in America, 'the welfare state' in Europe and Australia – and the differences between parties tended to be on the balance between welfarist ideals and market forces.

This approach held increasing sway until it ran into difficulties in the 1970s – difficulties that could only be described as minor in comparison to the depressions of earlier capitalism and, it cannot be said too strongly, far less than the difficulties we currently face. Nevertheless, some of those opposed to the welfare state developed a superficially forceful diagnosis of, and cure for, those problems. Governments had too much power, a power that public choice theory claimed was exercised by minorities against the interests of the majority. Even when wielded for the best of intentions, government interventions only made things worse because the wrong people were attracted to government and even the best lost their edge when they lacked a direct pecuniary interest. What was needed was a return to a simpler and purer form of capitalism in which virtually all goods and services would be allocated by the market.

In the sense that this view failed to address the objections and problems that had led so many to abandon such theories, it could be called 'primitive' (Galbraith's term),[27] 'infantile' or 'vulgar' capitalism. In preferring the last-mentioned term, I am not merely showing an aesthetic and moral distaste for the particular mixture of intellectual inadequacy and self-interest that characterizes the Anglo Saxon conservative reaction of the 1980s. The term is primarily chosen to highlight the parallels between it and what we used to call 'vulgar Marxism', whose decline has been going on for much longer and is now uncontested, and whose end is more clearly in sight.

Vulgar Marxism was based on a superficial reading of Marx that he would have totally disavowed. Similarly, vulgar capitalism was based on a superficial understanding of Adam Smith and John Stuart Mill, with which they would have been equally horrified. Both vulgarisms made claims to be a science. Both claimed to have discovered laws governing behaviour and the operation of society – vulgar Marxists on the basis of class and economic determinism of the base – vulgar capitalists on the laws of the market. Both views approach the world with a rigid set of assumptions and tend to blame the impurity of the real world when it does not behave as expected. Both find it easy to prove their conclusions within their own frame of reference because all their conclusions are already bound up in their assumptions. The Marxist pseudo-science went so far as to predict the imminent end of history. That has now been outbid by the claim that history has already ended![28]

Both vulgar capitalism and vulgar Marxism tend to compare the idealized version of their own system with the actual and imagined workings of their opponents' systems. Vulgar Marxists were notorious for comparing a highly overblown image of the West as a den of corruption in which money always won out to an ideal socialism, rather than to the grim societies they had produced themselves. Similarly, vulgar capitalists are always talking about how an ideal market is superior to the defects of actual public institutions. Where vulgar Marxists claim that the money power will always win out in the West, vulgar capitalists claim that public choice theory demonstrates that the interests of the majority will be frustrated by minorities. The Marxist ideal did not take into account the problem of the self-interest of those who were supposed to lead others for the benefit of all; vulgar capitalists ignore the influence of private power and ideology on the operation of markets.

Both views talk of democracy but seek to redefine or constrain it in the interests of the powerful groups who benefit from the implementation of their policies. The vulgar Marxists claimed they were true democracies in which all institutions were controlled by the people. However, the people were led by the party who made all relevant decisions. The vulgar capitalists like to claim that the market is 'democratic'. However, it is extremely important to distinguish the voting principles of the 'democratic' market. Instead of one person/one vote, the principle becomes one dollar/one vote. Unless the wealth distribution is extremely egalitarian, the latter is a denial of democracy on virtually any definition of, and justification for, democracy. This approach nevertheless enjoys an obvious attraction for those who possess more than the average number of dollars. Democratic institutions are a permanent threat to such people because the majority will have less than average wealth and income and may attempt to, at least partially, turn their votes into dollars.

Vulgar capitalists even share one of the vulgar Marxists' most criticized mistakes. Marx is often criticized for saying that the economy, which he called 'the base', determined 'the superstructure' of culture and law. This is regarded as nonsense because the economy cannot exist without the law. That is, the existing economy and its means of production are shaped by (even as they in turn help shape) the prevailing legal and ethical conditions. Vulgar capitalists make exactly the same mistake when they try to conceive of the economy separately from the law and complain of the way the law interferes with it. Both treat the economic base as given and prior; both dislike the law. The only difference is that vulgar Marxists dislike the base and blame it for the law, whereas capitalists love the base and blame 'socialists' for engaging in the unnatural act of legislation and passing all those terribly unnatural laws.

Vulgar Marxists and capitalists claim a degree of rigour and coherence and consistency. The dogmatic repetition of simplistic nostrums is consistent but it is neither clever nor sophisticated. It is merely the dogmatic repetition of simplistic nostrums.

Vulgar Marxists and capitalists share even less attractive features. They tend to be brutal, intolerant of dissent, bellicose and adventurist. This reflects another similarity. Vulgar Marxists predicted the withering away of the state, yet ran some of the most repressive and comprehensive states in human history. Vulgar capitalists excoriate the excesses of the state, portraying it as the enemy of liberty and arguing for a minimalist state. Yet, Margaret Thatcher concentrated state power, built up its repressive arms, tried to keep it beyond legal control, and used it more ruthlessly than any of her predecessors. Across the Atlantic, the Reagan administration also built up the state's overt and covert military capacity, attempted to avoid the legal controls that he could not remove, and used it contemptuously, ignoring international law and opinion. Thus, it would be wrong to dismiss either vulgar Marxism or vulgar capitalism as paper tigers on the grounds of their intellectual inadequacy. They both have real teeth and have generated enough supporters with a will to use those teeth.

Vulgar Marxism and vulgar capitalism are intended as examples of, and the latter a prime current manifestation of, ideologies to be displaced rather than philosophies to be discovered. In so doing, I am not intending to make a precise distinction and apply a pejorative to those things that fall on the disapproved side of the distinction. I am using the term as a reminder of how applied philosophy may lose its way and forget its prime purpose.

Philosophy emphasizes the question and analyses the alternative answers. It begins to degenerate into ideology when it presses an answer to the exclusion of everything else. It presses an answer that was carefully constructed in response to one question at one time and in one place to apply to all problems at all times and in all places. In its worst form, it presses the answer in ignorance of the question and to the forceful exclusion of all other answers. We must rediscover philosophy and we must be wary of its ready political degradability into ideology.

What can applied philosophy do?

Let me be more precise about what applied philosophy may do. Clearly we must be wary of claims that it can provide a ready solution to all of life's problems. That is the province of ideology – which philosophy must help to counter. However, in addressing and proposing some answers it can do much. Philosophy can:

- analyse the debate (in a manner similar to the above discussion of vulgar Marxism and capitalism);
- expose the unwarranted assumptions of those engaged in the political and ideological argument;
- note the illegitimate arguments;
- identify inconsistencies;

- identify some of the silly arguments;
- identify the apparent kernel of truth – the key insight that lies behind the long-term popularity of each ideology.

In so doing, it is possible to rescue the original philosophy from the ideology and begin to apply it to practical problems of the day.

Finally, and most fundamentally, philosophy can consider the possible syntheses of the eighteenth-century liberal ideals with the ideals propounded in the nineteenth-century reaction. There is not sufficient time to discuss and give examples of all of these moves. But I will mention a few examples before dwelling on the last.

Unwarranted assumptions

One example of a common and unwarranted assumption in current political discussion is that there is a clear distinction in virtue or efficiency between so-called ‘public’ and so-called ‘private’ enterprise. This has been subjected to much useful criticism from philosophers.[29]

Illegitimate arguments

That there are many illegitimate arguments in the current ideological debate hardly needs restating. Two that are deserving of particular attention are the 1980s catchwords: ‘there is no alternative’ (TINA) and ‘there is no money’.

‘There is no alternative’ – understood as the claim that there is no viable alternative to unregulated capitalism – is, and was, patently false. If you look around the rest of the Western world, it is clear that there are other alternatives. What is more, those alternatives are more successful than the path from which it is claimed there is no alternative. The only meaning that I can give to this common phrase is, ‘I can think of no other alternative’. This is not a statement of resolve and clear-sighted vision but merely of a lack of imagination and information-gathering. It is an admission of narrow-mindedness, ignorance and ideological obsession.

As to the ‘There is no money’ argument, this is put as an empirical statement about what you can do. In fact, it is a statement of priorities. It is perfectly legitimate to argue for priorities in government expenditure or between taxation/government expenditure and low taxation/individual choice. However, these are priorities that have to be argued for, rather than ignored by a claim of impossibility.

Asking embarrassing questions

Sometimes it is fun to turn an argument against those who use it. Most of the time it is just sport, but sometimes there is an important point to be made. Those who believe that everyone acts in their own selfish interests advocate free market policies as the best for the society. However, it is not unreasonable to ask whether those who advocate those policies are themselves pushing self-interest instead of truth – consciously or otherwise. Indeed, if they are not doing so then they would be acting, in their own terms, irrationally. If we are to take their theory seriously, then we must take their suggested prescriptions with extreme scepticism.

There is a potential reply. It is in the self-interests of such pundits to be right, as in the long-term they could be proven wrong. However, we should treat this riposte with care. First, the long-term is obviously *very* long-term. The many years of relative decline by the English-speaking democracies that have followed these policies is certainly long enough for me. Second, when they are proven wrong, as in the case of the float of the dollar, they always argue that the problems were caused by something else. Third, it must be pointed out that there are a lot of short-term advantages of telling people what they want to hear. In a market for ideas, people tend to buy the ideas that suit them and find plenty of eager, even sincere,[30] suppliers.

Identify some of the absurd arguments and concepts

Much of the talk about the market has an extraordinarily anthropomorphic ring to it. We hear of the 'judgement' of the market, the 'discipline' of the market, the view that the market will take. There is a clear reason why this is an attractive form of terminology. Having given up a form of regulation based on an attempt to further rational goals, it is comforting to think of the market as if it were some kind of rational, even if not benign, phenomenon.

However, it is completely contrary to the whole concept of the market that it would take a view. The whole idea of a market is that it is the result of many people taking different views. Where the market operates as a herd following the same view, then it will not work well. Indeed, it is clear that it does sometimes operate that way because opinion leaders affect the views of so many.

The synthesis

Most importantly of all, applied philosophers should attempt to rescue insights on which competing theories are based and build them into a new synthesis. I will not pretend that I can here offer you the synthesis of liberal, economic and social democratic theories underlying the contesting vulgarisms into which the ideas of Smith, Mill and Marx have descended. But I can offer some pointers.

1 We must look to the insights, the apparent kernels of truth, that lie behind the support for vulgar capitalism, vulgar Marxism and other ideologies that press their answers upon us:

- *The liberal ideal:* Human beings have goals, interests, and capacities. It is fulfilling for them to be able to plan their lives. It is good to maximize the range of actions citizens may choose to perform by the specification, elaboration and protection of the widest range of rights and liberties that can be enjoyed by all. This is not only good for the individuals who possess these rights but also for the interests of other citizens and society as a whole (as Mill's classic argument for freedom of speech goes).[31] Most fundamentally, the liberal ideal encapsulates the eighteenth-century realization that the purpose of society should be to serve its citizens, not the other way around.

- *The democratic ideal:* Rules should be made by those who are governed by them and decisions should be made by those who are affected by them. This is not only a right of citizens, it is also a more effective way of governing society and the institutions that comprise it because it mobilizes the ideas and wisdom of its members and generates support for the decisions reached.
- *The market ideal:* The stock of goods is maximized if citizens can exchange what they have for what they want more. The infinite variety of choices (and the diversity of lives that select these choices) can generally be better reflected by the market than detailed planning of production, distribution, exchange and investment.
- *The socialist ideal:* Human beings are social animals descended from social primates. This has both negative and positive dimensions. In negative terms, it is essential that we never were nor could have been individuals outside of society who could even conceivably contract with each other for the kind of society in which we should live, as both Hobbes and Rousseau (in different ways) believed. In positive terms, human beings can only achieve their potential and personal fulfilment through groups.
- *The institutional ideal:* We live our lives by and through institutions that simultaneously threaten individuals but also provide possibilities for the generation of ideas, experiences, effective action and fulfilment that are inconceivable for individuals acting alone.
- *The environmental ideal:* We are a part of our environment, not masters of it to dispose as we will.

2 While recognizing these fine values, we must look to the limitations of those ideals and the conditions of their fulfilment.

3 We may then begin to blend these insights together. Some of the most promising suggestions are as follows:

- *Extension of the concept of human rights:* Identify the key value underlying claims of human rights as the ability of individuals to further their life plans by ensuring that they can engage in activities that support and enrich their lives. This is not a matter of dignifying every claim by anybody to anything as a right. Indeed, it is the opposite, because these kinds of rights will necessarily be limited. This should not be seen as a retreat from rights but a preference for rights that all can enjoy over those rights that only a few can enjoy.[32]

- *Extension of the concept to group rights* but in a novel way: Group rights should not be seen as the rights of groups, which may be used against individuals. Group rights should be seen as flowing from the elementary fact of nature that human beings are social animals and can only be fulfilled through participation in group life. Accordingly, group rights should be seen as rights of individuals to the benefits of participation in group life that are respected and supported by the community. This means that those groups in which people find themselves by birth or traditional association should receive a degree of concern and respect.
- *'Guided markets':* Those as old as I may remember Indonesian President Sukarno's concept of 'guided democracy'. I have always considered that notion to be dangerous humbug and justifiably maligned. However, I have recently come to the view that guided markets make a lot of sense. The idea is that you establish conditions under which there will be vigorous competition within a field so that success is not guaranteed for any player but that a successful provider of a designated product or service will not be undermined by a sudden and major shift in the exchange rate or changed conditions of competition.
- We must look seriously at the interaction between what I call 'the democracy of the vote' and 'the democracy of the dollar': If we believe in the latter (that is, markets), we must be vigilant lest the unequal outcomes of the latter do not unduly intrude into outcomes of the former.

I am not suggesting that all these ideals can be comfortably synthesized. Even less am I suggesting that there is one correct synthesis – though, if I finalize my own construction and it survives my self-criticism, I will be as wedded to mine as anyone else's. But I would urge that the debate should be *between syntheses* rather than between vulgar capitalism and some other applied philosophy stripped for battle as an ideology.

Conclusion

At the end of this journey, I do not profess to give anyone the answers. I am sure that the former professor of philosophy would be pleased that I am at least holding my own in terms of questions asked and answers given; I am doing my bit to keep philosophers in work. But I can summarize the tentative conclusions I have drawn.

- Each theory encapsulates one or more insights into human beings, and/or the social arrangements in which they live. That apparent kernel of truth explains its popularity. But that kernel can rarely bear the burden of the theory which is constructed upon it.
- Legal theory and Western thought in general have inadequately engaged with the significance of institutions.

- The range, breadth and interrelationship of these issues means that they cannot be tackled by one person alone but need an institution.
- Philosophers use simple examples to generate theories that may face difficulties when confronted by real-life problems.
- Applied philosophy requires engaged academics and reflective practitioners.
- Applied philosophy is principally about questions, not about answers.
- The solution to many of the West's current problems requires a combination of legal regulation, ethical reflection and institutional design. Law can only provide part of the answer. We must take the dynamics of institutions far more seriously.

Legal, ethical, and political philosophy can and must assist in this process – not by providing all-pervasive answers but by emphasizing the question and analyzing the alternative answers. However, it is clear that the answers do not lie in simplistic versions of eighteenth-century philosophers. They lie in a synthesis of the insights found in the various theories that have been in constant competition since then.

Applied philosophy degenerates into ideology when it presses an answer to the exclusion of everything else – including, ultimately, the exclusion of the question. It presses an answer that was carefully constructed in response to one question at one time and in one place to apply to all problems at all times and in all places. We must rediscover philosophy and we must be wary of its ready political degradability into ideology.

I would say now, as I said to my students – consider the question, look at the alternatives, choose a tentative working answer on which to act, but be constantly self-critical of the answer adopted. Although I set out to profess, what I profess most earnestly is a wariness of those who profess too much.

I concluded the inaugural lecture by pointing out that what had started as an individual journey became an institutional journey. As such, it was not just my journey any more. Some others became intimately associated with that journey. Others were welcome 'fellow travellers'.

Notes

1 The DPhil thesis was entitled *Law Without Order* and the published book was: Charles Sampford, *The Disorder of Law* (Oxford: Basil Blackwell, 1989).
2 As expounded by Hart, McCormack, Harris and Raz – see ibid. Chapter 3.
3 Ibid. at Chapter 4.
4 Ibid. at Chapter 5.
5 I am not saying that this is a 'truth', a most problematic claim.
6 See above n. 3.
7 It hardly needs saying that rule and source remain, like most concepts in legal philosophy, fiercely contested and highly problematic.
8 Sampford, *The Disorder of Law*.
9 Based on the common reading of the Iliad that places Scylla and Charybdis in or near the Straits of Messina. See, E. Cobham Brewer, *Brewer's Dictionary of Phrase and Fable* (London: Cassell, 1963).

10 *Taxation (Unpaid Company Tax) Assessment Act 1982* (Cth).
11 Senator Crichton-Browne, 19 November 1982, Commonwealth Parliamentary Debates: Senate, vol. 96, 2599.
12 L.L. Fuller, *The Morality of Law*, Revised ed. (New Haven: Yale University Press, 1969): 59.
13 Although these ideas were formed during 1983 and formed the basis of a series of lectures I delivered to my classes, the research on the extent of retrospective rule-making and the final development of the argument was delayed until 1990. See Andrew Palmer and Charles Sampford, 'Retrospective Legislation in Australia: Looking Back at the 1980s', *Federal Law Review* 22 (1993–1994); and 'Judicial Retrospectivity', *Griffith Law Review* 4 (1995). The arguments are developed further in Charles Sampford, *Retrospectivity and the Rule of Law* (Oxford: Oxford University Press, 2006).
14 'The Dimensions of Liberty and Their Protection by Courts', *Law in Context* 4 (1986); and 'The Dimensions of Rights and Their Protection by Statute', in *Law Rights and the Welfare State*, ed. Charles Sampford and D.J. Galligan (Sydney: Croom Helm, 1986).
15 'The Senate and Supply: Some Awkward Questions', *Monash University Law Review* 13 (1987); and 'Responsible Government and the Logic of Federalism', *Public Law* 90 (1990). (Editor's note: this issue was still being debated on the fortieth anniversary of the dismissal – though the measures outlined in the first article to prevent a recurrence are still available to any government.)
16 '"Recognize and Declare" – an Australian Experiment in the Codification of Legal Conventions', *Oxford Journal of Legal Studies* 7 (1987); and Charles Sampford and D.A.R. Wood, 'Codification of Conventions in Australia', *Public Law* (Summer 1987).
17 *Cole v Whitfield* (1988) 165 CLR 360.
18 Charles Sampford, 'Coups D'état and Law', in *Shaping Revolution*, ed. E. Attwooll (Aberdeen: Aberdeen University Press, 1991).
19 Charles Sampford, 'The Future of Business Ethics: Legal Regulation, Ethical Standard-setting and Institutional Design', *Griffith Law Review* 1 (1992); and Charles Sampford and T. Coady, eds, *Law, Ethics and Business* (Sydney: Federation Press, 1993).
20 See Chapters 1, 3 and 5.
21 Charles Sampford and D.A.R. Wood, 'Legal Theory and the Law Curriculum', *Law Institute Journal* 61 (1987); Charles Sampford and David Wood, 'Theoretical Dimensions of Legal Education – a Response to the Pearce Report', *Australian Law Journal* 62 (1988) and 'Legal Theory and Legal Education – the Next Step', *Legal Education Review* 1, no. 1 (1989); Charles Sampford, 'Rethinking the Core Curriculum', *Adelaide Law Review* 12 (1989); and 'Editorial', *Griffith Law Review* 1, no. 1 (1992).
22 The last three issues were addressed in the constitutional theory project funded by the Australian Research Council centred on two books: Charles Sampford and Kim Preston, eds, *Interpreting a Constitution: Theories, Principles and Roles* (Sydney: Federation Press, 1996); Brian Galligan and Charles Sampford, *Rethinking Human Rights* (Annandale: Federation Press, 1997).
23 Nor are they because of adherence to the professional ethics of philosophers – which might amount to the same thing.
24 This is the terminology developed and explained in: Hugh Breakey, Timothy Cadman and Charles Sampford, 'Conceptualizing Personal and Institutional Integrity: The Comprehensive Integrity Framework', *Research in Ethical Issues in Organizations,* 14 (2015).
25 *Mabo v Queensland (No 2)* (1992) 175 CLR 1.
26 www.archives.gov/exhibits/charters/declaration_transcript.html (accessed 4 February 2016).
27 See, John Kenneth Galbraith, 'The Rush to Capitalism', *The New York Review of Books*, 25 October 1990.

28 Francis Fukuyama, 'The End of History', *The National Interest*, Summer 1989. Fukuyama's famous predecessor, Hegel, had already made a similar claim.
29 See discussion of some of those contributions and my own reworking of it in Charles Sampford, 'Law, Institutions and the Public Private Divide', *Federal Law Review* 20 (1991).
30 Though not always. The wealthy tend to pay better for the ideas they like.
31 John Stuart Mill, *On Liberty*, ed. Elizabeth Rapaport (Cambridge: Hackett, 2003).
32 For an example of this approach, see Sampford, 'The Dimensions of Rights and Their Protection by Statute'.

3 'Theoretical dimensions' of legal education

Charles Sampford (with David Wood)

One of the most striking criticisms that the 1987 *Pearce Report* makes of Australian legal education is that it is too 'rule-oriented'.[1] The report calls for greater emphasis on the critical and theoretical dimensions of law, and suggests that in designing their programmes law schools should 'look afresh at the theoretical dimensions of law'.[2] This call by legal academics to legal academics is not made by educational radicals out of the mainstream. The authors of the report recognize that for a long time legal academics have felt that legal education was not just a matter of 'learning the rules'. Most were inclined to follow the late Professor David Derham in characterizing this as a 'trade school'[3] approach to legal education and, as such, inadequate for a university.

What, however, is the problem with legal education? How is it that the general awareness of the importance of the theoretical dimensions has not been translated into legal education? What specifically are the theoretical dimensions of law that must be added, and how are they to be integrated into the legal curriculum?

This chapter concerns itself with these questions, and it starts by stating the problem with legal education as seen by us, and the causes of this problem (Section 1). The suggestion is then made that what is missing in legal education are the teaching of legal theory in its broadest sense, and an awareness of the questions it addresses (Section 2). In Section 3, we then sketch a solution, which sets out one way in which legal theory could be integrated into the undergraduate curriculum. Finally, we answer some objections to this proposal (Section 4).

1 The problem

Most of those who write about legal education, and presumably most law teachers as well, would agree that the aim is to teach the technical legal skills of finding relevant legal texts, and generating from them rule-based arguments of the kind used in courts. Another aim is to teach in detail the rules generated and used by lawyers in semi-arbitrarily defined spheres and to discuss the consistency and coherence of those rules. However, it is generally agreed that legal education should seek to achieve far more. This 'extra' is justified on broadly three grounds: that it is central to a university as opposed to craft-based education; that it is essential for any good legal training; and that law courses include students who will not enter the profession.[4]

On the first ground, it is argued that the 'extra'[5] is what makes law a university 'discipline', and what universities are best equipped to offer prospective lawyers, while also justifying law courses being placed in universities at all. Universities do not and should not seek to provide all of a prospective lawyer's education (and indeed the education is suitable for more persons than lawyers; see below), but only that part which a university approach to a phenomenon such as law can offer. On the second ground, following Llewelyn, it is often argued that knowledge of legal rules and skills is a hopelessly inadequate form of training, leaving the student with no knowledge of the context within which those rules and skills operate and no capacity to criticize them.[6] The best form of training for law is arguably a university education,[7] which should include the 'extra'. In particular, it includes an overview of law that is necessary for the student to conceive of the whole, not only to understand the context of legal practice better but also to enable her or him to choose whether to enter legal practice, the kind of legal practice entered and to understand any change in the context so that compensatory changes in practice can be made. The third ground appears less compelling. It is not obvious why law teachers should change what they teach merely because non-traditional students appear in their classes. Law teachers would not feel the least moved to start a discourse on plumbing just because some plumbers found their way into their jurisprudence classes,[8] nor would they spend time on maxims just because Latin scholars joined the classes on account of their interest in applied Latin. The point is that a broad university-style and university-based legal education, which is the best kind of legal education for lawyers, has attractions for others too. What a university can teach legal practitioners about law and legal institutions to enable them to interact more fruitfully and self-consciously with them is the same thing that universities can teach others to enable them to interact fruitfully and self-consciously with law and legal institutions.

Yet, despite this agreement on the need for something extra, it is a general lament from common room to CTEC (Commonwealth Tertiary Education Commission) that most law teachers seem to end up doing little more than teaching legal rules and technical skills.[9] The most that law teachers seem to add is perhaps some discussion of policy as either a part of received judicial opinion or as unsupported and unauthorized personal moral speculation.[10] In short, despite the best intentions, law teachers end up providing something close to the kind of education for which critical legal scholars damn American law schools.[11] Certainly, that is the perception of many students and it is a cause of trenchant criticism by some (and, unfortunately, praise by others).

How does this happen? Everyone can offer reasons and the following analysis necessarily incorporates much that has been said before. However, the point that needs to be made is that the causes are mutually reinforcing, which may explain why action to counter one cause is so frequently unsuccessful.

There are eight causes that we believe can be identified:

1 uncertainty over what the 'extra' is;
2 lack of teacher contact with developments in the field covered by the 'extra';
3 pressure of time and resources;
4 pressure from available texts;
5 perceived pressure from students;
6 pressure from assessment;
7 perceived pressure from the profession;
8 structure of the curriculum.

First, although the idea that legal education in a university involves a lot more than learning legal rules and developing legal skills is generally accepted, what that 'extra' is remains far from clear. The Deans' Report to CTEC refers to a vast and motley array of factors: 'the philosophical, scientific, economic, commercial, social, political, comparative or cultural dimension' and 'an understanding of the diverse concepts, values, rules and principles which underlie the fabric of the legal system', and 'the critical evaluation of law's suitability to contemporary conditions'.[12] Derham's 'academic principle' for university legal education is very limited, entailing scholarly competence and research by staff, student involvement in university life and the assertion that professional education in a university is based on a fundamental body of scholarly knowledge.[13] Others refer to: questioning what legal institutions are 'good for';[14] inculcation of moral responsibility and moral evaluation of law and the discovery of truth;[15] the self-conscious scrutiny of the bases on which concepts in law are selected;[16] and the uncovering and replacement of the ideology underlying the law school.[17] CTEC refers to the critical and theoretical dimensions of a legal education, but does not explain the concept, while listing a number of matters to which a student should be exposed in the process:[18]

> an understanding of the processes and functions in society of law and legal institutions, to the variety of modes of social control, to the moral and political outlooks embedded in law and conceptions of professional roles, to questions of justice, to the relevance of social, political and moral theories and forces to law, legal institutions and their change and development, and to the information and understanding to be drawn from the social sciences and social science research for the purpose of evaluating law.

It seems that what helps to make an academic discipline is not fixed, unique, determinate, or uncontroversial.[19] Indeed changeability, eclecticism and controversy are probably essential qualities of academic life and the continual questioning about what makes an activity academic is central to its academic nature.[20]

All this is well and good, but when we are faced with a certitude – that professional practice will require a knowledge of rules and the ability to generate those rules using generally recognized techniques – it is easy to defer the discussion of that less certain 'extra'. This approach sheds new light on the oft-remarked and oft-doubted conflict between professional and academic education. It is not really a question of fundamental incompatibility between professional and academic objectives but of a differential certitude about what is involved. It is axiomatic that lawyers have to use legal rules in argument and advice: but which of the many academic concerns about law is necessary for a university education is not so clear.

The second problem is that even where law teachers have a reasonably good idea of what is needed – for example, economic analysis, moral criticism – they may either lack the training or lack the contact with current developments to teach it confidently.

Third, there is the pressure of time and resources. If law teachers are teaching a large subject with few or no tutorials and if there are many important rules and principles that they feel obliged to get across, the uncertainty about what the 'extra' is and their capacity to teach it leads them to relegate the extra to a lower priority – a priority of which they may never manage to avail themselves.

The Deans of the Law Schools in their report to CTEC placed particular emphasis on the lack of resources. They claimed that fostering the reflective, critical and analytical capacity of students and assessing it is far more labour-intensive than teaching and assessing legal rules. They maintained that it is easier to assess 'objective' knowledge of rules but harder to assess understanding of those rules that involves knowing their rationale, history, operation, social context, alternative forms and permanence. Of course, they possess limited resources and this certainly makes it difficult to introduce the seminars, tutorials, and other small group programmes in which discussion and argument over theoretical issues are most fruitful. But the argument that lack of resources debars law teachers from doing this cannot be accepted. Critical issues are raised in lecture groups of some 250 in the arts faculty and are assessed in three-hour exams.

That is why we put it as a combination of, inter alia, uncertainty and resources. If law teachers had a clear idea of what extra they wanted to do and decided that it was central and crucial to any university law course, then they would devote appropriate proportions of resources thereto. Maybe they would teach fewer 'rules' or maybe they would not have to discuss the history, social context, and so on, of every rule, merely enough so that students could learn the relevant analytical skills. Maybe they could have larger lecture groups and more tutorials or otherwise alter their allocation of teaching hours. Maybe they would teach fewer optional subjects. If they had a clear idea of what was necessary, they could hardly justify ignoring it for what they decided was not so necessary.

The fourth pressure lies in the kind of texts and casebooks available.[21] Although the suffix 'and materials' is de rigueur for casebooks, the non-case law additions are limited in quantity and not directed to sustained academic inquiry.[22] This is peculiarly reinforced by the lack of teaching resources, which makes the generation of more relevant material a time-consuming and relatively thankless (and promotion-stifling) job – making it all too easy to slip back to teaching by the book.

The fifth pressure comes from the anticipated and perceived reaction of students. Many lecturers must have experienced the sound of pens dropping and the silent but perceptible click of minds switching off when some theoretical or critical question is raised – and sometimes even a hostility or impatience that time is being 'wasted'. This is partly due to current emphases on vocational training and the vocational choices of students, partly to the limited experience in other subjects of such theoretical and critical questions, thereby resulting in lack of expertise in handling such questions, and also making these appear more marginal[23] – 'not part of a proper law subject'. On the other hand, it is reinforced by the sixth pressure, namely, the form of assessment.

Where most of the assessment consists of problem questions, which merely seek statements of law, any lecture, tutorial or seminar that goes beyond that is bound to be seen as peripheral to the subject. Where essays are added they sometimes do call for theoretical or critical analysis, but such essays are usually optional and separate from a traditional examination. This segregation only serves to emphasize its apparently marginal place.[24]

As seen above, the Deans blame the problems as to assessment on lack of resources. However, this is based on a dubious claim that the testing of legal rules is 'objective' and that assessing the reflective, critical and analytical capacity of students is more difficult and time-consuming. This might be true if law teachers tested rote learning of statements and legal rules by named authorities, but what they test in the standard problem questions set in an examination is the student's skill in presenting legal arguments in respect of legal texts. To see the result of this as 'objective' is to have missed 60 years of jurisprudence. To test what the Deans call the 'understanding' of legal rules is no more difficult – it merely involves assessing the arguments students make for more complex conclusions based on legal texts, set theories and their own theoretical syntheses. The task for the student may be more difficult, but this makes assessment easier because of the inevitably greater spread of performance that more difficult tests produce.

The seventh pressure is provided by the perception that the profession requires that all or most subjects be taught in the traditional way. We emphasize this 'perception' because it is not at all clear that this is what the profession wants or that they would apply any pressure to achieve it. Certainly, we all have had an anecdotal encounter with those members of city law firms who are hostile to academia and complain that the 'products' of our faculties do not merely drop into their law offices and start billing. Yet, there is more than merely anecdotal evidence of contrary attitudes. For example, the Victorian Council of Legal Education strongly urged law schools to reintroduce jurisprudence as a compulsory subject. While not insisting on it as a prerequisite for practice, and while very properly suggesting that it was not their right as professionals to lay down prerequisites for a university law education, they did form a 'strong unanimous opinion' that it should be a 'basic part of a university law course'.[25] In the Melbourne Law Faculty, where professional representatives clearly do have a legitimate role in advocating such arguments, via the professional representative on the faculty, the Bar Council[26] has been much more forceful, arguing in no uncertain terms that jurisprudence or some other subject that discussed the 'nature and functions of law' should be compulsory in any law school.[27]

The eighth and final factor is probably the most important, not only as a cause but also as the source of the remedy, namely, the structure of the curriculum. Although we may all agree that a university education should involve a lot more than legal rules and techniques of argument, the curriculum appears to be structured around the opposite conclusion. The core of the law course appears to be the learning of the rules necessary for the practice of law rather than broader academic pursuits. This is reflected both in the criteria for distinguishing compulsory and optional subjects and in the nature of introductory courses. The curriculum includes compulsory subjects that are required for practice by the profession, but there are rarely compulsory subjects that the law school requires for the completion of a university legal education. This basis for choosing compulsory subjects is explicitly stated in both the current 'aims and objectives' statement of the Melbourne Law Faculty and in most reports that consider the issue – for example, the *Deans' CTEC Report*, the *Pearce Report*,[28] the *Lücke Report to ALEC*[29] and the *ALEC Report* itself.[30] The first document refers to a:

> core of subjects perceived to be needed for the practice of law by professional bodies and a range of optional subjects which reflect the resources, interests, strengths, and judgments of the Faculty.

There is no mention of subjects 'perceived to be necessary for the academic study of law by academic bodies'. The *Deans' Report* also perceives the core requirements in terms of the subjects needed for professional practice with optional subjects covering other areas and subjects that concentrate on the approaches such as jurisprudence, legal history, law and society, law and justice, and so on.[31] The *Pearce Report's* rejection of 'significance to professional practice' as the basis for compulsory subjects is to be applauded, but the doubts therein expressed seem based on the changing needs of practice (see 2.81). Subjects that deal with what is otherwise considered as the vital 'critical and theoretical dimensions' are still discussed in terms of electives. They are, in any case, uncritical of the present approach to core/elective subjects. Of course, it may be argued that there are no subjects necessary to a university education, merely a style of teaching of whatever subjects are chosen. Even if this were true, contrary to our claims below, the placing of subjects necessary for practice as the only compulsory core subjects marginalizes that which is not seen to be necessary for practice,[32] and undermines the theoretical efforts made in individual subjects.

This view of the law course as structured around the necessities of practice is set, reflected and reinforced in the content of most first-year introductory courses. This is certainly true in the case of the legal process course at the University of Melbourne. The core of the casebook, the final examination and the teaching time are devoted to learning formal techniques of legal argument.

Although legal history is taught at the University of Melbourne as part of the legal process course, it is marginalized by being taught at different times, with fewer resources and by being the subject of a separate examination. Some topical or critical issues are raised in the last six to seven weeks, but its lesser importance compared to the bulk of the course is emphasized by the lack of a casebook and the fact that a variety of issues are taught, subtly implying that none of them is necessary.

These eight factors also contribute to the marginalizing of that 'extra' that it is believed should be a necessary addition to the teaching of formal legal rules and techniques. Moreover, the eight factors are all mutually reinforcing. This explains why some of the suggested solutions seem so unsatisfactory.

The introduction of critical or theoretical elements into individual law subjects is frequently despaired of because of all the factors already mentioned. The addition of a single compulsory 'overview' legal theory subject is often criticized as further marginalizing critical and theoretical elements because of its presentation of these elements in a separate subject. This implies that such activities can be confined there. Thus, while partly alleviating the curriculum problem, it may increase all or most of the other problems. Furthermore, a single subject always seems to come at the wrong time. In the first year, students are insufficiently aware of that which is being criticized and theorized (the law), whereas in the final year, students may be too set in their ways seriously to question them. But the real reason why the introduction of a single overview subject is inadequate is that it tackles the problem at conceptually the wrong level. It is not a matter of what individual subjects should be taught, but what law school education as a whole should be like. It is not a question of which subjects should be the core or compulsory subjects or what should be included in all subjects, but of what the curriculum should be structured to reflect. The critical and theoretical extra is too important to be left to one compulsory subject and too extensive to be included in every one.[33]

In any case, the mutual reinforcement of causes means that the problem can only be resolved by measures that seek to tackle all the eight above-mentioned questions. As the problem is one that most of us face, and one that concerns the essential question of what we are doing as a university faculty, such coordinated action is not unreasonable. Such coordinated action is, in fact, called for by the *Pearce Report*.[34]

We would argue that the key to such action is the elucidation of what the 'extra'[35] is and its elevation (or restoration?) to the core of what the law school does by its incorporation within the structure of the curriculum.

If these problems are attended to, the rest may become manageable, 'wither away' or be reversed to become mutually supportive parts of the solution. Once reintroduced into the core of the curriculum, the academic 'extra' is seen as no longer extra but essential. As already indicated, even where resources are limited, law schools still have choices about their allocation, and a perception of a subject as part of a core of a law course is usually sufficient to justify choices in its favour.

If the 'extra' is a central part of the law course, then in the course of time, textbooks are likely to reflect it. Indeed, those that do not may face limited sales. Similarly, the students are less likely to drop their pens in class if they perceive the questions and the theoretical answers as a part of the core of law rather than a lecturer's 'frolic of his own', and law lecturers are unlikely to exclude it from their assessment! The likely professional reaction is canvassed in Section 4 but would be neither strongly nor uniformly negative. Finally, the staff contact with developments in the field covered by the extra is likely to be more extensive if they too see it as essential to their work. Thus, the identification of the 'extra' and its inclusion in the core of the law course can serve to turn these eight factors from 'causes' of the problem to 'supports' for the solution.

2 What is the 'extra'?

The ideal of the traditional, professionally-oriented legal education is perhaps best summed up by the fictional character of Professor Kingsfield, who is larger than life but all too representative of it.[36] He hopes to send out little American boys and girls who 'think like lawyers'.[37] However, the principal aim of a university legal education is for students to 'think about what it is to think like a lawyer'. The distinction is fundamental. Professional training or other forms of apprenticeship in general seek to teach people how to do things by practice in an environment where others are doing them. An academic training seeks to understand a way of doing things as a better preparation for doing them.[38] Academic training must be persistently 'reflexive' and self-conscious in a way that professional training need not be.[39] This involves asking important questions about law and attempting, at least, provisional answers to them. These include questions about the nature and organization of legal propositions, the nature of legal techniques and argument and the institutional context in which this occurs.

(a) Examples of questions about the nature and organization of legal propositions include:

- What is the nature of legal rules, norms, principles, policies, rights, powers and duties and how, if at all, are they structured into legal systems?
- If they are structured into systems, on what basis is this achieved and what are the forces within and without law which make this possible?
- If it is not possible to construct legal systems, what are the forces that frustrate its ordering?
- Is it possible to 'know' a legal rule and, if so, in what sense?
- To what extent and on what basis can legal doctrine be constructed?
- To what extent and on what basis can legal doctrine be compartmentalized?

(b) Examples of questions about the nature of legal techniques, argument and justification include:

- What is the nature of the legal skills we have?

- What is the basis of a good legal argument?
- What is it to think like a lawyer? Is it a distinct or autonomous mode of analysis, especially compared to other modes of analysis? What is the relationship between legal and moral reasoning? Is it possible to derive determinate answers from legal premises? If not, what has to be added to legal premises before a determinate answer is possible?
- How do judges decide cases?
- What is the difference between reinterpretation and reform?
- What is the relationship between moral values and law?

(c) However, the object of academic inquiry is wider than legal rules and techniques. It involves an inquiry into the social phenomena of legal regulation and the institutions in which and through which attempts are made to affect the interaction of others via the use of rules and decision procedures. The academic interest in the nature and use of legal rules is a vital part of that inquiry but only because of the relative importance of rules and rule-based arguments to the operation of those institutions. As these are the institutions in which law graduates typically practice, this kind of academic training is particularly valuable for them. All practice is enhanced by a knowledge of the context in which it operates and the medium through which it is effective. Those who study law without intending to practice have an even more direct interest in such knowledge.

This raises a series of more institutional, sociological and related historical questions such as:

- What is the institutional context in which legal rules and legal skills operate?
- What part do legal rules and skills play in the operation of those institutions? How do they interact and how are they affected by the personnel and practices of those institutions and the external social pressures on those institutions?
- What is the relationship between the historical development of doctrine and the development of certain institutions such as courts and universities?
- What is the relationship between the dynamics of social interaction, the generation of disputes, and the way cases are brought to court? What is the relationship between the conception and characterization of the dispute in the social context in which it arises, and the way in which the dispute is characterized and conceptualized by lawyers, jurors and judges?
- What is the relationship between legal institutions and other political institutions?
- What is the relationship between legal and other social phenomena such as power, economic relationships, gender relationships and ideology? To what extent does law reflect these phenomena? To what extent and in what ways does law help to reproduce them?
- What are the dynamic forces underlying institutional and doctrinal changes?
- Under what circumstances can and/or should legal rules be disobeyed?

- Can legal regulation provide a framework of social integration in increasingly pluralistic and fractured communities? Is it possible to articulate persuasive internal and external grounds for obedience as the forms of law become more varied and expand their regulatory fields? What capacity do legal mechanisms have as viable agencies of social change in the diverse struggles for human well-being and emancipation? How are legal mechanisms and institutions relating to the persistent inequalities of social power and conditions of life?[40]

These questions are not solely philosophical (compare Hunt's criticism of McCormick),[41] nor, as Hunt acknowledges, purely sociological.[42] These questions and the many others that are asked can be compartmentalized along many more and detailed lines, but the basis of such compartmentalization is, itself, an important question of high theory.

The 'extra', in fact, includes the full range of questions that academics have sought to ask about law and legal regulation because they are or should be of interest to those who work within, or are intimately affected by, legal institutions. Such persons include typically and especially, though not exclusively, practicing lawyers. They include all students of law from outside the profession and those who read or commission the research of legal academics.

These questions arise in their general form in jurisprudence and legal theory subjects. They also arise in more particular and limited forms in specific subjects. Thus in particular subjects, such as property or criminal law, we may ask deeper questions such as:

- Can this rule be justified?
- What is the origin of this concept?
- What particular moral values, interests, institutions affect the content of this doctrine?
- What moral values ought to be applied to this area of law?
- What are the proper limits of this kind of law?
- Should this law be changed, defied, obeyed?
- On this issue can we move from legal premises to determinate conclusions? If not, what can or ought to be added to do so?
- What is the relationship between a particular ideology, for example, liberalism, which is either identified or reconstructed, and the content of doctrine (whether as a way of seeing some pattern, or in fact as the key to its disorder)?
- What is the relationship between this area of law and other areas of law?

These are the sorts of questions law teachers are accustomed to asking, or at least wanting to ask about the areas of law they teach and research. They may not always be recognized as 'jurisprudential' or 'theoretical', but as we have seen they are, in truth, merely specific applications of the general questions raised in jurisprudence.

These lists of questions are not exhaustive. Indeed, it is in the nature of academia that the lists are never closed, and that there is no privileged source that can limit the range of questions asked.[43] Naturally, the academic endeavour does not end with the posing of these questions. Even though final and irrefutable answers are almost unknown to academia, answers to the questions are not a matter of idle speculation, uninformed or unanalyzed opinion, or intuitive reaction. In an academic environment, the answers must consist of, or be a part of, a theory. We mean neither to frighten nor impress by using this term. We are not attempting to drive away the dark spirits of 'black letter law' by the magical incantation of 'theory'. By theory, we mean no more than a coordinated series of answers to one or more of these questions – a set of claims, views, statements and/or propositions about law that are coherent and mutually reinforcing,[44] along with a self-conscious methodology and point of view. Such a theory will not answer all questions about law – although that may be the theorist's ultimate aim. It will also involve a relationship with other non-legal theories that the theorist has constructed or adopted to answer other questions about morality, humanity, society, etc.[45]

Academic attempts to answer the questions posed about law are in terms of competitions between, arguments over, and syntheses of, such theories. Thus, if a paper-giver or lecturer wants to ask what interests affect this particular rule, the academic answer is not to think what sorts of people would be affected and how they could influence the legislature. The academic answer uses a theory about the political process that includes claims about the way 'subjective' and/or 'objective' interests are reflected in its outcome. This theory may be 'off the peg'. Or it may be an amalgam of other theories and original insights to answer the question. Better still, the academic may contrast the answers that these theories would give.

Some might be tempted to say that the asking and answering of such questions makes law an 'academic discipline'. However, we resist the temptation because the concept of an 'academic discipline' can profoundly mislead. Discipline and rigour are essentially values for individual academics, not for academic institutions or areas of university teaching. They are the characteristics an individual academic attempts to bring to his or her thought processes. Indeed, it is only the very chaos of conflicting purposes, ideals, paradigms and theories that generates the variety and combinations of ideas from which students and academics can sift those that can fit into their changing, but coherent, synthesis.[46]

It might be objected that this view will still marginalize that which is central to the law course. It could be argued that this treats professional legal practice as given[47] and the questioning as separate – and hence severable during the law course and shreddable afterwards. However, genuinely asking some of the above-mentioned questions and generating the theoretical response to those questions is likely to change legal practice as engaged in by graduates. This might be called a process of reflexive equilibrium (with apologies to John Rawls) – 'reflexive' because asking questions and providing answers about the activity change the activity itself. However, in this case, the conclusions are probably too partial and hopefully too provisional and permanently alterable for an equilibrium to be reached; but this does not detract from the reflexive nature of the process, it merely means that it can, or at least should, be an ongoing process for the practice of graduates.

This view of the 'extra' shares much with the *Pearce Report,* which sees the critical and theoretical dimension covering many of these fields. Where we differ is that we cannot characterize the extra as the 'understanding of' these matters, as if these too could be taught. What we see as necessary is an awareness of the questions, the theoretical alternatives and the creation by students of their own defensible views.[48]

So far, we have been discussing this posing of questions and construction of coordinated answers as something 'extra' to the study of legal rules. It would certainly be an addition to what has been and to a large extent still is the general practice of legal education, but it is not seen by us as an 'optional extra'. Just as an engine, gearbox, steering and wheels might be additions or extras to a car that had none of these, they are no less necessary to the effective functioning of the vehicle.

Indeed, what we have been calling the 'extra' may be seen as more fundamental than that which we are used to teaching. Without the theories that such an education includes, the nature and point of legal rules cannot be established. And those theories may be challenged – including by theories that challenge the nature and point of those rules. Law schools must be prepared to accept that some may legitimately argue as such and may influence graduates to have a different understanding of legal institutions and the arguments within them.

Although we see the legitimacy of such a radical approach, we do not follow it ourselves. We envisage that students will still write down 'rules' in their case summaries, on their lecture pads and debate them in class (of course their understanding of the nature and use of those legal rules may not be so traditional). What is taught in a law school will vary with the theories adopted or used by the teachers. Indeed, what is taught can only be justified by such a theory about law and legal institutions.

3 Structuring theory into the core of the curriculum

Knowing what the 'extra' is deals with only one of those eight factors listed above. The key to dealing with the other factors lies in meeting the eighth problem – by placing legal theory and the questions it seeks to answer in the core of the law course.[49] We would suggest that this can be achieved by taking six interrelated steps.

First, the 'extra' should be introduced into the introductory course. There the questions should be posed, the main theories concisely expounded, and some practice gained in asking and answering such questions. The aim should be to make students 'jurisprudentially literate' rather than to bring forward the traditional mainstream subject of 'jurisprudence'.

Second, teachers of mainstream law subjects should ask, of the areas of law they cover, some of the questions posed in the introductory course and apply some theories to answer them. Obviously, the task of law teachers is made easier by knowing that the students are, at least, jurisprudentially literate in that they can recognize the questions, relate to the questions, and have some of the theoretical apparatus to deal with them. Third, jurisprudence should be retained as a penultimate year law subject in which some general questions and a few theories are dealt with in depth, and in which the relationships between the questions are discussed, and questions about law as a whole are asked.

Fourth, in the final year, advanced subjects' teachers should ask the questions they consider of most importance to their subjects. They will be able to raise these questions with students who will, by then, have a strong grounding in legal theory. Although the range of questions and theories considered in any one subject may be limited, the range covered in the course this way can be very significant.[50]

Fifth, optional jurisprudence or 'theory' subjects should be available to consider some of the more important questions, such as the relationship between law and society, the use of moral philosophy in law, and the justification of criminal law and punishment.[51]

Sixth, the opportunities for theoretical discussion among staff should continue to be fostered.

The posing of the questions, the perceptions of possible theoretical answers, and the personal choice of answers, constitutes a reflexive process that we would hope a university-trained professional would never abandon, and indeed would see as central to his/her professional activity. This reflection can operate at different levels at different times. Sometimes questions are considered in the abstract and general, covering all of law; sometimes questions are considered covering a single subject or a particular part of it. In the former case, a theoretical overview relates the questions together: in the latter case, the pluralism of questioning and theoretical answers is possible given the variety of teachers, subject areas, and points of view involved.

The answers reached in the abstract theory are applied to particular areas of law, and problems with respect to the theories raised by a particular practice are considered at the abstract phase. It is this natural rhythm that a legal education is intended to set up, nurture and reflect. The law course as a whole should express that rhythm.

We shall now turn to a more detailed discussion of the interrelated steps for reintroducing legal theory into the structure of the curriculum.[52]

First year introductory course

Our argument for a place for an essentially jurisprudential component in introductory law subjects is not only based on the view that it is a good place for this core process of posing questions and seeking theoretical answers. It also fits in with a view of what the subject should aim to achieve. This view sees essentially four aims for the subject:

a teaching students the formal techniques of legal reasoning;[53]

b helping students understand the institutions in which these techniques of argument are used (a kind of much-abbreviated legal sociology);[54]

c helping students understand legal history so as to have an idea of how we came to have those institutions and argumentative techniques;

d finally, posing the 'jurisprudential' questions and theoretical answers about those institutions and techniques.

This final aim should involve a fairly exhaustive posing of the questions, and should provide students with the major theories of law, legal reasoning and justice. The theories of law and legal reasoning could include natural law, positivism (Hart), Dworkin, Marx, economic analysis and critical legal studies.[55] The theories of justice could include Nozick, Rawls, and perhaps Miller or Green. Obviously, the lists would vary over time. The aim is, as already indicated, to make the students jurisprudentially literate. Not all of jurisprudence will be taught, but at least students will recognize a theoretical argument when they see one. In addition to abstract theories, there will be a few relatively self-contained problems or issues (preferably for discussion in tutorials) such as the possibility of immoral laws, or an experiment of asking students to place themselves in Rawls' 'original position' to consider its viability.[56]

It goes without saying that the theories in an introductory course should not merely reflect the predilections of the current lecturer in charge. They should reflect the range of questions and theoretical answers that other teachers want to raise and use in their own courses. This is one of those subjects where content has to reflect the interest and desires of the collegiate faculty compared to the individual rights of the subject teachers.[57]

The exact structure, organization and syllabus of such a modified legal-process subject is beyond the scope of this chapter. However, an indication of one possible such structure (which is a variation on the legal-process course, at time of writing, at the University of Melbourne) should be given in order to establish its feasibility. This structure envisages three lectures and one tutorial per week, with tight coordination between lectures and tutorials. Lectures would involve exposition and analysis by the teacher and extensive opportunities for questioning by students. Lectures would 'asterisk' or 'signpost' the issues to be covered by tutorials by stating the issues and some of the arguments that have been raised about them, and directing students to the relevant reading – thus ensuring that students were primed and ready for good quality debate in the tutorials themselves. The four aspects of the course would be taught sequentially in the order indicated above. Students would start with the 'skills' element, involving the formal techniques of legal argument. This would be particularly useful if later year entry were pursued because of the much greater volume of legal material covered in the first year's study of law. There is also the possibility that the first four weeks' tutorials of another subject (such as criminal law) might be devoted to the legal techniques forming part of the legal process – the first few weeks of a traditional law subject do not lend themselves to tutorials, but would certainly lend themselves to more intensive teaching of that part of the course in legal process. This would be administratively quite feasible provided students had the same tutor in both legal process and the other first year subject. For those who were not taking the legal-process course and the other subject at the same time, there would be one or two tutorials that would be given to the legal-process students for the first four weeks and to students of the other subject for the rest of the year. However, despite the additional benefit of such an arrangement, the structure of legal process would not have to depend upon it. Overall, the course would probably be divided along something like the following lines: eight weeks for formal techniques, seven weeks for history, five weeks for institutions, and six weeks for 'jurisprudence and legal theory'. Legal history would only change as much as the current teachers desired, subject only to the reorganization of material into 21 lectures and 7 tutorials rather than the current 26 lectures. The 'institutions' component would probably cover the courts, juries, the judiciary, the profession, regulatory bodies, administrative appeal bodies, lower courts and small claims tribunals. We do not intend to dictate the exact list, some may wish to include parliament, prisons or even a general study of the bureaucracy. However, the essential idea is to cover the kinds of institutions with which lawyers have to deal and to which their lawyering skills would be applied.[58]

Mainstream law subjects

The actual questions asked, the theories used and the extent and way in which the posing of questions and the offering and testing of theoretical answers is incorporated within other subjects, if at all, is up to the subject teachers. This chapter is predicated on the assumption that most law teachers want to teach more than the rules and legal debating techniques.

The solution suggested here is intended to make it easier for those who want to teach that 'extra' to do so.[59] The solution also justifies the range that that 'extra' will contain, without suggesting that the 'extra' is merely a matter of personal predilection or whimsy. The incorporation of legal theory into the structure of the course makes the posing of questions and the offering of theories as answers a natural part of any subject. Teachers can feel more confident of what they are doing and greater opportunities for contact with current theoretical development will improve their perceived capacity to do it. Textbooks are likely to be a problem initially, although the changed perception of law subjects that is likely to result will mean that the market for books with theoretical content will improve and the market for books without theoretical content will be reduced. The likelihood of pressure from students will be reduced. If this is seen as central to the law course, and something with which they have not only been familiarized but will come back to again, then students are less likely to become impatient. Such reaction is only likely if the assessment does not reflect the changes to the subject, but changes to what is assessed are the easiest part of all. Once a lecturer has incorporated something new into his or her course, it would be odd to ignore it when setting examinations on essay topics. If anything, the reverse is likely to be true.

Later year jurisprudence/legal theory

Jurisprudence, or whatever the general legal theory subject is called, would look at the process of posing questions and using theory to answer them. It would look at some of the problems posed in asking questions, such as problems of points of view and ideological assumptions. It would look at the relationship between the various levels of questions, something that would be possible given the students' experience of the general questions in the introductory course and the particular versions of those questions in particular subjects. For instance, if students have considered the impact of particular moral values and/or economic influences on contract law, they could turn this to considering the relationship between moral values, economic influences, political processes and law. This part of a jurisprudence subject would, naturally, be tailored to fit the particular questions that had been asked in the particular subjects. Jurisprudence would also look at the relationship between the various questions – between questions about the nature of law and the nature of adjudication, and whether one theory could do the job of both. Above all, it can focus on questions that apply to the whole of law (such as the relationship between law and other social and normative phenomena), and questions about legal practice.

Other subjects can use theories and test their applicability for discourse within or about law, but to include the general discussion of these issues in particular law subjects may lead to one of two fundamental problems. Either, on the one hand, discussion would be severely limited by time and distorted by the inevitable atypicality of any law subject or, on the other hand, the subjects in which the questions arose would be completely taken over by them. Only in a general subject can these issues be considered in depth and in detail. Only in a general subject that follows the introduction of the questions in the first year and their application to specific areas can these issues be dealt with at a suitable level of sophistication.[60] Only there can the skills of rigorous analysis and questioning of theory be adequately developed, and it is there that students have their best chance to form their own views about the general questions posed by jurisprudence and to frame their own attitudes to law and practice accordingly. In these senses, a general jurisprudence course can integrate the theoretical aspects of the law course and perhaps integrate the law course as a whole. This should not be seen as philosophical or theoretical 'imperialism' by jurisprudence teachers. Jurisprudence is not integrative because of what a jurisprudence teacher teaches, but because of the opportunity it gives to students to develop their own answers.

Other jurisprudential subjects

Most law courses have several other optional theoretical jurisprudence subjects. As the kinds of questions posed and the answers proffered by such theories are seen as more central to the law course, such subjects are likely to increase in number and popularity. The only change to these subjects is likely to be an increase in their theoretical sophistication as the students entering them improve through greater contact with similar analysis in courses on legal process, jurisprudence, and indeed, most or all other subjects.

Theoretical discussion among staff

Although not a part of the formal curriculum, the links between staff by which they become aware of theoretical developments are very supportive of this whole process. Fortunately, such links are (at time of writing) rapidly developing and expanding. Apart from the Victorian and Australian Societies of Legal Philosophy, there are a growing number of seminars and legal theory reading groups. An emphasis on legal theory as an essential part of the law course is likely to accelerate that trend – indeed, the current trend is the result of private acknowledgement of what the current curriculum denies: the centrality of legal theory to the understanding of law.

The analysis and solution outlined here suggest that the problem we often feel is a problem at the level of the law course and must be addressed at that level. Once this is done our problems at the subject level are much more manageable. This is because placing legal theory within the core of the law curriculum simultaneously deals with most of the other seven causes identified in the first section. The 'extra' is identified and its variety and uncertainty explained. The increased importance placed on legal theory will stimulate contact between teachers and the current state of legal theory. Time and resources will still be constrained, but if the posing of questions and the use of theory to answer them are seen as essential to the law course, it means that we can be more confident of including it in our subjects and excluding some areas of the subject that are not so essential. The area of law covered by each law subject, or the detail in which it is covered, may have to be reduced in favour of the greater depth of theoretical analysis that this new approach brings.[61]

Pressure from lack of appropriate texts will not be immediately relieved but pressure for such texts is likely to increase. In the interim, supplementary materials dealing with the theoretical questions and answers will be taken much more seriously by staff, faculty and students. Pressure from students is likely to abate if the theoretical excursions are seen as central to the law course, provided only that it is backed up by appropriate assessment. Our experience, and recent Melbourne University Law Student Society surveys, suggest that students are likely to accept the posing of questions and the theoretical discussion of them in legal process. We would also suggest that students would accept theoretical discussion in traditional subjects because this would be seen as part of what they expect to do in a law school. Furthermore, we believe that students would accept jurisprudence more because it would be seen as the focus of the theoretical part of other subjects. Of course, some will dislike the subject, but they will, in any event, feel less at home in a more theoretical law course. They will presumably have the same resigned attitude to it that many have towards other core subjects. We reject the view[62] that the majority of law students are not good enough to handle such questions and theoretical answers. This amounts to a depressing claim that the majority of law students are unfit for a university education. This not only sits ill with their high entry scores – it also contradicts their ability to handle the same kind of questions and answering in the arts subjects they so frequently take for non-law subjects. The profession is not, we suggest, a serious problem. Certain elements of it are clearly favourable thereto. The traditional subjects can still be taught and only a few subjects have to be added. The profession is likely to be circumspect in criticizing the new techniques as being properly the concern of a law faculty. In the long term, their graduate employees will simply be better and any opposition will die out (see further the discussion below).

A gradualist approach

Note that although we are talking of restoring these questions and the theoretical discussion of them to the core of the law course and in a sense 'integrating' it with doctrinal teaching, we are suggesting very specific changes that do not require an overnight revolution in legal education (although with luck it may well lend weight to a longer-term resolution). It thus avoids the kind of dilemma highlighted by the *Deans' Report to CTEC*[63] – we need integration of deeper analysis and doctrine; that cannot be achieved in all subjects and if it is achieved in a single subject or piecemeal in individual subjects, it is marginalized. The dilemma is largely avoided because the placing of legal theory self-consciously as part of the core of the law course and integrating it directly into its structure directly contradicts such marginalization. The problem of most gradualist approaches, that legal theory will be marginalized until it passes a threshold but that it cannot pass the threshold whilst it is marginalized, is avoided. The threshold is very consciously, deliberately and publicly crossed, making the further spread of theory much easier.

4 Objections

Some might object that this is an ambit claim:

> They can't really mean that we should expand jurisprudence from being one optional subject to include one core subject and an important part of another core subject.

In reply, we would deny that it is either an ambit claim or essentially a claim for jurisprudence. It is not just a claim about jurisprudence or legal theory as narrowly construed. It is a claim about legal education as a whole and how the reintroduction of a particular kind of questioning and theorizing is central to a good legal education. The claims for jurisprudence are merely a part of those wider claims. However, there is always a danger that a broad claim will, even if not seen as an ambit claim, be only partly met as a compromise and partial concession. The above discussion indicates why this is a danger, a lesser approach may still leave at the margin the questioning and theorizing which it is claimed is central to a good legal education still. The danger is that the failure of a half-measure may discredit the whole rather than emphasize the necessity of full measures.

We have not here dealt with the question of whether jurisprudence should be compulsory or not. Although we have quite clear views on it and those views derive directly from this chapter's main argument, we do not want to get bogged down in debate and do not want the debate to be distorted by it. This chapter has examined the question of what a good legal education consists in and has given an unequivocal answer. The next question is whether we are going to require all students to receive a good legal education. If there were no compulsory subjects, we might just advise students that they should do torts, constitutional law, legal process, jurisprudence, and so on. However, we do make decisions on what will be required for a law degree – currently these decisions are based on the sets of rules, concepts, etc., that are supposedly the foundation of legal practice. If the reasons for this are based on what we believe is necessary for a legal education, then the inclusion of other core subjects as compulsory ones is also justified and the refusal to do so perverse. The inclusion of only some of what we consider to be the core would falsely represent that part of the core as less important, less foundational. If the reasons for the current compulsory subjects are, on the other hand, based on what the profession requires for the graduates it takes, this discloses an inappropriate relationship between the university and the profession, a relationship which the profession does not expect and to which it is not entitled.

This leads us to the final objection. Some might deny our view of the profession as relatively benign towards the changes suggested. Our argument is not contingent on such benevolence. We would certainly try to retain the confidence of the profession,[64] arguing that a university-style education is at the core of a good legal education, and that in the twentieth century, the traditional conception of a profession as involving a body of knowledge and skills is no longer adequate. What is needed is a critical questioning and reflexive awareness of that knowledge and skill that is the hallmark of a good university education. In the final analysis, we would point out that it is also part of being a twentieth-century profession to have university accreditation. It is not just a question of the intellectual content of a university-style education, but a question of status too. Hunt has made the point that university law schools and the profession are partly dependent upon each other to maintain their respective status. In a sense, the profession is more dependent on the academy than we are on them. If they require more of students than we do for the law degree, they would either depend on us to teach it (as currently) or provide the teaching themselves. If we did the teaching (as we currently do for summer schools), we would be unaffected and probably richer. If they taught it themselves, they would still have problems. If the extra teaching were limited, then they would either have to make law a very minor diploma course with consequent loss of status, or teach it only to university law graduates, in which case we would be unaffected. Indeed, where bar examinations or separate, Part 2 legal education is required, as in the United

States and United Kingdom, respectively, the standing of law schools is undiminished. It would only be if the extra professionally provided teaching amounted to all that was required for law that we would suffer. However, the cost to the profession of setting up the institutions to provide that education would be enormous and it would take a very long time before those institutions earned the prestige of current law schools. We would only be placed in a difficult position if the profession could not gain support in the funding bodies and/or the university. The *Pearce Report* sees funding as being provided on the assumption that we will be training lawyers to meet the needs of the community[65] – the profession would have the difficult job of arguing that the questioning process proposed did not meet the needs of the community. But, in any case, funding is provided indirectly – via the university. As against that, the profession would have the equally difficult task of arguing that a university-style education was inappropriate for a university. Thus, we can reassure those doubters who believe such changes would bring about opposition from the profession by pointing to our considerable strength if conflict ensued. However, it is our contention that such conflict is unlikely.

There is, nonetheless, a danger if there is division among law schools. If all law schools introduced these kinds of changes simultaneously, or if the lead is taken by relatively secure, high-status university law schools, or if the lead is taken by newer law schools with the explicit and public support and goodwill of other law schools, there is unlikely to be a problem. However, if a newer or lower status law school attempts to introduce this questioning and theorizing (to which in various forms all law schools and their deans pay at the very least lip service, and to which we believe they are most certainly privately committed), but that new law school is criticized for this activity or is divided within itself over the legitimacy of that activity, then those within the profession who prefer a traditional legal education will receive support, and those who respect the decisions of legal institutions about legal education will, at the very least, stay out of the argument or, at worst, believe that there is something in it.

5 Conclusions

There seems to be a widespread feeling among law teachers that although a university legal education should be concerned with more than legal rules and technical legal skills, rules and skills are all we teach. Our analysis suggests eight mutually reinforcing causes of this problem, and explains how they contributed to the neglect of this necessary 'extra' to a proper legal education.

The solution was seen as an identification of the 'extra' and its reintroduction into the core of the curriculum.

In Section 2, we identified the 'extra' as the posing of questions about law and legal regulation and the construction and use of theories as potential answers to them. Questions about the nature and organization of legal propositions, the nature of legal techniques and arguments, and the institutional context of law are posed at the most general level about law as a whole and at more particular levels about specific areas of law. In a university, the answers to such questions should not be a matter of intuitive reaction or uninformed opinion. Rather, it is a matter of theory by which the answers to these questions are coordinated with each other and with answers to broader philosophical, sociological and political questions. The essentially academic skills in the construction and use of theories are among the most important skills a student can gain in a law school and provide the justification for the inclusion of law schools in universities.

In Section 3, we suggested how the 'extra', the development of theories to answer important questions about law, could be introduced into the core of the undergraduate law course. This could be done by introducing this questioning and theorizing in staff discussion and at five different points, namely, in the law curriculum in introductory courses, in mainstream law subjects, in a separate core of subject of jurisprudence (or some other general theoretical subject), in advanced law subjects, and finally in optional advanced jurisprudence subjects.

Finally, in Section 4, we considered some objections to our proposal.

Legal education remains a much debated topic. This has come about largely because of the kinds of problems outlined in Section 1. It has come to involve some searching questioning, and we hope the answers will involve the construction, application and reconstruction of theories about legal education. We suggest that the answers to the questions about legal education should involve an introduction of a similar questioning and theorizing about law into the core of the curriculum. This is not to say that solving the problem, identified in Section 1, should end the debate about legal education any more than the postulation of our own jurisprudential theories before our classes is intended to end the debate there. Much of the answer lies in the continuation of the debates themselves.

Notes

1 The four-volume report of the Committee of Review (Professor Dennis Pearce, Convenor, and Professors Enid Campbell and Don Harding) appointed to inquire into aspects of legal education for the Commonwealth Tertiary Education Commission, CTEC (see the note in (1985) 59 ALJ 589 as to the Committee's mandate). The report, which bears the title, *Australian Law Schools: A Discipline Assessment for the Commonwealth Tertiary Education Commission*, was submitted to the CTEC in March 1987 and made public in May 1987: Dennis Charles Pearce, Enid Mona Campbell and Don E. Harding, *Australian Law Schools: A Discipline Assessment for the Commonwealth Tertiary Education Commission (The Pearce Report)* (Canberra: Australian Government Publishing Service, 1987).

2 Ibid., 2:117. See also, for example, 1:142, 1:143, 2:108, 3:176.

3 Sir David Derham, 'An Overview of Legal Education in Australia', in *Legal Education in Australia: Proceedings of National Conference* (Sydney, 1976): 7, 14.

4 Ibid; Australian Law School Deans, '"Legal Education in Australia": Submission of Australian Law School Deans to the Commonwealth Tertiary Education Commission Assessment Committee for the Discipline of Law (Deans' Report to CTEC)' (Canberra: AGPS, April 1986); Pearce, Campbell and Harding, *The Pearce Report*, 1:146.

5 Although, as will be clear by the end of Section 2, this 'extra', though additional to what is currently taught, is foundational to a good legal education.

6 Pearce, Campbell and Harding, *The Pearce Report*, 1:80.

7 Consequently, there is no real tension between the need for university and professional education. The only conflict is with those who want the university to do what it cannot do well (teach all the rules used in practice and how to use them) instead of what it can and must do well. See Section 4, and ibid.
8 Although we might be tempted to use Anscombe's example of the man pumping poisoned water into the house so as to bring the Kingdom of Heaven on earth to illustrate points about action and its many descriptions: G.E.M. Anscombe, *Intention* (Oxford: Basil Blackwell, 1957): 41.
9 Pearce, Campbell and Harding, *The Pearce Report*, 1:142. For example, Duncan Kennedy, 'Legal Education as Training for Hierarchy', in *The Politics of Law*, ed. David Kairys (London and New York: Pantheon Books, 1982).
10 As Hunt calls it, 'A Question of Personal Taste and Value': Alan Hunt, 'Jurisprudence, Philosophy and Legal Education – against Foundationalism', *Legal Studies* 6 (1986).
11 For example, Kennedy, 'Legal Education as Training for Hierarchy'.
12 Australian Law School Deans, '"Legal Education in Australia": Submission of Australian Law School Deans to the Commonwealth Tertiary Education Commission Assessment Committee for the Discipline of Law' (Deans' Report to CTEC).
13 Derham, 'An Overview of Legal Education in Australia': 14. As will be seen, the questioning of such assertions is, for the authors, a key part of the extra.
14 Don Harding, 'Some Comments on the Role of the Law School and the Goals of the Legal Education Offered', (University of New South Wales, 1986).
15 A.T. Kronman, 'Forward: Legal Scholarship and Moral Education', *Yale Law Journal* 90 (1981).
16 Hunt, 'Against Foundationalism': 301.
17 M.J. Horwitz, 'Are Law Schools 50 Years out of Date?', *UMKC Law Review* 54 (1986).
18 Pearce, Campbell and Harding, *The Pearce Report*, 1:142, 2:08.
19 Ibid., 1:88.
20 For this reason, we are very careful about suggestions that law faculties should have agreed aims and objectives, and about criticism of those who cannot agree. It is in the nature of all institutions that aims and objectives are those that individuals hope can be achieved by or through the institution rather than of the institution itself. In an academic institution, this is particularly and, unlike other institutions, intentionally so. If there is an overall aim of the institution, it is the fostering of debate and the synthesis of individual answers by staff members and students. The most that can be agreed, and on which agreement should be sought, is the structure within which this debate can be furthered (pace ibid., 1:87.)
21 We would like to thank Lindy Jones, Lecturer in Legal Studies, La Trobe University, for raising the importance of this and its interrelationship to the other pressures.
22 Reports of commissions and inquiries are now often included, but these are still very much tied to a discussion of the bare rules, devoid of social, philosophical and textual analysis. They may raise principles, but little more.
23 This creates a dilemma – talk over the heads of the majority to the few who can cope with these, spending a great deal of time on the basics, and generating even more hostility from those who will not learn, or merely prefer to get back to the rules.
24 The suggestion that the appropriate assessment requires more resources has been discussed above.
25 Academic Course Appraisal Committee, 'Report: Legal Knowledge Required for Admission to Practice (McGarvie Report)', (Victoria: Council of Legal Education (COLE), 1982): 2, 41.
26 Through its representative, Peter Cummins.
27 See my remarks on the law lecturers pursuing a 'frolic of their own' in Chapter 1, above.

28 Pearce, Campbell and Harding, *The Pearce Report*, 1:141–142.

29 H. Lücke, 'Alec Committee Report on Core Subjects', (Australian Law Education Council 1982): 5–6; following Derham, 'An Overview of Legal Education in Australia': 16. The Lücke Report seems to equate compulsory subjects with a trade-school approach and optional subjects with an academic approach, but this cannot be accepted. Giving students options to allow some to specialize in particular areas or pick up subjects covering limited areas of law could be justified as providing a mix of graduates to meet a professional need for a range of specialists. The idea of a link between professional training and a basically compulsory curriculum assumes that there is only one type of practice. Similarly, academic disciplines may involve compulsory subjects.

30 Lücke, 'Alec Committee Report on Core Subjects': 2–5.

31 In suggesting that all students should do combined courses the *Pearce Report* may seem to imply an even greater degree of marginalization – out of the law course entirely (see Pearce, Campbell and Harding, *The Pearce Report*, 2:10.

32 It can also be argued that the choice of core subjects can be made on academic principles by asking what areas of law are necessary for a true understanding of the law and its place in society, but this assumes that such an understanding is possible by studying areas of law alone rather than asking the general questions in subjects designed to do so.

33 A third course often advocated is to require the choice of one of several 'perspective' subjects, for example, criminology, jurisprudence, law and contemporary social problems, law and technology, public international law, comparative law and judicial process. Pearce, Campbell and Harding, *The Pearce Report*, 1:112. This approach often includes subjects that merely cover areas of law that are different in some sense (for example, international law) or the theoretical, critical or sociological aspects of individual compulsory subjects (for example, criminology) simultaneously marginalizing those aspects and removing them from the subjects in which they should be taught.

34 Ibid., 2:117. Citing the *Michelman Report* with approval (1:112).

35 Pace the late Professor Kahn-Freund, we do not accept that it is unspecifiable into words (cited by ibid., 1:27).

36 Professor Kingsfield is the law Professor in the novel, film and TV series: *The Paper Chase*.

37 The traditional attitude to anything other than professional habits of thoughts is represented by his characterization of it as 'mush'.

38 We do not deny the obvious truth that a person can be a successful lawyer without having any appreciation of theoretical legal issues. This is just as feasible as a person being a successful artist even though he has no interest in theories of art. That said, awareness of context and larger perspectives can improve particular aspects of professional lawyering, such as adapting to and foreseeing changes to the law, and the capacity to see the law as clients see it. See, for example, Chapter 7, Sect. 8 below.

39 The *Michelman Report* refers to a lifelong critical reflectiveness about legal institutions, the profession and one's own work in the actual and changing conditions of society, law and legal practice (cited Pearce, Campbell and Harding, *The Pearce Report*, 1:112).

40 The last four questions are questions posed by Hunt, 'Against Foundationalism': 100.

41 Ibid.

42 Ibid.: 300.

43 Ibid.

44 Strict logical consistency may only be necessary (and possible) if the theory is couched in the form of a proposition – otherwise something equivalent to Dworkin's 'narrative consistency' is necessary: see Ronald Dworkin, 'No Right Answer?', in *Law, Morality and Society. Essays in Honour of H.L.A. Hart*, ed. P.M.S. Hacker and J. Raz (Oxford: Oxford University Press, 1977): 78.

45 The theory will almost certainly raise more questions. Indeed, any worthwhile legal theory is liable to generate further questions that will outstrip its capacity to find answers. The questions a legal theory must seek to answer are not limited to those the inquirer is aware of before he engages in the enterprise of developing a theory.

46 Thus, although students start by reading and discussing theory, they must, eventually, do theory.

47 Or, as Hunt calls it, 'an object of knowledge': Hunt, 'Against Foundationalism': 299. Hunt was criticizing MacCormick for thereby ignoring ontological questions. It may be queried whether the criticism is justified in relation to MacCormick. When he and Twining wrote about the subject again, they specifically included ontological questions among the questions asked by jurisprudence: Neil MacCormick and William Twining, 'Theory in the Law Curriculum', in *Theory of the Common Law*, ed. William Twining (Oxford: Oxford University Press, 1986). Certainly, we specifically include questions about the nature of law and the sense in which it exists as one of the key questions.

48 The *Michelman Report* comes closer when making reference to 'learning and argument' although, even there, the concept of learning is similarly too traditional.

49 As previously argued, this does not merely involve a single 'overview' or 'jurisprudence' subject nor attempting to broaden the scope of issues raised in class in all subjects. It offers both those things, but together in a package designed to provide both.

50 Indeed, it is only by spreading these theories and questions over several subjects that a sufficient range and depth of theories can be discussed and it is only by asking these questions in particular subjects that students can appreciate the value, or otherwise, of the theories in context.

51 These examples are chosen from those taught at Melbourne University (under the titles, 'Jurisprudence 2A', 'Jurisprudence 2B' and 'Criminal Law 2'). But the list of possibilities is much larger and will inevitably depend on staff cooperation and interest.

52 These ideas were developed more fully and linked to other needs in Charles Sampford, 'Rethinking the Core Curriculum', *Adelaide Law Review* 12 (1989). See also, 'The Griffith Law Curriculum (Appendix 1)', *Griffith Law Review* 1, no. 1 (1992): viii.

53 This includes, though in slightly different perspective, items c, d, e and g from the *McGarvie Report*, cited approvingly in Pearce, Campbell and Harding, *The Pearce Report*, 2.126.

54 This goes beyond the McGarvie recommendations a, b and f. The approach to legislation implicit in this would probably meet the *Pearce Report's* desire for more extensive treatment of the subject.

55 This could be criticized for providing inadequate 'potted' theories. There is a measure of cogency in this criticism. However, 'potted' theories can be very useful.

56 We are indebted to Christine Pederson for this suggestion.

57 There is much to be said for a range of different teachers posing these questions and offering their own views, although this would require extremely tight coordination to provide continuity and intelligibility for those studying such a subject.

58 The resources needed for teaching such a subject would be considerable, but depending on the number of lecture streams and sizes of the tutorials they need not be more extensive than that currently deployed in an under-resourced law school.

59 Certainly, the overall project depends on enough teachers wanting to do so but that is not seen as a problem given the wide interest in legal theory.

60 P.D. White, 'Teaching Philosophy of Law in Law Schools: Some Cautionary Remarks', *Journal of Legal Education* 36 (1986): 566.

61 We hold the view that some of the pressure could be relieved by an increase in the size of lectures in which rules can be expounded and an increase in the number of tutorials where the questioning and theorizing can go on. Lectures could involve essentially exposition – a talking textbook with an opportunity to ask questions of the

author and the delineation and signposting of the issues and possible responses for vigorous debate in tutorials. However, this view is unpopular in some quarters and it is certainly not essential to the approach taken in this chapter.

62 Put by Professor Kingston Braybrooke acting as devil's advocate, based on some depressing experiences he had with the high failure rate of unmotivated students in compulsory jurisprudence.

63 Australian Law School Deans, '"Legal Education in Australia": Submission of Australian Law School Deans to the Commonwealth Tertiary Education Commission Assessment Committee for the Discipline of Law (Deans' Report to CTEC)': 11.

64 See, Chapter 6, Section 1, for the campaign to 'sell' Griffith's curriculum to the profession.

65 Pearce, Campbell and Harding, *The Pearce Report*, 1:56.

4 *Reflection*

Philosophy in legal education – promises and perils

Hugh Breakey and Charles Sampford

Introduction

Since the late 1980s and early 1990s, when the foregoing chapters were first published, much work has been done on the role of philosophy, philosophical methods, and philosophical theory in legal education. Lawyers, teachers of law and philosophers have teased out the details of many aspects of philosophy's role, highlighting the benefits it can bring to a well-rounded legal education, while also alerting us to potential pitfalls.

Most contributions tend to focus on a handful of specific advantages or concerns. This chapter synthesizes this work, aiming to more comprehensively recount the many different ways philosophy can impact upon legal education for good or ill. More importantly, this chapter develops some of the themes in the previous two chapters that have still not been fully incorporated into the latest thinking. In particular, the chapter highlights the question of the substantive convictions that students may (or may not) come to hold as a result of their philosophical learning. In many subjects, it is a routine question to ask 'What do we want students to come out of this course believing and what skills and knowledges do we want students to acquire?' Yet, in reflections on philosophy, this question can fall to the background.[1] There are good reasons why this might occur; in some respects, the most important advantages of doing philosophy lie in learning its skills and methods (such as critical thinking) rather than the substantive theoretical beliefs the student acquires. Indeed, it is through those skills that they can choose the beliefs they will hold. An additional factor for resisting the focus on what beliefs the students should acquire is that teachers might be wary of indoctrinating students into specific theoretical beliefs, as this will stunt the student's own critical capacities.

Yet, not all substantive outcomes are equal. Legal education aims to provide certain benefits and qualities – in particular, those that will make for competent, principled, professional lawyers and legal practitioners.[2] The substantive convictions that a student comes to possess, and the way those convictions are held, impact upon these outcomes. The more that the student's legal education comes to facilitate convictions and understandings that drive their expertise and future professionalism, the more that university education is playing the role that students, professionals and the wider community demands of it.

Definitions

For our purposes here, we need to define a few terms. We take ‘philosophy’ to mean any studies that draw upon and enquire into abstract concepts and principles in a systematic and reasoned way. ‘Philosophical method’ describes the means by which philosophy aims to tackle these enquiries, especially through critical thinking, logical argument and careful conceptual analysis. We will use the term ‘philosophical theory’ to describe any systematic, comprehensive philosophical system aiming to explain or justify large-scale phenomena like law, language or morality.[3] In this way, we might talk about the philosophical theories of Aristotle, Bentham or Dworkin.

So understood, one can do philosophy without directly employing philosophical theories (though we do not doubt that knowing those theories usually empowers you to do it better). Applied ethics provides many examples of philosophy-without-theory. For instance, Peter Singer and Judith Jarvis Thomson both penned seminal articles on specific issues in applied ethics (on charity and abortion, respectively) without employing philosophical theories.[4] Instead, they operated at the level of moral principle; they drew on intuitions about analogous situations to support their advocated principle, and then showed the principle’s logical application to the issue in question. To be sure, large-scale moral theories lurked nearby in both their works (utilitarianism for Singer; rights for Thomson).[5] A reader who accepted their arguments would no doubt have taken the first steps towards agreeing with the philosophers’ larger theories. But the connection here is not necessary, and the arguments can be taken seriously on their own terms.

This possibility impacts on the question of philosophy’s role in legal education. It is possible to teach philosophically without teaching theory – and as we will see in more detail in what follows, it is possible for students to learn from engaging with philosophical theories, even if they do not wind up subscribing to any particular theory.

General desiderata for legal education

At the outset of our enquiry, it is worth sketching several of the main objectives that a university course in law aims to secure. If we are to weigh up the promises and perils of philosophy, then we require some criteria for what the degree course should aim to achieve.[6]

First, and most obviously, *expertise*. A degree course in law should provide the student with the intellectual skills and substantive knowledge to enter (at a beginning-level position) into the legal profession, and to practice law with competence, if not excellence. Naturally, a professional life is characterized by life-long learning, so the university course constitutes only one part (though usually the most intense part) of a larger journey of learning. But the degree should qualify the individual to begin the next phase of that journey, and to equip them with the resources to keep on learning as they progress. This involves at least two core elements:

a A general knowledge of the broad areas of law and their interconnections, to understand the place of their areas of expertise within the law and to know when to call in a colleague to advise on an areas of law relevant to the client but outside their expertise.

b The ability to identify relevant legal materials and how to analyse them in order to assist clients understand the legal effects of contemplated courses of action.

Second, *understanding*. University-level courses differ from other types of higher education by their intellectual depth and rigour. As befits a university education, degree courses in law should impart a deep understanding of the nature of law and legal practice, as well as generic intellectual skills such as critical thinking – a skill that is best learnt in general while being applied in particular cases. These qualities should be instilled in every graduate, but they will be of special value to the many law students who do not intend pursuing a career as a lawyer, as they help situate the law into its wider context, and hence facilitate the application of the learned legal knowledge to other sorts of careers.[7]

Third, *ethics*. The university cannot control the future choices – for good or ill – of its students in their professional life.[8] But it can aim to nourish and facilitate (or at least to avoid actively undermining) the type of values and perspectives that future clients, the wider community, and the legal profession itself, expects of professional lawyers.

Fourth, *meaning*. This last desideratum perhaps stands as the most controversial, but at least some law schools might aim to facilitate (or at least to avoid undermining) the types of values and character that will allow the student to draw meaning and significance from her future professional work as a lawyer. After all, a lawyer who finds her work enriching is likely over the course of their life to be a better lawyer – even if just in the straightforward sense that they are less likely to quit the profession, or suffer from mental breakdowns that can precipitate serious errors of judgment.

While these four criteria interrelate in many ways, they nevertheless remain distinct. For instance, cultivating *understanding* works in several ways to improve *expertise*. But, even if this was not the case (such as in areas of law where expertise alone will always suffice to perform one's professional role), imparting understanding remains an independently legitimate aim for any university degree. Equally though, teaching understanding might in some cases work against the process of instilling knowledge required for expertise, at least in the minimal sense that there are only so many topics that can be covered within a single degree course, and time spent fulfilling one objective must result in less time available for achieving some of the others.

Areas where philosophy can appear in legal education

Philosophy and philosophical method can be employed in myriad different areas within a law degree, sometimes within their own dedicated course, and other times as elements within other courses.[9] These areas include:

- *Jurisprudence*: Teaching legal theory and philosophy of law;[10]
- *Professional legal ethics*: Teaching the profession's required codes and ethical expectations – where this includes discussing the reasons, values and principles underlying and constituting those ethical codes;
- *Applied ethics*: Teaching the ethical issues arising in a particular area of law (such as property law) or pertaining to a specific feature of a system of law (such as the rule-of-law);
- *Doctrinal theorizing*: Cohering together and synthesizing the principles behind particular bodies of law (for example, equity, common law);
- *Conceptual analysis*: The law routinely draws on abstract terms, and often requires a precise and sophisticated rendering of those terms. Conceptual analysis allows a reasoned process of distilling the meaning of problematic terms like 'cause', 'objective', 'consent' and so on.
- *Political theory*: Teaching the theoretical debates about the political-cum-ethical foundations of law and the governance values underlying it.

As this list shows, the wide array of areas where philosophical thinking can enrich formal legal studies offers hope to proposals to integrate such thinking throughout the degree course.[11]

Some of these areas (jurisprudence, political theory) necessitate teaching philosophical theories. Some areas (conceptual analysis, doctrinal theorizing) usually will operate at a less abstract level of discourse, requiring philosophical thinking, but perhaps not full-blown theorizing. Other areas may or may not involve theory: for example, professional legal ethics might be taught through the use of mid-level principles and analogies, or by applying full-blown ethical theories like utilitarianism or Kantian deontology.

1 Teaching philosophy: generic advantages

Any teaching of philosophy – in any of the above-noted domains – promises an array of benefits. In the next section, we will consider some of the promises and perils from teaching philosophical *theories* in particular. This section describes the more 'generic' advantages that can follow from any teaching of philosophy, whether full-blown theorizing, discussion of mid-level ethical principles, conceptual analysis of legal ideas, synthesizing bodies of law, reasoned analogizing from one case to another, and so on.

Studying philosophy promises the following generic benefits

Understanding complex arguments: The core of the philosophical method involves wielding arguments about abstract ideas and principles.[12] This requires understanding logical interrelations, responding constructively to objections, clarifying explicit premises and identifying implicit premises, drawing reasoned comparisons, analyzing concepts, thinking laterally and creatively, dealing charitably with opposing standpoints, and more. While the philosophical method foregrounds such 'critical thinking' skills – often dealing with such skills explicitly and systematically through courses and texts in formal logic, informal logic and critical thinking – the well-honed capacity to develop and communicate well-reasoned, persuasive arguments applies to countless parts of law and professional lawyering.[13]

Reasoned reflection about values: Philosophy enables reasoned reflection and critical thought about issues of morality and personal values, and addresses the types of issues perennially thrown up by argument over these topics.[14] Principles and convictions, whether one's own, or found within the law or professional codes, are shown to be amenable to reasoned consideration.

Challenge uncritical acceptance: By applying reasoned reflection to the law itself, philosophy challenges those who hold an unreflective and unreasoned acceptance of the legal status quo.[15] Mounting this challenge can also serve to undermine implicit assumptions about lawyers' elite and privileged status; the moral status of law and lawyering can no longer be assumed.[16]

Highlight key concerns: Applied to hotspot social issues or legal areas, philosophical investigation reveals the types of ethical concerns different individuals perceive as important.[17] Such learning ensures that the student does not have any moral 'blind-spots', where they are simply unaware of the morally charged elements of a legal or policy controversy.

Inform personal decision-making: Upon completing their degree, law students face a major life-choice about whether or not to pursue a career in law and, if so, what areas of law to build a career in. The capacity for reasoned reflection about their own values, and an awareness of the social importance of law and lawyering, allows the student to make a more informed choice on such matters, connecting their own values to the type of career they wish to achieve.[18]

Historical awareness: The study of philosophy in application to morality and law often interweaves with the study of history. Philosophical theories and arguments are developed and popularized at different historical moments; awareness of this process can help students appreciate the role that philosophical arguments and concepts played in creating our present law, and also in understanding how ostensibly modern debates can rehearse well-trammelled legal–philosophical ground.[19]

Conceptual clarity: The law deals with abstract concepts (like 'event', 'cause', 'objective' and 'reasonable') as a matter of course. Philosophy can illustrate how to clearly form and wield such concepts.[20] This includes furnishing an awareness of definitional complexities, the problems of 'talking past' others, understanding that popular concepts can sometimes be muddled and confused – and at other times can betray considerable sophistication.[21]

Wonder and curiosity: Philosophical thought reveals that everyday matters prove more complex, sophisticated and interesting than most people tend to suspect. While at first this can seem intimidating, when combined with the reflective and critical tools to engage with these complexities, this realization can engender a sense of wonder and intellectual curiosity about one's world and one's practices within it. Rather than being repelled or defensive when faced with complexity, these traits can encourage a welcoming of intellectual and conceptual challenges, and so facilitate a lively interest that can constitute part of a lawyer's 'professional equipment'.[22]

Stepping-stone to theory: While the foregoing benefits apply whether or not the student confronts full-blown philosophical theories, they nevertheless serve to open the intellectual door to such theories. A student well-versed in critical thinking, reasoned reflection, conceptual analysis and applied ethical arguments will find herself well-placed to engage with the more comprehensive and abstract philosophical theories of law and ethics.

2 Teaching philosophical *theory*: advantages and perils

As aforementioned, the benefits of philosophy enumerated in the foregoing section can arise without introducing students to full-blown philosophical theories (though of course such benefits also arise from learning theory). Yet, there are certain advantages that derive from being introduced to large-scale, systematic philosophical theories of law or ethics. As well, however, potential pitfalls lurk within the realms of philosophical theory. Many of these promises and perils apply regardless of the specific substantive convictions that the student actually takes away from the course. This section will discuss such promises and perils – that is, those that apply *without taking into account* the specific substance and nature of the student's convictions on the philosophical theories in question. (The following section deals with that specific, and often unexamined, issue.)

Potential advantages of teaching theory

The advantages of teaching law students philosophical theories of law or ethics include:

Enriched understanding of law: Theories of law and ethics aim to synthesize specific laws and areas of law together, explaining their deeper workings and justifications. While this enriched understanding can be valued in its own right (the desideratum of *Understanding* from the first section), it can also feed into improving the practice of law (*Expertise*) in several ways. Philosophical theories can help in working out problem cases where the law or precedent do not provide definitive answers, in hypothesizing about likely future directions of law, in evaluating how issues of justice might impact upon judicial decision-making, in fashioning and evaluating proposed legal reforms, and so on.[23] In a nutshell, the world of ideas impacts upon the real world – this is after all how most progress happens – and understanding philosophical theory helps us predict how this process might impact on current law.

Systematic reflection on values: Understanding theory helps students reflect at a deeper level. They can move past the application of mid-level principles (say, of procedural justice or rule-of-law) to reflect on what justifies those principles and how they interact, cohere or exist in tension with other principles. Such deep reflection empowers the student to be comfortable in areas where definitive answers prove unavailable, and to be able to defend their position in a well-reasoned way when exposed to theory-based criticisms from one side or another.[24]

Autonomous position: Providing students with the tools of critical thinking, and offering them an array of theoretical alternatives to consider, empowers the students to come up with their own intellectual standpoint based on their own reasoned decision-making. In the next section, we will consider the content of some of these standpoints, but irrespective of their specific substance, the mere fact that the student has come to their own, well-reasoned standpoint may enhance both their likelihood of displaying professional integrity in future, and of finding meaning in their own careers in lawyering.[25] In short, they have a moral and philosophical position they can justifiably call their own, and with which they identify.

Avoiding the dangers of no theory: One further reason for teaching theory is that avoiding teaching theory can actually amount to teaching one particular theory, or at least a perspective based around, and inclining towards, one particular theory. In this context, Zerilli quotes John Maynard Keynes:[26]

> The ideas of economists and political philosophers, both when they are right and when they are wrong, are more powerful than is commonly understood. Indeed, the world is ruled by little else. Practical men, who believe themselves to be quite exempt from any intellectual influences, are usually the slaves of some defunct economist.

Arguably, there might be contexts where Keynes' claim overplays the impact of theoretical ideas.[27] But in *law*, itself an intellectual construct, undeniably influenced by past and present philosophies, Keynes' point finds its mark. To teach or practice law without any attention to theories of law or morality is itself to implicitly assume the correctness of certain theoretical perspectives on law, whether or not one knows about them.

This implicit inculcation invites several potential concerns. First, there is the matter of the content of the legal theory lurking in the background. As Zerilli goes on to argue: 'The true nature of law is apt to be obscured by its presentation as an independent, self-sufficient, self-referential body of knowledge.'[28] Many writers have argued that to teach black letter doctrine devoid of moral and other context amounts to assuming the truth of a version of legal positivism.[29] We consider in the following section how this result might impact upon the behaviour of practicing legal professionals. For now, the point is that any weaknesses in the underlying theory will be weaknesses in the understanding of law that the student possesses. Second, there is the problem of believing one is atheoretical when one is not. A practitioner's professed atheoretical stance can mean they fail to see that serious objections and concerns can be raised against their particular perspective – because they do not admit that they have, or are at least heavily influenced by, a theoretical perspective. Third, in teaching theory, law schools rightly may be wary of indoctrinating – or of appearing to indoctrinate – their students. But because the failure to teach theory often amounts to teaching a bowdlerized version of legal positivism, the possibility of indoctrination arises here as well – just as much economics (and economic theories of law) rely on bowdlerized versions of Friedman. Indeed, as Keynes' above reference to 'slaves' implies, the indoctrination concerns in this case prove more serious again. By occurring without any explicit admission, or without portraying alternatives or techniques of rational criticism, students are not well-placed to develop their own autonomous position. Teaching no theory allows indoctrination to occur beneath students' conscious and critical awareness.[30]

Summing up this concern, both the reigning contemporary methods of *teaching* law,[31] and the current predominating professional modes of *practicing* law,[32] imply and foreground quite particular theories about the nature of law, admittedly in an unreflective state. Eschewing teaching legal theory threatens to entrench – in an amorphous and implicit form – one particular philosophical theory of law.

Potential disadvantages of teaching theory

Just as teaching theory possesses benefits irrespective of the student's ultimate theoretical convictions, so too it encounters pitfalls. Such pitfalls must be taken seriously, for it may be that philosophical theory taught poorly, or unreflectively, would foment more trouble than it is worth.

Three main dangers loom here:[33]

Unhelpful abstraction: Unsurprisingly, the most commonly noted problems invited by philosophical theories lie in their level of abstraction, and their resulting inability to connect to real-world issues. There are several ways such abstraction can unhelpfully make its presence felt.[34] First, the theories may be so abstract that students struggle to see their connection to the real world.[35] The theories fail to provide illumination on concrete areas of law and legal ethics.

Second, while teaching philosophical theories can help encourage a historical awareness (as noted above), theorizing can also encourage a 'rough and rigorous logic'[36] that downplays the messy contingent factors – social, economic, religious, even military – that help explain the nature and substance of law. Shorn of history, students can also fail to realize that other generations also had their favoured and fashionable philosophical theories, and that future generations may well view our own philosophies with the same patient indulgence we grant our forebears.

Third, the applied instances the theory explores may differ from the ones that professionals usually encounter. Theories can tend to focus on exciting and high-profile ethical controversies rather than everyday professional dilemmas.[37]

A final possibility of over-abstraction emerges even if the theories are employed in commonplace professional contexts. Here, the problem may be that the description of the situation is too sanitized. Real-world ethical issues often arise in subtle and unforeseen ways, often demanding immediate attention in cases where the ethics poses obstacles to professional goals the lawyer has already been aggressively and inventively pursuing, and that attach directly to the client's interests. Though students may be capable of applying ethical thinking to obvious cases detached from their own goals, they may struggle to employ the same sensitivity where their professional goals are at stake.[38]

Indoctrination: Law students engaging with political theories in courses on legitimacy and justice, or legal theories in courses on jurisprudence, face the possibility of indoctrination into one particular theory or theoretical perspective.[39] Two dangers emerge on this footing. The first danger is that the students really are being indoctrinated; their teacher genuinely holds a particular theoretical position and intends – consciously or unconsciously, forthrightly or implicitly – to convert his students to that position. The choice of materials, the alternative theoretical positions offered, the nature of the presentation and (perhaps most tellingly) the marking of student essays, all press towards acceptance of the one 'true' answer. Sometimes, students can be so busy learning abstruse theoretical terminology that they can forget to ask questions about whether the theory is true or insightful.[40]

The second danger is that, even if the students are not being indoctrinated, for one reason or another they feel that they are being manipulated.[41]

Debilitating doubts: While we will consider ultimate positions like nihilism and relativism in the following sections, it bears mention here that philosophical scrutiny may call into question long-held values. Of course, if these values were themselves problematic (elitist or authoritarian, for example) then such questioning is welcome. But critical questions might start to erode students' positive ideals about the legal profession – perhaps based upon stories and role-models, rather than reasoning and theories.

As Jonathan Crowe stresses, however, often the types of problems sketched above do not derive from teaching philosophical theory per se, but rather derive from teaching it in a poor way.[42] Concerns about indoctrination often stem from students either not being presented with an array of alternatives to consider, or of not being equipped with the tools of critical thinking that empower them to engage reflectively with the theories confronting them. So too, philosophical investigation need not undermine students' positive views of the law and justice; at least some theories are bound to endorse the students' core concerns, and this study may open the way to further, deeper reflection in time. While philosophical abstraction remains an enduring concern, the students' critical reflective capabilities, along with improved teaching methods, can help bridge the gap between theory and action.[43] For its part, the 'ethics boom' has propelled far more literature on practical, applied ethics than was previously available, further reducing the problems of abstractness by systematically exploring the connections between abstract theory and concrete, real-world dilemmas.[44]

Teaching theory as inoculation for theory

Surprisingly, one final reason for teaching theory follows from attending to theory's potential perils. We have seen (and will continue to see in the next section) that philosophical theories can precipitate serious problems. At first, this can seem like a good reason to *avoid* teaching any sort of theory. But, as we noted above, teaching no theory can amount to teaching – or at least encouraging – a specific sort of legal theory, raising the possibility that the student is indoctrinated into a dogma beneath their conscious awareness.[45]

However, two other possibilities bear mention, both arising in the situation where the student is exposed to philosophical theory *from some other quarter*, either in their student years or their professional life. The first possibility occurs when the theory challenges the individual's beliefs and professional values. In such a case, the individual may wish (in a rational and informed manner) to defend herself and her position against the critique. However, without the tools of critical argument, and with no expertise in applying these tools to large-scale, complex theories, she may not possess the erudition to make an effective response – or even to rationally reflect on whether the criticism carries a genuine point. By not teaching theory, the student is left vulnerable *to* theory.

The second possibility arises when the student eventually encounters a theory for the first time, and is seduced by it. The well-crafted university course can expose the student to philosophical theories while concurrently providing the critical tools to evaluate the theories' arguments, and ensure that the student considers an array of theoretical alternatives. Outside of this carefully crafted crucible, the threat rears that the student will be exposed to a single theory that styles itself as *the* theory, confidently assuring the student that rival theories can be disdainfully ignored.[46] Enamoured of this theory, and without the critical skills and awareness of alternatives to appraise it, the student cannot come to an informed, autonomous position. Instead, she stumbles into an unreflective dogmatism.[47]

This can result in 'I have read a book' theorists. During the 1980s, most legal academics were trained in law and rarely studied other disciplines to undergraduate level – and even more rarely to honours or postgraduate levels. Those who were dissatisfied with the way law was taught sought insights elsewhere and often became enamoured of one or two books or articles. While this was very exciting for those concerned, it meant that knowledge of the theoretical tradition in which the book was written was a narrow and distorted view of that tradition – one that did not consider its limitations, variations and counter-arguments. Its application to law often would be done without the subtleties of the theorist who wrote the book (let alone those with whom the author was engaged). The legal academic who had 'read the book' could stumble into making too much or too little of the theoretical possibilities opened by the theory or philosophical tradition into which the book was a limited and distorted perspective.

Another version of this problem is the 'I have read a book about a book' theorist. It used to be extremely common for students in jurisprudence to learn of theories second-hand – sometimes through the descriptions of theories by critics of those theories. This was particularly true of legal positivism and 'liberal theories' whose supposed proponents would scarcely recognize their own theories in the descriptions taught to law students.

As a result, again, by not teaching theory, the student is left vulnerable *to* theory.

3 Substantive theoretical convictions: promises and perils

The foregoing section outlined the promises and perils that arise from any teaching of philosophical theories – irrespective of what substantive positions the student ultimately takes up. But what remains to be said about those substantive positions themselves? Are there some philosophical viewpoints that could degrade the student's understanding of law and their ability to practice it competently? Or are there certain standpoints that would even undermine the student's capacity to find meaning within her chosen career – or to practice it according to the full professional ethos?

The spectrum of students' ultimate epistemic positions

After completing any course that exposes the student to a variety of opposing philosophical theories, and equips them with the critical tools to interrogate and evaluate those theories, the engaged student might arrive at an array of different positions. We provide a rough map of these positions here, ranked on the dimension of the student's certitude in a given theory: how much the student thinks that one theory, several theories or theorizing in general, has something to offer.

1 *Nihilism* about reason: the student not only rejects all the proffered theories, but despairs about the prospects of all rational reflection.
2 *Scepticism*: the student doubts that any philosophical theory could ever adequately explain the world's complex, diverse and hard-nosed realities. However, the student acknowledges that various theories provide illuminating perspectives about aspects of law and ethics.
3 *Fallibilism:* the student doubts the ultimate truth of any of the theories on offer, but remains optimistic about theorizing in general; the student feels he or she has learned much from each theory's specific insights.
4 *Pluralism*: the student adopts his or her own synthesis or hybrid position, interweaving two or more theories.
5 *Conviction*: the student endorses one specific theory, on balance, but acknowledges the merits and attractions of others. The student remains open-minded to further argument and reflection.
6 *Dogmatism*: the student cleaves dogmatically to one theory, unable to conceive any rational criticism of it. He or she neither understands other theories nor credits their possible insights.

A final position is worth noting, though it does not sit neatly on the above continuum:

7 *Detached endorsement*: the student adopts one theory as an algorithm to run in obviously ethically charged situations to get the 'right' answer.

Some of these positions, and the terminology employed, require explanation

'Nihilism': Nihilism about reasoned reflection is the idea that all theories are, by their very nature, comprehensively wrong, that deep and systematic reflection is best avoided, and only a surface-level engagement with practice is worthwhile.[48] For our purposes, nihilism can also include what we might term 'naïve relativism'.[49] While the nihilist about theory at least finds solace in practice, the naïve relativist proves equally despairing of this appeal to practice. The naïve relativist thinks it is impossible to evaluate between theories, and also between holding theory and adhering only to practice. Each are as good (and bad) as the other.

'Conviction' versus *'Dogmatism'*: The student with conviction is convinced of the truth of one particular theory. However, the student remains open-minded about this belief; he or she understands other theories enjoy their own merits, and that reasonable people might not share the convictions in question. The dogmatist, on the other hand, is ideologically committed to her theory.[50] Such a student can hardly entertain the idea that reasonable people might reject or criticize his or her view.

'Detached endorsement': Detached endorsement describes a case where a student applies one theory (or perhaps a selection of theories) to paradigm ethical issues in an algorithmic fashion, with the view that doing so achieves the 'right' answer.[51] However, the student possesses no deeper connection to the theory or its values, nor an interest in the reasons and arguments for and against the theory. Because the student is not deeply committed to the theory's values, or its subtleties, he or she tends not to bother applying it in more everyday cases where it might interfere with the pursuit of significant goals. In a sense, the detached endorser treats the philosophical theory like a hard-nosed partisan lawyer treats black letter law. The student does not identify with it, or harbour any emotional or reflective attachment to its values or principles. Rather, he or she treats it as an algorithm to get the right answer, so as to avoid stumbling onto the wrong side of the moral law.

'Insights': Chapter 2 described a number of the insights that can be gleaned from different theories. Insights comprise valuable lessons about law or ethics, but do not (or at least may not) constitute the whole truth about the subject. Philosophical theories can betray a marked tendency to explode their core insights into comprehensive ontologies covering the entire domain of law or ethics. Of course, different people will have different ideas on what should count as a theory's insights. Generally, however, the insights can usually be found by reflecting on what particular questions the theorists initially sought to answer, and the main arguments and problem-cases that the theory uses to bolster its credibility.[52] For instance, if a theory takes its point of departure from a certain kind of ethical dilemma or question about law, then the theory will usually elegantly capture the crux of that dilemma or question. Thus, the insight might be 'partial', because it explains certain areas/features of law or ethics well, but does not work so well applied to other areas/features;[53] or, it deals well with explanatory matters of law, but not normative issues – or vice versa; and so on.

With that terminology explained, we can (without too much simplification) summarize the qualities of the student's different epistemic positions in Table 4.1.

Problems of nihilism: Given the four desiderata for university legal education canvassed in the introduction to this Chapter (expertise, understanding, ethics and meaning), legal education has strong reasons to try to avoid an outcome of nihilism about rational reflection. The nihilistic student's failure to understand and appreciate the arguments for various theories disables the student from seeing areas of law where that theory might provide illumination (for example, in foreseeing judicial responses to hard cases, or predicting the future development of the law). Nihilism deprives the student of a deep understanding of the topic of study, and may even hamper future professional work. Indeed, the nihilistic student is unlikely to have gained many of the earlier-noted benefits of philosophical methods, such as critical thinking and the capacity for rational reflection. As well, the inability to engage reflectively on his or her work may impede enthusiasm for holding professional legal ethics values, and corrode the student's future capacity to draw meaning and significance from professional work.

Problems of dogmatism: The dogmatist suffers from many of the problems encountered by the nihilist. Neither are open to rational reflection, nor empowered by the skills of critical thinking and dealing with complex arguments. That said, the dogmatist's values (depending upon their content) may still nourish his or her capacity to draw meaning from lawyering work, and inspire living up to professional ethical values.

However, dogmatism about philosophical theories invites a new set of dangers. Some of the most telling indictments of philosophical teaching concern the problems of individual philosophical theories. A consistent charge is that theories prove too comprehensive by purporting to cover the entirety of law or ethics: theories are *reductive* inasmuch as they reduce all values and phenomena exclusively into terms the theory employs; theories are *totalitarian* inasmuch as they ignore and marginalize values and phenomena that cannot fit into their theoretic confines; and theories are *top-down* inasmuch as they privilege abstract reasoning at the expense of local, lived detail.[54] Often theories aim to dismiss

Table 4.1 Qualities of different epistemic positions

Different epistemic positions	*Endorses Reflection*	*Endorses theorising*	*Endorses specific theories*	*Endorses one specific theory*	*Remains open-minded*
Nihilism	X	X	X	X	X
Scepticism	Y	X	X	X	Y
Fallibilism	Y	Y	X	X	Y
Pluralism	Y	Y	Y	X	Y
Conviction	Y	Y	Y	Y	Y
Dogmatism	X	Y	Y	Y	X
Detached endorsement	X	Y	Y	Y	X

other theories as catastrophically wrong – as built around obvious mistakes or ideological agendas, rather than reasonable reflections.[55] The theory's opponents are seen as misguided at best, ideological enemies at worst. Even philosophers in the business of developing and defending specific philosophical theories can be alive to dogmatism's dangers.[56]

As a result of the dangers of theory, a student enamoured by a specific philosophical position might be led to ignore, discount and spurn any factors that lie outside its narrow confines – potentially impacting upon the capacity to practice and understand the law (in cases where the nature and development of the law departs from what the theory predicts) – and degrading the student's future willingness to perform any professional legal duties that do not follow from the prized theory.

To an extent, these dangers might also apply to the student with conviction. But, in this case, the student's open-mindedness works to mitigate the dangers. The student with conviction acknowledges that other perspectives on law enjoy their own merits and that reasonable people might possess different views. He or she might thus prove more willing to compromise with others on matters such as a shared professional ethos.[57] So too, the student remains open to new evidence that the adopted theory might require revision or reform. Thus, while the *theory* itself might be reductive, totalitarian and top-down, the *way the theory is held* by the student means that his or her understanding and practice of the law and legal ethics may not possess these problematic qualities.

Problems of detached endorsement: The detached endorser employs the favoured theory (or a selection of theories) to get the right answers in class assignments, and perhaps can be expected to employ the theory when faced with obvious ethical dilemmas in the workplace. However, the detached endorser possesses little interest in the deeper reasons for the theory, nor any emotional connection to its values. As such, the student's capacity to wield the theory appropriately in sanitized situations does not derive from any genuine reflective capabilities, nor does it imply that he or she would be willing or able to employ the theory in more subtle cases, including cases where the client has compelling interests at stake.[58] The student furthermore garners none of the potential positive gains of learning philosophical theory, in terms of providing deeper understanding, increased critical reflective capabilities, and ethical responsiveness.

Aiming for the centre: from scepticism to conviction. As the foregoing discussion implies, teachers of philosophical theories would do well to aim for students to finish their studies with positions of either scepticism, fallibilism, pluralism or conviction. All these positions imply the student has learned critical-thinking skills and employed them in evaluating the philosophical theories. The student remains reflective and open-minded (and so a willing lifelong learner), but has gleaned insights that can deepen his or her understanding of the law and contribute to values that entrench professional ethical behaviour in future decision-making.

Lecturers aiming for their students to walk away with positions from scepticism to conviction cannot be accused of aiming to indoctrinate students. After all, these constitute the spectrum of positions that will arise if the student has learned and applied the skills of critical thinking, rational reflection and dealing with complex arguments. The student did not avoid reflection altogether (detached endorsement), did not despair in the face of an inability to rationally evaluate theories and insights (nihilism), and did not connect emotionally rather than rationally to a particular theory (dogmatism). Furthermore, the spectrum from scepticism to conviction allows an enormous window for myriad diverse positions. Not only does the sceptic about theory differ from the fallibilist, and both of these from the pluralist or the student with conviction, myriad differences are possible even within the same category. Students with conviction might embrace different theories, pluralists might synthesize different theories to unique combinations, and sceptics and fallibilists might disagree on the insights each theory has to offer. In short, aiming to avoid nihilism, dogmatism and detached endorsement still allows students to autonomously choose from an enormous diversity of positions.

What all these positions have in common is that their adherents acknowledge that many different theories possess important insights (even if their adherents reject that particular theory – or any possible theory – as providing the ultimate comprehensive truth on ethics or law).

How then can teachers of philosophy (inside or out of law courses) draw students' attention to these insights? While this is a large question, one clear strategy is to shift the types of questions students are asked in assessment pieces. Asking 'Which of these two theories is better?' or 'Are you persuaded by the arguments for this theory?' tend to encourage polarized answers: the student either accepts or rejects the theory *simpliciter*. But other sorts of questions can elicit a more nuanced response. Consider, for example, such questions as:

- What specific questions does this theory set out to answer? Does it illuminate answers to those questions (even if it fails to explain other areas of ethics and law)?
- If the theory fails as a comprehensive theory, are there applications or areas of ethics or law where it works well?
- If the arguments raised for the theory fail to vindicate its truth as a comprehensive theory of ethics or law, do they at least bolster a more limited, but nonetheless valuable, contribution?
- If two theories each possess important insights, are there any prospects for synthesizing the two theories, or must they remain in opposition? And, if synthesis is possible, how can the theories best be synthesized – through theoretical reflection or through their application to substantive subject matter?[59]

Dangerous convictions?

The foregoing arguments all targeted *ways of holding* a particular theory and the pitfalls or promises of different epistemic relations to the theory (scepticism, fallibilism, conviction, etc.). But what about the content of the theory itself? When it comes to the four desiderata noted in this Chapter's introduction, are all philosophical theories equally likely to fulfil those criteria?

This question threatens to open a can of worms. Deciding that some types of convictions are best avoided risks indoctrinating students rather than equipping them with the critical tools empowering them to come to their own autonomous position. On the other hand, a strong case exists that different theories' content are *not* equal with respect to the aforenoted desiderata. In particular, some convictions are more likely than others to bolster students' professional ethical values and to encourage a sense of meaning and worth in the professional's future lawyering.[60]

Margaret Castles hints at the problem looming here:

> The expectations of professional conduct emanate from underlying ethical norms. Professional conduct can be seen as the end product of a continuum that starts with (or without) an understanding of ethical norms and manifests itself in a manner of behaving.[61]

When students are taught legal professional ethics, this teaching will need to attach itself to certain ethical norms and perspectives if it is to provide the students with any reason to comply with the specific codes of conduct and to identify with them.[62] Yet, when it comes to teaching philosophical theories of ethics, politics and law, it is *an open question* whether or not those particular theories will vindicate the ethical norms that the course in legal ethics relies upon.

This tension should perhaps not be overplayed. Human beings are complex creatures, and their behaviour stems as much from their emotions and character, and from the qualities of their social communities and peer groups, as it does from their deep theoretical beliefs. Presuming that a student holds to a theory with conviction (rather than dogmatic certitude), they may well possess the resources to act with professional integrity even in cases where their deep theoretical beliefs would not align with certain professional obligations.[63]

Even so, teachers wishing to encourage professionalism in their students can profit by reflecting on the ways that certain theories of law attach – or fail to attach – to the reasons and norms underlying professional ethics and a sense of meaningful work. For example, neoliberal theories that strip legitimacy from any non-market values might call into question the nature of professionalism, inasmuch as the profession's monopoly status and practices depart from normal market operations.[64] Equally, some radical critical theories of law might see all law (or at least law in market, liberal democracies) as fundamentally illegitimate. While doubtless a legitimate position for a revolutionary or academic, such a standpoint might make it difficult for a lawyer to find meaning in their work, or to heed any professional values that derive from the law's social legitimacy and importance. Kevin Leicht details the worrying alliance between market fundamentalist theories seducing significant parts of the political right, and the certain types of postmodern scepticism fashionable in some quarters on the left.[65] While disagreeing on myriad other issues, both theoretical positions can work to undermine the legitimacy of a strong professional ethical code regulating lawyers' work.

Yet perhaps, the most persistent target of commentators' concerns on this front focuses less on ethical–political theories and more on the legal theory that implicitly undergirds much doctrinal (and ostensibly atheoretical) teaching: namely, the theory of legal positivism.[66] True, in principle, there exists no impediment to being a legal positivist and taking a forthright moral position on law and lawyering – the positivist, utilitarian reformer Jeremy Bentham provides only the first in a wealth of examples of such a creature. Yet, legal positivism's sharp division between law and morality, and with it the opportunity to teach law without justice, can pave the way for a vision of law – and then a subsequent practicing of law – purged of all social purposes and ethical reasoning.[67] Few notions could be more antithetical to the real Bentham.[68] But, there is a danger that a doctrinal focus on black letter law bereft of normative context and social purposes will not prepare students for discussion of law's social purposes and the significance of responsible lawyering in the context of instilling professional legal ethics.[69] Even if the students come to learn the content of their professional responsibilities, they may well adopt the 'detached endorsement' noted above – in effect treating their ethical responsibilities in same value-denuded and algorithmic way they treat black letter law.[70] Just as their de-moralized view of law encourages them to help their clients get whatever they can within the strict black letter of the law (or, worse, to get whatever they can while minimizing their legal risks and liabilities), the lawyer may take the selfsame spirit to their own professional 'responsibilities'.

The lesson here is not that teachers should strive to inculcate – or on the other hand to purge – certain legal and political theories in their students. Such a stratagem would undermine the values of critical and autonomous thought that comprise philosophy's (and, arguably, university education's) main benefit. Rather, the lesson here is to avoid teaching substantive philosophies (like legal positivism) implicitly. When theories like legal positivism are explicitly taught *as theories*, students are empowered to critically assess them – in all likelihood staving off the unreflective dogmatic commitments that they might otherwise have collected. Students are also empowered to explicitly consider sophisticated amalgams of different positions – such as how to incorporate tightly held moral commitments alongside a positivist theory of law (as Bentham himself did). Even if a student becomes convinced of the truth of a single theory, and even if that theory itself leaves little place for the ethics of law and lawyering, the student's open-mindedness and awareness of the merits of other perspectives may suffice to open a window into acknowledging the moral significance of lawyering and professional legal responsibilities. Again, the lesson here is to stress each theory's insights, and to empower the student with the types of critical thinking tools that free her from an implicit or explicit theoretical dogmatism.

Conclusion

Studying philosophy, philosophical methods and philosophical theories offers law students a wide array of important benefits. We have seen these include: understanding complex arguments and developing critical thinking; the capacity to systematically reflect on values and norms; avoiding uncritical acceptance of the status quo; highlighting key concerns in ethical hotspots; informing personal decision-making; historical awareness; conceptual clarity; wonder and curiosity; and developing a reasoned and autonomous position. Each of these outcomes can help legal education achieve its key objectives of inculcating expertise, understanding, ethics and meaning to students of law.

To be sure, the introduction of philosophy is not an unalloyed good (if there is such a thing). Philosophical theories carry their own risks, including unhelpful abstraction; indoctrination; debilitating doubts; detached endorsement; and ideological dogmatism. However, avoiding theory altogether is not an option. Failing to teach legal theory does not avoid theory but means that students – and probably their lecturers – do not (as Northrop and the 1991 Griffith brochure warned) know what their theory is. This unknown theory is likely to be a bowdlerized version of a theory with some insights but whose value is lost because the extent and limitations of that insight are not understood. The unknown theory could well be legal positivism but might also be bowdlerized 'realism', 'economic analysis' or mere scepticism. Instead, attention to teaching critical tools to engage with the theories, offering an array of theoretical alternatives, and working hard to stress each theory's unique insights can combine to ward off these dangers, allowing legal education to seize the benefits, and mitigate the dangers, of philosophical thinking and philosophical theory.

Notes

1 There are exceptions to this, as the later sections note.
2 Qualities that they are expected to take with them (even if they end up working outside the profession) to the benefit of those they work for.
3 See also Chapter 3, Sections 2 and 3.
4 Peter Singer, 'Famine, Affluence and Morality', *Philosophy and Public Affairs* 1:1 (1972); Judith Thomson, 'A Defense of Abortion', ibid., 1:1 (1971).
5 See Peter Singer, *Practical Ethics*, 2nd ed. (Cambridge: Cambridge University Press, 1993); Judith Jarvis Thomson, *The Realm of Rights* (Cambridge, Mass.: Harvard University Press, 1990).
6 See Chapter 3, Section 1 for a discussion of relevant desiderata.
7 See Chapter 3, Section 2.
8 Margaret Castles, 'Challenges to the Academy: Reflections on the Teaching of Legal Ethics in Australia', *Legal Education Review* 81, 84 (2001): 17. See also Chapter 12 below.
9 As well as Chapters 2 and 3 (especially Section 3), see Jonathan Crowe, 'Reasoning from the Ground Up: Some Strategies for Teaching Theory to Law Students', *Legal Education Review* 21, no. 1–2 (2011).
10 This is not to ignore the application of other disciplines to law (such as sociology, linguistics, economics, anthropology), which generate their own branches of jurisprudence (e.g. sociological jurisprudence and economic analysis of law) that are likely to

have a major place within jurisprudence courses. And philosophy plays, or ought to play, a key role in such 'jurisprudences'. However, this chapter deals with philosophy broadly (but not imperialistically) conceived.

11 See Chapters 2 and 3.

12 Chapter 2 (Sect. 3) enumerated many of the specific capabilities captured by this broad quality.

13 See John Zerilli, 'Reflections on Legal Education and Philosophy: The Critical Role of Theory in Practice', *Legal Education Review* 6 (2007): 116.

14 David Luban, 'Smith against the Ethicists', *Law and Philosophy* 9, no. 4 (1991): 421.

15 Roger Cotterrell, 'Pandora's Box: Jurisprudence in Legal Education', *International Journal of the Legal Profession* 7, no. 3 (2000). Of course, not all defences of the status quo are unreflective. Philosophy does not inevitably vitiate the existing system; it just maintains that the system is open to rational critique. See the exchange between: M.B.E. Smith, 'Should Lawyers Listen to Philosophers About Legal Ethics?', *Law and Philosophy* 9, no. 1 (1990); David Luban, 'Smith against the Ethicists', ibid., no. 4 (1991).

16 Nickolas John James, 'Expertise as Privilege: Australian Legal Education and The Persistent Emphasis Upon Doctrine', *University of Western Sydney Law Review* 8, no. 1 (2004).

17 Martha Nussbaum, 'The Use and Abuse of Philosophy in Legal Education', *Stanford Law Review* 45, no. 6 (1993).

18 Crowe, 'Reasoning from the Ground Up'.

19 Zerilli provides a case study pp. 114–116. Intellectual property furnishes another example, where modern debates routinely bring up arguments and counter-arguments present in the major eighteenth-century cases.

20 Zerilli, 'Theory in Practice', 111–112; Nussbaum, 'Philosophy in Legal Education'.

21 See, for example, Hugh Breakey, 'Who's Afraid of Property Rights? Rights as Core Concepts, Coherent, Prima Facie, Situated and Specified', *Law and Philosophy* 33, no. 5 (2014).

22 See Zerilli, 'Theory in Practice'; also Nussbaum, 'Philosophy in Legal Education'.

23 See Crowe, 'Reasoning from the Ground Up'; Zerilli, 'Theory in Practice'.

24 See Crowe, 'Reasoning from the Ground Up'.

25 Note the reflective requirements of professional integrity foregrounded in, e.g. Sharon Dolovich, 'Ethical Lawyering and the Possibility of Integrity', in *Professional Ethics and Personal Integrity*, ed. Tim Dare and W. Bradley Wendel (Newcastle upon Tyne: Cambridge Scholars Publishing, 2010); Noel Preston and Charles Sampford, 'Institutionalizing Ethics', *Encouraging Ethics and Challenging Corruption*, Charles Sampford, Noel Preston with Carmel Connors (Annandale: Federation Press, 2002).

26 Zerilli, 'Theory in Practice': 103.

27 Halpin considers some areas where practice carries its own expertise, and where any link to specific theories is more tenuous, before considering the merits of theoretical ideas.

28 Zerilli, 'Theory in Practice': 104.

29 Kim Economides, 'Learning the Law of Lawyering', *Current Legal Problems* 52, no. 1 (1999); James, 'Expertise as Privilege'.

30 Indeed, it may approach Marxist views of ideology in which it is more effective if it is not conscious.

31 James, 'Expertise as Privilege'.

32 Cotterrell, 'Pandora's Box'.

33 For some further, more extravagant concerns about theory, and sensible responses to them, see Andrew Halpin, 'Law, Theory and Practice: Conflicting Perspectives?', ibid. (responding to arguments by Stanley Fish). Note that the dangers of students arriving at particular substantive positions – such as dogmatism or nihilism – await the next section.

34 See Suzette Barnaby, 'Legal Ethics for the Real World: A Model for Engaging First Year Law Students', *QUT Law Journal* 4, no. 2 (2004); Crowe, 'Reasoning from the Ground Up'; Halpin, 'Conflicting Perspectives?'; Castles, 'Challenges to the Academy'. Each of these types of abstraction can lead to unreflective and 'algorithmic' application, where the theory is seen as a device for providing the right answer, but without genuine reflection, conviction or values. See the discussion below about 'detached endorsement' to moral theories. It should be noted that the Griffith Curriculum (foreshadowed in Chapter 2 and Charles Sampford, 'Rethinking the Core Curriculum', *Adelaide Law Review* 12 (1989)) addressed these problems by including ethical and theoretical issues in substantive subjects – starting with the law of obligations, the most theoretically fecund subject in the law curriculum.

35 Chapter 2, Section 1, noted one reason this can occur: because philosophical theories often take their bearings from deliberately simple examples (for example, of pains or chairs).

36 Zerilli, 'Theory in Practice'. A related concern might be that, from their perspective outside the profession, academic philosophers will inevitably misconstrue the operative facts and norms in any actual case. See Smith, 'Should Lawyers Listen to Philosophers?'; for a reply, see David Luban, 'Smith against the Ethicists', ibid., no. 4 (1991).

37 This issue also arises in other realms of professional education, and the lessons there can apply to legal education as well. See Rosamond Rhodes, 'Two Concepts of Medical Ethics and Their Implications for Medical Ethics Education', *Journal of Medicine and Philosophy* 27, no. 4 (2002).

38 See Castles, 'Challenges to the Academy'.

39 Crowe, 'Reasoning from the Ground Up'.

40 Nussbaum, 'Philosophy in Legal Education'.

41 Note that the Griffith curriculum, as set out in Chapter 3 above, took the approach that the students were introduced to questions and at least two different theories that tried to answer them – from which they could choose and revisit during their careers.

42 Crowe, 'Reasoning from the Ground Up'. See also Chapter 2.

43 Castles, 'Challenges to the Academy'.

44 Michael Davis, 'The Ethics Boom: What and Why', *The Centennial Review* 34, no. 2 (1990).

45 James, 'Expertise as Privilege'.

46 Nussbaum distinguishes sophism from philosophy on this trait. Nussbaum, 'Philosophy in Legal Education': 1641.

47 Indeed, one of the authors once engaged with a group of postgraduate criminology students, who thought that to be theoretical and philosophical effectively meant being postmodern. Postmodernism was the only theory they had ever been exposed to, and they were stunned by the idea that there may be philosophical arguments *against* it. As far as they were concerned, one had to choose between an unreflective trust of contemporary scientific method, and full-blown postmodernism.

48 Nihilism about rational reflection differs from adopting nihilism as a substantive philosophical position. The former despairs of the prospects of rational reflection; the latter has been led by rational reflection to a general existential despair.

49 Naïve relativism differs from sophisticated relativism (about ethics, law or truth in general). Sophisticated relativism is itself a defensible (and critique-able) philosophical theory, with many notable proponents. A sophisticated relativist may hold to their prized theory with *conviction* or *dogmatism*. (Note that relativism *contrasts* with fallibilism and, therefore, that a dogmatic relativist is altogether possible.)

50 See Chapter 2 and Nussbaum, 'Philosophy in Legal Education'.

51 This possible result derives from positions sketched in the work of Castles, 'Challenges to the Academy'; Barnaby, 'Legal Ethics for the Real World'. Moral psychology also allows for this possibility, in particular by noting that moral values (motives to do the right thing) can be distinguished from moral reasoning. See, for example,

James Rest, 'Morality', in *Handbook of Child Psychology*, ed. Paul Mussen (New York: John Wiley & Sons, 1992).

52 Crowe, 'Reasoning from the Ground Up'.

53 As Chapter 2 emphasized, the theory may be used in an attempt to address wider questions, which the insights cannot support.

54 Halpin, 'Conflicting Perspectives?'; Barnaby, 'Legal Ethics for the Real World'; Castles, 'Challenges to the Academy': 8.

55 Nussbaum, 'Philosophy in Legal Education'.

56 The libertarian philosopher Robert Nozick cautioned his readers against thinking of philosophical works as finished, elegant wholes, stressing at the outset that there is, 'room for words on subjects other than last words'. Robert Nozick, *Anarchy, State, and Utopia* (Oxford: Basil Blackwell, 1974): xii.

57 Benjamin describes how even people with strong convictions and personal integrity can still compromise in fair-minded ways (without changing their beliefs): Martin Benjamin, *Splitting the Difference: Compromise and Integrity in Ethics and Politics* (Kansas: University of Kansas, 1990). See also Andrew Edgar and Stephen Pattison, 'Integrity and the Moral Complexity of Professional Practice', *Nursing Philosophy* 12 (2011).

58 See Castles, 'Challenges to the Academy'. Note also Barnaby, 'Legal Ethics for the Real World'.

59 We note that Sampford's research centres emphasized the latter, especially where the theories came from different disciplines. This was also reflected in Chapter 3 and the 1991 Griffith curriculum, where subjects were characterized by questions to which two or more theories were offered rather than subjects based around a theory.

60 We must set aside the question of whether the theory in question promotes or disables deeper understanding (Desideratum Two) of the law or ethics, as compared with its rivals. Presumably, there is no way of deciding on this matter without begging questions of the truth of each theory. Each theory's proponents would not doubt feel that their theory deepened the understanding of ethics and law, and the other introduced false beliefs and confusions.

61 Castles, 'Challenges to the Academy': fn1.

62 Daniel E. Wueste, 'Promoting Integrity Integritively: Avoiding the Scylla and Charybdis of Abdication and Zealotry', *Research in Ethical Issues in Organizations* 12 (2014); Economides, 'Law of Lawyering': 393, 407.

63 See Benjamin, *Splitting the Difference* and Hugh Breakey, 'Compromise Despite Conviction: Curbing Integrity's Moral Dangers', *Journal of Value Inquiry* (2016 forthcoming).

64 On professional versus market values, see Michael Davis, 'Professionalism Means Putting Your Profession First', *Georgetown Journal of Legal Ethics* 2, no. 34 (1988): 353–354. On philosophical reasons to resist market fundamentalism see Chapter 2 above; its discussions of 'vulgar capitalism' remain as telling now as they were when first written.

65 Kevin T. Leicht, 'Market Fundamentalism, Cultural Fragmentation, Post-Modern Skepticism, and the Future of Professional Work', *Journal of Professions and Organization* (2015).

66 For further detail, see Chapter 9, Section 2.

67 Economides, 'Law of Lawyering': 393, 405.

68 Bentham wrote a book criticizing his lecturer William Blackstone. See Jeremy Bentham, *A Comment on the Commentaries and a Fragment on Government* (London: The Athlone Press, 1977). For Bentham, and the many English socialist positivists, positivism did not separate law from morality to place it above criticism but to locate it for moral attack, and to ensure that it could not claim any moral legitimacy just because it had become law.

69 See Castles, 'Challenges to the Academy': 13–17.

70 Economides, 'Law of Lawyering': 405. See also: Kim Economides and Julian Webb, 'Do Law Schools Care About Law Students and Legal Values?', *Legal Ethics* 3, no. 1 (2000): 9.

Part II

Australian law schools after Pearce

A case study in educating critical, theoretical and ethical lawyers?

5 Revisiting Pearce

Charles Sampford

This chapter reviews the impact study, *Australian Law Schools After the 1987 Pearce Report* by Craig McInnis and Simon Marginson, and reflects on changes to legal education in the dynamic period running from 1987 to 1995.[1]

The *Pearce Report* was commissioned by the Commonwealth Tertiary Education Commission (CTEC) as a review of the discipline of law in Australian universities. It reported early in March 1987 – just before the Dawkins revolution completely altered the higher education 'system'[2] and invalidated many of the assumptions on which *Pearce* had been based. In the five years that followed, Australian legal education changed mightily, perhaps even permanently. Many of the changes were due in part to *Pearce*; many of them were in spite of *Pearce*; and many were driven by the Dawkins reforms and institutional responses to them. In 1987, there were six so-called 'first wave' law schools and six post-war 'second wave' law schools. By 1992, many existing law schools had massively increased their numbers and a third wave of 14 law schools had either opened or were about to open (see Appendix A, below). Along with a change in numbers, there were huge changes in the institutional basis and approach to teaching, research, funding and organization.

To assess the effects of *Pearce* in this rapidly changing environment, the Department of Education, Employment and Training (DEET) commissioned Craig McInnis and Simon Marginson to do an impact study.

The impact study runs to some 500 pages – including 28 chapters in 5 sections with 6 appendices. It commences with an introduction (Section I) followed by a 'context' section (II), which looks at the radical changes to the HES and the extensive academic debate that *Pearce* stimulated. Section III contains 11 case studies on *Pearce*'s impact on individual law schools. Section IV looks at the main findings and Section V draws conclusions about the overall impact of *Pearce*, and critically assesses the form the review, and its report, took.

There are some extremely useful appendices including the results of various questionnaires administered by McInnis and Marginson and a tabulation of *Pearce*'s recommendations and suggestions with a short summary of its effect. One particularly useful Appendix (A2) for anyone reading in the area is the extensive annotated bibliography.

1 This review

In reviewing the impact study, I discuss its basic conclusions about *Pearce*'s impact and examine the weaknesses it finds in *Pearce* – suggesting that some of its apparent weaknesses explain its success and indicate the place of discipline reviews (and impact studies) in the development of dynamic disciplines.

However, in keeping with both *Pearce* and the impact study, I will state my overall conclusion at the beginning. That conclusion is that McInnis and Marginson have done a fine job in trying to tease out the effects of *Pearce*. The impact study is well written, insightful and packed with much valuable information. I believe that it is a study that legal educationists will turn to frequently, not so much for what it says about *Pearce* but, like the *Pearce Report* itself, for canvassing, in a single document, so many of the issues of importance to legal education today.

2 An admission of bias

In writing about either *Pearce* or its impact study, I have to indicate my own multiple biases. I studied and taught at a first-wave law school, won a Research Fellowship to a second-wave law school and was Foundation Dean at one of the third-wave law schools. These connections may be so numerous as to be self-cancelling – though they could just as well be mutually reinforcing!

I am bound to have a soft spot for any study which finds that Griffith is 'widely admired for its innovative curriculum and its developing approach to teaching, research and scholarship and relations with the profession'.[3] As to *Pearce*, it had certainly had a significant effect on my own career. It was the *Pearce Report* that first led me to write about legal education and it was Pearce himself who suggested Griffith should approach me when it was looking for a Foundation Dean. And the *Pearce Report* was of great assistance in planning a new law school. It listed and discussed many important issues and made it much easier to explain the need for resources. Finally, by lauding UNSW, it raised the possibility that the combination of ideas and resources could bring recognition to a new law school within a generation.

3 Significant effects

The impact study concluded that *Pearce* significantly affected law schools in six ways. These conclusions seem largely justified and are certainly in accordance with my experience – particularly the first three.

1 It set three 'standards' (or goals) that many law schools did not meet.[4]

1a Attention to the 'theoretical and critical dimensions of legal education' (Pearce's 'Suggestion no 1');

1b A student: staff ratio of 15/1 (and half that for skills teaching);

1c A library collection of 100,000 volumes or volume equivalents.

It should be emphasized that these were standards set rather than achieved. Most law schools attempted to address the first with varying degrees of commitment and success. The second was widely recognized and used – though with limited success against those universities which sought to apply the Relative Funding Model. The third became a key part of law school planning. Virtually all existing law schools made either good or spectacular progress while new law schools with strong institutional support like Bond, Murdoch, Flinders and Griffith aimed for, and achieved, around 50 000 volumes within a year of opening.

2 *Pearce* raised the standing of second-wave law schools, giving them greater self-confidence and encouraging third-wave law schools to follow their example in approaches to teaching and the profession. They might have added that it also provided an example of how the combination of ideas and resources might allow a new law school to lead its peers within a generation.
3 *Pearce* led to what the impact study calls the 'creation of a data base'. Although that phrase rather overstates the organization of material, *Pearce* certainly provided masses of previously unavailable information and created the conditions for further information gathering and scholarly debate.
4 *Pearce* encouraged a 'culture of continuous self-improvement', in which law schools examined their aims, their performance and looked to how they might improve themselves. This prepared law schools for the post-Dawkins environment and left them 'in charge of the process of change'.[5] While doubting whether any faculty (or anyone) could be said to be in charge of the process of change at any time over the last eight years, Australian law schools clearly coped better for the Pearce experience.
5 *Pearce* stimulated improvement in the first-wave law schools. *Pearce* forced most of these law schools to take coordinated action to improve themselves and to seek more university resources. This provided much-needed support for those within first-wave law schools who wanted change.
6 It stimulated greater cooperation between schools, particularly in the Committee of Law Deans.

4 Areas of limited effect

The impact study indicated a number of areas where it considered *Pearce* had little effect.

1 It failed to persuade first-wave law schools to adopt *Pearce*'s preferred small-group teaching methods – not least because its strong criticism of first-wave law schools was more conducive of alienation, defensiveness or counterattack than acquiescence.
2 Macquarie University did not agree to either close or fundamentally restructure the Macquarie Law School on account of the divisions within it – not least because the divisions ceased to be more marked than those in other law schools.

3 Although *Pearce* set a standard for resources, most law schools went backwards. With the exception of libraries, only a few of the most glaring resource limitations highlighted by *Pearce* were remedied. Some of the law schools identified by *Pearce* as better funded were actually cut back!
4 On postgraduate education, *Pearce* completely missed the trend of rising enrolments and the reasons for that trend. Accordingly, it was of little use on this issue.
5 *Pearce* is also seen as failing to make any contribution to issues of efficiency and management, how to improve relations with the professions (especially where *Pearce* saw them exercising far too much control over the curriculum), how to increase resources for research, student selection and the availability of places.

However, the area in which the Pearce report was most spectacularly ineffective was in the number of law schools. They recommended against new law schools and suggested the closure of Macquarie. Yet, the number of law schools has doubled.

5 Perceived weaknesses and limitations in *Pearce*

The impact study saw four weaknesses and limitations in the *Report* and the process that generated it.

Style

The impact study is highly critical of the style of the *Pearce Report*. *Pearce* is too detailed, looks only to Australian examples, fails to go back to first principles, fails to distinguish levels of importance, appeals to masses of evidence and authority, and is inconsistent in its voice (generally diffident but occasionally lapsing into the polemical in criticizing other law schools). When McInnis and Marginson choose to be 'blunt' they describe *Pearce* as reading like the text of a legal judgment – something they consider to be inappropriate to the non-legal audience and, in a discipline review, inappropriate for the legal audience.[6] *Pearce* failed to rule on forms of what was good teaching, or research, or collegiality. McInnis and Marginson readily admit that the committee was not asked to rule on these matters but then ask rhetorically, 'Who else was in a better position to do so?'[7] They go on to point out that the committee did have views on these matters and, 'the Committee's recommendations would have loomed larger if they had been built on a more solid platform'.

An unarticulated preferred model

Despite this, they see the committee's investigation and findings as shaped by an unarticulated preferred model of legal education exemplified by UNSW and Monash. This undermined the Pearce Committee's commitment to diversity, coloured their judgements of other institutions and led them to ignore or downplay strengths not found in the model (for example, some law schools were stronger on postgraduate study, had stronger publication records and/or were more successful in winning research grants than the preferred law schools). The impact study sees *Pearce* as having negative implications for UNSW and Monash. By indicating that UNSW or Monash were the ideal, those universities had no higher level to which they could aspire. By indicating that they were better funded than other law schools, their universities were tempted to conclude that they were giving their law schools too much rather than that they had made a good investment.

Composition

The above criticisms may derive, in part, from problems with the composition of the committee. The Pearce Committee included three professors from similar second-wave law schools. There was no representation from other types of law schools, let alone from other disciplines, the profession or from overseas.

Methods of enquiry

Pearce collected data, surveyed recent graduates and consulted legal academics. It lacked comparative work, a literature survey, a survey of longer-term graduates and feedback from the profession – elements that could presumably have gone some way to overcoming problems with its composition. More seriously, the impact study considers it to have been selective in those it consulted and in the way they presented the evidence.

Composition, methods and preferred model

Much of this criticism is clearly justified. The composition of the committee is clearly indefensible and gives the clear impression of bias. Here were professors from three second-wave law schools who praised their own institutions, castigated earlier ones and rejected any new ones.

However, the bias of the sample does not mean that UNSW, Monash and the ANU were not the best law schools at the time. It was certainly my view at the time, despite the fact that I was then at Melbourne.[8] It may even have been that similar perceptions by others had something to do with the selection of the committee.

The problem was not that the Pearce Committee recognized what was best at the time but that they gave too little credence to what was good in other law schools and to the possibility of new and emerging ideas about what would be better. Here, the impact study's criticism could be put even more starkly. Professors from the seventh, eighth and ninth Australian law schools criticized all six that came before, recommended the closure of the university-based school that followed them and suggested that the two most recent, CAE-based, law schools should conform to the mould of NSW and Monash. After that, there should be no more schools. Of the approved three schools from which the committee was drawn, the model was drawn from the two most recently established.

Read in this light, *Pearce* looks like a thesis about the end of history – in this case, an end to the history of legal education. Like so many such theses, it is embarrassed by the fact that it was written just before a revolution swept away so many of the assumptions on which it was based. Like so many such theses, it occurred at the end of a period of apparent stability that had been artificially enforced while forces for change were building (tertiary growth was stopped despite rising numbers and aspirations of year twelve students, and law school numbers were capped at the mistaken insistence of the profession).[9]

Timing

This brings us to the issue of timing. One limitation that is apparent throughout the impact study is that *Pearce* was based on assumptions and agendas that were radically altered by the Dawkins' changes. This severely limits its usefulness as a guide in dealing with a greatly enlarged university system that seeks to provide mass tertiary education to school leavers, mature age and graduate students who seem to want to study law.

The impact study refers to the changes that so drastically affected the context in which law schools must operate.[10] Numbers of university students increased dramatically; first by the stroke of a pen by which all CAEs became universities, and then by real increases in student numbers with which funding did not keep pace. This led to new money but declining funding-per-student and staff-student ratios. The demand for law graduates increased dramatically during the economic boom and most existing law schools expanded their intake (some by as much as two, three or even four hundred students). New law schools were established in part to meet student demand and in part for institutional reasons. When the economic boom ended and legal incomes dropped, many lawyers expressed concern over the number of law graduates (despite the high employment rates of law graduates and the range of careers that are opening up for law graduates).[11] There was an even greater explosion of demand for coursework master's degrees. Teaching and skills training were given renewed emphasis and research funding was increasingly redirected into competitive schemes.

Most important of all was a shift towards more corporate styles of management. Universities were required to compete for federal funds, to seek out non-government sources of income, and to provide an ever-increasing flow of information to Canberra in the name of accountability. However, at the same time, decisions on what courses were taught and how they were to be organized and funded were increasingly left to institutions. Thus, most of the issues on which CTEC sought advice from its discipline reviews were given to university central administrations. Agendas were now much more emphatically institution-based rather than discipline-based. In an important sense, the idea of a discipline review was alien to the new system. Thus, when quality reviews were introduced, this was on an institutional rather than a departmental basis (cf. UK).

Of course, the impact study does not criticize the Pearce Committee for the timing of its appointment, only for its failure to appreciate the changes that were already evident (most notably the growing demand for postgraduate coursework degrees and the changing role of such degrees). However, given the above catalogue of changes, it is surprising that it had any effect at all.

6 Unintended effects

That *Pearce* did have a significant impact is, in large part, because many of the most significant effects were largely unintended – either in outcome, in means, or in both. Given that some of the major effects intended by *Pearce* (no new law schools, closing Macquarie, improving staff-student ratios) so clearly did not come to pass, it is almost axiomatic that its major effects would have to be unintended. However, the predominance of unintended over intended effects is a constant feature of our complex world. Denis Wrong regards 'unintended influence' as a larger category than the 'intended influence' (that is, power) his book covered.[12]

In this, the style of the *Report*, so criticized by the impact study, was a strength rather than a weakness (see above). Had *Pearce* attempted to be more definitive and directive in the way that CTEC no doubt intended and in which the impact study would have preferred, I doubt that it would have been as influential or its influence as beneficial. Had it offered more specific recommendations, they would have proven either inadequate or dated by the rapid changes that followed. However, by providing a listing of issues, a variety of viewpoints on most issues, some examples of good practice, some suggested directions and a mass of information, it provided the base upon which others could work. It was, like many legal judgments, a storehouse of information and debating points that was used in future.

Different faculties and different academics made different uses of the *Pearce Report*. Where parts of the report were overtaken by events, irrelevant to the faculty or likely to be opposed point-blank by the university, they could be ignored and other elements emphasized. This is particularly appropriate where, as here, the *Report's* effects are not achieved across the system but in institutional contexts with particular politics driven by institutional goals, different agendas and management styles and rivalries based on entrenched interests, personal ambition and, occasionally, sheer bloody-mindedness. This is made abundantly clear by the 11 case studies in the impact study. In some of them, significant resource or accommodation constraints were identified by *Pearce*. Whether the law school got anything depended upon the unity of the faculty, the clarity of its voice and the reaction of the university.[13] Had it more explicitly insisted on the NSW or Monash model, new law schools could not have hoped to do more than replicate them. For those who did want to do more, *Pearce* could be particularly valuable in identifying the issues to be discussed and the approximate level of resources required. With the support of a sympathetic vice chancellor who realized that good legal education did not come cheap, much could be achieved.

In the system-wide recommendations, the prescriptions were less definitive than the impact study would prefer. However, this was their greatest strength. For example, *Pearce*'s first suggestion was that law schools pay attention to the critical and theoretical dimensions of legal education. Far from trying to set out the way this should be achieved, they left it up to other academics with a strong interest in theory to indicate what those dimensions were, and the best way of incorporating them into the curriculum. This is exactly what happened. Papers were delivered, articles were written, the 1988 ALTA conference and the first editions of the *Legal Education Review* were centred on the role of theory in law[14] – and a number of new and existing law schools implemented a range of answers that were not even contemplated by *Pearce*.

Similarly, with the emphasis on teaching, the impact study criticized the *Pearce Report* for failing to define good teaching.[15] But what they did was far better. They emphasized its importance, they recognized that it needed significant resources (especially a staff-student ratio of 1:15),[16] but after that they left it to teachers to debate, write about and experiment. The impact study seems right to see *Pearce* as over-influenced by the UNSW model, criticizing those who did not conform to it. However, *Pearce* stopped short of saying so, leaving the way clear for those who thought they could use the resources better to do so.[17]

It may be that what DEET wanted, and CTEC expected, were firm recommendations for the future of legal education. It may be that what they need is a vibrant discipline full of motivated people with ideas, a variety of institutions through which they may be pursued, and means of communications so that those whose interesting ideas appear to succeed may become influential in the development of legal education. The Pearce Committee was vital in generating that climate, just as the extra resources and the creation of new schools that resulted from the expansion in higher education were necessary to allow legal academics to put into practice the ideas that resulted.

Conclusion

This chapter is a review of an impact study of a report. I describe it as such with deliberate irony. It is but one example of the danger of bureaucratization in Australian higher education – that we will be so consumed by analyzing and discussing and planning what others do in teaching and research that we will cease to do it ourselves and stifle those who do do it.

There are moments in a student's life when it suddenly *clicks* – they have an insight, an experience that assists them to see themselves and their activity in a new light, in which they self-consciously develop themselves in a way they had not previously imagined. There are moments when an academic sees a new point, a new insight, a fruitful juxtaposition of ideas, and communicates it to her peers. These are the moments for which the billions of dollars are spent in higher education.[18]

The key goal must be to develop discipline reviews, and the entire higher education apparatus, to make those moments more numerous and, in the latter case, of more widespread effectiveness.

Such moments are intended effects but they cannot be planned – let alone managed. What planners and managers must do is to provide the environment in which they are more likely to occur, the resources to make them more likely (such as staff-student ratios that allow interaction and time to allow reflection),[19] the encouragement of debate, and the recognition of those who provide more of those moments.

Pearce succeeded because it encouraged legal academics to think about their discipline and gave them the confidence to act upon their thoughts. In so doing, it harnessed the thoughts, the ideas, the experiences of dozens, possibly hundreds of academic lawyers and, increasingly, sympathetic members of the profession and the judiciary.[20] It is no disservice to the three professors of the Pearce Committee to say that what was said and done went far beyond, and was in many ways contrary to, what they had envisaged. It is to their great credit that they promoted a process of reform that was, in a sense, highly academic.

This is what we should learn from *Pearce* about discipline reviews. They should be seen as key moments in an academic discipline review process.

It is academic in that it harnesses the ideas of academics and the results should have more to do with the outcome of academic debate than the authority of the review panel.

It should be focused on the discipline(s) within which we work rather than the larger institutions through which the work is done (I use the plural because, as *Pearce* emphasized, one of the key issues for any 'discipline' is the variety of disciplines relevant to it).

It should be a process in which issues-papers, reports and impact-studies provide key moments that draw attention to issues, collect and disseminate information, stimulate debate and concentrate the results of the debate but in which the centre of gravity is in the academic discussion and experimentation itself.

The one major improvement would be to be more self-conscious about these points and to reconceive reviews as a process lasting a number of years in which the formal moments are spread out to make the debate more thoughtful and sustained in the meantime.

Appendix A: a board-rider's guide to Australian legal education

McInnis and Marginson frequently refer to the various waves of Australian law schools:

First-wave (pre-war):
Sydney, Melbourne, Adelaide, Tasmania, Qld, UWA

Second-wave (post-war/pre-*Pearce*):
ANU, Monash, NSW, Macquarie, UTS (75), QUT (77)

Third-wave (post-Pearce):
NTU (87); James Cook, Bond (89); Murdoch (90); Wollongong (91); Deakin, Flinders, Griffith, Latrobe (92); Canberra, Newcastle, UNE, Southern Cross (93); Western Sydney (94)

The Pearce committee was drawn from the three italicized universities which were the seventh, eighth and ninth law schools, and the last members of the 'Group of 8' Universities.

Editor's Note: Since this essay, another 13 law schools have been opened. The law schools opened in pre-Dawkins universities may be contrasted with those established in post-Dawkins universities built on former CAEs – see Chapter 8 below for more detail.

Notes

1 C. McInnis and S. Marginson, *Australian Law Schools after the 1987 Pearce Report* (Canberra: AGPS, 1994).
2 I use scare quotes because I believe that in many cases, complex organizations are more usefully seen as unsystematic rather than systematic: see Charles Sampford, *The Disorder of Law* (Oxford: Basil Blackwell, 1989).
3 McInnis and Marginson, *Australian Law Schools after the 1987 Pearce Report*: 243. By way of contrast, at Griffith it seemed axiomatic that even the more limited task of establishing a new law school should include all the elements identified by the impact study as lacking in the Pearce committee. The steering committee included representation of three other disciplines and all branches of the profession. The selection committee I faced included Sir Zelman Cowen (former Melbourne Dean), Michael Crommelin (then current Melbourne Dean) and Bob Baxt (former Monash Dean) as well.
4 Ibid.
5 Ibid.: 244.
6 Ibid.: 248.
7 Ibid.: 259.
8 A law school that some would still have seen as Australia's best and was described as such by a senior ANU figure as recently as 1983.
9 See David Weisbrot, *Australian Lawyers* (Melbourne: Longman Cheshire, 1990); Charles Sampford and Christine Parker, 'Quality Not Quantity – the Key Issue in Legal Education', *Law Institute Journal* 67 (1993); Christine Parker, 'An Oversupply of Law Graduates? Putting the Statistics in Context', *Legal Education Review* 4 (1993).
10 McInnis and Marginson, *Australian Law Schools after the 1987 Pearce Report*: Ch. 2.
11 See Chapter 7 below and also: Parker, 'An Oversupply of Law Graduates? Putting the Statistics in Context'; Sampford and Parker, 'Quality Not Quantity – the Key Issue in Legal Education'.
12 Denis Wrong, *Power: Its Forms, Bases and Uses* (Oxford: Basil Blackwell, 1979); Sampford, *The Disorder of Law*: 170ff.
13 For example, a few universities were singled out by *Pearce* as failing to support their law schools. The language was remarkably blunt, saying that some universities had 'presumably diverted operating grants really made available because of the existence of the student load in law to other areas'. The law schools of Sydney and Tasmania used this to secure a substantial increase in their funding. Melbourne was not unified and faced a vice chancellor clearly opposed to giving law any extra money.

14 Chapter 3 (in its original 1988 publication) is an example of this. See also: John Goldring, 'The Place of Legal Theory in the Law School – a Comment', *Bulletin of the Australian Society of Legal Philosophy* 11, no. 3 (1987).
15 McInnis and Marginson, *Australian Law Schools after the 1987 Pearce Report*: 258.
16 McInnis and Marginson do not refer to this in their main findings but it does mean that the *Pearce* standard is for less than 15:1 for any law school that includes any skills training in its curriculum.
17 Marlene Le Brun, 'Law at Griffith University: The First Year of Study', *Griffith Law Review* 1 (1992).
18 Though I am not for one moment suggesting that it was necessary to double the number of schools for this purpose.
19 Unlike most modern academics, Archimedes had time to have a bath!
20 For example, Hon Mr Justice R.E. McGarvie, 'The Function of a Degree: Core Subjects', *Journal of Professional Legal Education* 9 (1991); Sir Ninian Stephen, 'Once and Future Law Schools', *Griffith Law Review* 1 (1992).

6 Reflections on a respectable revolution

Charles Sampford

On 6 March 1991, I was somewhat surprised to find myself Foundation Dean of Law at Griffith University. Not only was the process quick,[1] but it took my career in an unexpected direction. I had graduated in law just 12 years earlier and almost two-thirds of that time had been spent on full-time research – a situation I fully expected to continue.[2]

The diversion occurred because I had become very passionate about legal education and its possible improvement – sufficiently so to write about it,[3] talk about it and make some substantive suggestions for reform that were introduced into a number of Law schools. This passion was stimulated by the *Pearce Report*,[4] which (as we saw in Chapters 3 and 5) suggested that the first major failing of Australian law schools was that they lacked a 'critical and theoretical dimension' – without indicating what a 'critical and theoretical dimension' was, or how it might be incorporated into legal curricula. My writings on the topic appeared to make sense to Professor Pearce who, as a co-opted member of the Griffith selection committee, suggested I be approached.

So began a hectic term as Dean when the ideas for the law school were refined and implemented. Just under one year later, on 23 February 1992, Sir Ninian Stephen, former Governor-General and High Court Judge, delivered the keynote at the ceremony formally opening the Griffith Law School and hailed the curriculum as a 'revolution in legal education'. This was heady praise and accurately described our ambitions. However, I was a little nervous that this compliment might be too rich for a state whose conservatism was notorious.

It was soon apparent that I did not need to worry. We were not, and we were not seen to be, wild-eyed revolutionaries enraged at the wrongs of the world and wildly striking out at the perceived causes. We shared a passionate concern about the flaws in Australian legal education, an analysis of those flaws and a detailed strategy to address them. That strategy consisted of:

- a curriculum that had been refined through widespread consultation;
- a strategic plan to create a law school that could deliver that curriculum and take a national lead in interdisciplinary research; and,
- a brief campaign to promote the curriculum to the profession.

It was, indeed, a 'respectable revolution': informed by the literature, grounded in the needs of those it was intended to serve and, like all successful revolutions, timely.

At the urging of Peter Birks,[5] I have written at length about some of these matters, describing the academic and professional context in which the Griffith Law School was created.[6] I also said something about my own road to Griffith, a good deal about the curriculum and its development, setting up the library, recruiting staff and developing the new subjects to be taught.

As well as that work, much of that history appears in Chapters 1 and 2 above. In this chapter, I will describe the strategic goals we set and the campaign to promote the curriculum, and I will reflect on those goals and achievements in the light of today's changing legal and institutional context.

1 The strategic plan

With only 12 months to the opening of the law school, work had to proceed on all fronts simultaneously – curriculum consultations, staffing, library, relations with the profession and getting to know the university.[7] Sir Zelman Cowen, the Vice Chancellor's Advisor on Legal Education, had urged that the university should leave the major decisions until after the appointment of the Foundation Dean. (Indeed, he graciously told me he considered himself *functus officio* at that point, while saying that he was at my disposal in two senses – to help in ways I asked for as long as he could be of assistance. This was an offer that was, naturally, taken up with alacrity.) However, that good grace did mean that a lot of work had to be done.

Although I had already published a plan for a new core curriculum and had updated this for my interview by incorporating (with acknowledgement) some good ideas suggested by others, the strategic planning for the faculty that would deliver it started the morning after I was offered the job.

Resources

The first issue was that of resources – calculating what we needed and persuading the Vice Chancellor that this was a good investment for the university.[8] The calculations were simple but showed the problems of law school funding (even then). We would require 22 per cent more per student per year (A$1000 in 1990 dollars) at 'steady state'[9] than the then best-funded law school in Australia. I also wanted A$150,000 in seed money for an interdisciplinary research centre – believing that this was not merely necessary to support the research work of staff but to access the only source of funds that could make the difference between a modestly-funded law school and a well-funded one, and that team-based interdisciplinary research was not only the most important kind of research for law but would also attract the most funding. Quite naturally, the VC baulked. However, I was not just asking for this for the law school. I said – and I honestly believed – that Griffith could have Australia's best law school for the price of

Australia's cheapest science faculty. If that was an exciting prospect, then I would put my heart and soul into it. If not, it was not worth doing and I certainly would not be doing it.

Strategic plans

I also worked on a seven-year strategic plan, which was in place by July 1991. This was not formally required – indeed, there was no formal means by which faculty plans could be brought to the university for negotiation, endorsement and funding. However, I took the opportunity of our first budget submission for the next rolling triennium to provide a seven-year plan to bring the faculty to steady state.

There were three features of the strategic plan and the approach we took that I believe were crucial to all successful strategic plans. Good plans need to recognize the reasons why previous approaches are failing or falling short. I was particularly aware of three common reasons for such failure – and of three alternatives.

1. Seeking solutions to single problems. Many managers like to deal with problems and issues one at a time. This is particularly useful for day-to-day management within an effective structure. However, it is common that a solution to one problem exacerbates another. The most usual result is a regime of compromise solutions that cope with problems with minimum damage to other goals. The best plans are those that attempt to deal with both issues simultaneously – as I used to put it, complex plans often require complex solutions. Complex multifaceted problems require complex multifaceted solutions. It is not possible to deal with problems and issues sequentially when you are engaged in either the radical reform of an existing institution or the creation of a new one. What is needed is a strategy to achieve the multiple goals that any dynamic institution will be pursuing.
2. Dichotomy traps. One of the reasons we do not see our way out of problems is that we see alternatives in terms of false dichotomies, where the pursuit of one goal compromises another. Legal education was laced with such false dichotomies – with law schools apparently stranded between them, forced to make compromises. We were supposedly stranded between the academy and the profession, grappling with dichotomous choices between academic and practical, theoretical dimensions and clinical skills, content and context, educating for legal practice and educating for the range of careers to which law was put, teaching and research, breadth and depth, and so on. Resolving those dichotomies by developing strategies that would simultaneously address both was a key part of my previous writing and was a feature of the rationale for the curriculum.
3. A focus on individual rather than institutional issues. One of the greatest failings of our individualistic society is to conceive issues and problems in individual rather than institutional terms. By framing solutions in individual

terms, we fail to provide realistic institutional answers. This was evident even in the negotiations for my coming to Griffith. I was aware that law schools were prepared to offer some very high salaries to foundation deans (including Griffith and another that was seeking me at the time). However, the real issue was how to create a law school that could take the lead in legal education and research. This would require ideas and funding – with the funding of the faculty more important than the salary of the dean.

The 1991 plans

In broadest terms, the 1991 Strategic Plan set out a two-year goal 'to give Griffith's Law School a national reputation as an innovator in legal education and research' and a 10-year goal to 'give it a national reputation as a law school of the first rank [of Australian law schools]'. The plan aimed to do this by establishing Griffith as:

- The pioneer of integrated degree programmes;
- The leader in curriculum development, modernizing the law curriculum to meet the needs of the twenty-first century;
- The employer of high-quality staff;
- A centre of high-quality research, especially in applied legal and philosophical research and legal education;
- A national law school (although most students will initially come to Griffith from the Brisbane Gold Coast corridor, the Law School aims to be sufficiently distinctive that a growing proportion will come because of its programmes and reputation);
- A law school with an international focus in its research and its teaching programmes at both undergraduate and graduate level.

The rest of the strategy plan set out detailed plans for achieving those ends and the costs of doing so.

The aims of the curriculum were set out in more detail in a parallel document.[10] They were to:

- Cover the substantive areas of law identified by the professional admission bodies as necessary for practice;
- Develop a modern law curriculum to meet the needs of the twenty-first century, reflecting changes in the nature of law and legal practice since existing law curricula were designed in mid-century;
- Create a law degree that not only provides the academic stage of a professional lawyer's education but also an education that is of use in the many other purposes to which law degrees are increasingly put;
- Be a law school with an international focus in its research and its teaching programmes at both undergraduate and graduate level; and pioneer integrated degree programmes.

The key features of the curriculum designed to fulfil those aims were:

- Updating the core curriculum to incorporate areas of law that are of growing importance to law in general and professional practice in particular (for example, the property law course would include introductions to resources and intellectual property law);
- Teaching of related areas of substantive law in larger and broader subjects so that students will have a broader understanding of the law and its functions within society;
- Grouping of these larger subjects into annual themes for the first three years:
    - First year – laws that regulate interpersonal civil obligations
    - Second year – laws that regulate the creation and operation of organizations
    - Third year – laws that regulate the creation and transfer of property rights
- Incorporating the critical and theoretical dimensions of legal education as recommended by the *Pearce Report*;
- Introducing the consideration of ethical issues in all of the core areas of law;
- Improving clinical legal education and relevant skills training by placing them within the context of core subjects;
- Emphasis on the increasingly national and international dimensions of the areas studied;
- Pioneering of integrated degree programmes through a 10-point process of linking law and the disciplines with which we were integrating.

The campaign to 'sell' the curriculum

The curriculum was the public centrepiece of the Griffith Law School. Ethically, I believed that a radical departure from pre-existing practice needed to be justified. Pragmatically, we needed the support of the profession to accept our students on graduation and, more immediately, we needed to gain the approval of three professional bodies (Solicitors' Board, Barristers' Board and Supreme Court) as a degree that met the subject requirements for admission to legal practice. Bond University had experienced some difficulty in getting its course approved – with the process taking time and money.

Sir Zelman persuaded the Governor to provide a reception at Government House to formally introduce me, and the curriculum, to the Queensland profession. This would give a great deal of legitimacy and respectability to us revolutionaries. However, I did not want to rely on this. The reception was designed to be a centrepiece of the campaign. I announced that 'there is no such thing as overkill'. I did not want a strategy that merely delivered us a majority on the relevant approval authorities. I wanted to convert opponents into supporters, supporters into enthusiasts and both supporters and enthusiasts into potential employers. The reception was scheduled for the week before the October 1991 meetings of the Solicitors' and Barristers' Boards. The plan was to present the overview both through a speech and a 'takeaway' pack consisting of the Griffith Law School glossy brochure and a six-page document outlining the structure, main features and rationale of the curriculum. The full submission was some 60 pages long, with detailed subject descriptions and other information required by the board. With the approval of the secretary to the two boards, this full submission could be sent by us to the members of the relevant boards. My plan was to have them couriered to their offices while they were at Government House. When they came to look at the larger document, I hoped that they would already be enthused about the overall approach and would not question or niggle about details about which they might otherwise differ.

In the weeks leading up to the reception, I lunched with the opinion-leaders of the bar and the Law Society. I asked the members of the Advisory Committee for a list of those whom they considered to be opinion leaders and to rank them in order of influence and likely sympathy. The plan was to hold a series of lunches in which the board member and I would lunch with the most sympathetic first and the least sympathetic last, in each case bringing someone from the previous lunch with us. John Griffin QC joined me for the barristers' lunches and Peter Short, then president of the Law Society, organized (and hosted) the lunches for solicitors.

The Solicitors' and Barristers' Boards met and, of the 60-plus members, only one person suggested that accreditation not be given immediately – a suggestion with which he did not persist when it was clear that all others were in favour. A few days later, the Supreme Court unanimously approved it as well. Not content with an overwhelming majority, we 'lunched' the one potential dissident and he was fully on board. Thus it was that the 'revolutionary' curriculum passed through what some had imagined to be the most conservative profession in Australia with the toughest and most restrictive rules for accreditation.

2 The view from 2002 – 11 years on

Eleven years later, our original goals still seem worthy goals – all the worthier for having been so fulsomely achieved. The curriculum met its set aims and we managed to build in all the key features – although integrated degree programs proved to be very hard work, and introducing ethical issues into core subjects was initially patchier than I would have liked.

The curriculum was used to attract high-quality staff with congruent, if not identical, views on legal education. It was those staff who were responsible for winning more teaching awards and teaching grants than any other law school – and for consistently achieving the highest ratings for student satisfaction and employment rates. It was also those staff who made the research strategy so remarkably successful. From the beginning, we emphasized team-based interdisciplinary research. This delivered immediate results. In the next year, 1992, we won more new, nationally competitive grants than any other Australian law school. Throughout the 1990s, our research performance on a per-capita basis was better than any Australian law school. By the end of the decade, with

Australia's first Key Centre for Teaching and Research in Law to add to the rest of the faculty's research achievements, research centres run by Griffith's law academics were generating research income in excess of A$3 m a year.

Flexibility

Despite the detailed nature of the plan, it was not intended, or implemented, as a monolithic plan. It was not a rigid 'Schlieffen plan' that had to be implemented in full or fail. It was updated and modified each year. I expected my subsequent deans to actively do so and explicitly stated at the time I was appointed that I would 'not look over the shoulders of my successors'. The plan set ambitious goals – aiming to establish a reputation as the most innovative in two years and a law school of the first rank in 10. When we secured our two-year goal in the first year, the next version of the strategic plan 'fessed up' to the real goal – that the Griffith Law School could be to the third-wave of Australian law schools what the University of New South Wales Law School had been to the second, post-war wave. New South Wales gained a reputation for innovation in its first decade and become acknowledged as Australia's best in its second decade. Like all such goals, it was not all or nothing. I cheerfully admitted that we could live with failure – though second best would not be a result with which we would be satisfied. However, we would not get within range of second unless we had a vision and a plan for what best would be like and how we would get there.

All the evidence is that we are getting there. The strategic approach the faculty has taken seems to have built on, rather than being bound by, the ideas outlined in the original strategy plan – modifying, developing and responding to new opportunities.

3 'Great' universities and 'great' law schools

The Federal Minister for Education, Brendan Nelson, has suggested that Australia should seek to have one or two universities in the world's top 100 – that we should have at least one 'great' university. Few readers will expect much sympathy for that means of seeking academic excellence from a member of a university that lies between seventh and thirteenth on most competitive measures, and who is not only Foundation Dean of a Law School that aspires to be Australia's best but also the Foundation Director of Australia's only Australian Research Council-funded national centre in Law. However, this is no new revelation.

Twenty-three years ago, I graduated from Melbourne Law School and went to Oxford to commence my research there. The university I left was part of the group of universities that now like to think of themselves as the 'great eight'. I went to a university that had as good a claim to greatness as any. However, it was at Oxford that I first decided that the idea of a 'great' university was fundamentally misconceived – what philosophers call a 'category mistake'. I was very aware that there were some marvellous groupings – law and philosophy in particular. But there were a lot of academics who had turned out to be quite ordinary and departments that gained more from their association with Oxford than Oxford could ever gain from the fact that it contained them.

The conclusion I drew then, as now, is that it is not universities that are great. Qualitative compliments are more appropriately directed at the academics themselves and the academic entities in which they interact and develop their ideas. A university might be called great in a statistical sense if it has more great schools and centres than others. For the university to be meaningfully great, it has to have means by which it identifies and nurtures areas of very high quality.

While sceptical of the notion of a great university, I embraced the idea of 'great' schools and naturally harboured ambitions that this would be one of them. While Sir Zelman's caution led me to suppress such thoughts in writing the first version of the Strategic Plan, I was not so circumspect with my colleagues. When Professor Nancy Viviani took me out to lunch and asked what sort of a law school I was setting up, I simply answered 'a great one'. And when Sir Anthony Mason, then Australia's Chief Justice, asked why I had given up a great research job in an applied philosophy centre 'just to set up a law school', my reply was: 'Chief Justice, this is no ordinary law school'.

Of course, 'great' can just be an empty adjective heaped meaninglessly on themselves by those who have nothing new to sell. In the current context, any attempt to define some universities as 'great' or 'world class' and provide funding on that basis will not assist the search for excellence and world leadership. For one thing, the existing centres of national and international leadership are spread about the current university system. For another, giving preferential funding to some universities will stifle creative attempts to develop new and better schools and research groups.

What Australia needs to do is to recognize that the goal should not be a 'great' or 'world class' university but a 'great' or 'world class' university system (something for which ministers have the responsibility). In such a system, universities should be able to make strategic choices about where they will invest their money to maximize excellence in their universities and to provide funding mechanisms that reward such excellence.

In this, the experience of the Griffith Law School, with its curriculum and the research centres it spawned, provides a model. Universities should be given the resources to make strategic choices and be rewarded on the basis of the relative success of those choices on meaningful academic performance indicators. This will focus the minds of universities on the quality of their strategic choices and the strategic plans they make to achieve them – and not on the basis of reputation or some claimed diffuse general excellence based on past (generally well-funded) performance.

4 Globalizing of law: the coming issue for legal educators

One of the ways that we sought to create a first-rate law school and curriculum was to identify where we thought law and the legal profession were going and to provide the education of lawyers who would go there.

Law schools should regularly ask those questions. Research centres must certainly do so. Several of our projects concern the profound changes in national and international governance that are being wrought by the forces of 'Globalization'. These changes are as profound and far reaching as those of the seventeenth and eighteenth centuries, which saw the rise of the strong sovereign state and its gradual and partial civilization by enlightenment and post-enlightenment values of social and liberal democracy. We are now seeing the decline of strong sovereign states, a phenomenon with profound effects on many of our institutions and the assumptions that underlie them.

This is as true of the professions as it is of other institutions found in liberal democratic societies. In this context, it is notable that before the rise of the sovereign state, law and lawyering was a very cosmopolitan/international profession (at least through continental Europe) – supported by the cosmopolitan universities, which are, it should be noted, of far greater antiquity than sovereign states.[11] Indeed, the law and the military were the two most cosmopolitan/international professions. The rise of the sovereign state turned these into two of the most geographically bounded professions. With the relative decline of the sovereign state, we may wonder if law and lawyering will become far more international and transnational.[12] This would have profound effects on those teaching and researching such 're-globalizing' professions. Reflecting on this process and the kind of profession and professional ethics that will go with it is a fascinating prospect with far-reaching effects on the learned professions and the ways that universities provide for their education.

I suspect that the next great move in legal education will address this issue. I believe that Australia is in a particularly good position to make this contribution because we understand the world of strong sovereign states inhabited by the United States and the confederating states of the European Union. We also understand the vulnerabilities of smaller states that are not part of blocs. Our proximity to Asia provides us with an understanding of diversely different traditions. Therefore, Griffith University may well have a role to play in the rethinking of the theory and practice of law in a globalizing world – and eventually in the delivery of the results.[13]

Conclusion

During those first hectic years, I was asked if I was enjoying myself. My flip response was: 'I will enjoy myself in retrospect'.

When I do look back, it gives me immense pride to see how far the Griffith Law School has come. On 6 March 1991, I thought that it was possible for the Griffith Law School to do what the University of New South Wales had done and be the best of the new bunch in its first decade and the leader of Australian law schools in its second decade. I sought a curriculum that would attract and retain those with congruent ideas of legal education. I sought a research environment that would enrich the curriculum, support the research of its staff and provide a buffer in cash-strapped times. However, if this was to become a reality, it would require the work of several deans and dozens of staff; it would require the continued support of the university and the profession. The fact that we have clearly been the most innovative law school over the past decade and are challenging the best on most objective performance criteria[14] is a tribute to the hard work of all and their willingness to take risks that the ideas behind the Griffith Law School were more progressive and likely to produce better students and better research than their alternatives.

In retrospect, I am very glad to have played a part in this 'respectable revolution'. It was not always enjoyable, but it was worth doing and I am glad that it was done well.

Notes

1 Griffith had invited me to apply 37 days earlier and I had been offered it 17 days later.
2 See Chapter 1 for details.
3 Charles Sampford and David Wood, 'Legal Theory in the Law School', *Bulletin of the Australian Society of Legal Philosophy* 11 (1987); 'Theoretical Dimensions of Legal Education – a Response to the Pearce Report', *Australian Law Journal* 62 (1988); 'Legal Theory and Legal Education – the Next Step', *Legal Education Review* 1, no. 1 (1989). The last-mentioned, and later writings, are collected in John Goldring, Charles Sampford and Ralph Simmonds, *New Foundations in Legal Education* (Avalon, NSW: Cavendish Publishing, 1998).
4 Dennis Charles Pearce, Enid Mona Campbell and Don E. Harding, *Australian Law Schools: A Discipline Assessment for the Commonwealth Tertiary Education Commission (The Pearce Report)* (Canberra: Australian Government Publishing Service, 1987).
5 Challis Professor of Law at the University of Oxford and, for some time, Honorary Treasurer of the Society of Public Teachers of Law.
6 Charles Sampford, 'Reflections of a Foundation Dean – the Griffith Experience', *Queensland Law Society Journal* 26 (1996).
7 I began immediately but could only work half-time for the first eight months because of work I could not abandon at the Ethics Centre in Melbourne, for which I was still working.
8 As well as the below-noted resources, Griffith Law School also secured a higher ratio of administrative staff to academic staff than in other Griffith faculties. This was in line with a long-term view of mine that administration (where necessary) was best left to administrators because academics, (a) hate it, (b) are not good at it, and (c) cost more.
9 For example, when we reached the planned number of students after seven years – the initial figures were much higher, from 'infinity' in the first year when we had about A$300,000 for staff and expenses (as well as about a million dollars for books) with no students, to A$20,000 per EFTSU (effective full-time student unit not the most empathetic term for the raison d'être of academia) in our first year and dropping to A$5,600 per EFTSU.
10 The curriculum, its rationale, justification and structure were set out in Charles Sampford, 'The Griffith Curriculum', *Griffith Law Review* 1, no. 1 (1992): viii.
11 The first known law lecturer was the monk Pepo, who taught in Bologna nearly 1,000 years ago.
12 There is an alternative future to a world dominated by a single hegemonic empire. Despite the fears of some, and the unseemly enthusiasm of others, I doubt that this scenario will really come to pass. I have argued, and continue to believe, that the United

States has more to gain than lose from international law and a series of rules that applies to everyone, including them. See Charles Sampford, 'Sovereignty and Intervention', in *Congress of Legal and Social Philosophy* (New York, 1999). This was later published as Charles Sampford, 'Sovereignty and Intervention', in *Human Rights in Philosophy and Practice*, ed. T. Campbell and B. Leiser (Ashgate: Aldershot, 2001).

13 This theme was, of course, developed in my work over the following decade – see, especially, Chapters 17 and 18.

14 Griffith Law School was in middle of the top 100 law schools within 20 years of opening and the *Griffith Law Review* was ranked A* by the Australian Research Council. It also had a higher ratio of administrative staff to academic staff than in other Griffith faculties.

7 Law student numbers

Reassessing the issues

Charles Sampford (with Christine Parker)

Introduction

In the period from 1988 to 1993, 12 new law schools have opened in Australia.[1] At the same time, concerns about the number of law students grew, leading a number of media stories to warn of an impending 'glut' of lawyers.[2] These reports claim that the number of students will soon equal the number of lawyers, if it does not already. The implications seem horrendous – a doubling of Australian lawyers when the current number are having difficulty making a living. The legal profession will not be able to absorb all the graduates and they will be left, with an otherwise useless education, to become a social problem chasing ambulances in search of their hapless prey.

This picture is deeply flawed. Statistically, it is simply nonsense.[3] It is not true that there are as many university law students as there are practicing lawyers. The current ratio is approximately 59 students for every 100 lawyers, which is below the long-term average ratio of 65 to 66 students for every 100 lawyers dating back to the 1960s. Existing law schools have contributed as many new students as the new law schools. The proportion of law graduates who are unemployed is lower than any other graduate group except medical graduates. The difficulties that some graduates are experiencing in getting jobs in the profession is primarily related to the downturn in the legal profession, not the increase in student intakes that occurred in the height of a boom.

There are real problems with the education Australian law schools currently provide – but the crucial issue is the quality of that education. But improving Australian legal education requires consideration of issues much broader than the mere numbers of lawyers and law students. Changes in law, society and legal practice, and the variety of careers law graduates pursue, challenge law schools to keep their degrees relevant to the needs of students, the profession and the community they serve. To the extent that law schools do not respond to these challenges, they will produce too many graduates equipped only for the legal practice of the past and ill-suited to the range of work they will perform in the next century. Where large numbers of law students are educated cheaply or according to outdated assumptions, this will produce law graduates unequipped for performing useful functions in tomorrow's world. But, if universities discipline themselves to provide only education of the highest standard, then law graduates will be properly equipped to perform useful services in professional practice and elsewhere. The number of law graduates would incidentally be lower because of the increased cost of a better quality education.

The first part of this article summarizes the statistical evidence about the number of law students and lawyers in Australia and the historical trends into which these numbers fit.[4] (These figures were compiled in 1993 – for updated figures and commentary, refer to this Chapter's postscript). The second part of the article argues that the real issue is the quality of legal education, which, if addressed adequately, will make issues of quantity largely irrelevant.

1 Law students

Accurate counts of law students in Australia are not easy to come by.[5] For the purposes of predicting whether there will soon be a glut of law graduates, it is necessary to count students enrolled in bachelor law degree programs that lead to a qualification for legal practice. For 1992, the figure calculated in this way was 15,516. In 1993 the figure was 17,108. Figures calculated in the same way can also be found for 1989–1991, 1980–1984 and 1965.

We have not included people training as lawyers who are not university students in our figures. There are a small number of students enrolled in the Barristers Board course in Queensland (which is being phased out) and there are some 4,500 students estimated to be enrolled in the Barristers and Solicitors Admission Board Courses in New South Wales. Although the latter figure is substantial and amounts to nearly 25 per cent of the current number of university students, it is not included because we could not find comparative figures going back to the 1960s as we have for university students. The proportion of trainee lawyers that are not university students is lower now than it was in the 1960s when our statistical series commenced since it was historically far more common for lawyers to train outside of universities than inside of them. Therefore, even if we could include the number of non-university trainee-lawyers in all our figures, it would increase the proportion of students to lawyers more for the 1960s than for the present.

2 Lawyers

There are also difficulties with calculating the number of lawyers in Australia. First, who do we count as 'lawyers'?[6] Does it include only private practitioners? Or does it include government legal officers, corporate lawyers or legal academics? It is wrong to simply compare the number of students with the number of private practitioners and conclude there are too many students. Since many law graduates do not go into professional practice, the profession will not have to absorb all the law students presently being trained.

If we define 'lawyers' as those recognized as legal practitioners by the professional associations, there were approximately 29,165 lawyers in Australia in 1993.[7] Therefore, there are currently 59 law students for every 100 lawyers.

In 1987, Pearce found that only 64 per cent of law graduates took a private legal professional job as their first job. A further 13 per cent worked in government. After two to six years only 56 per cent were working in the private legal profession. A further 19 per cent worked in government.[8] In other words, within a few years of graduation around 25 per cent of graduates were neither in private legal practice nor working as government lawyers. Around 20 per cent were working for governments.[9] While there are no longer-term figures available, anecdotal evidence indicates that many lawyers move out of legal practice into a variety of careers.

3 But what will we do with 59 per cent more lawyers?

Fifty-nine students for every 100 lawyers may still seem excessive. One may wonder what on earth we could do with all these extra law graduates (anti-lawyer jokes aside!). It is easy to understand why the reports of there being as many students as practitioners forecast such doom and despair. But, even without doing much statistical research, the assumption that the number of lawyers will double in next to no time can be shown to be nonsense.

Even if the number of students in 1993 equalled the number of lawyers, the number of lawyers would not double in 1994 or even 1995. Most law students are doing combined or integrated degrees that take at least five years to complete. Many take more than the minimum time. Some never finish. The graduation rate of law students per year is only about one sixth of the number of law students.[10] Does this mean that the number of lawyers will double in about six years? No! Up to half of law graduates end up outside the profession in the medium term. So it would take up to 12 years to double the number of lawyers, even if none of the lawyers who remained in the profession retired. Taking retirements into account, it would take over 12 years to double the size of the profession. Taking into account the fact that the number of students is really only 59 per cent of the number of lawyers, not 100 per cent, it would take well over 15 years.

The question to ask is, 'how many years did it take for the Australian legal profession to double last time?' Very few people have seen the issue in that time scale. None have asked the question. It is to that historical context we now turn.

4 Putting the statistics in historical context

The ratio of students to practitioners has actually averaged almost two law students for every three practitioners since around 1965. Table 7.1 shows the ratio of law students to practitioners for the years for which an accurate figure for both is available. Figure 7.1 provides a bar chart of the same figures.

The rate of growth in the number of lawyers is not constant. It steadies or even slightly drops during recessions.[11] But the overall pattern, especially during economic booms, has clearly been of considerable growth in the legal profession both absolutely and relative to population, as shown in Figure 7.1.

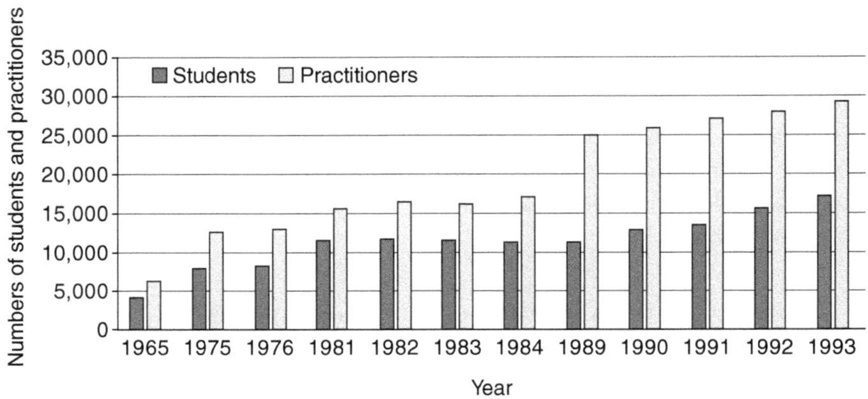

Figure 7.1 University LLB students and legal practitioners 1965–1993 Australia.

The Figure and Table show the number of lawyers has been doubling every 12–15 years for the last 30 or 40 years. For example, the figure for 1966 had doubled in the 10 years to 1976. This figure doubled again around 1988, 12 years later. In fact, if there are about two-thirds the number of students as lawyers, then – taking into account the factors described above – a doubling of lawyers every 12 years is not particularly surprising.

Australian law school projections of future enrolments suggest that the largest increases in students relative to lawyers are now over. In June 1993, we contacted all 25 Australian law schools and asked for their estimates of their numbers of law students for the next five years. Very few are planning to increase their intakes and those that previously increased their intakes to 400 or more are seeking to cut back significantly.[12] This suggests that enrolments will reach

Table 7.1 LLB students, lawyers, and ratio 1965–1993

Year	*LLB students*	*Lawyers*	*Students as percentage of lawyers*
1965	4,076	6,242	66
1975	7,917+	12,580	63
1976	8,249+	12,909	63
1981	11,467	15,524	74
1982	11,654	16,400	71
1983	11,535	16,100	71
1984	11,254	17,000	66
1989	11,297	25,000	45
1990	12,830	25,800	50
1991	13,370	27,000	50
1992	15,516	27,900	56
1993	17,108	29,165	59

approximately 20,000 by 1997, by which time most new law schools should have reached their steady state number of students.[13] This is a much lower increase in students than increases for the last five years (as Table 7.1 shows).

5 Recessions, new law schools and lawyer 'gluts'

The historical figures also put in context the claim that the recent increases in law students are due to the new law schools. One prominent practitioner was reported to have 'criticized universities for setting up law schools for prestige value and perpetrating a con job on law students as to their job prospects'.[14] But much of the recent expansion has been through the increases in intakes of existing law schools rather than the relatively small intakes of new law schools.

In fact, the high student and graduation rates of today are a legacy of the high demand for lawyers in the late-1980s after the government limited law student places in the early 1980s. In the mid-1970s a number of new law schools had been opened and existing ones became substantial in size, typically reaching intakes of 200 for the first time. Then came the early 1980s recession and the number of practitioners temporarily stopped growing. Student-to-practitioner ratios rose to 71 students for every 100 practitioners and concerns about lawyer gluts were prominent. The profession argued there were too many law graduates flooding the market. Presidents of Law Societies berated law schools, especially new ones, for flooding the market with lawyers who would never get jobs.[15] At this time, the Bowen Inquiry into legal education in New South Wales recommended that student places should be reduced as a matter of urgency.[16] Governments listened and put a cap on the number of law students for most of the 1980s. According to Weisbrot, because of funding cuts the total number of law places in Australia actually fell by about 200 during that time.[17] New law schools were vigorously resisted by the federal government.

In the meantime, coming out of the recession, the number of lawyers increased rapidly. A shortage of lawyers and high fees gave lawyers their highest incomes and starting salaries ever. Law societies complained there were not enough lawyers and encouraged immigration and new law schools. At this stage, the ratio of law students to lawyers had dropped to 45 per cent. Universities responded because it suited their own agendas. Some established law schools doubled or almost tripled their intakes in the early 1990s in response to the demand of the late 1980s.[18] But even this expansion not so much exceeded the long-term trend as returned us to it.

The wheel has now turned, with student and graduate numbers increasing just as another, more severe recession is slowing demand for private practitioners. This has occurred just as the really huge intakes of the late 1980s start graduating.[19] The present Australian ratio of law students to legal practitioners is still only 59 per cent and it is unlikely to exceed the long-term average of 66 per cent. It is clear that student numbers have been increasing regularly and considerably for the last 30 years. They doubled in the 1950s, in the 1960s, and again in the 1970s. There was a period of stasis in the early 1980s but this caused supply problems in the late 1980s. In comparison with the late 1980s, student-to-practitioner ratios and high demand for law graduates, there are now more students and graduates. But comparisons with the late 1980s are deceptive. That was an exceptional time driven by an artificial cap on law students earlier on.

It is the current ratio that is in line with recent legal history. In the light of that history, the growth in law schools and student numbers is an appropriate response. Universities that were denied law schools by government fiat are now establishing them.

Clearly, this history indicates the difficulties of synchronizing graduation rates and employer demand. But this is the case with all workforce planning. More research and coordinated planning on demand for lawyers and legal education may help in this context. Professor Duncan of the Queensland University of Technology has highlighted the 'ad-hoc isolated decision-making by the universities, government and professional bodies (barristers and solicitors)' in Queensland.[20] Intakes of all law schools should be examined and justified.

However, the possibilities of detailed workforce planning should not be overrated. Previous attempts to get teacher training in line with teacher demand failed miserably even though the government controls both student places and most employment. The major benefit of research should be to contradict erroneous information and to help participants understand the historical context in which they are operating, rather than guaranteeing accurate planning.

6 Employment of law graduates

Fortunately, it appears that detailed workforce planning is unnecessary. Employment rates for graduate lawyers are extremely good. Even in the depths of the latest recession, law graduates enjoy some of the highest rates of employment of any discipline. In 1992, six months after graduation, 96.3 per cent of 1991's graduates were employed or studying full time. This was second only to medicine and well above the national average of 70 per cent for all graduates.[21]

This is not because all of these graduates are working in the profession. Many law students never do, or want to, practice law. The percentage take up by the profession varies but averages around 64 per cent in the short term and 50 per cent in the medium term. During recessions the take up by the profession drops and the percentage pursuing other careers rises. Likewise, the net outflow from the existing profession increases at such times. For example, it is clear to any law dean that many of the profession turn to academia with longing eyes in times like these – including some of the most able!

Law is not one of those degrees for which employment prospects are limited to a single career leading to a need for workforce planning with all its vagaries. On the contrary, it appears to hold out the possibility of being a degree that, at least in combination with other degrees, can be of the highest prestige and enjoy a wide application.

7 Quality not quantity

The high employability of law graduates should not be taken as a reason for complacency in Australian law schools. The wide variety of careers that lawyers are coming to pursue, and the way that lawyers move to and from the profession, should make us focus on the kind of education we are offering them. We should ask ourselves whether current law schools are equipping law graduates for the variety of careers open to them. Indeed, given the criticisms of traditional legal education made by senior members of the profession, senior academics[22] and those detailed in the 1987 *Pearce Report* into legal education, we should question whether current law school curricula are adequately equipping their graduates for modern practice in a changing world.

These are questions about the kind of education we should be offering: questions of *quality* rather than *quantity*.

- What kind of careers are law graduates pursuing today and what kinds are they likely to pursue in the future?
- What makes a good lawyer? What are the skills, attitudes and knowledges they require?
- What curriculum is needed to help students acquire those skills, attitudes and knowledges?
- What teaching techniques are required for this purpose?
- What resources are required?

Law courses should not change merely because students with different career aspirations are attending law school. As Chapter 3 observed, just because a jurisprudence class is filled with plumbers it does not mean the lecturer is under any obligation to commence a discussion of water law. In the same way, the fact that some of our students will be future businesspeople or bureaucrats does not, of itself, mean that we have to start teaching special business or bureaucracy courses. Students come to law school to study law, not to study something else. But it does cause us to pause and ask: What is the something that we are or should be teaching? What is it about a training for law that should be attractive to those who work elsewhere and what are the legal skills that are transferable to other fields? Such questions put the ongoing dissatisfaction with traditional legal training in a new light. Perhaps the failings of traditional law schools are that they are not providing those skills, attitudes and knowledges.

These questions about the quality of legal education are also related to the public concern about the number of law students. There is a perception that law students are equipped only for conveyancing, drafting wills and, especially, suing others for negligence. In the public imagination, if there are too many law graduates they will descend upon the streets seeking potential clients on whose behalf they can sue others, regardless of the social utility of that action. Law schools are perceived to prepare students for only a narrow range of functions and those functions are seen as undesirable in any quantity. This underlying concern may be well-founded in some cases. It is therefore necessary to examine the legal education graduates have received and how it can be improved in the contemporary context. A high-quality legal education ought to be capable of producing law graduates who can find socially useful employment in many fields.

Part of the solution involves widening the areas of law covered in either the core or elective curricula. Law students need to be given an education that extends beyond 'vocational training' for a traditionally perceived narrow legal practice. Rather they need to be trained for government lawyering, policy development, corporate practice, family and criminal law as well as accounting, management consulting, and international business. For example, lawyers in a large commercial firm must be oriented to the needs and commercial realities of large corporations. They will also need to understand company law, securities, trade practices and environmental and town planning controls. Cottage conveyancing, drafting of wills and negligence will be, at best, of only marginal relevance. It may be useful for them to study some accounting and business so that they are conversant with the business methods and operations of their corporate clients. The huge growth in government lawyering means that many graduates will get jobs in government. But they will have much less orientation to an individual client than traditional lawyers had. They will also need to know different areas of law – administrative law, perhaps social security law and welfare law. It would also be good for them to have a chance to study government and social service organizations in a broader way than is normally done at law school.[23]

Part of the solution also lies in considering what is done within those courses. Traditional legal education involves a concentration on appellate court cases. However, most practice does not involve such cases. It involves advising clients on their problems, problems that are usually exacerbated by going to court, let alone making it to the Law Reports. What else does a lawyer need to know in order to adequately advise and represent clients? How much of that can usefully be taught in a university? Could it be that the extra that makes legal education of more use in advising a client may also make the education of more use if the law graduate ends up outside of private practice working for that client?

8 The potential contribution of new law schools

It is in addressing these questions and providing new answers that the *new* law schools are likely to make their greatest contribution. They will add to the education of law students, not by flooding the market, but by setting new benchmarks.

Sir Ninian Stephen has referred approvingly to a 'second revolution' in legal education.[24] In evaluating and reforming legal education, new, well-resourced law schools can play a particularly important, even 'revolutionary' role. When a new law school is built from the ground up, it can incorporate the best practices from Australian and overseas law schools, add some new ideas and consolidate them all within a coherent framework. It can evaluate the trends in legal education and go directly where other law schools are, sometimes painfully, sometimes reluctantly, heading. It can take notice of the present demands on law graduates and the careers they are moving into, and design a course to equip graduates with a range of skills and knowledges better suited to the future of law than its past.

A lot of time and effort must be spent in constructing curricula. Law schools will have to seek input from the profession, the judiciary and other academics. The criticisms of existing law schools made by the Pearce committee, and the standards recommended by that committee should be considered carefully. Student evaluation procedures should be put in place. Finally, the school must be willing to continue to make changes in accordance with student (stakeholder) comments and reactions.

The curriculum should be specifically designed to equip students with both the traditional legal skills and an understanding of the broader context within which law operates. The substantive content of the subjects required for admission to practice needs to be updated, supplemented and reorganized in several important ways. For example, in the past the kind of property that was most important for lawyers was real estate. However, the nature of the economy, law and legal practice have now changed so that while real property is still important, other types of property are also important. Intellectual property is important in an increasingly knowledge-based society. In an economy dependent on mineral exports, resources law is vital, and in an economy in which most economic activity is performed by companies rather than individuals, securities needs to be included in an enlarged property subject. Law is an increasingly international phenomenon, so the national and international dimensions of areas studied have to be emphasized.

Most law schools recognize that graduates need more than a training in traditional legal skills. Graduates also need a broad legal education to better understand the context in which those skills are used. Practitioners do not practice law in a vacuum. They practice law in the context of their clients' needs and problems. Therefore, it is necessary for a legal education to look at the human, institutional, historical and social context in which law operates. Some see this as a very academic thing to do, and in a sense this is true. But these are not just academic questions. In establishing the Law School at Griffith University, we gained support from the highest lawyers still practicing to suburban solicitors. They agreed that if we educate lawyers only in the traditional legal skills, then they will not be able to adequately serve their clients. But if law students learn another discipline and learn to look at law in a broader way, they will be better practitioners because they will understand the context in which the law operates. This will make them better lawyers because they understand the context of their clients' problems and the way their clients see those problems. That understanding will also make them particularly well-equipped if they choose one of the careers outside law.

These are some of our ideas for improving legal education. We offer them not as the only solution but as examples of how new solutions can be tried. It is hoped that several new law schools will offer curricula that are designed to build and improve on existing law schools, to offer new models from which other new and existing law schools can borrow, and ultimately to set new benchmarks for legal education in Australia.

It is in that spirit that Griffith was opened. We did not plan to flood the market with more lawyers but to educate what we considered to be better lawyers more attuned to the range of careers they are likely to follow. We and our professional advisors may or may not be right. But what we are attempting could not even be contemplated in an existing law school. It is in these experiments that the value of new law schools lies.

9 The effect of quality on quantity

This is not to say that quantity is irrelevant in legal education. There are a number of ways quality can be sacrificed for quantity. It is very difficult to maintain quality when there are massive intakes leading to poor staff-student ratios or weak staff. It is impossible to maintain quality without considerable expenditure of resources. Some law schools are expected to get by with two-thirds of the national average of dollars per student, and some new law schools have virtually non-existent law libraries. It is also extremely difficult to modernize curricula when you are expanding rapidly. Conversely, where quality is maintained, there are unlikely to be too many law students.

But sacrifices are all too obvious in some Australian law schools. For example, Weisbrot comments that:

> The central message of the *Pearce Report* on Australian Law Schools was that legal education in Australia is being run on the cheap, and this is a Bad Thing. The moral for Vice Chancellors, University Councils and Governments, however, is that legal education in Australia can be run on the cheap, and this is an Absolutely Splendid Thing.[25]

If we can ensure the quality of legal education, the quantity of law graduates is unlikely to be a problem. This is partly because the resources required for a good legal education will discourage some universities from offering new programs 'on the cheap' and existing universities from offering overly large programs. But, it is largely because their graduates will have received the kind of education that both equips them for legal practice in a changing world and for work within that world outside of the law. It is only if their education is limited to that which is good for nothing more than a traditional practice that the spectre will become a reality. To the extent that law schools teach a narrow traditional curriculum, they *are* producing too many lawyers – lawyers who cannot be competitive in seeking work or lack the ability to translate their skills into non-legal careers.

Postscript: law student and lawyer numbers 1993–2014

In 1993, we concluded that the long-term ratio of students to practitioners stood at a little less than two-thirds, and that the 1993 ratio of 59 students for every

100 lawyers was actually a little low given long-term trends – and that the ratio was still in the process of recovering from its low-water mark in 1989. Current figures suggest that the trends we identified have continued.

Table 7.2 shows the ratio of law students – including LLB and JD students – to legal practitioners from 2001 to 2014.[26]

Correspondence with law deans had indicated that they expected growth in numbers to merely reflect the effects of new and higher intakes in the early 1990s. By 1997, the numbers of LLB students was a little higher (21,680) than our estimate of around 20,000. Numbers of LLB students continued to increase because of higher intakes in some universities (notably QUT, with intakes of over 600 in the mid-1990s). With some further new law schools and the phasing out of 'Board courses', the number of LLB students grew to 27,109 by 2001. While the number of lawyers increased, the ratio of LLB students to lawyers reached 67 per cent – still within the range of figures for 1965–1984 (though the earlier figures did not include the then significant number of those studying law through Board courses). From this high-water mark for the ratio, LLB student numbers continued to rise but at a lower rate than the number of lawyers. The ensuing years saw a significant drop in the ratio of LLB students to lawyers. This was partly due to the introduction of Juris Doctor (JD) offered as a postgraduate degree. As Table 7.2 shows, the overall ratio of all law students to lawyers slips from its high of 67 (in 2001–2002) to a low mark of 61 to 62 (from 2006–2008), before levelling out at 64: not far from the historical average (of 66) estimated in 1992. In general, the ratio remains remarkably constant, despite the shift from undergraduate LLB to postgraduate JD courses from 2001 to 2014, by which time the latter accounted for over 12 per cent of law student enrolments.

Table 7.2 Law students per 100 lawyers

Year	*LLB students*	*JD students*	*Total students*	*Lawyers*	*Law students per 100 lawyers*
2001	27,109	143	27,333	*40,701*	67
2002	28,755	265	29,020	*43,019*	67
2003	29,649	479	30,128	*45,730*	66
2004	30,464	536	31,000	*48,164*	64
2005	31,379	535	31,914	*50,647*	63
2006	31,875	553	32,428	*52,236*	62
2007	33,227	698	33,925	*54,715*	62
2008	33,489	1,375	34,864	*57,280*	61
2009	35,501	1,872	37,373	*59,562*	63
2010	36,575	2,818	39,393	*62,297*	63
2011	37,066	3,922	40,988	64,948	63
2012	37,614	4,927	42,541	*66,855*	64
2013	39,085	5,392	44,477	*69,448*	64
2014	40,605	5,633	46,238	72,216	64

Note
Italicized figures are estimated from NSW Law Society members.

While this percentage has remained fairly steady, if the 1993 rate of 'lawyer-doubling' every dozen years mooted earlier had continued, we would have substantially more lawyers than we currently have.[27] Given that the law-student to legal-practitioner ratio has stayed stable, while the doubling-rate has fallen more towards the slower 15-year doubling also raised,[28] this suggests that law graduates are increasingly moving into other career paths, either immediately upon graduation, or after a brief stint as legal practitioners.[29] However, hard data on law graduate career destinations is not available.[30]

Commentary

When I first delivered the 1993 paper, I was relatively relaxed about the increased number of law students to that date as law schools caught up with the decade of capped places, the economic recovery and the broader opportunities for law graduates outside the profession. This message helped calm others. In 1994, in the midst of the 'panic over numbers', I published an op-ed based on the paper and met the new Australian Attorney General, Hon Michael Lavarch, over lunch. He made an off-hand comment about the huge numbers of law students. I summarized the paper. He not only asked me to send the paper but it was clear from the time I next met him that he had read and absorbed it.

My concern about quality remained. *Pearce* was concerned about resourcing of existing law schools. While some of the new law schools provided an example of how law schools could be funded (Griffith and, to a lesser extent Wollongong and Murdoch) in the way that Monash and UNSW did in the 1960s and 1970s, the examples of new and existing 'cheap' law schools seemed more compelling to many universities. With most of the new law schools operating at the third-level of university management, deans found it harder to argue in favour of Griffith levels of funding – even at Griffith!

While the Committee of Australian Law Deans initially shared information on funding and tried to establish minimum standards, it was difficult to take collective action and even more difficult to urge accrediting bodies to make such minimum funding standards a condition of accreditation.[31] However much as the law deans would like to have the resources enjoyed by colleagues, they feared charges of insubordination for signing up to such a document, and they were concerned that the outcome would be that they would lose accreditation. There was also a concern that law societies might demand other conditions and that the profession should be making contributions to improving legal education rather than demanding that government and students fund those improvements.

If offering law was a relatively cheap form of prestige, adding numbers to an existing law school at marginal cost could be extremely cheap. For a university whose law school is securing significant numbers of entrants with significantly higher entrance scores than any other sizable faculty, it is a huge temptation to take students at the next lower cutoff mark.

At the same time, law is becoming recognized as the new prestige generalist degree: what undergraduates do instead of an honours degree to credential themselves. Our approach to legal education has (and those who followed us have) made law courses more suitable for this purpose as well as giving a broader view of law to those who do go on to practice.

Given this role, it is not surprising that law student numbers have been growing alongside overall student numbers. The above figures indicate that law students have increased by 119 per cent between 1993 and 2013. Total university enrolments have increased by a roughly similar amount (125 per cent) over the same period.[32] While the dynamics of legal jurisdictions and university systems will naturally vary, it would not be surprising that similar factors are at work where lawyers and administrators suffer 'panics over numbers'.

Notes

1 Bond University, Deakin University, Flinders University, Griffith University, James Cook University, La Trobe University, Murdoch University, Newcastle University, University of Canberra, University of New England, University of New England (Northern Rivers), Wollongong University.

2 For example, J. Gagliardi, 'Queensland Faces Jobless Lawyer Glut', *Courier Mail*, 5 February 1993; C. Jones, 'Law Dean Warns of Graduate Glut', *The Australian*, 9 September 1992; G. Thompson, 'Jobs Will Be Hard to Find in the Brave New Republic', *Australian Financial Review*, 5 May 1993; J. Faine, 'Lawyers to Spare', *Australian Lawyer*, 1993.

3 See Christine Parker, 'An Oversupply of Law Graduates? Putting the Statistics in Context', *Legal Education Review* 4 (1993).

4 The 1993 statistics have been dealt with in more detail in ibid.

5 For some of the challenges Christine Parker and I encountered in collecting this data see: ibid.

6 In fact the term is notoriously difficult to define in a way that satisfies everybody. See David Weisbrot, *Australian Lawyers* (Melbourne: Longman Cheshire, 1990): 57–58.

7 This figure is the membership of the Law Council of Australia, the umbrella professional association for lawyers. Its membership covers all solicitors and barristers in traditional private practice, as well as a few government solicitors and barristers. Law Council of Australia membership figures were found for 1975, 1982 and 1986–1992. It is difficult to find any other series of statistics on lawyer numbers that have been collected in a consistent way. But for 1957, 1961, 1966, 1971 and 1981 census figures on lawyers are comparable with Law Council of Australia membership. See Parker, 'An Oversupply of Law Graduates? Putting the Statistics in Context'.

8 Dennis Charles Pearce, Enid Mona Campbell and Don E. Harding, *Australian Law Schools: A Discipline Assessment for the Commonwealth Tertiary Education Commission (The Pearce Report)* (Canberra: Australian Government Publishing Service, 1987): 74.

9 Many government lawyers would not be members of professional associations, and thus would not be counted in Law Council of Australia membership. This is consistent with Weisbrot's analysis of 1981 Australian census data, which showed only 72 per cent of Australians with legal qualifications worked directly in the law. After 20 years of work, the figure drops to 66 per cent. Weisbrot, *Australian Lawyers*: 64.

10 This ratio is taken from the graduation rates for law students 1988 to 1991, *Selected Higher Education Statistics*, Department of Education, Employment and Training, 1988–1991.

11 For example 1981–1982 but not, interestingly, 1991–1993.

12 We know of some large law schools planning to cut intakes by over 100.

13 See Parker, 'An Oversupply of Law Graduates? Putting the Statistics in Context' for more details on this figure. The actual figure was 19,500, but we have rounded it up to be safe.
14 George Fox, Queensland Law Society President, reported in *Courier Mail* 5 February 1993. See also S. Matchett, 'Too Many Lawyers Spoiling the Tort?', *The Australian Higher Education Supplement*, 7 October 1992.
15 See for example, W. Pincus, 'Future Employment of Lawyers', *Queensland Law Society Journal* 10 (1980).
16 *Legal Education in New South Wales: Report of Committee of Inquiry (The 'Bowen Report')* 1979: 61.
17 David Weisbrot, 'Recent Statistical Trends in Legal Education', *Legal Education Review* 2 (1991): 223.
18 According to both ibid. and J. Crawford, 'The Future of the Public Law Schools', *Journal of Professional Legal Education* 9, no. 1 (1991): 3, Monash University, University of Western Australia, Australian National University and the University of Adelaide all increased their intakes considerably at this time.
19 The new law schools will be happily graduating our first students in four years' time right in the middle of the next boom!
20 W. Duncan, 'It's Time for a Queensland Council for Legal Education', *Proctor*, November 1992.
21 These are the latest figures available at time of writing. Graduate Careers Council of Australia, *Graduate Destination Survey*, 1993.
22 For example M. Chesterman and D. Weisbrot, 'Legal Scholarship in Australia', *Modern Law Review* 50 (1987): 718, argue that Australian legal education 'has undoubtedly altered to a significant extent, away from the "trade school" aspirations that wholly dominated the field until the 1960s, and towards the classic, liberal model of university education, with law taking its place among the social sciences'. They see this movement as desirable, but point to a number of undesirable constraints on the change at pp. 718–719.
23 J. Goldring and G. Hawker, 'Lawyers in a Government Department: A Report and Suggestions for Further Research', *Australian Journal of Public Administration,* 14, no. 3 (1985): 290. For a similar attempt to look at what family lawyers actually do and what this should mean for legal education, see also J. Wade, 'The Behaviour of Family Lawyers and the Implications for Legal Education', *Legal Education Review,* 1 (1989).
24 Sir Ninian Stephen, 'Once and Future Law Schools', *Griffith Law Review* 1 (1992): 11.
25 Weisbrot, 'Recent Statistical Trends in Legal Education'.
26 Data for law student numbers – using enrolment figures (rather than commencements) – was supplied by the Department of Education.
27 Lawyer doubling each 12 years from 1993 would imply that by 2017 we would have 116,600 lawyers. As the figure for 2014 stands at 72,216, we are clearly a long way from achieving that total.
28 The 15-year doubling (which was based on the above assessment of the total figures at 1993) would have yielded 58,330 legal practitioners by 2008 – a little above the actual number of lawyers that year: 57,280. Again, this suggests that the 'doubling-rate' is slowing, and the curve is evening out.
29 Graduate employment rates have fallen considerably from their position in the high-90 per cent area in the early 1990s. The 2015 graduate employment rate stands at 74 per cent. This would explain some – but by no means all – of the lowering of the 'doubling-rate'.
30 The most recent hard figures on this topic were created way back in 1998, from a 1997 survey of a 1995 graduate cohort. In that study, the percentage of 1995 graduates who were legal practitioners (understood as both holding and being required to

hold a practicing certificate) stood at 41 per cent. Sumitra Vignaendra and The Centre for Legal Education (CLE), *Australian Law Graduates Career Destinations* (Canberra: Evaluations and Investigations Program Higher Education Division, 1998). This figure stands lower than the equivalent figures in the *Pearce Report* of 1987, again suggesting that law graduates are increasingly moving into careers outside legal practice.

31 As was attempted by the Council of Australian Law Deans, CALD, 'Standards for Australian Law Schools' Final Report, prepared by Christopher Roper, with input from the CALD Standing Committee on Standards and Accreditation, (March 2008).

32 See A. Norton, 'Mapping Australian Higher Education 2014–15', Grattan Institute, see http://grattan.edu.au/wp-content/uploads/2014/10/816-mapping-higher-education-2014.pdf.

8 *Reflection*

Developments in legal education

Charles Sampford

It is now 25 years since I commenced my work as Foundation Dean and nearly 30 years since my first paper on the reform of legal education in Australia. This comment cannot aim to document and analyse all the changes in legal education in Australia, let alone globally. But I will seek to highlight and reflect on several of the major changes.

1 Critical and theoretical dimensions are generally not seen as optional

Most Australian deans (and most of those in law schools I visit beyond our shores) would now claim to incorporate a version of what *Pearce* called 'the critical and theoretical dimensions' of legal education and research. While jurisprudence was thought to be an optional extra, there is now not often an option to exclude it. (Though see Sect. 5 below for some sobering considerations.) The mainstreaming of legal theory in legal research and curriculum development has made it commonplace to appoint legal philosophers and jurisprudes to deanships. Not only was I approached several times to be a dean but so were others with similar backgrounds.[1] And the inclusion of critical and theoretical dimensions into the course was, for most, not just a matter of scheduling a theory subject into the law school but instead the incorporation of these dimensions into mainstream subjects.[2] We are more likely to see debates about *how* theory is built into law than *whether* it should be.[3]

The idea that there should be two kinds of law schools – those for those who would practice and those for those who did not – was quickly abandoned. Indeed, legal studies departments were folded into law schools.[4] It was recognized that a broader legal education was better for both kinds of students. Future legal practitioners understood the law much better when seen from the viewpoints of politics, economics, philosophy and so forth. And those who did not practice secured a wide range of transferable skills. This was particularly true of those doing combined or 'integrated' degrees.

It has become clear that senior members of the judiciary and the bar/law society recognize, and frequently emphasize, the importance of legal theory. Indeed, occasional anecdotes of support from senior members of the profession turn up from time to time.[5] One partner in a very large commercial firm told me that there was an awful lot of justice to be done.

2 Legal education as an object of research

One of the meta-results of *Pearce* and the writing that I and others did about legal education in its aftermath was the rise and legitimation of legal education as an object of research. For me, it was natural that activities in which I was involved stimulated my curiosity and led me to formulate research questions about that activity, to discuss them with practitioners and write about them. Not only did the *Pearce Report* stimulate me to write about legal theory and the law school but appointment to the curriculum committee at Melbourne led not only to proposals for reform of that curriculum but to Australian legal curricula in general.[6] I continued to write and encouraged others in the Law School to do so.[7] Of course, we were neither the first nor the only ones contributing to the growth of this research, which provided the basis for the Griffith curriculum.

3 Lifelong learning

It is now widely recognized that an LLB is just a stage in lifelong legal education – a stage that must concentrate on what can best be taught at what is now recognized as the 'university stage' of that education. Large law firms engage in highly sophisticated graduate education programs, bars and law societies require continuing legal education (frequently with a mandatory ethics component), and judicial education long institutionalized in civil law jurisdictions has become an increasing part of common law jurisdictions. Clinical education became common with the institutionalizing of student participation in legal advice centres. In some jurisdictions, coursework LLMs came to be seen as a key element in developing skills and specialization (though this trend was curtailed by fee increases and punishing workloads for young lawyers). On the other hand, the post-degree educational requirements for admission to the profession have been radically cut back. Where it was common to require one to two years of articles, or a six month, full-time hands-on practical legal training, a web-based course is now considered sufficient. And, while the need for lifelong learning is recognized, there are no evident plans for a comprehensive strategy for achieving it. As a Foundation Dean with a medical background, I wondered if a medical model of hospital internships between university and practice might serve a range of purposes: boosting clinical legal education, the provision of legal advice to the many who needed it but could not afford it, an understanding of the legal problems of ordinary people, and a commitment to the contribution that the legal profession can make to creating a more just society under law. It was not long before I realized that this was a reform too far for me to drive and I confined myself to legal education and legal research.

4 Some underlying trends?

One way of thinking more broadly about these changes is to revisit the eight causes I suggested for why the critical and theoretical dimensions are downplayed. In each case, I contrast the 1987 problem with the 2016 situation.

1987 problem 1: Uncertainty of what the 'extra' critical and theoretical dimensions were.

> *2016 reality*: The extra is now seen as coming from a smorgasbord of other disciplines and increasingly within law has meant that there is much to choose from and legitimacy in the choice.

1987 problem 2: Lack of contact by law teachers with developments in the fields covered by the extra critical and theoretical dimensions. This was partly a matter of education – few law teachers had strong backgrounds in other disciplines (with few having first class honours and even fewer having higher degrees outside of law – let alone having interdisciplinary doctorates). This generally led to timidity in engaging leading researchers in the relevant disciplines. Those who were interested and knowledgeable in those disciplines were likely to be discouraged and were as likely to follow their interests through the other disciplines as to pursue them through law. This reflected my own uncertainty (as related in Chapter 1) of whether to pursue my own interests through law or philosophy.

> *2016 reality*: There are now many more aspiring legal academics with good qualifications in law and another disciplines. They are now much more welcome in law schools and they are likely to find other kindred spirits. At the same time, law schools have expanded and other humanities and social science disciplines have been cut back, at least in relative terms.

1987 problem 3: Pressure on time and resources.

> *2016 reality*: the pressure is greater but there is a greater clarity about how to incorporate the 'critical and theoretical dimensions' into law courses and law subjects with a lot of material available. At Griffith, I aimed to have staff teaching new courses to arrive at least six months before they had to start teaching and to have provided a full-time research assistant to chase material for our new subjects. I would be surprised if law deans could adopt that policy now, though the availability of interdisciplinary texts makes it easier to manage without it.

***1987 problem 4*:** Lack of available texts that include material covering the critical and theoretical dimensions. At the time, the excellent *Law in Context* series was produced by Weidenfeld and Nicholson with Professor William Twining as general editor. However, this could only be supplementary as they did not cover Australian law.

2016 reality: The *Law in Context* series continued to expand and has now provided a role model for other books. More conventionally, most subjects will include at least one cases-and-materials book in which the latter involves materials that address that subject's critical and theoretical dimensions.

1987 problem 5: Perceived pressure from students: Students were not used to seeing critical and theoretical dimensions.

2016 reality: Students are now used to seeing critical and theoretical dimensions material. In Griffith, this was planned. In other law schools, it just happened. To the extent that standard textbooks started including critical and theoretical dimensions, it became commonplace and expected by students.

1987 problem 6: Pressure from assessment. Part of this was the reliance on 'problem' questions rather than essays with critical and theoretical issues which were more likely to be optional. The law deans' report to Pearce complained that legal rules could be tested more objectively and cheaply than assessments.

2016 reality: Students are used to answering essay questions and there has been a move towards them in the continuous assessment process that has emerged. Few, if any, current law deans would subscribe to that part of the deans' submission to Pearce.

1987 problem 7: Perceptions of what the profession required. Many educators felt institutional and senior peer pressure against inclusion of theoretical material.

2016 reality: Law schools and senior staff are generally supportive, and – as the Melbourne and Griffith experiences (see Chapters 1 and 6) reveal – the profession can be, itself, the source of progressive pressures.

1987 problem 8: Curricula were structured in ways that made it difficult to incorporate critical and theoretical dimensions.

2016 reality: Griffith provided a model and its success gave the incorporation of critical and theoretical dimensions into law schools legitimacy. Since then, all law schools have gone through major curriculum reviews and have, almost universally, incorporated critical and theoretical dimensions into their curricula.

Before I dealt with the listed problems, I faced a general one: the multiple challenges of law schools at the time could lead to paralysis. Not for the last time, I suggested that when facing multiple-problem situations, the problems cannot be tackled severally but need to be addressed strategically and simultaneously.

Some new law schools merely sought to replicate existing law schools, producing cheap imitations of outdated models. I remember one Foundation Dean who told me that he drew up the curriculum on the back of an envelope on a two-hour flight; he saw my scowl and lamely added that he had been thinking about it for a long time. However, those law schools that took up the opportunity provided by a blank sheet showed what could be done and provided models for others to follow, adapt or build on. Griffith was certainly such a case and its widely recognized success[8] made borrowing from our approach respectable. More generally, the responses to some of these problems made answers to other problems easier (as more academics were educated and interested in interdisciplinary and transdisciplinary approaches to law they engaged in more research in these areas and this fed into the text books).[9]

5 An incomplete revolution

This chapter is, and remains, very positive about the extent to which law schools have responded to the challenges of the 1980s discussed above. That said, the extent and duration of the response by law schools naturally varies. Reformers in some law schools may well feel, as I did in 1988, that the glass was very much half empty and that there was pressure to drain it rather than top it up. In corresponding with me over this book, one colleague who had been dean in more than one law school regretted that all he could do was to make jurisprudence compulsory, a change that was reversed after he left. In the terms of my 1988 article (that formed the basis for Chapter 3), they had not even asked the right question.

Certainly much writing is predicated on the general acceptance of the importance of theory, and discusses what theories should be deployed for what purposes and at what level.[10] However, some contemporary writing provides a sense of déjà vu, in which law schools seem to be facing the same challenges as we did in the 1980s, with relatively limited awareness of the responses that various law schools developed to meet those challenges. To take one example (a 2014 work), Stolker lists a number of challenges including curriculum content textbooks;[11] law school numbers; the place of the law school in the university (discussed above); the supposed failure to bring the fruits of legal education research into the classroom;[12] the transition from law school to the profession;[13] the place of the law school in the university and dichotomies between academic and professional education;[14] the competition for good staff and students;[15] and the difficulties others have had in generating funds for legal research from granting bodies.[16]

While I was not the one to coin the term 'revolution' in terms of what we were trying to do in the early 1990s,[17] the above does lead us to reflect on various theories of revolution. In the mid-seventeenth century, revolution was as often seen as a return to an earlier order (and hence *revolving*) as the basis for an entirely new one. This has largely given way to the idea of a revolution as involving the overthrow of a previous order and its replacement with a new and progressive one. However, such revolutionaries are always on the watch for a 'counter-revolution'.[18] In Marxist dialectics, this was a recurring phenomenon (at least until the 'end of history'). An order would generate contradictions, which led to a new order that transcended both the previous order and the contradictions it developed.[19]

I would not suggest that law schools have reverted to the status quo ante or that some malign counter-revolution has been staged. However, Marx's insight does suggest that 'revolutions', if they occur, are rarely complete. The contradictions, issues or 'challenges' (my preferred term in this book) from the old order are not completely resolved in the new.[20] Even as we need to meet the new challenges of the globalization of law, lawyering and legal education, the old debates continue because the challenges that generated them are still, at least to an extent, present.[21] Indeed, the new challenges may provide new ammunition for old debates. Some might argue that we need to drop legal theory because globalization means there is more content to teach and competition between law schools means that we have to have shorter courses in which to teach it. Unsurprisingly, I would argue that we need interdisciplinary and transdisciplinary work that encompasses the various governance disciplines at the 'vortex' to understand the nature, process and challenges of globalization, so that law schools know what to communicate to students and members of the profession engaged in their lifelong learning. This approach will not substitute for the teaching of specific areas of law, but it will help us identify what areas of law we should teach and help new and old graduates identify what they should seek to learn. Whether such a coordinated and strategic response should be called a 'revolution' (as Sir Ninian Stephen did) or not is beside the point. Law schools will need to address the challenges and opportunities created by the globalization of law, lawyering and legal education by addressing long-standing issues that will never completely go away. I would not claim that our approach has resolved, for all time, the issues we addressed, nor put an end to ongoing debate about those issues. However, I hope that our example and approach at Griffith continues to provide useful ways of thinking about those issues, and some practical ways of dealing with them.

6 Resourcing universities and law schools

Pearce reported to a body that was soon after abolished – the Commonwealth Tertiary Education Commission (CTEC). CTEC was established after the Whitlam Labor government abolished student fees and took over all funding for universities and Colleges of Advanced Education ('CAEs') which, like British polytechnics, did tertiary teaching but not research. CTEC advised the Commonwealth Government on a wide range of issues from the courses taught to the buildings built – along with recommendations for consequential triennial funding. Of course, the Commonwealth Government was the ultimate arbiter of those funding levels so CTEC had to adjust as required. From the mid-1970s to the late-1980s, student levels were largely static and universities were under financial pressure as a large group of young staff appointed in the 1970s moved up salary and promotion scales. Academic vacancies were almost entirely just that – vacancies created by retirement and resignation (one reason why I was so fortunate that the then dean of Melbourne Law had secured the approval of the vice chancellor to create a position for me in 1982). Universities wanting to create new law schools had to ask CTEC and the answer was likely to be 'no'. This was partly because of lack of funding; partly because various law societies had been objecting to what they saw as a glut of lawyers coming from the four law schools established in the 1970s (UNSW, Macquarie, NSWIT and QIT)[22]; and partly because CTEC liked funding non-traditional faculties.

Within this funding envelope, universities had a great deal of autonomy as to how they deployed those resources and which degrees to concentrate on. Monash and UNSW put a great deal of funding into law to fund the strategies outlined by their foundation deans and, when Pearce reported, the 15-year-old UNSW law school was widely considered the best law school in Australia. Latrobe recruited exceptional professors in philosophy and political science. It was possible for new university schools to excel.

The *Pearce Report* did not recommend any new law schools because of the priority the report gave to resourcing. Establishing an adequate library involved very high fixed costs and only a small number of existing law schools had the recommended minimum of 100,000 volumes. And quite a few law schools had what were considered very high student-staff ratios (up to double those in arts faculties).

The context completely changed with the radical 'Dawkins reforms' to higher education: the distinction between universities and Colleges of Advanced Education (CAEs) was abolished (though funding for former CAEs did not increase); CAEs were encouraged to merge with each other and with universities on the basis that larger institutions were more efficient;[23] universities were given much more autonomy over the courses they taught; some money was taken away from tertiary institutions and redistributed by competitive research grants; and a new deferred fee scheme was introduced in which students were expected to contribute 20 per cent of the cost of their education, but only after reaching average weekly earnings. The last allowed an expansion of funding for universities because the universities did not have to wait for that 20 per cent (later to increase to as much as 100 per cent of the real cost of legal education).

Universities were in a more competitive environment with differential resources. The long-established universities had high funding bases, high prestige and professional schools that attracted the best students. The new universities had similar per student funding bases but generally far fewer students, because growth had stalled soon after their establishment, they enjoyed lower prestige and offered few if any professional courses. Former CAEs were worst off on all three counts but at least could call themselves universities. The 'unification' of higher education in fact generated a tripartite division of: older universities (who formed the 'Group of 8'); universities established in the 1970s; and, former CAEs that became post-Dawkins universities. The second group generally sought to incorporate CAEs, which gave them numbers but with lower funding per student and a large body of academics with little or no research experience. Most of these universities opted to establish law schools (James Cook, Wollongong, Charles Darwin, Murdoch, Deakin, Griffith, Flinders, Latrobe, University of New England and Newcastle). It was, perhaps, a little more surprising when the rest of the Australian universities decided to start law schools – (University of Canberra, University of Western Sydney, Southern Cross, Notre Dame, Victoria, RMIT, Australian Catholic University, University of Southern Queensland, Northern Queensland, Central Queensland, Sunshine Coast, John Curtin, Edith Cowan, Southern Australia, Canberra).[24] The year 1993 was something of a crossover point, with the last two pre-Dawkins universities opening law schools and the first two of the post-Dawkins universities opening theirs. From then on, all new law schools were the post-Dawkins universities that were built on former CAEs. One might consider the new law schools from post-Dawkins universities a 'fourth wave' that was bigger than any other, and bigger than the first two waves combined.

Some sought to fund their law schools reasonably well. Others did not. After being invited to apply for the Foundation Deanship at Griffith, I was interviewed by a panel of 22. After answering all questions, I was, as is usual, asked if I had any questions. I had but one: 'Is this going to be a cheap law school?' The vice chancellor immediately answered 'no!' We spent three weeks negotiating what 'no' meant. I saw the opportunity for a law school (funded a little better than UNSW, with staffing at the same levels as a good arts faculty, a new curriculum, support from the profession, and engaging in interdisciplinary research) that could do for this wave of law schools what UNSW had done for the previous one. With the new money coming in to universities, this was an investment a vice chancellor could afford to make. This was the origin of my suggestion that it was quite possible to create Australia's best law school for the price of the worst science faculty. If that prospect excited him, then I was his man. If he asked if I could do it cheaper, he was asking the wrong question – the right one being, who else he should approach to do it. After three weeks of negotiations, he had still not 'bitten the bullet' and, during a lunch with Sir Zelman Cowen and his deputy vice chancellor, he asked a little insouciantly, if there were any other issues. 'As you know vice chancellor,' I reminded him, 'there is this question of resources.' At that point, he declared that he would do everything he could to ensure I had the best-funded law school in Australia. I agreed to accept the post and Sir Zelman triumphantly exclaimed 'in front of witnesses'. The vice chancellor was true to his word for as long as I was dean. Indeed, when I came back for an extra 5 per cent per 'EFTSU' ('effective full time student unit'), he agreed. Within months, he had agreed to a new fully air-conditioned building, the first such Australian law school building south of the tropics. (My view was that this would encourage staff to come to work rather than stay at home on hot days, building collegiality.)

During our first decade, we were seen as national leaders in our curriculum and in our research – exceeding all other Australian law schools in per-capita research output and in research funding won (regardless of size). The National

Institute for Law, Ethics and Public Affairs, the ARC Key Centre for Ethics, Law, Justice and Governance, and the ARC Governance Research Network were a key part of this group. The dean of the UNSW law school privately told me that he knew exactly what we were doing and that it was the best thing for the law faculty in a decade because it was stimulating others to improve. In the end, we were clearly the most successful of the third-wave law schools. Indeed, we outperformed some first-wave law schools in global rankings and the national 'ERA' rankings (Excellence in Research Australia).

The failure to reach even more ambitious targets can be put down to a number of factors. It was partly because of the much more competitive environment and partly because Griffith restructured in 1998, moving the law school from the second level of university governance reporting to the vice chancellor (equal with eight other faculties) to the third level of university governance, reporting to one of four pro vice chancellors. This approach was popular in the post-Dawkins universities and the vice chancellor was persuaded by his 'pro vice chancellor administration'[25] to introduce this system after he had failed in an attempt to reverse the vice chancellor's successes in distributing staffing and funding to the faculties.[26] The result was, as I predicted, that law's unique contribution to the university and what it needed to make that contribution, was not represented at the highest levels. I put it to him that law schools are too big to be a traditional department but too small to be a traditional faculty. Universities could, of course, choose which level they would place law at, but it was a fact that there were no great law schools at the third level of university administration and that this was explained by the lack of voice such relegation would give it. In 1994, I was initially successful in persuading him not to proceed. However, several years later, after I ceased to be dean, the restructuring went ahead and Griffith went from the best-funded law school in Australia to around the average and below. The only Australian law schools that are ranked higher than Griffith are long-standing law schools at the second level of university management. I bear nothing but good will towards the vice chancellor who supported all my later research initiatives. The Dawkins revolution provided opportunities for new law schools but, in making it possible for universities to get much larger, it created incentives to restructuring which limited those opportunities.

Two other developments in the 1990s should be mentioned. First, the Commonwealth Department of Education developed a 'relative funding model' to compare the costs of teaching various disciplines. Given the low funding of some law schools, the average placed law in the lowest grouping of university courses – made worse because law libraries were generally funded from the university central management and therefore did not show up in the model. Universities above the average were tempted to reduce funding to that 'average'. Law schools with below-average funding were generally powerless to demand more (their powerlessness being demonstrated by how little funding they had hitherto been able to secure). The second development was the vast expansion of full fee-paying, largely undergraduate, foreign students, which saved universities from the serial cuts in real government funding. Given the geographical limits of most laws, law schools received limited benefits from this. And given the globalization of law, lawyering and legal education, the numbers of international students studying first degrees in law is limited. However, the globalization of law and lawyering is likely to change this – though Australian law schools will need to ensure that they can match the competition from better-funded universities in the region. While Australian law schools have some remarkably good rankings (typically with 5 in the top 50 worldwide), it is important to recognize that rankings are a lagging (and potentially unreliable) indicator of quality.

7 The changing face of law schools

In my piece on *Pearce*, I suggested that legal education had changed potentially permanently. Another 20 years later, there can be no doubt of it. Staff-student ratios got worse across the Australian system (and many other systems). If the differential between law schools and arts faculties closed, it was only because the latter deteriorated at an even faster rate. The model of teaching that was the basis for my estimates of how much a good law school would cost, initially achieved at Griffith in the 1990s, is now considered utopian. Large lecture theatres overflowing with students are a thing of the past – but only because an even larger number of students are watching online between the part-time jobs they take to pay their fees and rent. While this opens up the possibilities of MOOCs (mass open online courses), it does cut down important points of interaction that benefit student and teacher alike. Of much more concern is the demise of the small-group tutorial (which I would have preferred to set at 12 but which I was prepared to compromise up to 18) taught by full-time members of staff. In theory, it would be possible to transcend the traditional lecture with a multimedia tour de force and switch resources to small-group face-to-face teaching. The problems of MOOCs sourced in one jurisdiction that do not recognize the differences in various jurisdictions could be handled, at the very least, by comparative commentary and other materials by experts in other jurisdictions. Better still, the material could be reordered in each jurisdiction to be structured around the local law. With the globalization of law, there would be common international material and access to local material in a range of jurisdictions. Such MOOCs could take curriculum development much more seriously, adopting a coordinated and cooperative response. Unfortunately, it is at least as likely that lectures will be standardized and tutorials cut further.

No discussion of the changes, challenges and opportunities for law or legal education would be complete without reference to technology and access to information. While the 'law in the books'[27] is not the only form of law that we need to study, it has remained a key part since Pepo's time. In 1076, books were laboriously reproduced by hand and were both incredibly expensive and valuable. Students hired them out from commercial operators with the cheapest period being overnight. Printing empowered the wider and more detailed dissemination of legislation and case law – changing the law, lawyering and law schools. Law libraries came to be seen and justified as our 'laboratories'.

Pearce had set the minimum standard of 100,000 volumes for Australian law schools. However, by early 1990s a range of forms of legal retrieval had been marketed, including microfiche, microfilm and various CD collections. So my first call as dean was to Professor Colin Tapper. He had supervised me at Oxford and was the academic who proved the effectiveness of full-text retrieval long before computers could deliver it; he was also a key figure in the development of Lexis. 'Do I still need books?' I asked. His view was that, for a long time to come, we would need books and the latest form of information retrieval (with the second-latest being a white elephant).[28] I accordingly set about getting the *Pearce*-mandated 100,000 volumes through a multimillion dollar Griffith budget, supplemented with donations of law reports and the journals of other law schools, which we got in return for copies of the *Griffith Law Review* (which also served as an outlet for high-quality interdisciplinary legal research and became the youngest law journal to secure an A* ranking from the Australian Research Council).

We also sought to maximize the quantity of material that was free online – recognizing that the content of journals and law reports was created by those on the public payroll, assessed by those on the public payroll, and edited by those on the public payroll. With respect to journals, and to a lesser extent with cases and materials, the public purse paid for the published outputs. The publishers, who had once played a critical role in making dissemination both quicker and cheaper, were now having the opposite effect.

Printing was much cheaper than the hand-copied books that Pepo's students had to hire overnight. It allowed widespread dissemination of knowledge. However, the costs of setting up the presses and the relatively large runs that were needed to make them economical meant that choices had to be made on what was printed based on expected demand and, for university presses, quality. (The two are linked as university presses expected that the higher quality work would generate more academic sales.) Copyright protected authors but also meant that those who first took the risk of publishing could profit from reprints of successful books.

However, by the time I was building the law collection it was obvious that this system was creating a break on dissemination of ideas. Most of what we bought was written by academics paid by the state, assessed for quality by academics paid by the state, and available at great cost to the state a year or so later. It was obvious that it was time to cut out the intermediaries. However, most academics preferred to write and referee for long-standing journals operating under the old system. While recognizing that this was not going to change soon, we did all we could to get information for free from the creators to the ultimate users. I persuaded the High Court to send all judgements before their release to law deans for distribution to relevant staff – by fax. My fellow deans and I encouraged governments to release the intellectual property (IP) for all case law and legislation, paving the way for AustlLII (the Australasian Legal Information Institute).

8 Final words on Pearce and Griffith

My essay on *Pearce* recognized one major criticism: the panel members were too much impressed with their own universities and there were few international comparisons. Nor did the report really look to future changes in legal education. Instead, the authors saw the future as the more widespread adoption of what was best in their own institutions – as well as the inchoate appeal to incorporate the 'critical and theoretical dimensions'. I remarked earlier (in Chapter 5) how the *Pearce Report* read a little like the end of history of legal education. In fact, the globalization of law, lawyering and legal education was just starting. Moreover, incorporating those critical and theoretical dimensions had widespread implications. Nevertheless, the *Pearce Report* was, for me and for others, a mine of information.

I note Chow's criticisms that *Pearce* and other legal education reviews in commonwealth jurisdictions tended to investigate what is lacking and what needs to be changed – rather than how to make those changes.[29] However, I think that this misses the point. I would stick with my previous conclusion (from Chapter 5), that *Pearce* succeeded because it encouraged legal academics to think about their discipline and have the confidence to act upon their thoughts, supported by the many sympathetic members of the judiciary and the profession.[30] The report certainly did have this effect for me and my colleagues at Griffith, providing the launching point for our 'respectable revolution'. By asking the question about critical and theoretical dimensions, the *Pearce Report* helped legitimize a comprehensive answer that recognized the importance of traditional legal skills and the broad perspectives that allowed lawyers to ask important questions about those skills. *Pearce* and the senior lawyers made the 'revolution' respectable – though its success to date is measured by the extent to which it is no longer seen as revolutionary but simply part of what law schools do. Another measure of the success of Griffith's revolution is the large number of those appointed to junior posts in the first four years who went on to become chairs – generally within a decade of first appointment.[31] The next test is when the graduates reach the peak of their careers.

But the final test – and the challenge that all law schools now face – will be how they handle the next great challenge: the globalization of law, lawyering and legal education. As indicated in Chapter 1, I saw this as an opportunity in 1999 and a necessity by 2002, when it formed the last section of Chapter 6. It is, of course, the core of the final section of this book, especially Chapters 17 and 18.

Notes

1 With at least six others who were primarily jurisprudes being appointed to deanships in Australian law schools since, and with more who had a strong interest in jurisprudence.

2 This point was first made in Charles Sampford and David Wood, 'Theoretical Dimensions of Legal Education – a Response to the *Pearce Report*', *Australian Law Journal*

62 (1988). (Chapter 3 above), but is frequently repeated: see, e.g. Jonathan Crowe, 'Reasoning from the Ground Up: Some Strategies for Teaching Theory to Law Students', *Legal Education Review* 21, no. 1–2 (2011).

3 See, for example, the special edition edited by Avrom Sherr and David Sugarman, 'Theory in Legal Education', *International Journal of the Legal Profession* 7, no. 3 (2000).

4 In another highly symbolic move, the Department of Jurisprudence in Sydney, set up as a refuge for legal philosophers from the Department of Law in the 1950s was merged with the Department of Law. I was consulted on the move and my view was that it was once necessary to preserve jurisprudence but, now that protection was no longer necessary, its merger would allow each to be enriched.

5 On my sixtieth birthday, Professor Roy Webb disclosed that, although the selection process was supposed to be completely confidential, a particularly senior barrister had told Griffith I was the only one to appoint – and I had never even met him.

6 Charles Sampford, 'Rethinking the Core Curriculum', *Adelaide Law Review* 12 (1989).

7 For example, Mary Keyes and Richard Johnstone, 'Changing Legal Education: Rhetoric, Reality, and Prospects for the Future', *Sydney Law Review* 26, no. 4 (2004): Mary Keyes and Graeme Orr, 'Giving Theory a Life: First Year Student Conceptions of Legal Theory', *Legal Education Review* 7 (1996); Mary Keyes and Michael J. Whincop, 'The Moot Reconceived: Some Theory and Evidence on Legal Skills', ibid. 8 (1997); Richard Johnstone and Sumitra Vignaendra, 'Learning Outcomes and Curriculum Development in Law', in *A Report Commissioned by the Australian Universities Teaching Committee (AUTC)* (Canberra: Higher Education Group Department of Education, Science and Training January 2003); Christine Parker, 'An Oversupply of Law Graduates? Putting the Statistics in Context', *Legal Education Review* 4 (1993); B. Dick *et al.*, 'A Case Study of the Offices Project (Teacher-Less, Cooperative Learning Groups) at Griffith University: Implementing Educational Theory', ibid.; Marlene Le Brun, 'Law at Griffith University: The First Year of Study', *Griffith Law Review* 1 (1992). Charles Sampford, '*Pearce* Revisited', *Australian Universities Review* (1995); 'Starting a Law School from Scratch: The Griffith Experience', in *New Foundations in Legal Education*, ed. John Goldring, Charles Sampford and Ralph Simmonds (Avalon, NSW: Cavendish Publishing, 1998); 'Reflections of a Foundation Dean – the Griffith Experience', *Queensland Law Society Journal* 26 (1996); Charles Sampford and Sophie Blencowe, 'Educating Lawyers to Be Ethical Advisers', in *The Ethical Challenge to Legal Education and Conduct*, ed. Kim Economides (UK: Hart Publishing 1998); Charles Sampford, 'What's a Lawyer Doing in a Nice Place Like This? Lawyers and Ethical Life', *Legal Ethics* 1 (1998); John Goldring, Charles Sampford and Ralph Simmonds, 'New Foundations in Legal Education' (Avalon, NSW: Cavendish Publishing, 1998); Charles Sampford, 'Educating Lawyers for Changing Process', in *Educating Lawyers for a Less Adversarial System*, ed. Charles Sampford, Sophie Blencowe and Suzanne Condlln (Sydney: Federation Press, 1999); Charles Sampford, Sophie Blencowe and Suzanne Condlln, eds, *Educating Lawyers for a Less Adversarial System* (Sydney: Federation Press, 1999).

8 Referred to in C. McInnis and S. Marginson, *Australian Law Schools after the 1987 Pearce Report* (Canberra: AGPS, 1994), documented in Chapter 4, and recognized with its world #43 ranking in its twentieth year and consistent recognition in the middle of the top 100.

9 Though I note that, in some jurisdictions, academic lawyers still need to emphasize its importance: Paul Maharg, *Transforming Legal Education: Learning and Teaching the Law in the Early Twenty-First Century* (Burlington: Ashgate, 2007).

10 See, for just one example, Avrom Sherr and David Sugarman, 'Theory in Legal Education', *International Journal of the Legal Profession* 7, no. 3 (2000).

11 C. Stolker, *Rethinking the Law School: Education, Research, Outreach and Governance* (Cambridge: Cambridge University Press, 2014): 6, 7, 42, 45.
12 A challenge that Griffith and other law schools addressed by encouraging that research so that we had experts on hand and we had legal education focus groups for our lecturers.
13 See Stolker, *Rethinking the Law School* and N. Hamilton and V. Monson, 'Legal Education's Ethical Challenge: Empirical Research on How Most Effectively to Foster Each Student's Professional Formation (Professionalism)', *University of St. Thomas Law Journal* 9, no. 2 (2012). This was something we addressed through an understanding of lifelong learning.
14 See Stolker, *Rethinking the Law School*: 7, 42; and Chapters 3 and 4.
15 These were addressed (along with Stolker's 'pentagon' of teachers, students, programme, regulatory programme and culture) in our strategic plan, as they should be in others. See ibid.: 191; and also Chapter 6 above.
16 We found that interdisciplinary research was very well-funded.
17 It was the former Governor-General who used the term as high praise, as we saw in Chapter 6.
18 Karl Marx, 'The Eighteenth Brumaire of Louis Bonaparte', *Die Revolution* 1 (1852): 31–127.
19 In Hegelian terms, *thesis* generated *antithesis* which was transcended by a new *thesis*.
20 This is in line with Avineri's reinterpretation of Marx, which I found useful as a partial insight into one of the reasons why law and society were not as ordered as some thought they were, and had to be. See Charles Sampford, *The Disorder of Law* (Oxford: Basil Blackwell, 1989).
21 See, for example, Chapter 12, Section 2, which gives the example of the large-scale and perennial factors arrayed against reform efforts in improving legal education on ethics.
22 New South Wales Institute of Technology (now University of Technology in Sydney) and Queensland Institute of Technology (now Queensland University of Technology).
23 Something that was generally true of single campus universities but not necessarily true of the multi-campus monstrosities that frequently emerged.
24 Indeed, only three have not given in to the temptation – see David Baker, 'An Avalanche of Law Schools: 1989 to 2013', *Journal of the Australasian Law Teachers Association* 6, no. 1 & 2 (2013). If Baker had wanted to ramp up the 'wave' metaphor, he could have used the term 'tsunami' – though both are overstated; while the article offers little in analysis (beyond repeating that found in M. Chesterman and D. Weisbrot, 'Legal Scholarship in Australia', *Modern Law Review* 50 (1987). See also, various chapters in John Goldring, Sampford and Simmonds, *New Foundations in Legal Education*) that provides very basic details on the new law schools.
25 This renaming of what had traditionally been a 'registrar' was an early indication of the problem.
26 He was a very good micro-economist and he had practiced what he preached.
27 Compared to the American Realists' 'law in action'.
28 The soundness of his advice with regard to microfiche and microfilm is attested by the fact that few under 40 know what they are.
29 W.W.S. Chow and F. Tiba, 'Professional Legal Education Reviews: Too Many "What's", Too Few "How's"', *European Journal of Law and Technology* 4, no. 1 (2013).
30 Including the Lord Chancellor's Advisory Committee for Legal Education and Conduct (ACLEC), 'First Report on Legal Education and Training', (London: ACLEC, 1996). I was invited as a participant.
31 Brian Fitzgerald, Michael Whincop, Brad Sherman, John Devereux, Christoph Antons, Lee Godden, Mary Keyes, Haig Patapan, Tracey Robinson, Mike Robertson, Graeme Orr and Christine Parker.

Part III

Legal ethics

Opportunities and challenges in education and practice

9 What's a lawyer doing in a nice place like this?

Charles Sampford

Ethics currently enjoys a place in the academic lawyer's landscape that was scarcely conceivable in the early 1980s.[1] In this chapter, I shall consider how the role of ethics in teaching, research and practice has grown and some of the intellectual fallout from that growth – in law, jurisprudence, legal practice, applied philosophy in general, and legal ethics in particular.

I will conclude by suggesting some of the implications and opportunities for ethicists.

In drawing the brush so quickly over so many issues and arguing for such linkages, I am bound to offend many. In some areas, I have argued the positions taken in some detail (though not, I hope, to the satisfaction of my adversaries).[2] In other areas, I am reaching beyond the detail of my argument to potential new arguments, the defence of which (if they be defensible) will await more sober reflection.

My remarks are primarily based on my knowledge of the Australian legal academy and its interaction with the legal profession in that country. I cannot comment authoritatively on the experiences of British law academics – and I am aware that many take a far gloomier view of the potential support of, and contribution from, the English practicing profession than I. However, I would be wary of any suggestion that the forces at work are fundamentally different in our two countries.

1 A remarkable change: the rise of ethics and jurisprudence

Theory in the curriculum

The early chapters have discussed what it was like to start a new law school from scratch, incorporating legal theory and legal ethics into the curriculum.[3] Theory made a comeback in most law schools, either through the efforts of individual lecturers in their subjects or through curriculum reviews supported by law deans. While the English profession does not seem to have been as supportive, the work of the Lord Chancellor's Advisory Committee on Legal Education and Conduct – which includes judges and professionals – has provided strong support for reform in this area.[4]

Research

Once the importance of jurisprudence and legal theory for the education of future law students was appreciated, it is not surprising that it was supported by the profession and, eventually, by senior legal academics. However, it might be imagined that the profession might have less interest in research incorporating jurisprudence, legal theory and legal ethics. In fact, the support of the profession has been as strong for the incorporation of jurisprudence, legal theory and legal ethics into research as it was into teaching. In retrospect, it seems clear that research led to much of the change in attitudes, with academics asking new questions about old material and looking for answers from a range of modern theories. This led to a profusion of work in the traditional academic sense of papers and publications, and appellate judges increasingly referred to the views of academics in their judgments.[5] During his term as Chief Justice of the High Court, Sir Anthony Mason made it clear that he was less interested in traditional doctrinal exegesis by academics than in their ability to provide reasoned arguments as to the direction the court should take, particularly when the courts did not have time to research and reflect upon the issues in such detail.[6]

The emerging respect for academic research that brought to bear the potential insights of legal, ethical and political theory to practical issues led to some stimulating collaborative projects that go beyond traditional methods of individual academic research. Australian research centres such as the National Institute for Law, Ethics and Public Affairs (NILEPA) managed to bring together academics engaged in law, philosophy, politics, sociology, criminology and economics as well as reflective practitioners from law societies, the bar, the bench, government and industry. Such projects have helped legal academics to secure substantial research funding from the Australian Research Council, law reform bodies, law societies, and government.[7]

Again, the encouragement and support initially came from the profession rather than senior law academics[8] – exemplified by my then dean rejecting my proposal for a centre in law and ethics on the basis that there was 'no money in it'.

Legal ethics – a slower progress

Legal ethics has been rather slower than jurisprudence and legal theory in securing a core place within the teaching and research of the law school. At of time of writing in 1998, legal ethics courses remain comparatively rare in Australian law schools and advanced legal ethics courses virtually non-existent. There is very little attempt to incorporate legal ethics into substantive law subjects and there is no equivalent of the Australian Pearce Committee urging law schools to introduce it into the 'core of the curriculum'.

This slower start can be attributed to a number of factors. First, legal ethics was seen as part of 'professional responsibility' subjects, which are taught as part of the professional year in the United Kingdom. Similarly, in Australia, it is one of only three subjects that students must take after completion of their law degree as part of what is, in other respects, practical training. Legal ethics was traditionally taught by practitioners as, essentially, another set of legal rules governing conduct within the profession. Since these teaching practitioners had little contact with legal theorists within law schools, ethics was not linked to the teaching of jurisprudence and legal theory from either direction. Jurisprudence teachers did not consider legal ethics to be part of their responsibility.[9] Teachers in substantive law subjects rarely raised the ethical issues that arose in their areas of law (especially in family, tax and litigation) and teachers of professional responsibility subjects did not relate their subject matter to general theoretical issues arising within the law course.

The second factor was that there seemed to be fewer law academics with interests and expertise in ethics (let alone applied ethics) than in legal and political philosophy, sociology or even history.[10]

These two factors combined to produce a lag in research into legal ethics. In comparison to the profusion of texts and articles on general and applied legal theory, little was published in ethics and virtually none of this work originated in the United Kingdom or Australia. In the absence of such research, finding material to incorporate into mainstream curricula has been a major effort for law lecturers who are already under pressure to cover other material and to get on with their own research.

At Griffith University, a three-part strategy to incorporating ethics was employed. In first year, we introduced students to the basic questions asked about law and lawyering by jurisprudence and legal ethics. This material was taught as part of a major substantive law subject (Law and Legal Obligations) rather than part of a segregated 'History and Philosophy of Law' subject. This would ensure that students were aware that such questions were part of the central agenda of the law school and the life of a lawyer. In second and third years, lecturers revisited those questions as part of the teaching of other substantive law subjects according to the nature of the subject and their own interests. This worked very well with respect to most areas of legal theory, including feminism, critical legal studies and general issues of political philosophy and justice. However, the limited expertise of staff and the difficulty of finding suitable material meant that our goal of including ethical issues in casework was only achieved in a few subjects (most notably taxation and litigation). Fortunately, the recent growth in legal ethics research, most prominently in the USA and more modestly in the United Kingdom and Australia, has alleviated many of these problems.[11] Some of the subjects of greatest interest to the judges and practitioners with whom we interact are ethical issues. The issues involved generally require the input of professional lawyers as well as academic lawyers and philosophers but we have found that such teams can find support in professional as well as government funding bodies.

Lawyers as contributors to applied ethics

The incorporation of legal, ethical and political theory into legal academia not only improves its quality and its relevance for lawyers, it makes law more capable of contributing to the resolution of ethical and social problems. For many, the involvement of lawyers in ethical issues seemed to be an oxymoronic joke. Even where lawyers were not the direct source of the problems, their black letter solutions, involving ever more detailed regulations, confused or obscured the core issues of ethics and principle that needed to be highlighted for solutions to be found and implemented. In addition, when ethics took what has been commonly referred to as its 'public turn', the means by which it could contribute to public debate and the evolution of the law was not initially clear.

One traditional model was clearly inappropriate. Philosophers could not expect to descend from their ivory towers and echo Plato's suggestion for an ideal Republic ruled by philosopher kings by telling politicians, businessmen and ordinary citizens how to behave and what to do. Nor was it sufficient to take the theories that were the result of philosophical speculation and debate and apply them directly to modern day problems and attempt to deduce the correct answer.[12] Instead, applied philosophy units needed to accept they needed lawyers: Not only is legal regulation a part of the solution to many problems of applied philosophy (most notably in bioethics); the methodology is similar to that of legal reasoning.

Lawyers as ethical problem solvers

While ethically informed legal academics may contribute to applied ethics research, it is notable that lawyers with a strong grasp of ethics and principle have been playing an important role in major ethics reforms and, more generally, in producing practical responses to critical social and political problems. In the USA, lawyers played a key role in establishing and running the Office of Government Ethics and other institutional responses to the Watergate watershed. In the United Kingdom, the Committee for Standards in Public Life was led by a law lord, Lord Nolan – and a legal academic, Lord Neill, has recently been appointed as a member. In Australia, corruption-fighting bodies such as the Independent Commission against Corruption in New South Wales and the Criminal Justice Commission in Queensland have typically been led by lawyers. The Fitzgerald Inquiry into official corruption in Queensland was chaired by a lawyer with a high ethical reputation who set in chain a process of institutional and ethical reform within government and the police force.[13] This contribution is not only recognized in public life. Corporate clients will often go to their lawyers for advice on particular ethical issues and in setting up systems for dealing with ethical issues. Despite the oxymoronic knee-jerk reaction against the idea, as we will see in the following chapter (Chapter 10), lawyers should be the major source of such advice.

In the remainder of this article, I will suggest what some of the potential intellectual fallout of the changes outlined above might be – in law, jurisprudence, legal practice, and philosophy in general.

2 The ethicization of law and jurisprudence

Values in law

Laws involve statements of value. These may be implicit or even deliberately obfuscated by those who seek to further their interests and preferences through litigation or legislation. They may be explicit in the pursuit of social ends through those same means. Whether those values are explicitly recognized in legislation, judicial interpretation of legislation, judicial exegesis and application of the common law, and in the documents drawn by individuals or groups to give effect to their preferences in wills, deeds, contracts and articles of incorporation, depends in part on style.

While there was confidence in judicial method to resolve issues without recourse to values, judicial style tended to concentrate on an apparently technical discussion of precedents, despite the values underlying them and the values of litigants that brought the cases to court. However, with the decline of legal positivism and the realization of the inevitability of value judgements in law, judges became more willing to openly discuss issues of ethics and justice in their judgments. This trend has its origins in constitutional litigation, initially confined to countries with entrenched bills of rights.[14] It gradually spread to other jurisdictions and areas of law. One of the early Australian examples of a value-based judicial jurisprudence was *Commercial Bank of Australia Ltd v Amadio*,[15] with the reintroduction of equity into contract law to protect guarantors from unconscionable action by powerful creditors such as banks.

In general, as judges grapple with difficult issues in litigation they have turned to jurisprudence and ethics to resolve them. In so doing, the values involved have been more explicitly recognized as the only means by which they have been able to find intellectually acceptable solutions. These changes are not confined to the common law. Legislative styles also seem to have displayed signs of more explicit recognition of values. There appear to be two forces at work. First, attempts to prescribe rules in detail have been widely seen as failures. This was especially the case where widespread avoidance and non-compliance led to further detailed prescription – producing acts of monstrous proportions.[16] This led Australian legislatures to encourage judges to take a 'purposive' interpretation of legislation.[17] Later, statements of principle were incorporated into legislation against which the detail of the legislation and regulations could be assessed.[18]

The second source of more explicit value recognition lies in the increasing volume of legislation governing human rights since the Second World War, irrespective of whether these rights were explicitly incorporated in a constitution and protected by a constitutionally entrenched court. In addition to specific human rights and antidiscrimination legislation providing mechanisms for the protection of rights, there has also been significant welfare rights legislation. However, the tendency to treat welfare as a form of state charity rather than an individual right has tended to limit the effectiveness of the latter.

Finally, in a particularly interesting Australian experiment, parliamentary committees have been established to scrutinize legislation for its adherence to a number of principles. This has been developed furthest in Queensland where legislation establishes a scheme for the pre-legislative scrutiny of all legislation to ensure, as far as possible, its conformity with so called 'fundamental legislative principles' (or FLPs)[19] including, but not limited to, the respect for the human rights of individuals[20] and respect for parliament and, by extension, other key public institutions such as courts and local government. Under this scheme, all those involved in developing legislation, including bureaucrats, the parliamentary draftsman, the cabinet, parliament and its bipartisan Scrutiny of Legislation Committee,[21] consider whether or not proposed legislation complies with those FLPs. This tends to focus debate on the principles governing legislation and reinforces the aforementioned trend by encouraging legislators to explicitly state within the body of the statute the principles it is intended to fulfil and to justify, as a matter of principle, any conflicts with FLPs. Whether or not legislative and judicial style explicitly recognize value conflicts, those value conflicts remain the source of litigants' and interest groups' interest in litigation and legislation respectively. This gives the law and lawyers a general role for articulating and institutionalizing values and dealing with the conflicts between such principles.

Jurisprudential separation of law and morals

Despite this, for the past 200 years, most jurisprudence has been wedded to a separation of law and morals. This has been much criticized by scholars influenced by the critical legal studies movement and postmodernism.[22] This was not, as some imagine, because positivists accepted the law uncritically and urged blind obedience to its dictates. Such views may have been held by some positivists but should be seen as based on other grounds (general conservative self-satisfaction in the USA and Hegelianism in Germany). In fact, the original motivation for positivists like Bentham was to criticize law, not to legitimate it. Bentham saw no 'majesty' in the law,[23] and was contemptuous of Blackstone for arguing that English law was a fine logical creation of the common law judges in accord with reason. Bentham found it deeply flawed and in need of fundamental change. Rather than mixing it with his own values and developing a persuasive interpretation of his own, as Blackstone had done, Bentham thought to fix his target by identifying the law on the basis of objective facts about the behaviour, verbal or otherwise, of officials and subjects. Once fixed, it could be criticized and reformed or, if found adequate, justified.[24] The critique was in terms of an ethical and political philosophy. In Bentham's case, the critique took the form of a radical form of utilitarianism in which the pleasures and pains of all human beings were treated equally and all laws and social institutions were to be judged in terms of whether they increased the 'felicific calculus' of human pleasure minus human pain.[25] Thus the jurisprudential separation of law and morals was really a separation between ethical and political philosophy on the one hand and legal philosophy on the other.

This approach continued with realists like Llewellyn, who argued for a temporary separation of law and morality, and Hart, who sought to rediscover the subtlety of Bentham's analysis and to refine the positivist approach. Although Hart hoped that this would be an exercise in social theory, it was left to the Marxists and various sociological theories of law to use broader social and ideological factors to understand the phenomenon of law. However, those who sought to separate the analysis of law and the values underlying it did so in order to criticize it. The reasoning was simple. If you use your values to assist you in determining the content of the law, it will inevitably appear better to you than it might and not appear to be in immediate need of reform. However, the problem was that other interpreters might not be so 'enlightened' in their values, so that the law, as actually implemented, will be worse than you imagine it.

There were two problems with the essentially positivist separation of jurisprudence from ethical and political philosophy. It became increasingly apparent that any interpretation of the law sufficient to generate answers to real legal problems required a resort to values. Second, even if it were possible to separate law and morals in order to use the latter to criticize the former, such separation would only be the precursor to the moral debate about what the law should be. This debate inevitably enters the fields of ethical and political philosophy.[26] If legal issues cannot be resolved without resort to essentially ethical and political debate, then the question becomes the means by which such reintegration is to be achieved.

Various attempts at reintegration have been made. For example, Finnis sought to incorporate a modernized Thomian natural law within Hartian positivism.[27] Dworkin's empire of law involved judges, lawyers and citizens seeking an interpretation of the whole of their law that made it appear in the best possible light.[28] Some critical legal scholars and postmodernists sought to collapse the distinction by claiming that law was indistinguishable from politics and that in any case 'all values were equal, or in the slightly milder version, there was no privileged way of determining which values were more significant than others'.[29] These views have been rightfully criticized by subsequent commentators as dangerously close to totalitarianism. Instead, the subsequent commentators articulate a 'philosophy of otherness', based on consideration of the other before making an ethical (or legal) decision.[30]

While agreeing that a rigid separation of law and politics or ethics is neither possible nor desirable, I have long thought that, to rephrase Clausewitz, law is politics carried on by other means.[31] Although the combatants seek power, advancement and advantage through arguing their cases through the courts, the ground is different and the different weapons and field of battle fundamentally affect the nature of the contest and its outcome. I would now add that, in an important sense, law is ethics carried on by other means. If ethics involves discussion of how we should live our lives, then law involves attempts to ask and answer that question within the forum provided by legal institutions. Ethics involves debate and discussion about the values underlying behaviour and the means for their realization. The same can be said of law. However, legal means involve state sanctions and generally involve more formal, complicated and unwieldy processes. These affect the nature of the norms produced and the means by which they are interpreted. The use of state sanctions also requires the protections implied within the rule of law that would not be either as necessary or appropriate in ethics. Both ethics and law involve debate and discussion leading to different forms of norms about the means by which we should live our lives. These norms are partially different and, at best, partially supportive and complimentary forms of norms. But they are not the same, nor should they be identical.[32]

Such an approach resonates strongly with views of republican communitarians and postmodernists who, each in their own way, emphasize the importance of law as a form of public debate and/or contest of values. Such scholars see law as a forum for debating values in the context of past and current communal decisions about values.[33] In the legislative context, the political debate involves a direct invocation of political and ethical values to determine what old laws should be changed and what new laws should be added. In litigation, the debate is over the interpretations that are placed upon previous decisions of legislatures and courts. In making these arguments, traditional jurisprudence is inadequate. In seeking to comprehend legal institutions and the nature of legal arguments carried on within them, the ethical and political nature of those institutions and arguments has to be appreciated. Thus, Critchley states that he understands democracy as:

> An ethically grounded form of political life which is continually being called into question by asking of its legitimacy and the legitimacy of its practices and institutions: what is justice?... However, *democracy does not exist*.... One must not restrict oneself to conceiving of democracy as an existent political form (and, once again, certainly not as an apologetics for Western liberal democracy). Rather, one must begin to think of democracy as a task, or project, to be attempted.[34]

Realists have helped us to appreciate the political content and context of legal argument. Postmodernists have helped us to appreciate the ethical content and context of legal argument. The institutional aspect must be appreciated as well. Legal institutions need to be seen as formally rather than substantively ethical. They are formally ethical because they provide a forum for the debate of ethical ideas. However, the real challenge is to make institutions substantively ethical. Powerful interests argue ethical positions that are congenial to themselves but do so under a backdrop of legislation that has been pushed through by power politics in which the assuaging of interests is legitimated. To put it another way, if jurisprudence seeks to understand law as politics and ethics carried on by other means, it will, at the very least, need to incorporate political and ethical philosophy. Indeed, it is hard to see how this task can be accomplished without a reintegration of legal, ethical and political philosophy.

3 Reintegrating legal, ethical and political philosophy

As someone interested in the vortex where law, politics and philosophy met, I was never particularly concerned with supposed divisions between their various subject matters. I never thought of legal philosophy as separate from social, political and ethical philosophy.

The separation of legal, ethical and political philosophy is partly a result of the general tendency to academic specialization and the reduction of complicated theories and knowledge bases to simplistic models. The philosophies of Plato, Aristotle, Aquinas, Hobbes, Locke and Bentham involve elements of what are now seen as political, legal, ethical and social philosophy and they may be studied in the separate courses devoted to each. Bentham was one of the last to attempt to cover all of them. However, as previously argued, his positivism provided the basis for a separate legal philosophy that subsequently left out the other areas of philosophy that he pursued vigorously.

A similar phenomenon has occurred in economics – in which a particularly rich political economy as seen in the works of Smith, Ricardo and Marx gave way to a specialized version of economics that ignores politics, institutions, ethics and law except when these other phenomena can be reduced to its own terms.

While such specialization may seem inevitable in various branches of physics and chemistry, it seems deeply problematic for law and economics. Highly specialized disciplines relying on simplistic theories/models of social life lack the perspective to tackle major and complicated social problems. After the failure to solve major social problems in the 1960s by 'throwing money' at them, governments tended to 'throw laws' at them with masses of legislation in the 1970s, then increasingly to apply simplistic neoliberal economics to every issue in the 1980s and 1990s. If either law or economics are to provide solutions to legal and social problems, they must escape their specialization either by becoming broader themselves or by working in combination with other disciplines.[35] If, as I have argued earlier, legal solutions are only likely to be successful if pursued in combination with ethical standard-setting and institutional reform, there is no alternative to law reformers working with ethicists.[36] However, as argued in the first section, attempts to do so have shown considerable promise.

If law is to live up to its promise, jurisprudence, the philosophy which seeks to understand and guide law, must incorporate or at least understand ethical and political philosophy. This may only be achieved with a reintegration of legal, ethical and political philosophy, which, if achieved, would amount to the most exciting intellectual fallout from the changes described above. Signs of this reintegration are not lacking. Unger,[37] then Raz,[38] have engaged in serious political philosophy, and Douzinas and Warrington have been working on integrating ethics into legal philosophy.[39] If linked to jurisprudence, ethical and political philosophy would appear different. Political philosophy would not be seen as generating a single set of values (either a mythical 'classical consensus'[40] or a set of political ideals derived from reason as in Plato, Aquinas, Hobbes, Locke,

Rousseau or, indeed, Bentham). The political philosophy would be seen as helping to supply, articulate and refine the various principled arguments to be used by various parties and other political participants in debates over framing laws (while emphasizing those viewpoints which are not always heard). It would also place the legal institutions in which this debate took place in their social and economic context.

Ethical philosophy would also discuss values – for persons as well as institutions – as we seek to consider how we should live our lives. Legal philosophy would emphasize the role of law as involving attempts to provide authoritative statements of value on behalf of a community that is constantly involved in debate over such values. It would be conscious of law as a set of norms and its relationship to other sets of norms. It would be particularly conscious that law and ethics form (partially) different and (partially) complimentary forms of norms for three reasons: for the purposes of comparing different kinds of norm sets; to understand the partial and incomplete distinction; and better to understand law (the basic task of jurisprudence).

4 Ethics and lawyers' practice

If, as argued above, law and ethics form (partially) different and (partially) complimentary forms of norms, this has significant consequences for practice. An understanding of each set of norms would assist in understanding the other. Indeed, lawyers should be good at each – provided that they are good at both. In fact, barristers have always had to appeal to the ethical sense of judges. In many cases, they may not have been very good at ethical argument. But the same could be said of judges. The barristers appealed to the same ethical senses that the judges held. This was ethics by osmosis rather than intellect.[41]

However, if judges continue to seek more principled bases for their judgments, barristers will either have to develop their abilities as ethicists and, particularly in constitutional cases, political philosophers, or, more sensibly, to team up with them in developing their arguments in major cases. I have argued elsewhere that the first litigants to do so will be surprised with their success, leading to a much greater involvement of ethicists and jurisprudes in major cases.[42] The further the other developments outlined above progress, the more likely the (successful) use of ethics in legal disputes.

Some lawyers are already seeking solutions to practical problems that involve both law and ethics. Paul Finn successfully argued for the reinvigorating of equity in Australian law and, through the acceptance of his views by the High Court, became the most influential legal academic in Australia before being appointed directly to the federal court bench.[43] However, as argued earlier, the solution to contemporary social and legal problems requires more than a link between law and ethics. It needs a combination of ethical standard-setting, legal regulation and institutional design.[44] The last mentioned does not come easily for most lawyers – or, indeed, Anglo-Saxon intellectuals – who tend to see issues, problems and solutions in individual rather than institutional terms.[45]

However, the closer lawyers get to understanding the nature of law and its interactions with other social phenomena through the appreciation that an enriched jurisprudence makes possible, the greater the possibility of lawyers playing a key role in this tripartite process. This is not a new role. Dworkin once suggested that lawyers have a 'unique genius' in creating institutions to meet social needs.[46] He is right as a matter of history – from the American founding fathers, to the drafters of other important constitutions, to those who established the United Nations, to those who are drawing the rules and structures for new forms of corporate interaction.

On a smaller scale, and as we will investigate further in the next chapter (Chapter 10), as clients seek 'whole of business advice', and do not confine their questions to 'what is the law?' but 'what should I/we do?', lawyers could become the natural providers of ethical advice. Corporate clients will often go to their lawyers for advice on particular ethical issues and in setting up systems for dealing with ethical issues.[47]

Of course, the kind of lawyers who do such work and are asked for such advice are not typical (and certainly not the stereotypical amoral zealous advocate). However, this merely reinforces the importance of ethics in law and the role that such ethically informed law can play. In any case, as the boundary between law and ethics becomes more problematic, it is more important that those who advise in either field understand or, preferably, know the other. Lawyers are the natural profession to develop as the quintessential experts in the analysis, interpretation, application and institutionalization of norms – ethical, legal and mixed.

5 The content of legal ethics

So far, I have concentrated on the exciting possibilities for the incorporation of ethics into jurisprudence, law and legal practice, indicating the current positive trends and the future possibilities. This suggests the possibility of building ethics into law and law into ethics as the interrelationship between the two sets of norms are better appreciated. I have said little about the traditional area covered by legal ethics – the values and norms governing the practice of the legal profession.

It might be argued that lawyers need to set their own house in order before they can assist in ordering the houses of others. While this is tidier, more logical and more modest, life and social change do not work that way. I would suggest that the ethics of the legal profession is likely to develop in tandem with the ethicization of law and legal practice, with developments in each supporting and assisting developments in the other. The involvement of lawyers in advising governments and clients on ethical issues is likely to be as great a stimulus to lawyers' ethical thinking about their own lives as their ordering of their own ethics will make them attractive as advisers on ethics.

However, I do suggest that legal ethics will have to deal with a number of challenges and that meeting them will not only improve the moral value of the profession but also assist lawyers to perform the enhanced ethical role outlined above. Specifically, law must deal more effectively with its own institutional bases; it must deal with the fact that legal practice involves a series of overlapping sets of ethical norms and paradigms; it must learn to recognize and deal with the interconnecting values of the individual lawyer, the client and legal institutions.

First, although legal ethics has concentrated on the ethics of lone practitioners, more and more lawyers are becoming partners or employees of large firms that constitute very large businesses. These businesses have to be organized and managed. This does not mean handing the organization over to technocratic 'experts'. The running of any business raises questions of business ethics. To set and internalize appropriate ethical standards for that business requires the involvement of the staff in determining the ethical dilemmas, challenges and temptations that arise in that business and determining the norms, sanctions and institutional supports required to minimize the dilemmas and temptations. Thus, the work of lawyers is going to involve an interesting amalgam of professional ethics and business ethics. This is not an easy challenge.[48] However, the exercise will not only make legal ethics more relevant to the institutional realities of large firms, it will also provide lawyers with a greater understanding of the ethical issues confronting large institutional clients and make them far more able to give composite, 'whole of business' advice incorporating business ethics as well as law.

This parallels a long-acknowledged tension between government lawyers' ethical responsibilities as practitioners and their responsibilities to the state as public servants – a topic we will return to in later chapters.[49] The tension has also generated different sets of norms for different types of lawyers employed by the government, such as prosecutorial ethics and judicial ethics, as well as supportive institutional arrangements protecting prosecutorial and judicial independence. These sets of norms involve a resolution of issues arising from an interaction between legal professional ethics and public sector ethics. As government lawyers providing legal advice are forced into competition with private firms, they will also need to resolve the interaction with business ethics as well. Although the resolution of such interactions is far from easy, the attempt to do so will give such lawyers a vital insight into the problems of each, assisting them in advising government on public sector management and ethics as well as business regulation. All lawyers, as officers of the court, owe important duties to the court and the law.

These include duties of candour, honesty and disclosure, which are incorporated, however inadequately, into the rules of professional ethics. In addition, the demands of modern practice are such that all lawyers are required to merge professional, public sector and business ethics into their practice. If legal ethics can meet the challenge of the changing nature of legal practice and the lawyer–client relationship, it will assist lawyers to become normative experts with a deep understanding of the interaction of different sets of norms, including, but not confined to, the interaction of ethical and legal norms. It is also to be hoped that lawyers will appreciate that they are operating through large and powerful organizations and that they will be confronted by their own power. Lawyers are a powerful group within society. There are two responses to such power. The traditional response is to deny it, and see lawyers as mere individuals acting as agents for their clients. The second is to recognize this power and use it responsibly for the purposes for which it was given and which justify its continued exercise.

Second, legal ethics must develop its capacity to deal with a number of concurrently important values. The tension between the duty to court and the duty to client has generally been resolved by placing the duty to the client as paramount, subject only to exceptions provided by the duty to court and the law. This fails to give full value to the latter duties but marginalizes them and leads lawyers to exercise their skills, particularly well developed with regards to tax and regulatory avoidance, in reading rules narrowly. Seeing legal practice as involving a merging of business ethics, public sector ethics and traditional legal ethics may offer a better way of dealing with the long-standing tensions between different values within legal ethics.

The third challenge/opportunity for legal ethics is for lawyers to appreciate and deal with the interaction between their own values, those of their client or employer, those of the profession and those of the law itself.[50]

The final challenge is to develop legal and institutional supports to make the ethical solutions more effective, even with those of our brethren who would prefer to maximize profit rather than virtue. As I have long suggested, the key to this is to look to the justification of our professional activity and use that justification to provide the values that inform our ethics, the principles guiding the laws that regulate us and the design of the institutions in which we work.[51] None of these challenges will ever be either perfectly met or fully resolved.[52] However, in seeking to confront them and 'do our best', legal ethicists and ethical lawyers can do much to improve the profession and its ability to benefit the public it claims to serve, to make it a more genuinely noble calling.

Conclusion

In this chapter, I have outlined some of what I see as exciting possibilities for an expansion of the role of ethics within law and some of the trends that might support such changes. None of these possibilities will 'just happen'. They will only happen if ethicists and ethical lawyers work for them to happen.

There are, naturally, many contrary indicators available for the pessimists to emphasize and even the greatest of efforts might not produce success. However, there would have been far greater justification for pessimism in the early 1980s when I was just starting as a legal academic and considering whether it would be better to pursue my work in the more insulated ivory tower of a philosophy department. If we remind ourselves how far jurisprudence and legal ethics have come in the last 15 years (the subject of the first section), the long-term hopes of the remaining sections might not seem overstated.

Of course, some may consider that the suggested developments are undesirable. Others would want to give the suggested developments different focus, priority and so on. As the years pass, our images of what is possible and desirable will change and with that the objects of our optimism/pessimism. I do not seek to predict or guide the future, merely to think optimistically of the possible and thereby make the unlikely a possibility and a version of the possible a future reality.[53]

Notes

1 This chapter is based on an article originally published in 1998.

2 I would not want any fellow legal philosopher to abandon the habits of philosophers to which I have previously drawn attention – that being a philosopher means never having to say you are wrong (without apologies to *Love Story*). Philosophers never admit that they are wrong and merely invent new arguments to defend old positions.

3 As well as Chapters 2, 3, 4 and 6, see Charles Sampford, 'Reflections of a Foundation Dean – the Griffith Experience', *Queensland Law Society Journal* 26 (1996).

4 Lord Chancellor's Advisory Committee for Legal Education and Conduct (ACLEC), 'First Report on Legal Education and Training', (London: ACLEC, 1996). Part of the problem in the United Kingdom may be the separation of law teaching into two stages (a law degree and a professional year). This tends to limit interaction and communication with the profession, not least because law schools do not hand over their students directly to the profession.

5 For example, in *Theophanous v Herald and Weekly Times Ltd* (1994) 182 CLR 104 at 171–172, Deane J referred to the views of Inglis Ozark regarding the role of the constitutional text.

6 Sir Anthony Mason, 'Preface: Universities and the Role of Law in Society', in *New Foundations in Legal Education*, ed. John Goldring, Charles Sampford and Ralph Simmonds (Avalon, NSW: Cavendish, 1998). Also see Hon Mr Justice R.E. McGarvie, 'The Function of a Degree: Core Subjects', *Journal of Professional Legal Education* 9 (1991).

7 NILEPA secured major support from the Queensland Law Society, the Office of the Public Service, the Australian Law Reform Commission, the Australian Defence Forces and the Australian Federal Police (the last two being involved in our project on 'Preserving and Restoring the Rule of Law in the Asia Pacific').

8 See Chapter 1 for the story of my former dean who thought there was no money in it.

9 This is most unfortunate. If jurisprudence seeks to ask questions about the nature of law and lawyering, ethical issues must take centre stage. Some of the links between these are described in Chapters 2, 4 and 12.

10 During the 1980s, there seemed to be a fair number of young academic lawyers with undergraduate (and in the USA, graduate) degrees in politics, philosophy and sociology, with a disappointing decline in those with degrees in history. Of those with training in philosophy, political philosophy seemed far more popular than ethics (since ethics tended to emphasize linguistic philosophy and meta-ethics rather than the substantive issues covered in normative and applied ethics).

11 Journals publishing such work include *Proctor*, *Ethos*, and *City Ethics* as well as the traditional university-based law journals.

12 See Chapter 2.

13 G.E. Fitzgerald, *Commission of Inquiry into Possible Illegal Activities and Associated Police Misconduct* (Brisbane: Queensland Government Printer, 1989).

14 This can be found in the grand style of Holmes but became the norm in the Warren Court. It was quickly adopted in Canada with the introduction of the Charter of Rights and Freedoms.

15 (1983) 151 CLR 447.

16 The unified Australian Corporations Law, *Corporations Act 2001* (Cth) contains 1410 sections and the *Income Tax Assessment Act 1936* (Cth) contains 624 sections.

17 The *Acts Interpretation Act 1901* (Cth), s. ISAA states that

> in the interpretation of a provision of an Act, a construction that would promote the purpose or object underlying the Act (whether that purpose or object is expressly stated in the Act or not) shall be preferred to a construction that would not promote that purpose or object.

Section 15AB permits recourse to extrinsic material to assist in the ascertainment of meaning. Equivalent State and Territory legislation contains similar provisions.

18 For example, the *Public Service Act 1996* (Qld).

19 See Charles Sampford, 'Fundamental Legislative Principles: Their Meaning and Rationale', *Queensland Law Society Journal* 24 (1994).

20 *Legislative Standards Act 1992* (Qld) s. 4. This formulation was intended to ensure that human rights protection was confined to natural persons rather than corporations, which in other jurisdictions seek and gain protection of their 'human' rights, potentially to the detriment of real persons whose rights might be furthered by legislation.

21 Of which – at initial time of writing in 1998 – I had the honour to be the legal adviser.

22 See C. Douzinas and R. Warrington, *Justice Miscarried: Ethics, Aesthetics and the Law* (London: Harvester Wheatsheaf, 1994): Ch. 1.

23 Ibid.: 4.

24 Although much discussion in the 1960s concerned civil disobedience and the rights of the citizen to disobey the law, this was always a secondary issue. The first question was whether the law could be justified!

25 Bentham must be distinguished from the far cruder economic analysis of law in which dollars are treated equally rather than pleasure and pain. The difference is summed up in Bentham's law of diminishing marginal utility in which provision of goods that provided pleasure to one who already had such goods (or, indeed, other pleasures) would increase the felicific calculus far less than the provision of those goods to those with the least.

26 Even if one takes the generally laudable democratic line that the content of the law should be determined by the representatives of the people (or an improved version of their assembly), this merely shifts the locus of the political and ethical debate.

27 John Finnis, *Natural Law and Natural Rights* (Oxford: Clarendon, 1980).

28 Ronald Dworkin, *Law's Empire* (Cambridge, Mass.: Harvard University Press, 1986).

29 Douzinas and Warrington, *Justice Miscarried*: 9–10.

30 Ibid., Chs. 4–5. Also see Simon Critchley, *The Ethics of Deconstruction: Derrida and Levinas* (Oxford: Blackwell, 1992): 28; and D. Cornell, *The Philosophy of the Limit* (London: Routledge, 1992): 63.

31 M. Howard, *Clausewitz* (Oxford: Oxford University Press, 1983): 34.

32 I have argued elsewhere how they may support and complement each other. See Charles Sampford, 'Law, Institutions and the Public Private Divide', *Federal Law Review* 20 (1991); and Charles Sampford and Christine Parker, 'Legal Ethics: Legal Regulation, Ethical Standard-setting and Institutional Design', in *Legal Ethics and Legal Practice: Contemporary Issues*, ed. S. Parker and C. Sampford (Oxford: Oxford University Press, 1995).

33 See Cornell, *The Philosophy of the Limit*: Ch. 2.

34 Critchley, *Ethics of Deconstruction*: 239–240.

35 The relative decline in the use of law may, in part, explain both the rise of law and economics (giving in to the enemy) and the almost pathological hatred of 'economic rationalism' by many senior Australian judges and lawyers.

36 See Chapter 2.

37 R.M. Unger, *Knowledge and Politics* (New York: Free Press, 1975).
38 J. Raz, *Ethics in the Public Domain: Essays in the Morality of Law and Politics* (Oxford: Clarendon Press, 1994).
39 See C. Douzinas and R. Warrington, *Postmodern Jurisprudence: The Law of Texts in the Texts of Law* (London: Routledge, 1991) and Douzinas and Warrington, *Justice Miscarried.*
40 See *Justice Miscarried*, Ch. 1.
41 In making this less than gentle gibe, I am not seeking to give pure intellect too great a role – there lies totalitarian ideology. I am, however, suggesting that it has a role greater than the bit part previously assigned to it. See Chapter 2.
42 See Charles Sampford, 'Academy and Practice', in *Sir Zelman Cowen: A Life in the Law*, ed. Charles Sampford and Carol-Anne Bois (Sydney: Prospect Media, 1997).
43 P. Finn, 'Commerce, the Common Law and Morality', *Melbourne University Law Review* 17 (1989).
44 See Chapter 2 and Sampford, 'Public Private Divide'.
45 Ibid.
46 In Roland Dworkin, 'Address on the Value of Integrity', in *17th World Congress of the International Association for Philosophy of Law and Social Philosophy (IVR)* (Bologna, 1995).
47 See Chapter 10.
48 For a start, see Chapter 11 below.
49 See Chapters 11, 14, 15 and 16.
50 See Amy Gutman, 'Can Virtue Be Taught?', *Stanford Law Review* 45 (1993).
51 Sampford and Parker, 'Institutional Design'.
52 True legal ethicists would not avoid doing their job for fear of putting themselves out of work. However, the inherent difficulties of the issues involved will ensure a long-standing and noble pursuit.
53 This chapter was based on my contributing article to the inaugural issue of *Legal Ethics*. At the time, I took the opportunity to wish its contributors and editors well. Looking back, I am pleased to recount that the journal did, indeed, prosper – first under the editorship of Professor Kim Economides and now under Professor Christine Parker – who was my research assistant and co-author in the first legal ethics essay I wrote (Sampford and Parker, 'Institutional Design').

10 Educating lawyers to be ethical advisers

Charles Sampford (with Sophie Blencowe)

Introduction

The subject of this essay was first suggested in 1993 when Griffith University was designing its coursework Masters in Law. In consulting the local profession as to what was lacking in the LLM courses then available, we were intrigued when Elizabeth Nosworthy, a senior partner of one of Australia's largest and most successful law firms, suggested that lawyers should be taught ethics – not so much for themselves but for their clients. Her view was that clients needed more than just legal advice. They needed, and were increasingly seeking, 'whole of business' advice. They had gone beyond asking lawyers for the legal consequences of potential decisions and accountants for the financial consequences. Some of them were asking: 'what do you think I should do?' In her view, lawyers should be the natural profession to whom clients should turn for such advice – and should be educated accordingly.

This is a tantalizing suggestion because it is so contrary to the received image of lawyers as the most amoral of professions – yet so suggestive of what a nobler role for lawyers might entail.

In this essay we examine the arguments against the capacity and appropriateness of lawyers as sources of ethical advice and suggest that these arguments are based upon a number of flawed assumptions about the nature of law, ethics, legal practice and the lawyer–client relationship. We will consider the reasons why it might be in the interests of clients to receive a richer mix of ethics in their legal advice, citing a number of case studies. The implications of these changes for the role of lawyers and the ways in which legal education might be modified to equip them more effectively for this role are considered next. We will conclude by considering how lawyers might convince clients of the need for ethical advice and the legal profession's ability to provide it.

1 Knee jerk and beyond – the case against lawyers giving ethical advice

The ethical incompetence of lawyers

The grand jury of public opinion would have us believe that lawyers are the last people to whom clients should turn for ethical advice – from the myriad of (often very funny) anti-lawyer jokes to the higher points of English literature. Luban cites Macauley's indictment that a lawyer 'with a wig on his head, and a band round his neck [will] do for a guinea that, without those appendages, he would think it wicked and infamous to do for an empire'.[1] Shakespeare's Dick the Butcher simply passes sentence and urges: 'The first thing we do, let's kill all the lawyers'.[2]

Less savagely, some would argue that lawyers lack the competence to offer advice beyond the strictly legal. They are not, with very few exceptions, professional philosophers or astute businesspeople.[3] Thus, Morris argues that:

> It is not ... clear that someone who wanted moral or political advice would or should seek it from a lawyer. There is no reason to believe that lawyers have special moral or political expertise. In fact, general public opinion would probably suggest the contrary.[4]

This argument supports the need for the better education of young lawyers but does not establish that lawyers lack the potential to offer valuable advice on the social and business consequences of a client's proposed course of conduct.

We do not seek to contradict the popular disenchantment with past legal practice. Legal education has generally failed to adequately equip lawyers to go beyond a discussion of legal consequences to broader social and ethical consequences. However, the assumption that lawyers should not offer ethical advice (even if they could do so with confidence) rests upon a very limited understanding of the role lawyers can, and in some cases do, play in advising clients. As the case studies in this chapter indicate, the clients of lawyers who confine themselves to aggressive interpretations of law and procedure may suffer very badly. As Lake quips, 'good advice is rarely as short-sighted and narrowly drawn as helping Scrooge fire his employees on Christmas Eve'.[5]

The subjectivity of ethics

A related justification for leaving questions of ethics, justice and morality for the philosophers is that these concepts are sometimes seen as inherently subjective and unstable.[6] What may be abhorrent and socially unacceptable behaviour to some people may be perfectly legitimate in the eyes of others, particularly where there is no law prohibiting the conduct, or the relevant law is seldom enforced, provides no effective sanction, or a good lawyer can find a way around it. However, as both Ramsay and Haskell point out, there is a broad consensus amongst philosophers and even lawyers regarding the basic elements of moral action: doing good, avoiding harm to others, keeping promises and telling the truth, among others.[7] Simon argues that within the legal profession, these basic norms have 'observable regularity and are mutually meaningful to those who refer to and engage in them'.[8]

Disagreements at the margin, especially involving moral dilemmas and clashes between important principles, should not disguise the fact that most ethical philosophers, indeed most rational people, will agree on the correct behaviour in most everyday situations. Despite the different bases of ethical theories, there is convergence on many real-life issues. Lawyers who think that the law allows their clients to do what the vast majority of ordinary citizens believe to be unethical are the ones who have given the profession a bad name. As we shall see in this chapter, it may be bad advice as well.

Overdrawn contrasts between law and ethics

These arguments are based on assumptions about the differences between law and ethics. Howitzer Ethics is not as subjective as is suggested nor is law as clear as these criticisms would suggest. In recent years, legal theory has emphasized the indeterminate nature of rules and the inability of laws to regulate all aspects of human affairs.[9] Indeed, legal theory mirrors ethical theory in ranging through, but generally avoiding, the two extremes of 'one right answer' and complete indeterminacy. The margins of indeterminacy are very broad and both law and ethics are subject to bouts of scepticism. However, the strength and consistency of our moral conclusions belie the shaky theoretical foundations of our moral arguments. Similarly, legal theory is more controversial than the relevant law in the vast majority of what were once called 'easy cases' (in most legal disputes, the majority of lawyers will be able to predict with reasonable accuracy the relevant law).

This outcome should not surprise. Both law and ethics involve the application of values to human action. They involve general rules subject to varying formulations, conflicts and uncertainties in interpretation. The logical, ontological and moral status of both legal and ethical rules is subject to a number of controversial and conflicting theories. There are differences – of which the most important is the establishment of legal hierarchies for both the making and interpreting of law. These, in turn, produce texts that are expected to have legitimate as well as persuasive authority – whereas the texts produced by ethical philosophers have to rely purely on their capacity to persuade (and the interests of audiences that appear to make them more persuasive).

Yet, this important distinction does not undermine the continuity and links between law and ethics. Law provides a forum through which differences over values can be formally debated and through which attempts are made to reach tentative solutions. Despite its highly formalized manner, law is, in effect, a continuation of ethical debate by other means.[10] Although justice, ethics and common values are the language in which debate over legislation or the common law is fought, the battles are not concluded with the passage of legislation or judicial decisions at final appeal. Such decisions involve significant compromises and lawyers rarely completely succeed in either articulating the values that drive the decisions or in expressing them in language that can apply to the infinite variety of human experience. Accordingly, competing values lie at the heart of the interpretations of authoritative texts However, textual interpretation would benefit from courts, citizens and their counsel articulating those values and the relationship to the interpretations they are proposing.

This intertwining of law and ethics in both the formulation and interpretation of law makes it possible for law and ethics to be mutually supportive. According to Warren CJ:

> Law floats in a sea of ethics. Not only does law presuppose ethical commitment; it presupposes the existence of a broad area of human conduct controlled only by ethical norms and not subject to Law at all.[11]

Simon sees so-called moral options as competing legal values.[12] But not all of ethics is incorporated into law. Some ethical concepts are too general to be effectively encompassed by laws. For example, it may not be cost-effective or efficient to enforce some norms as laws if we adopt Mill's harm principle that laws should not enforce morality where no harm is done to others. Laws tend to respond to temporary ethical issues rather than lead them,[13] and ethical behaviours and cultures cannot generally be created by law.[14]

For these and other reasons, law and ethics are not identical. However, at their best they are mutually supportive, with ethical principles providing the principled justification for legal rules and offering valuable interpretive tools for legal rules as well as the basis for a supportive ethical culture.[15]

The similarities between law and ethics lead to similarities in the nature of legal and ethical argument and advice. Both involve imprecise general rules in need of interpretation that are applied to complex real life situations. Unsurprisingly, this has led to an interest by ethicists in common law modes of reasoning and to the jurisprudence that attempts to explain the nature of such reasoning.[16] The applicability of legal reasoning to applied ethics underlines the potential of lawyers as ethical advisers.

Even if lawyers attempt to provide only good legal advice, it will not be without ethical content. Explaining the law and the possible interpretations of it that a court might take necessarily involves an explanation of the ethical values that are likely to inform those interpretations. A lawyer who pretends that the law operates, for the court, in an ethical vacuum is misleading his or her client.

Good legal practice depends upon the making of complex judgments about a variety of matters not strictly related to the law. As Eberle points out, the lawyer applying a body of technical rules to practical business problems must exercise 'a capacity for sound judgment and practical wisdom, a process of imagination, careful deliberation, and intuitive comprehension'.[17] These skills can be and are harnessed to offer advice that goes beyond the black letter of the law to the psychological, social, public relations, monetary and business consequences of a particular transaction or course of conduct. Indeed, those lawyers who possess such skills may be almost uniquely suited to the role of ethical adviser.

The imperatives of modern practice

Several attributes of legal practice are said to limit the potential of individual lawyers to raise ethical issues with clients: the self-interest of lawyers, institutional and market pressures, and the financial dependence of large law firms on corporate clients.[18] Nelson argues that the institutional pressures of large firm practice and the competition to attract clients in a contracting market for legal services means that lawyers are more likely to further the client's self-interest than engage in discussion about the ethical implications of a proposed legal strategy.[19] Wilkins considers that 'like other self-interested actors, lawyers frequently overestimate their own abilities and privilege their own interests'.[20] According to Langevoort, lawyers cope with the pressures of daily practice and the need to achieve marketplace success through the use of heuristics, mental shortcuts and blind spots (making positive assessments of clients and ignoring evidence to the contrary).[21]

It is easy to see the nature of modern legal practice as hostile to the exercise of moral judgement and ethical persuasion. The income and reputation of individual lawyers and their firms may be substantially dependent on keeping clients through furthering their short-term interests. One of the major reasons for the general malaise affecting so many lawyers is said to be the feeling that they are employed to be no more than mere 'tools of their clients', possessing no 'duty to tell the client that he's wrong'.[22] This sense of powerlessness is reinforced by the structuring of work within large firms, with little personal interaction with clients (except for senior partners) and the handling of various aspects of the client's problem by discrete, specialized departments.[23]

However, the tension between 'doing good and doing well' may well be exaggerated.[24] It is too simple to see lawyers as the pawns of greedy corporate clients, as slaves to their firm's time sheets and driven solely by a market-driven legal culture. Such images give too little credit to the power and independence of lawyers and understate clients' respect for the expertise of lawyers (why else would they pay hundreds of dollars per hour for their services?) and the importance of ethics. It also assumes strong distinctions between business, legal and ethical advice.

The powers of a lawyer include the power to define what the law is and how it applies to client conduct and relationships.[25] Felstiner and Sarat argue that in any lawyer–client relationship no party dominates the other. Rather, the relationship is characterized by a process of negotiation in which power is constantly shifting and is never exclusively in the possession of either the lawyer or the client.[26] The relationship is one of shared interest, cooperation and mutual benefit. Lawyer client relationships are not zero-sum games. Cooperation and respect are important and clients generally recognize the advantages of resolving and, better still, avoiding, disputes.

Furthermore, lawyers do not so much simply object to a client's proposal on philosophical or public policy grounds as use a number of strategies to bring the client around to their way of thinking. Nelson observes that the lawyer's evaluation of legal options itself shapes client behaviour by suggesting what is possible and able to be accomplished legally.[27] Levin lists the practical strategies used by lawyers to dissuade clients from particular courses of conduct including limiting the duration of discussion, controlling the direction of dialogue and warning of the possibility of legal sanctions and other adverse social or business consequences.[28]

The rules of professional conduct, the risk of malpractice litigation and the threat of externally imposed sanctions also affect the nature of advice given to clients, ensuring that other considerations than the short-term interests of clients are taken into account.

Model Rule 2.1 of the American Bar Association states that 'a lawyer may refer not only to law but to other considerations such as moral, economic, social and political factors, that may be relevant to the client's situation'.[29] Although the rule does not oblige lawyers to provide such advice to clients, the Comment to the Rule acknowledges the potential benefit of broad advice:

> Advice couched in narrowly legal terms may be of little value to a client, especially where practical considerations, such as costs or effects on other people, are predominant. Purely technical legal advice, therefore, can sometimes be inadequate. It is proper for a lawyer to refer to relevant moral and ethical considerations ... [that] impinge upon most legal questions and may decisively influence how the law will be applied.[30]

There is an increasing possibility that a failure to provide the client with broad advice may amount to negligence or a breach of fiduciary duty.[31] For example, taxation authorities now expect a lawyer's advice to conform to government policy and the standards expressed in taxation legislation, which Philipps sees as effectively 'conscript[ing] the lawyer as part of the government's enforcement mechanism'.[32]

In isolation, such external requirements might only intensify the potential conflicting demands on lawyers. Fortunately, there are some hopeful signs that modern legal practice includes some developments favourable to the giving of ethical advice by lawyers. The emphasis is shifting from a model of pure technical expertise to an understanding of the nature of the client's business. Major clients like to deal with a single partner who will bring in other experts as necessary. This generates the possibilities of interpersonal relationships in which lawyers can understand the clients and their business needs and can be trusted in their advice. Finally, the greater emphasis lawyers now give to preventative action in areas where the law is uncertain is based upon a conception of lawyering that emphasizes the avoidance of questionable behaviour rather than promotion of clients' short-term self-interests.

These developments are breaking down the distinctions between business and legal advice and between legal and ethical advice. They also shift attention from the immediate needs of the client in a particular matter to long-term interests. Although there may be apparent conflicts between short-term interests and ethical action, conflicts between long-term self-interest and ethical action are extremely rare. Some might even be tempted to see a necessary connection because, in the long run we are all dead and must either face the judgement of an ethics-conscious deity or our own judgement of whether the life we are about to depart is one of which we can be proud (in one sense, our inability to 'take it with us' means that only those good works that outlast us can constitute a long run that outlives us). However, we do not attempt to *equate* ethics with long-term self-interest. Because of the vagaries of the future predictions and the varieties of interests any 'self' may have, what is in the long-term self-interest is not susceptible to certainty. However, ethical behaviour is rarely against long-term self-interest; it is a safe choice. It is also generally simpler – honest people do not have to remember the particular lies they have told different people, fair dealers do not have to watch out for revengeful victims, and those who try to live by the spirit of the law are unlikely to be pursued by officials who are determined to get them next time. Those who try to defeat the purpose of the law may find that their luck runs out as their overly clever lawyers find that the judge neither agrees with their interpretation of the law nor has sympathy for the client who has sought maximum advantage from it.

The proper role of lawyers

Another argument that lawyers should not give ethical advice rests upon a common view of the proper function of the lawyer, variously called the libertarian, client advocate or amoral model.[33] According to this model, lawyers should set aside their own or community conceptions of ethical behaviour from their dealings with clients. Bradley Wendel describes lawyers who engage in such role-differentiated behaviour as 'Teflon professionals – none of their client's slime sticks to them'.[34] The lawyer is simply there to maximize the client's interests, using whatever means, so long as those means are within the letter of the law (if not its intent) including the laws and rules of professional conduct.

The client advocate role may have been based on the idea that justice is best served by a rigorous competition for the truth. It sits well with liberal economic theories relying on competitive amoral markets in which self-interested behaviour by clients and their lawyers will result in overall gains for the community.[35] It centres on obligations to the client arising from the conception of the lawyer as a zealous advocate[36] and prefers relations based upon contract and economic interest over relations based upon duties to institutional and higher ideals.

The flaws in this view are many. It marginalizes the lawyer's duty as an officer of the court. It is based upon a paradigm of individual clients rather than large organizations.[37] It is also founded on the paradigm of the criminal defence lawyer's valiant defence against the state's attempts to deprive the underdog of his liberty. Both paradigms paint a distorted picture of the reality of much legal work – the pursuit and defence of complex civil litigation and the creation of long-term legal devices (corporations and trusts) and business relationships.[38]

We find it hard to accept that the role of lawyers is to ensure that their clients can prosper despite acting in a way that the majority see as unethical and contrary to values of justice and ethics underlying the law. Even if success is achieved in using the law in this way, large corporations are dependent on their success on much larger issues. An unsympathetic legislature may seek to change the laws that are misused and in any case will not take kindly to corporate representations. Even more fundamentally, as Pitt and Groskaufmanis point out: the litigator's syndrome overlooks the crucial fact that the preservation of a company's credibility – and perhaps even its survival in the marketplace – often will turn on the company's capacity to tell the truth, admit fault and make amends.[39]

Of course, once litigation is joined, the client has a strong interest in avoiding adverse findings. However, it could be argued that litigation frequently arises because long-term ethical advice to clients has been deficient or non-existent, a fact that seems to be ignored in much of the literature that supports the amoral role of the lawyer.[40] As noted above, this literature relies on arguments that presume a separation between ethical and legal advice and that law is not itself 'a source of moral limits'.[41]

Margulies warns of potentially undesirable consequences for the legal profession if the amoral role of the lawyer is abandoned. Lawyers may have to provide ethical advice at no cost because clients will not wish to pay for it and lawyers could leave the profession after feeling the effects of additional (uncompensated) ethical responsibilities.[42] Although it may be true that some clients will have to be persuaded that it is in their best interests to consider ethical issues, it is unlikely that they will refuse to pay for such advice, particularly as so much of legal advice is inevitably bound up with the ethical values that are required to explain and interpret the law. It would be highly artificial (if not impossible) for a lawyer to offer advice to a client with the proviso that only technical advice is included within the services to be paid for. Furthermore, we have seen that lawyers are changing careers because they are *disillusioned* with the amoral role. Finally, the decision to refrain from providing ethical advice is, itself, a moral choice. As Bradley Wendel observes:

> Lawyers *qua* professionals cannot avoid asking moral questions merely because they are difficult to answer. Lawyers routinely confront moral quandaries as persons undifferentiated by role, and probably do not believe that moral argumentation is worthless in the context of their own private morality. In addition, the decision to become an amoral actor is a moral judgment, and must be justified in moral terms. Attempting to justify one's non-accountability requires a rather sophisticated argument that belies the contention that one is not capable of making ethical judgments. Lawyers do not accept radical moral scepticism. Lawyers assume that ordinary citizens can make ethical judgments, such as whether they are dealing fairly and in good faith, or exercising due care.[43]

This challenges the assumptions on which the client advocate role is based: that the lawyer's duty to the client can be distinguished and separated from his or her duty as an officer of the court and obligations as an individual moral citizen *and* that the client is solely interested in monetary gain. These presumptive images of a schizophrenic lawyer and a sociopathic client are at the heart of the client advocate model's rejection of the lawyer's giving of ethical advice. The lawyer's duty becomes a matter of advancing and defending the selfish interests of the 'bad man'.

Advising Holmes' 'bad man'

This immediately raises Oliver Wendel Holmes' 'bad man' – one of the most evocative images of modern jurisprudence.[44] The bad man was not concerned with ethics or principle but with 'what the courts would do, in fact'. In the client advocate model, the lawyer should not judge or preach but advise what actions would avoid the court's wrath.

But let us consider the best advice that would be given to a bad man. If lawyers want to know what the court will do, in fact, they have to consider the values that will be used to interpret the law and make sense of it (not to mention the values that the judge will bring to bear in imposing sentences or awarding damages should the client lose). This does not mean that those values need be adopted by either lawyer or client. It is possible to treat them as mere facts about the beliefs of others – important in explaining and predicting behaviour. However, such detached observation and prediction is no easy task. Judges do not generally have the time, the inclination or the training to systematically consider their values or articulate them. The values judges bring to bear are to be found embedded in their judgments and then only to the extent that they are necessary for the case at hand. Those values are, in any case, likely to vary substantially from judge to judge and be subject to development through exposure to different cases, life experiences and changing community opinion.[45]

Rather than try to stay fully detached and second guess the values particular judges will bring to bear, the lawyer will find it easier to seek an approximate understanding of those values, adopt them and use them to interpret the law and advise the client how to act. Both lawyer and client will find it much easier to adopt the values that underlie and justify the law than to stand outside of them and attempt to keep just outside the range of actions that courts will penalize. The prediction game is time-consuming and unreliable. The more precisely the lawyer and client try to judge what the courts will do, the more often they will lose – and the less sympathy the court will have for their breaches. On the other hand, someone who is trying to follow the values underlying the law is far less likely to fall foul of it and will be treated far more leniently, by official and judge alike, if their action inadvertently strays into that which the law, as interpreted by the judge, prohibits.

Thus, we find the great irony. The best advice of the lawyer to the 'bad man' is to attempt to be 'good' according to the lawyer's best understanding of the values underlying the law. The most efficient behaviour is generally that in compliance with the law and its principled justification.

Of course, individuals are free agents and may have principled disagreements with the values the lawyer sees as informing the law. The underlying rationale of the client advocate model is to protect client autonomy. However, the necessary protection for independent moral judgement is rarely relevant in the case of large corporate clients. In any case, if the values underlying the law are enunciated, it is easier for the client to identify that the law has different standards from his or her own and then to decide whether to defy the law as a matter of principle.

Where clients' values are in line with a controversial interpretation of the law, they can be advised of this fact and tailor their actions accordingly, knowing that they run the risk of losing in court.

The best legal advice to bad men, good men and principled rebels highlights the underlying ethical values (and any conflicts within or among them) to make compliance easier for the majority who wish to comply and to make principled opposition easier for those who are genuinely offended by the values the law seems to espouse.

2 Why clients need ethical advice from lawyers

Far from suggesting that lawyers are inappropriate dispensers of ethical advice, the nature of law, the nature of practice and the role of the lawyer all indicate that lawyers need to be able to advise on ethics merely to give good legal advice.

A striking illustration of why clients need ethical advice from lawyers comes from the Federal Sentencing Guidelines in the United States.[46] Since 1991, federal judges have been required to take into account an organization's 'culpability' when imposing fines on companies whose primary purpose was not to engage in criminal activity. A firm can reduce its culpability score and escape with a significantly reduced penalty if it can satisfy certain requirements. The most important requirement is that prior to the conduct occurring, compliance standards and procedures were in place that were reasonably capable of reducing criminal conduct. Furthermore, a senior employee (who will often be an in-house lawyer) must have been made responsible for managing the compliance programme. The existence of a written code of conduct will not be sufficient to prove that the company had diligently sought to prevent and detect criminal conduct. Rather, the company must have undertaken active monitoring and auditing of its operations to ensure that they complied with the purposes of legislation, provided mechanisms for employees to report breaches in confidence and educated employees at all levels about the policies and procedures in place.[47]

Of course, courts will tend to take these matters into account irrespective of the existence of explicit sentencing guidelines. Courts are increasingly embracing a purposive interpretation of legislation, particularly in relation to the environment, public safety, health, privacy and the conduct of corporations overseas.[48] Judges inevitably bring values such as justice and good faith to the interpretation of the law, and are often influenced by the concept of corporate social responsibility, 'the notion that corporations [and their employees] have an obligation to constituent groups in society other than stockholders'.[49]

However, clients and lawyers should not confine their discussion of ethical issues to the imponderable values a judge may apply in determining the validity of the client's actions, should the matter get to court. Rather, a proper consideration of ethical considerations requires both lawyers and clients to bring their own values into conversations about the law and then to attempt to live by them.

Australian case studies

In Australia, the reputation of a major mining corporation has been badly scarred by its willingness to operate in another country in ways unacceptable at home and then to engage in questionable tactics to avoid paying compensation. In June 1996, BHP Limited finally agreed to an out-of-court settlement of a class action brought by landowners affected by the company's joint-venture mining operations in the western highlands of Papua New Guinea. Since 1984, following the collapse of the original tailings dam, all the waste from the mine had simply been dumped into the Ok Tedi and Fly River systems, with devastating environmental consequences. The tailings had washed downstream, settling on the lower reaches of the river. The resultant silt build-up had killed fish and also destroyed trees and market gardens.

During the two-year legal battle, BHP embarked on a massive publicity campaign to win over the Australian public. BHP's public relations campaign was not helped by the finding by Justice Cummins that the company was in contempt of court for its role in drafting legislation before the PNG Parliament. The legislation would have restricted landowners' ability to access courts of a foreign jurisdiction, thus placing an immediate halt to the litigation in Victoria. It would also have made it a criminal offence for landholders to seek further compensation through the courts once they accepted a settlement package from BHP. Although Cummins was reversed on appeal,[50] the damage had been done. BHP's experience indicates that a 'legal win' (the avoidance of formal legal sanctions) may be truly pyrrhic in terms of a corporation's reputation. The former chief executive of BHP publicly admitted that management's failure to ensure that 'there was proper understanding (in the legal team) of all the values necessary' had played a critical part in BHP's loss of standing in the Australian community.[51]

By contrast, an Australian biscuit manufacturer's response to a recent extortion threat provides an example of the benefits of ethical behaviour for companies. Arnott's Biscuits Ltd quickly responded to a threat by an anonymous letter-writer to contaminate its biscuits with enough poison to kill a young child by recalling its products from approximately 2,500 supermarkets and shops in two states and then destroying the 800 truckloads of biscuits that had been stockpiled.[52] The biscuits were off the shelves for two weeks, costing the company a million dollars a day at a time when it faced intense competition in the food sector and declining profits.[53]

Arnott's placing of the safety of its consumers above immediate financial considerations paid off in terms of minimizing long-term damage to the company's market position. Arnott's managing director held daily media conferences and the company put together a team comprised of senior executives, including the head of its legal division, to oversee the company's response to the crisis, which included the provision of a telephone call-in service for concerned customers and retailers. Arnott's prompt and public reaction to the extortion crisis and its well-planned crisis-management strategy has clearly earned it the respect of the media, investors and the broader Australian community.[54] In the not so long-term, it also advanced that company's interests.

3 Alternative models of lawyering

If the artificial dichotomies between law and ethics are rejected, it becomes relatively easy to locate the giving of ethical advice within the lawyer's overall duty to his or her client. However, this will require an alternate model of lawyering to the simple client advocate model discussed above. In so doing it will need to avoid the mistaken dichotomies between legal and business advice; the short-term and long-term consequences of action; the lawyer's duty to the court and duty to the client; and the lawyer's duty as a moral citizen and as an advocate.

In helping to rethink the lawyer's role, Eberle lays down three foundations: the 'autonomy foundation' (client advocate role of lawyer); the 'community foundation' (lawyer's obligations to the broader community, including the courts); and the 'morality foundation' (the lawyer's and client's duty to use ethical means to achieve ethical ends).[55] He observes that lawyers tend to give only secondary consideration to community and moral interests, despite the fact that:

> Interests relevant to clients involve duties to themselves in achieving their rights under the law, duties to community arising from their connections and sense of belonging to others, including lawyers and our system of law, and duties to conscience as given content by fundamental moral norms.[56]

Critics of the narrow client advocate role have embraced alternative models of lawyering that require the lawyer to establish a moral dialogue with his or her client to give more weight to these community and moral interests. The moral dialogue approach is based on the assumption that not only is it often in the client's interests to receive ethical advice, it is also the lawyer's duty to consider ethical issues (whether the client wishes to or not) and that the lawyer has an interest in the outcome as an independent moral actor and member of the community. However, these various duties should not be viewed as mutually exclusive. Rather, they should complement each other to achieve a result that 'empower[s] clients to achieve autonomy in an ethical manner within the context of a just community'.[57] An example of this approach is the lawyer who suggests realistic structural solutions to environmental or occupational health and safety problems instead of encouraging clients to evade their legal and moral responsibilities.[58]

Proponents of the moral dialogue school differ in the weight they give to each type of interest and the degree of autonomy they allow the client to exercise. Under Simon's model, the lawyer should assess the relative merits of the client's interests and the interests of others and then attempt to resolve the competing claims, taking 'those actions that, considering the relevant circumstances of the particular case, seem most likely to promote justice'.[59] He argues that it is legitimate to give this degree of discretionary judgment to a lawyer because, among other things, any increase in the lawyer's capacity to frustrate client goals is balanced by a reduction in the lawyer's capacity to frustrate goals of third parties and the public.[60]

However, others point to the risk of paternalism or domination of the client inherent in this model. Heller suggests that after providing the client with a 'full picture' of the law, its purposes and the possible consequences of the client's preferred course of conduct, the lawyer should allow the client to be the final decision-maker.[61] Ellmann argues that the lawyer should privilege the client's views even if this requires the lawyer to either exploit a legal loophole or a lack of legal regulation in the area, or to argue for an interpretation of the law that does not accord with the lawyer's.[62] Although the client-centred approach recognizes that, from the client's perspective, the lawyer is employed to act as his or her agent (one of the many roles of the lawyer) it overestimates the extent to which lawyers can dominate clients, particularly where the client is a corporation.[63] As Morris notes, not all clients can be classified as 'frightened and uninitiated'.[64] In fact, the economic power of clients often poses a significant barrier to lawyer's ability to retain ethical autonomy from their clients.[65]

A more moderate approach is taken by Margulies, who sets out a list of factors to guide lawyers in the exercise of their discretion to undertake ethical counselling.[66] These factors include morality (the action or decision may harm others, involve lying or misleading, violate the equality norm or be one that the client would not wish for everyone in society); psychology (the action or decision may engender guilt or regret, perhaps the client should be advised to seek the services of a mental health professional); and policy (unintended consequences and net cost to society). He argues that the lawyer should have a duty to advise the client to modify his or her position when the factors in his list are present, and a right to withdraw altogether if the client is not convinced of the lawyer's advice. Margulies' proviso is that the client's interests must not be 'immediately and irrevocably' prejudiced by this latter action.[67] However, even if the lawyer is 'the last lawyer in town', a refusal to assist the client is unlikely to affect the interests of justice unless the client's *rights* (as opposed to the client's ability to manipulate the law to suit its own business interests) are at stake. As even Fried observes, the last lawyer in town should not feel morally obliged to help the finance company repossess a widow's refrigerator.[68]

There is much merit in these views. However, there is a common strand that emphasizes conflicts between client interest and ethical action. As we argued above, long-term self-interest is strongly correlated to ethics.

Most clients want to be ethical, they want to 'be able to sleep with themselves at night'. The divorce of legal and ethical advice seems to operate on the assumption that clients are sociopaths. The lawyer assumes a duty to act as if client's interests are to be pursued whatever values inform the law. Unfortunately, some company directors think that they have a similar duty with respect to their shareholders – as if they really were sociopathic warriors for stockholder interests.

As suggested above, the best legal advice highlights the underlying ethical values (and any conflicts within or among them) to make compliance easier for the majority who wish to comply and makes principled opposition easier for those who are genuinely offended by the values the law seems to espouse. In so doing, the best legal advice assists clients to integrate rather than separate their roles as corporate executive and moral citizen. The way to resolve and integrate the roles of lawyers and business executives with their values as citizens and human beings lies in the individual lawyer seeking to justify his activity as a lawyer on the basis of the benefits it provides to the society as a whole.[69] Such justifications emphasize the importance of ensuring advice to, and representation of, individual citizens and the organizations to which they belong. Such justifications are based on human rights and the rule of law. Such justifications tend to unify rather than dichotomize the lawyer's various duties as a lawyer, a professional, a citizen and an officer of the court. Similarly, corporations and their executives need to justify their activity on the basis of the benefits it brings to society as a whole rather than to their shareholders in particular – through increasing the economic output of society and the benefits that this brings to all citizens, whether or not they are shareholders in their or any other corporation.

Role of the in-house lawyer

Most of the above models are based on outside lawyers advising clients. However, in-house lawyers have a particularly important role to play in giving whole-of-business advice, particularly as their relationship with their employers (as 'clients') and their method of lawyering is likely to be distinctive. As the above case studies indicate, in-house lawyers who provide broad advice are more likely to serve the interests of the corporation and ensure its long-term survival in the marketplace. Mackie notes that in-house lawyers must observe how 'public policy considerations' enter case-law and legislation; of how narrow commercial goals have long-term repercussions in community perceptions of business and in business liabilities.[70] They must see that the consequences of a proposed course of action for the company's external relations with customers, suppliers, competitors and the government and its internal relations with employees and shareholders are at least as important as legal ramifications.

Accordingly, one of the in-house lawyer's most important roles is to promote corporate compliance with legislation and to predict possible developments in the law. This requires a consideration of broad moral and ethical issues and the potential future reaction to current corporate practices.

The in-house lawyer can play a vital role in helping to institutionalize ethics within a corporation by counselling employees at all levels, influencing the decision-making of senior management and 'creat[ing] the facts of the client situation rather than react[ing] to the situation imposed by the client'.[71] In a large corporation, the in-house lawyer who successfully combines a preventative role with a counselling role has the potential to combat the risk, identified by Solomon, that: 'ethics will degenerate into a set of abstract rules rather than remain a living community of interpersonal relations … compromised (or reinterpreted) under the pressures of the corporate hierarchy'.[72]

However, the important role that in-house lawyers can play in framing ethical corporate policy and changing the behaviour of both employees and management needs to be balanced against the risk of the lawyer also succumbing to 'the pressures of the corporate hierarchy'. Aibel notes that it requires considerable strength of character to give advice that conflicts with accepted management practices, particularly if such advice places at risk the lawyer's career path within the company.[73] On the other hand, if the lawyer does not provide such advice, both the reputation of the company and its lawyers may be adversely affected. Corporations that do not admit different values and opinions are not only impoverished but are less adaptable to change – especially when confronted by laws informed by different values to those of management. As Murphy notes, corporations cannot justify their existence to the community if they do not adhere to broad social values, even if this adherence is largely for customer relations or profit maximization purposes.[74]

Nonetheless, the in-house lawyer is even more clearly a candidate for a moral adviser to businesspeople than the outside lawyer. He is more than a 'friend', as Fried would see him. He is part of the family. As a good employee, he has the long-term interests of the company to look to and has no pecuniary interest in expensive protracted adversarial litigation.

4 Ethical education of lawyers

So far, we have set out the needs of clients for ethical advice, the strong relationship between ethical advice and good legal advice, the particular suitability of lawyers to provide such advice and the models of lawyering that emphasize that suitability. However, we have also acknowledged that many lawyers are not equipped for this role, highlighting the importance of developing legal education to so equip them. Fortunately, most of the changes that are necessary to make lawyers effective ethical advisers are already occurring for other reasons in some of the more progressive law schools and are advocated by major reports into legal education.[75] What is needed is a reinforcement and, in some cases, extension of these changes to attitudes and curricula.

Avoiding mistaken assumptions

The first change to legal education is to ensure that educators do not suffer from the same mistaken assumptions against lawyers giving ethical advice identified above. Law should not be seen as divorced from ethics. Legal advice should not be divorced from ethical advice or general business advice. Duties to court and clients should not be separated from each other or from the students' ethics and values as moral citizens. Clients should not be seen as sociopaths nor lawyers as moral schizophrenics. Instead, the role of ethical values in forming the law and interpreting it should be emphasized. This is not a difficult message to sell to young academics – it merely needs to be emphasized that this is not a matter of individual moral musings but a central element to law. This is not to say that values should be the only factors external to the legal texts which are studied and emphasized. The role of history, culture, power, economics and other disciplines in the development and interpretation of the law is important for all law schools. However, values are generally the medium, the mechanism, through which other forces affect the law. The examination of values will remedy a weakness of theories that seek to demonstrate the relationship between the content of laws and the interests of powerful social groupings but do not convincingly indicate how the one affects the other.

Law schools should reverse the idea of separating law and students' sense of morality, through making them appreciate that the morality is contestable and is, indeed, the stuff of legal debate. As Shaffer observes, for far too long legal educators have followed Llewellyn's advice 'to treat ethics, social policy, and their students' sense of justice as 'woozy thinking'.[76]

Attempts should be made to identify the moral conflicts in law and in legal practice. Matasar identifies some of the most important reasons for integrating the teaching of law with the teaching of ethics:

> First, exploring the various contexts in which ethical questions underlie … decisions exposes the moral dimension of everyday lawyering. Seeing that dimension helps us to understand better the consequences of our decisions and allows us to balance client, personal, and societal interests. Second, examining whether some of our solutions to ethical problems are culturally contingent, whether some problems have only one right answer, and whether we have correctly perceived our problems reveals a range of ethical dilemmas and solutions that makes morality and doctrine functions of each other, not separate matters. Delimiting dilemmas and solutions shows that morally and technically sound lawyering often merge. Third, studying ethics and doctrine together allows us to confront directly the difficult questions lawyers face. Fourth, understanding that all players in the legal system – clients, lawyers, judges (and even students and teachers) – are moral actors who must take responsibility for their decisions suggests that we must all share the pain of ethical practice.[77]

Open discussion of the ethical issues involved in key areas of law and of the potentially competing values involved should be encouraged in all subjects. If the law is taught as involving certain clashes of values, then it will not only serve to assist students to understand legal doctrine and argument,[78] it will assist them in anticipating and understanding future changes and in advising clients of the law and of what to do under it.

Curriculum changes

These changes of attitude need to be supported by, and reflected in, the curriculum. As with other elements of theory, this does not involve merely adding an optional or even a compulsory subject to an otherwise unchanged curriculum. As we saw in Chapters 2 and 3, it involves building ethics into the core of the curriculum. Like other elements of theory, we would argue that this is best done by a three-pronged strategy.

First, students should be introduced to ethics in the first year and given the tools to analyse ethical problems. The ethics taught should not be limited to legal ethics but should include general issues of ethics of relevance to ordinary moral citizens so that students may think through their own moral positions and assist clients to do so.

Second, ethical issues should be incorporated within a proportion of the problems discussed in every subject of the degree.[79] Nothing should seem more natural than that ethical issues are raised by law and that clients will need to be advised of them. This should also counter the possibility of the unethical character of an end result being obscured by fascination with legal techniques.

Third, students need to revisit ethics towards the end of their legal education to think again more generally about the relationship between law and ethics and to engage in some deep reflection on their own values. This is the approach taken in some thoroughgoing reforms to the curriculum in existing law schools[80] and in some new law schools such as Griffith.[81]

In corporate law courses, students need to be introduced to the ethical dimension of corporate behaviour and the institutional dimensions of corporate ethics. We do not want to compound the mistake of separating law and ethics by the mistake of seeing ethical problems and solutions as merely individual concerns. By showing them how many ethical problems arise from institutional weaknesses that subject staff to ethical dilemmas or ethical temptations, they will not only learn much of use in advising corporate clients but also understand more generally the institutional dimensions of most organizational ethics.

Change should not be limited to the first degree stage (LLB or JD). Subjects in master's degrees could be of great interest to members of the profession. Ethics should also play a significant role in continuing legal education, once the profession is convinced of its utility in advising clients.

Other measures

To support these attitudinal and curriculum changes, it is highly desirable that law schools encourage research into ethical issues concerning a wide spectrum of law subjects (preferably in conjunction with ethically attuned lawyers in the profession) and to generate materials and cases. Both assist in 'pervasive' teaching of ethics and in increasing academic awareness of, and sensitivity to, ethical issues.

In developing and selling the new curricula to the profession, academics should seek out the ethically attuned members of the profession. The profession does not appreciate being preached to. Yet, academics who are used to deriding the crassness of the profession may be pleasantly surprised at the significant minority of ethically aware practitioners who will welcome academic allies – as we should appreciate professional ones.

5 Selling ethical risk management to clients

Although introducing ethics into the law course is valuable in its own right, the aim of educating and encouraging lawyers to be ethical advisers counts for nothing if clients are not interested in receiving the advice. Likewise, if lawyers do not believe that clients are interested in receiving advice, they will be reluctant to embrace the educational opportunities. Given the negative attitudes of many to the ethical credentials of lawyers, this requires more thought than a change in letterhead.

Increasing client awareness of the value of ethical advice will often be incremental – adding on to existing service. Lawyers may do any one or more of the following:

- incorporate ethical dimensions in more effectively explaining the law (especially in major litigation involving significant value questions);
- add ethical advice to the legal advice they are otherwise asked to give;
- incorporate ethics into compliance regimes that lawyers are increasingly being called upon to establish within corporations to protect them against large potential liabilities imposed by government regulation or trade practices law;
- incorporate ethical elements when asked for broad-based, whole-of-business advice, or when the client asks 'what should I do?'; and,
- when clients find themselves in messy and difficult litigation, especially through the unethical behaviour of their staff or business associates, lawyers may be able to offer to suggest ways of avoiding similar problems in the future.

There is also scope for a proactive marketing of ethical services to clients. Large law firms are now used to promoting their capacities to clients in a number of ways and contexts, such as in:

- tendering for work;
- advertising directed at particular clients or in the form of general information about services the firm offers;
- newsletters and client briefings on current developments within the firm's areas of expertise; and
- promotional activities such as sponsorship of public events and in media coverage of the firm's activities.

The range of services of use to clients that could be packaged and offered by these means could include the following:

a Ethics management advice

This entails advice on the various means of incorporating sound ethical practice into a client's management processes and includes:

- providing awareness seminars for senior staff;
- advising on the role of a code of conduct;

- advising on suitable structures and processes for promoting ethics for new and existing staff; and
- advising on dealing with ethical issues as they arise.

b An ethics audit

This is a process for examining the ethical issues facing the organization, their current means of resolution and the needs of the organization for ethics development.

c Assistance in drafting or redrafting a Code of Conduct *for the organization*

This includes:

- advice and/or training sessions on developing codes of conduct;
- generation of internal case studies to focus code development on real problems;
- consultation with staff; and
- follow-up training to increase staff understanding of the code's purpose, meaning and effect.

d Ethics Education *for staff (including induction training, training of trainers, ethics awareness sessions)*

e Ethics maintenance

This includes:

- provision of ongoing advice on the operation of ethical programmes and sustaining the ethical performance of the organization;
- monitoring code awareness and effectiveness;
- provision of confidential advice on ethical issues as they arise.

In all of this, law firms might emphasize both the positive advantage of improving the ethics of a client's organization as well as the potential damage caused by not taking ethical considerations into account.

A firm that successfully decided to offer ethical advice would establish a marketing edge over others. Not only would the firm be meeting an important client need, its clients' public image would benefit from being seen to be advised by the 'ethics firm'. Other firms would need to compete to maintain their own clients and to avoid being branded one of the 'no ethics' firms. This competition would generate expectations within the business community that at least some lawyers were suitable persons to whom they might turn for ethical advice. The increasing expectation would be met with increasing provision in what is potentially a virtuous circle (or rather a virtuous spiral). Even if the spiral does not reach its full felicific potential, it would mean that at least some lawyers were offering ethical advice and assisting themselves and their firms towards a more noble profession in which they are proud to serve and which we are proud to educate.

Notes

1 D. Luban, *Lawyers and Justice: An Ethical Study* (Princeton, NJ: Princeton University Press, 1994): xxi.
2 William Shakespeare, *Henry VI Part II*, Act IV Scene II. Dick the Butcher was a follower of the rebel Jack Cade, who is probably modelled on fourteenth-century rebel Wat Tyler.
3 Ian Ramsay, 'Ethical Perspectives on the Practice of Business Law', *Law Society Journal* 30, no. 5 (1992): 62.
4 John K. Morris, 'Power and Responsibility among Lawyers and Clients: Comment on Ellmann's *Lawyers and Clients*', *UCLA Law Review* 34 (1987): 808.
5 P.F. Lake, 'Make Lawyers, Not Lethal Sheep', *Journal of Legal Education* 42 (1992): 272.
6 Ian Ramsay, 'Ethical Perspectives on the Practice of Business Law': 62.
7 Ibid.; P.G. Haskell, 'Teaching Moral Analysis in Law School', *Notre Dame Law Review* 66 (1991): 1031.
8 William H. Simon, 'Ethical Discretion in Lawyering', *Harvard Law Review.* 101, no. 6 (1988): 1120.
9 See Richard Tur, 'An Introduction to Lawyers' Ethics', *Journal of Professional and Legal Education* 10, no. 2 (1992).
10 This is not to say that law is only about values. I do not wish to convey that law is not about power. Like all complex institutions, law reflects much that occurs in society. In the case of ethics and value debate, this is the most proximate medium through which other social forces influence law.
11 R. Murphy, 'Defining and Practicing Business Ethics', in *Business Ethics in Australia and New Zealand: Essays and Cases*, ed. K. Woldring (Melbourne: Nelson, 1996): 46.
12 According to Simon, this reflects the fact that the ethical conflict arises within legal culture itself: Simon, 'Ethical Discretion in Lawyering': 1114.
13 Murphy, 'Defining and Practicing Business Ethics': 46.
14 J.F. Dalton, 'Boardroom Ethics', in *Business Ethics in Australia and New Zealand: Essays and Cases*, ed. K. Woldring (South Melbourne: Thomas Nelson, 1996): 179.
15 Charles Sampford and David Wood, 'The Future of Business Ethics', *Griffith Law Review* 1, no. 1 (1992); P. Finn, 'Commerce, the Common Law and Morality', *Melbourne University Law Review* 17 (1989); Hon Sir Gerard Brennan, 'Commercial Law and Morality', ibid.
16 See Chapter 2.
17 E.J. Eberle, 'Three Foundations of Legal Ethics: Autonomy, Community, and Morality', *Georgetown Journal of Legal Ethics* 7 (1993): 123.
18 See G.C. Hazard, 'Ethical Opportunity in the Practice of Law', *San Diego Law Review* 27 (1990); R. Nelson, 'Symposium on the Law Firm as a Social Institution', *Stanford Law Review* 37 (1985); D. Arron, *Running from the Law: Why Good Lawyers Are Getting out of the Legal Profession* (Berkeley: Ten Speed Press, 1991).
19 Nelson, 'Symposium on the Law Firm as a Social Institution': 537–539.
20 D.B. Wilkins, 'Practical Wisdom for Practicing Lawyers: Separating Ideals from Ideology in Legal Ethics', *Harvard Law Review* 108 (1994): 470.

21 D.C. Langevoort, 'Where Were the Lawyers? A Behavioural Inquiry into Lawyers' Responsibility for Clients' Fraud', *Vanderbilt Law Review* 46 (1993).
22 Arron, *Running from the Law*: 46. (Interview with 'Kate').
23 See P. Joy, 'What We Talk About When We Talk About Professionalism: A Review of Lawyers' Ideals/Lawyers' Practices: Transformations in the American Legal Profession', *Georgetown Journal of Legal Ethics* 7 (1994): 1007. However, most lawyers in Nelson's survey felt they had ample opportunity to give non-legal advice to clients, irrespective of the size of their firm. Nelson, 'Symposium on the Law Firm as a Social Institution': 532.
24 Wilkins, 'Practical Wisdom for Practicing Lawyers': 472.
25 Hazard, 'Ethical Opportunity in the Practice of Law': 132.
26 W. Felstiner and A. Sarat, 'Enactments of Power: Negotiating Reality and Responsibility in Lawyer-Client Interactions', *Cornell Law Review* 77 (1992).
27 Nelson, 'Symposium on the Law Firm as a Social Institution': 548. Also see W. Bradley Wendel, 'Lawyers and Butlers: The Remains of Amoral Ethics', *Georgetown Journal of Legal Ethics* 9 (1995): 173.
28 L.C. Levin, 'Testing the Radical Experiment: A Study of Lawyer Response to Clients Who Intend to Harm Others', *Rutgers Law Review* 47 (1994): 123–126.
29 United States American Bar Association Model Rules of Professional Conduct (1983). See S. Ross, *Ethics in Law: Lawyers' Responsibility and Accounting in Australia* (Sydney: Butterworths, 1995): 173–174. There is no equivalent in Australia. However, Ross notes that the *Family Law Act 1975* (Cth), s 17 and Family Law Regulations, 19, require lawyers to declare that they have given their client a copy of a prescribed document, informing the client of 'the legal and possible social effects of the proposed proceedings' and the counselling and welfare facilities available. Ibid.: 174.
30 Ibid.
31 P.S. Menell, 'Legal Advising on Corporate Structure in the New Era of Environmental Liability', *Columbia Business Law Review* 1990, no. 1 (1990); T. Greenwood, 'Ethics and Avoidance Advice', *Law Institute Journal* 65, no. 8 (1991): 724.
32 J.T. Philipps, 'It's Not Easy Being Easy: Advising Tax Return Positions', *Washington and Lee Law Review* 50 (1993): 621. See also, G.S. Cooper, R.L. Deutsch and R.E. Krever, *Income Taxation: Commentary and Materials* (Sydney: Law Book Company, 1993), Ch. 24. An Australian tax adviser may be subject to a variety of sanctions for unethical conduct, including criminal liability under the *Crimes Act 1914* (Cth) the *Taxation Administration Act 1953* (Cth) and the *Crimes (Taxation Offences) Act 1980* (Cth).
33 The chief proponents of this view are Fried and Pepper. See S.L. Pepper, 'The Lawyer's Amoral Ethical Role: A Defence, a Problem, and Some Possibilities', *American Bar Foundation Research Journal* (1986); C. Fried, 'The Lawyer as Friend: The Moral Foundations of the Lawyer-Client Relation', *Yale Law Journal* 85 (1976); R.A. Wasserstrom, 'Lawyers as Professionals: Some Moral Issues', in *Ethical Issues in the Professions*, ed. Peter Y. Windt *et al.* (New Jersey: Prentice Hall, 1989): 88.
34 Wendel, 'Lawyers and Butlers': 165. See J. Allegretti, 'Shooting Elephants, Serving Clients: An Essay on George Orwell and the Lawyer-Client Relationship', *Creighton Law Review* 27 (1993).
35 Robert W. Gordon, 'Corporate Law Practice as a Public Calling', *Maryland Law Review* 49 (1990): 258; Wendel, 'Lawyers and Butlers': 176. This assumption ignores the reality of inequality of bargaining power and resources between the opposing sides and of social barriers such as race, gender and class.
36 N. Cahn, 'Forward: Responsible Lawyers', *George Washington Law Review* 63 (1995): 926. Cahn notes that the term 'zealous' is itself ambiguous: a lawyer can be zealous either by putting the client's interests first, or by putting the lawyer's own interests above those of the client.
37 J. Leubsdorf, 'Essay: Pluralising the Client-Lawyer Relationship', *Cornell Law Review* 77 (1992).

38 P.L. Rizzo, 'Morals for Home, Morals for Office: The Double Ethical Life of a Civil Litigator', *Catholic Lawyer* 35 (1991): 82, 90.
39 H.L. Pitt and K.A. Groskaufmanis, 'When Bad Things Happen to Good Companies: A Crisis Management Primer', *Cardozo Law Review* 15 (1994): 967.
40 Cahn, 'Forward: Responsible Lawyers': 926, n.22.
41 Pepper, 'The Lawyer's Amoral Ethical Role: A Defence, a Problem, and Some Possibilities': 626.
42 P. Margulies, 'Who Are You to Tell Me That? Attorney-Client Deliberation Regarding Non-Legal Issues and the Interests of Non-Clients', *North Carolina Law Review* 68 (1990): 246, n.118.
43 Wendel, 'Lawyers and Butlers': 177–178.
44 M.D.A. Freeman, *Lloyd's Introduction to Jurisprudence* (London: Sweet & Maxwell, 1994): 670–676.
45 For example, many Australian judges' attitudes towards Australia's indigenous people would have been affected by growing public awareness of past injustices. See *Mabo v Queensland (No 2)* (1992) 175 CLR 1; and *Wik Peoples v Queensland* (1997) 141 ALR 129.
46 United States Sentencing Commission Guidelines, 52 Fed. Reg. 44,675 (1987). See P.E. Fiorelli, 'Guideline Amendments Dramatically Change the Structure of Organizational Fines', *Catholic Lawyer* 35 (1991).
47 Ibid.: 189–191.
48 See D.L. Rhode, 'Ethics by the Pervasive Method', *Journal of Legal Education* 42 (1992): 38; T. Donaldson, 'Moral Minimums for Multinationals', in *Business Ethics: Readings and Cases in Corporate Morality*, ed. W.M. Hoffman and R.E. Fredrick (New York: McGraw-Hill, 1995), Ch.12; and *The Ethics of International Business* (New York: Oxford University Press, 1989).
49 M. Cash Mathews, *Strategic Intervention in Organizations: Resolving Ethical Dilemmas* (Newbury Park: Sage Publications, 1988): 28.
50 *BHP v Dagi* (1996) 2 VR 117.
51 'BHP Visits the School of Hard Knocks', *Weekend Australian*, 15–16 June 1996.
52 'Biscuits Back on Shelves', *The Age*, 26 February 1997.
53 'Arnott's Gears up for Big Climb Back', *The Age*, 15 February 1997.
54 'Arnott's Agenda', *The Age*, 22 February 1997. Arnott's response seems to have been modelled on that of Johnson and Johnson's to the Tylenol scare in the United States over 15 years ago. See Pitt and Groskaufmanis, 'Crisis Management Primer': 951.
55 Eberle, 'Three Foundations of Legal Ethics': 91. Also see R.W. Painter, 'The Moral Interdependence of Corporate Lawyers and Their Clients', *Southern California Law Review* 67 (1994).
56 Eberle, 'Three Foundations of Legal Ethics': 97.
57 Ibid.: 125.
58 Gordon, 'Corporate Law Practice as a Public Calling'; and Menell, 'Legal Advising on Corporate Structure'.
59 Simon, 'Ethical Discretion in Lawyering': 1090.
60 Ibid.: 1127.
61 J. Heller, 'Legal Counselling in the Administrative State: How to Let the Client Decide', *Yale Law Journal* 103 (1994): 2504; S. Ellmann, 'Lawyers and Clients', *UCLA Law Review* 34 (1986). Ellmann embraces a similar approach.
62 'Lawyers and Clients': 2518.
63 Thus, Hazard argues: 'A lawyer is an agent, not a principal. Having taken on a client, a lawyer is not free to pursue the client's objectives only to the extent that the lawyer may see fit. The lawyer has to go forward to the point that the client sees fit, within the limits of the law'. Hazard, 'Ethical Opportunity in the Practice of Law': 135.
64 Morris, 'Power and Responsibility': 783.
65 Hazard, 'Ethical Opportunity in the Practice of Law': 136.

66 Margulies, 'Who Are You to Tell Me That?': 221–222.
67 Ibid.
68 Fried, 'The Lawyer as Friend': 1086–1087.
69 Charles Sampford, 'Law, Institutions and the Public-Private Divide', *Federal Law Review* 20 (1991). This has been developed in Charles Sampford and D.A.R. Wood, eds, *Business, Ethics and the Law* (Sydney: Federation Press, 1993); and Charles Sampford and S. Parker, eds, *Legal Ethics and Legal Practice* (Oxford: Oxford University Press, 1995).
70 K.J. Mackie, *Lawyers in Business: And the Law Business* (Hampshire: MacMillan, 1989): 185.
71 Ibid.: 98.
72 R.C. Solomon, *The New World of Business: Ethics and Free Enterprise in the Global 1990s* (Maryland: Rowman and Littlefield, 1994): 114.
73 H.J. Aible, 'Corporate Counsel and Business Ethics: A Personal Review', *Missouri Law Review* 59 (1994): 431.
74 Murphy, 'Defining and Practicing Business Ethics': 44. See B. Kaye, 'The Real Issue in Business Ethics? Institutional Ethics and the Free Market', *Australian Journal of Management* 19, no. 1 (1994): 131.
75 Dennis Charles Pearce, Enid Mona Campbell and Don E. Harding, *Australian Law Schools: A Discipline Assessment for the Commonwealth Tertiary Education Commission (The Pearce Report)* (Canberra: Australian Government Publishing Service, 1987); C. McInnis and S. Marginson, *Australian Law Schools after the 1987 Pearce Report* (Canberra: AGPS, 1994); and Lord Chancellor's Advisory Committee for Legal Education and Conduct (ACLEC), 'First Report on Legal Education and Training', (London: ACLEC, 1996). The issue is naturally linked to the question of educating ethical lawyers – for which (as well as the following pointers) see Chapter 12.
76 T.L. Shaffer, 'On Lying for Clients', *Notre Dame Law Review* 71, no. 2 (1996): 196.
77 R.A. Matasar, 'Teaching Ethics in Civil Procedure Courses', *Journal of Legal Education* 39 (1989): 588.
78 See Chapters 2 and 3, as well as Charles Sampford and David Wood, 'Legal Theory and Legal Education – the Next Step', *Legal Education Review* 1, no. 1 (1989).
79 This is sometimes referred to as the 'pervasive' method. See Rhode, 'Ethics by the Pervasive Method'. However, it is best linked to specific core subjects for reasons given in Chapter 3 and Charles Sampford, 'Rethinking the Core Curriculum', *Adelaide Law Review* 12 (1989).
80 D.T. Link, 'The Pervasive Method of Teaching Ethics', *Journal of Legal Education* 39 (1989). Link discusses curriculum changes at Notre Dame Law School.
81 The curriculum is available from the Griffith law school and has been published in Charles Sampford, 'Reflections of a Foundation Dean – the Griffith Experience', *Queensland Law Society Journal* 26 (1996). See also Chapters 6 and 9 (esp. Ch. 9, Sect. 1.3).

11 The ethics of employed lawyers

Charles Sampford

Traditionally, lawyers (like doctors) have operated as sole practitioners or in small partnerships. This has affected such professions' images of themselves and the way their ethics have been conceived and written. But doctors' practices are increasing in size and reach and an increasing number are working for hospitals that have become very large and employ a range of professions to achieve their goals. Lawyers are increasingly being employed by large organizations – corporations and, increasingly, the creation of mega practices that are incorporated and even listed on the stock exchange.

For some, these problems are exacerbated by the intense competition for clients (not only between law firms but between legal, accounting and mixed firms), and the rise of litigation funders who effectively give instructions to the litigators. In this environment, lawyers will face 'multiple duties which need to be deciphered and weighed against each other' and may have to 'reconcile the ascendance of commercial considerations over older notions of professionalism'.[1]

As more and more lawyers are employed by large corporations (whether incorporated law firms or directly for large corporations), there is a risk that they and their employers may think they must respond to the corporate values, goals and ethics. However, I would argue that these are merely new versions of old challenges to the profession and that the answers lie in reemphasizing what it is to be a profession and the consequence of how we live our lives as lawyers.

The problems of lawyers acting unethically because they are too influenced by those who pay them (particularly when they are employed rather than retained or briefed) are not new. David Luban quotes Macaulay's essay on Francis Bacon that a lawyer is someone who 'with a wig on his head and a band round his neck, would do for a guinea what he would otherwise think it wicked and infamous to do for an empire'.[2] You may well take issue with this bipolar view of lawyers – and insist that it will not ground an insanity defence before the ethics board. You may well say that the lawyer in private practice is likely to earn a lot more guineas – even taking account of inflation since Macaulay's time that makes his 1840 guinea worth $1,000 – or Bacon's time when it represented one fortieth of his annual income.[3]

Ironically, given the subject matter of this discussion, what the lawyer Macaulay was thinking of was a lawyer with an employer far more powerful than any modern law firm, litigation funder or multinational corporation. Macaulay was talking about one of the greatest minds of the last millennium,[4] who worked as a QC and judge for Elizabeth I and James I/VI. The risks of judges serving their sovereign masters with greater attention to the wishes of their sovereign than the rule of law are long-standing and continue in many jurisdictions. However, they can be, and largely are, managed in modern liberal democracies. This gives hope that lawyers can manage to be ethical lawyers despite working for large employers – government agencies, defence forces, international agencies, multinational corporations and incorporated law firms.

Part of the answer lies in conscious and conscientious attention to ethics by the relevant branches of the profession involved. A second part of the answer lies in the institutional context within which those lawyers work including:

- a recognition by the lawyers' employers that they can only employ lawyers to do what lawyers can ethically do; and,
- a profession that emphasizes, to lawyers and employers alike, that all lawyers only remain lawyers as long as they do what lawyers must do and refrain from doing what they must not.

1 Professions and professional ethics

Law and medicine are the two oldest and enduring 'learned professions' with strong classical roots going back to Cicero and Hippocrates.[5] Other groups with a claimed expertise for sale have sought to be recognized as 'professions' – with the prestige, autonomy, power and ability to charge higher fees.[6] The great learned professions of medicine and law were joined by dentists, architects, accountants and engineers in the nineteenth century and 'allied health professions' (nurses, pharmacists, psychologists) in the twentieth. There have been moves to professionalize other areas (for example, journalism) and to re-professionalize the military.

There are several attempts to articulate the elements of a profession. To me they all centre on service to the community whose delivery constitutes what is seen by the profession, and generally regarded as, a public good. A profession involves a body of knowledge, institutions for imparting it, a dedicated and identified group of experts who apply that knowledge for the benefit of the community they claim to serve, a set of processes for determining who enters and leaves the profession, and a code of ethics/conduct with a strict set of priorities in which the public good comes first, the client comes second, and the professional comes third.

The public good, which the profession claims to deliver and is the basis for the privileges accorded the profession, may be expressed in a number of slightly differing but convergent ways. Doctors emphasize the health of the community and its members. Engineers emphasize safe and effective structures and systems. Lawyers talk about the rule of law, the preservation of liberty, and justice under the law.

Public good

The dedication to the public good does not make professions into charities or government agencies and professionals can charge fees (or be paid salaries) for the service they render. Those who serve best may earn particularly high fees or salaries, in line with the service they do and the public good they promote.[7] But generating those fees can never be the central rationale or justification of the profession. A professional should never design or recommend services in order to maximize fees. A doctor must not recommend a procedure because he makes more money out of it. A lawyer must not recommend tactics to increase cost or delay – even if the client wants this to intimidate or bankrupt the opponent. This addresses another vital point. Even though most professionals work for corporate or individual clients, they are not supposed to serve their clients at the cost of the public good to which the profession is dedicated. Even when lawyers are employed by a large organization like a multinational corporatized law firm, a multinational corporation, the state, or an international body, the public good to which they are dedicated must still be at the centre of their professional life.

Body of knowledge

A learned profession relies on a 'body of knowledge', which it develops, communicates and applies. The best professions have multiple means for challenging that body of knowledge – through public contestation in the academy, in professional bodies and, in law, through the structure of adversarial court processes. Such challenges are critical to the development of that body of knowledge and its application in the service of the community. While no profession lives up to the above ideals in full, all acknowledge them and try to do so – and part of the body of knowledge is to reflect upon its practice to consider how it can better realize the ideals of the profession and the public good it claims to deliver. A profession must always interrogate and challenge the ideas that form part of its knowledge and is particularly careful about those propositions that suit its own practitioners. If something appears to be too good to be true, it probably is too good to be true and should be tested. The testing of legal propositions is hardwired into the legal profession and the legal institutions in which it operates (though the exposure and testing of fundamental assumptions has traditionally been weaker).

Ethics

Ethics are generally seen as central to any genuine profession. While codes of conduct and means for enforcement are important means for promoting professional ethics, they are not the core of professional ethics. That core lies in the profession reflecting on its work, asking questions about its values and how those values can be furthered. This can be expressed in a number of ways but I find it most useful to conceive it as a version of Peter Singer's fundamental ethical question: 'how should I live my life?'[8]

Answering that question involves asking yourself hard questions about your values, giving honest and public answers, and trying to live by those answers. If you do, you have integrity in the sense you are true to your values, and true to yourself. In fact, if you do not live up to the answers you give, the first person you cheat is yourself. However, many ethical questions are not just matters of individual action. As social animals descended from social primates, much of our life is lived in and through groups and institutions (including public agencies, corporations and, of course, professions). Institutional ethics involves asking the same set of questions to that group activity.[9] Legal professional ethics starts with asking hard questions about the values of the profession, giving honest and public answers and living by them. Doing so for a profession is more complex than for an individual, but it is both possible and necessary. It requires leadership in posing questions and seeking answers from members. This process starts with the vital questions that must be asked of any profession (indeed any institution): What is it for? Why should it exist? What justifies the profession to the community in which it operates given that the community provides privileges such as immunities, funding, monopolies (professions)? Why is the community within which it operates better for the existence of the profession? Asking those questions involves a collective effort under its own formal and informal processes.

A profession has integrity if it lives by its answers. However, it does so in a different way. It cannot merely be a personal commitment but an institutional commitment, which involves creating mechanisms that make it more likely that the organization keeps to the values it has publicly declared and to which it is publicly committed. These generally and appropriately include the debating, making and communicating of ethical codes; the provision of education, mentoring and advice; and they include disciplinary mechanisms. As indicated above, these mechanisms make professional ethics more effective but they are not ethics and cannot be substituted for it.

2 Ethical professionals in large organizations

In the strongest professions, medicine and the law, this process has been developed over millennia with formal processes being in place for well over a century. It was developed when most doctors and lawyers were individual practitioners thinking about what individual doctors and lawyers should do.

Other professions have emerged from groups who were already employed in large organizations – journalists, nurses and engineers. It has been harder for them to develop strong traditions of professional ethics that resist the demands of their employers.[10]

In fact, an increasing number of doctors and lawyers are employed by large organizations. While the image of these professionals is of sole practitioners exercising independent judgment, some of the most critical roles played by professionals are within very large organizations whose decisions cannot be effective without the deployment of major capital and personnel resources. Indeed, the doctors with the greatest prestige, influence and respect operate (often literally) in hospitals and large research teams. This claim is particularly true of decisions about diagnosis, prognosis and treatment of hospital patients. However, long-standing traditions of the profession that developed while most were individual practitioners mean that such decisions are made on the basis of their professional ethics rather than dictated by the hospitals that employ them. Of course, the individual doctor cannot expend unlimited hospital resources and the hospital has to decide the kind of services it offers. Such decisions have to be taken institutionally and involve a number of different professionals. But they are not determined by the owners of the hospital based upon their economic interests or even religious beliefs. It would be regarded as utterly outrageous for someone to buy a private hospital and start to dictate (or even influence) the diagnoses, prognoses and treatments of patients or to override or direct the professional duties and decisions of the medical professionals (whether by individuals or professional oversight committees).

Like doctors, lawyers were traditionally sole practitioners or members of small professional practices even if they shared facilities and services (as in chambers). Like doctors, they are increasingly likely to work for large organizations and this is particularly the case with the most able practitioners (other than barristers in divided professions). More and more lawyers are working for governments, corporations, corporatized law firms or mixed professional firms. But it would be considered utterly outrageous for a corporate law firm to instruct employed lawyers on how they should fulfil their professional duties to the court.[11]

Even though many professionals work for large and often profit-making corporations (engineering firms, private hospitals, corporatized legal practices), they are employed as professionals. Their employers should realize that they cannot be expected or required to compromise their professional standards and service to the public good that their profession claims to deliver for the sake of higher profits. Even if some professionals may breach these requirements and some professions develop a range of excuses for practices that might otherwise be seen to breach them, there is, for most, a genuine commitment to these principles by the profession and the vast bulk of relevant professionals.

Those who employ lawyers should expect high professional standards from their employed lawyers. If they want someone to do legal work for them subject to the highest standards of professional ethics, then they have chosen the right person. If they want that lawyer to work contrary to the ethics of the profession, they should discover that they have made the worst employment decision of their lives. They should find that they have not only wasted their money but, if they persist with acting in ways their employed lawyers have told them are illegal, then they may find that their lawyers are duty bound to report them under 'delinquent client' rules.[12]

This raises the question of how lawyers should act when they are working for a large organization. Should they be seen as lawyers or public servants/corporate executives? Should they be seen as having dual and conflicting loyalties? Or should they be seen as lawyers who contextualize their responsibilities and interpret what it is to be a good lawyer working within that organization?

3 Institutional ethics of the employing institution

If the employer instructs an employed lawyer to act contrary to legal professional ethics, the answer is easy. They must fulfil their ethical duties as a lawyer. A more subtle concern might arise where the institution in which they are employed has its own ethical standards and 'institutional ethics' – either corporate ethics or public sector ethics of the relevant corporation or public agency. There could be concern that the ethical duties as an executive of a corporation or an official in a public agency were not compatible with the professional ethics of a lawyer.

Warren refers to the profit motive of corporations and some proponents of corporate ethics put 'shareholder value' at the pinnacle of corporate ethics.[13] If so, it might be argued that a lawyer employed by a corporation would have a duty to the shareholder to increase shareholder value even if it clashed with the lawyer's duty to the court and the administration of justice. I have long argued that this view of corporate ethics is fundamentally mistaken.[14] It is based on the assumption that corporations are a form of institutionalized sociopathy in which corporate profit is to be pursued whatever damage to the community might arise. But the reasons why limited liability joint stock companies were not only permitted to operate but facilitated were not so that they could pursue profit against the public good. It was assumed that allowing the easy formation of limited liability joint stock companies would benefit the community in which they operated. I would argue that corporate ethics should start with the same collective questioning as professional ethics – asking hard questions about the values of the corporation, giving honest and public answers and living by them. The values questions should centre on the way in which the corporation can prosper by providing something that the wider community values.[15] Lawyers should be able to assist corporations to engage in this practice, helping corporations to become more ethical – rather than the lawyers becoming less ethical because they are employed by a corporation.

Similarly, lawyers employed in the public sector might be seen as having a duty to carry out the policy of the government that clashes with their duties as lawyers. However, public sector ethics does not put obedience to the commands of the executive government above other duties. They are expressed in a number of ways but they all emphasize values similar to those found in the Queensland *Public Sector Ethics Act 1994*: integrity and impartiality, promoting the public good, commitment to the system of government as well as accountability and transparency.[16] It could be argued that there still may be a clash between public sector ethics within a jurisdiction and the legal ethics of employed lawyers. This is not a duty to ignore ethics in the pursuit of profit but of potential between the ethical traditions of two long-standing professions.[17]

There are two answers to this. The first is to treat professional and public sector ethics as involving a series of 'don'ts', negative duties about actions that should be avoided. If so, the two sets of ethics can be entirely reconciled. If either code of ethics requires those subject to them to refrain from an action they must so refrain. The second is more positive. There are great synergies between the legal profession and the civil service. Their codes tend to be mutually reinforcing. For example, the values of the Queensland public service were set out in the *Public Sector Ethics Act* as described above.[18]

The duties to the court are entirely compatible with the system of government and the public good – certainly the kinds of public good that lawyers might be expected to pursue within government. The duties of a civil servant to give frank and fearless advice (reflected in the Queensland values of integrity and impartiality) is in line with the duties of professional lawyers to give clients the advice they need to hear rather than the advice they want to hear. Being a lawyer provides an extra reason to be frank and an extra reason to be fearless.

Lawyers who work for other institutions (corporations or public agencies) do not so much face contradictory ethical duties. It is more a matter of contextualization of their professional ethics to the particular work that they do and a recognition of particular temptations and potential dilemmas that such work is likely to generate. This contextualization is a particularly appropriate subject for the kind of institutional questioning and development that I see as central to being a 'reflexive' lawyer.[19] I will consider some issues of contextualization of legal ethics relevant to the judiciary, public service and corporations.

Those who employ lawyers should recognize that they are employing members of a long-standing profession. As such, they should be seen as committed to a vital public good and a very strong set of values, norms and practices designed to increase the chances that that public good will be secured. While the legal profession needs to reflect on, and occasionally vary, the way they express that public good and the derived values, norms and practices, they are not subject to renegotiation with their employers. If the employer wants to employ a professional exercising the skills of a legal professional, then they have come to the right place. If they want a lawyer to deviate from those values to suit the employer's interests, then it should be seen as one of the worst decisions they could make. Employed lawyers should say: 'sorry, I cannot and will not do that'. The profession needs to back lawyers up when they do and sanction them when they do not. It is much easier to do this if the employed lawyers have, and are required to have, formal membership of the legal profession and be subject to its discipline.[20]

4 Judicial ethics – from Bacon on

In Bacon's time, power was being centralized within the institutions of the state. The pre-Westphalian order had involved multiple sources of law (canon law, common law, manorial law, Roman law, law merchant etc.) and multiple sources of military power (the various tenants in chief whose duty it was to raise forces for the king but who sometimes used those forces against him – becoming 'overmighty subjects').[21] Sovereigns around Europe were centralizing power with a monopoly on law making, standing armies (and the claimed monopoly of legitimate force), centralized courts, and the power to appoint bishops. The English

Tudors were leaders in these developments. They expected their QCs/KCs to do their bidding and judges to deliver the outcomes they wanted. Most obliged as readily as a Soviet judge accepted guidance from the Communist Party exercising its 'leading role in society' (or guidance by the aristocracy, the monarch, the military in post-coup regimes, the Führerprinzip).

Bacon was a classic example. The actions for which Trevelyan[22] censured him were his acts as a public lawyer.

- Arguing the case against his patron and good friend Essex using his personal knowledge;
- Using torture to extract a confession of someone who was innocent;
- Judge of the Star Chamber and various abuses as a prosecutor;
- Used star chamber to throw Coke into the Tower of London;
- Lobbied judges in a capital case where he was appearing for the crown;
- As a judge, he took directions from the king's favourite;
- In other cases, he took bribes. Bacon's view of doing justice under law was: 'I take a bribe from the plaintiff and an equal bribe from the defendant and then I decide the case upon its merits.' He was impeached for taking bribes – and fined £40,000 pounds – in several cases taking bribes from two or more parties.

Of particular interest is Bacon's great fight with Coke, one of the most fascinating clashes in legal history. Two highly gifted and flawed men rose to fame under the last of the Tudors and took part in the critical legal battles of the first Stuart. It commenced with a battle for the heart of a woman and ended up as a fight for the soul of law. Under the Tudors, English law claimed supremacy over all other forms of law – canon law, law merchant, local law. Under the Stuarts, Coke and Bacon fought over whether the law should have supremacy over the crown. It was a near run thing, but Coke spent little time in the Tower and the three great cases he decided and reported on shaped English common law.[23] Those who value the Rule of Law are thankful that Coke ultimately bested Bacon.

While no modern Australian judge would dream of seeking to emulate Bacon and would see themselves doctrinally on the side of Coke, it is important for judges, as very special lawyers, to consider the values that justify their branch of the profession and which they should commit to. While individual judges do this consciously or unconsciously,[24] it is important for judges, like other branches of the profession, to do this collectively. This action should be done whether or not there are formal enforcement mechanisms. Indeed, I would emphasize that asking the questions about values and the generating of answers is the most important part of ethics whether or not there are means of enforcement. Even without those means of enforcement, the judiciary is and should be judged – by other judges, by counsel and by the people judges claim to serve. It is better for judges to be proactive in setting out what judges think those answers should be – and being open to feedback from other elements of the profession and the polity more generally.

This kind of collective reflection on professional values and the way they should be built into the practice of judging is particularly important when judicial standards are under attack – from latter day Bacons or their would-be sovereign clients and patrons. This gives individual judges strength and confidence in their actions and confidence that they know the right and wrong things to do. They should know when they will be supported by their judicial colleagues in their own jurisdiction and outside of it. They should also know when they are likely to be shunned by those colleagues. I emphasize two points from this formula.

First, the asking of questions and answering them should be both jurisdictional and international. The most immediate source of advice, support and, if necessary, censure, should come from judges in their own jurisdiction. This is especially the case when it comes to certain issues with jurisdictional variation like the practice of sitting as Royal Commissioners or giving gubernatorial constitutional advice.[25] While there is likely to be some variation in ethical values, standards and particular norms between jurisdictions, those variations are merely contextual, institutional and constitutional variations on larger, common themes. Judges within any one jurisdiction can gain a great deal from the contributions of judges and commentators in other jurisdictions and from participation in national, regional or global consideration of judicial ethics. The Australasian Institute of Judicial Administration (AIJA) assisted the Australian judiciary in its consideration of judicial ethics and the Australian Chief Justices signed off on the result. Since then, the Bangalore principles have been signed to set standards for judicial independence and behaviour.[26]

Second, other judges should not only provide positive support for those who act in the best traditions of judging but should deliberately shun those whose behaviour falls so far below what is expected of a judge that you do not recognize him as one. Judges who are known to take bribes or take instruction from a politburo or junta should be shunned by fellow judges and should not expect invitations to the Australian Bar Association (ABA) or judicial conferences.

5 'Government' lawyers

As we have seen, judges are employed by the state and in many jurisdictions, in Bacon's time and since, they have accepted guidance or direction from other state or party officials. However, where the separation of powers and the rule of law are respected, judges can be treated as a separate case.

But the state employs lawyers in many other capacities. Government is not just about making and enforcing laws, but those activities are always important. Furthermore, government actors are subject to a very different closure rule to individual citizens, which means that public officials and their legal advisors must always be concerned about legality. While citizens know that what is not prohibited is permitted, public officials should know (and sometimes have to be reminded) that what is not permitted is prohibited. They can only act where there is a statutory or prerogative power that enables them to do so.

The following is a (not necessarily exhaustive) list of the variety of roles that lawyers play within the various institutions of the executive:

1 The Attorney General;[27]
2 The solicitor general;
3 Crown law and or Attorney General's department;
4 JAG lawyers within the military;
5 Lawyers within particular agencies and departments;
6 Parliamentary draftsman;
7 Department of Public Prosecutions;
8 Administrative tribunals;
9 Ombudsman;
10 Law Reform Commission;
11 National legal services ombudsman.

The last six are all statutory authorities whose CEO and/or Chair must be legally qualified and in which many or most officials are lawyers. Most jurisdictions have several such bodies. While these statutory bodies are classified as part of the executive under a tripartite separation of powers, this says more about the limitations of the theoretical tripartite separation than the danger of their subversion by the executive. Statutory bodies are not under the control of the ministry or the bureaucracy and can have degrees of independence approaching that of the judiciary.[28] In this context, Warren's concerns that the establishment of the national legal services ombudsman and the National Legal Services Board involves 'bringing the legal profession under the control of the executive arm of government'[29] are somewhat overstated. Given the fact that the members will be appointed by the attorneys general of the states, territories and Commonwealth this is even less of a concern.[30]

The position of the solicitor general, as second law officer, is one clearly modelled on the role of a lawyer giving advice to his client with clear responsibility to the court. As such, is it largely unproblematic whether employed full-time (as is the Commonwealth Attorney General) or part-time as in some jurisdictions.

The position of Attorney General, as first law officer, is not so straightforward. There are conventions requiring independence and the certificates he or she provides for the legality of decisions put to the governor or governor-general-in-council clearly require the exercise of legal professional judgment. In the past, prime ministers have sometimes required the same for cabinet decisions. Traditionally, Australian attorneys have signed off on major legal advice (and still must for the governor-general-in-council). They also have several functions that they are expected by convention to exercise independently and professionally reflecting the highest standards of the profession. However, the position of the Attorney General as a member of cabinet can raise difficulties. Hon Daryl Williams, QC MP, a very fine lawyer, thought that the administration of a very large department and membership of cabinet meant that he did not have the time or the space to provide independent legal advice. In his view, that was much better done by the solicitor general. Other attorneys have respectfully disagreed and Hon. Matt Foley (the Attorney General who followed Mr Beanland in Queensland) secured legislation codifying the conventions of the independence of the Attorney General.[31]

With all these government lawyers, high and low, our expectation should be that they will be appointed/employed on the understanding that they will act ethically in the best traditions of the profession. Those who expect government lawyers to compromise those traditions should find that they have not only wasted money but, if they ignore the advice they are given and act beyond power or contrary to law, they will face sanctions themselves.

While the solution is simple and principled, some governments may put pressure on government lawyers – from the Attorney General down to a humble crown law solicitor – to come up with the legal advice they want to hear. As I have argued,[32] the temptation to seek and the temptation to give such advice in domestic matters is significantly reduced by the availability of courts that can pass judgment on the advice in future court cases where those who are aggrieved by the decision are given better advice by their lawyers. I once recall a vice chancellor, unhappy with a legal view I had expressed in a committee meeting,[33] declaring that, 'I am not going to be told by my dean of law what I can or cannot do'. My response was: 'It is better to be told by your lawyer today that you should not do something tomorrow than be told by a judge afterwards that you should not have done it.' He smiled and graciously conceded. As I hinted and he readily acknowledged, if you give the advice your client wants to hear rather than needs to hear, the client will not thank you later and your reputation and possibly practicing certificate may be at risk – indeed, *should be* at risk.

This vital check on the temptation to seek and give poor but convenient advice can be limited if:

- the courts are reluctant to review (for example, because of executive privilege or, more generally, respect for other arms of government in general and/or the office of president in particular);
- the likely or confected delay in the court's hearing the matter may render the litigation pointless;
- the jurisdiction of the relevant court is not compulsory, in particular matters of international law before the International Court of Justice.

The Iraq war provided a number of examples where governments and lawyers succumbed to this temptation – most famously John Yoo's 'torture memos' and Lord Goldsmith's public advice on the legality of the invasion.[34]

6 Lawyers in corporatized law firms

This should be the easiest. Lawyers in corporatized law firms are solicitors doing the work of solicitors for clients and with overriding obligations to the court, the law and the quest for justice that are the same as those for other solicitors.

Corporatized firms collect skills and earnings and share them in particular ways just as firms of solicitors do. A part of the earnings go to the shareholders. But a share of income has gone to various trusts under Philips schemes for a long time and, in any case, a good deal of the income generated by lawyers has gone to employing paralegals and other staff, landlords and lease companies among others.

The size of the firm and the paradigms of some of their clients might mislead them to think that their responsibilities might be altered. But this would be an amazing example of self-delusion.

The case made for permitting law firms to be corporatized did not make any mention of a reduction in ethical responsibility or for a new set of rules or subset of rules for them. If it had, the proposal would have been immediately rejected and a big question mark placed over the lawyers who had made the proposal.

What they should do is to recognize particular temptations and dilemmas (in fact, almost entirely temptations) as well as the risk of the above-mentioned delusion and devise governance mechanisms to reduce the temptation and enhance detection and punishment of those who are tempted. This is the approach taken by Mark who argues that regulators have sought to promote 'ethical behaviour and encouraged to remain a true profession as well as operate like a business'.[35] Each incorporated legal practice is required to

> implement an ethical infrastructure – that is, formal and informal management policies, procedures and controls, work team cultures, and habits of interaction and practices – that supports and encourages ethical behavior. This requirement brings benefits not only to the profession, in terms of good ethical behavior, but also to the community.[36]

Mark and Gordon conclude that this has been largely successful:

> The legal profession has always aspired to maintain the highest of ethical standards as a testament to the great privilege that attaches to a position as an Officer of the Court. With incorporation and public listing, the concomitant financial privilege of that position may be even further enhanced. Our experience in NSW has shown that the benefits of such a reform can outstrip the challenges. The challenges are manageable so long as appropriate standards are systematically applied and monitored. To date the system devised in New South Wales has proved adequate to the task.[37]

The regulators and judges (who have ultimate oversight of the profession) should be vigilant to make sure that this is a fact rather than a pious hope. The profession must ensure that it is so and recognize that its duty to the court, the administration of justice and the community they serve is to report those who give in to temptation, delusion or both. If someone thinks that joining a corporation means ceasing to put their legal professional ethics first, their erstwhile colleagues must expose and expel them from the ranks of lawyers among whom they should not seek to be counted.

A note on litigation funders

One of those temptations is the rise of litigation funders who may want to substitute themselves for the client whose litigation they are funding. The answer is and must be simple. They cannot expect lawyers to operate outside their ethical duties. The legal profession must be absolutely clear on this and say to litigation funders:

> you are welcome to fund our clients. But funding does not entitle you to give instructions in place of the client. You believe that you will make a profit under permissible rules employing lawyers to act as lawyers. That is for you to judge. However, we are not responsible for assisting you to make that profit and cannot take that profit into account in acting as lawyers. If our action as lawyers means that you fail to make a profit, we cannot cease to be lawyers. We could not then act for the client you are funding or any other client. If our acting as lawyers leads you to make less money than you otherwise might, we recognize that you will be disappointed – and that you must live with that disappointment.

Conclusion

There are several branches of the legal profession. More and more of the most able are employed by large organizations – including the Commonwealth, the states and large multinational corporations (some of which are now corporatized law firms). They should see themselves as part of a great profession with particular critical roles to play within the law. Those different roles should lead to various branches of legal ethics that spell out that role, values and norms and address potential challenges, temptations and dilemmas. Employed lawyers should, for their own protection, be subject to legal ethics and professional bodies, and should be overseen by courts. As indicated, there is an advantage to lawyers who continue to hold practicing certificates. This gives employed lawyers another reason to stick to principles.

Notes

1 Hon. Justice Marilyn Warren AC, 'Legal Ethics in the Era of Big Business, Globalization and Consumerism', in *Joint Law Societies Ethics Forum* (Melbourne, 2010): 5.
2 David Luban, 'Introduction', in *Legal Ethics Stories*, ed. David Luban and Deborah L. Rhode (New York: Foundation Press, 2006): 5.
3 Bacon was a QC with an annual income of 40 guineas.
4 Among other achievements, he outlined scientific method.
5 The clergy were the third 'learned profession'. A lot could be said about the differences between the clergy and other professions – including the fact that it was always part of a large organization.
6 Sociologists describe this effort as the 'professional project'. See Keith M. Macdonald, *The Sociology of the Professions* (London: Sage, 1999).
7 Chief Justice Mason says that a profession is dedicated to public service rather than profit. Sir Anthony Mason, 'The Independence of the Bench', *Australian Bar Review*

10 (1993): 9. This does not mean that profit is ignored. It is merely that the way a lawyer should profit is through serving the community well in delivering the identified public good.

8 See for example, Peter Singer, *Practical Ethics*, 2nd ed. (Cambridge: Cambridge University Press, 1993); *How Are We to Live?*, 2nd ed. (Oxford: Oxford University Press, 1997).

9 For further explanation of the links between personal and institutional integrity, see Hugh Breakey, Timothy Cadman and Charles Sampford, 'Conceptualizing Personal and Institutional Integrity: The Comprehensive Integrity Framework', *Research in Ethical Issues in Organizations* 14 (2015).

10 I have argued that this is a particularly critical issue for journalists, see Charles Sampford and R Lui, 'Australian Media Ethics Regime and Ethical Risk Management', *Journal of Mass Media Ethics* 19, no. 2 (2004).

11 To a large extent, it would be seen as similarly outrageous for the owners of a large construction company to instruct employed professionals to sign off on engineering plans. (Though I note the discussion of the Challenger disaster in Michael Davis, 'Thinking Like an Engineer: The Place of a Code of Ethics in the Practice of a Profession', *Philosophy & Public Affairs* 20, no. 2 (1991).) Unfortunately, it seems to be considered entirely within the rights of those who buy the bulk of the newspapers (by circulation) to dictate the editorial direction of those papers. (While Rupert Murdoch inherited the *Adelaide Advertiser* and built the *Australian*, virtually all of the 59–70 per cent of Australian capital city newspaper circulation was acquired in takeovers). This is, of course, contrary to the editorial charter of the Fairfax newspapers and should, as I have argued, be utterly unacceptable in a democracy.

12 See Chapter 16 below.

13 See my discussion in Charles Sampford and V. Berry, 'Shareholder Values, Not Shareholder Value: The Role of "Ethical Funds" and "Ethical Entrepreneurs" in Connecting Shareholders' Values with Their Investments', *Griffith Law Review* 13, no. 1 (2004).

14 Indeed, some argue that Milton Friedman himself did not hold such a view: Christopher Cosans, 'Does Milton Friedman Support a Vigorous Business Ethics?', *Journal of Business Ethics* 87, no. 3 (2008). However, it is perhaps better to say that Friedman failed to hold such a view *consistently*.

15 See Sampford and Berry, 'Shareholder Values'.

16 Sections 6–9, *Public Sector Ethics Act 1994* (Qld).

17 While corporate executives would not see themselves as a profession, the same kind of argument could be made for lawyers employed by a corporation with a highly developed ethical code.

18 I developed this in a keynote on 'Ethics Navigation for Government Lawyers' Invited Keynote, Legal Officers Conference, Canberra, 2012. While I make some points from that address below, I cannot fully address these issues here.

19 See Chapter 3, Sect. 2.

20 One way would be to issue a modified form of practicing certificate. Another is to have a requirement that anyone claiming to be a lawyer or with legal expertise be subject to the relevant ethical code and disciplinary proceedings.

21 See M Hicks, 'Bastard Feudalism, Overmighty Subjects and Idols of the Multitude During the War of the Roses', *History* 85, no. 279 (2000).

22 See G. Trevelyan, *England under the Stuarts* (New York: Methuen, 1980).

23 The *Case of Prohibitions* [1607] EWHC KB J23, (1607) 77 ER 1342; the *Case of Proclamations* [1610] EWHC KB J 22, (1611) 12 Co Rep 74; *Thomas Bonham v College of Physicians* (1610) 8 Co Rep 107 (commonly known as Dr Bonham's Case).

24 A tendency bolstered by the previous experience of most judges at the bar, the habit of giving individual judgments and the tradition that a judge is the court.

25 While I would prefer that judges avoided both activities, I recognize that such practices could develop with appropriate ethical safeguards and benefit from strong judicial traditions of impartiality.
26 While it might be argued that international standards for judges might cover human rights, the Bangalore principles were rather wider and probably more directly concerned with the rule of law – the most fundamental concern of all lawyers.
27 The Attorney General does not have to be a lawyer and Queensland Liberal/National Party governments traditionally did not appoint lawyers as Attorneys General. Some sought to defend this approach by analogy (the Minister for Health does not have to be a doctor) or by breadth of perspective (lawyers may not understand the way the law operates in practice for citizens). Some pointed to the limited number of lawyers (indeed, graduates in general) in previous governments. The last non-lawyer to hold the post of Queensland Attorney General was heavily criticized for his handling of the Connolly Ryan Commission. The Legislative Assembly passed a motion of no confidence in him in 1998. The incoming Newman government had significant numbers of graduates, including lawyers, and there was no indication that the old practice would be revived.
28 While the tenure of statutory bodies' officials is generally shorter than those of judges, that will depend on their age. While they might like to be reappointed or appointed to another post and might therefore favour the government's view, there is potential danger for judges now that it is becoming much more common for judges to be promoted to higher courts.
29 Hon. Justice Marilyn Warren AC, 'Legal Ethics in the Era of Big Business, Globalization and Consumerism', in *Joint Law Societies Ethics Forum* (Melbourne 20 May 2010): 7.
30 However, I do share her concerns about the constant reference to 'consumers' – something that is discussed in the section on professional ethics.
31 Karen Sampford, 'Legislation Note', (Brisbane: Queensland Parliamentary Library, August 1998).
32 See Chapter 14 below.
33 This was not a formal opinion and I was not, at that stage, a legal practitioner.
34 For further discussion, especially on the latter, see Chapters 14 to 16 below.
35 Steve Mark, 'Views from an Australian Regulator', *Journal of the Professional Lawyer* 2009 (2009): 46.
36 Ibid.
37 Steve Mark and Tahlia Gordon, 'Innovations in Regulation – Responding to a Changing Legal Services Market', *Georgetown Journal of Legal Ethics* 22 (2009): 533.

12 *Reflection*

Educating ethical lawyers

Hugh Breakey and Charles Sampford

Introduction

The prevailing literature on educating ethical lawyers tends to either stress one pedagogical initiative (for example, clinical training) and explore the multiple benefits it promises, or stress one professional characteristic (for example, emotional intelligence), and then detail a portfolio of teaching initiatives that further that result. This chapter aims to provide a synoptic perspective, synthesizing the wealth of recent literature with the foregoing chapters to provide an overall map charting the many different pedagogical alternatives available to reformers, and the embedded characteristics and specific outcomes such reforms may seek to cultivate.

We begin in Section 1, reflecting on the outcomes for which education reformers might aim, before turning in Section 2 to provide a quick sketch of the usual suspects – institutional, political, sociological, economic and psychological – that combine to stymie reform efforts. Section 3 describes the toolbox of mechanisms that universities may employ to promote professionalism, noting also the embedded characteristics and specific outcomes that these mechanisms aim to bring about. An important lesson here is that many of the standard characteristics we aim for in teaching law can overlap with nurturing ethical professionalism. With this analysis in tow, the final section considers prospects for the reformer working in contexts where explicit, wholesale and pervasive focus on professionalism is not possible (at least in the short term), and looks at more gradual and piecemeal improvements.

1 What outcomes should reformers aim for?

Professionalism and moral psychology

We will understand 'professionalism' in this paper as a moral quality involving: a) a commitment to the public good which justifies the profession (see Chapter 11); (b) scrupulous adherence to all relevant legal rules; c) adherence to all relevant professional and ethical codes regarding conduct and competence – including the code's more aspirational statements of values and virtues as well as its detailed black letter obligations that have disciplinary consequences.[1] Lawyers will generally adhere to the basic moral norms held by the local community where the lawyer practices but recognize that a lawyer's commitment is to the values of the profession and the public good it seeks to further, even, and especially, when they conflict with public sentiment.[2] Professionalism does not require mere conformity with these rules, but an intrinsic, internalized respect for them[3] – the ethical professional would live up to these ideals even if no-one was looking.

What is required for such internalized moral compliance to occur?[4] To answer this question, we borrow from James Rest's influential four-component theory of moral psychology.[5] Rest observes that four sorts of things can go wrong when an agent is faced with an ethical requirement.[6] First, the agent may simply fail to recognize their situation as one requiring moral considerations; they are oblivious to the moral issues in play, perhaps because the agent fails to notice the interests of others being harmed, or fails to apprehend the potential risks and consequences their action sets in train. Second, even when the agent manages to recognize the situation as morally significant, they may fail to reason appropriately about what they should do, and so come to a mistaken conclusion about what morality requires. Third, even if the agent comes to the right conclusion, when it comes to making their decision the agent may be insufficiently motivated by a concern to do the right thing – or their other values may swamp their moral concerns. Fourth, and finally, even if the agent decides to do the right thing, they may through weakness of will, or other human frailty, fail to follow through on their decision.

Thus, four broad (though interwoven) psychological components are necessary to ensure genuine moral action in general – and professionalism in particular. That is, the agent must possess: (1) *Awareness* of the moral aspects of their situation, requiring empathy and other social and emotional qualities to interpret it effectively; (2) *Judgment* in being able to reason about what morality requires; (3) *Values* that ensure they pay appropriate heed to morality's demands; and, (4) *Character* that empowers them with the courage and grit to resist temptations and follow through on their moral decisions.

The dimensions of legal professionalism

A lawyer's ethical behaviour stretches across several dimensions. That is, we can rank the lawyer by considering how scrupulously they act vis-à-vis different groups.

Three dimensions warrant mention here, each with a 'normative continuum' running from exemplary professionalism that represents and furthers the highest standards of the profession and the values that underpin it through to outright malfeasance that requires discipline, expulsion or even gaol:[7]

I Lawyers' obligations to the community(ies) they serve. This is often summarized as the 'duty to the court'. This duty goes well beyond recognizing the role of courts in supervising lawyers practicing within their jurisdiction. It reflects the fact that lawyers are 'officers' of that court with duties to that institution arising from the office held within it. However, the duty to the court goes much further than that. It represents and/or encompasses the duties to further justice under law that judges and lawyers take on as officers of the court. As one of Australia's most conservative Chief Justices said:

> It is the duty of the barrister to stand between the subject and the crown, and between the rich and the poor, the powerful and the weak, it is necessary that, while the Bar occupies an essential part in the administration of justice, the barrister should be completely independent ... The activities at the Bar are greater than those on the Bench, and the responsibilities are no less.[8]

For Sampford, such obligations arise out of the justification to the community for the recognition and privileges the profession enjoys and is the source of the other obligations – to clients, third parties, and to the profession. Others put it as a lawyer's responsibilities towards justice and the commonweal.[9]

Lawyers may live up to these ideals to different extents and there is a very long normative continuum. This may well involve lawyers performing pro bono work in ensuring access to justice for the poor. (Indeed, some codes set standards and expectations bordering on duties to provide pro bono work.) It may also involve contributing to just law reform initiatives, and other civil society-related efforts that lawyers are well-placed to execute. The normative continuum runs through lawyers holding firm to the aspirational decrees of professional codes regarding third-party obligations, through lawyers willing to conform at least to the black letter of the professional code, to those willing to breach the professional code but not violate more serious laws (such as criminal laws), and finally – at the morally worst pole – to those lawyers who pay no attention to their responsibilities to third parties save for a pragmatic concern with the risks of getting caught.

II Lawyers' relationship with the client: This dimension considers how lawyers comport themselves to their client's actions and purposes. At its most ethical pole, the lawyer may adopt a role of wise counsellor, ethical adviser,[10] or internalize an ethic of care (insofar as such caring avoids inappropriate and unhelpful emotional attachments).[11] At the next position on the continuum stands the lawyer who dutifully and competently represents and advises all their clients, but invests their most zealous efforts and council towards those who have justice and morality on their side. Next comes the lawyer as 'zealous advocate': acting without any consideration of the justice of clients' interests and endeavors.[12] Approaching the less ethical end of the spectrum come two different sorts of immoral lawyers. The first is the lawyer who exploits their clients, milking them for billable hours and encouraging actions and litigations that enrich the lawyer at the client's risk or expense. The second type shifts in a contrary direction, becoming complicit with their client's wrongdoing and rule-breaking. Their complicity may range over different types of rules the lawyer is willing to be complicit in breaking (aspirational, codified, 'victimless', civil, criminal). Evaluating complicity also includes assessment of the degree to which the lawyer rigorously ensures the activities they facilitate are not illegal; that is, if a contract or litigation looks suspicious, how far does the lawyer go in ascertaining its full conformity with the law?[13]

III The lawyers' relationship with colleagues and employers: This dimension tracks the relationship with other professionals but extends to those they work with (ethics of workplace relations), spanning from the lawyer who works well in a team and treats their colleagues and employers with respect and probity – to the cutthroat competitor aiming to climb the corporate ladder at any cost.

Different lawyers may achieve divergent scores on each of these three dimensions. For example, an over-zealous client advocate might be scrupulous towards their client, sparing no effort in achieving the client's best outcome – but may happily violate professional codes as part of those efforts. Equally, a corporate lawyer might prove all-too-loyal to their employer – even to the point of facilitating their malfeasance.

Just as different lawyers may score differently on each dimension, certain types of educational interventions might promote increased compliance on one dimension without improving the others. For example, increased justice-based reasoning might increase the lawyer's respect for their duties toward the justice system – but not help them become more sensitive to a client's difficult predicament. Conversely, interventions aiming to nurture an ethic of care might make the lawyer foreground their ethical duties to the desperate client depending upon them – but fail to enhance their respect for abstract duties of justice to the court.

Still, without too much simplification we can suppose that most of the initiatives canvassed in the literature (and noted below) will tend to improve each dimension, at least insofar as the intervention makes serious ethical breaches in each dimension less likely. That is, most of the initiatives considered below do not target specific moral considerations, but instead aim to make generic improvements in one or other of the four components of morality noted above, such as improving development in moral reasoning (Component Two of Rest's system), raising empathy to improve moral awareness and influence personal values (Components One and Three), or raising emotional intelligence to bolster awareness and character (Components One and Four). Since these are coarse-grained improvements in the relevant capacities, such initiatives – if they succeed in influencing the trait in question – should bring about broad improvements in professionalism across all three above-noted dimensions.

How much moral diversity is a good thing?

The foregoing discussion opens a question about whether a shift in this pro-ethical direction should be uniformly welcomed: What degree of diversity in moral approaches would we ideally wish for the legal community? While we might wish for high ideals from all lawyers, a certain diversity of moral perspectives may still prove worthwhile – especially at the top of the normative continua where there is room for diversity in how the profession might move forward and what new behaviour is exemplary. Different areas of law may make different types of approaches more effective. For example, defence attorneys in criminal law work within in an adversarial system that envisages a zealous defence for all those accused of serious crimes. This combative approach might be less helpful for a corporate in-house lawyer giving prospective advice on how the corporation should behave. So too, even within a specific area of law – and even within a single employer – a diversity of perspectives might prove valuable. A large corporation might benefit from having some lawyers capable of offering an ethically sensitive perspective, favouring negotiation and alternative dispute resolution, while others provide a more adversarial viewpoint.

Turning to the issue of dynamism, a lawyer's moral standpoint (or just practical *modus operandi*) can shift over time, impacting on their behaviour in unforeseen ways. Approaches that sail 'close to the wind' – aiming to run right up to the limits of legality without ever stumbling over the line – might prove unstable, prone to stepping onto a slippery slope. For example, a lawyer might routinely ask: 'Strategically, and setting aside all ethical concerns, what is the best I can get for my client *within the bounds of the law*?' Over time, however, this question – and the mentality driving it – might shade into: 'Strategically, and setting aside all ethical concerns, what is the best I can get for my client *given the risk–reward set of payoffs the legal system presents*?' This latter is an altogether different question, allowing violations of the law provided they carry a low chance of detection and punishment. But the lawyer might barely notice the difference. They have merely slipped from making instrumental cost–benefit analyses *within* legal constraints, to making instrumental cost–benefit analyses *about* legal constraints.

While the slippery slope from amoral advocacy to illegal complicity might be real enough, the education reformer also must be alert to other, less obvious, dynamics. In an influential paper, Susan Daicoff considers whether large-scale efforts to make lawyers more feeling and caring might – somewhat counterintuitively – lead to *less* ethical compliance.[14] Daicoff worries that if hard-nosed, competitive character traits are adaptive to legal practice, then a lawyer's heightened emotional sensitivities may engender a potential increase in psychological problems such as stress, substance abuse and depression. These factors play a role in many serious breaches of ethical and legal codes. In this way, Daicoff directs our attention to the fact that reform efforts have to deal with existing realities, and that merely having good intentions does not suffice to guarantee good outcomes.[15]

In a 2003 paper, David Luban took a different tack, and considered how everyday lawyering, combined with basic psychological mechanisms such as cognitive dissonance, can push lawyers towards unplanned departures from their moral compass.[16] While Luban stresses that lawyers possess few tools to inoculate themselves against these pressures, one solution he advocates is for aspiring lawyers at the beginning of their career to set down in concrete terms their own moral limits. These can then work as a mental 'tripwire'. When the lawyer later finds herself crossing that line, she knows she has strayed too far from her own limits, and it is time to step back from the brink – or perhaps even to get out of the game. Luban's suggestion alerts us that it is not only the *content* of a moral approach that matters – it is also the *way it is held*.

Summing up this first section, reform efforts do not need (and possibly should not even try) to purge every self-interested or materialistic ambition of student lawyers. Within bounds, a diversity of approaches, personalities and moral worldviews may prove welcome. Two sets of limits delineate these bounds: The first limit rules out any approaches that would countenance breaches of the spirit and letter of legal and professional obligations. The second calls into question any approaches that will predictably degrade – under the pressures of ordinary legal practice – into such unwelcome outcomes.

2 Why are desirable outcomes difficult to achieve?

Myriad theorists stress the dire state of the ethics of the legal profession.[17] Given the extent of this long-standing view, and given that legal education is one obvious site for reform, why has progress proved so difficult? This section provides a snapshot of several general features – stemming from psychology, philosophy, sociology and economics – that conspire to frustrate efforts at ethical improvement.

Let us begin by defining some terms.

Codes comprise codes of conduct or professional ethics. Most will include disciplinary elements (black letter rules whose breach may lead to disciplinary consequences) and aspirational statements of values, principles, ideals or virtues, which are not enforceable in themselves and which may inspire professionals to think of new ways to excel.

Values constitute goods that people are or should be pursuing. Values provide the reason communities have codes in place, and capture the spirit animating those codes. Values may be made explicit in professional codes' more aspirational parts. As we defined the term, a lawyer with *professionalism* holds the relevant values, as well as conforming to the specific codes.

Fundaments refer to the deeper metaphysical, theoretical, personal or faith-based reasons for holding and understanding values. Often, the same value can be vindicated by different fundaments.[18] For example, two lawyers might both be committed to the *value* of respecting the rule of law and the parts of the lawyers' professional code that realize that value; however, one lawyer may hold to the value for religious reasons, while the other might be a humanist who follows the work of Immanuel Kant.

With this terminology laid down, the following points can be made:

1 *Learning about codes is not controversial*: While various aspects of codes may be controversial insomuch as certain groups might wish to review,

reform or repeal specific directives, there is little controversy that would-be professionals should learn about the professional duties and legal obligations they will undertake to uphold.

2 *Values are somewhat controversial*: Beyond the simplest, most common-sense values in their signature applications, values prove at least somewhat controversial. Different subcultures and political positions (across the normal spectrum in liberal democracies) may possess diverging values, and prioritize them differently. Often, there is room for difference and development.

3 *Inculcating values is quite controversial:* Even in cases when the values themselves enjoy widespread acceptance, it can be controversial that a tertiary educational institution should be in the business of inculcating them.[19] Some would rather leave such work to the profession, or to society more generally. What some theorists would see as the welcome professional enculturation of aspiring lawyers, others may view as moralizing, indoctrination, politicization, elitism or cultural assimilation. Some would even question whether a university *can* or *should* inculcate values.[20] Even, if in principle, it was allowed that universities may influence student values – there remains a question of priority. Class time and resources spent inculcating values mean less time and resources remain available for other (uncontroversial) priorities, such as covering legal doctrine.[21] If students perceive themselves as paying consumers purchasing a commodity[22] – rather than apprentices learning their roles in a professional community – they may themselves resist the course prioritizing values. The issue of prioritization may also depend on the professional community's influence on university curricula. While various professional groups may laud (or even author) reports stressing the importance of ethics in legal education,[23] such recommendations can be swamped by employers' desires for graduates sufficiently steeped in the relevant doctrine to start racking up billable hours.

4 *Fundaments prove highly controversial*: The truth of any given fundament (whether philosophical theories or religious doctrines) remains hotly disputed. Such controversies are unlikely to be resolved in the near future – or, perhaps, ever.[24] For reasons of intellectual honesty, no university should teach any controversial theory as if it were unvarnished truth. Indoctrinating fundaments also can wade into treacherous secular vs. religious waters. That said, teaching *about* important philosophical theories (of ethics and law) invites less controversy.[25]

5 *Inculcating values requires significant resources:* The types of pedagogical activities that improve professionalism (enumerated below) tend to be resource intensive. Such activities usually require higher staff–student ratios, as well as time and effort in redesigning courses, developing pedagogical expertise, and institutional learning. These economic and time pressures occur in an environment that is (arguably, at least) already under-funded.[26]

6 *Codes without values fail to motivate*: Being informed about one's professional duties as delineated in the reigning code of conduct – with no discussion or explanation of the values undergirding the code and providing its

rationale – fails to encourage spirited compliance with that code.[27] Even if such teaching does induce compliance, it may impel a thoughtless, legalistic interpretation that leads to absurdities.[28]

The controversies noted in points 2–4 (especially 3) conspire to create a 'weakest link' quality. That is, in the face of such controversies, any one of an array of groups may decide to resist methods aimed at promoting professionalism in law students. These groups include: (i) professional organizations (wielding control through accreditation, and indirectly through the bar exam); (ii) major graduate employers; (iii) law deans and university administrators; (iv) university lecturers and tutors; and, (v) the student body itself. The weakest link phenomenon arises because if *any one* of these groups decides to actively resist professionalization, then they can stymie others' efforts. For example, if major employers and professional organizations insist on the priority of doctrinal learning, then it may prove difficult for any single university to introduce extra objectives that leave their students at a competitive disadvantage to professional entry and employment. Likewise, if teachers and university administrators resist the objective, then they may find it within their power to scupper reform attempts. And students themselves can be hostile to pedagogies they do not like, that may impact deleteriously on their grade-point-average, and that they are (after all) often paying for.

These six factors combine to generate the following results. Universities encounter few problems in teaching the content of professional ethical codes (because of 1). Through subjects like jurisprudence, universities can usually broach – though not *inculcate* (because of 4) – various fundaments that support those codes. But (because of the controversies of 2–4, and their 'weakest link' property), universities may shy away from the fraught business of promoting values and professionalism – especially once its costs are factored in to the equation (as per 5). As a result, students learn the letter of codes, but are not given the awareness, judgement, motives or character (Rest's four components) to enact them. This encourages a legalistic-compliance response at best, or a lack of any respect for the rules at worst (because of 6).[29]

Worse still, years of teaching legal doctrines while eschewing the fraught business of values can disconnect existing student values from the law and the profession they are studying. Even without deliberate intentions, universities can inculcate perspectives that arise in the absence of explicit concern for and teaching of ethics and theory, such as certain brands of legal positivism. As we saw in Chapter 4, avoiding theory can also render the student vulnerable to the first pieces of theory she encounters (for example, neoliberalism and critical theory/postmodernism – both of which can undermine professionalism.)[30]

Furthermore, because this is the usual result, there are less academics, course-materials, accepted pedagogies, and tried-and-true curricula for inculcating values. This makes educational reform more difficult and time-consuming again. As well, without explicit training in education, new lecturers typically emulate the way they themselves were taught. These various factors conspire to create a vicious circle exacerbating the costliness of these teaching methods (as per 5).

Summing up, while a barrage of voices may call for increased lawyer professionalism, an array of perennial pressures resist reforms. Reform initiatives must be pursued with a clear recognition of these challenges – especially of the 'weakest link' quality that they may possess.[31] For this reason, reformers might require access to a wide portfolio of reform alternatives, and pay heed to various clusters of interweaving educational objectives. The next section details these possibilities.

3 Content, character and outcome

This section enumerates the many levers of reform that promoters of professionalism may wield, and the different outcomes that result from them. Section 3.1 describes the key educational options available – including changes to curricula, teaching methods and culture. Section 3.2 surveys the embedded changes to the student (in terms of character traits, knowledge and skills) that legal degrees may aim to produce, while Section 3.3 describes the specific outcomes in the graduate's professional life that the degree aims to facilitate. Finally, Section 3.4 reflects on the various causal links between these initiatives, embedded changes, and graduate outcomes

Teaching initiatives

'Teaching initiatives' make up the university's toolkit, comprising aspects of education that lecturers, course-designers, deans and university administrators have at their disposal in launching reform efforts. The breadth of the listed initiatives is important, as any given initiative may not be amenable to introduction in a particular context. Initiatives coalesce into three main groups: course content (curriculum); teaching methods; and faculty culture.

Course content

Course content can be organized into several clusters: legal doctrine; socio-legal studies; philosophical studies; professional studies; and practical skills. While we separate these here for expository ease, it should be clear from the previous chapters that specific courses may – and often should – smear these neat divisions.[32]

Detailing these clusters:

Legal doctrine: Legal doctrine constitutes the mainstay of any university degree in law. It covers, for any given area of law, legislation and relevant case-studies, and the capacity to understand and analyse these.

The next three clusters can be seen as various elements of the 'critical and theoretical dimensions of legal education' (as Chapter 3 detailed).

Socio-legal studies: This cluster covers all content that expands the student's breadth of knowledge about the nature of law, bringing in new perspectives. It includes all 'law and legal' studies, linking law with economics, history, statistics, sociology, politics and social sciences. The practice in some countries (for example, US) of having the LLB as a postgraduate degree encourages the breadth of perspective and interdisciplinarity that lies at the core of socio-legal studies. This cluster also includes comparative law, and some parts of international law – inasmuch as they provide tension with, and alternatives to, domestic law. Other studies, such as of biography and fiction, may likewise feature under this rubric.

Philosophical studies: Law raises questions of moral, political and legal philosophy. Law students will encounter philosophy when they study jurisprudence, but may also engage with it in the form of political theory (for example, on the moral foundations of law) and applied ethics (for example, on legal hotpots such as immigration, euthanasia, taxation, abortion and bioethics).[33]

Professional studies: Professional studies requires, at minimum, teaching the content of the applicable professional codes of conduct. It can also include such matters as: consideration of specific case-studies and everyday professional dilemmas; the psychological vulnerabilities lawyers face;[34] consideration of rationales for the professional code;[35] reflection on students' personal ideals for their lawyering future – what the student aspires to 'stand for'; and so on.

Practical skills: This category covers coursework designed to improve student knowledge of, and the acquisition of skills involved in, practical legal activities such as negotiation, dispute resolution, interviewing, public speaking, legal argument, and so on.[36]

Teaching methods

Some types of content imply certain types of teaching methods. However, a certain modularity often exists between content and method, allowing even a single course to employ different teaching methods at different times or with respect to different topics.

We group teaching methods into three groups: Traditional; Experiential and Reflective.

Traditional: In law, traditional practice covers two teaching modes. The first method constitutes the common (and cost-effective) 'chalk and talk' university lecture format, with a single lecturer, often back-dropped by a power-point presentation, imparting knowledge to a large student audience. Aspects of almost all course content – including philosophical and socio-legal studies – can be conveyed through this method.

The other mode is the 'case-study', 'casebook' or 'Socratic' method, beginning in Harvard under the influence of C.C. Langdell and celebrated in the image of Professor Kingsfield and would-be imitators (see Chapter 1). This pedagogy involves students learning an area of legal doctrine from studying a selection of key cases, and then being interrogated in class to uncover their underlying logic or deeper principles.[37]

Experiential: Experiential methods provide learning through direct experience: this can include the use of clinical training and apprentice-style/internship work experience, simulations and role-play, and interactions with successful practicing lawyers through mentoring, dialogue or interviewing. There is, of course, a long-term use of mooting which has been extended to a wide range of specific areas (most famously the Jessup International Law Moot) and techniques (for example, negotiation competitions) and with different levels of simulation (for example, Griffith initially had one moot per student per year with first and second year moots replicating fewer stages in litigation than the typical moot and more stages in the final year). Experiential learning also covers the use of small-group work focused on specific assessment tasks, such as drafting contracts, advice to clients and legislation.[38]

Reflective dialogue: This method involves students reflecting critically on their experiences or on content initially conveyed through traditional means or selected readings. It can involve exercises in perspective-taking, or focus on the student's own values and beliefs – such as reflection on what sort of lawyer they aspire to become. The activities might cover moral and/or philosophical dialogue, where students learn to argue their position (and perhaps change their position) in terms of principles, analogies and moral theories. Students may engage in guided reflection on their own – such as through self-reporting instruments, journal-keeping and workbooks – or in groups – such as discussions reflecting on student's analysis of moral dilemmas). Inns of Court, debating and mooting can encompass both experiential and reflective-dialogue modes of learning.

Faculty culture

Faculty and university culture can impact upon desired graduate outcomes. Three factors warrant attention:[39]

Modelling professionalism: The teaching faculty – and the administrative support they receive – can exemplify the types of behaviour and ethos that future professionals would ideally possess. One obvious place where values can be modelled is through processes safeguarding academic integrity. If students see that the academy takes seriously its commitments to confront cheating and plagiarism, then they can be introduced to an institutional model that prides itself on integrity.[40]

Branding: Universities and their law schools aim to market themselves in attractive ways, often seeking through their branding to distinguish themselves from competitors. These public relations efforts can help establish community and student expectations about what students will be taught. As Kim Economides notes, enrolling in a school of *law* may conjure up different expectations from participating in a school of *justice*.[41] If the school's marketing and orientation-activities foreground social and ethical issues, then students are primed for later encounters.

Personnel: The staffing of the law school can make a difference to the portfolio of content, culture and teaching methods available. Law schools in large, urban universities may have access to psychology lecturers and behavioural scientists (who can be helpful in teaching or advising about social/emotional skills), social scientists, historians and economists available for teaching interdisciplinary, and cross-disciplinary courses, and philosophers for teaching jurisprudence, political theory or applied ethics.[42] Alternatively, university schools can employ lecturers who are interested in and committed to teaching emotional and ethical skills. The school's research focus can also help shape student interests and expectations, even as it impacts on the nature of the faculty more broadly.[43]

All this said, aspects of culture may be difficult to budge, even from within the university. Student culture may be influenced by large-scale political and economic factors with respect to how course funding occurs. In cases where the user pays, it may be difficult to dislodge a consumerist mentality within the student body.[44]

Character: embedded graduate characteristics

Through the use of its curriculum, teaching methods and faculty culture, legal education can embed a wide variety of qualities, characteristics and traits in its graduates. These potential objectives (not all schools can prioritize them all) may be grouped under four rubrics: knowledge content; social and emotional skills; ethical traits, and; personal qualities.

Knowledge content: Perhaps the most obvious quality one would expect from any university graduate is their possession of substantial knowledge. The law graduate's expertise must encompass comprehensive knowledge of legal doctrine in key areas, as well as associated doctrinal skills such as searching, understanding and analyzing court cases and legislation. Their embedded knowledge may also include a broader understanding of law's nature, limitations, possibilities and role in society, particularly through being well-versed in aspects of its relationship with economic, philosophical, historical, political, psychological and sociological factors.

Social and emotional skills: Graduates may possess a wide portfolio of practical social capacities of use in future lawyering. These include skills and qualities regarding listening, interviewing, understanding, negotiating, persuading, cooperating, leadership, teamwork, collegiality, empathizing and eliciting empathy. These qualities overlap with 'emotional intelligence', which we understand here as the capacity to understand the emotions of oneself and others, and to influence both sorts of emotions to achieve larger goals.[45] These generic skills may also exist in a more targeted form, in terms of practical legal skills such as legal negotiation, alternative dispute resolution, legal counselling, and the ability to influence juries through persuasion and appeals to emotion.

Ethical qualities: From the perspective of this chapter, the key traits to nurture[46] will be those that we have termed 'professionalism', a moral core comprising Rest's four components of moral awareness, reasoning, values and character.[47] Different parts of legal education may extend (or, alternatively, degrade) each of these distinct components. For example, the law degree might increase the second component covering the cognitive development of moral reasoning – indeed, most formal education tends to increase the sophistication of graduates' moral reasoning[48] – but fail to improve students' moral values or awareness.

Personal and intellectual qualities: Graduates may acquire a variety of other personal attributes that overlap with the above-noted qualities. These include intellectual and cognitive capacities such as: critical thinking (including reasoning, lateral thinking, logical and rational cognitive skills, capacity for analysis and synthesis); academic research (and other evidence-gathering and informational skills); and familiarity with social science, natural science and statistical methodologies.

Acquired personal qualities may also include characteristics like grit, resilience, assertiveness and possessing a work-ethic (often collectively expressed as 'ego-strength'[49]) as well as qualities of mind encompassing reflectiveness, introspectiveness, curiosity and wonder – perhaps especially with respect to law's nature and social role.

Ultimate outcomes and specific effects

By instilling various embedded graduate characteristics, legal education alters the likelihood of specific outcomes later in the graduate's life. Setting aside academic success, the following clusters of outcomes – sorted under rubrics of 'effective lawyering', 'ethical outcomes', 'quality of life' and 'other occupation outcomes' – describe the types of events that legal education may aim to elicit.

Effective lawyering: Perhaps the central outcome intended by every law school is that their graduates enjoy professional success as lawyers. Hamilton and Monson advance a metric of overall lawyer 'effectiveness': the lawyer bringing about results that the lawyer's clients and colleagues' value.[50] Such overall effectiveness covers a myriad of specific outcomes, such as: wielding knowledge of relevant areas of doctrine to a standard demanded by the profession and its entrance requirements; success in professional socio-personal interactions (counselling, communication, negotiation, gaining clients' trust, gaining juries' sympathy, working in a team, listening and understanding in interviews); and their achievements in lifelong professional learning.

Depending upon the type of law practiced, effective lawyering outcomes might also include efficacy in employing empirical, scientific and quantitative evidence in one's work (such to assist the court's fact-finding);[51] and achieving flexibility and foresight with respect to changes in the law (such as in international, cross-jurisdictional or politically charged areas of law).

Ethical outcomes: This outcome means that over the course of her professional life, the lawyer lives up to the letter and spirit of all laws and professional codes – not only avoiding legal and professional transgressions, but helping her employers, clients and colleagues to resist transgressions. Deeper outcomes may be also desirable. These include the ability to give effective ethical advice to clients,[52] and to wisely direct and guide clients' ends (as well as advising on the best means to those ends).[53]

Quality of life: Graduates' quality of life encompasses two distinct areas. First, it covers the graduate making wise and informed career choices, for example about whether they wish to pursue a career in law, the area of law they should pursue, whether to favour a private business or a corporate career, how to achieve a constructive work/life balance, and so on. Second, quality of life includes the graduate's long-run capacity to find fulfilment, achievement and enjoyment in their practice of law. Rather than just providing professionals with material and status benefits, the practice of law can be apprehended as worthwhile itself. The lawyer feels fulfilled in defending the needy, helping people pursue worthwhile projects, and making a positive difference in the world.

While significant in any employment area, quality of life issues are magnified in their significance in law, given the documented high rates of stress, depression and substance abuse.[54]

Other occupational outcomes: As well as undertaking careers as lawyers (or judges), an increasing number of law school graduates – in some cases a majority of graduates – proceed toward cognate careers. These may include employment as public servants, legislators, politicians, regulators, serving on ethics boards, and so on. Alternatively, some graduates may move into academic research and teaching. While graduate success in these areas would not be a central objective of the law school, the capacity to instil such success nevertheless adds to the degree's overall value (personal and economic).

Links between initiatives, qualities and outcomes

No single work can detail all of the permutations interweaving between the myriad reform levers within curricula, methods and culture, the embedded characteristics with which graduates leave the university, and the specific outcomes that occur later in their lives. However, this section aims to convey some of the most important links as they apply to nurturing professionalism.[55]

An exclusive focus on doctrine can undermine social and moral qualities

The exclusive teaching of doctrine and the explicit or implicit inculcation of legal realism/positivism does little to advance law students' professionalism. If anything the evidence indicates the reverse: that placing an overriding priority on traditional teaching of law actually works to erode students' moral values and sunder their ethical and personal connections to their learning and future professional work.[56] A lack of reflective and philosophical thought may feed these problems.[57] In particular, some theorists hold that an exclusive focus on legal doctrine cements an unhelpful view of law as academically unique – and hence beyond external understanding and critique.[58]

Case-study method ambiguities

The verdict on the 'case-study' method proves hard to render. Different scholars form conflicting assessments of this method, with some lauding its capacity to strengthen moral imagination, and others countering that it encourages technicist moral ratiocination, stripping away values and emotions by emphasizing indifference and abstraction.[59] As with other doctrinal methods, some scholars argue it cultivates a sense of law's uniqueness, and thereby acts as a roadblock to reform and worthwhile interdisciplinary and occasional trans-disciplinary connections.[60]

Emotional intelligence promotes professionalism

Many scholars stress the link between developing emotional intelligence and facilitating professionalism. To some extent, the link between the two is constitutive.[61] That is, key parts of emotional intelligence make up elements of Rest's four components. For example, empathy stands as a key part of emotional intelligence (awareness of others' emotions) and as an important factor in moral awareness and values.[62] So too, emotional intelligence's elements of self-awareness, reflectiveness and the capacity to regulate one's own emotions would feature in any account of character (Rest's fourth component). Emotional intelligence also possesses features that contingently link with professionalism, such as improved coping and communication capacities, including through enriched interviewing and negotiations skills.

Some sceptical voices query links between emotional intelligence and lawyer effectiveness. In particular, Daicoff mounts a multi-faceted argument questioning whether lawyers' aggressive personality traits could be changed, and questioning whether pro-social changes would be beneficial, especially if lawyers' hyper-competitive personality traits were adaptive and helped them cope with their challenging occupation.[63] However, since Daicoff made her argument in 1998, scholars have argued that the empirical evidence points the other way: (a) pro-social traits *can* be altered by education,[64] (b) emotional and moral qualities correlate with *more* (rather than less) effective lawyering,[65] and, (c) such qualities *improve* rather than degrade emotional coping.[66]

Methods can achieve powerful results

How something is taught can prove more important than *what* is taught. In the terminology employed above, changes in 'teaching methods' may create greater impact than changes in course content itself (at least, once a value-crushing focus on doctrine has been removed).

In particular, experiential and reflective methods loom large in analyses of how to promote emotional intelligence, lawyers' social skills, and professionalism.[67] Basing their work on empirical evidence from psychology and education studies, scholars from a variety of pedagogical perspectives hammer home the significance of experiential methods such as simulations, role-play, and imagining and discussing typical problem cases;[68] mentoring and other interactions with successful ethical exemplars;[69] and reflective methods such as self-reporting instruments, class discussions and journal-keeping.[70] Many writers similarly stress the significance of in-house clinical training or externships – provided that there is space for classroom discussion and critical reflection.[71] And almost all note the need for moral dialogue and teacher-facilitated exploration in small groups,[72] especially when focusing on ethical dilemmas occurring in the subtle and contested forms they typically arise in professionals' lives.[73] Faculty culture can also help by modelling the values and integrity teachers aim to instil.[74]

Moral outcomes correlate with effective lawyering

Perhaps the most important link highlighted in the literature is that between professionalism (understood as an internalized moral core) and effectiveness. Even setting aside the social science on this correlation, the earlier chapters have already noted several ways in which ethically good lawyering promotes effective results. For example, Chapter 9 (Sect. 4) noted how barristers prosper when they can tap into the moral reasoning of judges, while Chapter 10's discussion of advising Holmes' 'Bad Man' observed that the best advice of the lawyer to the 'bad man' is to attempt to be good according to the lawyer's best understanding of the values underlying the law.[75]

The reason this multifaceted link is so important is that, as Hamilton and Monson stress, a significant subset of students, 'will adopt ideas and skills to the extent they find them useful and efficient in solving practical problems'.[76] In other words, so long as experiential and reflective methods can be demonstrated to improve how future lawyers handle serious problems, otherwise sceptical students have a rationale for investing in these activities. So too, future employers and professional organizations – and in turn university administrators – might be less supportive of ethical objectives in the curricula if they felt that such interventions would weaken the workplace effectiveness of graduates.

Summing up, the literature demonstrates a virtuous spiral between social skilling, professionalism and overall effectiveness, and suggests that – while attention must be paid to the curriculum content – the significant levers of effective reform lie in experiential, reflective and cultural shifts.

That said, distinct types of content impact on certain aspects of professionalism and effective lawyering. An example of the first (impacting on professionalism) is studying history to dramatize the 'ancient and honourable enterprise' of lawyering, and the traditional standards upheld by famous historical lawyers.[77] An example of the second (impacting on effective lawyering) are socio-legal studies on statistics and science which facilitate lawyers grappling with courts' increasing engagement with factual and social-scientific questions (especially in the US).[78]

Figure 12.1 portrays some of the major links. The Figure's first three columns cover the three types of potential teaching initiatives (Curriculum Content; Teaching Methods; University Culture). The remaining two columns list Embedded Characteristics and Specific Outcomes.[79] In its grey ovals, the Figure illustrates the narrowness of the traditional approach (in curriculum content and teaching method) – showing that it tends to promote only a single Embedded

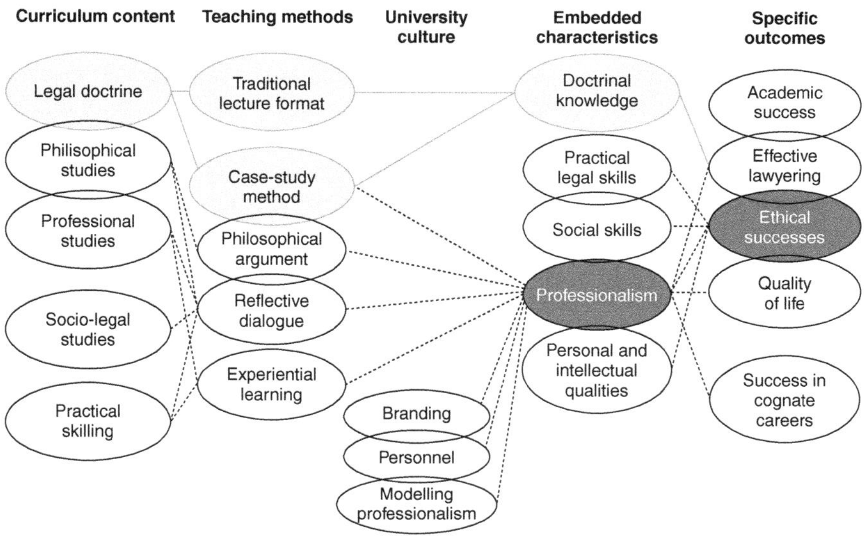

Figure 12.1 Initiatives and outcomes linking professionalism and ethical outcomes.

Quality that can lead to Effective Lawyering, and altogether fails to impact on Ethical Successes. In contrast, the dotted-line links show the main paths to Professionalism (as an Embedded Quality) and Ethical Successes (as a Specific Outcome). These links illustrate how alternative curriculum content and various teaching methods encourage Professionalism, and how a wide array of Embedded Qualities improve the likelihood of Ethical Successes.

4 Ways forward

Reformers must be realistic when surveying tools, limitations and potential student outcomes. The equation necessitates trade-offs and hard prioritizations. Myriad teaching models exist within different national cultures and economies – and no model can accomplish every desirable outcome.[80] Quality sometimes comes at a cost, and in a world with finite limits, a breadth of education inevitably weakens the depth of narrow specialization.[81] Equally, funding limitations must loom large in any reckoning.[82] These limitations include not just the costs shouldered by the student and/or the state, but also consider graduates' job prospects; in a user-pays system these prospects provide the economic return students can expect from their investment in the law degree.[83] So too, jurisdictions will differ with the type of pressure professional groups apply to universities. For example, professional bodies might prove strong supporters of universities prioritizing ethical values in students. At other times, the profession might pressure universities to prioritize doctrine, and so limit the training that would otherwise fall to employers or the professional body itself.[84] As we saw earlier in Section 2, forthrightly inculcating ethics might spark controversy, meaning professional, industry or student-led pressures might necessitate more indirect reforms.

These different pressures, influences and constraints mean there is no one-size-fits-all approach to expanding professionalism in law students. With this in mind, this section provides three separate ways forward.

The *Ameliorative Approach* outlines a limited intervention capable of being introduced with little fanfare, even in cases where explicit values promotion might trigger unhelpful controversy. The *Educating the Effective Lawyer Approach* prioritizes the social-emotional skilling required by effective lawyers, and so requires greater freedom and resources for reform. Finally, the *Educating the Whole Lawyer Approach* implies a holistic and public pursuit of inculcating ethical values.[85]

The Ameliorative Approach

In working largely within the bounds of traditional curricula, the Ameliorative Approach's core motto is 'First, do no harm (to existing student values)'. Even if it eschews pervasively inculcating values, the Ameliorative Approach aims to avoid eroding them. The Ameliorative Approach provides a piecemeal and surreptitious approach to nurturing students' latent professionalism. Aspirations regarding professionalism and overall effectiveness are not explicitly publicized. As Silver observes, while reformers must plan and act pervasively to inculcate professionalism, 'we need not always do it explicitly ... [Values] can be conveyed through modelling and mentoring'.[86]

Drawing on Section Three, Ameliorative Approach initiatives include:

- *Eschewing claims of uniqueness:* The law school resists any suggestion of law's autonomy and uniqueness, or the 'distinctiveness of legal reasoning'. While such distinctiveness can help build a specific role-identity, an emphasis on specialness can foster an unwarranted sense of status and pride, and immunize legal practice from lay and interdisciplinary moral challenge or enrichment.
- *Increasing positive industry contact:* Courses aim, wherever possible, to increase student contact with, and teaching/mentoring from, successful lawyers who are themselves models of professionalism, in order to show that professional achievement can accompany personal values.
- *Exemplifying values:* Teachers and academic protocols model professional values: for example, in teaching and maintaining academic integrity.
- *Dispelling myths:* Students may harbour counterproductive assumptions about professionalism in lawyering: for example, that most successful real-world lawyers are unscrupulous. Such myths should be confronted with reason and evidence.[87]
- *Employing alternative pedagogies:* Teachers can employ processes and procedures that encourage moral thinking and behaviour (habitualizing

feedback, dialogue and reflection), stressing the complexity and diversity of moral issues. Political philosophies and legal theories can illustrate this complexity, but so too can well-taught applications of the Socratic Method.

- *Stressing insights, not ideology:* Teachers can be sensitive to the prospects of inculcating schemas of legal practice and theories of legal philosophy that marginalize ethics from law, and that thereby erode the sense of ethical lawyering. More positively, teacher can teach legal-political philosophy theories so as to showcase the normative insights that each has to offer; allowing students to settle on philosophical positions that will not hinder, and might well burnish, their moral character.[88]

'The Effective Lawyer' Approach

The Effective Lawyer Approach follows the Ameliorative Approach in resisting an explicit appeal to ethics (perhaps to avoid controversy or student hostility). Unlike that narrower approach, however, it highlights that effective lawyering requires social-emotional skilling. Because these types of skill acquisition, and the pedagogies promoting them, impact on student's moral awareness and character, such practices can promote ethics even as they equip future lawyers with key social and emotional resources.

As well as employing the Ameliorative Approach's techniques, Effective Lawyer Approach initiatives include:

- *Practical and social skilling:* Coursework inculcates social skills relevant to interviewing, negotiating, dispute resolution and teamwork – especially through employing reflective dialogue and experiential learning.
- *Teaching about the effective lawyer:* Students can be explicitly taught how social skills and ethical values impact upon effective lawyering.[89] So too, the school's commitment to creating effective lawyers can be foregrounded in its branding and orientation materials.

'The Whole Lawyer' Approach

The final approach occurs when the school is in a position to publically prioritize its stance on the importance of inculcating ethical values.[90] Because of this forthright stance, the Whole Lawyer Approach can – in addition to the above-noted initiatives – include:

- *Publicizing its values*: The school can be up-front (including in marketing and orientation materials) about teaching values and educating 'the whole lawyer'. This forestalls the student's sense that they 'didn't sign up for this'.
- *Pursuing a holistic or pervasive approach:* The school can aim for something of a synthesis across its many courses and pedagogies, with all the elements pushing in the same general direction, rather than ethics being 'bolted on' to the core business.[91]

- *Inculcate basic values:* The school can teach 'low-level' values (such as honesty and respect for the rule of law) that can be embraced by a wide overlapping consensus. Similarly, it can demand appropriate student values (such as academic integrity), which may set the platform for cognate professional values.
- *Encourage personal ownership:* Using reflection and discussion, coursework can encourage students to think for themselves about the type of lawyer they want to be, and the type of role for law that they want to encourage.[92]
- *Forewarning students:* Students can learn the common pitfalls and psychological 'traps' endangering lawyers, and how to recognize danger signs in their own practice.

Conclusion

This chapter provided a synoptic view of the tools available to reformers aiming to instil professionalism in graduates. The wide array of curricula options, teaching methods and cultural shifts allows differently placed reformers to adopt strategies tailored to their specific context. So too, reformers can reflect on exactly what types of embedded qualities and specific outcomes they aim to promote. As a general theme, we highlighted that reflective and experiential teaching modes tended to improve both overall lawyer effectiveness and professionalism.

Notes

1 To be clear, we mean that professionalism requires meeting these codes in more or less their standard form. Some authors imply that professionalism can be improved by altering the *codes* to fit the existing (lack of) values. See, for example, Susan Daicoff, 'Asking Leopards to Change Their Spots: Should Lawyers Change? A Critique of Solutions to Problems with Professionalism by Reference to Empirically-Derived Attorney Personality Attributes', *Georgetown Journal of Legal Ethics* 11 (1998). To the contrary, as many theorists have stressed, all professional codes share certain constraints precisely because the clients or community's vulnerabilities to the profession's practice makes such constraints necessary. The constraints are the price the profession pays for its licence to practice. Repealing the constraints is thus not a morally acceptable option. See, for example, Hugh Breakey, 'Supply and Demand in the Development of Professional Ethics', in *Australian Association for Professional and Applied Ethics Annual Conference* (Auckland, 2015).

2 This goes beyond moral norms that are patently unjust, discriminatory or in violation of human rights. In a community where the vast majority share moral norms against a particular kind of sexual practice, lawyers are statistically likely to share those norms. However, as lawyers, they have particularly important duties to ensure that even the morally condemned receive a fair trial by a combination of vigorous and totally committed defence counsel and a prosecution constrained by the higher standards of prosecutorial ethics.

3 See N. Hamilton and V. Monson, 'The Positive Empirical Relationship of Professionalism to Effectiveness in the Practice of Law', *Geo. J. Legal Ethics* 24 (2011); 'Legal Education's Ethical Challenge: Empirical Research on How Most Effectively to Foster Each Student's Professional Formation (Professionalism)', *University of St. Thomas Law Journal* 9, no. 2 (2012).

4 In this chapter, we treat the terms 'ethical' and 'moral' as synonyms.

5 Developed over a series of works: James R. Rest, 'Morality', in *Handbook of Child Psychology*, ed. Paul Mussen (New York: John Wiley & Sons, 1992); James R. Rest, 'A Psychologist Looks at the Teaching of Ethics', *The Hastings Center Report* 12, no. 1 (1982); and in the context of the professions in: James Rest, 'Background: Theory and Research', in *Moral Development in the Professions*, ed. James Rest and Darcia Narvez (Taylor & Francis, 1994).

6 'Morality'.

7 See, Charles Sampford and Sophie Blencowe, 'Raising the Standards: An Integrated Approach to Promoting Professional Standards and Avoiding Professional Criminality', in *Crime in the Professions*, ed. Russell Smith (Aldershot: Ashgate, 2002): 251–267.

8 Sir Owen Dixon, 'Remarks by Sir Owen Dixon on His Swearing in as Chief Justice of the High Court of Australia', in *The Role of Barristers* (Melbourne: Chancery Chambers, 1952).

9 Strictly, one could separate the professional community from the general commonweal, as the community may benefit from collective codes that run counter to social interests. See, for example, David K. McGraw, 'A Social Contract Theory Critique of Professional Codes of Ethics', *Journal of Information, Communication and Ethics in Society* 2, no. 4 (2004). See also, Michael Davis, 'Professionalism Means Putting Your Profession First', *Georgetown Journal of Legal Ethics* 2, no. 34 (1988).

10 See Chapter 10 above.

11 Marjorie A. Silver, 'Emotional Intelligence and Legal Education', *Psychology, Public Policy, and Law* 5, no. 4 (1999): 1195. It provides a nice analogy to porcupines nestling together in cold weather: close enough to benefit from the others' warmth – not so close as to get pricked.

12 A converse immorality would be lawyers who are paternalistic to their clients – acting without heeding how best to realize this specific client's actual wants and needs.

13 These two elements of complicity may diverge; for example, a lawyer who would never be complicit in any obvious illegality placed before her eyes might remain less than rigorous in ascertaining the status of dubious activities she facilitates.

14 Daicoff, 'Asking Leopards to Change Their Spots'.

15 That said, research since Daicoff's (1998) work implies that professionalism makes for *more* effective lawyers, weakening the casual chain she envisages. See below n. 64–67.

16 David Luban, 'Integrity: Its Causes and Cures', *Fordham Law Review* 72, no. 2 (2003).

17 Daicoff puts forward an interlinked tripartite crisis: of (i) professionalism, (ii) lawyers' quality of life, and (iii) public opinion about lawyers. Daicoff, 'Asking Leopards to Change Their Spots'.

18 Borrowing Rawls' terminology, we can have an 'overlapping consensus' on values, despite differing fundaments ('comprehensive doctrines'). John Rawls, *Political Liberalism*, Expanded ed. (New York: Columbia University Press, 2005). See also Sunstein's 'incompletely theorized agreements': Cass R. Sunstein, *Legal Reasoning and Political Conflict* (New York: Oxford University Press, 1996): Ch. 2.

19 Modern education shies away from values and emotions generally, prioritizing intellectual development. See Hamilton and Monson, 'Relationship of Professionalism to Effectiveness': 142; Silver, 'Emotional Intelligence and Legal Education': 1202.

20 See Daicoff, who argues that lawyers' and law students' personalities are resistant to the types of changes envisaged by enthusiastic reformers. Daicoff, 'Asking Leopards to Change Their Spots'. Sampford's approach in the Griffith curriculum was to put the values as answers to questions about the nature of the profession rather than to teach the values themselves.

21 See Chapter 3 (Sect.1). In Australia, several theorists stress the significance of the 'Priestley 11': the areas of doctrine mandated by the profession. See, for example, the work of two Griffith professors: Mary Keyes and Richard Johnstone, 'Changing Legal Education: Rhetoric, Reality, and Prospects for the Future', *Sydney Law Review* 26, no. 4 (2004).
22 See ibid.
23 See the reports considered by John E. Montgomery, 'Incorporating Emotional Intelligence Concepts into Legal Education: Strengthening the Professionalism of Law Students', *University of Toledo Law Review* 39, no. Winter (2008); Compare, however, Kim Economides and Julian Webb, 'Do Law Schools Care About Law Students and Legal Values?', *Legal Ethics* 3, no. 1 (2000).
24 Rawls opines that pluralism and disagreement about comprehensive doctrines stands as an irremovable feature of liberal democracies. Rawls, *Political Liberalism.*
25 For more discussion, see Chapters 2 and 4.
26 See, for example, Keyes and Johnstone, 'Changing Legal Education'.
27 Kim Economides, 'Learning the Law of Lawyering', *Current Legal Problems* 52, no. 1 (1999); Margaret Castles, 'Challenges to the Academy: Reflections on the Teaching of Legal Ethics in Australia', *Legal Education Review* 6 (2001); Daniel E. Wueste, 'Promoting Integrity Integritively: Avoiding the Scylla and Charybdis of Abdication and Zealotry', *Research in Ethical Issues in Organizations* 12 (2014); Hamilton and Monson, 'Relationship of Professionalism to Effectiveness': 151. Daicoff also notes lawyers' resistance to authority/lack of subservience. Daicoff, 'Asking Leopards to Change Their Spots'.
28 Wueste, 'Promoting Integrity Integritively'.
29 That this is a consistent outcome in all teaching of professions, see Hamilton and Monson, 'Relationship of Professionalism to Effectiveness': 185.
30 Kevin T. Leicht, 'Market Fundamentalism, Cultural Fragmentation, Post-Modern Skepticism, and the Future of Professional Work', *Journal of Professions and Organization* (2015).
31 This helps explain the efforts (see Chapter 6) at Griffith to bring the profession on board with the 'revolution'.
32 See especially Chapters 2 to 4.
33 Applied ethics differs from the separate category of professional ethics, which deals with dilemmas and issues faced by lawyers in their professional capacity. The two topics, and the educational challenges they raise, remain quite distinct. Discussing the analogous domain of medical ethics, see: Rosamond Rhodes, 'Two Concepts of Medical Ethics and Their Implications for Medical Ethics Education', *Journal of Medicine and Philosophy* 27, no. 4 (2002).
34 See, for example, Luban, 'Causes and Cures'.
35 These need not involve philosophical justifications. See, Suzette Barnaby, 'Legal Ethics for the Real World: A Model for Engaging First Year Law Students', *QUT Law Journal* 4, no. 2 (2004).
36 For discussion, see Keyes and Johnstone, 'Changing Legal Education': 550.
37 Langdell saw this method as establishing the 'science' of law, based on the theory of 'legal formalism/doctrinalism', which holds that the common law consists of an interconnected system of broad principles and specific doctrines. In the twentieth century, the predominance of legal positivism purged this method of any search for underlying 'transcendent' principles, but left the substance of the method intact. See Steven Dow, 'There's Madness in the Method: A Commentary on Law, Statistics, and the Nature of Legal Education', *Oklahoma Law Review* 57 (2004).
38 One of the most interesting of these was the creation of mini law 'offices' where students got used to the kind of documents created by lawyers and the challenges in generating them – understandings that helped them understand the disputes over such documents in the cases they read.

39 Others could be mentioned: for example, different mechanics within the way coursework is offered and explained can give students different senses of their own level of choice, investment and control over their learning. This can provide students with a greater sense of autonomy. Kennon M. Sheldon and Lawrence S. Krieger, 'Understanding the Negative Effects of Legal Education on Law Students: A Longitudinal Test of Self-Determination Theory', *Personality and Social Psychology Bulletin* 33, no. 6 (2007).
40 Wueste, 'Promoting Integrity Integritively': 25.
41 Economides, 'Law of Lawyering': 411.
42 See, generally, Montgomery, 'Strengthening Professionalism': 351.
43 Chapter 1 observed how Griffith Law School's interdisciplinary research centres dovetailed with its interdisciplinary approach to education.
44 Keyes and Johnstone, 'Changing Legal Education'.
45 See Silver, 'Emotional Intelligence and Legal Education'; Colin James, 'Seeing Things as We Are: Emotional Intelligence and Clinical Legal Education', *International Journal Clinical Legal Education* 8 (2005); Montgomery, 'Strengthening Professionalism'.
46 Related embedded qualities contribute to professionalism. For instance, nurturing students' sense of *integrity* – of having them reflect on what they want to stand for and how they can live up to those chosen ideals – will usually work to enhance their professionalism. See Hugh Breakey, Timothy Cadman, and Charles Sampford, 'Conceptualizing Personal and Institutional Integrity: The Comprehensive Integrity Framework', *Research in Ethical Issues in Organizations* 14 (2015); Sharon Dolovich, 'Ethical Lawyering and the Possibility of Integrity', in *Professional Ethics and Personal Integrity*, ed. Tim Dare and W. Bradley Wendel (Newcastle upon Tyne: Cambridge Scholars Publishing, 2010). Similar benefits can arise from encouraging students to *identify* as lawyers – as members of a specific group with its own role-identity. However, this latter quality can also carry its own concerns. See, for example, D.B. Wilkins, 'Practical Wisdom for Practicing Lawyers: Separating Ideals from Ideology in Legal Ethics', *Harvard Law Review* 108 (1994); Nickolas John James, 'Expertise as Privilege: Australian Legal Education and The Persistent Emphasis Upon Doctrine', *University of Western Sydney Law Review* 8, no. 1 (2004).
47 This concept is that employed and developed in: Hamilton and Monson, 'Relationship of Professionalism to Effectiveness'; 'Legal Education's Ethical Challenge'.
48 Rest, 'Morality'.
49 The purpose here is to gather together the types of useful attributes universities may aim to instil in their graduates. That said, it remains noteworthy that less obviously desirable attributes can be instilled or selected by university legal education, including ambition, competitiveness, aggression and individualism. See, Daicoff, 'Asking Leopards to Change Their Spots'.
50 Hamilton and Monson, 'Relationship of Professionalism to Effectiveness'.
51 Dow, 'Madness in the Method'.
52 See Chapter 10 above.
53 For example, Kronman's idea of the lawyer-statesman, with practical wisdom capable of helping clients come to a better understanding of their own interests. See Wilkins, 'Practical Wisdom for Practicing Lawyers'.
54 See, for example, Daicoff, 'Asking Leopards to Change Their Spots'.
55 Our earlier discussion already noted some links. For example, Section 2 noted that teaching the content of professional codes without explaining their rationale fails to motivate compliance. Equally, we noted tensions between professionalism and assumed role-identities (see above footnote 47). Previous chapters (esp. Chapters 2 and 4) also interrogated the links between the teaching of philosophical theories (of ethics, politics and law) and subsequent promises and dangers.

56 See, for example, Rest, 'Teaching of Ethics': 30; Deanell Reece Tacha, 'Training the Whole Lawyer', *Iowa Law Review* 96 (2011): 1703; Economides and Webb, 'Do Law Schools Care About Law Students and Legal Values?': 8; Keyes and Johnstone, 'Changing Legal Education'.
57 See Chapter 4.
58 James, 'Expertise as Privilege: Australian Legal Education and The Persistent Emphasis Upon Doctrine'; Wilkins, 'Practical Wisdom for Practicing Lawyers'. Privileging law in this way can foster the wrong sort of professional pride: see, in the context of another profession, Tetsuji Iseda, 'How Should We Foster the Professional Integrity of Engineers in Japan? A Pride-Based Approach', *Science and Engineering Ethics* 14 (2008).
59 See Wilkins, 'Practical Wisdom for Practicing Lawyers'; Tacha, 'Training the Whole Lawyer'; Silver, 'Emotional Intelligence and Legal Education'; Dow, 'Madness in the Method'.
60 James, 'Expertise as Privilege: Australian Legal Education and The Persistent Emphasis Upon Doctrine'.
61 In fact, some argue a satisfying account of emotional intelligence requires claims about the rightness of certain emotions in certain situations. See Sophie Rietti, 'Emotional Intelligence and Moral Agency: Some Worries and a Suggestion', *Philosophical Psychology* 22, no. 2 (2009).
62 That is, components one and three of Rest's system. For detailed analysis of the links between various initiatives and elements of Rest's system, see Hamilton and Monson, 'Legal Education's Ethical Challenge'.
63 Daicoff, 'Asking Leopards to Change Their Spots'.
64 See Silver, 'Emotional Intelligence and Legal Education'; M Neil Browne, Carrie L. Williamson and Linda L. Barkacs, 'The Purported Rigidity of an Attorney's Personality: Can Legal Ethics Be Acquired?', *Journal of the Legal Profession* 55 (2006).
65 Hamilton and Monson, 'Relationship of Professionalism to Effectiveness'.
66 James, 'Seeing Things as We Are'.
67 Almost all the methods noted in the forthcoming paragraphs were noted or anticipated regarding their importance in advancing components of Rest's model of moral psychology, in Hamilton and Monson, 'Legal Education's Ethical Challenge'. *Inter alia*, the authors note: teacher-facilitated discussions accompanied by position-reversals; service-learning experiences; creating and supporting the student through a cognitive disequilibrium; linking professional formation pedagogy to the standard 'case-dialogue pedagogy'; and the significance of faculty culture.
68 Silver, 'Emotional Intelligence and Legal Education': 1195–1196; Barnaby, 'Legal Ethics for the Real World'.
69 Rest, 'Teaching of Ethics'; Tacha, 'Training the Whole Lawyer'.
70 James, 'Seeing Things as We Are'; Montgomery, 'Strengthening Professionalism'. For pedagogical initiatives promoting emotional intelligence, see the collected references in ibid., 350–351.
71 For example, Silver, 'Emotional Intelligence and Legal Education'.
72 Browne, Williamson and Barkacs, 'The Purported Rigidity of an Attorney's Personality: Can Legal Ethics Be Acquired?'.
73 Castles, 'Challenges to the Academy'.
74 Tacha, 'Training the Whole Lawyer'; Hamilton and Monson, 'Legal Education's Ethical Challenge'; Wueste, 'Promoting Integrity Integritively': 25.
75 Section 2. Chapter 10, Sect. 1, also noted further potential problems for the zealous 'client advocate' role.
76 Hamilton and Monson, 'Legal Education's Ethical Challenge': 384.
77 Davis notes how earlier ethical courses in law (in previous ethics 'booms') had foregrounded this method. Michael Davis, 'The Ethics Boom: What and Why', *The Centennial Review* 34, no. 2 (1990): 173. In a more modern context, Barnaby highlights

the use of biography to inspire moral response and reflection: Barnaby, 'Legal Ethics for the Real World'.

78 Dow, 'Madness in the Method'.

79 To highlight links with Part I of this volume (especially Chapters 2 and 4), Figure 12.1 puts Philosophical Argument as a separate Method.

80 As Jakab observes in his comparative overview of US, UK and Continental law schools. András Jakab, 'Dilemmas of Legal Education: A Comparative Overview', *Journal of Legal Education* 57, no. 2 (2007).

81 Ibid. As well as the trade-offs in monetary and student-time costs, Jakab notes that quality pedagogies often eat further into teachers' time constraints: marking essays takes more time than exams. That said, Chapters 3 and 8 above noted various methods for navigating these compromises in curricula.

82 Though law deans and law schools should develop strategic plans that demonstrate how investments in quality can generate a return. That return should include serving the community by helping the profession serve the community though delivering justice under law and move higher up the normative continuum. But it is not unethical to point out that it will also serve the prestige of the university, secure better staff, and generate higher research funding and ultimately alumni donations.

83 In the US context, Sullivan estimates the economic costs of a law degree have outstripped its falling benefits, especially given the weak employment prospects. E. Thomas Sullivan, 'The Transformation of the Legal Profession and Legal Education', *Indiana Law Review* 46, no. 1 (2013).

84 As some argue the 'Priestley 11' has done in Australia.

85 'The Whole Lawyer' terminology in this context is from Tacha, 'Training the Whole Lawyer'.

86 Silver, 'Emotional Intelligence and Legal Education': 1200.

87 See Chapter 10, Sect. 4.

88 See Chapters 2 and 4.

89 For example, Hamilton and Monson, 'Relationship of Professionalism to Effectiveness'. See also James, 'Seeing Things as We Are'.

90 Chapter 10, Sect. 4, provided a clear example of the 'Whole Lawyer' approach, noting Griffith's pervasive approach to ethics across and beyond the curricula.

91 See especially Chapter 3.

92 See especially Chapter 2.

13 *Reflection*

New challenges to ethical practice

Charles Sampford

The first two sections of this book deal with the search for the 'critical and theoretical dimensions' of law and their incorporation into mainstream legal education and research. Two of the longest standing elements of those critical and theoretical dimensions have been 'jurisprudence' and 'legal ethics'. However much 'jurisprudence' was marginalized in the past, 'legal ethics' was much more so. And while jurisprudence was rehabilitated in the late 1980s and early 1990s, this underlined how far legal ethics had to go and the low base from which it started. Indeed, the discussions about the inclusion of an 'ethical dimension' in legal education in the 1990s seemed similar to those about theory in the 1980s[1] with debates about whether it should be a required part of the LLB still ongoing in this decade.[2] In Australian law schools, legal ethics was not generally taught as part of the law course but as part of a set of subjects taken during practical legal training (PLT) and marked to pass – suggesting that there was nothing to be gained from high ethical standards and all you had to do was to avoid failing by not knowing the rules and getting caught.

This chapter will briefly compare the progress of legal ethics into mainstream academic law courses before considering some of the issues in legal ethics that have either emerged or changed focus over the last 25 years. It will do so through a process of storytelling which is valuable for introducing issues[3] though not necessarily for fully answering them.[4] It starts with an old issue – lawyers' role in tax and regulatory avoidance, which has been writ large by globalization. This leads to a discussion of the under-recognized role of lawyers in governance. The bulk of the chapter will be taken up with the discussion of three emerging issues:

1 Lawyers' participation in asset stripping (whether to avoid tax, the payment of workers' entitlements or the compensation for negligence).
2 The ethics of confidential settlements where confidentiality may lead a defendant to pay one plaintiff a premium on their loss to prevent other potential plaintiffs learning of facts relevant to the defendant's liability to them.
3 'Ex curia' campaigns in which lawyers seek, through publicity, outcomes they might not secure in court.

1 Legal ethics in the law curriculum

As indicated in Chapter 9, the solitary ethics subject was almost always taught by a practitioner who had little or no contact with the ethicists in philosophy departments (though the kind of ethics taught and researched at the time would not necessarily have been particularly congenial until the rise of applied ethics in the 1980s). At the time, most law subjects were taught doctrinally, concentrating on the content of the rules rather than the philosophical principles and/or the social, political, economic and cultural forces behind that content – or on competing contents. Accordingly, it was not surprising that legal ethics was taught on the basis of rules that had to be complied with if you were going to enter the profession. For many, this led to a compliance-based approach to legal ethics. There can be debates between compliance- and ethics-based approaches to regulation – which I have argued for 25 years needs to be ethics-centred with the back-up of regulation, incentives and institutional design.[5] However, one should have thought it a little bizarre that compliance approaches to ethics trumped ethics approaches to ethics! That said, it should not be that surprising. Lawyers in the British Commonwealth emphasize the paramountcy of the duty to the court over the duty to the client. American lawyers do not always state it in the same terms.[6] American lawyers are more likely to talk about 'balancing' the two or facing 'dilemmas' because of the dual responsibilities. For some, it appears that a lawyer's duty is to the client provided the lawyer is not actually breaking the law or in breach of the ABA code. At times, it seemed that duties to the court are read as if they are a tax act. In some American companies, this is the general approach to ethics. It is common for American companies to give the management of ethics to their general counsel. This would be a perfect fit if they took the kind of view advocated by Elizabeth Nosworthy (who, as we saw in Chapter 1, provided the impetus behind Chapter 10's discussion of lawyers as ethical advisers). However, the result is less attractive where the general counsel operates on a take-no-prisoners approach to legal rules in which all obligations, legal or otherwise, are read as narrowly as possible.[7] I remember well a speech given by the retiring White House ethics counsel at the Ethics Resource Centre in Washington in the early 2000s. He started his speech by saying that he had not known much about ethics when appointed to the job but had rung his predecessor who said he did not have to worry – 'just know the law'. No one seemed to see the problem with this. Ethics is not the same as law and if you think that it is confined to law you have missed the plot. He was treating the ethical duties of the White House as merely complying with the formal rules.

The institutional separation of the teaching of jurisprudence and legal ethics by law schools and PLT helped reinforce two intellectual divisions. First, one of the mainstays of jurisprudence courses in the 1950s and 1960s was the Hart–Fuller debate over the 'separation of law and morality' (see discussion in Chapter 12). While morality and ethics are not the same, this debate tended to highlight differences rather than promote unity between legal philosophy and the philosophies that looked at the issues within morality. Second, legal, ethical and political philosophy tended to be specialized and few were examining them (or the vortex where they met) in a unified way.

However, if the US is the source of the most strident form of zealous advocacy, it has also been the source of important developments in legal ethics – including the applied ethics movement and some who took its messages to legal ethics within law schools – none more than David Luban. Critical and post-modern scholars renewed interest in ethics – though not in a way that was always understood by the profession.

This has led to a flowering of research and scholarship in legal ethics – exemplified by the journal *Legal Ethics*, in which Chapter 9 had the honour of constituting the first article – though the journal also devoted considerable space to a discussion forum that generated debate involving academics and practitioners. The journal has covered issues as diverse as judicial conduct; gendered discourses in the legal profession; the tempering of the adversarial imperative in mediation; perceptions of professionalism; ethical challenges for criminal defence lawyers; Islamic finance; legal ethics and the media; ethics in legal education; ethics in organizations and legal practice; and professional values for the twenty-first century.

We are still a long way from the reintegration of legal, ethical and political philosophy that was in evidence in the time of Smith and Bentham. But the article on which Chapter 9 is based did discuss attempts at integration including my approach to relating definitions of ethics and integrity;[8] that is now a key part of our long-term 'integrity project', which aims to link individual integrity, institutional integrity and integrity systems.[9] Other promising avenues are opened up by insights such as my suggestion that law is ethics carried on by other means.[10]

2 Ethics, tax and the GFC

My first work on legal ethics took a bird's eye view of the field. The one specific ethical issue I raised, tax avoidance, was itself raised as a systemic issue – suggesting that the privileges and protections of the profession 'cannot be justified unless the legal profession serves some general, and important, interest'.[11] The ethical issues concerning tax avoidance have continued but with much lower levels of public prominence until they exploded again with the concerns over BEPS ('base erosion and profit shifting') in G20 meetings. The lower prominence of tax avoidance, in Australia at least, was because tax avoidance ceased to be mass marketed through tax avoidance schemes for rich 'taxpayers'[12] re-emerging as bespoke creations for much richer ones. It was after the Global Financial Crisis, as governments were expected to bail out some corporations, that it was realized just how little large global firms paid in tax because of the far greater opportunities for tax minimization, avoidance and evasion in international taxation. The Global Financial Crisis raised other issues more directly. The Collateralized Debt Obligations (CDOs) and Credit Default Swaps (CDSs) and other financial instruments that Warren Buffet called 'financial weapons of mass destruction'[13] were drawn up by lawyers. The 2009 Adam Smith conference[14] illustrated this very well. The lawyer who drafted the first CDO said a little nervously that a lot of people had used this model and trillions of dollars of transactions had been conducted on them. They were now being litigated and he 'hoped the judges got it right'. I was a little alarmed at the reversal of the usual roles between judge and lawyer in determining what is 'right'. I thought about what I had written on ethical advisors (see Chapter 10, Sect. 2), where 'overly clever lawyers' might 'find that the judge neither agrees with their interpretation of the law nor has sympathy for the client who has sought maximum advantage from it'.[15]

This rather alarming ethical question transmutes into an even more alarming economic one: that trillions of dollars of an instrument could be traded when its legal meaning had not been determined by law, courts or even regulators. This should have sent alarm bells to anyone who was evaluating them and advising on them. Lawyers were not solely to blame. Among other professionals, accountants drew up financial reports and auditors gave a tick to balance sheets loaded with these instruments. Outside of the professions, members of the finance industry sought to profit from rather than fulfil the trust others had in them, and ratings agencies made a lot of money out of classifying this financial rubbish 'AAA'.[16] The multiple ethical failures underlying the Global Financial Crisis have been emphasized by many. Republican Senator Tom Coburn, co-chair of a bipartisan senate investigation into the meltdown said at the press briefing on the report[17]:

> It shows without a doubt that lack of ethics in some of our financial institutions who embraced known conflicts of interest to accomplish wealth for themselves, not caring about the outcome for their customers.[18]

As Christine Lagarde, MD of the IMF later put it:

> Trust is the lifeblood of the modern business economy. Yet, in a world that is more networked than ever, trust is harder to earn and easier to lose.... To restore trust, we need a shift toward greater integrity and accountability. We need a stronger and systematic ethical dimension ... the link is clear – ethical behaviour is a major dimension of financial stability.[19]

The legal profession certainly needs to consider its part in the ethical meltdown – not just for its own role but whether it should have been providing a lead to other professions and guidance to the relevant banking executives. Should it have been a better 'friend' in Fried's term? Should they have sought to take an active role in offering their client's advice on 'what they should do'?[20] If members of the legal profession thought more about their own ethical role, they might be in a better position to advise others. If lawyers thought more about their roles, they can make the contribution to improved governance that professions can and often do perform.

3 Lawyers and governance

This last point should be emphasized. Much governance reform involves changing regulations and sanctions, raising the bar below which sanctions are imposed. However, as I pointed out in 'Raising the Standard' (discussed in Chapter 12), the point of ethics and governance reform is to raise standards of individual and institutional behaviour well above the minimum below which sanctions are imposed. I saw behaviour as a 'normative continuum' ranging from exemplary behaviour that is recognized as setting the highest standards of a group, through behaviour that earned high praise, promotion, increased pay/fees, and holding your job, all the way down to behaviour that generates sanctions from reprimand to demotion to dismissal and to criminal prosecution. Effective change on this approach thus involves governance reforms that reward good behaviour and make it easy to do the right thing, hard to do the wrong thing and easy to find out who has given in to temptation (something which, in itself, radically reduces the temptation). Professions are one of the few groups that are formally dedicated (and the best professionals fully so) to improving standards. This is where lawyers can and should take a lead and be able to advise their business clients – not just on formal rules and ethical standard-setting but also contributing to institutional design (which makes it easy to do the right thing and hard to do the wrong thing[21]).

Of course, there are many who insist on the zealous client advocate model in which 'the lawyer is simply there to maximize the client's interests, using whatever means, so long as those means are within the letter of the law'[22] and that the client will not pay, and should not be billed for, ethical advice. Except where specifically required to do otherwise by law or the letter of the ethics code, such advocates will sublimate their ethical views to the expressed interests (generally financial) of the client. This image of the 'schizophrenic lawyer and the sociopathic client'[23] remains. But the idea that ethics should play a more central role in business is becoming more widely accepted (and bolstered by every major scandal – of which the Global Financial Crisis is merely the largest).

Part of this is the recognition of the long-term risks of the sociopathic pursuit of profit at the expense of customers, suppliers, employees and the community.[24] But there is a much broader commitment to values beyond and above 'the bottom line'. In the 19 years since I wrote those essays, a range of business groups have agreed on principles to guide their behaviour: the UN Global Compact, the UN Principles of Responsible Investment, UN Guiding principles on Business and Human Rights, Caux Roundtable, Green Cross, the Earth Charter, triple bottom line reporting and ideas like 'stakeholder theory'[25] and the 'social license to operate'.[26] I have had the privilege to speak at events organized by these groups and to organize some others (for example, the World Ethics Forum and the Global Integrity Summit). While the principles vary in detail and modes of expression, they are all generally 'congruent' and all make clear that there are values other than profit at the heart of business.[27] Lawyers can, and do, advise clients on how they can 'comply' with these provisions and build it into what they do. Some, such as the UN Guiding Principles on Business and Human Rights,[28] have attracted quite a few lawyers.[29]

Some clients may not want to pay their lawyers to provide such advice and fail to recognize that ethical advice may be the best and the cheapest, and that the best lawyers are those who give you practical advice based on moral reflection. The last 19 years have seen the demise of many of the most unethical companies. While there is no guarantee of retribution (from communities, markets or regulators) for the unethical, each year adds more examples of huge losses generated by unethical behaviour – pointing to ethical risks and the potential value of ethical risk management.

4 Emerging ethical issues for lawyers

Dilemmas and temptations continue to arise in ethical practice – generating more issues that the legal profession needs to consider. The most interesting issues go to duties to court, client and, more broadly, to justice through the law. I will highlight three.

Asset stripping

One of the most egregious Australian tax avoidance/evasion schemes in the early 1980s was the so-called 'bottom of the harbour' scheme. The scheme's promoters bought companies with cash and tax liabilities (generally left over after their owners had sold corporate assets to trusts to minimize tax), stripped out the assets, appointed members of the notoriously violent Painters and Dockers Union as directors and dumped the papers (hence 'bottom of the harbour'[30]). The reason for appointing members of that union as directors was to deter any tax office officials from digging too deeply. The former owners would 'save' 80 per cent of the tax they would otherwise have paid, giving the promoters 20 per cent. The scam/scheme was exposed by the Costigan Royal Commission[31] into the union that appeared intended by the Liberal government to discredit unionists but 'boomeranged' back when it was discovered that quite a few of those who benefitted were closely associated with the Liberal Party. This caused a furore, fatally weakened the government and led to retrospective legislation to recoup the tax avoided.

In 1998, Patrick Stevedores decided to terminate the employment of its existing unionized workforce (who were members of the Maritime Union of Australia) and replace it with non-union contract workers trained in Dubai under new terms and conditions.[32] At the same time, there was a company restructuring in which all the assets of the companies that employed the existing workforce were transferred to other companies in the group. The new asset-holding companies contracted with the employing companies to provide labour then terminated the contracts. This left the employing companies with liabilities of up to A$350,000,000 for termination and outstanding leave payments, which they could not meet, and the entire workforce was sacked on 7 April 1998. The next day the Dubai-trained employees attempted to start work – along with security guards with Alsatians who ordered the unionized workforce out. On the very same day, Mr Peter Reith, the Workplace Relations Minister, produced legislation to pay the redundancies through a levy on all stevedores.[33] Recently passed industrial relations legislation[34] had made sympathy strikes illegal, with crippling fines for breaches along with restrictions on picketing. However, picketing was done by those not involved in the union and the unions applied to the Federal Court seeking interlocutory orders to impose interventions on the actions of the Patrick group until a full hearing of the matter based on an alleged conspiracy between various Patrick group companies and the government. The judge accepted that there was a likely conspiracy in breach of the *Workplace Relations Act 1996* (Cth) and issued an interim injunction ordering reinstatement.[35] On appeal, three judges of the Federal Court unanimously upheld his judgement and six of the seven judges of the High Court did as well[36] – meaning that 10 out of the 11 judges hearing the case concluded that there was a sufficiently high probability of a conspiracy to give and uphold the injunctions. Enormous pressure was put on the union to settle, with the threat that the insolvent employing companies would be liquidated – turning a win in court to a Pyrrhic victory for the union. The union settled on the basis that the majority of their members were given jobs by the new Patrick companies on radically changed terms, with the rest being funded by A$181,000,000 from the redundancy legislation.[37] The government loan to Patrick's financed the employment termination packages that were funded by the stevedoring levy.[38] The Dubai-trained workforce were left to fend for themselves with no contracts and no union.

Frank Costigan drew the analogy to the 'bottom of the harbour scheme' in that assets were stripped to avoid liability.[39]

> The behaviour of Patrick in relation to its reorganization of its corporate structure deserves the strongest condemnation. Whatever the courts may decide about the legality of such conduct it is, in my view, as unacceptable for a company to shift assets around between subsidiaries, and to strip assets from those particular subsidiaries which are likely to be faced with claims from employees and creditors, as it was for companies to bury their assets in the harbour to avoid the payment of tax.

In 2001, James Hardie Industries (JHI), which had supplied asbestos-based building products, was being sued by many who were dying from the effects of that asbestos. JHI decided to relocate the company and its financial assets to the Netherlands, leaving a trust fund to cover the asbestos-related liabilities that they claimed to be adequate. JHI was found to have engaged in misleading conduct[40] and its executive directors were found to have breached their directors' duties under the *Corporations Act 2001* (Cth).[41]

All three forms of asset-stripping involved taking money out of a company and leaving it with liabilities it could not meet. The first involved liabilities to pay tax. The second involved liabilities to pay employees' wages and entitlements. The third involved liabilities to pay for injuries inflicted on workers and consumers. None would have been possible without lawyers – and generally other professionals, including accountants and actuaries.

The ethics of confidential settlements

It is a central tenet of civil litigation in common law jurisdictions that the proceedings are to resolve disputes between the parties. There is no 'matter' unless the two parties have a dispute. Once they have resolved that dispute that is an end to the matter – with no need for more expenditure of time by judges, courts, lawyers and clients. The settlement, like the litigation, is between the parties and few judges would dream of intervening. Settlements will usually involve confidentiality clauses and there are many very good reasons for them. One of those is that parties will frequently not settle without them. However, there are some cases where a party is willing to settle to avoid a trial in which important facts about its conduct will be of great and legitimate interest to others. I will discuss a generalized compound 'hypothetical' and a real but disturbing example.

The hypothetical involves a company (D) being sued by a plaintiff (P) in a product liability case in which P claims damages for pain and suffering from using the allegedly dangerous product. Let us suppose that the liquidated damages are $250,000 and the usual amount that plaintiffs would secure for the degree of pain and suffering in such cases was between $200,000 and $400,000. Let us suppose that P finds damning evidence to prove the product is dangerous and is likely to have harmed hundreds of consumers. D will naturally not want this evidence to become public knowledge because it would expose it to liabilities in the hundreds of millions. If it would be difficult for other plaintiffs to secure the evidence, D would be more than happy to pay $5,000,000 in pain and suffering as part of a confidential settlement. Many plaintiffs would be more than happy with such a deal. So there would be a temptation to offer, and a temptation to accept, the settlement. Both P and D are much better off than if there was a trial (or settlement) in which the facts came out. So the agreement is one that benefits both at the expense of the other consumers. D might even decide to continue marketing the product.[42]

What should the law in general, and the judge in particular, do? The first question is potentially simple. Settlements are contracts. Contracts can sometimes be set aside as against the public interest. A strong case could be made that this contract was against the public interest, and that it overrides the public interest in the finalization and settlement of disputes. A case could be made that judges should seek to see settlements after they are made and, if they are suspicious, to call counsel before them, hear argument and determine whether to strike out the confidentiality clause as against the public interest. In any case, codes of ethics should address this issue.[43]

Another example, involving a different kind of public interest was a very real one. The June 1998 Patrick's settlement mentioned above prevented the airing of the union's case (which would have been bolstered by discovery) alleging a conspiracy by the government and Patricks. This was a matter of great and legitimate public interest. Although the trial judge had already issued an injunction that required him to determine that there was strong evidence of such a conspiracy, that is not the same as a judicial determination of fact. It was of immediate public interest to the voters at the election held in December that year in which the incumbent government lost the popular vote but managed to hold the swing against them in marginal seats to retain power. This raises many ethical issues – from the lawyers advising government and in government who derived the original scheme, to those who designed the tactics to put pressure on the union to settle. Even more than the first case, this is an issue in which the information held by the parties should not be sealed permanently because of a settlement. Should judges be able to order that certain documents that are discovered by the parties be made available publicly even if the trial does not go ahead? Should third parties have standing to seek their release? To some extent, the fact that so much that is relevant involves government documents suggests alternative approaches. Should there be limits to privilege where there is a strong public interest in their release? Perhaps judges should have the power to order that certain documents be released under Freedom of Information (FOI) and Right to Know legislation? Or should it just be part of the FOI process quite separately from judicial process?

The ex-curia campaign – arguing the case in public before the decision

The traditional concern about arguing the case in public has been that the lawyer might affect the views of the judge or jury so that they do not hear the evidence and/or law with a fresh and open mind – hearing all the evidence the judge accepts as relevant and in a context where evidence adduced by one side is open to timely (often immediate) challenge. To argue the case in public may result in the decision-maker prejudging the evidence and the law. If this is done deliberately, it is seen as a contempt of court and could be seen as an attempt to pervert the course of justice. To argue that it was not done with an understanding of the consequences of what they said is to argue negligence. There is arguably less concern about judge-only trials than about jury trials. However, prejudicing the decision-maker is only one of the consequences that might be sought.

The general concern is that the lawyer is seeking, for the client, an advantage that they could not otherwise secure just through the process of the courts of which he is an officer. I suggest two recent Australian examples – one criminal and one civil.

Dr Haneef[44]

In June 2007, Dr Mohammed Haneef was working as a registrar at the Gold Coast hospital on a skilled worker visa. He bought a one-way ticket back to India to see his wife who had given birth to a jaundiced child in an emergency caesarean operation. Ten thousand miles away a second cousin (Dr Khafeel Ahmed)[45] drove a bomb-laden Jeep Cherokee into Glasgow airport. Khafeel's brother Dr Sabeel Ahmed who lived in Liverpool was arrested. Haneef was stopped from boarding the plane on 2 July, arrested and held in custody for 12 days prior to being charged. The period of detention without charge was permitted to allow questioning of suspected terrorists in Part 1C of the *Crimes Act 1914* (Cth) as inserted by the *Anti-terrorism Act 2004* (Cth). On application to a magistrate, questioning time can be delayed or suspended during the investigation of a terrorism offence.

The prosecutors claimed that:

- he had no explanation for buying a one-way ticket,
- he had, while working in England, shared a flat with the terrorists,
- he had associated with terrorists,
- there were incriminating entries in Haneef's diary, and,
- that he recklessly provided assistance by leaving a SIM-card and the balance of a two-year phone contract with Sabeel to use and pay off himself and that the phone containing the SIM-card had been found in Khafeel's burnt-out Jeep.

These claims were included in court submissions and widely publicized.

While Haneef was being interviewed by the police, the prime minister announced the arrest and, while saying we should not jump to conclusions, claimed that: 'there are people in our midst who would do us harm and evil if they had the opportunity of doing so'.[46]

In fact, the transcript of Haneef's interview provided a cogent explanation for the one-way ticket and the phone (handed over to avoid surrender costs). He had not shared a flat with terrorists, the extent of his association was that he was a second cousin and the claimed incriminating entries in his diaries were actually police notes. Finally, by 8 July, Scotland Yard had informed the Australian Federal Police (AFP) that Sabeel, who had received the phone, was no longer a suspect in the bombing. Also at that time, the Yard notified the AFP that the phone was not in Khafeel's jeep at all but found in Sabeel's flat.

ASIO, the AFP and the Queensland Police all concluded that there was insufficient evidence to charge the doctor and on 13 July the prosecutor, AFP's lead investigator and the two arresting officers expressed their views that the evidence was inadequate to lay charges. However, the first two changed their minds after contact with their superiors and insisted on charges being laid on 14 July. Under the anti-terrorism law, Haneef's lawyers were not allowed to hear the evidence against Haneef or be present when the magistrate made the decision.

The magistrate was unimpressed by the case and asked some embarrassing and pertinent questions before granting bail on 16 July. The immigration minister revoked Haneef's visa, with the consequence that he would be taken to an immigration detention centre in another state. Haneef decided not to post bail so that he could stay in remand in Brisbane where he had better access to his lawyers who were finally given the police evidence.

Instead of backpedalling on the untenable charges, newspapers were fed stories by 'law enforcement agencies' suggesting that the government had evidence against Haneef that they could not reveal – though those sources did clearly imply that Haneef had been looking at blowing up Gold Coast skyscrapers.[47] To counter this barrage of prejudicial publicity, Haneef's barrister, Steven Keim QC, released the transcript of Haneef's first police interview. He was attacked by the prime minister and federal Attorney General, and the AFP commissioner initiated disciplinary action (Keim was cleared by the Queensland Legal Services Commission – finding him in technical breach but exonerated him and dismissed the complaints in the public interest[48]). On 27 July, the DPP dropped the case, but the immigration minister insisted that the visa cancellation stand because Haneef had failed the character test based on his association with terrorists. Justice Spender quashed the minister's decision because it was premised on an unacceptably wide interpretation of 'association'. The minister said Spender's decision was wrong and appealed – an appeal that was rejected unanimously by a very powerful full bench of the federal court (Chief Justice Black of the Federal Court, Justice French who was to become Chief Justice of the High Court and Justice Weinberg a former Commonwealth DPP).[49]

Many Australian lawyers were shocked at the combination of a misleading public campaign of vilification, the persistence with claims before the courts that had already been discredited (exacerbated by the initial refusal to provide them to the defence team) and the attempted use of the *Migration Act 1958* (Cth) to incarcerate someone bailed by the courts. These concerns were heightened because: (a) an election was due to be called within weeks;[50] (b) the government was trailing badly in the polls and there was pressure on the prime minister to stand aside for his ambitious but reticent treasurer;[51] and, (c) because the prime minister had managed to turn around his fortunes in 2001 through, inter alia, post 9/11, the vilification of Muslim asylum seekers as potential terrorists and parents willing to throw their children overboard.[52]

In the end, judicial ethics held. However, this safeguard constitutes the last line of defence – a line that should never have been reached. Police should have recognized an ethical duty to ensure that the prosecutors were appraised of the holes in their case. Prosecutors should have been mindful of the higher ethical standards expected of prosecutors because of the human rights of defendants – heightened in this case because the exclusion of defence counsel meant that they were effectively making ex parte submissions in criminal matters. The public servants who were leaking false and misleading information should have been constrained by their ethics, and the journalists had a duty to check and to avoid being manipulated (though they should be able to put a high degree of trust in what public servants tell them, and the abuse of that trust is very dangerous).

This emphasizes that integrity systems work best when all participating institutions have strong integrity measures backing strong codes of ethics – and those ethics should be mutually reinforcing.[53]

In this case, lawyers working for the government were not the ones pursuing the ex-curia campaign. Lawyers may advise against it for a number of reasons, including any potential contempts. If they are allowed, they may give ethical advice, as discussed in Chapter 10. They must certainly insist on their independence in making prosecutorial decisions and in what they bring to court, noting that, as officers of the court they must not mislead it. In the next case, the ex-curia campaign was a speciality of the leading lawyer involved.

Speaker Slipper

Whereas Haneef was the innocent pawn in a political power game, Peter Slipper, the now-disgraced former Speaker of the Australian House of Representatives demonstrates that injustices can be perpetrated on the unworthy as well as the worthy.

Peter Slipper held the Sunshine Coast seat of Fisher for the National Party from 1983 to 1987 and returned to win it for the Liberal Party in 1993 and in six subsequent elections.[54] He was a parliamentary secretary from 1998 to 2004 but was otherwise a backbencher of limited distinction. Like many others, he claimed expenses that the Department of Finance found were in excess of his 'entitlements'[55] and had to repay a total of A$14,000 over 21 years as an MP between 1983 and 2010.[56] It is not clear whether he was a particularly serious offender or whether he was targeted by party enemies (including Hon Mal Brough, a former Howard government minister who lost his own seat in 2007 and who was seeking a new, safe seat). In June 2010, Brough told the Sunshine Coast daily local newspaper that Slipper should stand aside for the election due by the end of the year.[57] On 8 July, a raft of new claims of abuses of expenses were made by that paper but the issue was not pressed by Liberals after the election was called on 17 July. The 2010 election led to a hung parliament in which the government relied on independents to secure a two-seat majority reduced to one seat after they provided the speaker. In 2011, the government announced that the Labor speaker was stepping down and Slipper was elected in his place on 24 November, raising the government's majority to three.[58] The 2010 complaints were countered by the Department of Finance and Slipper was reported as having been cleared in January 2012.[59]

In December 2011, Slipper hired James Ashby as an aide, who earned Slipper's praise for 'masterminding a social media campaign against Brough'[60] and on 20 March congratulated Ashby and another staffer (Miss Doane) on a 'successful tactic devised by Ashby and Doane to deflect Steve Lewis, a reporter for News Limited's *Sydney Telegraph*, from running a story critical of Slipper'. However, on 23 March 2016, Ashby approached Mal Brough, reporting that he had been sexually harassed by Slipper, made claims of expense abuse and expressed concern that working for Slipper might make it difficult to secure a job with the newly-elected Liberal National government in Queensland. This was a day before Slipper left for overseas with a parliamentary delegation on which Ashby had proposed he accompany Slipper at Ashby's own expense.[61] On 29 March, Ashby was asked to provide copies of Slipper's diary entries for days relevant to the alleged expense abuses and provided them to Mr Brough in three separate forms. There are conflicting claims about whether Brough himself asked for the diary entries.[62] On 30 March, Doane met with Brough, who offered to assist her in seeking employment with the new Queensland Government.[63] On 2 April, Doane texted Ashby saying she wanted to 'balance' Mr Ashby's harassment charge with one of her own concerning Mr Slipper's behaviour towards her which she considered unprofessional.[64] On 4 April, Ashby met Lewis, after which Lewis texted Ashby 'we'll get him'.[65] Ashby was referred to Harmers Workplace Lawyers, who had 'gained a reputation as an aggressive workplace relations litigant bringing claims against high-profile defendants … known for actively seeking out media coverage and filing broad-ranging statements of claim'.[66]

Until Ashby–Slipper, Harmers were most famous for suing David Jones (DJs), a major upmarket department store chain, for sexual harassment of 27-year-old publicist Kristy Fraser-Kirk by DJs' CEO. DJs had already sacked the CEO and offered A$850,000 but Harmers claimed A$37million in punitive damages. The media splash generated by publicist Anthony McClelland put the spotlight on the victim and claimed that there were 14 other victims. When Fraser-Kirk's integrity was questioned by DJs and the other victims did not provide the evidence promised, Fraser-Kirk settled for what is reported to be well under the A$850,000 offered.[67] The *Australian Financial Review* (AFR) quotes one lawyer saying that Harmers are 'willing to use bad publicity or the threat of it to gain payouts that would not be awarded if a matter goes all the way to a court decision'. The AFR reported Harmer as responding that he needed to use the media in a legal system that is stacked against sexual harassment victims and quoted him as saying: 'the sad reality is some of these matters settle more because a corporate has a great fear about potential public relations rather than the paltry outcomes from courts'.[68] He was quoted as saying: 'I don't mind that people say we are feral ankle-biters. If that's a means to an end for our clients then so be it'.[69]

After asking Doane to get copies of further dates from Slipper's diary, Ashby took sick leave (eliciting a sympathetic email from Slipper who was still overseas and had no inkling of what was going on). He then flew to Sydney and stayed at News Limited's expense during which time he spoke to Lewis but spent most of his time at with Harmers lawyers.

On 15 April, McLelland was retained by Ashby and Doane on a 'deferred fee' basis at A$605 per hour. On 16 April, the *Daily Telegraph* and *Courier Mail* published a piece with Lewis' byline alleging Slipper had 'splurged $75,000 in taxpayer funds on lavish limousine and taxi travel in an 18-month period'.[70] On 20 April, Harmers filed an originating application about alleged sexual harassment of Ashby along with two other claims: having sworn evidence of an alleged 2003 harassment by Slipper of another male staffer by a Ms Hobson, and that Ashby was intending to go to the federal police with claims of fraudulent use of Cabcharge vouchers. As required under federal court rules, Harmers filed a 'genuine steps' statement (outlining the steps taken to attempt a resolution or the reasons why they have not taken any). They claimed that the matter was urgent and that alerting the respondents to the matter would only increase the opportunity for victimization.[71]

Harmers emailed Slipper attaching the application at 3:54 p.m. Sydney time – the day Slipper was due to leave New York (I note that he was not formally served until about 11 May). As it was 2:00 a.m. in New York, it was unlikely that Slipper would wake in time to consult his lawyers before close of business on Friday even if he had worked out who they should be. At 7:18 p.m. Sydney time, Lewis emailed Slipper saying that they were running a story on sexual harassment allegations and mentioned allegations of fraud against the Commonwealth. As Slipper flew to Los Angeles, the first stories were run in the News Ltd papers and he 'was met at Los Angeles airport by representatives of the Australian media, including television crews and questioned about these proceedings', with a 'large group of journalists' waiting in Brisbane when Slipper arrived on the Sunday morning.[72] Justice Rares later inferred 'that Mr Ashby or Ms Doane caused it to be provided to the media and that each of them planned that, as a result, the media would be waiting for Mr Slipper when he arrived'.[73]

I was unaware of any of this background when the news broke on 21–22 April. Much was made of the fraud claims, as conviction would make Slipper ineligible to sit. I caught a glimpse of what was going on when a journalist from *The Australian* rang me on Sunday morning asking me if I would call for Peter Slipper to stand down because of the accusations included in the papers lodged with the federal court. An analogy was drawn to the defence minister's desire for the head of ADFA to resign. I knew the reporter though, from a completely different area of work. It seemed obvious that *The Australian* must have brought in quite a few journalists and got those who knew relevant academics to ring them. The first question I asked was where Peter Slipper was; I was informed that he was still on his way home. I then asked if I could see the court documents. (I wanted to see whether Ashby had gone through the usual procedures in cases of alleged sexual harassment; I wanted to see if Ashby had signed an affidavit; and I wanted to see how the alleged criminal misuse of Cabcharges were relevant to the cause of action.) He told me that they would not be publicly available until the next day.

I told him that no reasonable academic could make the call requested. When he told me the names of two academics who had made the call requested, I repeated my comment. But I sent him an off the record comment. He asked if he could use parts of it, but I did not want my comments to be put at the mercy of *The Australian's* sub-editors and we agreed that it would be better as an op-ed. I sought to compare it to accusations against a Labor prime minister, a Conservative premier, and a High Court judge. I sent it to him, he passed it on – and I did not even get the courtesy of a reply. The text read as follows:

> Sexual harassment claims need to be carefully and fully investigated – to do justice to those who suffer it and for those who are wrongly accused of it. While I suspect that there are more who falsely deny it than falsely assert it, one cannot presume in any particular case before it is fully investigated – and if one did, it would encourage more false allegations.
>
> I was asked to draw an analogy to the calls for the head of ADFA to be dismissed. He was not and should not have been dismissed. He was stood

> down on full pay and was reinstated. This was controversial but probably justified. The head of ADFA had commenced disciplinary proceedings against the alleged victim. Some might have been worried that the alleged victim might feel pressured into retracting her allegation. There is no similar issue here.
>
> As I understand it, there are accusations against Mr Slipper contained in a statement of claim filed in civil proceedings under privilege.[74] I have only had second-hand reports of their contents and the evidence. I do not know if these are backed by sworn statements (which are not required at this stage). In my view, Mr Slipper has a *right* to stand aside to fight the allegations but no *duty* to do so. If those against whom accusations were made had a duty to stand aside it might encourage the making of allegations at critical times (elections, crucial votes). In this respect, we should recognize that not every claim made under privilege against legal and political figures ultimately proves to be well founded (e.g. those against Justice Kirby, Mr Rudd and Mr Newman).[75]
>
> Accusations in parliament against Rudd and Kirby were based on concocted evidence (though not, I emphasize, concocted by their accusers who ended up the primary victims of those concoctions). Accusations against Campbell Newman were found to have no evidentiary basis. If Rudd, Kirby or Newman had been forced to resign because of those accusations, it would have been a travesty. If Rudd or Newman had had to stand aside, any political benefits gained during their absence would have tainted the beneficiaries. This is why we have the presumption of innocence and the requirement of a proof before a criminal court before a parliamentarian loses his seat in parliament.
>
> There is good reason for this. When monarchs controlled the courts and the predecessors of the police, they sometimes sought to exclude opponents from parliaments. This led some countries to give parliamentarians immunity during their tenure of office. With our confidence in the independence of police and judiciary we do not go that far. However, parliamentarians do not lose office without conviction for a serious offence. While the tenure of a speaker or party leader is determined by a simple majority in the relevant house or party room, it is generally wise for fellow MPs or party members to avoid a rush to judgment and wait to hear the evidence of both sides.

I frankly told him that I thought the story stank. On 15 May 2012, Ashby finally submitted a statement of claim; the 2003 allegation and the Cabcharge allegations were not included. The Commonwealth (who was, as the employer, named as first respondent) argued that the case be struck out as an abuse of process. There was also an argument over whether the content of some of Slipper's texts to Ashby would be released. The kindest description of them was that they were 'puerile observations on female genitalia'.[76] I would not be that kind. Once the texts were released, the government decided to settle with Ashby for A$50,000, with each side bearing its costs, and it stopped funding Slipper's defence. On 9

October, Slipper resigned after surviving a no confidence motion by one vote. Slipper now had to represent himself. The Commonwealth's QC offered to assist the court but the offer was declined by Justice Rares. On 12 December, Rares J delivered a damning judgement dismissing the case as an abuse of process:

> Mr Ashby's predominant purpose for bringing these proceedings was to pursue a political attack against Mr Slipper and not to vindicate any legal claim he may have for which the right to bring proceedings exists... The originating application was used by Mr Ashby for the predominant purpose of causing significant public, reputational and political damage to Mr Slipper. It contained the scandalous and irrelevant 2003 allegations and assertion that Mr Ashby intended to report to the police Cabcharge allegations.[77]

He found that Brough, Doane and Ashby shared that purpose and that Harmer,

> breached his professional obligation not to misuse his privilege to make allegations under absolute privilege in Court documents. Mr Harmer knew that Mr Ashby had the right, if not the duty, to go to the police with any concerns he genuinely had about Mr Slipper's use of Cabcharge vouchers. But, the pleading of Mr Ashby's intention to do so had no legitimate forensic purpose.[78]

Costs were awarded against Ashby.

On appeal, the court was split with two judges (Mansfield and Gilmour JJ) finding that Rares J should not have dismissed the case for abuse of process. The key reason was that sworn evidence by Harmer and others that was 'not inherently improbable or unreasonable'[79] was rejected on the basis of other facts without the evidence being challenged in cross-examination. The accusations against Harmer were 'at the extreme end of those which might be raised against a solicitor' and should have been put to Harmer.[80] Of course, Slipper would not have been able to effectively pursue the cross-examination and the majority's suggestion that Rares J be the one to 'put his concerns' to Harmer is something that judges avoid for fear of bias accusations. The third judge (Siopis) issued a strong judgement in favour of Rares' use of the evidence. The majority reversed the costs order and so the substantive matter was returned to the primary judge. When the Commonwealth announced that it would fund Slipper's defence, Ashby dropped the suit, saying that it was unfair to have to fight on when the Commonwealth was paying Slipper's bills. (I note that, when they had managed to render Slipper lawyerless in October 2012, they had refused to agree to an adjournment.) When they sought to enforce the costs order, they were in for a rude shock. Flick J pointed out that:

> The discontinuance of the proceeding by Mr Ashby left Mr Slipper in the position where his rebuttal of the allegations remained unresolved and the allegations made by Mr Ashby left untested by cross-examination. It also

> left Mr Slipper in the position that his contention that the proceedings instituted by Mr Ashby were an abuse of the process of the Court had not been resolved on a final basis. Had he been ultimately successful in respect of that contention, he may possibly have secured an order in his favour that Mr Ashby pay the costs of the proceeding.[81]

Ashby appealed Flick's finding on costs which was unanimously rejected by the same court that heard the earlier appeal (Mansfield, Gilmour and Siopis JJ). They pointed out that Rares J and Siopis J had found abuse of process and put less emphasis on the two judges in the majority.

> Although, in the view of Mansfield and Gilmour JJ, Slipper's evidence did not 'get him over the line', the Court (as we have noted) did not then make findings of fact in Ashby's favour and it remains the case that the Court is not prepared to do so on this application ... [It is] not established to our satisfaction that Slipper's summary dismissal application was so obviously untenable that it could not succeed, or that it was manifestly groundless, or that it was vexatious or oppressive.[82]

This left Harmers with a reported million-dollar costs bill in what was apparently a contingency fee basis. I do not know whether McLellan's 'deferred' fee of A$605 per hour was ever billed to Ashby.

Slipper was finally charged for the misuse of Cabcharge vouchers in that he used them to visit wineries in January, April and June 2010. He was charged under s135.1 (5) of the Commonwealth Criminal Code[83] which makes it an offence for a person to dishonestly cause a loss to a Commonwealth entity. The total amount was A$954. On 24 September 2014, he was sentenced to 300 hours of community service (a curious punishment for a politician whose 30-year career had secured 1.6 per cent in the 2013 election – indicating an almost unanimous desire by the public that he no longer serve them). However, on 26 February 2015 his appeal was upheld, and conviction and sentence were set aside. Slipper was angry at being charged when MPs had, for years, been allowed to repay excessive expense claims – including then Prime Minister Abbott who had been allowed to repay A$609 for claiming attendance at Peter Slipper's 2006 wedding (along with A$1095 for attending another politician's wedding the same year).[84]

On the issue of politicians' expenses, I am in favour of a consistent approach to all politicians involving prior advice, repayment in the first instance, repayment with an added administrative charge in the second instance, escalating to criminal prosecution for the incorrigible recidivists.

However, the issue for consideration is the combination of litigation and an extra-curial campaign – especially where there are serious accusations made against individuals under privilege. The matter was not judicially resolved, with two judges finding an abuse of process and three warning that a full testing of the claims might lead to that conclusion.

Some are sanguine: Charles Power of Holding Redlich warns that clients may often want to generate adverse publicity for the other side. But,

> at all times you have got to satisfy yourself, as a legal practitioner, that there is a genuine belief in the facts that are alleged in the case by your client, and that the allegations that you are making have a reasonable relationship with the claim that you are making.

He did not think, 'these tactics are part of mainstream practice anyway and this just emphasizes why they are not'.[85]

That may be the case but the question is how far it can be pushed by self-styled 'feral ankle-biters' looking for a means to their client's ends. In this area, as others, the profession should consider these issues, set high standards, reward those who meet them, warn those who fall a bit short, and punish those who are well short. The courts should only be responsible for dealing with the very worst behaviour.

The other point that is crystal clear is that the lawyers are not the only ones making ethical decisions. The PR consultants and the journalists/editors have ethical choices as well. Good ethics by one group bolsters good ethics by others. In this, lawyers should take the lead.

Notes

1 Avrom Sherr and David Sugarman, 'Theory in Legal Education', *International Journal of the Legal Profession* 7, no. 3 (2000): 167.

2 Kim Economides and Christine Parker, 'Roundtable on Legal Ethics in Legal Education: Should It Be a Required Course?', *Legal Ethics* 14, no. 1 (2011).

3 Kim Economides and Majella O'Leary, 'The Moral of the Story: Toward an Understanding of Ethics in Organisations and Legal Practice', *Legal Ethics* 10 (2007).

4 A process that may require not only extensive analysis and debate but also empirical analysis and debate to understand the scope of the problem and the threats it may provide to the community, to clients and the profession.

5 C. Sampford, 'Law, Institutions and the Public Private Divide (Keynote Address)', in *Australasian Law Teachers Association Conference, Brisbane* (Brisbane, 1990).

6 Elements of a duty to clients in the United States can be found in several sections of the Model Rules of Professional Conduct, as opposed to there being an explicit duty of loyalty to a client. Previously, Canon 7–1 of the Model Code of Professional Responsibility stated the duty of a lawyer, both to his client and to the legal system, is 'to represent his client zealously within the bounds of the law'. This is replaced by the Model Rules of Professional Conduct 1.3, which instructs lawyers to 'act with reasonable diligence and promptness in representing a client'. The Model Rules are underscored by the Commentary directing lawyers to 'pursue a matter on behalf of a client despite opposition, obstruction or personal inconvenience to the lawyer, and take whatever lawful and ethical measures are required to vindicate a client's cause or endeavor' and to 'act with commitment and dedication to the interests of the client and with zeal in advocacy upon the client's behalf, stating also that '[a] lawyer is not bound . . . to press for every advantage that might be realized for a client'.

7 I had direct experience of this with two large American corporations.

8 Charles Sampford, 'What's a Lawyer Doing in a Nice Place Like This? Lawyers and Ethical Life', *Legal Ethics* 1, no. 1 (1998): 40, 43.

9 Hugh Breakey, Tim Cadman and Charles Sampford, 'Conceptualizing Personal and Institutional Integrity: The Comprehensive Integrity Framework', in *The Ethical Contribution of Organizations to Society*, ed. Michael Schwartz, Howard Harris and Debra Comer (Emerald Group Publishing, 2015).
10 Sampford, 'What's a Lawyer Doing in a Nice Place Like This? Lawyers and Ethical Life': 44.
11 C. Sampford and C. Parker, 'Legal Regulation, Ethical Standard-Setting, and Institutional Design', in *Legal Ethics and Legal Practice: Contemporary Issues*, ed. S. Parker and C. Sampford (Oxford: Clarendon Press, 1995): 21.
12 In writing about tax avoidance, I have long felt compelled to put the word 'taxpayers' in inverted commas.
13 Warren E. Buffet, 'Berkshire Hathaway Inc., 2002 Annual Report' www.berkshirehathaway.com/2002ar/2002ar.pdf.
14 Charles Sampford, 'Adam Smith's Dinner', in *Future of Financial Regulation Conference, Glasgow, held to celebrate the 250th anniversary of the publication of Adam Smith's Theory of Moral Sentiments* (March 2009). My keynote was later published as C. Sampford, 'Adam Smith's Dinner', in *The Future of Financial Regulation*, ed. J. O'Brien (Oxford: Hart, 2010).
15 Charles Sampford and Sophie Blencowe, 'Educating Lawyers to Be Ethical Advisors', in *Ethical Challenges to Legal Education and Conduct*, ed. K Economides (Oxford: Hart Publishing, 1998).
16 Charles Sampford, 'Closing Keynote: Integrity in Finance and Accounting: A Key Role in Saving Capitalism from Itself 2.0', in *Australian CPA Conference* (2011).
17 C. Levin and T. Coburn, 'Wall Street and the Financial Crisis: Anatomy of a Financial Collapse. Majority and Minority Staff Report', (Permanent Subcommittee on Investigations, United States Senate, 13 April 2011).
18 Kevin Drawbaugh, 'Senate Panel Slams Goldman in Scathing Crisis Report', www.reuters.com/article/2011/04/13/us-financial-regulation-report-idUSTRE73C8JR20110413 2011.
19 Christine Lagarde, 'Economic Inclusion and Financial Integrity – an Address to the Conference on Inclusive Capitalism', (27 May 2014), https://www.imf.org/external/np/speeches/2014/052714.htm.
20 See Chapter 10 for the account by the senior lawyer where lawyers form the natural profession to whom clients should turn for 'whole of business' advice – and lawyers should be educated accordingly.
21 Noting that other professions can assist as well – especially accountants, auditors and IT engineers who design reporting and management systems that have that effect.
22 See Chapter 10.
23 See Chapter 10.
24 Explored in C. Sampford and V. Berry, 'Ethical and Socially Responsible Investment: From Oxymoron to Tautology?', *GovNet eJournal* 1, no. 1 (2007). and in the next book in this series *Doing Just Business* (Routledge).
25 Originally outlined by R. Edward Freeman, *Strategic Management: A Stakeholder Approach* (Boston: Pitman, 1984); and more recently by Robert Phillips, *Stakeholder Theory and Organizational Ethics* (San Francisco Berrett-Koehler, 2003); Thomas Clarke, ed. *Theories of Corporate Governance: The Philosophical Foundations of Corporate Governance* (London; New York: Routledge, 2004).
26 Neil Gunningham, Robert A. Kagan and Dorothy Thornton, 'Social License and Environmental Protection: Why Businesses Go Beyond Compliance', *Law & Social Inquiry* 29, no. 2 (2004): 308.
27 'How to Raise Business above the Bottom Line; Maintaining Business Integrity in Corrupt Business Environments; Ethical Business, Human Rights and Corporate Values', (paper presented at the Global Integrity Summit, Brisbane, Australia, 2015).
28 Endorsed by the Human Rights Council, Resolution 17/4 of 16 June 2011.

29 The Guiding Principles formed a central component of discussion at the Global Integrity Summit, particularly in the Ethical Business, Human Rights and Corporate Values session involving speakers Dr James Gifford, Senior Fellow, Initiative for Responsible Investment at Harvard University; Dr Stuart Palmer, Head of Ethics with Australian Ethical Investment; Carly Nyst, Fellow and former Legal Director of Privacy International and advisor to Amnesty International's Technology and Human Rights Programme; Greg Vickery AO, Special Counsel, Norton Rose Fulbright; and Vanessa Zimmerman, Chair, Global Compact Network Australia's Human Rights Leadership Group.

30 Our family accountant, who was always trying to sell tax avoidance schemes to my father despite the fact that I was a director and was totally opposed, told us about one of the earlier versions of this scheme in 1979 (up to the point where they would pay for the company and the share of tax 'saved' that the promoters expected). When I raised the obvious point about the tax liability of the new owners, he told me that it was better not to ask but that the papers might be dropped off a bridge.

31 *Royal Commission on the Activities of the Federated Ship Painters and Dockers Union: Final Report: Ordered to Be Printed by the Legislative Assembly*, ed. Painters Royal Commission on the Activities of the Federated Ship, Union Dockers and Frank Costigan, Parliamentary Paper (Victoria. Parliament). (Canberra: Government Printer, 1984).

32 Recruited by a newly formed company Fynwest. News broke of the training of recruits (many former army personnel) in Dubai, resulting in the United Arab Emirates revoking visas: Katharine Murphy, Mark Davis and Mark Skulley, 'The Docks of War: A $10m Plan to Break Unions', *The Australian Financial Review* 4 December 1997. For background to the dispute, see Gerard Griffin and Stuart Svensen, *Industrial Relations Implications of the Australian Waterside Dispute*, Working Paper No. 62 (Monash University: National Key Centre in Industrial Relations, 1998); Chris Mcconville, 'The Australian Waterfront Dispute 1998', *Politics & Society* 28, no. 3 (2000).

33 *Stevedoring Levy (Collection) Act 1998* (Cth) and *Stevedoring Levy (Imposition) Act 1998* (Cth) – meaning that the other stevedores had to fund the elimination of their competitors' workforce.

34 *Workplace Relations Act 1996* (Cth).

35 *Maritime Union of Australia & Others v Patrick Stevedores No. 1 Pty Ltd (under administration) (ACN 003 621 645) & Others* [1998] FCA 378.

36 See *Patrick Stevedores Operations No. 2 Pty Ltd & Ors v Maritime Union of Australia & Ors* [1998] FCA 397 (23 April 1998); *Patrick Stevedores Operations No 2 Pty Ltd v Maritime Union of Australia* [1998] HCA 30. The exception was Hon Justice Ian Callinan who had been appointed by the federal cabinet because the National Party wanted a 'big C conservative' instead of the nominee of the Attorney General who had proposed John van Dousa after consulting the profession.

37 According to the agreement terms, the Maritime Union of Australia agreed to more than 600 redundancies. Security, cleaning and line-marking functions were contracted out. The redundant employees were given preference for these contracting jobs. Higher base wages were agreed to in return for reductions in overtime. See Griffin and Svensen, *Industrial Relations Implications of the Australian Waterside Dispute*.

38 Richard Morris, 'A Watershed on the Australian Waterfront? The 1998 Stevedoring Dispute', *Maritime Policy & Management* 27, no. 2 (2000); Rick. Brown, 'Patrick Waterfront Fight: Where It Finished [Who Won the Settlement and Who Didn't]', *News Weekly* (25 July 1998). The final figure of A$181,000,000 was provided by the Australian National Audit Office 17: 2000–2001.

39 F. Costigan, 'How Dare Howard Applaud Patrick', *The Age,* 23 April 1998.

40 *James Hardie Industries NV v ASIC* [2010] NSWCA 332.

41 *Australian Securities and Investments Commission v Meredith Hellicar & Ors* [2012] HCA 17.

42 As I was finalizing this essay, the US Supreme Court delivered a judgment in a relevant case *Campbell-Ewald Co. v. Gomez*, No. 14–857, Supreme Court of the United States (20 January 2016). Gomez had received nuisance calls in the form of text messages that violated federal law from Campbell-Ewald (CE). Under the federal law, recipients of the texts could recover up to $500 per call. When Gomez sued CE, he stated that this would be part of a class action. Before other plaintiffs joined the class action, CE offered Gomez $1,500 per call and, when Gomez did not accept, argued that there was no longer a 'matter' between Gomez and CE because he had been offered all he could get under law. CE was unsuccessful. However, it was not decided what would have happened if Gomez had accepted the offer.
43 Shirvington deals with the possibility that a letter demanding money not to disclose information could be blackmail if a solicitor accepted instructions to write to a respondent in a class action (in which the client was not involved) demanding a sum of money in return for the client's nondisclosure of information which could be harmful to the company. Virginia Shirvington, 'Turning a Blind Eye: Professional Liability and Responsibility', in *NSW Law Society* (Sydney February 2001): 18.
44 The account provided here is based on the Clarke Inquiry, M.J.R. Clarke, 'Report of the Inquiry into the Case of Dr Mohamed Haneef', (Canberra: Attorney-General's Dept., 2008). Michael Head, 'The Haneef Inquiry: Some Unanswered Questions', *Journal of the Australasian Law Teachers Association* 2 (2009).and newspaper reports at the time.
45 Jeremy Page, 'Investigation Turns to Family Ties That Link Eight Suspects in Custody', *Times Online,* 5 July 2007.
46 Brendan Nicholson, Cosima Marriner and Tom Allard, 'Local Suspects Linked to UK Plots', *The Age,* 4 July 2007.
47 Paula Doneman and Lincoln Wright, 'Picture Puzzle', *The Sunday Mail,* 22 July 2007.
48 Evan Schwarten, 'Haneef's Lawyer Cleared over Leak', *The Age,* 2 February 2008.
49 *Minister for Immigration & Citizenship v Haneef* [2007] FCAFC 203.
50 The previous election had been held on 9 October 2004 and it is usual for elections to be held within three years of the previous one. However, the three-year term formally runs from the return of the writs from one election to the writs for a new election giving the government some extra time – which they did in this case, holding the election on 24 November 2007.
51 In early September, many called for the prime minister to stand down but he refused and the treasurer did not challenge.
52 Michael Leach, '"Disturbing Practices": Dehumanizing Asylum Seekers in the Refugee "Crisis" in Australia 2001–2002', *Refuge* 21, no. 3 (2003).
53 See Chapter 11.
54 His last win, in 2010, was for the merged Liberal National Party.
55 This is an unfortunate term because it builds expectations that the relevant funds are for a personal right rather than a scheme for reimbursing work-related expenses.
56 Senate Standing Committee on Finance and Public Administration, 'Media Articles Concerning Mr Peter Slipper, Member for Fisher: Alleged Misuse and Repayments of Entitlements', in *Supplementary Budget Estimates Hearing* (October 2010). www.finance.gov.au/sites/default/files/foi_11–109_ministerial_briefing_slipper-Document_4.pdf.
57 Nick Bryant, 'Mal Brough Crashes Through', *The Monthly,* 2013.
58 Bryant claims that Slipper did not think he could survive Brough's challenge to his pre-selection: ibid.
59 'Peter Slipper Cleared over MP Expenses Following Investigation', *Herald Sun,* 30 January 2012.
60 'Mal Brough Crashes Through'.
61 *Ashby v Commonwealth of Australia (No 4)* [2012] FCA 1411 at 48.

62 Including by Brough, who claimed he had asked for them in a TV interview then denied in parliament that he had – though he had to withdraw a slur on the TV producers that his apparent admission had been the result of editing by the TV programme. The Age Editorial, 'Mal Brough Is Setting a Terrible Standard over Peter Slipper Diaries Affair', *The Age,* 4 December 2015. I note that, at time of writing, this is subject to a criminal investigation.

63 This offer emerged from an email from Doane on 2 April that included her updated resume and portfolio preferences. See *Ashby v Commonwealth of Australia (No 4)* [2012] FCA 1411 at 62.

64 *Ashby v Commonwealth of Australia (No 4)* [2012] FCA 1411 at 67. He also noted that on 6 April Ashby and Doane met David Russell QC, former President of the National Party, who warned them that party members could not offer them employment or any other inducement. On 10 April, Doane emailed Brough with a resume for consideration by Clive Palmer, a major donor to the Liberal National Party, seeking a position at his golf course resort. Palmer later fell out with the party and formed his own 'Palmer United Party'. Under parliamentary privilege, Palmer later claimed that Mr Brough asked him to fund Mr Ashby's legal case, which he said he understood to be worth around A$200,000. Brough rejected the claim. Latika Bourke, 'Clive Palmer Revives Explosive Claims against Mal Brough over James Ashby Affair', *The Sydney Morning Herald,* 25 November 2015.

65 Lewis claimed this was a reference to contacting someone who hired a car for Slipper, while Justice Rares found that it referred to Slipper. *Ashby v Commonwealth of Australia (No 4)* [2012] FCA 1411 at 71.

66 Cara Waters, 'Peter Slipper Case: Why Mark Mcinnes Is Grinning', *Crikey,* 13 December 2012.

67 Ian McIlwraith, 'How Fraser-Kirk Went from Victim to Villain', *Sydney Morning Herald,* 21 October 2010; Samantha Maiden, 'Dream Team Harmers Workplace Lawyers Swings Back into the Action', *Sunday Telegraph,* 22 April 2012.

68 Rachel Nickless, 'Meet the Sexual Harassment Game Changer', *Australian Financial Review,* 30 July 2014.

69 Ibid. I hope that he pointed out that he had a higher duty to the court.

70 Steve Lewis, 'Slipper's Got Form on Travel Spending', *The Courier-Mail,* 16 April 2012; 'A Huge Feat to Fit Slipper in Fleet of Chauffeured Cars', *Daily Telegraph,* 16 April 2012.

71 Rares J noted the less public means specifically created by legislation for staff complaints by those employed by members and the Human Rights Commission had not been taken, and that the urgency of allegations largely relating to conduct before 1 February, and Ashby's subsequent proposal to travel overseas, threw doubt on the urgency. *Ashby v Commonwealth of Australia (No 4)* [2012] FCA 1411 per Rares J at 192.

72 *Ashby v Commonwealth of Australia (No 4)* [2012] FCA 1411 at 102.

73 *Ashby v Commonwealth of Australia (No 4)* [2012] FCA 1411 per Rares J at 102.

74 As we now know, there was, as yet, no statement of claim.

75 Kirby was the High Court judge who had been accused of using Commonwealth cars to hunt for rent boys in Sydney (to be cleared when the documents supporting Senator Heffernan's claims of misuse of Comcar entitlements were found to be unauthentic). Australian Senate, 'Parliamentary Debates Official Hansard' (Tuesday, 12 March 2002); Darren Gray, 'Faked Record Handed to Federal Police', *The Age,* 20 March 2002. Rudd was the PM who was accused of favouring donors through a post-GFC stimulus scheme based on evidence from a doctored email. Emma Rodgers, 'Ozcar Scandal: Controversy Explained', www.abc.net.au/news/2009–06–21/ozcar-scandal-controversy-explained/1327966; Misha Schubert, 'Rudd, Swan Cleared over Ozcar Affair', *The Age,* 4 August 2009. An accusation of corruption was made against Newman to the Crime and Misconduct Commission when he was opposition leader

about to enter an election campaign. The Commissioner found that there was insufficient evidence and cleared Newman. Crime and Misconduct Commission, 'CMC Concludes No Official Misconduct by Newman in Assessment of Three BCC-Related Matters – 16.03.2012', www.ccc.qld.gov.au/news-and-media/cmc-media-releases/statement-on-matters-concerning-brisbane-city-council.

76 Bryant, 'Mal Brough Crashes Through'.

77 *Ashby v Commonwealth of Australia (No 4)* [2012] FCA 1411 per Rares J at 196–197.

78 *Ashby v Commonwealth of Australia (No 4)* [2012] FCA 1411 per Rares J at 190.

79 *Ashby v Slipper* [2014] FCAFC 15 per Mansfield and Glimour JJ at 155.

80 *Ashby v Slipper* [2014] FCAFC 15 at 140, 146.

81 *Ashby v Slipper* [2014] FCA 973.

82 *Ashby v Slipper* (No 3) [2015] FCAFC 9 (09 February 2015) (Mansfield, Siopis & Gilmour JJ).

83 *Criminal Code Act 1995* (Cth).

84 Jonathan Swan and Michael Bachelard, 'PM Caught up in Expenses Row on Slipper Wedding', *Sydney Morning Herald*, 8 October 2013.

85 Waters, 'Peter Slipper Case: Why Mark McInnes Is Grinning'.

Part IV

Legal ethics in a globalizing world

14 Get new lawyers!

Charles Sampford

Introduction

In James Rubin's account of the Kosovo war, he describes an exchange between Secretary Albright and Robin Cook (the British Foreign Secretary).[1] Cook was explaining that it was difficult for Britain to commit to the war without UN Security Council approval because the legal advice he had received was that such action would be illegal under international law. Albright's response was, simply, 'get new lawyers'. Rubin 'credits' Blair with a 'push' that swung the British to 'finally agree' that a UN Security Council resolution was 'not legally required'.[2] Robin Cook later stated in Parliament that the war was legal.[3] Interestingly, Blair did not.

At the time of writing (in 2003), I cannot verify whether the exchange took place. There is certainly other evidence on the public record[4] and I have good reason to believe that Rubin is correct to assert that the initial legal advice was unequivocally negative. However, my purpose is not to establish exactly what advice was sought and how those advised behaved – either in the Kosovo war or in the Iraq war.[5]

What I want to do is to discuss the ethical issues that such a situation would generate. In doing so, I will suggest what the ethical obligations of the key legal players in such institutional dramas should be – including governments seeking advice, the lawyers giving it, the ministers reporting it and the opposition in parliament.[6] As can be seen by the list of players, I am going to set out what I consider to be the particular responsibilities of the lawyers and officials of a Westminster system. I will also set out some of the institutional mechanisms for making it more likely that those obligations will be fulfilled – as always through the interaction of obligations by different players that make it more risky for any player to breach his or her ethical obligations. Analogous duties would be faced by the relevant actors in other systems.

1 Starting point – soldiers and politicians going to war

I begin with the obvious and tautologous statement that going to war involves the deliberate killing of others. Enemy combatants are killed through deliberately executed war plans. Non-combatants are sometimes killed deliberately or recklessly. In all other cases, they are killed as a predictable consequence of the actions taken to kill combatants or to destroy infrastructure. This is not to take a pacifist position and I am no pacifist. I learnt about war from my father who was a decorated intelligence officer in the Pacific War.[7] He knew all the secrets of that war and had access to all the transcripts of the Pacific version of 'Ultra' as well as the opportunity to debrief those who had directly experienced its horrors. War can sometimes be justified – even obligated.[8]

However, going to war is a decision whose seriousness challenges even the most Roget-enriched nuances of the English language. War is not 'politics carried on by other means'.[9] It is a form of organized, pre-meditated mass killing. It can only avoid being mass murder several orders of magnitude above Columbine by being legally justified. It can only avoid moral condemnation and obloquy by being morally justified. Jurisprudence has long contemplated the difference between a group of highway robbers stealing from travellers and a state collecting taxation. The question here is more pressing: what is the difference between a mass murderer and the Commander-in-Chief of a country's armed forces? Some deny that there is any difference – anarchists mouthing 'taxation is theft' in the first case and pacifists insisting that all violence, even in self-defence, is wrong. The answer to both is legality, legitimacy and morality.

The issues of legality take two different forms. First, there are the constitutional and statutory arrangements for conducting war that form part of a country's domestic law – which may authorize the commencement of war and what procedures must be followed to do so.

Second, there is the body of international law on when and how war may be waged (that is, *ius ad bellum* and *ius in bello*). These bodies of domestic and international law are related in a variety of ways. In some countries, treaties become a part of domestic law without enabling legislation, so that a war waged contrary to the UN Charter may well be contrary to domestic law. In other countries, the effectiveness of treaties is dependent on the implementation of legislation or on the willingness of courts to use international legal instruments as means for interpreting domestic law.

2 Politicians

The rise of international law, the growing jurisprudence of the International Court of Justice (the ICJ), the creation of the International Criminal Court (the ICC), the extension of universal jurisdiction for certain kinds of war crimes and the Nuremberg precedent all give politicians pragmatic reasons to consider their decisions to engage in 'armed conflict' – that is, go to war. The United Nations Charter outlaws armed conflict except in very limited circumstances (essentially self-defence or with United Nations Security Council (UNSC) backing).[10] Any other attempt to engage in international armed conflict involves the crime of aggression – already recognized by the Nuremberg and Tokyo war crimes trials. The Rome Statute establishing the International Criminal Court (ICC) does not yet define the crime of aggression and thus does not yet give the ICC jurisdiction over such a crime. However, listing it in Article 5 of the Rome Statute confirms the existence of the crime prosecuted in Tokyo.[11] A prime minister, cabinet member, Queen or governor general may take comfort that they will probably not be prosecuted by an ad hoc tribunal or – at least not yet – through the exercise of the jurisdiction of the ICC. Even that comfort may be circumscribed in the future by the potential of prosecution in a rapidly growing number of nations – making future tourism, health care or international grandstanding much more risky.[12] But, in any case, the avoidance of prosecution does not entail innocence. Indeed, the clear words of the UN Charter and the recognition of the crime of aggression will mean that many will decide that those who authorize aggression are guilty of a crime. If they were prepared to defend the legality of their action in the ICJ, then they would be able to assert their innocence – for there is no crime of aggression if the war is in conformity with international law. However, if they are not prepared to defend their action in the ICJ, they can hardly complain if others read the UN Charter and decide for themselves. The presumption of innocence is a legal presumption of all well-ordered courts. It does not apply to those who refuse to accept the relevant courts!

3 Soldiers

The same set of laws and institutions applies to the soldiers who are sent off to fight. This raises important moral and practical issues for those with a will to war. Democracies expect their soldiers to be loyal and to follow orders. In most countries (and certainly in democracies like the UK and Australia), they are a highly professional group who, unlike other professionals, are prepared to die in the course of their professional duty (something even the most dedicated lawyers rarely have to contemplate). In countries like Australia, adherence to international law is a core part of military doctrine for normative and pragmatic reasons. Normatively, it fits with an image of the military of a democratic state committed to the rule of law as supporters of international order. Pragmatically, the military thinks that this approach works better – especially in peacekeeping operations where the Australians have a reputation second to none.[13] When Lieutenant Col Michael Kelly calls the Australian Defence Force the 'largest human rights organisation' in the country,[14] this is not intended as an idle boast but a proud claim of the values they live for and, if necessary, die for. I can think of few greater betrayals of the Australian soldiers I know than transforming such a fine group of internationally responsible professional soldiers into a band of international outlaws and potentially into individual war criminals.

This is not to say that soldiers will automatically become war criminals through participation in an illegal war. From its origins in the sixteenth century, international law has distinguished between participation in an illegal war and committing a war crime in the conduct of war. Such conduct is covered by *ius in bello*. The legality of the war is covered by *ius ad bellum* and the war crime of initiating a war of aggression is committed by those involved in the decision to go to war – the PM, the cabinet, the head of state who accepts their advice – and presumably any accessories before the fact.[15] However, forcing soldiers to participate in an illegal war threatens serious damage to the morale and international reputation of the armed forces. It may also increase the likelihood that they will be charged with *ius in bello* war crimes.

Since Nuremberg, most would say with complete certainty that a soldier's only real concern was with the legality of the way they fight a war rather than the legality of the war itself.[16] While they might worry about the former, they could follow orders blindly on the latter. This view sits at odds with traditional concepts of domestic law and reflects the traditional distinctiveness of international law based upon strong concepts of sovereignty. International law has accepted that obeying orders is no defence to the commission of war crimes that are governed by the principle of *ius in bello*. This would be the case even if domestic law required obedience to such orders. To a domestic public lawyer, it is not immediately clear why superior orders should be a defence to participation in an illegal war. In domestic criminal law, an illegal enterprise confers no powers on its leaders to give lawful orders to others. Those who carry out the orders of the ringleaders are likely to be guilty as principals – not just accessories. In domestic public law, the use of a power for improper (never mind illegal!) purposes is ultra vires making the exercise of that power void (or possibly voidable). No one can rely on such exercises of power in such trivial matters as authorizing a licence for a fruit cart, let alone mass killing. It is only traditional assumptions about sovereignty that maintain this chasm between the approaches of domestic and international law. This view of sovereignty assumes that it is the right of sovereign states to order their armed forces to fight illegal wars. As sovereignty weakens, the chasm between the approach taken by domestic and international law to participation in illegal mass killings is likely to be bridged. By that time, participation in an illegal war will have direct legal consequences for the participants.

A second, more direct, way in which the legality of the war may affect the likelihood of being found guilty of war crimes lies in the elements of the crimes outlined in the Rome Statute. Crimes include: 'unlawful deportation or transfer or unlawful confinement ... in particular when committed as part of a plan or policy or as part of a large-scale commission of such crimes'.[17] Another, relevant given the massive bombing launched in past wars against Iraq and Serbia, is

> intentionally launching an attack in the knowledge that such an attack will cause incidental loss of life or injury to civilians or widespread, long-term and severe damage to the natural environment which would be clearly excessive in relation to the concrete and direct overall military advantage anticipated.[18]

It is conduct of this kind that has raised the concerns of Australian lawyers in relation to the potential liability of Australian troops under the ICC statute – whose provisions are reflected in the *Criminal Code Act 1995* (Cth).[19] If the war itself is unlawful, a court might more easily decide that deportations or bombings carried out in furtherance of its objectives are unlawful. Similarly, the Statute criminalizes actions not required by 'military necessity'.[20] It would not be hard to see a court deciding that there can be no such thing as military necessity in prosecuting a war that should not be happening in the first place. Even if the court does conclude that military necessity is possible under such circumstances, it may be hard to convince that this defence has been made out in a particular case.[21]

A third way in which participants in illegal wars may be more likely to find themselves war criminals is that states which commit the crime of aggression (thus failing to observe the requirement of *ius ad bellum*) may have little compunction in ordering action that would breach the requirements of *ius in bello*. This is true of dictators such as Adolf Hitler and Saddam Hussein. It also seems true of modern democracies – with the US the most willing to engage in wars that are contrary to international law and the most willing to select targets that their allies believe to be contrary to international law.[22]

Even if a politician has no compunction in giving soldiers orders to engage in an illegal war, he should consider how professional soldiers will be affected by being given such orders. Politicians, commanders and lawyers will comfort them with the *ius ad bellum/ius in bello* distinction. However, many soldiers in a democratic society proud of its adherence to the rule of law may have real qualms about taking part in a war that most international lawyers considered to be illegal.

No democrat who values the soldiers who defend us, as I value ours, should ever place professional soldiers in that position. First, it is unfair to them. Second, it puts huge strains on the military and their capacity to act effectively and cohesively. Third, if soldiers are expected to take part in illegal wars of aggression, we may find that the best soldiers will be sickened and take the first opportunity to resign. Those who are attracted to join the forces in their place are not likely to be as admirable. It changes the force into one that merely obeys orders – my country right or wrong, or rather, 'my government, right or wrong'. Fourth, if soldiers are prepared to accept orders to take part in illegal wars of aggression, can we rely on them to refuse orders to break the *ius in bello* laws? Finally, if they are prepared to accept orders to take part in illegal wars, can we rely on them to refuse to break domestic laws prohibiting coups d'état or to refuse to engage in human rights abuses under a 1970s style 'state of siege'?[23] We value civilian control of the military, especially in a strong democracy such as ours. However, civilian control is not the sworn obedience to a Fuhrer. It is obedience under law: laws which determine who has the right to issue orders on behalf of the democratic majority and laws which determine the scope of the power to give such orders. Civilian control does not mean that those who temporarily hold power because of the last election and the continued confidence of a majority of their fellow parliamentarians can use military power against their domestic opponents. Civilian control cannot now mean using military power in breach of one part of international law (*ius in bello*). Civilian control is better preserved if civilian authorities take the consistent line that it is exercised within the authority the government has under international law to make war (*ius ad bellum*). How can we insist that soldiers show adequate respect for domestic law when we are telling them that they must ignore international law when told to do so? To maintain a distinction in commitment between domestic and international lawfulness will become increasingly difficult as international and domestic law are increasingly intertwined. Where international treaties are directly incorporated into domestic law (as in the United States following Senate ratification), some would argue that the distinction is no longer valid. However, countries which claim to be good international citizens are estopped from making that distinction. This is certainly a claim that Australia makes: 'Let me make it very clear to this parliament that this government will never act in breach of international law'.[24] That is certainly a claim we should seek to live up to for our soldiers as well as for ourselves.

These points go to the nature of the armed forces we have. Democracies like Australia have developed highly trained professional armed forces where even section commanders are expected to understand the purposes of the mission and apply them in the real-time dilemmas faced in complex peacekeeping (and, where necessary, war-making) operations. This is very much in the mould of a profession whose members are instilled with core values that justify the profession and apply those values to the actions they take. Part of the core values is legality, both domestic and international. Statements such as that quoted above bolster the armed forces. Our military has seen itself as the armed forces of a good international citizen seeking to support international law and order. This is a noble ideal which would be destroyed by Australia's participation in illegal wars. Using our armed forces for illegal wars challenges the legitimacy of the armed forces and their image of themselves. From being a force to protect the weak against aggression, they would become a force of aggression against the weak. For a soldier who joined for the ideals expressed by the force and reinforced in all its recruiting campaigns, this is a terrible betrayal. It is like ordering a doctor who joined his profession to save lives to kill patients because the hospital told him to. It is like ordering a lawyer who joined the law firm to do justice according to law to break and undermine that law because the senior partner told him to. This is to assume that the only basis for their responsibilities is solely in domestic law. Nuremberg emphatically rejected that claim.

Since Nuremberg, it is clear that, legally and ethically, a soldier must refuse to commit a war crime even if ordered to by his democratic government. We may well find that international law changes to make it their legal duty to refuse to take part in an illegal war. Some might argue that it is already the ethical duty of a modern professional soldier in a world in which international law is taken seriously to refuse participation in illegal wars.[25] This would not be a matter of allowing individual soldiers to exercise personal preferences about the wars they fight; it is a matter of excluding personal preferences of politicians to order wars which their countries have foresworn waging. This is why the duties of democratic governments and the lawyers who advise them are so important. It is their duty to ensure that none of their soldiers ever has to consider the terrible choice between following orders and their ethical duties.

Exceptions?

There may be occasions when wars that are contrary to international law are justified. I have to say that I am very sceptical about such claims and it may well be that there are no cases where such justifications can be made out. In a paper delivered to the final plenary of the 1999 *World Congress on Legal and Social Philosophy*[26] (held in the World Trade Centre!), I argued that those who intervene in other countries should be bound by international law and accept the compulsory jurisdiction of the ICJ. The ICJ would have an important role whether the war was fought pursuant to a UNSC resolution or in claimed self-defence. In the latter case, it could determine if the claim is made out. In the former case, it could determine whether the action was authorized by the UNSC resolution.[27] Nevertheless, for most people and for most ethical theories, the law is not the highest morality and there may be cases where democratic politicians genuinely believe that war contrary to international law is justified. However, if that is their view, they owe it to their people, and especially their soldiers, to justify the action on that basis, not to pretend that it is legal as well. Such a view is behind those who say that the Kosovo war was illegal but morally justifiable – though this is not a judgement for lawyers to make, it is one for ethicists to debate and politicians to justify to their electorates. However, such countries should do so publicly and acknowledge that this course of action may ultimately lead to legal sanctions against them.

One of the exceptions that may be argued is that the 'other side' does not respect these same laws. However, that is not an argument for abandonment of the rule of law. The willingness of others to break the law is not an argument within the debate about what to do with lawbreakers: it is the ground upon which the debate begins. The domestic arguments about the treatment of those accused and convicted of breaking the law commence with the fact that others break the law and that the institutions with the authority to deal with lawbreakers are constrained by a set of rules about how they treat the accused and the convicted. I will not go through the many rule of law arguments for officials responding to law breaking within their legal authority.

On the basis of this analysis, let us examine the ethical responsibilities of some of the actors in a Westminster-style liberal democracy.

4 The lawyers

Secretary Albright's reported statement about 'getting new lawyers' will strike many as a reasonable, unproblematic, knee-jerk response. It is often said in the context of domestic law and I do not condemn her for reacting in that way. However, when we unpack and reflect upon the domestic analogy, some important issues arise for the lawyers involved in giving advice on the legality of war.

Normal cases – giving advice on domestic law (that is, the law of the sovereign state). Clients regularly go to lawyers for advice on the legal consequences of their intended course of action.[28] It is their duty to their clients to give honest advice on the meaning and content of the relevant laws and how they will be interpreted and applied by the relevant court or courts who have had the authority to adjudicate on such matters. If there are alternative means of achieving the same ends, they will advise on them. If the client is determined to follow through with a course of action that may have adverse legal consequences, the lawyer will outline the interpretations of the law that could be adopted, the arguments that would be raised against them and their honest view of the chances of their success in court. Where the client is a corporate entity considering a course of action, the lawyer may have to consider the interests and legal rights of shareholders who comprise the corporation. These ethical duties are backed up by the possibility of professional negligence if the advice fails honestly and diligently to state the law and the prospects of success as known to the legal adviser. In the case of corporate entities, those suing lawyers may extend beyond the staff who formally seek the advice but could run to the directors, shareholders and others who rely on the advice (under Hedley Byrne principles).[29] If the lawyer considered that action which a corporate client wanted to pursue was criminal yet gave the client advice that it was legally permissible, those employees of the corporation who acted on that advice would have the 'mother of all actions' for professional misfeasance!

In summary, it is their ethical duty to the client to try to find a legal means to achieve the client's ends, to anticipate any challenges that might be made to the legality of the client's proposed course of action, to identify the arguments that they could use to defend the client's proposed course of action, to identify the opposing texts, precedents and arguments, and to give an honest assessment of the probability of those arguments being successful in court.

Of course, the client is not obliged to accept this legal advice. The client can go to as many lawyers as it likes. Under all but a few circumstances, the advice of earlier lawyers is entombed in the vault of lawyer–client confidentiality. The client may well find different opinions on the likely success of a particular action. This is a function of the complexity of much law and the inherent contestability of many legal norms. The client may find a lawyer who thinks they have a greater chance of success than another and ask them to act for them. Alternatively, the client may ignore the advice of the first lawyer, commit to the course of action that they had been advised against pursuing and other lawyers will defend them in court, putting the best possible defence that they can. All of these factors give the common impression that you can get a lawyer to say anything you like and that the response to adverse legal advice is to 'get more lawyers'.

However, it is not nearly as easy as that. First and foremost, each lawyer has the obligation to give honest and diligent advice. If the lawyer were to give the client the advice he knew the client wanted to hear, but which the lawyer knew to be wrong or incomplete, then that would be a failure in his duty to the client. If he did it in order to secure favour with the client and to secure more fees (especially in pursuing a hopeless case on behalf of the client), the lawyer is in serious breach of his ethical duties. In most cases where a good lawyer gives unequivocal advice that a proposed course of action is illegal, others will give similar advice. Sometimes, they may be able to identify a different course of action to achieve the result desired that the first lawyer had not conceived. They may also see a way of characterizing it that the first lawyer had not conceived and which may have a very good chance of success. More often, they see an argument may succeed that pushes the existing law to the fullest extent, but which, they will have to advise in all honesty, will probably fail. Thus, the actual advice given by the second lawyer may be much closer to the first lawyer's advice than it at first appears. Corporate executives may boast that they can get a lawyer's opinion in favour of any proposition but if you looked at the different opinions the variations would be of nuances and the probabilities of success.

Similarly, the fact that there will generally be lawyers on each side of any action does not mean that their views of the law are fundamentally different – merely that they have a duty in litigation to put the best case they can and to try to win for their client, however hopeless the case may seem and however much they believe that the client's interests would have been served by taking the legal advice first tendered. Thus, the divergence of views ultimately expressed in court masks the convergence of the likely advice tendered by ethical lawyers who are diligent and competent.

The most critical factor underlying this convergence is that the advice can ultimately be tested in court. Lawyers have fertile minds and all forms of law have leeway and uncertainties that they know have been exploited in the past. They have different views of where the law should go and may be keen to test how far it can be pushed. But, however keen they are to run an argument, they know that there is an ultimate judge of the race and it is their duty to assess the likelihood of that judge coming down in favour of the argument.

A related factor is that lawyers are officers of that court and owe a primary duty to that court[30] and, more generally, to law and the system of justice.[31] That duty does not constrain the legal arguments they make,[32] but it does constrain their actions in a number of important ways. The major set of constraints relates to abuse of court process, especially the duties not to knowingly mislead the court, not to argue a client's innocence when that client has admitted his guilt to the lawyer, not to destroy evidence or to refuse discovery. A rarer set of constraints operates to limit client confidentiality where the lawyer reasonably believes that the client is seeking to flee the jurisdiction or to commit a serious crime.[33] Client confidentiality is to advise clients how to obey the law and to allow them to best defend those who have been charged with breaking the law. It does not require the lawyer to be silent about future crimes that the client is determined to commit. The classic examples given involve kidnapping and violent crime. Family law provides examples where the client decides to seek custody by killing his wife or to avoid the issue entirely by taking the child out of the jurisdiction. Lawyers who advise organized crime figures provide other examples. Lawyers may not advise their clients how to nobble jurors or which courts to blow up. They have a duty to report their clients should it be clear that their clients are engaged in such activities. The purpose of legal advice is to advise on proposed courses of action to further and protect their interests through the law. It is not a means to pursue illegal activities.

Accordingly, clients can 'get more lawyers'. However, if they employ ethical lawyers, they will rarely get fundamentally different advice. If the lawyer gives whatever advice the client wants to hear, they are in breach of their duty to give honest and competent advice and could well be sued for negligence. If the client seeks out lawyers who will give them bad advice, their foolishness will be amply demonstrated. Lawyers may follow instructions and write to the client's adversaries with claims about the legal rights and duties of the various parties. However, competent lawyers from the other side will laugh at the claims and simply say: 'See you in court'. If the client's lawyers seek to abuse the court process, the response may be: 'See you in the ethics committee'. If the client's lawyers are too close to, or too knowledgeable about the client's violent criminal activities, the lawyers may themselves face court from the other side of the dock.

Giving advice on international law

When a lawyer gives advice on a matter of international law, most of the above applies. There is a body of international law from recognized sources.[34] There is a court (the ICJ) with the authority to make authoritative statements of international law in resolving disputes between nations. There is also the ICC. Ethical and competent legal advice should be based on the established sources of international law recognized by the court with honest advice as to the way the ICJ and ICC is likely to find in cases brought before them.

The differences concern the power of these courts, the ability of plaintiffs to get cases before the court and to enforce its decisions. Not all countries accept the compulsory jurisdiction of the ICJ – notably the United States, following actions against Nicaragua in the mid-1980s that few lawyers could have considered legal under either domestic or international law. Certainly, the ICJ found against the United States in unequivocal terms. It is a matter of some regret that the response was not to recognize the law and comply with it but the avoidance of future adverse findings. The US has even threatened to forcibly remove any American soldier from a court that it does not recognize.

The voluntary nature of submission to the jurisdiction of the ICJ creates a temptation for governments and lawyers. First, there is the temptation for governments to block the jurisdiction of the ICJ, to refuse to defend their action in the only competent court available and to pretend that the action is legal rather than in gross violation of international law.

Second, there is a temptation for lawyers (freed from the pressure of potential litigation) to give the 'advice' the client wants. However, if they do that, they are not giving legal advice in the normal sense – how to conform to the law and how to defend themselves in court. The role of the lawyer is then justifying the illegal, and potentially criminal actions of their clients. They are not acting as lawyers but, as best, public relations advisers and 'spin doctors'. If one cuts legal opinion adrift from what would actually happen in a court of competent jurisdiction, it becomes 'spin'. The purpose of legal advice is not to bolster the position of a client in public debate – let alone in defiance of the relevant court. If they choose to take such an approach, they should certainly make it clear that they are not acting as lawyers. Bar associations and law societies should consider whether such action is incompatible with the action of lawyers.[35] The reason for this is that others might easily mistake the activities for genuine legal advice. Indeed, there is no point going to lawyers unless others are so mistaken and thereby misled. My view tends towards a stronger line.

In any case, lawyers should collectively recognize this problem. Lawyers as a group, through their professional associations, should remove the temptation that their clients might act illegally and seek the cloak of respectability by seeking compliant and unethical lawyers and pressuring lawyers to act unethically to suit their own interest. The relevant professional bodies should not only provide guidance to lawyers giving advice on international law but should also protect lawyers from the pressure that might be applied to them by governments anxious to secure a favourable 'opinion'.

There are a number of approaches that could be taken:

1 Law societies and bar associations might refine and apply their ethics rules to counter such conduct and seek to disbar those who abuse it. They should be particularly harsh on lawyers in government who bully, threaten, cajole or induce other lawyers to deliver an opinion that the latter do not hold.
2 Law societies might set up independent panels of international lawyers to give the public independent advice on the legality of any proposed war that the government was not prepared to defend in the appropriate court. The panel might recommend disciplinary proceedings against those lawyers who gave what the panel consider to be advice that is not deemed diligent.
3 Restrictions might be placed on professional negligence cover.
4 Lawyer–client confidentiality might be erased where the government is not prepared to defend its action in the ICJ – especially where they are likely to attack the court. The lawyer's duty to law and the system of justice mean that they must report the planned commission of a crime.[36]

It is important that this disconnection between the lawyers and the courts that determine the legal issues on which they are giving advice should not disconnect them from their duties as lawyers to the law. Where lawyers are giving advice to governments who represent free and democratic peoples and who give orders to loyal soldiers, they have an even greater responsibility.

In the medium term, we should strive for an international code of ethics for lawyers that would help to properly internationalize the profession. A duty to respect international law would be included in the duties required of all lawyers. This would be a radical shift for lawyers – reflecting the decline of sovereignty and the globalization of law and lawyering. I used to say that the legal profession is one of the most localized professions because its subject matter is almost universally the law of sovereign jurisdictions. That is no longer true. Lawyers need to develop a working knowledge of international legal norms and a commitment to the international rule of law.

If a liberal democracy decides to go to war without the authorization of the UNSC and without being prepared to subject its proposed actions to the scrutiny of the ICJ, I would hope that lawyers around the world and in the country concerned would speak out.[37] I would like to think that lawyers working for such a government would threaten to resign and would carry out that threat if their country persisted with such unsanctioned action. The analogy is that of the lawyer who knows that their client intends to commit a criminal act. In most jurisdictions, the lawyer is under a duty to advise the client of the illegality, to refuse to represent him and to report him (lawyer–client privilege explicitly excludes the intention to commit a subsequent criminal act). Few criminal acts are more heinous than the illegal taking of a large number of lives.

Lawyers have a particular responsibility not to aid and abet criminal activity where the client will refuse to accept the jurisdiction of competent courts. If a false or reckless statement of its legality makes it more likely that the criminal act will be committed, the lawyer may be an accessory in some legal regimes. They are certainly, in the moral sense, an accessory. In a democracy, a statement that a proposed war is legal may be practically necessary before the war can be launched. Lawyers should take this into account in what they say about law. Ethics codes and bar associations should consider the issue too.

This may seem hopelessly idealistic. What lawyer would give up his job? However, that is exactly what every code of ethics tells lawyers to do in some circumstances. Where the majority of lawyers practice outside of government and the right to appear before courts is decided by the courts themselves, there is hope. As law becomes more international and international tribunals become more important, the hope may be fanned from a faint glimmer to a distant beacon.

I can envisage a day when lawyers who have been found to act unethically according to norms of the international bar may be disbarred from the international bar and would not be able to appear before any international judicial forums – including those covering international contract disputes, international trade disputes and so on.

These are strong suggestions and their implementation would have to await further institutional development of an international profession of lawyers. In general, however, lawyers should treat the rule of law as one of the most fundamental values of the legal profession and should be prepared to provide the strongest institutional support for its full, and international, implementation.

Lawyers advising governments should be particularly careful where the government refuses the jurisdiction of the international courts and has threatened to act violently against the relevant international court.

The role of lawyers to which the legal profession and their ethics are dedicated is to advance justice and the system of law. Lawyers do this by providing advice to clients before they act so as to enable them to keep within the law and to defend them after they act in litigation. Their role is not to assist them to break the law and to act as spin doctors for their illegal activity.

The lack of compulsory jurisdiction and enforcement mechanisms is, of course, hardly a new issue in international law. This is being addressed, and institutional supports for international law are stronger now than at any time in the past. International law has generated sources of law independent of the international equivalents of legislation (for example, the UN Charter), precedent (ICJ decisions), executive authority (UNSC) and contract (treaties between nations). Other critical sources of international law are the decisions of relevant tribunals and the writings of international law professors. International advisers should take these into account. Senior academic lawyers contribute to the latter and should be aware of the responsibility which that role imposes on them. It also means that, where the vast majority of academic experts supports a particular proposition, lawyers representing governments should take this into account in giving honest advice.

When lawyers give advice, governments publish it and newspapers report it: we should never forget what legal advice is. It is not determinative of international law but a view of it. Lawyers for the different sides of a dispute do not determine the law. They advise their clients on it and they defend their clients using legal arguments in court. Given the duty of lawyers to defend clients with even the most desperately hopeless cases, there will be a wide range of views expressed in the latter case (although the confidential legal advice provided to clients will differ less in reality). However, lawyers retained by either side do not determine the law. (If so, the law would be hopelessly inconsistent.) Other lawyers determine the law, independent of the parties whose role it is to determine such issues. The most usual set of lawyers are to be found on the bench of the courts of competent jurisdiction. However, refusing to go before such a court does not mean that the action that a country refuses to test in court is legal. The lack of such courts in the past has meant that the views of law professors provide an alternative source of law. Accordingly, if the majority of senior international law professors state that a particular war is illegal, avoiding the court does not make the action legal. The reverse is true. In the absence of a court case determining the issue, the majority of senior international law professors are, by definition, right under clause (38)(1)(d) of the *Statute of the International Court of Justice*! It is only through going to court that a weak case can be successfully made out. Nothing seems more natural to a lawyer!

5 Employed lawyers

Where the client employs the lawyer, the lawyer's duties remain. If a corporate lawyer is threatened with the sack or with breach of his contractual obligations if he blows the whistle on planned corporate criminality, then he must act on his ethical obligations as a lawyer if he is still to consider himself one. He may well have some protection from the court in the interpretation of the contract and the voiding of clauses so clearly contrary to public policy. However, a lawyer may no more consider his employment in deciding his ethical duties than he may the loss of a client's fee.

Where the lawyer is employed by the military and bound by (in Australia) *the Criminal Code Act 1995* (Cth) or the *Defence Force Discipline Act 1982* (Cth), the lawyer's problems in following his ethical duties are compounded by the fact that he might be prosecuted for revealing that his employer is planning to act illegally. My view is that the use of these provisions by a government to protect themselves from exposure as lawbreakers in parliament and in public should be struck down as a matter of administrative law as such use furthers a purpose that is most improper. If a minister does act to mislead parliament, it is the convention that that minister must resign.

Unless a lawyer observes these principles, there is little difference between him and a shameless paid 'sophist',[38] lying for his client. The lawyer is then merely a gun for hire, indifferent to the larger requirements of justice, and ready to trample the legitimate claims of other interested parties.

In the case of a lawyer for a corporate entity (and even more so when it is the democratic polity of which he is a part), the issue arises as to 'who is the client?' The CEO of a corporation or the Prime Minister of the country may well seek legal advice. However, in asking about the conduct of the company or the polity, the 'client' is the company/polity. If the client's agent uses the advice to mislead the client, I do not see that the lawyer's duty is to remain silent while the company/polity commits a serious crime.

The ethical lawyer does not face a dilemma so much as face a clash between international law and the laws and orders of regimes that break international law. It is merely a less extreme version of the position faced by German soldiers ordered to take part in war crimes during World War Two.

6 The government

The prime minister has the responsibility of tendering advice to the crown as to how it should exercise its statutory and prerogative powers in making war. In doing so, he knows that there is a very powerful convention that such advice will be followed with very few exceptions. The PM is accountable for the advice given, and hence actions taken by the crown, to the democratically elected parliament.

MPs have the right to question the government and governments have the duty to avoid misleading parliament in their responses. Parliament has the right to demand that the government give a public justification for any action taken by the government, let alone such a momentous decision as going to war and thereby engaging in mass killing. However, accountability to the older Westminster parliaments does not require formal or prior endorsement. There is no constitutional requirement for a formal declaration of war or a war powers declaration. Parliament might wish to indicate that its confidence is conditional on seeking prior approval for certain actions, including going to war other than in self-defence. However, it is not clear that the British crown or Australian Governors-General should or would enforce such conditions.

The role of the executive is not to make law but to act within its confines. This is institutionalized in the strongest possible way in domestic law. The executive can be held accountable in the courts if it acts beyond that law. In international law, the position is not so clearly articulated. The executive can make law in the form of treaties. It is accountable to parliament in the normal way for its actions. Australia has added a requirement that treaties be considered by the Joint Standing Committee on Treaties,[39] but does not go so far as to require ratification of treaties by the upper house (the Senate) before they take effect. Treaties become part of domestic law through the passage of ordinary legislation.

Depending on the terms of the treaty and the intention of the parties, signatory nations have the right to abrogate treaties. This is also a right of the executive in a Westminster system. However, if the alteration of Australia's commitment to international law in becoming party to treaties is expected to be the subject of scrutiny by the joint parliamentary committee, it is arguable that the alteration of Australia's commitment by abrogating a treaty should equally be subject to that safeguard.

The point of this is that Australia and the UK have signed up to a number of important treaties – such as ANZUS and NATO. Under Article 1 of ANZUS, the parties:

> undertake as set forth in the Charter of the United Nations, to settle any international disputes in which they may be involved by peaceful means in such a manner that international peace and security and justice are not endangered and to refrain in their international relations from the threat or use of force in any manner inconsistent with the purposes of the United Nations.

(NATO has an almost identical provision.) To do otherwise would be to be in breach of the treaty that has had the strongest bilateral support for nearly a half a century. The fact that another party is planning to breach this treaty would not mean that our obligations are extinguished, not least to the other party to the treaty.

Honesty demands that if a democracy decides that treaties it has ratified will not bind it, the country should renounce the relevant treaty. In most cases, there are means for doing so – although abrogation itself is governed by international law.[40] If no attempt is made to withdraw from the treaty, we presume that the parties will keep to their word and accept adjudication by independent tribunals as to whether or not they have kept it. This is formalized in relation to trade matters through the WTO and in other matters through the ICJ.[41]

It goes without saying that war must never be embarked upon for partisan political reasons. 'Wedge' politics have no part in this equation. Political advantage is insufficient reason to kill one person, let alone many. Indeed, the very thought is obscene. No ethical person should have any part in it and any minister or public servant who became aware of such a reason would have a duty to blow the whistle on the government.

The government makes the decision and is accountable for it to the parliament and, through it, the electorate. In my view, the government must either provide a formal opinion of the first law officer that the war is in compliance with international law as well as accepting the compulsory jurisdiction of the ICJ against any who wish to challenge the legality of the war *or* it must provide a justification for going to war even it is not legal.

There is another obligation. Those who seek to enforce international law should be bound by international law for deontological and consequentialist reasons. I have argued this before[42] and will not do so here.

7 The Attorney General

In Westminster systems, the Attorney General has a key role to play. I have argued before that, before a Westminster democracy goes to war, the attorney should make a statement to parliament about the legality of the war on the basis of:

- his status as the first law officer with a partially independent role;
- his status as a lawyer subject to legal ethics;
- his obligation not to mislead parliament – a fundamental constitutional obligation; and
- his ethical obligations as a minister.[43]

Note that the House of Representatives Standing and Sessional Orders for the Australian Parliament state that questions to ministers must not seek a legal opinion or even an opinion.[44] That is as may be. However, the parliament should satisfy itself as to the legality of actions proposed to be taken by the government and if the advice relied on by the first law officer is not tabled, then the parliament may take note of the government's failure to table it and draw its own conclusions.

While, at the time of writing, the Iraq war is just beginning, it is good to note that Westminster governments have been more willing to release legal advice than in 1999 and the attorneys general are more prepared to make statements to parliament. The British Attorney General provided an opinion and backed it in parliament. The Australian government provided a written and signed opinion claiming that the war was within international law – following the prime minister's welcome insistence in parliament that Australia would never act in breach of international law.[45] In neither case is it possible to say whether this was the advice of the first lawyers or 'new lawyers' (although a report in the *Guardian* suggested earlier contrary advice being received by various ministers in the UK).[46] The position that the war was legal does not have much support from professors of public international law. However, as argued above, the key test is whether they are prepared to defend their position in the International Court of Justice.

Conclusion

Going to war is a momentous decision. I do not argue that democracies should never do it nor that they should never do it in contravention of international law. Indeed, one must accept the possibility that there might be cases where war is justified despite its illegality (just as we may find ethical justification for breaking other laws). However, democratic governments should justify any wars to their own people – giving the substantive reasons for going to war as well as the legal justification *or* the reason for going to war despite international law.

However, statements of legality should not be mere rhetoric. Because governments can generally avoid having to defend their position before a court of competent jurisdiction, there is a temptation for governments to seek, and lawyers to give, advice that the government wants to hear. Thus, governments may prefer congenial advice to competent advice.

This raises ethical issues for all the lawyers involved. Whether or not they are the 'first lawyers' or the 'new lawyers', lawyers giving advice to the ministers of democratic governments should consider their ethical responsibilities to the law, to the system of justice, to the democratic peoples whose governments they are advising and above all to the members of the military whose professionalism requires greater sacrifice than any lawyer is likely to have to make. More than ever, they should not only cite the texts, precedents and arguments that support the government's preferred course of action but deal with the contrary arguments and give their honest views of the prospects of success should their opinion be challenged in a court of competent jurisdiction. They are not absolved from those responsibilities by the unwillingness of the government to defend its position in the relevant court of competent jurisdiction. The reverse is the case and they should consider their ethical responsibilities in the light of other precedents of clients who will not be bound by the law.

These issues are not easy and lawyers should give collective consideration as to how they should deal with such occasions. As always, a collective institutional response is more effective and reliable than individual ethical heroics. It would be even better if democratic governments did not act to give ethical lawyers such grief and put temptation in the way of unethical lawyers. Whether the legal right to make war is alleged to derive from clear UNSC authority, disputed UNSC authority, self-defence, an emerging humanitarian intervention or some other justification, democratic nations who are confident of their case and their claims to act within international law should have no fear of defending their positions in the International Court of Justice. As I have argued elsewhere,[47] this allows them to counter-sue those against whom they are acting and get substantive orders against them. Furthermore, this makes it possible for the ICJ to develop the law slowly, reflecting changes in the international community.

Ethical reflection is most effective if backed by institutional supports. This article effectively suggests a number of such institutional supports entirely consistent with the Westminster system.

1 Updating of codes and advice by professional associations of lawyers.
2 Tabling of advice and the AG taking personal responsibility for it as a lawyer.
3 Democratic governments should be prepared to defend their claims of legality in the International Court of Justice and be proud to do so. It is the real test of their commitment to act within international law.

There are other institutional mechanisms that might be suggested. First and foremost, I would argue that the UNSC should only authorize the use of force if those proposing to use such force are prepared to subject their actions to ICJ and ICC scrutiny.

In conclusion, I would suggest that we remember that Law and the Rule of Law are not absolutes. However, they are central to the professional ethics of lawyers. Lawyers should treat them very seriously, even at the margins of enforceability found in international law.

Notes

1 James P. Rubin was the press secretary of the then Secretary of State, Madeleine Albright during the Kosovo War. He published his account of the machinations leading to the war under the title, 'A very personal war' in *The Financial Times* on 30 September 2000.
2 See Rubin's article cited above. This is a rather amazing statement. The legality or otherwise of attacking Yugoslavia in the absence of a UN Security Council resolution is not determined by the British cabinet or the American government. It is interesting to note that they refused to defend their claims in the International Court of Justice – no doubt because of the strength and cogency of the first lawyers' advice.
3 See I. Brownlie and C.J. Apperley, 'Kosovo Crisis Inquiry: Memorandum on the International Law Aspects', *International and Comparative Law Quarterly* 49, no. 7 (2000).
4 Ibid.
5 The Iraq war began during the final stages of drafting the initial (2003) article this chapter republishes. For consideration of these later events, see Chapter 15 below.
6 Other key individuals will have ethical responsibilities – including members of the cabinet, the opposition, the crown (as legal head of the armed forces) and the armed forces who are ordered to go into battle. Ideally, their ethical obligations should be congruent with, and reinforcing of, the ethical obligations of those listed (as always, the best integrity systems have a number of mutually reinforcing legal and ethical norms as well as mutually reinforcing institutions). However, this chapter cannot accommodate a listing, let alone a meaningful discussion, of their roles and ethical responsibilities.
7 He was seconded to General Macarthur's headquarters and was decorated by the United States in recognition of his work.
8 Much has been written on just war theory. For a recent look at the issues as they relate to humanitarian intervention – note that Saddam's domestic atrocities have been highlighted by the US and the UK to justify intervention in Iraq – see C.A.J. Coady, *The Ethics of Armed Humanitarian Intervention* (Washington: United States Institute of Peace, 2002).
9 Carl von Clausewitz, *Vom Kriege [On War]*, trans. James John Graham (London: N. Trübner, 1832; repr., 1873).
10 Note that even these exceptions are limited. Article 51 defines the right of self-defence quite narrowly, providing as follows:

> Nothing in the present Charter shall impair the inherent right of individual or collective self-defence if an armed attack occurs against a Member of the United Nations, until the Security Council has taken measures necessary to maintain international peace and security. Measures taken by Members in the exercise of this right of self-defence shall be immediately reported to the Security Council and shall not in any way affect the authority and responsibility of the Security Council under the present Charter to take at any time such action as it deems necessary in order to maintain or restore international peace and security.

United Nations (UN), 'Charter of the United Nations', (San Francisco, 1945). Thus, those countries defending themselves are still expected to take the matter to the UNSC. Chapter VII of the Charter provides for coercive intervention by UN member states. The UNSC may authorize military intervention under Article 42 if it decides under Article 39 that the conduct of the target state is such as to amount to a threat to the peace, a breach of the peace or an act of aggression.

11 If some government believes that the lack of definition and jurisdiction in the Rome Statute means that there is no crime of aggression, they are welcome to suggest that the UNSC refer the case to the ICJ for an advisory opinion. They should be able to get a majority without suffering a veto. Alternatively, they could accept the compulsory jurisdiction of the ICJ in any war they fought and defend their case there! If the amendments to the Rome Statute agreed at Kampala in 2010 (and now ratified by the required 30 states) are allowed to commence by the state parties after 1 January 2017, the matter will be put beyond any residual doubt.

12 General Pinochet found a routine operation almost cost him his freedom when a Spanish judge sought to have him indicted for the crimes he committed during the long period of his treasonous rule: it commenced with an act of high treason, the murder of the head of state and the forceful taking from the people of Chile the sovereignty that belonged to them. The first time the people were given a choice they rejected him. Henry Kissinger has to be more careful where he travels and Ariel Sharon now knows that Belgium should be crossed off his itineraries following the end of his term as prime minister.

13 Some might say that they have been the only successful peacekeepers in the 1990s – first in Cambodia under General Sanderson and then in East Timor under General Cosgrove. The view expressed to me is that, if the Australians stick by the rules, then others will know that if they stick to the rules, they will be left alone. But, if they break the rules, they will face a violent and highly effective response.

14 Spencer Zifcak, ed. *Globalization and The Rule of Law* (London: Routledge, 2005).

15 I see no reason why accessories before the fact should not include those who clamour for the war. To take a fictional example, Citizen Kane's newspaper campaign for the Spanish American war should, if translated to the present day, make Kane an accessory. It might also be argued that lawyers who give the politicians indefensible advice about the legality of prospective military action that allows them to 'snow' their colleagues, their parliaments and their people should also be considered accessories: but more of that later.

16 The principle of *ius in bello* applies whether or not the war is legal. The Nuremberg International Military Tribunal (IMT) declared in its 1948 Hostage trial, for example, that:

> whatever may be the cause of a war that has broken out, and whether or not the cause be a so-called just cause, the same rules of International Law are valid as to what must not be done, may be done, and must be done by the belligerents and neutral States. This is so, even if the declaration of war is ipso facto a violation of International Laws…

Cited in. W.G. Sharp Sr., 'Revoking an Aggressor's License to Kill Military Forces Serving the United Nations: Making Deterrence Personal', *Maryland Journal of International Law and Trade* 22, no. 1 (1998). However, the status of this proposition may have been qualified. It has been argued, for instance, that:

> The reason for this separation [of the principles of *ius ad bellum* and *ius in bello*] is to be found in the fact that humanitarian law of armed conflict is intended to protect individuals, primarily vulnerable and helpless individuals such as civilians, the sick, and the wounded. Such a purpose is better achieved by avoiding any considerations about how the conflict originated. Considering this principled background, it would not, however, be unreasonable to let *ius ad bellum* justifications, such as humanitarian intervention, influence, or aid in the interpretation of *ius in bello* rules, as long as the goal and objective is a better, more comprehensive protection of individual persons.

See A. Laursen, 'Nato, the War over Kosovo, and the ICTY Investigation', *American University International Law Review* 17 (2002). See also Hilary Charlesworth, 'Interview', *ABC Insiders Program*, 9 March 2003, who states that 'if you are going in under the guise of humanitarian intervention and you end up killing either immediately, or in the longer term, many, many Iraqi civilians, it immediately undercuts the legal rationale of using humanitarian intervention'. Note however, that in the context of the Kosovo conflict, the Final Report of the ICTY itself noted that 'the precise linkage between the *ius ad bellum* and the *ius in bello* is not completely resolved'. Cited in A. Schwabach, 'Nato's War in Kosovo and the Final Report to the Prosecutor of the International Criminal Tribunal for the Former Yugoslavia', *Tulane Journal of International and Comparative Law* 9 (2001).

17 ICC, 'Rome Statute of the International Criminal Court', (Rome, 1 July 2002). Art 8(2)(a)(vii)

18 Ibid. Art 8(2)(b)(iv).

19 See Chapter 8 of the Code, which reflects the provisions of the ICC Statute. In particular, see section 268.38: War crime – excessive incidental death, injury or damage:

1 A person (the perpetrator) commits an offence if:

a the perpetrator launches an attack; and
b the perpetrator knows that the attack will cause incidental death or injury to civilians; and
c the perpetrator knows that the death or injury will be of such an extent as to be excessive in relation to the concrete and direct military advantage anticipated; and
d the perpetrator's conduct takes place in the context of, and is associated with, an international armed conflict.

Penalty: Imprisonment for life.

2 A person (the perpetrator) commits an offence if:

a the perpetrator launches an attack; and
b the perpetrator knows that the attack will cause:

i damage to civilian objects; or
ii widespread, long-term and severe damage to the natural environment; and

c the perpetrator knows that the damage will be of such an extent as to be excessive in relation to the concrete and direct military advantage anticipated; and
d the perpetrator's conduct takes place in the context of, and is associated with, an international armed conflict.

Penalty for a contravention of this subsection: Imprisonment for 20 years.

20 See Art 8(2)(a)(iv), which defines as a war crime as: 'Extensive destruction and appropriation of property, not justified by military necessity and carried out unlawfully and wantonly'.

21 Examples of offences to watch for following recent conflicts include:

a Grave breaches of the Geneva Conventions of 12 August 1949, namely, any of the following acts against persons or property protected under the provisions of the relevant Geneva Convention:

- i Wilful killing;
- ii Torture or inhuman treatment, including biological experiments;
- iv Extensive destruction and appropriation of property, not justified by military necessity and carried out unlawfully and wantonly;
- vi Wilfully depriving a prisoner of war or other protected person of the rights of fair and regular trial;
- vii Unlawful deportation or transfer or unlawful confinement;

b Other serious violations of the laws and customs applicable in international armed conflict, within the established framework of international law, namely, any of the following acts:

- i Intentionally directing attacks against the civilian population as such or against individual civilians not taking direct part in hostilities;
- ii Intentionally directing attacks against civilian objects, that is, objects which are not military objectives;
- iv Intentionally launching an attack in the knowledge that such attack will cause incidental loss of life or injury to civilians or damage to civilian objects or widespread, long-term and severe damage to the natural environment which would be clearly excessive in relation to the concrete and direct overall military advantage anticipated;
- v Attacking or bombarding, by whatever means, towns, villages, dwellings or buildings which are undefended and which are not military objectives;
- xiii Destroying or seizing the enemy's property unless such destruction or seizure be imperatively demanded by the necessities of war;
- xxi Committing outrages upon personal dignity, in particular humiliating and degrading treatment.

22 Disputes about the legality of targets were rife during the Kosovo war. At the commencement of the Iraq war, the Australian government emphasized that it had different rules of engagement and made a point of stating that an Australian FA–18 pilot had decided against attacking a target that had been allocated to him.

23 The term is taken from South America – in particular, Argentina's dirty war. However, similar issues arise in Westminster countries where the military is called out in aid of the civil power.

24 John Howard, *Hansard*, House of Representatives, 6 March 2003: 12428.

25 Some I have spoken to are nervous about even suggesting what I set out here. They insist that raising the legality of wars as an issue for professional military ethics is dangerous. It is up to the government to decide when we go to war, even if it is illegal. In a democracy, the military must follow orders lest we see them usurping the role of the democratic leadership. I find this unconvincing. Once you acknowledge the need for soldiers to recognize the law independent of orders in the case of *ius in bello*, it is not clear why you should eschew it in cases of *ius ad bellum*. Indeed, in practical terms, it is much easier to require compliance with *ius ad bellum* because decisions on the latter do not have to be made in real time under fire. As immediate self-defence is clearly within international law, the wars where difficult decisions have to be made can generally be considered carefully. Even if military ethics were stretched to

refusing to take part in an illegal war, this would not get the military involved in policy. It is a matter of law. This is standard fare for other public servants. It is their duty to tell their ministers when they want to act outside the law and their duty to refuse to follow such orders. It is not clear why politicians should be able to give illegal orders in matters of war and peace but not in the issuing of dog licences.

26 Charles Sampford, 'Challenges to the Concepts of "Sovereignty" and "Intervention" (Closing Keynote)', in *World Congress on Philosophy of Law and Social Philosophy* (World Trade Centre: New York, 1999). Reprinted as: 'Challenges to the Concepts of "Sovereignty" and "Intervention"', in *Human Rights in Philosophy and Practice*, ed. T. Campbell and B.M. Leiser (Aldershot: Ashgate, 2001).

27 I argued that one of the reasons for the reluctance of the UNSC to give mandates for the use of force by a permanent member is that any abuse of that mandate is unreviewable because the permanent member could veto any clarification of the mandate by the UNSC.

28 I am not here discussing lawyers' duties to clients who have already acted and seek to defend themselves against claims that their action is criminal, beyond power, negligent or exposing them to consequences that they find uncongenial – like exposing them as liable for more tax than they would like to pay. The nature of the ethical duties is essentially the same but there are some differences that I need not discuss now. However, it is important to note that the idea of zealous advocacy is the approach taken to defend the client's interests in court rather than to advise them on how to keep out of court.

29 *Hedley Byrne v Heller* [1964] AC 465, in which the House of Lords decided that there can be liability for economic loss arising out of negligent misrepresentation, where there is a duty of care to the plaintiff.

30 It is often said that a lawyer has a duty to the client and a duty to the court (or to law and the administration of justice). While some American legal ethicists may see this as a conflict of duties, the standard view in Anglo–Australian legal ethics is that the duty to court takes priority where there is a conflict. My own view is that the duty to the client should be read as part of the lawyer's duty to court (that is, to law and the system of justice). The way that a lawyer employed by a client serves law and the system of justice is by honest and confidential advice to clients before they act and zealous advocacy of their clients' interests in litigation. Those cases that are traditionally seen as the duty to court overriding the duty to the client are, in my view, better seen as cases where the client confidentiality or the zealous advocacy do not run because they so clearly compromise law and the system of justice.

31 The professional conduct rules of the Law Society of the Australian Capital Territory is typical in requiring that 'practitioners should not, in the service of their clients, engage in, or assist, conduct that is calculated to defeat the ends of justice or is otherwise in breach of the law'.

32 At least until they are told to 'move on to their next point'.

33 The general rule of confidentiality of communications passing between lawyer and client has been qualified in Australia by the High Court in Re Bell; Ex parte Lee (1980) 146 CLR 674. In this case (where a mother had absconded with a child of the marriage, of whom the father had been awarded custody), the High Court held that the confidentiality of lawyer–client communications needs to be balanced against other public interests bearing on the administration of justice. In this case, the privilege did not apply when the communication (here, the mother's address) was made to the lawyer as part of a criminal or unlawful proceeding or made to further an illegal objective. See generally S. Ross, *Ethics in Law: Lawyers' Responsibility and Accounting in Australia* (Sydney: Butterworths, 1995): 235–236.

34 The sources of international law are described in Article 38(1) of the Statute of the International Court of Justice: this provides as follows:

'The Court, whose function is to decide in accordance with international law such disputes as are submitted to it, shall apply:

- a international conventions, whether general or particular, establishing rules expressly recognized by the contesting states;
- b international custom as evidence of a general practice accepted as law;
- c the general principles of law recognized by civilized nations;
- d subject to the provisions of Article 59, judicial decisions and the teachings of the most highly qualified publicists of the various nations, as subsidiary means for the determination of rules of law'.

35 Such conduct certainly appears to be inconsistent with (for example) the Model Rules of Professional Conduct and Practice of the Law Council of Australia, which requires honesty to clients and the court as well as competence, and imposes a duty not to engage in conduct that is calculated to defeat the ends of justice.

36 In any case, the argument about confidentiality is a complex one that is not resolved as automatically as it might be assumed. If the client wants confidential advice, this can be kept confidential. If the client wants to publish the advice, they should not do so in a misleading way – especially to those to whom they are accountable (CEO to directors, directors to shareholders, politicians to parliament and to the electorate).

37 This has occurred in Australia. A group of 43 international legal experts warned the Australian government of the illegality of a pre-emptive strike against Iraq, and, in any case, the limits placed by international humanitarian law on any strike even if it can be justified. See letter to *The Sydney Morning Herald,* 26 February 2003. Similar points were made by George Williams in an address to the National Press Club on 31 January 2003. Legal critics have also raised similar issues elsewhere. See, for example, the letter by James Crawford and others to the *Guardian,* 7 March 2003; and the letter by Simon Chesterman and Michael Fullilove to the *International Herald Tribune,* 5 March 2003, which warned Australia against playing 'fast and loose' with international law.

38 In the colloquial rather than classical meaning of the term.

39 A Joint House Parliamentary Committee which tables a report with recommendations to the government on the desirability of becoming a party to the treaty in question.

40 Art 54 of the Vienna Convention on the Law of Treaties (which entered into force in 1980) provides that: The termination of a treaty or the withdrawal of a party may take place:

- a in conformity with the provisions of the treaty; or
- b at any time by consent of all the parties after consultation with the other contracting States. Art 56 provides that:

1 A treaty which contains no provision regarding its termination and which does not provide for denunciation or withdrawal is not subject to denunciation or withdrawal unless:

- a it is established that the parties intended to admit the possibility of denunciation or withdrawal; or
- b a right of denunciation or withdrawal may be implied by the nature of the treaty.

2 A party shall give not less than twelve months' notice of its intention to denounce or withdraw from a treaty under paragraph 1.

While the ANZUS Treaty contains provision for withdrawal from the Council of Foreign Ministers established under the treaty, it has no specific provision allowing for withdrawal or denunciation. Article X of the ANZUS Treaty provides that:

> This Treaty shall remain in force indefinitely. Any Party may cease to be a member of the Council established by Article VII one year after notice has been

> given to the Government of Australia, which will inform the Governments of the other Parties of the deposit of such notice.

Contrast article 13 of the North Atlantic Treaty, which provides that:

> After the Treaty has been in force for twenty years, any Party may cease to be a Party one year after its notice of denunciation has been given to the Government of the United States of America, which will inform the Governments of the other Parties of the deposit of each notice of denunciation.

41 Where there is sensitive intelligence information on which the decision to go to war is based, the PM should brief the leader of the opposition. He must trust him with the information. It is not open to the PM to decide that the leader of the opposition cannot be trusted with it. The system is designed so that he may be the leader of the government. Accordingly, the PM and senior officials are estopped from denying that he can be trusted with it. It goes without saying that the leader of the opposition must keep that trust.

42 See, for example, Charles Sampford and Margaret Palmer, 'The Theory of Collective Response', *US Council on Foreign Relations* (1999), www.cfr.org/pdf/Dem_TF_International.pdf.

43 For the Australian position, see 'A Guide on Key Elements of Ministerial Responsibility', which provides that 'Ministers must be honest in their public dealings and should not intentionally mislead the Parliament or the public. Any misconception caused inadvertently should be corrected at the earliest opportunity': 10.

44 Rule 144 of the *Standing and Sessional orders of the House of Representatives* states that Questions should not ask Ministers:

- a for an expression of opinion;
- b to announce the Government's policy, but may seek an explanation regarding the policy of the Government and its application and may ask the Prime Minister whether a Minister's statement in the House represents government policy; or
- c for legal opinion.

45 The Australian Attorney General did not originally table any legal opinion upon which the government relied to assert that military action against Iraq does not have to be approved by the Security Council. In response to a question from the opposition as to whether the attorney could provide the house with a formal assurance that any decision taken by the government to deploy Australian military forces in a combat role in Iraq will be in full conformity with international law in the absence of a second Security Council resolution, the AG merely stated that the prime minister 'has already given the assurance publicly that no further resolution is required'. He then dismissed the published view of 43 international lawyers as 'political in nature (and using) exaggeration and selective quoting of the law to achieve conclusions that are both wrong and offensive' (Hansard, 6 March 2003: 1250). The government tabled its advice in mid-March. The advice was not signed by the Attorney General or the solicitor-general but by two senior government lawyers. It was criticized by a number of international lawyers, including Charlesworth, who accused the government's lawyers of selectively using phrases from UN resolutions to support their case. See Cynthia Banham, 'Experts at odds as PM releases legal advice', *The Sydney Morning Herald*, 19 March 2003.

46 See White and Wintour, 'No Case for Attack Say Lawyers', the *Guardian*, 7 March 2003.

> Some senior ministers have been alarmed that legal opinions circulated within the cabinet challenge the legality of the looming scenario for war, not least the prospect of a US-led reconstruction of a post-Saddam Iraq. It would be illegal, Whitehall lawyers say, without direct UN authority.

47 Sampford, 'Challenges to the Concepts of "Sovereignty" and "Intervention"'. See above n. 25.

15 More and more lawyers but still no judges

Charles Sampford

As we saw in the previous chapter, at the time of the Kosovo war, I argued that before a democracy went to war, the Attorney General (or equivalent official) should declare in parliament that, in his independent judgment, the war was legal *and* that the government be prepared to defend that view in the ICJ.

In the Kosovo war,[1] neither occurred, although there were some statements by Robin Cook and others that the war was legal. One of the most pressing issues raised therein was whether the inability to have the legality of a war tested in a court of competent jurisdiction might provide a temptation for governments to seek, and some lawyers to give, convenient but untenable advice.

In the Iraq war, the British and Australian governments did provide parliament with legal advice (though not, of course, in response to any of my musings). This chapter discusses some parallels and contrasts between the legal roads to war and suggest that the case is stronger than ever for adjudication of the matter before an independent tribunal where the competing views can be tested.

The published opinions

The British Attorney General, Lord Goldsmith, tabled a 365-word argument that the war was legal on 17 March 2003. The Australian Prime Minister told parliament on 6 March 2003 that there was ample authority to go to war,[2] and on 18 March tabled a 2,000-word memorandum by two government lawyers dated 12 March.[3] The Australian Attorney Solicitor General and the next most senior government lawyer, Henry Burmester AO QC, provided no opinions. As in the Kosovo war, Britain had its 'first lawyers' and 'new lawyers'. In Australia, much less is publicly known and I only have a single verbal report about the existence of earlier 'highly equivocal' advice of the kind freely flowing in England. The only basis we have for suspecting that there was such advice is the statistical one that so few international lawyers, senior or otherwise, agreed with the views expressed in the tabled memorandum. In Britain, debate raged about whether Lord Goldsmith held more equivocal views and had expressed them in an opinion dated 7 March 2003 (published in April 2005)[4] and whether he agreed with legal advice to Cabinet dated 8 March 2002 (published in August 2004).[5]

Potential litigants (and judges)

However, the debate about Lord Goldsmith's views and whether and why he changed them to be both a 'first lawyer' and a 'new lawyer' distracts us from the fact that the legality of an action is not determined by the legal counsel employed by the initiator of the action. It is determined by a court of competent jurisdiction. While there was considerable debate about the war's legality, very few international lawyers said it was legal at the time and, to my knowledge, no lawyers who backed the war have ever argued that their views would be backed up by a court competent to hear such matters (the most obvious being the International Court of Justice). Neither Goldsmith's answer of 17 March[6] nor the Australian memorandum of 18 March make such a claim. The Goldsmith omission is all the more remarkable because his, then unpublished, advice of 7 March 2003[7] had, most appropriately, addressed a variety of ways in which the matter might be litigated and the difficulties of mounting a successful defence. The most he could do was to say that he accepted that: 'a reasonable case can be made that resolution 1441 is capable of revising the authorization in 678 without a further resolution'. However, even this weak 'acceptance' of a 'reasonable case' was immediately followed by the caveat that the argument would 'only be sustainable' with 'hard evidence of non-compliance and non-cooperation', indicating that the views of the UN inspectors would be highly significant and pointing to the recent reports of those inspectors. He correctly emphasized that a 'reasonable case' did not mean he was confident that the court would agree with what he called 'this view' (rather than his view). Some might think it ominous that he dwelt on the chance of avoiding a hearing rather than the chance of winning the case if it was heard. The case could come before the ICJ via a reference from the General Assembly (which the UK could not veto) or by the suit of another country that had accepted the compulsory jurisdiction of the ICJ (although he doubted the basis on which this could be done, any NATO country could do so because of Article 1 of the North Atlantic Treaty). He also mentioned the possibility of prosecutions for murder and the crime of aggression, which he did not doubt was part of the domestic law of the United Kingdom. Even if Goldsmith changed his mind between 7 and 17 March, it is hard to see that a dispassionate assessment of the chance of winning in court could have changed.

Lord Goldsmith was correct on one matter – that Iraq could not bring a case before the ICJ. Serbia had tried in 1999 but had failed on procedural grounds. Although the Iraqis approached at least one London-based international lawyer to mount a case, they were in a worse position than Serbia in 1999. The ICJ can only hear cases where both parties accept jurisdiction – either for the purposes of that dispute or because they have accepted the 'compulsory jurisdiction' of the court. The United States no longer accepts the compulsory jurisdiction of the ICJ and Britain accepts it only where the other litigant has accepted that jurisdiction for at least a year. By March 2003, when the war began, Australia had adopted the same position on compulsory jurisdiction as the United Kingdom. However, on 8 March 2002, when the British cabinet received legal advice that the contemplated war would be illegal, there was no such impediment. Since 1975, Australia had been one of those countries that accepted the compulsory jurisdiction of the ICJ against all comers, on the basis that it would have nothing to fear from accepting law suits from all comers (and something to gain as it could, thereby, counter-sue the other party for breaches of international law – including human rights). However, in a move that must now raise eyebrows, Australia altered its acceptance of the compulsory jurisdiction of the ICJ on 22 March 2002, just two weeks after the 8 March advice. Eyebrows were not raised at the time for three reasons. First, the Iraq war was then seen as a mere possibility raised in the 'State of the Union' address two months earlier, in which Bush referred to Iran, Iraq and North Korea as an 'axis of evil'. Second, the clear views of the British lawyers about the legality of the war and the likelihood of a loss in an international court were not then known. Third, Australia's introduction of a time-bar in its acceptance of compulsory jurisdiction was accompanied by another change – the exclusion of seabed disputes. This was what grabbed attention, as there was already a dispute with East Timor over seabed rights to oil and gas.

This is most unfortunate. The legality of an action is not determined by the legal counsel employed by the initiator of the action. It is determined by a court of competent jurisdiction. The inability of such a court to hear the case does not make the action legal – although it may create temptations for politicians to seek, and for some lawyers to give, advice that is wrong, misleading or otherwise inadequate. In international law, the opposite may be the case. The longstanding limitations of international tribunals have been one of the factors that have given greater weight to academic opinion – raising it to a source of law. Where the vast majority of international law professors (and an even larger majority of the senior ones) endorse a legal proposition and are not contradicted by a superior source of law, we can say that international law includes that proposition. It may be that the only way that it can be displaced by the minority who differ is if the matter is taken to an international court of competent jurisdiction. Given this, one may wonder why the minority of international lawyers who claim that the war was legal have not urged their governments to seek vindication in the ICJ by a United Nations Security Council reference or through the request to a friendly country in a position to get the matter before the court. The majority of lawyers are not always right. Law develops when the majority view is challenged – but only when it is challenged, and challenged successfully.

Although I think that the majority of international lawyers are probably correct on Iraq, I would be happy to be proven wrong for two reasons. First, I support the Australian prime minister's stated view to parliament that Australia should never go to war contrary to international law. The only point of disagreement is that, theoretically at least, there could be circumstances where war contrary to international law might be justified, not least because no one should surrender their conscience to the law.[8] Second, I have argued that international law should evolve to encourage stronger actions to protect peoples against their oppressors through a process of treaty-making and judicial decisions.[9] The Treaty of Westphalia was, in some important ways, a tyrant's charter. International law needs to develop to recognize the primacy of peoples over sovereigns in the same direction as the domestic law of most nation states has progressed over the last three centuries. But it can and should be developed rather than ignored. I understand the argument that sometimes laws must be broken through civil disobedience and even revolution, and that much of the domestic progress has been made by such means. The powerless must sometimes resort to such means but in the hands of the powerful they take on a more sinister connotation. However, such arguments are irrelevant because neither UK nor Australia said they were breaking the law and both insist that they were acting lawfully.

A common flaw

Both the Australian and UK opinions rely on an argument that the right to use force included in Resolution 678 (1990) either continues or is revived. It is common ground that the only authorization for the use of force is found in Resolution 678 paragraph 2:

> Authorizes Member States co-operating with the Government of Kuwait, unless Iraq on or before 15 January 1991 fully implements, as set forth in paragraph 1 above, the foregoing resolutions, to use all necessary means to uphold and implement resolution 660 (1990) and all subsequent relevant resolutions and to restore international peace and security in the area.[10]

Resolution 687[11] sets out the ceasefire conditions, including the obligations to destroy a wide range of nominated weapons. Subsequent resolutions clearly state that Iraq has failed to meet its obligations under resolution 687 and has breached the ceasefire terms contained in that resolution.

Those arguing for the legality of the war claim that resolution 678 is continuing and can be reactivated by any breach of resolution 687 or subsequent resolutions. Lord Goldsmith's 7 March opinion indicates that this view was supported by few academics and only one state, the United States. This would imply that not only the British lawyers disagreed but that the Australians did as well – raising questions about whether a different view had been expressed by Australian government lawyers from that which was later published.

There are many arguments to be made against the cryptic justifications put on 17 and 18 March. However, the opinions of 17 and 18 March share a common flaw. If you are going to rely on resolutions for your justification, you have to look at all relevant resolutions. Although citing Resolutions 678 and 687, they fail to cite the intervening Iraq resolution. Resolution 686 was the first ceasefire resolution put in place when the fighting stopped and before the details of 687 could be determined.

Resolution 686 'notes the suspension of combat operations', affirms the previous 12 resolutions on Iraq, demands Iraq comply with them and highlights the most important actions required. The Resolution:

> 2 Demands that Iraq implement its acceptance of all twelve resolutions noted above and in particular that Iraq:
>
> a Rescind immediately its actions purporting to annex Kuwait;
> b Accept in principle its liability for any loss, damage, or injury arising in regard to Kuwait ... as a result of the invasion and illegal occupation...;
> c ...release all ... Kuwaiti and third-state nationals detained by Iraq...;
> d Immediately begin to return all Kuwaiti property seized by Iraq, the return to be completed in the shortest possible period;

It also sets out some specific measures to do with implementing the ceasefire and making it effective:

> 3 Further demands that Iraq:
>
> a Cease hostile or provocative actions by its forces...;
> b Designate military commanders to ... arrange for the military aspects of a cessation of hostilities at the earliest possible time;
> c Arrange for immediate access to and release of all prisoners of war...; and
> d Provide all information and assistance in identifying Iraqi mines, booby traps and other explosives ... in areas of Iraq where forces of Member States cooperating with Kuwait pursuant to resolution 678 (1990) are present temporarily, and in adjacent waters.[12]

It is then that Resolution 686 seems to offer a critical clue in interpreting Resolutions 678 and 687. Paragraph 4 of 686 states that the UNSC:

> Recognizes that during the period required for Iraq to comply with paragraphs 2 and 3 above, the provisions of paragraph 2 of resolution 678 (1990) remain valid.

This would seem to clearly contemplate that the validity of the authorization for force is limited and was about to end in early 1991 – once Iraq had complied with the obligations contained in those two paragraphs. As resolution 686 was passed just before 687 and only a few months after 678, it would presumably be particularly important in interpreting the other two resolutions.

Like many legal arguments, it could work both ways. If Iraq had still been in breach of one of those first 12 resolutions, and in particular if it were in breach of paragraphs 2 and 3 of resolution 686, it could provide an exceptionally powerful justification for the revival of the right to use force under resolution

678. No such argument has been made and it would seem difficult to make one. Although the list of obligations is relatively long, it would be difficult to argue that Iraq was in breach of any of those conditions 10 years later. Certainly, I could find no UNSC resolution over the last decade claiming a breach of those first 12 resolutions or the provisions of paragraph 3. All the arguments have been about breaches of resolution 687.

Resolution 686 recognizes that the right to use force remains valid until certain conditions have been met. Those conditions have been met. Many judges might conclude that it is logical to conclude that the right to use force is no longer valid.

It is also totally inconsistent with statements made by the Australian government lawyers:

> 16 Operative paragraph 2 of SCR 678 set out above itself contains no limitations in terms of time.... There is no finite time under the Charter in which the authority given in a Security Council resolution expires. Nor is there *any indication in resolutions subsequent to SCR 678 that the authority for the use of force contained in that resolution has expired.* Indeed, subsequent resolutions indicate to the contrary.[13] [emphasis added]

SCR 686 is one of the clearest possible indications to the contrary and one has to wonder how anyone reading 686 could confidently make such a statement.

What should be done?

A number of intriguing questions remain and much that can usefully be done.

Questions for government

1 Did the British government pass on the 8 March 2002 advice to Australia? If so, who received it and to whom was it passed on? If not, did Australia have similar advice prior to the variation of its acceptance of ICJ compulsory jurisdiction?
2 Was other advice provided to the relevant decision-makers?
3 Why did the governments choose advice and/or advisors whose views were so clearly in the minority?

Questions for lawyers who claimed the war was legal at the time

1 Had they believed and/or claimed, at the time, that their views would be endorsed by a court of competent jurisdiction?
2 If not, then on what basis had they made the claim that it was legal and in what sense did they use the term?

3. Had they read resolutions 678, 686, 687 and 1441 at the time they made their public statements on the war's legality?
4. If they were unaware of resolution 686, the first ceasefire resolution, at the time, do they consider that their research was adequate to make a public statement as a lawyer?
5. If they no longer think that it is legal, are they prepared to state so as publicly as they had previously asserted that it was legal?
6. If they think that it was legal, will they join me in urging the British and Australian governments to seek vindication in a court of competent jurisdiction or before a genuinely independent Royal Commission?

Recommended actions for concerned lawyers

1. Challenge the governments of the UK and Australia to do one of three things:

   a. withdraw their statements that the war was legal;
   b. defend their view before the ICJ through seeking a General Assembly resolution or requesting a NATO ally to bring the case to the ICJ; or
   c. agree to an international arbitration established in the usual way, with them nominating an arbitrator, those who believe the war to be illegal nominating another arbitrator and the two of them choosing a chairman of the arbitration.

2. If they refuse to do the above, then an NGO should establish a separate commission established as in 1c.
3. Refer any advice that appears substandard to professional tribunals.
4. Encourage the professional bodies of the United Kingdom and Australia to establish panels to advise on changes to the relevant ethical codes to provide very clear guidance to lawyers advising governments professionally or publicly on issues of the legality of wars.

Is all of this made irrelevant because of the re-election of the Blair and Howard governments? Did the voters choose them despite invading Iraq without lawful sanction? There are three clear responses. First, there are many issues in any election and Iraq was not the only one. Neither Blair nor Howard emphasized Iraq (though they both asked to be trusted to deliver lower interest rates on home mortgages). Second, neither electorates nor the legislatures they elect are courts of law. Finally, they are estopped from saying that they were elected despite having acted illegally because they asserted at the time, and since, that they were acting legally.

Let them test their case before an independent tribunal. If there was 'ample authority', then they have nothing to fear. They and the lawyers who claimed that the war was legal should be pleased to be vindicated. The case would set an important precedent and the ICJ may help develop international law on the circumstances under which intervention against tyrants oppressing their people is legally justifiable.

Notes

1 See, for example, House of Commons, 'Debate on Kosovo', *Hansard* (23 March 1999), www.publications.parliament.uk/pa/cm199899/cmhansrd/vo990323/debtext/90323–06.htm.
2 See Hansard (House of Representatives), Thursday 6 March 2003: 12428.
3 Campbell and Moraitis, *Memorandum of Advice to the Commonwealth Government on the Use of Force against Iraq*, Prepared by the Commonwealth Attorney-General's Department and the Department of Foreign Affairs and Trade on 12 March 2003. (Published as: Bill Campbell and Chris Moraitis, 'Memorandum of Advice to the Commonwealth Government on the Use of Force against Iraq', *Melbourne Journal of International Law* 4, no. 1 (2003).) Prepared by the Commonwealth Attorney-General's Department and the Department of Foreign Affairs and Trade on 12 March 2003. Tabled by the Prime Minister in the House of Representatives, Parliament of Australia: Commonwealth, Votes and Proceedings of the House of Representatives, 18 March 2003: 788 (John Howard, Prime Minister); and by the Leader of the Government in the Senate, Parliament of Australia: Commonwealth, Journals of the Senate, 18 March 2003: 1577 (Senator Robert Hill, Leader of the Government in the Senate and Minister for Defence).
4 See, 'The Full Text of the Advice About the Legality of War with Iraq Given by the Attorney General, Lord Goldsmith, to the Prime Minister, Tony Blair, on March 7 2003: Iraq: Resolution 1441', *Guardian (UK),* 29 April 2005, www.theguardian.com/politics/2005/apr/28/election2005.uk.
5 See, The Iraq Inquiry, 'Declassified Documents', (2015).
6 'Full Text: Written Answer on Iraq Advice in Response to a Question Asking Attorney General Lord Goldsmith His View of the Legal Basis for the Iraq War, Posed by Baroness Ramsay of Cartvale on 17 March 2003', *BBC News*, 28 April 2005.
7 'The Full Text of the Advice About the Legality of War with Iraq Given by the Attorney General, Lord Goldsmith, to the Prime Minister, Tony Blair, on March 7 2003: Iraq: Resolution 1441'.
8 See Chapter 14.
9 See Chapter 14.
10 United Nations, 'Resolution 678 Adopted by the Security Council at Its 2963rd Meeting', (S/RES/0678, 29 November 1990).
11 'Resolution 687 Adopted by the Security Council at Its 2981th Meeting', (S/RES/0687, 8 April 1991).
12 'Resolution 686 Adopted by the Security Council at Its 2978th Meeting', (S/RES/0686, 2 March 1991).
13 See, Campbell and Moraitis, 'Memorandum of Advice to the Commonwealth Government on the Use of Force against Iraq': 181.

16 Goldsmith's delinquent client

Charles Sampford

This chapter is the third in a trilogy on the role of lawyers in giving prior advice on the legality of wars being contemplated by sovereign states – stimulated by the Kosovo and Iraq wars in 1999 and 2003. It considers the ethical issues confronting Lord Goldsmith in advising the government of which he was a part on the legality of the latter. His long advice provided on 7 March 2003,[1] was by far the best advice by a senior government lawyer that has so far come to light, canvassing both sides, pointing out that only the Americans took the view that the invasion would be legal and addressing some of the ways in which the matter might come to court.[2] What should a lawyer in his position do – as a lawyer, as a member of the government, as the first law officer of the crown (and to what extent do these multiple roles either produce different answers or modify the answers provided in each)? This chapter argues that the answers to these questions can be most helpfully framed by the arguments about how lawyers should deal with 'delinquent clients' who tell their lawyers, in advance, that they intend to engage in activity that the lawyer considers to be a crime, fraud or tort – especially those acts which are likely to lead to serious harm to another. Examples discussed in the case law and literature range from where clients plan to commit fraud by submitting a claim to which they were not entitled, taking a child out of the jurisdiction following a custody visit, committing perjury, planning to sell a stolen car to pay for a lawyer's fee, to murdering a spouse's boyfriend.[3] In this discussion, I will refer to other wars and other countries and build on other work about the legality under domestic and international law.[4] I will also canvas the question of how we might improve our procedures for going to war. But I should begin with the impetus for the first of these three essays.

1 Meeting a 'first lawyer'

Like a number of other essays in this volume, the central ideas arose from an interaction with a practicing lawyer. As I indicated in Chapter 1, that lawyer was a young JAG officer (a Lt Colonel) who spoke at a conference organized by my research centre. After giving the official UK line, he was apparently affected by the derisive laughter it generated. He approached me and said that he had been tasked with developing the advice on the legality of the bombing campaign. He said that he had done his job as a lawyer to find a legal justification but he came to the conclusion that it would be unlawful and, as a good lawyer, that is what he told his client who then sought other advice. For some time, I was concerned that he had committed a very serious breach of legal professional privilege until James Rubin's account of his 'very personal war' put the existence of the first lawyers in the public domain.[5]

The first two essays in this trilogy dealt with more general issues without making clear recommendations or discussing what the first lawyers should do. I was much troubled by the idea that this knowledge should be permanently entombed in the privilege of the first lawyer–client relationship just because the client had sought a second lawyer who was less fastidious about the client's intended criminality (at least according to the majority of lawyers).

After much consideration, I have come to a clear and simple answer that not only absolves the Lt Colonel but paints a path to what ethical lawyers can and should do both individually and, most importantly, collectively. That solution starts, with all the respect I can muster for those who started the Kosovo and Iraq wars, with the recognition that they were delinquent clients. The 'delinquency' of the client raises a number of issues, which would justify 'first lawyers' and 'second lawyers' to not only do what my 'first lawyer' did but go much further – and for state, national and international bar associations to provide clear guidance to other lawyers in such situations.

Delinquency-related issues include:

1 The crime-tort-fraud exemption to confidentiality and privilege;
2 Misprision of a felony;
3 Lawyers' complicity in the crime;
4 Waiver of privilege;
5 'In-house' lawyers and privilege;
6 More general duties to the court, the rule of law and the administration of justice;
7 Perjury and lying to parliament;
8 Duties to other parties;
9 Who is the client – is it the delinquent office-holder or the otherwise innocent institution in which the delinquent holds office.

2 The crime-tort-fraud exemption to client confidentiality and legal professional privilege

Ethical rules in the US and Commonwealth generally involve strict rules covering client confidentiality and legal professional privilege to allow clients to speak freely with their lawyers and for lawyers to give confidential advice on the law and on tactics that can be pursued in current or potential litigation and pursue their clients' ends in an adversarial system of justice. As discussed in Chapter 14, there are limitations on confidentiality and privilege. One set of limitations relates to where the lawyer comes to know that the client had engaged in wrongdoing that is the subject of litigation – whether through admission or otherwise. The lawyer is not permitted to disclose that admission and cannot decline to represent the client without the client's permission. However, the lawyer cannot ignore it and cannot make representations in court inconsistent with it. The lawyer can require the crown/state to prove its case but cannot mount a defence, or cross-examine witnesses, on the basis that conflicts with the admission. However, in some cases positive action can be required. The US Rules of Professional Conduct require not only that a lawyer must not knowingly 'offer evidence that the lawyer knows to be false' but,

> if a lawyer, the lawyer's client or a witness called by the lawyer offered material evidence and the lawyer knows or comes to know of its falsity, the lawyer shall take reasonable remedial measures, including, if necessary, disclosure to the tribunal.[6]

In these cases, the lawyer's duty to the court, the law, and/or the administration of justice overrides any duty to the client. Or, as I would put it, the duty to the court includes the vigorous pursuit of the client's interests through the law and the system of justice, but not contrary to the law and system of justice.

However, the limitations on confidentiality and legal professional privilege are more significant when the client expresses an intention to commit a crime-fraud-tort in the future. As indicated in Chapter 14, the High Court held that the confidentiality of lawyer–client communications did not apply when the communication was made to the lawyer as part of a criminal or unlawful proceeding or made to further an illegal objective (in this case where a mother took a child from the father who had been awarded custody).[7] The US Code provides that

> a lawyer may reveal information relating to the representation of a client to the extent the lawyer reasonably believes necessary:
>
> 1 To disclose the intention of the lawyer's client to commit a crime and the information necessary to prevent the crime;
> 2 To prevent reasonably certain death or substantial bodily harm.

An example is provided by *Shorter v. State*[8] where a client called his divorce lawyer and said he planned to kill his wife's boyfriend. The lawyer immediately called the police but the client killed the boyfriend before the police could get to him. The lawyer was not only allowed to report the client's statements but the lawyer's report of the conversation was admissible at the defendant's trial. Broadbent argues that the prosecution could compel a defence lawyer to testify to a client's statement about a future crime.[9]

In most jurisdictions, where a lawyer cannot represent a client in matters where the lawyer could become a witness, this would mean the lawyer would have to cease to act for the client. However, that cessation does not end the remaining duties of confidentiality. It might be argued,

> that a solicitor who is informed by a client of the client's intention to perform an illegal act should be discharged from any continuing contractual duty to maintain the client's confidence if the solicitor's silence would enable the illegal purpose to be accomplished.[10]

Shirvington regrets how common it is for the NSW Ethics Section to be asked about 'the appropriateness of the solicitor reporting the possible crime ... notwithstanding the obvious detriment the disclosure of the making of the threat will have on the client'.[11] She recognizes that it may be in the client's interests to do so because it prevents the client from doing something that will have severe consequences not only for another party but also for the client.

While there seem to be clear cases for the waiver of confidentiality in cases of future wrongdoing, there are likely to be areas of uncertainty and room for judgement. In most jurisdictions, the ethics rules *permit* disclosure; they do not *require* it (compulsion may come from the state but not the Bar). Disclosure is only allowed 'to the extent the lawyer reasonably believes necessary' to accomplish the purpose of the exceptions, that is, to prevent the crime or harm. This will limit both what is disclosed and those to whom it is disclosed. And, there is also the question of how certain the lawyer is of the client's intent to commit the crime – mere suspicion is not enough.[12] To this should be added the question of whether the lawyer believes that the client is likely and capable of carrying out that intent – and whether he will heed the solicitor's advice not to do it. Caution will point the solicitor in two directions – not wanting to blow the whistle on their clients too readily but not wanting to take the risk that the client commits a serious crime that the solicitor knew about and could have stopped. The Massachusetts Legal Ethics Committee recommended reporting where it was reasonably likely that the crime would be committed, saying that the standard should not be so high that the important goal of preventing serious harm to third persons will be defeated, but also not be so low that the mere possibility of a crime triggers its application.[13]

Millar argues that rules should be discretionary, leaving it to the lawyer to balance the various factors.[14] However, there is also merit in clarity for lawyer and client alike. It is easier for the lawyer to tell the client that he has to report it and clients are less likely to feel let down by their lawyer who chose to report them. At the very least, ethics rules should seek to provide guidance and examples. And, they should address the application of the ethics rules to international law advice.

I am mindful that one of the reasons for privilege is so that clients can seek advice about the lawfulness of the conduct they are considering. Nicolson and Webb query whether 'confidentiality leads to more clients eschewing illegal or immoral acts'.[15] For me, the key question is what happens next. If a client asks, the lawyer advises it is illegal and the client decides to eschew, then privilege has served its purpose very well. If he knows that it is his lawyer's duty to report him if he does not eschew, even stronger incentives apply.

Application to war advice

In some ways this is straightforward. The criminality is of a very different order of magnitude. Its consequences in terms of loss of life, horrendous injuries and suffering dwarf the worst mass murders, including those committed by terrorists. Aggression, once the sovereign right of every king, has been outlawed since 1928 and forswearing it has become a pre-condition of statehood. It was first tried in Nuremberg where the chief prosecutor emphasized that it bound us all:

> Let me make clear that while this law is first applied against German aggressors, the law includes, and if it is to serve a useful purpose it must condemn aggression by any other nations, including those which sit here now in judgment.
>
> (Robert Jackson, Chief US Prosecutor, Opening Address at Nuremberg)[16]

Goldsmith suggested that it had been incorporated into British law and could lead to charges of murder (a point he kept to himself rather than referring to the police when his colleagues embarked on the invasion).

The difficulties of enforcing the law do not mean that it is not a crime. They merely emphasize the importance of more effort to enforce it. If a lawyer will report on prospective parental kidnappings and even small frauds, aggression should surely warrant the most extreme action by lawyers collectively or individually. The only way to suggest otherwise is to appeal to something that is very different about international law or the client.

What is different about international law?

It is now rare to claim that international law is not 'law',[17] though some treat it as a lesser form of law or a kind of law that can be ignored because some nations ignore it. To the extent that it is not law, then advice concerning it is not legal advice and is not subject to the protections that surround it.

The biggest differences are the means by which law is made (states are generally only bound by the laws to which they have signed up, compared to citizens in strong democracies, who are bound by the decisions of a majority of voters, and those in dictatorships or oligarchies who are bound by laws in which they have no say at all) and the limited and inconsistent means of enforcing it. The first gives international law a great deal of legitimacy which is one of the reasons why international law is, while limited in coverage, generally effective despite the difficulties of enforcement. As to the latter, the difficulties of enforcement may be a reason for acting *more* quickly and decisively (in the example above, before the child was taken out of the jurisdiction).

It might once have been said that international law is not as important as domestic law, so that the rule of law does not apply to it. However, this has been rejected by Lord Goldsmith and Lord Morris (his predecessor who was AG during Kosovo). They agree that the AG is the guardian of the rule of law, which involves compliance with the law: 'that means domestic and international obligations'.[18] The question inevitably arises of 'who guards the guardians'. I would prefer the Bar Council to perform this task as a professional body – rather than a political body like the House of Commons/Representatives or one of its committees. Since then, the UN General Assembly in the Global Summit have agreed on the equal importance of the rule of law in domestic and international affairs.[19]

One potential difference is that the confidentiality is not about the facts but about the law. In the custody case, the law is clear but the intention to take the child out of the jurisdiction is secret. In Iraq, the intention to invade was clear and the debates were about the legality. I am not inclined to put too much weight on this distinction. For the parent to succeed, they must keep the authorities uninformed about what they are going to do. For Blair to succeed, he had to keep authorities (including his cabinet colleagues and chiefs of staff) in the dark about the legalities. The production of this advice involves misleading those authorities and entails a more active engagement by the lawyer (which raises other questions about misleading third parties, elements of the client and participation in the crime discussed below).

What is different about the client?

Some lawyers may not like ascribing the word 'delinquent' to their client – especially if the client employs them, their employer is the sovereign state and the person who is seeking their advice is the democratically elected head of government in a long-standing democracy. It may seem disrespectful. In response, I would say that 'delinquent' (or 'rogue') are euphemisms when we are looking at a war of aggression that could kill hundreds of thousands. Lawyers should recover from their surprise that they have criminals for their clients and act accordingly, lest they cease to act as lawyers should and begin to resemble their clients. Prime ministers are entrusted with more power than any other official. The greater the power, the greater the potential abuses and the greater the consequences of such abuse. This is the reason why we need greater integrity measures for governments than for other institutions – and attorneys general should recognize that they have a critical role in those integrity measures.

3 'Misprision of a felony' and other duties to report crime

In many jurisdictions, there is a legal obligation to report a crime that has been committed. The common law misdemeanour of 'misprision of a felony' was committed when someone knew that a felony had been committed, and failed to disclose that knowledge to those responsible for the preservation of the peace within a reasonable time, having had a reasonable opportunity to do so. This has been replaced in many jurisdictions by particular responsibilities for some to report crime (including senior civil servants with respect to corruption or professionals who become aware of child abuse). There is often a general statutory offence that replaces the misprision. One example is provided by s316 of the *Crimes Act 1900* (NSW).[20]

> (1) If a person has committed a serious offence and another person who knows or believes that the offence [defined as one that is punishable by imprisonment of five years or more] has been committed and that he or she has information which might be of material assistance in securing the apprehension of the offender or the prosecution or conviction of the offender for it fails without reasonable excuse to bring that information to the attention of a member of the Police Force or other appropriate authority, that other person is liable to imprisonment for 2 years.

However, under 316 (4) and regulations passed under 316 (5), professionals who learn of the offence in their professional capacity can only be prosecuted with the approval of the Attorney General. Lawyers are included, along with doctors, nurses, psychologists, social workers, clergy and academic/professional researchers.

The duties of confidentiality might seem a 'reasonable excuse'. However, the issue is complicated by the fact that the relevant ethics rules make two exceptions to confidentiality where:

1 The practitioner is permitted or compelled by law to disclose.
2 The practitioner discloses information in circumstances in which the law would probably compel its disclosure, despite a client's claim of legal professional privilege, and for the sole purpose of avoiding the probable commission or concealment of a felony.

Accordingly, the ethics rule and the act both provide that the other can be an exception to its own rule.

In a real case, the NSW Law Society Ethics Unit was asked by three lawyers who, after seeking the advice of two QCs considered the lawyer's duty of confidentiality a 'reasonable excuse', at least when it came to past crimes.[21]

Application to war advice

In his long advice of 7 March 2003, Goldsmith raises the question of whether the crime of aggression is part of UK law and that it might, in any case, be murder (he did not consider the possibilities that this might also be seen as terrorism – see section 9 below). This proves that he was aware of the possibility that potential felonies under UK law were being planned and, afterwards, committed. Of course, he changed his mind. But it is not clear that that would help him. Suppose a client is convicted of a felony and the lawyer is then charged with misprision. Suppose the lawyer had formally agreed with the position of more or less all of his colleagues (later confirmed by the judge) but switched to an extreme minority view after it was clear that the client and his co-conspirators were determined to go ahead and one of the co-conspirators had a lawyer in that extreme minority. I am not sure that this would count as a defence to misprision.

While I think that this issue needs careful consideration, I would tend to the view that such lawyers should have a duty to report under the preceding section or possibly be treated as having complicity under the next.

4 Lawyers' complicity in the crime

Depending on the text of the relevant offences, lawyers can become principals in offences committed by their clients, co-conspirators in conspiracies to commit a crime, or guilty of other related crimes.

We are used to concerns about 'mob lawyers' who allegedly know their client's business (as a good lawyer should in giving the 'whole of business' or 'ethical advice' discussed in Chapter 11). However, their 'whole of business advice' will be how to pursue criminal activity with impunity by creating a veneer of legitimacy, advising what documents are inconvenient, which witnesses/investigators/officials/politicians/judges could be a problem or helpful. Having given that (verbal) advice the client will then choose what to do to ensure the absence of documentation, the silence of witnesses, the ineffectiveness of investigations and the inaction of courts through intimidation, bribery, political interference and the odd murder or bombing. However, in some 'jurisdictions' lawyers acting for criminals are directly involved in bribery of court officials to lose documents and judges to make favourable decisions on the evidence that remains. After the proceeds of crime are collected, they also give advice on how their mob clients can launder criminal proceeds into 'legitimate business', drawing documents that create sham transactions and bogus owners. We would hope that such lawyers would swap their plush chambers for a bare cell.

But lawyers do not have to work for the mob to be personally criminally liable. In 1999, a sitting judge of the High Court warned[22] that some actions that could be seen as encouraging client's unlawful activities, generating either a conspiracy to defraud the revenue or aiding and abetting a breach of the law.

> In the present context of the relationship between a commercial solicitor or accountant and his client, I think … that it is unreal to suggest that the professional adviser is not 'in any real sense encouraging the client to act or proceed in a particular manner.' … The lawyer, and in an appropriate case the accountant, has a vested interest in the matter proceeding … much professional advice in commercial situations extends beyond the field of their legal advice.… An inference of encouragement would usually be open even when the client simply asks whether a particular course of commercial conduct is lawful. It would be open to a jury to conclude that the client was relying on the lawyer's advice and was encouraged to carry out the prohibited conduct by reason of it.

His Honour pointed out that the danger was particularly great

> when the lawyer goes beyond advice and draws documents for the purpose of enabling a client to achieve an objective, it is, I think, almost impossible to contend that the adviser does not aid the commission of any offence which results.

Others argue that this goes too far.[23] One suggested that McHugh's approach would mean 'That no citizen could obtain guidance from those qualified to give it as to the lawfulness of a proposed course of action'.[24]

I am not as troubled as McHugh's critics. The lawyer should give their honest and independent opinion[25] of the law. If it is uncertain, he should say so and warn the client of the uncertainty and the consequences of a case going against them – including the fact that ignorance of the law is no excuse and even less so if they have just been advised of it. The lawyer should provide a lead by refusing to have any involvement – the warning bells should be even stronger to the lawyer than the client. Lawyers will not be prosecuted for advising their clients to avoid potentially illegal activity. If they genuinely believe that it is legal and so advise, the client is in no way immune from prosecution. The client will naturally consider the lawyer grossly negligent. The victims of the crime will have even more legitimate complaints – especially if the nature of the crime was such that a more competent lawyer who recognized the criminality of the proposed action would have had a right or a duty to report it and try to stop it.

The kinds of crime that McHugh had in mind did not involve violent crime and direct harm to human beings – but the elaborate schemes for the avoidance of tax and other regulatory requirements.[26] These are conceived by accountants and lawyers and offered to clients.[27]

But what if the contemplated crimes did involve harm or violence? To secure a hypothetical in a domestic setting, let us vary the child custody example. Suppose the client hankered after the traditional canon law approach to custody[28] and the lawyer used this to try to find ambiguity in the matrimonial law of the jurisdiction where the custody was granted and the custody visit was being held (J1). Suppose he knew that the client had already gone to other lawyers who had advised the client that canon law had been superseded by matrimonial law. Suppose that lawyer advised that there were other countries where J1's laws were not enforced in custody matters. Suppose that the lawyer drew up an unequivocal legal opinion that the non-custodial parent was legally entitled to take the child out of the country for the non-custodial parent to present to the airline desk on departure. Would the lawyer be an accessory before the fact to the abduction?

Let us similarly manipulate the murder of the wife's lover into a new hypothetical. Suppose the client hankered after the nineteenth century when it was generally thought that no man who killed his wife's lover would be convicted by a jury[29] because of an 'unwritten law'.[30] Suppose that he had sought advice whether he would be convicted if he killed the lover while he was in his house. Suppose that, having received unequivocal advice against that course of action, a second lawyer concocted an argument for justifiable homicide or merely jury nullification that was bolstered by isolated cases in the US (such as Wald's 2013 acquittal in Tampa Bay).[31] Suppose that the lawyer provided written advice to this effect so that he could get a licence to carry a concealed weapon (which is required in a number of states).[32] Suppose, in either case, that the second lawyer thought that a 'reasonable case could be made' (or, slightly weaker, that it was arguable) and proceeded to give an unequivocal written advice so that the client could pursue his goals. Suppose, that the lawyer thought that the client's planned action was 'illegal but legitimate'. Again, would the lawyer be an accessory before the fact?

Application to war advice

In these hypotheticals, few would have any difficulty arguing that law and ethics should prevent the second lawyers acting as they did – and recommending changes if legal and ethical rules were ambiguous on the question. I have, of course, manipulated these examples to make them closer to the situations faced by the 1999 and 2003 lawyers. Many will claim that the legal arguments were stronger, at least in 1999. However, as far as I can see, none of those publicly arguing for the legality of the war in 2003 claimed that it would, or even could, succeed in the ICJ and, as in 1999, they sought to avoid the jurisdiction of the ICJ. The right of sovereign states to initiate wars of aggression is as outdated as the idea that husbands have unequivocal rights to custody of the children their wives give birth to and to kill their wife's lovers.[33] For the coalition of the willing, the right to wage aggressive war ceased in the 1928 Treaty of Paris (if not already extinguished by the logic of the Treaty of Versailles). Whereas, the right to wage war was the quintessential sovereign right, foreswearing it is a condition of statehood because the UN and the international community will only recognize, as states, those who sign the UN Charter.

5 Waiver of privilege

Confidentiality and privilege have the limits described above. However, it can also be waived by the conduct of the client that is inconsistent with exercising that privilege. Where a client voluntarily discloses all, or more usually some, of the gist, substance or a summary of the advice to a third party or the public at large, this is inconsistent with treating it as confidential and privileged.[34]

Application to war advice

Given the release of the advice, it is hard to see how privilege had not been waived.

More generally, a larger question must be asked if the refusal to accept the jurisdiction of the ICJ might remove the very basis for any confidentiality and privilege. Such confidentiality and privilege are a core part of the relationship between officers of the court and those whom they assist to understand the law and legal process in that jurisdiction and to assist them to secure or defend their rights. But does this apply to cases where the client is not seeking that assistance but is seeking to avoid those courts and the laws they adjudicate? Can the privilege be claimed in the absence of the structures that deliver it? This might be seen as irrelevant as there is no formal process for appointing counsel as officers of the court.

Technically, privilege is something accorded by the court so that if you are not appearing before the court it cannot be claimed. Confidentiality is generally provided by the professional ethics of the relevant bar. However, these are all conceived as the duties of lawyers performing the said functions. The Hague Principles on Ethical Standards for Counsel Appearing before International Courts and Tribunals, endorsed by the International Law Association, have strong confidentiality provisions. However, as the name implies, they only apply to counsel appearing before international courts and tribunals. The Hague principles state that they are standards of professional conduct for counsel in proceedings before international courts and tribunals with a view to ensuring the integrity, justice and fairness of the international judicial process. If the client is actively undermining that integrity, justice and fairness and wants to avoid that process, it is not clear that confidentiality is relevant. Of course, the lawyer may appear for the client to point out that their client has not signed up to the compulsory jurisdiction for that matter. Confidentiality could attach to communications about the jurisdictional point (subject, of course, to any rules of the relevant international court and the issues discussed above). But, as the client has no intention of the substance being adjudicated, it might be argued that confidentiality does not apply to communications about that substance.

6 'In-house lawyers' and privilege

Privilege does not necessarily apply to communications between in-house lawyers and their clients. For a document to be privileged it must be:

- a communication between lawyer and client, or between two lawyers;
- prepared with the dominant purpose of providing legal advice to the client; and
- a 'confidential communication', prepared in such circumstances that either the writer, the intended recipient or both was under an express or implied obligation not to disclose its contents.[35]

An employer can be a client but the relationship may not be found to be sufficiently independent. In-house lawyers do not have to have practicing certificates, but it helps.[36]

Application to war advice

This is relevant to war advice in that government lawyers do not have to have practicing certificates and neither of the Australian lawyers did. While the degree of independence of government lawyers was traditionally high, Attorney General's departments have not been immune from the politicization of the public service and pressure to provide what governments want to hear. Daryl Williams is known to have stepped in to protect lawyers in some cases but there is no evidence that he did so in this case. Indeed, according to the governor general's account, he did not respond to the governor general's question about the legality of the proposed war and allowed the prime minister to take over the process.

There is also a genuine question about the dominant purpose. Was the purpose to advise the government of the substance of the relevant law or was it designed as publicity material? As it missed such obvious elements of advice as the arguments that could be put against and the likely success of those arguments in relevant courts of competent jurisdiction, it is not so much legal advice as an argument. Legal advice is generally defined as the assessment and application of principles of law to a particular factual situation. It involves the application of legal principles to facts in a manner that: (1) in effect predicts a specific resolution of a legal issue, or (2) directs, counsels, urges, or recommends a course of action by a disputant or disputants as a means of resolving a legal issue. Neither the Australian nor the English advice contained either.

One might argue more generally that giving a client what they want to hear is not sufficiently independent and fails both privilege and legal advice tests. However, my principal, and principled, argument is about the professional responsibilities of ethical lawyers and the standards that the profession should place on themselves and those who give in to the temptation of giving clients (especially delinquent clients) the cover they want.

7 More general duty to court

It is central to legal ethics that the duty to the court trumps the duty to the client. As outlined in earlier chapters, I see the duties to clients are derived from a duty to court and the system of justice under law. We do not have two masters. It is as officers of the court that we assist clients and advise them of substance, process and how they may advance their interests within the law and court processes or through the bargaining under the shadow of that law and those processes.

Of course, lawyers may represent clients under different courts, laws and systems of justice. It is common for lawyers to be admitted in different jurisdictions – either within the same sovereign state (especially if it is a federation without a nationally unified profession) or in different sovereign states. This does not automatically lead to a conflict for two reasons. First, most matters are within a single jurisdiction and it is the bar and ultimately the peak court in that jurisdiction that will determine ethical standards. Where matters involve multiple jurisdictions, the advice given on the laws and procedures in that jurisdiction should be consistent with legal ethics of that jurisdiction. Second, the ethical rules do not vary much from jurisdiction to jurisdiction, so conflicts are going to be unlikely.

Application to war advice

Legal ethics in international law is, like much else in international legal institutions, not nearly as developed or as coherent as it is within well-run national and sub-national jurisdictions. The courts do not constitute a uniform system and the volume of work means that lawyers are not practicing before them on a full-time basis. Nevertheless, the ICC has developed a code of ethics under the control of that bench and the International Law Association (ILA) developed a code of ethics for lawyers appearing in other tribunals which was adopted in September 2010.[37]

The latter code provides explicit backing for most of the conclusions above. Under clause 2.1, 'Counsel has a duty of loyalty to his or her client consistent with a duty to the international court or tribunal to contribute to the fair administration of justice and the promotion of the rule of law'. Under 2.2 Counsel 'shall maintain independence of conduct in the performance of his or her duties and shall act without regard to personal interests or external pressure'. Under 3.2 Counsel must not take part in criminal or fraudulent behaviour nor 'advise or assist a client to engage in conduct that he or she knows or ought to know is criminal or fraudulent or otherwise in conflict with these Principles'. Under 3.4 Counsel are required to respect confidentiality, subject to rules of the court.

These codes provide a strong start and they are, unsurprisingly, generally consistent with national codes of ethics. Neither deals effectively with some of the issues raised in this book – leaving the exceptions to confidentiality to the relevant courts. In particular, the ILA standards deal with counsel appearing before the tribunals on behalf of clients rather than advising clients who are actively avoiding the jurisdiction of the court.

This raises an important question: what duties and loyalties are there to a client who defies the court and its attempt to administer justice under law and subject to the rule of law – let alone one who plans to engage in criminal conduct of a massive extent? So much of legal ethics is prefaced on lawyers assisting their clients to achieve their ends through law and the system of justice with the courts at their apex and the profession as guardians. In most jurisdictions, defying those courts is not an option unless you are the mafia who may bomb courts that cannot be bribed or a junta which stages a coup d'état. While only the United States has claimed a right to do the latter,[38] sovereign states can reject or limit the jurisdiction of the ICJ more or less at will.

What does a lawyer do when the client rejects the jurisdiction and its courts in which the relevant lawyer is giving advice (in this case, international law) and is determined to act in breach of the law? Where that determination involves massive and fundamental criminality one could use the principles outlined above with duties to report. However, one could also argue that once the client has made it clear that they will seek to defy the jurisdiction of the court to whom the lawyer owes his primary duty, the duties to the client are at an end. That defiance means that the client is no longer playing a legal game but a non-legal game (whether or not it involves massive criminality). It could be cogently argued that the rejection of the jurisdiction makes a lawyer–client relationship impossible and voids all obligations that the lawyer might have – while activating duties to report the planned crimes that arise directly as a lawyer in general and an international lawyer in particular.

This may be too strong a position to take. It might be that the lawyer can continue to act for the client in a limited number of ways (as they can when a client confesses to a crime). It might terminate the lawyer–client relationship but not void it so that some duties from the earlier engagement remain. These are the issues that should be debated by lawyers – and the results of those debates endorsed by international courts.

8 Perjury

Of all the crimes that a delinquent client may commit, perjury is one of those in which the duty to court most clearly overrides the duty to client. Lawyers must not mislead the court, must not be a party to misleading the court and must not allow the court to remain misled. For example, the US Rules of Professional Conduct state:

> A lawyer shall not knowingly: . . . offer evidence that the lawyer knows to be false. If a lawyer, the lawyer's client or a witness called by the lawyer offered material evidence and the lawyer comes to know of its falsity, the lawyer shall take reasonable remedial measures, including, if necessary, disclosure to the tribunal.[39]

Application to war advice

In the cases being discussed there will be no perjury because the client is going to ensure that the matter never comes before the court. However, the client will probably be making statements to parliament as may the Attorney General. Both have very strong duties not to mislead the parliament – the quintessential 'hanging offence' for any minister. It is true that the conviction rate is small and recidivism endemic and it is generally thought that ministers only resign when the political inconvenience of their staying exceeds that of their removal. However, a statement by senior government lawyers that the prime minister is lying to parliament about a matter as serious as the legality of the war he is proposing is likely to go beyond inconvenience. There is little doubt that the vote on the 2003 Iraq war would have gone against the government and resignation would have been almost inevitable – even without the likely effect on the willingness of the chief of staff to commence hostilities, which was unknown at the time.

The question is whether the analogy could and should be drawn between perjury (the worst offence a client can commit in court) and misleading parliament (the worst offence a minister client can commit in parliament). Is this, should this, be an exception to confidentiality and privilege? And, if so, should reporting be mandatory or discretionary? And, to whom should the report be made?

I would argue that:

a Ministers must not mislead parliament;
b This is one of the most serious cases of misleading parliament one can imagine;
c The minister is under a duty to correct any statement that even unintentionally misleads parliament;
d A minister who fails in this duty should receive no support from the law or the ethics of the government's advisors;
e It is very wrong for the minister to seek to conceal his misleading of parliament;
f Any use of a minister's powers to prevent the revelation of information that provides evidence of his misleading parliament is a serious abuse of those powers amounting to corruption under most definitions.[40] I have previously argued that this is the case with respect to FOI requests and the use of the Official Secrets Act (UK). I am more than happy to argue that it would also apply to the ministers. Indeed, it is an abuse of his power as ministerial client to refuse to release the lawyer of his duties of confidentiality (if they can be argued to exist in these cases);
g To the extent that a minister has been delegated power to seek legal advice on behalf of the state and to the extent that this delegation includes making decisions about whether or not to release the lawyer from any duty of confidentiality, the protection of the minister from evidence that he misled parliament is an irrelevant consideration and an improper purpose.

Given the variety of circumstances, the argument for discretion rather than an obligation to report the minister is strong. However, leaving the decision solely in the hands of the lawyer puts a great deal of pressure on him or her and a temptation for governments to approach the weak and promote them afterwards – leading to a misallocation of senior government legal jobs towards those with less integrity and more 'adaptability'. I would favour a system of mandatory reporting to a bar ethics committee, which would decide what, if anything, should be reported to parliament. If members' ethics committees were genuinely objective and non-partisan, one could consider reporting only to them. In the absence of such reform, it is better that this become, effectively a collective response of the legal profession rather than the lonely duty of a lawyer.

My preference is that these matters be debated and discussed by international lawyers, endorsed by the ICJ and then lawyers can collectively enforce them on those lawyers who want to practice internationally.

The question of Blair's misleading parliament on the legality of the war was raised by Chilcot who asked whether 'the Prime Minister's words were compatible with the advice you had given him', he replied: 'No'. Stephen Glover concluded that this meant that Goldsmith knew that Blair was misleading Parliament.[41] Glover suggests that Goldsmith should have resigned and given this as his reason and that Goldsmith put love of or for office ahead of his duty. In my view, there was no need for him to resign – nor was there a need for Wimshurst to do so. Whistle-blowers should have protection and it should be the person on whom the whistle is blown who should resign. Wimshurt's resignation should have been treated as constructive dismissal to be compensated for lost income under the jobs to which she should have been appropriately promoted. I would not suggest Harmers as her solicitors (see Slipper case in Chapter 13) but if the British government sought to recoup damages from Blair's speaking fees and Goldsmith's directors' fees, I would not demur.

9 Duties to other parties

Lawyers must not only avoid misleading the court but also third parties and even opponents. For example, rule 34.2 of the NSW Law Society's code of conduct forbids lawyer to 'make any statement that is calculated to mislead or intimidate the other person, and which grossly exceeds the legitimate assertion of the rights or entitlement'. Shirvington warns that such action might not only be a breach of the code of ethics but the criminal offence of blackmail. She cites an actual example where a client wanted the solicitor to demand a sum of money in return for the client's nondisclosure of information that could be harmful to a defendant in a class action to which the client was not a party.

While there is a very strong duty not to mislead the court, a similar duty to third parties is recognized. The Queensland Bar puts it very strongly:

> when acting as advocate and counsel, while pursuing a client's case by all legitimate means, a barrister must not mislead the Court or an opponent and must acquaint the Court with the true state of the law whether or not it favours a client's case.[42]

The point is that lawyers serve their clients by advising and arguing about the rights they have and assist the development of the system of justice through litigation between those who cannot agree and/or settle. They should not be using the system to threaten what the system would not deliver.

Application to war advice

The war advice was entirely for third-party consumption. The coalition/conspiracy of the willing did not prepare the advice for presentation in court or for tactics to be used in court. The advice proffered was grossly misleading and hence, prima facie, a breach of professional codes including such a provision. Where the advice or communication is produced to mislead or intimidate other states it might be seen as a deadly form of blackmail – or even state terrorism.

The latter possibility should not be dismissed lightly. Under the UK's Terrorism Act 2000, terrorism is defined in section 1.1 and 1.2 as the:

use or threat of action ... designed to influence the government or to intimidate the public or a section of the public and the use or threat is made for the purpose of advancing a political, religious or ideological cause AND it:

a involves serious violence against a person,
b involves serious damage to property,
c endangers a person's life, other than that of the person committing the action,
d creates a serious risk to the health or safety of the public or a section of the public, or
e is designed seriously to interfere with or seriously to disrupt an electronic system.

Under sub-section 1.4.d, 'government' includes the government of any state.

10 Unmeritorious or unfounded arguments that would not run in court

In filing cases and drawing pleadings, lawyers must not make claims which they believe have no prospect of success but are made for other reasons – such as to delay payment or to put pressure on the other party. Where those pleadings involve allegations that will 'do great harm to a party before a word of evidence has been offered and submitted to the searching scrutiny of cross-examination or to rebuttal',[43] lawyers have to be particularly careful. Courts have been particularly concerned about allegations of fraud where courts have held that it is not sufficient to be instructed by the client that a fraud has occurred but must decide for themselves that there is an adequate basis for making the allegation.

> No enthusiasm for his client's case, no specious assurance from his client that the insertion of some strong allegations will coerce a favourable settlement, no desire to fortify the relevance of his client's case, entitles the advocate to trespass, in matters involving reputation, a hair's breadth beyond what the facts as laid before him and duly vouched and tested will justify. It will not do to say lightly that it is for the Court to decide the matter. It is for counsel to see that no man's good name is wantonly attacked.[44]

These issues were given a significant airing in a 1998 cause célèbre, *Flower and Hart,*[45] in which the eponymous law firm was found, 10 years earlier, to have manufactured a claim of fraud against a building company that was owed money by their client – a development company owned by George Herscu, whose infamy was about to be enhanced by a conviction for paying a A$100,000 bribe to a senior Queensland minister. Documents that were subsequently bought from the developer's liquidator provided proof Flower and Hart had initiated the claim to gain a 'temporary bargaining stance' even though he advised that 'you could not win any litigation if put to the test'.[46] Justice Goldberg found against Flower and Hart and ordered them to pay indemnity damages (that is, all costs rather than the more limited 'party to party' costs that are usually awarded) to the builder, a decision confirmed on appeal.[47]

Application to war advice

The insight that cases like *Flower and Hart* bring is in the judicial consideration of the ethics of lawyers making highly prejudicial claims about the clients' opponents without any adequate basis. While judges are concerned about a waste of court time, greater concerns are generated by the abuse of process and the long-term damage to the client's opponents.

First, the legal process involves bargaining under the shadow of the law followed, if necessary, by litigation in which the issues between the parties can be refined and judicially determined. The raising of baseless arguments that the lawyer believes cannot succeed in litigation cannot aid their client in an eventual win in litigation and must be done for another reason.[48] Using a process for another reason might be seen as a prima facie abuse of process (see discussion of *Slipper* case in Chapter 13).

Second, pleadings that include these accusations are made under privilege and will remain unchallenged by cross-examination until heard in court and may be very damaging to the person against whom the accusations are made. Lawyers should not do so lightly and should satisfy themselves that there is an evidentiary (and legal) basis for it. Where the damage to the client's opponent is very great and the evidentiary standard higher, this has to be taken into account.

It might be argued that there can be no abuse of process because the client has no intention of going to court and will do everything it can to prevent the matter going to court.[49] This means that there will be no Justice Goldberg to excoriate and impose orders against the lawyer making statements that he knew, or ought to have known, could not have succeeded in court. However, avoiding the court does not avoid legal ethics. The duty to court is not as narrow as that even if the formulation chosen is 'duty to court' rather than something like 'duty to justice under law' which most legal ethicists would prefer. The avoidance of court does not avoid legal ethics but should make the lawyer all the more alert to the temptation to seek and the temptation to provide the advice the client wants.[50] In any case, lawyers should realize that their formal advice is sought because of the gravitas and legitimacy provided by the law and the courts from which its officers (especially the most senior law officers) derive their credibility. For a lawyer to make a claim that he knows would not get up in court is not excused because his client will prevent the issue going to court. He should be all the more vigilant. Lawyers know that extra responsibilities fall on them when they are arguing *ex parte* (that is, before the judge but without the other party). They should be even more responsible when they are arguing *ex judice*[51] as well! Whereas Goldsmith's first advice canvassed the grim prospects some of the arguments would have in court, the second advice (and the Australian advice) did not even address what would happen in court.

On the second point, it might be argued that because the client intends to avoid court or enter pleadings, then there is no privilege generated by the pleadings and therefore no issue. However, if the subject of the accusation has no legal opportunity to sue for damages caused by the accusations (against which privilege would usually be led), then the person accused is in a much worse position. It is not a matter of making accusations that will not be subject to cross-examination. It is making accusations that will *never* be subject to cross-examination.

Of course, the allegation that Goldsmith made on behalf of his client was not the same as in *Flower and Hart* – misleading statements about the price of a contract. But it did claim that Iraq has been involved in massive deceptions and ongoing breaches of UN Security Council resolutions that justified military action.

The damages done because of those claims was not limited to the reputation of the person accused but the unleashing of a war that Goldsmith must have known would kill tens of thousands and risked, as any war must, many more.

Goldsmith did tell Blair in the 7 March advice that the UK and US

> would need to be able to demonstrate hard evidence of non-compliance and non-cooperation… [T]he views of UNMOVIC and the IAEA will be highly significant in this respect. In the light of the latest reporting by UNMOVIC, you will need to consider very carefully whether the evidence of non-cooperation and non-compliance by Iraq is sufficiently compelling to justify the conclusion that Iraq has failed to take its final opportunity.[52]

He might have had his doubts given two facts: (a) the 'dodgy dossier' produced by the British government that was almost instantly discredited; and (b) the UN investigations had unearthed no evidence despite having the ability to go anywhere in Iraq, including the places the US claimed they knew were weapons sites. I am not suggesting that he had to conclude his client was a liar. I am suggesting, as Goldberg did to Flower and Hart, that it was his duty to determine that there was a sufficient factual basis to make the allegations. Of course, if he had concluded, as most international lawyers did, that even if true the accusations did not provide a legal basis to go to war, the factual claims were moot. But, having only recently changed his mind on that, he had, in my view, a duty to satisfy himself that there was a reasonable basis to make the accusations and a reasonable basis that the standard of proof that would be required by the ICJ had been met.

In making this analogy, I am not suggesting that all jurisdictions should draw identical conclusions on the ethics of war advice. However, I am suggesting that the international and local bars should consider the issue of war advice and that this is the kind of analogy they should consider.

11 Who is the client?

Goldsmith was advising Blair – sometimes at his request, sometimes, it appears, not. Goldsmith was treating the PM as his client, with duties to confidentiality and privilege a matter for the prime minister as his client.

Even putting aside the limitations on privilege and confidentiality discussed above, *is the PM his client*? Is it cabinet, the government, the parliament as a whole, the house of parliament that determines the ministry, the 'crown', the 'sovereign' people, the state or, in presidential systems, the head of state? As in all complex organizations, there are numerous officers with various delegations, formal or implied through which various individuals are entrusted with some of the powers of the overall organization. The British government, 'asserts that the AG's advice to government is no different from advice to a client – such that it should always be subject to legal privilege (and thus not disclosable unless the government chooses to effect disclosure)'.[53] Lord Bingham is not convinced.

> There seems to me to be room to question whether the ordinary rules of client privilege, appropriate enough in other circumstances, should apply to a law officer's opinion on the lawfulness of war; it is not unrealistic in my view to regard the public, those who are to fight and perhaps die, rather than the government, as the client.[54]

Even if the British government's view is preferred to Bingham's, it does not necessarily answer the question as government and parliament are, themselves, complex organizations with various delegations of power – formal and conventional (especially the power to determine the government).

If we look to the analogy of a lawyer advising a corporation, the corporation is created by its constitution with the shareholders holding the ultimate power to alter the constitution and approve major changes as well as appointing the board which appoints the CEO. The directors have a fiduciary responsibility to the shareholders who act as their agents and have a duty to act in the best interests of the shareholders, subject to law and various other debated constraints to other 'stakeholders' under a 'license to operate'.[55]

The powers of the CEO and senior managers will include seeking legal advice on the legality of potential actions. The shareholders have a right to expect that the agents of the corporation will act legally and to check if there is any doubt. That advice may be sought from in-house lawyers, external lawyers and may be up to the individual manager or coordinated/directed by the general counsel. Suppose that the CEO is planning joint action with another CEO. (To bring this closer to the Kosovo/Iraq examples, they may have tried to structure the deal so that it will avoid the jurisdiction of the courts and regulatory authorities that have held such practices illegal in the past.) If the legal advisor tells the CEO that his planned action is criminal and it is clear that the CEO intends to continue with it, he may have a duty to report it to the authorities under the principles outlined above. However, a preliminary question is whether he should notify other officials or groups of officials within the corporate client. Should he notify the chairperson, the board, a board committee or the chair of that board committee? Should he notify the shareholders?

This could be a more effective way of stopping the crime under the above principles. It even could be part of the duty to the client to advise them. If the

CEO forbids the lawyer from informing these other officials or groups of officials, is this an invalid exercise of his entrusted power that is, accordingly, void? Is it a breach of the CEO's fiduciary duty that should, itself, be reported? If the lawyer's letter of engagement requires that all decisions about confidentiality and privilege be decided by the CEO, is this a valid exercise of power?

The same issues arise with a lawyer advising the prime minister (or other cabinet ministers). Should the lawyer notify the cabinet, a relevant subcommittee, the parliament, the speaker or a relevant parliamentary committee? Should he notify the Queen (for UK) or Governor-General (in Australia)? Should he inform the minister of defence, the chief of staff or the appointed field commander?

The PM is not acting in a personal capacity but in his official capacity within the state, exercising powers delegated/entrusted to him. It would be a gross abuse of his power to seek to enforce confidentiality to refuse the lawyer permission to notify at least some of the above. The attempt at suppression would be void for taking into account irrelevant considerations and acting on an improper purpose. As such, it should be treated as ultra vires at least and possibly corrupt.

In one of the more benign 'Catch 22s', if the PM is misleading the parliament then the lawyer may have a duty to report it either as a third party being misled or because parliament is part, and a superior part, of the client.

Other analogies are available which I will not explore here. If we are going to apply stakeholder theory, there are other important stakeholders – allies going to war as part of the coalition of the willing, residents in the country being invaded, and soldiers.[56] It could be argued that states have a 'licence to operate' from the United Nations which recognizes them as sovereign states on the basis that they accept the UN Charter.

12 The English lawyers: Goldsmith before the Bar Council and Chilcot

A number of complaints were made to the Bar Council about Goldsmith's advice (including from Clare Short who had been a member of cabinet at the time), MPs, senior barristers and the father of a soldier killed in Iraq. The complaint was that he had permitted 'his absolute independence, integrity and freedom from external pressures to be compromised', or acted so as to 'compromise his professional standards in order to please his client, the court or a third party'.[57]

The bar's professional conduct and complaints committee referred the issues of jurisdiction to a constitutional lawyer,[58] who advised that the Bar Council had no power to investigate the provision of legal opinions to ministers by the government's law officers.

I find it hard to agree with that conclusion. A lawyer who works for a corporation or a government does not cease to be a lawyer and no employer should ever expect them to cease to be a lawyer or to cease acting ethically. Goldsmith was a lawyer acting as a lawyer. He was the first law officer and, as such, should only be appointed if he lived up to the highest standards[59] and continued to lead by example rather than (like a Hobbesian monarch) not subject to the rules he oversees.

If there is a view that there is a conflict between his duties as a lawyer and his duties as a cabinet minister, then he should have chosen between them – either refusing the appointment or ceasing to be and practice as a lawyer. As I argued earlier, adequate ethical rules for public servants and lawyers are mutually reinforcing rather than contradictory.[60]

Had a professional conduct hearing gone ahead, Lord Goldsmith would have had to explain why his advice changed so radically from the 13-page advice and the unequivocal statement he produced 10 days later. That very question was put to him by Chilcott,[61] to which Goldsmith eventually offered three answers.

The first was that the earlier advice was 'overly cautious'. This is astonishing and beggars belief. Indeed, it undermines his credibility as a witness. An argument in line with the vast majority of international lawyers (and the unanimous view of the Foreign Office lawyers) could never be 'overly cautious'. His initial analysis of the likely views of English courts was underlined by Lord Bingham, who later stated that Goldsmith's advice contained 'no hard evidence' that Iraq had defied UN resolutions 'in a manner justifying resort to force'. (He also drew the conclusion that the invasion was 'a serious violation of international law and of the rule of law'.)[62]

The second response was that he was persuaded by the revival argument that he had previously said only the Americans believed in.[63] He did not explain how he overcame the weaknesses of the position that he had, himself, identified nor addressed the question of what a court of competent jurisdiction would think of it (something that he had addressed in the earlier advice). As I indicated in Chapter 15, there are fundamental obstacles to this view. This Damascene conversion (though, in this case, possibly blinded more by the dark than the light) was only to the point of deciding that 'a reasonable case could be made' that the war was lawful, a standard that he claimed had been sufficient for earlier attorneys general in earlier limited bombing campaigns in Iraq (1998) and the Kosovo War (1999). This is confirmed by Rt Hon John Morris, Lord Abrovon, the Attorney General at the time who said that 'sometimes the best one could do was to say that I believed we had a 'respectable argument or an 'arguable case'.[64] However, if he came to this view, he should have stated it. If he needed to give short advice, he could say that, in his view, a reasonable case can be made but that this was very risky and the weight of legal opinion would make the government and the chiefs of the armed services war criminals.

The third response was that the armed services had asked for a yes or no answer.

> I very quickly saw that actually this wasn't satisfactory from their point of view. They deserved more. Our troops deserved more, our civil servants who might be on the line deserved more than my saying there was a reasonable case.... So therefore it was important for me to come down clearly on one side of the argument or another, which is what I proceeded to do.[65]

As he put it later, Boyce wanted 'an unambiguous black-and-white statement saying it would be legal for us to operate if we had to'.[66] 'Rightly the armed services – as did the civil service – needed to know that they were covered by a clear statement of lawfulness.'[67] With respect, admirals who are about to gives orders to commence a war that the vast majority of international lawyers think is a crime of aggression deserve better than to be told it is legal. Consider the case where most of my colleagues thought that a financial transaction that a client wanted to do was fraudulent and I thought that the best that could be done would be that a reasonable case could be made that it was not. The client presses me: is it fraudulent or not. It would be utterly irresponsible for me to say: 'it is not fraudulent'. This would be both negligent and a clear example of permitting my 'absolute independence, integrity and freedom from external pressures to be compromised', or compromising my 'professional standards in order to please his client'.[68] But engaging in a war of aggression is so much worse than drawing a fraudulent document. He was asked for a yes or no answer.

Like any lawyer, he should have said that such answers can only be given by courts. In purporting to give a yes or no answer in these circumstances, he purported to act as a judge in a matter concerning the conduct of the government of which he was a part. Few acts could be more fundamentally a breach of his duty to that court. It is now more than 400 years since the Case of Prohibitions[69] established the separation of judicial and executive power by stating that the King could not act as a judge. The Attorney General should know that the crown could not delegate to him a power that it did not possess.

Finally, it should be noted that his changing his advice (by simplifying it) because of this request establishes the factual basis of the allegations before the Bar Council that he gave in to pressure – as well as trashing the independence necessary for legal advice and the independence necessary for an ethical lawyer.

Wimshurst, who had quietly resigned over Goldsmith's change of mind, was highly critical of the 'lamentable' process he followed in reaching it. However, she did say she understood that 'Goldsmith was put into an impossible position'. I think she was too kind. He was not in an impossible position. He was in a position where doing his duty as a lawyer would not be popular with his client. The youngest barrister would recognize the responsibility to give quality independent advice. If the fact that his client was a colleague who had appointed him has any effect on the advice that is given, he should not have agreed to give it. Some, like Glover, think he should have resigned, indicating, at the very least, that this was because the government was not following his advice on the legality of the war.

I do not agree that either had to resign. As first law officer, he should have said to the PM what our Lt Col had said to his superiors. He should have reiterated his view that this was probably criminal and should have told him, that if Blair persisted with his planned course of action, Goldsmith would have to inform the police or the DPP. He should have pointed out that his client was not the PM personally but either the government, the crown, the parliament or the state. Even if his instructions purported to limit the advice to the PM, the cabinet, parliament and the Queen were other parties that should not be misled and who might, themselves, suffer criminal liability.

Advice to the Queen raises a couple of issues. The power to make war is a prerogative power (it was listed as such by the UK government in 2004 and the Queen was advised to refuse consent to the debate on a bill to delegate the power to authorize strikes against Iraq to parliament).[70] Although this prerogative would only be exercised on the political advice of the PM (or possibly by the PM with an implied delegation of prerogative authority), legally, the decision is the Queen's so that, if she acted on his advice she would be criminally liable as well (even if she was not generally liable as the head of state). The Queen's reserve powers are virtually never used but they do include requiring more information, especially as to the legality of what is advised and they do run to dismissing a PM acting illegally[71] – though she would be expected to counsel, advice and warn[72] before doing so.

Had Goldsmith thought about some of the other issues, he could have added that:

- his duties of confidentiality stopped at the point of future criminality, especially on a scale inherent in the invasion of Iraq;
- he would have to avoid any question of misprision of a felony and would feel it incumbent on himself to refer the criminal law issues he had raised in his first advice with the relevant authorities;
- he had to ensure that he was not complicit in the crime Blair was going to commit;
- the publication of the one-page advice would waive privilege on all the other advice he had given;
- it had become apparent to him that the dominant purpose of the advice sought was not legal advice but as a cover for the above illegal acts;
- his duty to court, justice, the rule of law and the administration of justice required him to report this activity;
- Blair was only a part of the government and he had a duty to inform the cabinet, the parliament and the Queen;
- The advice sought was misleading to other parties (to the extent that they were parties other than the government/crown/state;
- If Blair lied to parliament about the legality of the war, he could not keep silent.

However, he would only have to have given one or two of the above reasons to have prevented the United Kingdom committing what the vast majority of international lawyers considered a crime of aggression.

The above amounts to an argument that lawyers in Goldsmith's and Wimshurt's positions were not bound by confidentiality and privilege to keep silent on the legality of the proposed Iraq war. While Millar and others argue that the decision to report should lie with the lawyer, the greater the magnitude of the consequences and the higher the office, the stronger the case for a duty.

I would suggest that the right lay with Wimshurst and the duty on Goldsmith. This is partly a matter of seniority and partly because the reaction that could have been anticipated from Campbell and others in the Prime Minister's office and the ferocious attacks that could be expected from the Murdoch press and media interests (which we now know had been pledged to Blair if he decided to go to war).[73]

If either had done so they would have been whistleblowers. This is one of those areas where public sector ethics and legal ethics are largely reinforcing – though I would still analyse the issues for lawyers in terms of legal ethics.

However, I would argue that lawyers exercising their right/duty to report should be guided by best-practice whistleblowing – attempting to report it internally to relevant superiors of the person whose misconduct they are reporting, offices set up to receive complaints, law enforcement authorities and finally the media.

Lawyers should also be able to avail themselves of the protections available to whistleblowers. Any retaliatory action should be unlawful in both senses – void for improper purpose and subject to disciplinary and criminal sanction. Any attempt to stop a lawyer from reporting a crime that is being planned or in progress should be seen as part of a conspiracy to commit the crime.

Where the lawyer resigns because of reasonably expected retaliation, it should, in principle, be treated as a case for constructive dismissal. As in other cases of justified whistleblowing, the whistleblower should be protected and it is the person on whom the whistle is blown that should lose their jobs.

That was not what happened here. Neither Goldsmith nor his delinquent client were sacked or were forced to resign. Goldsmith retained his office for another four years before becoming a solicitor on one million pounds a year and was put on the board of an apparently sympathetic billionaire's company.[74]

13 The Australian lawyers

The only advice that has ever been published was the Campbell-Moraitis advice discussed in Chapter 15. We do not know if other lawyers were consulted or gave other advice. Professor Ivan Shearer had thought that there would be a number of lawyers giving advice to the various ministers. As indicated, I was told that there was a highly equivocal draft advice in circulation but have not seen it and cannot confirm the report.

As in the Sherlock Holmes story 'The Silver Blaze', one of the most significant facts was the dogs that did not bark – the lawyers that did not advise. The then Attorney General thought that his responsibilities in a very large portfolio and his membership of cabinet meant that advice to the government was best delivered by the solicitor general. While I do not entirely agree, and the Cabinet Handbook obliges the AG to sign off on the legality of recommendations for action by the Governor-General-in-Council, I certainly respect his view. However, in this case, the solicitor general was not asked for an opinion and no published opinion came from the next most senior lawyer Henry Burmester QC, the Chief General Counsel of the AG's department and former Head of the Office of International law.[75]

The Campbell/Moraitis advice was widely criticized. Chapter 16 identified one flaw (which Professor James Crawford, Australia's most distinguished international law professor and now a member of the ICJ, confirmed). To this, I would point out that the advice did not make any mention of the counter arguments that would be put by others or the likely success of the arguments put forward in a court of competent jurisdiction.

Williams and Hovell's opinion to the leader of the opposition clinically dismembers the Campbell/Moraitis opinion. Byrnes and Charlesworth were even more critical:

> In our view, the arguments advanced to support the lawfulness of the government's action are unpersuasive. They depend on a distorted reading of the language of the relevant Security Council resolutions and of the context in which they were adopted. They also neglect the rationale of the role of the Security Council under the charter in dealing with threats to international peace and security.[76]

Gavan Griffith was absolutely scathing:

> I cannot characterize the advice as an opinion. The short paragraphs 14 to 18 of the brief seven-page advice read as weak best arguments for the use of force. Para 34 of SCR 678, cited in para 18, denies the continued authority of that resolution to support present action by individual states, as does the entire SCR 1441.
>
> It is significant that the authors of this Advice, on the important issue of giving legal sanction to war, do not even entitle it as 'Opinion'...
>
> The Australian and United Kingdom legal advices are entirely untenable. They are arrant nonsense.[77]

While only one opinion was published by the government, many international lawyers who were not directly employed by the Australian government did provide their views.

Forty-three Australian international lawyers published advice that the proposed war would be illegal as did 15 international lawyers based in the United Kingdom (including the two of the most prominent Australian international lawyers, James Crawford, who was later appointed to the ICJ, and Christine Chinkin).[78]

The only Australian international law professor who argued in favour of the legality of the war was Emeritus Professor Don Greig who suggested that a good case could be made on the basis that the coalition of the willing were repudiating part of the ceasefire agreement between them and Iraq in 1991.[79] I do not think that this novel approach would stand up in court because it assumes that the termination and recommencement of hostilities was within the discretion of the leaders of the 1991 intervention rather than the UNSC and that the right to continue hostilities was open-ended despite the specific wording of the relevant resolutions.

Shearer criticized the 43 international lawyers for conflating *ius in bello* and *ius ad bellum*, but he was Delphic in expressing his own views:

> While it is always essential, except in the case of immediate self-defence, to refer situations threatening international peace and security to the Security Council, the failure of the council to act decisively cannot in the end deprive states, especially those acting collectively and with transparent motives, from using armed force to advance the wider objectives of the charter, especially the protection of human rights.[80]

The question was whether the coalition of the willing was transparent in its motives and was using armed force for the protection of human rights. As Australia explicitly eschewed humanitarian intervention, this argument failed. According to Hon Kevin Rudd (then shadow minister for foreign affairs), Shearer's own views were pretty close to those of the 43 international lawyers.

This is not to say that a number of lawyers without expertise in international law were not free with their opinions and were given space by the Murdoch press. Most scandalous of all was a joint letter by 18 lawyers published in *The Australian* under the title 'a group of international lawyers: the case for a legal attack'.[81]

Gavan Griffith dismissed them as follows:

> I know few of the American signatories. The Australian signatories have, with but slight exception, common interests more in areas of taxation, defamation and commercial law and none is known in the field of public international law (excepting Professor Waller who has a reputation in the specialized area of humanitarian law).[82]

My own analysis showed the vast majority made no claims on their websites to knowledge of international law. When one of the signatories rang me about another matter, I asked him if he had read the UN resolutions and he said he had not but had signed it because he was asked to. I briefly outlined my views on the ethics of what he had done and have not spoken to him since.

An attempt to bring the two authors of the report before a disciplinary hearing fell at the first hurdle – of whether the authors had practicing certificates. While government lawyers can apply for practicing certificates, they do not have to, even QCs. So neither has been held to account. Campbell has remained in his position. But Moraitis has done very well. The Abbott government appointed him to head the Attorney General's department. He achieved fame when Professor Gillian Triggs, the president of the human rights commission, gave evidence that Moraitis had told her that she had lost the confidence of the Attorney General, asked her to resign and offered her another job. If this was an 'inducement' to resign, it would have been a criminal offence. Triggs defused the situation by saying that the word 'induce' was a term of legal art and she was not going to use it.

14 What has changed?

Since 2003, when I first began writing on these issues,[83] there have been some positive developments.

1. In 2005, the UN General Assembly endorsed both the rule of law in domestic and international affairs. It also endorsed the Responsibility to Protect (R2P), though limiting it to the most serious offences and making it clear that the authority for R2P only comes from the UN Security Council.
2. The Rome Statute conference of parties defined the crime of aggression and voted to activate that section of the Rome Statute from 2017 if sufficient parties ratify the changes. Even if they did not ratify, the resolutions would be an important reminder and text for those practicing universal jurisdiction.
3. The wide recognition (despite occasional denials) that the 2003 Iraq war was a disaster.
4. The declining power of the United States and the rising power of China mean that the benefits of a rules-based order are being more widely recognized – especially given controversies over the South China Sea.[84] However, many of those who call for China to accept a rules-based order do not acknowledge their own countries' failures to do so in Iraq.
5. The torture memos in the United States focused on the professional ethics of lawyers advising governments. While the use of force was intended to be non-lethal and directed against individuals rather than states, that hardly rules it out as a precedent for lawyers advising on war. In 2009, the Justice Department's Office of Professional Responsibility recommended that the advice provided by John Yoo and signed off by Jay Bybee amounted to professional misconduct and should be referred to bar disciplinary processes. While the recommendation was not endorsed by the US Attorney General because David Margolis considered it was 'merely' flawed and demonstrated poor judgement, it raises the risk for US lawyers and makes lawyers in other states wonder why government legal advisors should be immune from professional misconduct.
6. In the UK, Goldsmith and his delinquent client are under a permanent cloud for the advice one gave and the other took (though in Australia, Moraitis has prospered and his client fared rather better).
7. While the power to make war remains a prerogative power in the United Kingdom, a constitutional convention is, at the very least, emerging that a parliamentary vote will precede any choice by the United Kingdom to go to war. There is a practice, a norm and a real risk of adverse consequences in breaching it.[85] There have been votes on Iraq in 2003, Libya in 2011 and Syria in 2013 and 2015. The fact that the first Syria vote was lost means that this is

no mere formality and may be a greater effective constraint than the power the US Congress has under its Constitution. Legal advice has been provided. The 2011 and 2015 advice had the backing of UN Security Council resolutions. The 2013 advice did not, and the House of Commons voted against war.

8 Enquiries have been conducted by the Dutch and British Governments. The former concluded that the war was illegal and, while the Chilcot Enquiry is yet to report,[86] the evidence produced has meant that parliaments are going to be cautious of government advice.

On the other hand, little progress has been seen on the possible directions set out in Chapters 14 and 15, and the original articles on which these were based.[87]

15 What should be done?

Ethical guidance to lawyers

This chapter started with a deeply disturbing ethical challenge faced by one highly ethical lawyer trying to do his duty. It has looked more generally at some of the ethical challenges lawyers have in advising those clients who wish to do something that is, in the view of the lawyer, probably or certainly illegal. It has applied them to lawyers advising governments on the legality of wars. It has recognized that lawyers advising governments planning to go to war may face the alternative of becoming mob lawyers or whistleblowers. Lawyers in government employ will generally not see themselves as either. But that may be the real, if possibly impossible, choice that they have.

While we can recognize courage in individual lawyers (from the unnamed Lt Col to Elizabeth Wimshurst), we cannot leave it to individuals to solve these issues. Not only does it place too much strain on individual saints, individual action is likely to lead to unnecessary and unsuccessful sacrifices. I am mindful of Edmund Burke's quote (which is often misquoted in a much milder form).[88]

> When bad men combine, good men must join together or fall one by one, an unpitied sacrifice in a contemptible struggle.[89]

The point is not merely that good people should avoid doing nothing: they must act collectively or they will individually reach their point they can no longer tolerate and then take individual action – a sacrifice that others will neither pity nor thank them for in a struggle that is held in contempt because it can get nowhere.

I entirely agree with this conservative emphasis on the need for call to collective action. It is much better for the profession to collectively consider these questions, and identify the principles to be followed, the rules to be adopted and the means for guidance and the resolution of doubt. This clarifies issues as much as possible in advance while providing means for resolving those issues not adequately anticipated and covered. It also limits the opportunities to 'get new lawyers' who will give in and tell their clients what they want to hear. One should not leave individuals to confront those dilemmas and expect them to be saints. The ethics of professions is a form of institutional or collective ethic – where groups agree on the right thing to do as individuals but collectively commit to doing the right thing, collectively refusing to do the wrong thing and throwing out those who choose the latter course.[90] In this sense, a profession becomes a kind of 'conspiracy of virtue'.

Bar associations consider the first set of challenges from quite minor frauds to serious harm or illegality, with the veil of confidentiality and privilege thinning even in the fraud cases and liable to completely dissolve as the harm and illegality escalate with debates turning on whether reporting is discretionary or not.

The harm and the illegality escalate when we look to the waging of aggressive war. I would argue that national and international bar associations should meet and consider the issues of advising on aggressive war, issuing international ethical rules and seeking involvement and approval from the ICC and ICJ as well as national bar associations. Breach of the agreed rules should involve the loss of rights to appear before international tribunals and, preferably disbarment at the national level as well.

As always, I think that it is would be useful to have a set of principles that explain the more detailed rules. I offer a potential draft as follows:

> *Draft Principles for International Lawyers employed by Governments*
>
> The first duty of lawyers is to do justice through law and the institutions through which it is administered – including international law and international legal institutions. The principal means by which this duty is fulfilled is by assisting clients to advance and protect their interests through the law and legal institutions. This includes providing advice as to how their interests can be advanced and protected by acting in conformity to international law as interpreted by international legal institutions and other sources of international law.
>
> This duty includes assisting clients to assert and defend the legality of their actions through international legal institutions. It includes a vigorous defence of the client's interests and assertion of their rights in pleadings and arguments before courts of competent jurisdiction. It does not include assisting clients to avoid international law and international legal institutions while claiming to act in conformity with international law.
>
> Respect for the justice, the law and the relevant international courts precludes the lawyer from seeking to substitute his own judgement for that of the court and should not allow his or her opinion to be used in substitution for the court's judgement where the client refuses to accept the jurisdiction of that court.
>
> Lawyers advising clients under such circumstances should ensure that their judgements reflect their opinion of the likelihood of the court finding for or against the client and should not allow their opinions to be released in anything but their full form. If the client refers to the lawyer's advice, it should be treated as a waiver of confidentiality/privilege rights.

Where clients have the opportunity to refuse jurisdiction of courts of competent jurisdiction, there is a temptation for clients to seek, and lawyers to give, the advice the client wants to hear rather than the advice they should be given. This 'advice' may then be publicly paraded by the client. To succumb to that temptation is to substitute the role of a spin doctor for that of a lawyer. Lawyers cannot be both.

Lawyers should appreciate the important distinction between duties to clients before and after they act. Once they have acted in an area which is marginal or probably illegal, they assist them to defend it. But beforehand, they should explain the law and warn them of the limitations of confidentiality and the duties they have to report and prevent planned criminal behaviour.

Opinions are for clients, not for the public. They should be independent, open, honest and frank to avoid unnecessary litigation and fees. If the client provides the opinion to the public or makes statements inconsistent with that opinion while refusing to accept the competent jurisdiction of a relevant court, the client waives lawyer–client privilege and it is the right and duty of the lawyer to correct the impression.

Lawyers must recognize the consequences of actions illegal under international law and recognize the foreseeable damages that others might suffer as a result. Lawyers should be personally liable for those foreseeable damages and professional indemnity should be limited.

Recommended changes to improve procedures for going to war

I have argued that lawyers should collectively confront these issues to give clearer guidance and collective support to those who follow it and collective condemnation to those who do not. However, while lawyers have a responsibility to take a leading role in this and other activities to develop the rule of law in international affairs, the solutions should not just be left to them and the conspiracy of virtue they should pursue. As always, we need more than just ethics – we need a mutually supportive mixture of legal and institutional reforms – bringing to bear the four governance disciplines of the 'vortex'.

Parliamentary vote

The reform most often proposed is to require a prior vote in one or both houses of parliament – as is required in the US by the somewhat compromised Constitution but has become something of a convention – preferably by legislation. I am cautious about how effective this will be by itself. For example, those who put faith in this mechanism to prevent Australia joining in American-led wars must face the irony that such wars cannot start without clearing the same (indeed stronger) constitutional hurdle in the US. Parliaments as political bodies are often swayed by perceived political advantage and frequently operate on inadequate information and advice. While it is not clear that we can or should attempt to address the former, much can be done about the latter by providing better legal, military and intelligence advice. Where necessary, this can be done in secret session (as practiced during World War Two) or through multi-party confidential committees (as is common in the US).

Legal advice

There is much to be said in favour of the second option where a parliamentary committee comprising government and opposition members could receive the legal advice provided by the Attorney-General, Solicitor-General and others that members or their parties might call. This committee should seek to come up with a shared view to put to parliament. But, if doubts remain as to the legality of the proposed action, this would inform the position taken by the parties in the parliamentary vote. This will become particularly important once the ICC has jurisdiction over the crime of aggression in 2017 or thereafter. Those who put a tendentious and one-sided legal argument to sway parliamentarians would be severely embarrassed in front of an Australian court or, if Australia had not adequately investigated and prosecuted the alleged crime, in front of the ICC.

All those giving legal advice should have practicing certificates that would be in jeopardy if their advice did not meet appropriate professional standards.

Military, intelligence and security advice

Of course, just because something is legal does not mean it should be done. The same committee that heard legal advice could also receive confidential briefings on military, intelligence and security assessments. These assessments must, of course, be professional, independent, reliable, frank and fearless.

The Federal Executive Council, Privy Council or like body

Her Majesty's most Honourable Privy Council is the formal body through which many prerogative powers are exercised – and similar bodies are found in many Commonwealth and parliamentary systems. It does not appear that British decisions to go to war are put to the Privy Council. The Australian government has used a statutory power of the defence minister to enter armed conflicts, side-lining the Federal Executive Council in a way that surprised at least two Governors-General. I have argued for the re-inclusion of the Governor-General in the process of going to war and the use of the crown's uncontroversial boiler-plate constitutional authority through the Federal Executive Council. Under Cabinet Handbook procedures, the Attorney-General has to provide a certificate as to the legality of what he is advised to do. There is also an opportunity for the Governor-General to perform the role Bagehot identified for a constitutional monarch – 'the right to be consulted, the right to be encouraged, the right to warn'.[91]

Rule of law commitments

Since the 'Sovereignty and Intervention' paper delivered at the twin towers,[92] I have suggested that governments deciding to use force should recognize the compulsory jurisdiction of the ICJ and the jurisdiction of ICC for that use of force and agree to be bound by any decisions. They would accept suit from any other country – subject only to the country against whom force is used agreeing to ICJ jurisdiction over the issues that led to the intervention.[93]

A combination of safeguards

Safeguards often work well in combination. Implementing all of the above would not add more time to the processes that government would need to engage in before taking part in a 'war of choice' initiated by ourselves or our allies. If a state subscribing to the above principles were a victim of aggression, its institutions would have to move quickly (possibly requiring prior agreement by only the leader of the opposition with a subsequent ratification in parliament). But the legality would not be in question and a response is unlikely to be politically controversial.

Notes

1 'In Full: New Goldsmith Statement', *BBC News*, 26 May 2006.
2 This advice followed up on earlier advice such as that on when he said he remained of the view that Resolution 1441 did not authorize the use of military force without a further determination by the Security Council. Lord Goldsmith QC, 'Memo: Lord Goldsmith to PM Blair (Iraq)', 30 January 2003, www.iraqinquiry.org.uk/media/46496/Goldsmith-note-to-PM-30January2003.pdf.
3 The Association of the Bar of the City of New York, 'Formal Opinion: Client Confidentiality and the Intention to Commit a Crime', March 2002, www.nycbar.org/ethics/ethics-opinions-local/2002-opinions/831-client-confidentiality-and-the-intention-to-commit-a-crime. (Accessed 20 January 2016).
4 Charles Sampford and Margaret Palmer, 'The Constitutional Power to Make War: Domestic Legal Issues Raised by Australia's Action in Iraq', *Griffith Law Review: A Journal of Social and Critical Legal Studies* 18, no. 2 (2009): 350–384. C. Sampford, 'Legality and Legitimacy: A Dozen Years after Goldstone', in *Responsibility to Protect and Sovereignty*, ed. Charles Sampford and Ramesh Thakur (Surrey: Ashgate, 2013): 143–170.
5 James Rubin, 'Countdown to a Very Personal War', *Financial Times*, 30 September 2000.
6 New York State Unified Court System, 'Rules of Professional Conduct: Part 1200', ed. Department of State (New York: The New York State Bar Association, 2013): Rule 3.3.
7 *Re Bell; Ex parte Lee* (1980) 146 CLR 674.
8 33 So. 3d 512 (Miss. Ct. App. 2009).
9 www.nolo.com/legal-encyclopedia/the-crime-fraud-exception-the-attorney-client-privilege.html.
10 V. Shirvington, 'Turning a Blind Eye: Professional Liability and Responsibility', in *NSW Law Society* (Sydney, February 2001). Quoting Riley's *NSW Solicitors' Manual*.

11 While this is anecdotal, it is reinforced by many others. I particularly recall at a lunch at a law firm in 1991 when a partner joined us, apologized for being late and said that he had suddenly realized that the client he had been meeting with was a criminal – and that he was not alone.
12 Helen Hierschbiel, 'Disclosing Client Confidences: When Doing the "Right" Thing May Be the Wrong Thing to Do', *Oregon State Bar Bulletin,* 2011.
13 Ibid. Quoted Massachusetts Ethics Op. No. 90–92.
14 T.J. Millar, 'The Attorney's Duty to Reveal a Client's Future Intended Criminal Conduct', *Duke Law Journal* 33, no. 3 (1984): 582–600.
15 Donald Nicolson and Julian Webb, *Professional Legal Ethics: Critical Interrogations* (Oxford: Oxford University Press, 1990): 260.
16 The International Military Tribunal, *Trial of the Major War Criminals before the International Military Tribunal (Blue Series) 14 November 1945–1 October 1946*, vol. 2 (Nuremberg: Hein, 1947; repr., 1995): 146.
17 Samantha Besson and John Tasioulas, 'Introduction', in *The Philosophy of International Law*, ed. Samantha Besson and John Tasioulas (Oxford: Oxford University Press, 2010).
18 Constitutional Affairs Committee, 'Constitutional Role of the Attorney General: Fifth Report', (London: House of Commons 19 July 2007): 12. See, reference to Lord Morris, ibid.: 37.
19 UN General-Assembly, 'Res. 60/1: World Summit Outcome Document', (2005), esp. paras 21, 114.
20 Others will be found in various 'whistleblowing' statutes – where the issues are likely to be a similar need for careful consideration and detailed provisions.
21 Shirvington, 'Turning a Blind Eye: Professional Liability and Responsibility'.
22 J. McHugh, 'Jeopardy of Lawyers and Accountants in Acting on Commercial Transactions', *Australian Bar Review* 5, no. 1 (1989): 1.
23 S. Davies (QC), 'Revenue Offences Generally: Can the Professional Adviser Be a Party or Conspirator', *Queensland Law Society Journal* 19, no. 3 (1989): 207; R. Gyles (QC), 'Criminal Liability of Professional Advisers', *Taxation in Australia* 23, no. 7 (1989): 480.
24 'Criminal Liability of Professional Advisers'.
25 Shirvington quotes Samuel Johnson:

> A lawyer has no business with the justice or injustice of the cause which he undertakes, unless his client asks his opinion, and then he is bound to give it honestly. The justice or injustice of the cause is to be decided by the judge.

'Turning a Blind Eye: Professional Liability and Responsibility': 24. While Shirvington is correct to query the first proposition, the last two are axiomatic.
26 Denying tax revenue may do indirect harm to human life through government programs with inadequate funding due to corporate tax avoidance – especially in health and especially in developing countries whose people are in greater need and who are more reliant on corporate tax revenue because of the poverty of the vast bulk of their citizens. See for example, D. Itriago, 'Owning Development: Taxation to Fight Poverty', (2011), https://www.oxfam.org/sites/www.oxfam.org/files/rr-owning-development-domestic-resources-tax-260911-en.pdf.
27 I remember well my father's accountant and lawyer coming to me in 1978 while I held his power of attorney to tell me about a tax avoidance scheme. As I was studying tax at the time, I listened with interest and asked a number of questions before my single word reply – a firm and testy 'no'. They got nothing. As McHugh rightly indicated, they only got their fees if I agreed.
28 I could use examples of Sharia law or Talmudic law but use canon law because it was a large part of the British and European legal tradition.

29 Mark E. Kann, *Taming Passion for the Public Good: Policing Sex in the Early Republic* (New York: NYU Press, 2013): 84.
30 Lawrence Friedman, *Crime and Punishment in American History* (New York: Basic Books, 1993): 221.
31 'Peter Jamison Jury Acquits Brandon Man in Killing of Wife's Lover', *Tampa Bay Times*, 30 May 2013.
32 Including Florida.
33 The possibility of the latter is the reason for the terminology for the former.
34 *Mann v Carnell* (1999) 201 CLR 1 at 29.
35 *Commonwealth of Australia and Air Marshall Errol John McCormack in his capacity as Chief of Air Force v Vance* [2005] ACTCA 35.
36 *Commonwealth v Vance* [2005] ACTCA 35. At first instance, the right to practice was held to be necessary for privilege. While this was rejected on appeal, no test was set for such independence.
37 The Study Group of the International Law Association on the Practice and Procedure of International Courts and Tribunals, 'The Hague Principles on Ethical Standards for Counsel Appearing before International Courts and Tribunals', 2010, www.ucl.ac.uk/laws/cict/docs/Hague_Sept2010.pdf. I was a member of this group.
38 American Service Members' Protection Act (ASPA, Title II of Public Law 107–206, §§ 2001–2015 approved Aug. 2, 2002) 22 U.S.C. §§7421–7423 and colloquially called the 'Hague Invasion Act' see John Sutherland, 'Who Are America's Real Enemies?', *Guardian*, 8 July 2002. (Accessed 18 January 2016) invites comparison to the domestic case of a client who does not choose to flee the jurisdiction but informs his lawyer that he plans to bomb the family court. The lawyer might think that these threats are idle talk. But, can the lawyer be sure?
39 New York State Unified Court System, 'Rules of Professional Conduct: Part 1200', Rule 3.3.
40 Transparency International's definition of corruption is the abuse of entrusted power for personal gain – noting that party political gain has long ago been accepted by Transparency International as part of their understanding of 'personal gain' See, Transparency International (TI), 'What Is Corruption', 2015, www.transparency.org/what-is-corruption/.
41 'At Last, the Damning Evidence That Should Bury Blair for His Lies over Iraq', *Daily Mail*, 19 January 2011.
42 https://www.qldbar.asn.au/#/barrister-about.
43 *Minister Administering the Crown Lands (Consolidation) Act and Western Lands Act v Tweed Byron Aboriginal Land Council* (1990) 71 LGRA 201 in the following terms at 203–204.
44 Lord Macmillan, 'The Ethics of Advocacy', in *The Law and Other Things* (Cambridge: Cambridge University Press, 1937; reprint, 2015): 191–192.
45 *White Industries (Qld) Pty Ltd v Flower & Hart* (1998) 156 ALR 169.
46 Stephen Warne to The Australian Professional Liability Blog, 25 January 2014, http://lawyerslawyer.net/2014/01/25/white-industries-v-flower-hart-unfounded-allegations-of-fraud/.
47 The case secured a high profile because the barrister briefed, Ian Callinan QC, had just been controversially appointed to the High Court because the Attorney General's recommendation, based on wide consultation, was discarded when the National Party demanded a 'big C' conservative.
48 This reflects the mischief behind the concerns of blackmail and misleading third parties above.
49 In the US case, going so far as to threaten illegal military action against court.
50 See Chapter 14.

51 That is, without a judge present. This is not a manufactured term but was apparently used by Cicero. See, S.M. Cerutti, *Cicero's Accretive Style* (Lanham: University Press of America, 1996): 15.
52 March 7 2003 advice para 29.
53 Khawar Qureshi QC, 'Constitutional Renewal or Re-Packaging?', *New Law Journal*, December 2008.
54 Jonathan Peterson, 'Lockean Property and Literary Works', *Legal Theory* 14 (2008).
55 For more detail see, Charles Sampford and William Ransome, *Just Ethical Business* (London: Routledge, 2016 (forthcoming)).
56 See Chapter 14.
57 Clare Dyer, 'Attorney General Spared Trial by Bar', *Guardian*, 14 July 2005.
58 'Attorney General Subject of Bar Complaint', *Guardian*, 2 May 2005.
59 See 'Raising the Standard' discussed in Chapter 12.
60 See Chapters 9 and 11.
61 Chilcot Inquiry, *Transcript of Evidence to the Iraq Inquiry by Lord Goldsmith*, 27 January 2010: 170–171.
62 Peterson, 'Lockean Property and Literary Works'.
63 This implies that the disbelievers were not confined to the Europeans, the Foreign Office lawyers and himself – but also the Australian lawyers who were in constant contact with the English ones; unless, of course, he thought that the Australians were nobodies.
64 Lord John Morris, *Fifth Years of Politics and the Law* (Sydney: University of New Press, 2011): 213.
65 *Transcript of Evidence to the Iraq Inquiry by Lord Goldsmith*: 171.
66 'In Full: New Goldsmith Statement', para 19.
67 Lord Goldsmith QC, 'Government and the Rule of Law in the Modern Age', in *Clifford Chance Lecture series on Rule of Law* (London: LSE Law Department, 22 February 2006): 13.
68 Clare Dyer, 'Attorney General Spared Trial by Bar', *Guardian (Australia)*, 14 July 2005.
69 12 Co Rep 64, [1607] EWHC KB J23, 77 ER 1342.
70 Robin Theobold, 'So What Really Is the Problem About Corruption', *Third World Quarterly* 20 (1999).
71 This was the explicit grounds for the dismissal of Premier Lang by Sir Philip Game in 1933 and formed part of the reasoning by Sir John Kerr in his dismissal of Prime Minister Whitlam in 1975.
72 'The Sovereign has under a constitutional monarchy such as ours – the right to be consulted, the right to be encouraged, the right to warn'. Walter Bagehot, *The English Constitution*, 1st ed. (London: Chapman & Hall, 1867): 103.
73 See, Nicholas Watt, 'Rupert Murdoch Pressured Tony Blair over Iraq, Says Alastair Campbell', *Guardian (UK)*, 16 June 2012.
74 See, Westfield Corporation, 'Annual Financial Report for Westfield Corporation', (Sydney: AXS, 2008).
75 Gavan Griffith, the previous solicitor general described Burmester as 'the most senior and experienced international lawyer in commonwealth service'. See, 'Notes on the Legal Justification for the Invasion of Iraq and Security Council Resolutions 678 and 1441', (Fairfax Digital, 2003).
76 Andrew Byrnes and Hilary Charlesworth, 'The Illegality of the War against Iraq', *Dialogue* 22, no. 1 (2003): 4.
77 Griffith QC, 'Notes on the Legal Justification for the Invasion of Iraq and Security Council Resolutions 678 and 1441'.
78 Quoted in ibid.
79 Don Greig, 'The Case for a Legal Attack', *The Australian*, 18 March 2003; 'War, Legality and Iraq', *Canberra Times*, 17 March 2003.

80 'The Case for a Legal Attack': 15. See also, 'War, Legality and Iraq': 11.
81 Cited in, Griffith QC, 'Notes on the Legal Justification for the Invasion of Iraq and Security Council Resolutions 678 and 1441'.
82 Ibid.
83 In the article republished as Chapter 14: Charles Sampford, 'Get New Lawyers!', *Legal Ethics* 6, no. 1 (2003).
84 'Dreams and Nightmares of Alternative Powers' Futures', in *Shifting Global Powers and International Law*, ed. R. Maguire, B. Lewis, and C. Sampford (Abingdon, Oxon: Routledge, Taylor & Francis Group, 2013).
85 Charles Sampford, 'Responsible Government and the Logic of Federalism: An Australian Paradox?', *Public Law*, Spring 1990.
86 John Chilcot, 'Letter to Prime Minister David Cameron Suggesting Date of Publication of Iraq War Inquiry Report', (UK Government, 28 October 2015). Chair suggests a publication date of May/June 2016.
87 Sampford, 'Get New Lawyers!': 97; 'More and More Lawyers but Still No Judges', *Legal Ethics* 8, no. 1 (2005): 21–22.
88 'All that is needed for evil to prosper is for good men to do nothing.'
89 Edmund Burke, 'Thoughts on the Cause of the Present Discontents', in *Thoughts on the Cause of the Present Discontents and the Two Speeches on America*, ed. E.J. Payne (Oxford: Clarendon, 1926): 146, Line 34.
90 This is a general feature of professions. See: Michael Davis, 'Professionalism Means Putting Your Profession First', *Georgetown Journal of Legal Ethics* 2, no. 34 (1988); 'Thinking Like an Engineer: The Place of a Code of Ethics in the Practice of a Profession', *Philosophy & Public Affairs* 20, no. 2 (1991).
91 Bagehot, *The English Constitution*: 107.
92 Charles Sampford, 'Challenges to the Concepts of "Sovereignty" and "Intervention" (Closing Keynote)', in *World Congress on Philosophy of Law and Social Philosophy* (World Trade Centre: New York, 1999).
93 For example, if the use of force was to prevent gross abuse of human rights, the ICJ would have jurisdiction to make findings and give orders. I note that Lord Morris said he was relieved to win the jurisdictional point in the Kosovo case but was disappointed that there was no opportunity to judge the legality of actions. I was also disappointed. However, it was within the power of his government to accept the jurisdiction of the ICJ and argue its case.

17 Professions without borders

Global ethics and the international rule of law

Charles Sampford

> The time has come for mankind to make the rule of law in international affairs as normal as it is now in domestic affairs. Of course the structure of such law must be patiently built, stone by stone. The cost will be a great deal of hard work, both in and out of government particularly in the universities of the world. Plainly one foundation stone of this structure is the International Court of Justice ... [and] the obligatory jurisdiction of that Court.... One final thought on rule of law between nations: we will all have to remind ourselves that under this system of law one will sometimes lose as well as win. But ... if an international controversy leads to armed conflict, everyone loses.
>
> President Dwight D. Eisenhower[1]

Introduction

Those who believe that good governance should start at home and extend abroad will easily agree, but may be surprised at the source of the quote and be more optimistic about its achievement. In this chapter, I will argue that the emergence of strong sovereign states after the Treaty of Westphalia turned two of the most cosmopolitan professions, the law and the military, into the least cosmopolitan. Sovereign states determined the content of the law within their borders – including what elements of ecclesiastical law, law merchant and international law applied. Similarly, states sought to ensure that all military force was at their disposal in national armies. The erosion of sovereignty in a post-Westphalian world may significantly reverse this process.

The erosion of sovereignty is likely to have profound consequences for the legal profession and the ethics of how, and for what ends, it is practiced. As we shall see, lawyers have played a major role in the civilization of sovereign states through the articulation and institutionalization of key governance values – starting with the rule of law. An increasingly global profession must take on similar tasks – and may find unexpected allies within the profession of arms. This chapter applies these ideas to the rule of law, reviewing the concept of an international rule of law and its relationship to domestic conceptions and outline the task of building the international rule of law and the role that lawyers and soldiers can and should play in it.[2]

1 Westphalian states and two cosmopolitan professions

Pepo, Bologna and pre-Westphalian professions

The gradual evolution of the institutions that gave rise to universities means that there is no precise date for when particular institutions became 'universities' and which can claim the mantle of the 'first'.[3] Some ancient bodies might claim as much right to call themselves 'universities' as the eleventh and twelfth century European centres of learning in Bologna, Paris and Oxford. China's Nanjing (*c.*200), Morocco's Al-Karaouine (859) and Egypt's Al-Azar (975) could claim to be the oldest continuing universities while India's Odantapuri (BC *c.*550 to *c.*1040 AD) and Jalanda (BC *c.*450 to 1193 AD) have respectable claims to being the earliest institutions that could be called universities. Although predated by a medical school at Salerno, the institution with the claim to be the first university in Europe is the University of Bologna, and there is evidence of law lectures being given by the monk Pepo as early as 1076.[4] Universities and university law teaching thus predated the modern state by nearly six centuries (and predate the joint stock company, which they have latterly been encouraged to emulate, by nearly eight centuries). They were originally among the most cosmopolitan of institutions.

The students of the time learnt Roman law, canon law and, as it developed, the law merchant.[5] Such law was not made by territorial sovereigns but was developed by jurists, priests and traders and covered most of mediaeval Europe. Indeed, the re-emergence of international trade involved issues which the existing local laws were not equipped to address, but which the preserved Roman law could. Accordingly, the legal education gained by students at Bologna and, later, Paris, Oxford and other mediaeval universities allowed them to work for any of the princes of Western Europe and to argue in many courts – making the profession of law highly cosmopolitan. There was no 'dingo fence' in mediaeval Europe.[6] Indeed, most professions were cosmopolitan – not just the oldest profession but also the most venerated profession: medicine. This applied not only to medicine and law but also the profession of arms, where there was a claimed transnational affinity between knights and a code of chivalry setting out how one could and could not fight. Most soldiers did not fight directly for kings but for local lords or as mercenaries following 'captains' of 'military bands' or 'military companies'. They might be part of armies organized by kings. But they might also fight against kings or in civil wars – or for foreign princes as individuals or groups who would fight in return for land or money.

However, the rise of strong sovereign states in the seventeenth century turned these two, most cosmopolitan, professions into two of the least cosmopolitan. Those who like a convenient date look to the Treaty of Westphalia in 1648, which provided the basis for state sovereignty. These transitions arguably commenced long before Westphalia and were not fully completed 300 years later when the United Nations (UN) Charter enshrined key aspects of the Westphalian system.[7]

The Westphalian legal profession

The claim of sovereign states to determine the content of the law within their borders – including which, if any, ecclesiastical law, what form of economic regulation and what, if any, international law was to apply – meant that those who sought to study law would study the law of a particular sovereign state. Admission to practice was determined by domestic institutions – courts, Inns of Court and various forms of apprenticeship and professional examination.[8] In common law countries, universities were not initially engaged in educating lawyers for such practice. English law was not even taught at Oxford until 1758 when William Blackstone commenced his series of lectures on English law.[9] However, after six centuries, even Oxford came around to teaching primarily English laws.

Two other developments profoundly affected the law and lawyering:

1 The rise of printing, which allowed legislation and case law to be disseminated more widely and in far greater detail than had ever been possible.
2 The decline of feudal land tenure, the gradual decline in the importance of land in European economies and the extension of the market led to the idea that landholding typically involved an 'owner' with sole dominion over it.[10]

Over some 300 years, these developments came to be seen as so entrenched that they were perceived to be natural, and the legal pluralism of pre-Westphalian Europe seemed contrary to the very nature of law.[11] However, the last 10 to 15 years have seen the emergence of trends that involve profound challenges to the nature of law in Westphalian sovereign states. The challenges to sovereignty include the rise of transnational law – including traditional international law based on treaties and the judgments of international tribunals, laws made by regional bodies, Security Council 'legislation',[12] free trade treaties,[13] investor state dispute settlement, the extra-territorial reach of United States (US) law and the development of universal jurisdiction.[14] Whether lawyers are working for law firms, governments, corporations, NGOs or as teachers and researchers in university, they will increasingly need to take into account laws from a range of sources that amount to what might be called 'global law'.

The rise of international and transnational organizations in the public, corporate and voluntary sectors has also increased the move towards pluralism. The growth of the UN and the other pillars of the UN system (the International Monetary Fund (IMF) and World Bank) have led to a profusion of international organizations for global public purposes. The International Court of Justice (ICJ), the International Criminal Court (ICC) and now the World Trade Organization (WTO) are international judicial institutions capable of enforcing an increasing volume of international law, and universal jurisdiction allows domestic courts to apply international law in certain circumstances. While the WTO has real 'teeth', the growth of transnational supply chains and global corporations led to calls to establish internationally acceptable norms to bind corporations to international human rights norms. In response to the growth of corporations and their increased recognition as actors under public international law, the UN established the Global Compact.[15] The Global Compact is a corporate social responsibility scheme where corporations agree to be bound by 10 principles in return for the perception of being a good corporate citizen. This scheme is the largest corporate citizenship group in the world with approximately 40,000 stakeholders across 100 nations.[16] Despite the current limitations on the enforcement of international law, states have created regulatory vehicles to hold non-state actors accountable for unethical business practices. The *Organisation for Economic Cooperation and Development (OECD) Guidelines*, for example, provide voluntary guidance for corporations in their international affairs and are enforced by member states.[17] While these guidelines have limited impact upon many corporations to which the guidelines are directed, they do represent moves by states to impose universal standards across jurisdictions.[18] There is no barrier to OECD member states agreeing to implement similar ethical guidelines for the way lawyers conduct themselves in international affairs and they should be encouraged to do so.

In the not-for-profit sector, the growth of international and transnational NGOs from the Red Cross to Greenpeace and Transparency International has given such NGOs a larger place in the global community than in most sovereign states. On the other hand, institutionalized religion has a more limited place than in pre-Westphalian Europe, despite attempts by fundamentalists in the 'middle east' and 'mid-west' whose aspirations for states dominated by particular religions are distinctly pre-Westphalian.[19]

More generally, the challenges of globalization, involving the movement of people, goods, services and ideas across boundaries, have increased the growth of a global community. One important aspect of this is the emergence of the internet, which has created substantial difficulties for states that desire to regulate their citizens' access to information.[20]

The issue of sovereignty has been substantially challenged by the environmental problems facing the global community. Arguably, the greater ease of movement of organisms that damage flora, fauna and people, and the unintended effects on the environment of human activity, are leading to an awareness that the land is, once again, too important to be the subject of the private dominion of individual citizens. The perception that the environment should be regarded as a global issue arguably gained traction with the UN Framework Convention on Climate Change and has obtained increased recognition with the Kyoto Protocol.[21] The Kyoto Protocol, 'creates significant responsibilities for the participating countries, and brings together many of the most industrialized countries of the world to limit gas emissions in an unprecedented way'.[22]

Sovereignty is also challenged by the flow of debt (toxic or otherwise), political ideology (toxic and otherwise), capital (mostly legitimate but including the proceeds of corruption) and viruses of varying degrees of virulence. None of these problems can be addressed by sovereign states attempting to act alone within their borders – though they can contribute to global solutions.

Most of these trends will intensify over the next few decades and could lead to fundamental changes to the nature, practice, structure and content of law over the professional lifetimes of contemporary students studying law. By the time that current students entering law schools today reach the peak of their careers in the mid-twenty-first century, the law and the legal profession may be as different from its Westphalian sovereign paradigm as that paradigm was to the world of Pepo's students.

The Westphalian profession of arms

The profession of arms was also transformed by the rise of the nation state. The European feudal system involved direct loyalty to local lords rather than to princes, kings or, in the Holy Roman Empire, the emperor. Outside of the feudal system, mercenaries had been a common feature[23] – particularly in pre-Westphalian Europe where soldiers' loyalties were often to their immediate captain rather than to a sovereign.

The growth of sovereign states resulted in standing armies that claimed the loyalties of their soldiers directly, rather than through their lords or captains. States claimed a monopoly of legitimate violence. If the soldiers' loyalty and duty were to the nation state, it was inappropriate for them to give their loyalty to, and fight for, one part of the state against another, risking the newly established order which it was the prime responsibility of the state to engender for the protection of its citizenry. Professional soldiers saw themselves as maintaining order rather than contributing to disorder. Similarly, 'mercenaries' became a dirty word as it was also totally inappropriate for a soldier to fight for another state. These principles were not always followed. Occasionally, the military would break up and join opposing sides in a civil war – something that was seen as the ultimate tragedy for a professional military force. More often, the military would remain unified in suppressing insurgency – or unified in overthrowing governments in coups d'état – one of the curses of the modern state. On the external front, some states continued to recruit mercenaries, but they were generally looked down upon as not real soldiers.[24] The use of mercenaries became less popular and in the twentieth century there were national and international steps taken to outlaw the use of private military forces.[25]

The forces of globalization are changing the profession of arms as surely as the profession of law. The last 20 years has seen the rise of private military forces associated with the US military, corporations and criminal gangs.[26] The largest remaining forms of private military forces exist in private military companies (PMCs). These PMCs can provide training, security or direct military support. The 'Sandline affair' involved an attempt to bypass the Papua New Guinea military in suppressing a secessionist movement.[27] Where PMCs perpetrate human rights abuses within a sovereign state on behalf of that state or an invading state, these forces have largely been immune from prosecution. More recently, the international community has been examining vehicles to hold PMCs responsible under international law.[28]

While the monopoly of legitimate force was a matter of definition, in most states, most of the time, the military forces of the state could prevail over any and all other coercive forces ranged against them. For mainstream military forces, the development of the laws of war has entrenched codes of behaviour that can now be enforced by the International Criminal Court. The increasing range and intensity of cooperation between military forces through participation in each other's training programs, joint exercises and UN deployments are reinforcing the sense that soldiers are part of a common global profession of arms. Indeed, their common code of conduct is in some senses far more advanced than that of lawyers, being distilled into a number of international agreements – with the four Geneva Conventions and the three amendment protocols the most significant.[29]

2 Building global professions as important institutions in a globalizing world

Global values and global institutions

The trends towards globalizing the legal and military professions and others are important. Indeed, given the absence of any equivalent to national governments within the international order, such professions may need to play a disproportionate role in building and sustaining that international order. The basis for this argument is a narrative that has much influenced my thinking over the last 10 years, briefly outlined in Chapter 1 and summarized here. Good governance requires the articulation of governance values (for example, liberty, equality, citizenship, community, democracy, human rights, the rule of law and environmental sustainability)[30] and the institutions that can realize those values. Since the seventeenth century, governance debates have centred on sovereign states rather than relations between them. Late seventeenth-century states were generally highly authoritarian and justified as such. Hobbes argued that rational people would mutually agree to subject themselves to an all-powerful sovereign to avoid a 'state of nature' in which the life of man would be 'solitary, poor, nasty, brutish and short'.[31]

Once internal order had been restored, this social contract did not seem such a good bargain. The eighteenth-century enlightenment sought to civilize these authoritarian states by holding them to a set of more refined and ambitious values – notably liberty, equality, citizenship, human rights, democracy and the rule of law. Some of these values were adaptations of classical city-state ideals to the much larger polities of the time. Nineteenth-century thinkers extended the range of rights championed and added concern for environment and for practical and social equality.

Most importantly, the key to the enlightenment governance project was a 'Feuerbachian' reversal of the way rulers and ruled related to each other first noted in my work on coups (see Chapter 1). Before the enlightenment, 'subjects' had to demonstrate their allegiance and loyalty to their 'sovereign'. The enlightenment proclaimed that 'governments' had to justify their existence to 'citizens' who chose them. Once the reversal of the relationship was suggested, it was very hard to go back.

Values are rarely self-implementing: they require institutions to realize them. Institutional innovations included an independent judiciary exercising judicial review of the executive, representative institutions, bicameral parliaments, federal division of functions, government and civil society watchdogs, universal education, questioning media and 'responsible' (or 'parliamentary') government.[32] This development of governance values and the institutions to realize them can be seen as an 'enlightenment project'.

Debates have rightly continued over the precise meaning and relative importance of these governance values and the best institutional means of achieving them. However, the centre of gravity in governance debates has remained the sovereign state, with the 'enlightenment project' becoming a 'UN project' in which all the peoples of the world might become members of strong sovereign states securing their citizens' universal human rights.[33]

This 'UN project' has been shaken by the 'globalizing' flow of ideas, people, goods and services flooding over international borders and weakening many sovereign states. Liberal democratic values were formed *in and for* strong states. Citizenship, democracy, welfare and community have clear meaning *within* sovereign states but lack apparent application in a broader, more diffuse, globalized world. The institutions that sustain, promote and realize those values are very much state-based. The rights, duties and 'sense of belonging' that citizenship carries are attached to state institutions. Democracy is realized through citizen participation in national and sub-national legislatures – and loses mileage if the real power and range of choice open to those legislatures is restricted. Welfare rights like education and healthcare are only implemented through the institutions of strong, sovereign (and wealthy) states – and even their capacity to do so is increasingly questioned.

Two common responses are to abandon inconvenient governance values such as democracy and welfare or to resist globalization and strengthen the state. I have long argued for a third approach, because globalization exposes a flaw in the 'enlightenment project' and later 'UN project'. How can universal rights be secured by geographically limited entities? Why should the welfare rights of the citizens of some states be a tiny fraction of the welfare rights of others? This approach suggests a fundamental rethinking of our governance values and the mix of institutions that can achieve them – a 'global enlightenment' in which, as in the eighteenth century, the ideals will come first and the practical institutional solutions will come later.[34] As in the eighteenth century, when city-state values and institutions were reworked and recombined for nation states, sovereign state values and institutions may need reworking and recombining.

I have argued that the institutional arrangements that are most likely to emerge and which are most likely to secure such values will not resemble 'sovereign states writ large'. It is more likely to look like pre-Westphalian Europe. States and multilateral institutions will be important but other institutions – corporations, superannuation funds,[35] professions and NGOs – may play a larger role.[36] In this light, I will consider the roles of the legal and soldierly professions in a future order and I will suggest that lawyers and the military should see themselves as part of an international profession, respecting international values.

Towards global professions

I suggest that the legal profession is, and should be, breaking free of its Westphalian shackles. Professions are not bound by their employers, let alone their states. This principle is the whole point of an independent profession.[37] As discussed in Chapter 11, the concept of a profession involves a group who develops and deploys a body of knowledge and skills for a public purpose. Such knowledge and skills can be used for good or ill – for the ostensible purpose which justifies the powers and privileges of the relevant profession, or abused for other purposes. As I argued elsewhere,[38] the justification of a profession (indeed, institutions generally) should be in terms of the values it furthers on behalf of the community in which it operates. Those values provide the core for ethical standard-setting (both aspirational and disciplinary), legal regulation and institutional reform.

The importance of ethical guidelines is axiomatic in the case of the military – whose knowledge and skills may involve the deployment of organized deadly force against other states in defiance of international law or deployed against the state itself (and generally the human rights of its citizens) in a coup d'état. The oft-asked question about the difference between a government and a band of robbers is repeated in asking the difference between the army and an organized group of violent gangsters. The answer cannot simply lie in following orders of the civilian 'commander in chief' as to which groups of people are to be killed en masse, as that does not guarantee that the military is more than a reliable accomplice. The answer must lie in the values the military forces claim to espouse, the codes of honour and ethics they develop to realize those values, the commitment to that code and the institutional means that they provide in order to make that realization probable – including mechanisms for reviewing the actions of soldiers and applying appropriate sanctions.

While lawyers cannot directly deploy lethal force, if they are not bound by ethical restraints they can provide advice that can result in spectacular individual and social harm. Where lawyers give advice on the legality of wars or torture, the consequences can be catastrophic for those who suffer invasion and/or torture. The fact that those who sought selective legal advice may leave office with their reputations shattered is small consolation and an insufficient deterrent.

The abuse of the knowledge and skills of lawyers is not as spectacular as the deployment of military force, it is potentially insidious if the knowledge and skills of lawyers are used to deny justice. Sometimes globalization makes this task of denial easier – when lawyers forum-shop for jurisdictions wherein their clients can engage in lawful practices, which would be regarded as criminal in their home state.[39] A similar question arises with regard to the difference between a lawyer and a 'spin-doctor' – saying whatever suits the client's interest and, in effect, making lawyers figuratively rather than literally 'guns for hire'. As we saw in Chapters 14 to 16, where the client refuses to have disputes heard in a court of competent jurisdiction, there is a temptation for clients to seek, and lawyers to give, advice they want to hear. As with the military, the answer for lawyers must lie in values, ethics, commitment and the institutional means for keeping lawyers to their task.

In both cases, the professionals act, with very few exceptions, on instructions by the commander-in-chief or client. However, they do so in an institutional context designed to further the core values of that profession and reduce the likelihood that the professionals' knowledge and skills will be abused. In the case of the military in Western states, the core values are the protection of the civil population and constitutional authority from external attack and (rarely) internal insurrection. For lawyers, the core values are the rule of law, due process, and human rights – sometimes packaged under an overall value of doing justice according to law. For the military, it is civilian control by constitutional authority (only using force when legally permitted) and that force should be used against citizens under very strict rules and specific safeguards. However, there is considerable overlap. The core values of the military reflect core values for lawyers. Likewise, the rule of law and human rights can be central to some conceptions of the role of the military. Hon Mike Kelly, Parliamentary Secretary for Defence, had argued that the military would be more likely to be successful if it subjected itself to the rule of law in interventions, because others knew when force would be used and when it would not.[40] In a workshop on 'Reconceiving the Rule of Law in a Globalizing World' in 2001, he argued that the Australian army was the largest human rights organization in Australia because it did more to further human rights through its peacekeeping operations than any other organization.

I emphasize *furthering* core values of the relevant profession. It is not sufficient for a profession to avoid actions that compromise their core values. Professions take a lead role in promoting certain values. Lawyers were critical in developing and proselytizing the rule of law and the institutional mechanisms to make it effective within strong sovereign states. The military have taken a lead role in the strongest democracies in emphasizing their subordination to the constitution, to law and to constitutional authority. Lawyers and soldiers should now do the same in international affairs, recognizing that the profession of arms may be an ally. In some of my earlier writings,[41] I set out an approach to the rule of law – as a contested concept with largely reinforcing and supportive meanings. It stands for a fundamental value or ideal, an ethic for lawyers and officials, the basic principles of constitutionalism and a set of institutions that supports its attainment. In those writings, I also argued for a 'thin' theory of the rule of law based on the approaches of Fuller, Hayek and Raz, which identified human rights as a distinct if reinforcing 'virtue', law or governance value.[42] These meanings are appropriate for both the 'domestic' and 'international rule of law'. The rest of this chapter discusses how the globalizing professions of arms assisted the former and may play a critical role in developing the latter.

3 Role of the legal profession in developing the international rule of law

If one looks at the various difficulties in developing and institutionalizing the international rule of law, one could conclude that, in many areas where the rule of law seems most needed, it is as distant as it would have seemed to those living under the largely absolutist regimes that emerged in Western Europe after the Treaty of Westphalia. The fact that the heroic efforts by lawyers and revolutionaries over several centuries led to a remarkable transformation in those states may offer little comfort. The international community cannot wait that long and cannot sustain the violent struggles that were often necessary for the rule of law to emerge domestically. However, the rule of law is a very strong domestic ideal on which we can build support. It is an ideal that is not only endorsed, but in many cases sincerely so, by various leaders' summits.[43] To make the attainment of an international rule of law realistic, there needs to be coordinated action to address some of the institutional limitations of international law. Lawyers can and should take a lead in such action – just as they did in the development of the domestic rule of law and the institutions that underpin it. This is not the time or place to set out a comprehensive strategy for building the rule of law in international affairs to match the rule of law in domestic affairs (something we hope to be closer to at the end of the above-mentioned projects). However, I will suggest some things lawyers may do and the reasons they may find unexpected allies in the military.

Developing and promoting the rule of law as a fundamental governance value in international affairs

Just as lawyers were major contributors to the development and promotion of the rule of law in domestic affairs, so they should be in international affairs. However, they should not be so as narrow lawyers, but as lawyers who understand the philosophical, political and economic issues it raises. Indeed, they should recognize that the rule of law was developed at a time when those disciplines had not yet become distinct. While mastering these disciplines in their entirety is not a realistic goal for individuals, it is for groups of lawyers who respect those disciplines and bring their insights to bear.

If the rule of law becomes a fundamental value of the profession and a value that it uses to justify the profession, lawyers need to reflect carefully and debate publicly its meaning, value and relationship to the nature of the profession and its work to a global community.

Ethical standard-setting through codes

Lawyers can contribute to the articulation of more specific codes for lawyers and others – not least the military who are, as we have seen, potential allies in building the international rule of law. Lawyers should begin by developing a code of ethics for international lawyers and lawyers operating across borders. However, this should not be done in isolation. One of the most important underpinnings of the rule of law in modern states is the importance it plays in the ethics of key participants. Lawyers have 'duties to the court' or, more generally, to 'the law' or 'justice'. Civil servants are concerned with ensuring that all action taken in the name of the state has legal authority. More generally, the rule of law is an ethic for the wielders of power – to exercise powers they have for the purposes that are entrusted to them. Codes need to be developed for:

- *International lawyers; international judges and tribunal members; and international civil servants.* Such codes cover a variety of issues but centrally concern how entrusted power is handled and a commitment to international law and the rule of law in international as well as national affairs. Lawyers have made a good start on developing voluntary codes. The International Bar Association consulted with the American Bar Association and the Council of Bars and Law Societies of Europe in October 2008 to create an anti-money laundering code that provides a risk-based approach to avoid participation in money laundering, including monitoring processes and training for lawyers. The International Bar Association has a two page 'International Code of Ethics'[44] and the Union Internationale des Avocats has developed the 'Turin Principles for the Legal Profession in the 21st Century' (2002). The only area with developed codes that are authorized and (in theory at least) enforced by courts are in the International Court of Justice and the various ad hoc criminal tribunals for Rwanda, Sierra Leone and the Former Yugoslavia. The NYU/UCL Project on International Courts and Tribunals (PICT)[45] developed a code of ethics for lawyers appearing before international tribunals. The committee (on which I was honoured to serve) met in London, Geneva and Utrecht between June 2009 and April 2010, finally reporting to the International Law Association in August 2010.
- *Member states and their delegates to General Assembly* (GA), *United Nations Security Council* (UNSC) and *international bodies*: analogous to codes of ethics for parliamentarians in domestic systems.
- *Military forces* which are acting under UN authority and military forces engaging in international action – reflecting the same kind of respect for international law and particularly the UN Charter that they are expected to show for domestic laws and domestic constitutions.

The nature of the code development would vary depending on the work already undertaken and completed by others. In all cases, the code development should consider the dilemmas, apparent and real conflicts of duties, as well as the pressures and temptations of practice that may lead participants to 'read down' their ethical duties. However, the focus of the work will vary depending on the codes and principles already in place and the degree to which those codes and principles are controversial. For example, where there are rival codes or principles, it is very important to tease out the reasons for disagreement and make suggestions.

Also, where most of the relevant ethics codes are domestic (for example, practicing lawyers and, to a lesser extent judges), it is important to deal with issues involving the extension of existing codes, potential conflict between codes, the relationship between the duties to domestic courts and clients and relevant duties to international courts and clients.

In all cases, the relationships between the codes must be considered carefully by examining the ways in which they may unintentionally conflict and ways in which they may be mutually supportive (for example, in the complementarity of the ethics of judges and advocates).

Once relevant international codes for lawyers acting and advising in international matters are developed, their principles should be incorporated into domestic legal ethics codes so that respect for international law and the rule of law in international affairs is built into the codes by which most lawyers practice. Similar domestic implementation should be followed in professional civil service codes and military ethics.

Other forms of ethical standard-setting

The creation of codes is a high priority for a number of reasons. The Project on International Courts and Tribunals (PICT) provides an example of a recent opportunity to perform this work. Additionally, there is a great deal of disquiet about the 'torture memos' briefly discussed in the previous chapter. Further, the creation of an international code will emphasize the responsibilities of international lawyers to the international legal system separately from their responsibilities as lawyers within their domestic jurisdictions; and such codes can provide inputs for those who want to reform the domestic legal ethics codes following the torture memos.

While the creation of codes is a high priority and is a natural activity for lawyers, it should be recognized that this does not exhaust the ethics of this or any other profession. If legal ethics were co-extensive with codes of ethics, two counterintuitive consequences would follow. First, it would mean that there would be no sense in complimenting or criticizing the ethics codes. Second, it would make no sense to criticize the ethics of some and praise others. It would be pointless to compliment Lord Goldsmith for the first advice and to criticize him for the second advice.[46] It would also be pointless to refer to the temptation for clients to seek, and lawyers to give, the advice the client wants to hear rather than the advice the client should hear if they are facing court. If the client has no intention of accepting the jurisdiction of a court of competent jurisdiction, lawyers should make it clear that they will not give such advice or, if they do, they will not be acting as lawyers and there should be no privilege.

Before there are codes, people can debate what kind of conduct they admire as ethical and what they criticize as unethical. They can advocate new rules to bolster these normative claims. Even where there are codes in place, they generally set minimum standards of behaviour. There is room to articulate and practice according to what the proponents believe to be higher standards. These will help set standards even while they are supererogatory. While they may affect code development, there will always be room for such higher standards, and they are part of a dynamic profession.

In all cases, the pressures for and against compliance should be considered. While the initial focus of code development would involve the clarification of ethical standards for those subject to the pressure, and those who may be applying the pressure, suggestions would also be made for institutional changes that remove or reduce dilemmas, temptations and pressures for unethical behaviour.

Simultaneously, the legal profession should be actively involved in strengthening institutions that will support the international rule of law and the participation of all states in it. Lawyers made tremendous contributions to the institutionalization of the rule of law domestically – not always succeeding, and risking occasional death or imprisonment.

4 Role of the military in developing the international rule of law

I will not spend as much time on the role of the military, as my research and expertise lies primarily in the profession of which I am a part. However, the following thoughts may be helpful.

As I have emphasized throughout this chapter, lawyers should seek suitable allies within the military. During the lead-up to the Iraq war, two of those most implicated in what seems to most international lawyers to be a serious breach of international law were lawyers turned prime ministers. Prime Minister Blair appears to have been instrumental in persuading Lord Goldsmith to produce a short and misleading opinion claiming the proposed war would be legal, omitting the caveats in his original advice.[47] On 6 March 2003, Prime Minister Howard told the Australian parliament that there was ample legal authority for the war, although virtually no legal authorities supported it.[48] Some members of the military behaved much more creditably. Admiral Sir Michael Boyce, the Chief of the UK armed forces, refused to cross the Kuwait border without written legal advice that the war was legal.[49] If the lawyers providing written advice for public consumption had been prepared to acknowledge the limited support their arguments had and the unlikelihood of being able to succeed in a court of competent jurisdiction, the British military may have stopped the war.

Later in the Iraq war, it was serving soldiers who first reported and then leaked what had happened at Abu Ghraib.[50]

While soldiers who are also lawyers may play an important role, it is the respect for international law by other soldiers that is determinative. In the Kosovo and Iraq wars, JAG officers in the armed forces advised against some targeting.[51] The differential response of different militaries indicates the importance of their role and the extent to which the adherence to international law is built into their ethics and the way they see themselves serving their countries. In the Iraq war, this respect for JAG advice could have been motivated by an awareness of the ICC and the possibility of criminal conviction. However, the differential response in the Kosovo war indicates a difference in ethics of different militaries.

The idea of professional obligation is deeply entrenched in the military – so deep that they are prepared to die for it – something other professions are rarely called upon to do. But this is cross-fertilized by the fact that a number of military officers are members of two professions – with engineers and doctors being more numerous than lawyers. While being a member of two professions may be potentially confusing, it is more likely to help in developing codes in underdeveloped areas. Some cross-fertilization between professions in the military may assist.

Conclusion

This chapter endorses the idea that the rule of law should become as fundamental a governance value within the international community as it is within sovereign states. The legal profession should take a lead in developing our understanding of that value and the ethical and institutional means of realizing that value. The military profession is a potential ally and Americans have traditionally been, and hopefully will again become, natural allies in this process. Our good work in the twentieth century has been tarnished by a poor end to the twentieth century and a poor start to the twenty-first. However, those who are either unduly optimistic or pessimistic about major institutional change might do well to recognize that history is, what I call, a 'long game'. But the way that long game will play out is not a matter of prediction but of action. What lawyers and soldiers do during the next 50 years will be crucial to how it plays out. Lawyers were critical to the crystallization of the rule of law in seventeenth-century England – soldiers all but undid it, and a bloody civil war almost destroyed the country. This century – or more likely quarter-century – we are playing for much bigger stakes. The international rule of law has been sufficiently conceptualized. This is the time when the international rule of law may be articulated, advocated and institutionalized. But we cannot afford a global civil war along the way. This is why the international rule of law must be a key goal of the newly cosmopolitan and globalizing legal profession – and the increasingly cosmopolitan profession of arms must go along with them – not just to avoid conviction in the ICC, but because of their conviction that internationally, as well as domestically, their use of force must be lawful.

At the 1999 World Congress on Legal and Social Philosophy,[52] I drew a link between domestic and international rule of law and suggested that it was a great tragedy that the US, so long a leader in articulating and practicing the domestic rule of law, was setting such a bad example in the international rule of law. When I described illegal bombing from 15,000 feet as a new 'high crime and misdemeanour', I was told I must be a Republican. Had my interlocutor known of Eisenhower's quote, with which this chapter opens, he might have pressed me. But the answer is that the rule of law is neither Republican nor Democratic, Liberal or Labour, Left or Right. It is a fundamental governance value, a basic rule of the game – indeed, it is the commitment to the idea that the game *has* rules. This over-arching idea can be expressed as a 'rule-based order' – a term that is currently popular, including among those who appear to have broken those rules in 1999 and 2003.

One truly disturbing trend that has emerged is the abandonment of the rule of law by some who consider themselves conservative – or the oxymoronic category of 'neo-conservative'. The corollary of this trend is that the argument for the rule of law has so often to be run by the left, and those genuine conservatives who fight for it are often ranged against those who call themselves conservatives – and those conservatives who fight for it are treated as if they are left-wing radicals.

Let us hope that the apparent implosion of the oxymoronic 'neo-conservatism' allows conservative, liberal and social democratic lawyers to make common cause on the rule of law – and take a lead in its realization internationally as well as domestically, bringing with them the profession of arms and the vocation of politics.

Notes

1 Dwight D. Eisenhower, 'Remarks Upon Receiving an Honorary Degree of Doctor of Laws at Delhi University', (11 December 1959), www.presidency.ucsb.edu/ws/?pid=11617. Quoted with the kind permission of the American Presidency Project. Those who are surprised by the source of the quote should recall that this soldier turned politician used federal troops to protect a black student in Little Rock and warned of the military industrial complex. In Delhi, the old warrior who had masterminded the 6 June Normandy landings of the 'United Nations' (a phrase used in newspapers on that day) made his plea for law not war.

2 In so doing, I will expand on views expressed above in Chapters 9, 14 and 15, and also in Charles Sampford, 'Challenges to the Concepts of "Sovereignty" and "Intervention"', in *Human Rights in Philosophy and Practice*, ed. T. Campbell and B.M. Leiser (Aldershot: Ashgate, 2001); *Retrospectivity and the Rule of Law* (Oxford: Oxford University Press, 2006).

3 See, http://en.wikipedia.org/wiki/List_of_oldest_universities_in_continuous_operation for Wikipedia's discussion of the issue with the claims of Nanjing and Academy of Gundishapur in Iran as well as University of Al-Karaouine in Morocco and Al-Azar in Cairo.

4 C. Phillipson, 'Andrea Alciati and His Predecessors', *Journal of the Society of Comparative Legislation New Series* 13, no. 2 (1913).

5 For a discussion generally see: W. Mitchell, *An Essay on the Early History of the Law Merchant* (Cambridge: University Press, 1904).

6 The 'dingo fence' was erected in Australia to keep dingoes (wild dogs that were present in Australia before European settlement) out of south east Australia. The restrictive practices for keeping southern lawyers from appearing before Queensland courts were colloquially referred to as a 'dingo fence'.

7 For example, United Nations (UN), 'Charter of the United Nations', (San Francisco, 1945). Chapter 1, Article 2, principles 1 and 7:

> The Organization is based on the principle of the sovereign equality of all its Members

and

> Nothing contained in the present Charter shall authorize the United Nations to intervene in matters which are essentially within the domestic jurisdiction of any

state or shall require the Members to submit such matters to settlement under the present Charter; but this principle shall not prejudice the application of enforcement measures under Chapter VII.

The concept of universal standards provided increased support for the human rights instruments which accompanied the Charter. The preamble of the United Nations General Assembly, 'Universal Declaration of Human Rights (UDHR)' (1948) explains that human rights are a 'common standard of achievement for all peoples and all nations'. Article II of the UDHR explains the universal application of human rights by stating:

> Everyone is entitled to all the rights and freedoms set forth in this Declaration, without distinction of any kind, such as race, colour, sex, language, religion, political or other opinion, national or social origin, property, birth or other status. Furthermore, no distinction shall be made on the basis of the political, jurisdictional or international status of the State or territory to which a person belongs, whether it is independent, trust, non-self-governing or under any other limitation of sovereignty.

The UN General Assembly, 'International Covenant on Civil and Political Rights (ICCPR)', No. 16 (New York: United Nations, 1966) and the 'International Covenant on Economic, Social and Cultural Rights (ICESCR)', ed. UN General Assembly, No. 16 (United Nations, 1966) both support the notion of universality in their preambles when they state that nations are obliged to give 'universal respect for, and observance of, human rights and freedoms'. On the links between the UN Charter and the UDHR, see: Hugh Breakey, 'What Human Rights Aren't For: Human Rights Function as Moral, Political and Legal Standards – but Not as Intervention-Conditions', *Research in Ethical Issues in Organizations* 13 (2015).

8 See, e.g. Introduction to P. Lemmings, *Gentlemen and Barristers: The Inns of Court and the English Bar 1680–1733* (Oxford: Oxford University Press, 1990).

9 See William Twining, *Blackstone's Tower: The English Law School* (London: Sweet & Maxwell, 1994).

10 This development is in sharp contrast to feudal law when land was at the centre of life and likely to be subject to a range of rights. In a sense, it was 'too important' to be simply owned by one person.

11 Which was, since Austin, seen as norms emerging from a sovereign.

12 Vesselin Popovski and Trudy Fraser, eds, *The Security Council as Global Legislator* (Abingdon: Routledge, 2014). My contribution argues against this trend: Charles Sampford, 'The Coming "Coke Moment"', in *The Security Council as Global Legislator*, ed. Vesselin Popovski and Trudy Fraser (Abingdon: Routledge, 2014).

13 Or 'Preferential Trade Treaties' as a sceptical Productivity Commission calls them: Productivity Commission (PC), 'Trade and Assistance Review 2013–14', (Australian Government, 2015).

14 See, e.g. R. O'Keefe, 'Universal Jurisdiction: Clarifying the Basic Concept', *Journal of International Criminal Justice* 2, no. 3 (2004).

15 The UN General Assembly on 5 December 2007 unanimously adopted a Resolution which supported the work of the UNGC Office: UN General Assembly, 'Towards Global Partnerships', (General Assembly, 2007); United Nations, 'UN General Assembly Renews and Strengthens Global Compact Mandate', *Compact Quarterly*, 2007. See, for a comprehensive discussion: A. Rasche, 'A Necessary Supplement' – What the United Nations Global Compact Is and Is Not', *Business & Society* 48, no. 4 (2009).

16 United Nations Global Compact (UNGC), 'Annual Review 2006', 2 (2007).

17 S. Cooney, 'Improving Regulatory Strategies for Dealing with Endemic Labour Abuses' (JSD thesis, Columbia University, 2005): 155–158; 'A Broader Role for the Commonwealth in Eradicating Foreign Sweatshops?', *Melbourne University Law Review* 28 (2004): 315–316.

18 For a criticism of the *OECD Guidelines for Multi-National Enterprises* (2000) see: J. Ruggie, 'Protect, Respect and Remedy: A Framework for Business and Human Rights: Report of the Special Representative of the Secretary-General', (United Nations, 2008).

19 The caliphate predated Westphalia by 800 years and the establishment of religiously defined colonies predated it by 30 years.

20 See for a discussion on attempts to regulate the internet: S. Deva, 'Corporate Complicity in Internet Censorship in China: Who Cares for the Global Compact or the Global Online Freedom Act?', *George Washington International Law Review* 39 (2007).

21 United Nations (UN), 'United Nations Framework Convention on Climate Change', (1992). Opened for signature on 4 June 1992, 31 ILM 849 (entered into force on 21 March 1994); 'Kyoto Protocol to the United Nations Framework Convention on Climate Change', (1992). Opened for signature 16 March 1998 (entered into force on 16 February 2005); See for discussion of the impact: D.G. Victor, *The Collapse of the Kyoto Protocol and the Struggle to Slow Global Warming* (New York: Princeton University Press, 2001).

22 H.D. Shumaker, 'The Economic Effects of the European Union Carbon Dioxide Emission Quota on the New Member States of the European Union: Can They Become Equal Economic Partners of the European Union While Complying with the 2008–2012 Quota?', *Pennsylvania State Environmental Law Review* 17 (2008): 99.

23 D. Stinnett, 'Regulating the Privatization of War: How to Stop Private Military Firms from Committing Human Rights Abuses', *Boston College International and Comparative Law Review* 28 (2005); The main instruments banning mercenary activities are the ICRC, 'Protocol Additional to the Geneva Conventions of 12 August 1949, and Relating to the Protection of Victims of International Armed Conflicts (Protocol I)' (Geneva: International Committee of the Red Cross, 1977): 42; and the UN General Assembly, 'International Convention against the Recruitment, Use, Financing and Training of Mercenaries (UN Mercenary Convention)', (General Assembly, 1989). (Entered into force 20 October 2001).

24 While some would argue that the Ghurkhas are a potentially contradictory example, there were attempts to avoid considering them as mercenaries and their rights were never as extensive as Britain's citizen soldiers.

25 P.W. Singer, 'Corporate Warriors: The Rise of the Privatized Military Industry and Its Ramifications for International Security', *International Security* 26 (2001/02): 191.

26 See P.W. Singer, *Corporate Warriors: The Rise of the Privatized Military Industry* (New York: Cornell University, 2003).

27 S. Dinnen, R. May and A. Regan, eds, *Challenging the State: The Sandline Affair in Papua New Guinea* (Canberra: ANU, 1997); S. Dorney, *The Sandline Affair: Politics and Mercenaries and the Bougainville Crisis* (Sydney: ABC Books for the Australian Broadcasting Corporation, 1998).

28 D. Morgan, 'Professional Military Firms under International Law', *Chicago Journal of International Law* 9 (2008); D. Ridlon, 'Contractors or Illegal Combatants? The Status of Armed Contractors in Iraq', *The Air Force Law Review* 62 (2008).

29 ICRC, *Convention (I) for the Amelioration of the Condition of the Wounded and Sick in Armed Forces in the Field* (Geneva: International Committee of the Red Cross, 1949). (first adopted in 1864, last revision in 1949); *Convention (II) for the Amelioration of the Condition of the Wounded and Sick in Armed Forces in the Field* (Geneva: International Committee of the Red Cross, 1949). (First adopted in 1906); *Convention (III) for the Amelioration of the Condition of the Wounded and Sick in Armed Forces in the Field* (Geneva: International Committee of the Red Cross, 1949). (First adopted in 1929, last revision in 1949); *Convention (IV) Relative to the Protection of Civilian Persons in Time of War* (Geneva, 1949). (first adopted in 1949, based on parts of the 1907 Hague Convention IV); *First Protocol*; *Protocol Additional to the Geneva*

Conventions of 12 August 1949, and Relating to the Protection of Victims of Non-International Armed Conflicts (Protocol II) (Geneva: International Committee of the Red Cross, 1977); *Protocol Additional to the Geneva Conventions of 12 August 1949, and Relating to the Adoption of an Additional Distinctive Emblem (Protocol III)* (Geneva: International Committee of the Red Cross, 2005).

30 Though not as recently as might be imagined: nineteenth-century environmentalists sought to clean up the Thames and protect the countryside via the National Trust.

31 Thomas Hobbes, *Leviathan,* 1 ed. (Cambridge: Cambridge University Press, 1991): 89.

32 A feature shared by all long-standing democracies other than the United States.

33 Charles Sampford, 'Challenges to the Concepts of "Sovereignty" and "Intervention" (Closing Keynote)', in *World Congress on Philosophy of Law and Social Philosophy* (World Trade Centre: New York, 1999).

34 While deferring the institutional issues, I would emphasize that this does not amount to an argument for global government – the sovereign state writ large. A more likely result is a mix of institutions reflecting both pre-Westphalian Europe and the modern ideal of an integrity system made up of public, corporate and NGO bodies.

35 Especially if driven to engage in sustainable investment that meets the values and interests of their unit holders who have longer-term interests than the investment managers.

36 There is also likely to be a place for unions or faith-based organizations – though I am not sure that their role will be larger or smaller. It is relevant to observe that faith-based NGOs have been involved in pressuring corporations to date on good corporate citizenship: L. Allen, 'Religion and Corporate Social Responsibility: The Interfaith Centre on Corporate Responsibility and the Corporate Withdrawal Movement from Burma' (Boston University, 2003).

37 In describing the profession as 'independent', this does not mean that it is entirely self-regulating; see Fred C. Zacharias, 'The "Self-Regulation" Misnomer', in *Reaffirming Legal Ethics: Taking Stock and New Ideas*, ed. Kieran Tranter, *et al.* (London: Routledge, 2010). Zacharias points out the central role played by legislation and, especially, the judiciary. However, the main impetus for enunciating and developing legal ethics and the structure and role of the profession comes from lawyers, with many of the regulatory and most of the disciplinary decisions in the hands of the judicial branch of the profession.

38 See Charles Sampford, 'Law, Institutions and the Public Private Divide', *Federal Law Review* 20 (1991). Charles Sampford and Christine Parker, 'Legal Ethics: Legal Regulation, Ethical Standard-setting and Institutional Design', in *Legal Ethics and Legal Practice: Contemporary Issues*, ed. S. Parker and C. Sampford (Oxford: Oxford University Press, 1995): 11.

39 For a discussion of where this has occurred in relation to bribery and medical trials see: P. Ala'i, 'The Legacy of Geographical Morality and Colonialism: A Historical Assessment of the Current Crusade against Corruption', *Vanderbilt Journal of Transnational Law* 33 (2000); D. Fidler, '"Geographical Morality" Revisited: International Relations, International Law, and the Controversy over Placebo-Controlled HIV Clinical Trials in Developing Countries', *Harvard International Law Journal* 42, no. 2 (2001).

40 Discussions with the then Lt Col Kelly in 1999 during our work on an ARC linkage grant on 'Preserving and Restoring the Rule of Law in the Asia Pacific'.

41 Charles Sampford, 'Globalizing the Rule of Law', in *Legislative Council Chamber* (Brisbane: Queensland Parliament, 2000), later published as 'Reconceiving the Rule of Law for a Globalizing World', in *Globalisation and the Rule of Law*, ed. Spencer Zifcak (London: Routledge, 2004). This was further developed in '"Thin Theories" of the Domestic and International Rule of Law', in *International Rule of Law and Professional Ethics*, ed. Vesselin Popovski (Surrey: Ashgate, 2014).

42 'Reconceiving the Rule of Law'.
43 Such as the UN General Assembly, 'Res. 60/1: World Summit Outcome Document', (2005), clause 134.
44 First adopted in 1956, last amended in 1988.
45 See www.pict-pcti.org/ (last accessed 13 Jan 2016).
46 See Chapter 15 for discussion and sources.
47 R. Whitaker, 'The Crawford Deal: Did Blair Sign up for War at Bush's Texas Ranch in April 2002?', *The Independent*, 27 February 2005.
48 Chapter 15.
49 A. Barnett and M. Bright, 'British Military Chief Reveals New Legal Fears over Iraq War', *Observer*, 1 May 2005.
50 Suzanne Goldenberg, 'Abu Ghraib Leaked Report Reveals Full Extent of Abuse', *Guardian*, 17 February 2006.
51 Confidential but reliable source.
52 Sampford, 'Sovereignty and Intervention'.

18 *A final reflection*

New challenges and opportunities for law, lawyering and legal education

Charles Sampford

1 Challenges and opportunities for law schools: then and now

When I first started writing about legal education, the big issues were whether and how to incorporate theory (the critical and theoretical dimensions) and practical skills into legal education – as well as whether to offer separate law degrees for the then 50 per cent who were not in legal practice three years after graduation. Resourcing constraints in some older law schools raised questions over the relative roles of research and teaching. But some of the greatest constraints arose from the conceit that a law degree could or should provide a full legal education rather than the most intensive section of lifelong learning.

We argued that understanding practice helped theory and vice versa – whether a graduate ended up as a lawyer serving clients and community or part of that community understanding the role of norms in their own activity. The pursuit of quality teaching and research was a matter of resources and timing. Curriculum design was not 'something done in February' but supported by a clear structure, early appointment of staff, stable teaching allocation, research assistance, externally won teaching grants, mentoring and feedback. At Griffith, high expectations of research excellence were supported by stable teaching allocation, staff–student ratios matching that of good Australian Arts faculties, strong appointments of professorial staff but particularly sub-professorial staff in the first four years,[1] support for securing external grants, and a model for research based on interdisciplinary teams.[2]

We emphasized the importance of understanding, researching and teaching the context in which law is practiced and in which our graduates and their clients operate. The greatest challenge for law schools today is the rapidly changing context that their graduates will face. As we saw in Chapter 17, that context changed radically from the 'cosmopolitan' and legally pluralistic world of Pepo's graduates to the world of the strong sovereign state where the only law that counted was that approved by the sovereign institutions of the state. That remained largely so in the 1980s but is now being radically changed by globalization. As I suggested in the last chapter,

> by the time that current students entering law schools today reach the peak of their careers in the mid twenty-first century, the law and the legal

profession may be as different from its Westphalian sovereign paradigm as that paradigm was to the world of Pepo's students.

How might the law and the legal profession change? One possibility is that there will be a return to a form of legal pluralism[3] as existed in pre-Westphalian Europe. Fifteen years ago, some of my colleagues were concerned about a globally imperial American law. I suggested that the model might be more like the 'middle kingdom' where other countries avoided doing what the United States clearly did not want them to do. Earlier this decade, it seemed more likely that China might secure that role as the original middle kingdom recovers from its 'two bad centuries'. There are other less drastic alternatives – recognizing that international law and the international system are not determined by the number one economic or military power.[4] One change that is highly likely is that in advising clients, resolving disputes and setting new directions, lawyers will need to resort to legal rules and practices arising at the international and regional level, as well as the national and sub-national laws of several jurisdictions. This combination may be seen as 'global law'. This increasing combination of laws at multiple levels is already at the forefront of responses to the Global Financial Crisis, to the Global Carbon Crisis, to intellectual property, to disease control, to oil spills, to taxation, and to refugees. I suspect that this will increasingly happen in what are now seen as mundane areas of practice – I have suggested that the suburban lawyer may find standard conveyancing done by others, with clients needing skilled advice concerning time-shares in Thailand!

Even with the best research, law schools cannot be expected to predict how law and lawyering will change. But they should help students understand some of the directions of current and possible future changes, recognize emerging trends and not be too surprised at the outcomes. As always, the philosopher in me suggests that the key is to help students ask questions, reach tentative answers and revisit those questions during their careers. The Foundation Dean in me recognizes that law schools must consider the skills and knowledge that might be required by lawyers in likely legal futures as they determine which skills and knowledge they include in their curricula and the kinds of research they pursue.

This might return us to the 1980s' laments about impossible levels of required teaching content. As always, the answer is not to teach everything but to provide an overview of the law and 'legal systems', delve deep into a few areas to understand not only the legal norms but the normative issues and the dynamics of change. It is never possible to know it all, but we can teach where to look and how to look. In a global legal profession, it will involve teams of lawyers chosen not just for the areas of law in which they specialize but the jurisdictions in which those specializations have been developed. And lawyers will not be the only professionals involved – whether it is because they work in a law firm that brings in other experts, in a multi-professional firm, in a corporation, in government, an international body, an NGO, or a range of institutions that may emerge.

2 Challenges and opportunities for the globalizing profession

Pepo's students had what we would now call highly 'portable' law degrees in what was a more cosmopolitan profession in a far less bordered world than ours. Our graduates are entering an increasingly global profession and are taking their degrees to continents Pepo did not know existed. The law firms I worked with in developing the Griffith Law School were local firms based in Brisbane and the Gold Coast. In the following decade, they became national firms through mergers and the opening of branch offices. In the most recent decade, they have become global firms. My own lawyers provide a vivid example. They started out as the Brisbane firm Cannan and Peterson, merged with a Sydney firm (Sly and Weigall) to form a national firm Sly, Weigall, Cannan and Peterson. This Australian mouthful became part of Deacon Graham and James that was formed by the merger of Hong Kong (Deacons), US (Graham and James) and other Pacific-rim firms. Deacons split with Graham and James and then was taken over by a London-based global firm (Norton Rose) which merged with Fulbright and Jaworski to become Norton Rose Fulbright.

While larger law firms are globalizing, the global profession is still under construction. Most lawyers involved in representing and advising clients are trained and admitted in one jurisdiction and may then move from that jurisdiction to others. This not only remains the case for the vast majority of lawyers working outside mega-firms but is also true of the 3,800 lawyers at Norton Rose Fulbright. Formal professional institutions, accreditation, codes of ethics and disciplinary procedures are in national or, in many cases, sub-national bodies. In many federations, the national bodies are merely coordinating or collaborative. International bodies are even looser.

Other branches of the profession have a similar mixture of globalizing interests within institutions that largely grounded in the domestic jurisdictions of sovereign states. That grounding was a result of the long-claimed monopoly in law-making based on a tenuous claim to a monopoly on legitimate force.[5]

Corporate lawyers often work for global organizations but their professional associations are those of their colleagues in law firms. The same is true of those working for NGOs and international or regional bodies – as well as those government lawyers who are members of professional associations.

Judges are members of courts which are almost all state-based. The rare disciplinary procedures are tied to the courts of which they are members. Their professional associations are loose at a domestic level and even looser internationally.

Law schools are very much tied to the jurisdictions in which they are located and the bulk of their students seek admission. They concentrate on teaching the law in the state and sub-national jurisdictions in which they operate and traditional legal research concentrates on the law in those jurisdictions. In another sense, they are globally connected by shared questions in international law, the branches of jurisprudence, and comparative studies of the laws and their context. In leading law schools, students can be connected by their increasingly international student body to other jurisdictions, cultures and faiths. Academic lawyers are increasingly taking part in international academic associations and conferences. However, these global connections are far more limited than they are for other disciplines whose core questions are generally not jurisdictionally bounded like philosophy and the natural sciences. In this, law schools are following rather than leading the universities of which they are a part – and within law schools, interdisciplinary research and international law often take a leading role in that movement.

Accordingly, all branches of the profession are rooted in institutions that reflect the domestic nature of Westphalian law. But all of them possess the global associations in which to debate, discuss and form a more global profession. I would argue that law schools should take a lead role in that debate, discussion and consequent professional institution-building. They do so as the centre of legal research, as those responsible for the most intensive part of lifelong legal learning, and as those who should be engaging with other members of the profession in their own lifelong learning. Indeed, if the careers of our current students are going to span the coming challenges and changes, this last element may be crucial – and may involve a more dynamic and intense relationship with alumni than is common. Traditionally, alumni are reminded of how much they value the law school that provided the core of their education and how much they want it to continue for other students. I would suggest that alumni would be reminded of how they can work with law schools to simultaneously change themselves, the profession, the organizations in which they work, and law schools as well.

I will conclude by suggesting and briefly discussing some of those issues which the emerging global profession will need to address. Such issues are best addressed with the active participation of national, regional and international lawyers' associations, along with judges and law schools. However, this does not mean that any of these groups should wait for the others to come on board before engaging with the issues. Law schools should always see their role in pioneering the identification and understanding of issues, challenges and opportunities for the larger profession.

3 Values and institutions

Eisenhower identified one clear goal: building the rule of law in international affairs. This, he said, would involve, 'a great deal of hard work, both in and out of government particularly in the law schools of the world'.[6] Chapter 17 emphasized that, like the development of the domestic rule of law, this needed the contribution of a range of professions, not least Eisenhower's own profession of arms. As we have seen, building the rule of law is not just a matter of promoting the rule of law's value but building it into the ethics of key groups and building institutions that support it. Lawyers should not be just involved in the normative articulation of the value of the rule of law and the supporting ethics, but also involved in building the institutions that will realize those values. Dworkin reminded us of the 'unique genius' in creating new kinds of institutions to meet new kinds of needs.[7]

But the rule of law stands as the governance value which lawyers have a special duty to foster. Whether included in a 'thick' theory of the rule of law, or as separate values, lawyers are also expected to take an interest in other values listed in Chapter 17: human rights, democracy, citizenship, liberty and, we would hope, equality and environmental values.

Indeed, lawyers should be able to make a critical contribution to the core questions identified in Chapter 1: 'What are the values that should inform this emerging order and what are the institutions that will deliver them?' This is not a task that lawyers can fulfil on their own as part of a monodisciplinary approach to the challenges of the emerging global order. Those challenges need to be addressed using the insights of all four 'governance disciplines' of the vortex to which I was attracted, namely, law, philosophy, politics and economics. As argued in Chapters 1 and 2, those disciplines emerged in the nineteenth century from a common intellectual space inhabited by the great thinkers of the eighteenth century and the original 'North Atlantic' enlightenment. In addressing the challenges of a globalizing world, those insights must be reintegrated – not in the mind of individual philosophes but by transdisciplinary groups of 'engaged academics' and 'reflective practitioners'. As such, lawyers are a critical and necessary part of the solution – but cannot be sufficient for a solution.

On this basis, law is not the only university-based discipline that needs to be deployed and law schools will not be the only university elements to be involved. Law schools will make their best contribution if they bring in the philosophers, political scientists and economists.[8] As in the debates of the 1980s that we began with, the law school can contribute most to the profession as part of the university – rather than as an element largely detached from it.

These global governance values will not be mirror-images of North Atlantic enlightenment values that were conceived in and for strong sovereign states. They need to build on a values dialogue that brings together long standing cultures to reach global governance values that will modify, replace or transcend the North Atlantic enlightenment values.[9] Nor will the institutions be replicas of those found in such sovereign states. However, when lawyers exercise their 'unique genius' in institutional design, they need to recognize that the institutions are for realizing those global governance values, not for favouring their richest clients at the expense of such values.

One example of an institutional development that the emerging legal profession should examine closely is investor state dispute settlement (ISDS). These were initially incorporated in a number of bilateral free-trade agreements in the 1990s.[10] They were a core of the proposed OECD Multilateral Agreement on Investment (MAI) which was shelved after widespread protests but reappeared in major regional trade agreements such as the North American Free Trade Agreement and the even bigger Trans-Pacific Partnership and Transatlantic Trade and Investment Partnership. An ISDS allows an investor from one state party (the home state) who had invested in another state party (the host state) to sue the host state if it alters its laws or policies in a way that reduces the value of the investment.

There have been concerns about many of the tribunals – their transparency, their procedures, the revolving door between counsel and arbitrators, and the absence of a doctrine of precedent or avenues of appeal. There are concerns that they favour multinational investors over local ones[11] and might block legislation to promote health and protect the environment. There are also concerns that tribunals may effectively overrule some of the most respected courts in the world – as Philip Morris sought to do when their loudly declared claims that plain paper packaging laws took away their property were rejected by the Australian High Court 6:1. Philip Morris failed,[12] but there can be little doubt that the action was intended to have a chilling effect on other jurisdictions – enhanced by the fact that in threatening letters sent to Togo, Namibia and Solomon Islands citing the sole dissenting judge (Heydon J), there was no acknowledgement that he was a dissenting judge.[13] After the plain packaging law was passed, Philip Morris transferred its Australian subsidiary to its Hong Kong subsidiary (the old Hong Kong–Australia Free Trade Agreement had an ISDS clause – whereas the US–Australia agreement did not). However, the United Nations Commission on International Trader Law (UNCITRAL) unanimously rejected the case on Australia's jurisdictional point that the move was done to attempt to attract UNCITRAL's jurisdiction, and hence an abuse of process. Following the decision, Marc Firestone, Philip Morris International Senior Vice-President and General Counsel, brazenly stated that

> there is nothing in today's outcome that addresses, let alone validates, plain packaging in Australia or anywhere else ... It is regrettable that the outcome hinged entirely on a procedural issue that Australia chose to advocate instead of confronting head on the merits of whether plain packaging is legal or even works.[14]

Abuse of process is not a procedural issue and the substantive law had been covered in the High Court case.

My response to the MAI push was that, while protecting the property rights of investors was often justified in enhancing the general welfare, they were not human rights and were not on the list of rights enunciated in the Universal Declaration of Human Rights. Where basic rights were still being abused in the host country, corporations should not seek to 'jump the queue' and expect protection of their property rights in host countries while political prisoners rotted in the jails of that host – in contravention of the 1948 UN Declaration of Human Rights. However, if corporations sought to pursue both rights simultaneously, they might secure support for reasonable claims from those who so vigorously opposed them.[15]

Subsequent to those debates, I recognized that ISDS is based on a false assumption – that anyone can have a legitimate expectation that the law not be changed in ways that affect their interests.[16] It is one of the legislature's functions to deal with new issues and to adjust laws as more is learnt about the issues those laws seek to address and their degree of success in addressing them (not least because of the attempts of some lawyers to limit their intended effects on their clients). Most changes in law are intended to be a positive-sum game but not many are fully Pareto efficient. Investors who really do not know this are poorly advised fools who should not be entrusted with the money of others. No credibility should be given to those who pretend not to know.

ISDS also fails to take into account another fact about legislation: it is very rare for any particular group to always lose out or always gain. If an investor were to be compensated for any losses caused by legislation subsequent to the investment, they would have to deduct from that the benefits accrued because of *gains* caused by other legislation (which can sometimes be massive, as in the reductions of company tax in most jurisdictions). But, if the sole issue is loss or gain, then those who benefit from government legislation should make a payment to the government for the gains in excess of losses (something that is not unknown but generally proposed for betterment taxes[17] arising from zoning and other government decisions that increase the value of a particular individual's property).

While this chapter is not intended to resolve the disputes over ISDS, I would argue that the emerging global profession should take a key role in those debates – with the voices of those lawyers who make money for themselves and their ISDS clients being leavened by the wisdom of those who do not. Investors have legitimate interests against discrimination after they have invested (just as citizens have legitimate interests that their governments not be subject to undue influence, or worse, from foreign investors). If there are to be ISDS provisions, they should be subject to appeal to the ICJ or some other body, which should take into account whether the legislation was a bona fide exercise of legislative power for the 'peace, order and good government' of the host state's residents. Better still, we might conceive of an international arrangement similar to the Rome Statute. The principal responsibility for protecting investors from discrimination should lie with state agencies (such as a Human Rights and Anti-Discrimination Commission backed by the courts) and a right to go to an international tribunal only when it can be argued in that tribunal that the states have failed 'or are unable' to diligently carry out their duties[18] under the relevant treaty. But even then, should investors' rights get these sorts of protections before human rights, which are one of the core governance values from the North Atlantic to the Global Enlightenment and, for some, a part of the rule of law? This is acutely the case where the legislation challenged has been enacted to further the long-standing internationally recognized human rights of the residents in the jurisdiction, which both the home and host state have committed to uphold.

Perhaps the most appropriate way for these issues to be handled is for the rights of companies to avoid discrimination to be made subject to an international rules-based order which places their demands in the context of other long-recognized human rights and the duties of states. Many of these rights and duties have higher priority than the disappointed expectations of profits that would accrue in the absence of legislative change. The first priority for the duties of states is to the Kellogg-Briand Pact incorporated into the UN Charter in which all states must formally commit to forswear wars of aggression in order to be even recognized as states (what might be seen as the core of a state's licence to operate within the global community).

The next highest priority is the 1948 Universal Declaration of Human Rights.[19] Some corporations may see the Trans Pacific Partnership as a corporate Magna Carta (this is perhaps a less inappropriate analogy than some might imagine as the real Magna Carta made demands on the sovereign to respect the rights of its over-mighty subjects).

But a perhaps more appropriate document to cite is the United Nations Global Compact, which emphasizes the duties of corporations to the communities in which they operate and draw their profits. I am not saying that corporations should have to wait as long as the victims of state aggression and human rights abuses for redress under an international rules-based order against those states which have not honoured their 1928 and 1948 commitments. We lawyers should not object to the international rules-based order providing corporations ISDS redress *at the same time* as redress is given to the victims of aggressive wars and human rights abuse. What seems impossible to justify is that they should secure redress under ISDS before that time – or that their rights of redress should be asserted and granted independently of their duties under UNGC duties. To be specific, proper respect for the international rule of law would at minimum demand that a state may not seek ISDS redress for its corporations (or those substantially based in them) unless it has signed up to the compulsory jurisdiction of the ICJ, the ICC and courts that enforce international human rights.[20] We have long been urged to accept gradualism in the protection of human rights. Corporations should accept gradualism in the rights they want. If they know they have to wait their turn in the queue after the victims of aggression and torture, they may become a force for the protection of those victims ahead of them in the queue. If find yourselves behind others in a queue there are three things you can do – insist on greater need or urgency; push those in front aside; or press for those in front to be served so that you can be served in turn. The first is untenable and the second is outrageous. The third is courteous and can earn you friends you might one day need.

4 Establishing a genuinely global profession

If we follow the approach set out in Chapter 11 that a profession is centred on:

1. A service to the community whose delivery constitutes what is seen by the profession, and generally regarded as, a *public good*;
2. A *body of knowledge*, institutions for imparting it, and a dedicated and identified group of experts who apply that knowledge for the benefit of the community they claim to serve;

3 A set of processes for *entry and exit* of the profession, and;
4 A *code of ethics*/conduct with a strict set of priorities in which the public good comes first, the client comes second, and the professional comes third.

While some approaches to professions may differ in formulation, few would exclude those four elements, so let us consider these severally as they might apply to the global profession of law.

The public good is likely to be very similar to the public good claimed by lawyers in systems with strong traditions of the rule of law, human rights and democracy – such as 'justice according to law'. As in domestic legal professions, justice is likely to seen as a matter of avoiding a set of manifest injustices and providing a means of contestation between different claims to justice, through legal argument in legal institutions. The key differences will be that a global profession must serve a global community rather than a national or sub-national community, and the law is global law – with international law having the central role rather than a bit part determined by the national sovereign.

The body of knowledge will be 'global law' – that combination of international, regional and domestic laws, the way they interact and the conflicting forces of change and stability that drive them. The body of knowledge will also include other 'critical and theoretical dimensions'. The *institutions* for imparting that knowledge will centre on universities and law schools recognizing their global role. It will also include a largely (but not entirely) familiar array of institutions that contribute to an enriched process of lifelong legal learning.

The existing processes for *entry and exit* are rudimentary, even for those practicing before international tribunals. The one exception is the ICC, which admits lawyers as defence counsel,[21] has a professional code of conduct and a disciplinary board drawn from those who are accredited to appear before it.[22] In other courts and tribunals, lawyers do not even have to be accredited to their local bars. However, the lack of formal mechanisms for accrediting and, importantly, withdrawing accreditation should not stop a profession from forming a membership group in which membership is granted on the basis of a level of legal training and adherence to ethics – and where membership is withdrawn for those who do not live up to the required standards of ethics, integrity and competence. This membership group could be based on the practitioner members of the International Bar Association, the International Law Association, the International Commission of Jurists or a new body. Those whose membership has been withdrawn would not be recognized as lawyers by other members, be able to attend legal conferences or hold adjunct positions in law schools.[23] This would also apply to judges who breach the Bangalore principles,[24] as determined by a panel of judges.

The *Code of Ethics* needs to be developed to take into account debate and formal consideration of some of the ethical issues facing lawyers in international and global practice. Some of these have been discussed in this book, most notably the temptation to give government clients the advice they want to hear, international tax minimization, abuse of ISDS process and misleading statements to third parties with limited resources.[25] But there are others and many more will emerge. The codes developed for the ILA and the IBA[26] provide a potential start but do not yet address the above and many other important issues. Indeed, their unqualified insistence on confidentiality without the clear criminality exceptions in other codes might make them a bad start.[27]

One such area (with similarities to the above discussion of ISDS) is advising clients how to avoid paying taxes and/or meeting regulatory requirements in the jurisdictions in which they operate (Chapter 13). This is a long-standing issue in legal ethics,[28] whose excesses threaten the legitimacy and acceptance of the profession. The opportunities in international tax transactions for virtually eliminating tax are so much greater now than they ever were in the past.[29] Indeed, the lawyers who are designing complex international strategies to more or less eliminate tax may be the first large group of truly global lawyers – deploying international law, regional law and the laws of multiple national and sub-national jurisdictions. And it is much easier for them because of the enormous difficulty in changing double tax treaties and securing coordinated state action (not least because of the logic of collective action[30] and attempts by beneficiary companies to block such action).

It would be a great pity if the international legal profession came to be identified with the attempt to undermine the effectiveness of the revenues on which the security and welfare of the peoples of the world partly depend. It would be even worse if this were seen to be linked to the undermining of national regulation by ISDS and global regulation was rendered ineffective by their clients. This interaction between duties to clients and duties to the wider legal system is not new. It constitutes the core of the traditional question of duty to clients and the duty to court – sometimes formulated as 'justice under law'. The interaction reflects the fact that duties to clients must be constructed in a way that is ultimately supportive rather than destructive of justice under law. An international legal profession must address this issue just as domestic professions have long-recognized the need to do (and to a significant, but never perfect, extent have tried to do).

The emerging international profession needs to talk law to power, not just power to law.

Individual and groups of lawyers can do a great deal. One senior partner in a very large and conservative law firm surprised me in 1992 with the statement that 'there is an awful lot of justice to be done'. Some of that justice is done pro bono (as was much of the work for Guantanamo inmates and refugees). There is little of the equivalent of government-funded legal aid – though there is definitely a role for state and non-state donors. But lawyers who find ways that they can do justice and get their fees paid ethically should also be recognized and celebrated. Injustice does damage to human beings and, while not all of that damage can be monetized, damages can ameliorate some injustices and those doing damage can be deterred. Lawyers who recover those damages can advance justice in an economically sustainable way. To be sure, there will be competing views about the justice of the pleaded causes – and providing a forum to deal with these is one of the functions of law. Those who are accused of damaging the rights of others not only deserve their day in court; they need their day in court so that the legitimate arguments they have to make are debated in front of courts that are, as far as possible, independent and drawn from a wide variety of experiences and wisdoms. As I have said about quite a few leading politicians over the last 20 years: 'they deserve a fair trial – no less, but no more'. Lawyers should be available to argue both sides. Whether via the 'cab rank principle' of the independent bars of many Commonwealth countries or by other processes, there should be lawyers to do so.

But it should be clear what lawyers may and may not do. Lawyers will use the knowledge of their profession to help clients get to where they want to go. This is particularly apt a decade after the UN's 'great compromise' of agreeing to the importance of the rule of law at *both* national and international levels and when Western countries increasingly talk of a 'rules-based international order'. I am not entirely sure how seriously the US, the UK and Australia will be taken until they acknowledge that the Kosovo war and (especially) the 2003 Iraq invasion were a denial of that order.

In helping get clients where they want to go, lawyers should only go along legal pathways. They will not go off-road, they will not go the wrong way down one-way streets. They will help you navigate the law. They will give you a choice of routes. But they will not take you out of the law. They are not outlaws and will not assist you to become one. That is the key to the law and lawyering – and something that legal educators should never forget, at whatever stage of the lifelong learning process for lawyers they contribute.

I hope that Pepo taught his students that before they left the walls of Bologna to become cosmopolitan lawyers in Europe. We must teach our students that before they leave our halls to become global lawyers – and to demand it of their fellows who seek to call themselves 'lawyers'.

Notes

1 Twelve of Griffith Law School's staff at this level secured chairs, most within a decade of their first academic appointments.
2 See Chapter 6.
3 Prof William Twining has suggested that the term 'normative pluralism' might be more appropriate as the boundaries of legal and other norms are less clear in the absence of a sovereign state to determine the sources of law and the inability of courts to enforce the law on all those who claim to be bound by it.
4 Charles Sampford, 'Dreams and Nightmares of Alternative Powers' Futures', in *Shifting Global Powers and International Law: Challenges and Opportunities*, ed. Rowena Maguire, Bridget Lewis and Charles Sampford (Abingdon, Oxon: Routledge, 2013).
5 The monopoly claim on legitimate force might be true by definition if legitimate force was definitionally confined to that of the state: see, Andrew Palmer and Charles Sampford, 'Retrospective Legislation in Australia: Looking Back at the 1980s', *Federal Law Review* 22 (1993–1994).

6 Dwight D. Eisenhower (1959) *Remarks Upon Receiving an Honorary Degree of Doctor of Laws at Delhi University* 11 December 1959, www.presidency.ucsb.edu/ws/?pid=11617. See Chapter 17.
7 Roland Dworkin, 'Address on the Value of Integrity', in 17th World Congress of the International Association for Philosophy of Law and Social Philosophy (IVR) (Bologna, 16–21 June 1995).
8 With more than occasional contributions from sociologists, criminologists, social psychologists and organization theorists.
9 Charles Sampford, 'Sovereignty and Intervention', in *Congress of Legal and Social Philosophy* (New York, 1999) republished as: Charles Sampford, 'Sovereignty and Intervention', in *Human Rights in Philosophy and Practice*, ed. T. Campbell and B. Leiser (Ashgate: Aldershot, 2001).
10 William Maley, Charles Sampford and Ramesh Thakur, eds, *From Civil Strife to Civil Society: Civil and Military Responsibilities in Disrupted States* (Tokyo: UNU Press, 2003): 1.
11 See, for example, Charles Sampford and David Wood, 'The Future of Business Ethics', *Griffith Law Review* 1, no. 1 (1992).
12 *JT International SA v Commonwealth of Australia; British American Tobacco Australasia Limited v The Commonwealth* [2012] HCA 43.
13 As reported by, John Oliver, 'Last Week Tonight', *HBO*, 16 February 2015.
14 Quoted by Kristen Gelineau, 'Court Rejects Case against Australian Cigarette Logos Ban', *The Associated Press*, 18 December 2015.
15 Charles Sampford, 'Business and Human Rights: Reflections and Observations', in *Business and Human Rights*, ed. Wesley Cragg (Cheltenham: Edward Elgar, 2012).
16 The same problem afflicts much posturing by tax avoidance lawyers, occasionally backed by some academic writing, that any laws changing rights are retrospective. See, *Retrospectivity and the Rule of Law* (Oxford: Oxford University Press, 2006): 21.
17 See box E–4.2 in Australia's Future Tax System. Final report http://taxreview.treasury.gov.au/content/FinalReport.aspx?doc=html/publications/Papers/Final_Report_Part_2/chapter_e4–5.htm.
18 See, Michael Kirby *et al.*, *Through the World's Eye* (Sydney: Federation Press, 2000), Article 17 (3).
19 Many might also think that the 1992 UN Framework Convention on Climate Change is growing in priority with each passing year, and clearly has relevance to ISDS provisions.
20 This should preferably be regional, like the EU court, and ultimately global. However, in the interim, national courts of human rights with state-imposed limitations on the Universal Declaration of Human Rights could be accepted – provided that state-imposed limitations on corporate rights under ISDS are equally accepted.
21 Rule 21(2) of the Rules of Procedure and Evidence.
22 Articles 36 and 44 of the Code of Professional Conduct.
23 We note that New York Law School (not NYU) has appointed Firestone an Adjunct Professor.
24 Brian Galligan and Charles Sampford, *Rethinking Human Rights* (Annandale: Federation Press, 1997).
25 See Chapters 14 to 18.
26 A. Boon and J. Flood, 'Globalization of Professional Ethics? The Significance of Lawyers' International Codes of Conduct', *Legal Ethics* 29, no. 1 (1999). They also refer to a regional code approved by the Council of the Bars and Law Societies of the European Union (CCBE). Boon and Flood locate both problems (pp. 43–46) as well as opportunities (p. 47) in globalization of the profession and its ethics.
27 For example, the only exception in the CCBE requirement to always act in the client's best interests is that he should not compromise his professional standards to please his client. See ibid.: 34.

28 An issue to which (as well as Chapter 13's more recent reflections) I directed attention in my first essay on legal ethics: Andrew Palmer and Charles Sampford, 'Judicial Retrospectivity', *Griffith Law Review* 4 (1995): 11–24.

29 Charles Sampford, 'The Coming Coke Moment', in *The Security Council as Global Legislator*, ed. Vesselin Popovski and Trudy Fraser (Abingdon: Routledge, 2014).

30 Mancur Olson, *The Logic of Collective Action: Public Goods and the Theory of Groups* (Cambridge, Mass.: Harvard University Press, 1965).

References

'Arnott's Agenda', *The Age*, 22 February 1997.

'Arnott's Gears up for Big Climb Back', *The Age*, 15 February 1997.

'At Last, the Damning Evidence That Should Bury Blair for His Lies over Iraq', *Daily Mail*, 19 January 2011.

'BHP Visits the School of Hard Knocks', *Weekend Australian*, 15–16 June 1996: 54.

'Biscuits Back on Shelves', *The Age*, 26 February 1997.

'The Full Text of the Advice About the Legality of War with Iraq Given by the Attorney General, Lord Goldsmith, to the Prime Minister, Tony Blair, on March 7 2003: Iraq: Resolution 1441', *Guardian (UK),* 29 April 2005. www.theguardian.com/politics/2005/apr/28/election2005.uk. (Accessed 12 February 2016).

'Full Text: Written Answer on Iraq Advice in Response to a Question Asking Attorney-General Lord Goldsmith His View of the Legal Basis for the Iraq War, Posed by Baroness Ramsay of Cartvale on 17 March 2003', *BBC News*, 28 April 2005.

'The Griffith Law Curriculum (Appendix 1)', *Griffith Law Review* 1, no. 1 (1992): viii.

'How to Raise Business above the Bottom Line; Maintaining Business Integrity in Corrupt Business Environments; Ethical Business, Human Rights and Corporate Values', Paper presented at the Global Integrity Summit, Brisbane, Australia, 2015.

'In Full: New Goldsmith Statement', *BBC News*, 26 May 2006.

'Peter Jamison Jury Acquits Brandon Man in Killing of Wife's Lover', *Tampa Bay Times*, 30 May 2013.

'Peter Slipper Cleared over MP Expenses Following Investigation', *Herald Sun*, 30 January 2012.

Royal Commission on the Activities of the Federated Ship Painters and Dockers Union: Final Report: Ordered to Be Printed by the Legislative Assembly. Parliamentary Paper (Victoria. Parliament); Edited by Painters Royal Commission on the Activities of the Federated Ship Painters and Dockers Union and Frank Costigan, (Canberra: Government Printer, 1984).

Academic Course Appraisal Committee, 'Report: Legal Knowledge Required for Admission to Practice (McGarvie Report)', (Victoria: Council of Legal Education (COLE): 1982).

Aible, H.J. 'Corporate Counsel and Business Ethics: A Personal Review', *Missouri Law Review* 59 (1994): 427–440.

Ala'i, P. 'The Legacy of Geographical Morality and Colonialism: A Historical Assessment of the Current Crusade against Corruption', *Vanderbilt Journal of Transnational Law* 33 (2000): 877–932.

Allegretti, J. 'Shooting Elephants, Serving Clients: An Essay on George Orwell and the Lawyer-Client Relationship', *Creighton Law Review* 27 (1993): 1–24.

Allen, L. 'Religion and Corporate Social Responsibility: The Interfaith Centre on Corporate Responsibility and the Corporate Withdrawal Movement from Burma', Boston University, 2003.

Anscombe, G.E.M. *Intention*. (Oxford: Basil Blackwell, 1957).

Arron, D. *Running from the Law: Why Good Lawyers Are Getting out of the Legal Profession*. (Berkeley: Ten Speed Press, 1991).

Australian Law School Deans. '"Legal Education in Australia": Submission of Australian Law School Deans to the Commonwealth Tertiary Education Commission Assessment Committee for the Discipline of Law (Deans' Report to CTEC)', (Canberra: AGPS, April 1986).

Australian Senate 'Parliamentary Debates Official Hansard', 573–577, Tuesday, 12 March 2002.

Bagehot, Walter *The English Constitution*. 1 ed. (London: Chapman & Hall, 1867).

Baker, David, 'An Avalanche of Law Schools: 1989 to 2013', *Journal of the Australasian Law Teachers Association* 6, no. 1 & 2 (2013): 153–166.

Barnaby, Suzette. 'Legal Ethics for the Real World: A Model for Engaging First Year Law Students', *QUT Law Journal* 4, no. 2 (2004): 1–26.

Barnett, A. and M. Bright. 'British Military Chief Reveals New Legal Fears over Iraq War', *Observer*, 1 May 2005.

Benjamin, Martin. *Splitting the Difference: Compromise and Integrity in Ethics and Politics*. (Kansas: University of Kansas, 1990).

Bentham, Jeremy. *A Comment on the Commentaries and a Fragment on Government*. (London: The Athlone Press, 1977 [1776]).

Besson, Samantha and John Tasioulas. 'Introduction', in *The Philosophy of International Law*, edited by Samantha Besson and John Tasioulas. (Oxford: Oxford University Press, 2010): 1–27.

Boon, A. and J. Flood. 'Globalization of Professional Ethics? The Significance of Lawyers' International Codes of Conduct', *Legal Ethics* 29, no. 1 (1999): 29–57.

Bourke, Latika 'Clive Palmer Revives Explosive Claims against Mal Brough over James Ashby Affair', *The Sydney Morning Herald*, 25 November 2015.

Breakey, Hugh. 'Who's Afraid of Property Rights? Rights as Core Concepts, Coherent, Prima Facie, Situated and Specified', *Law and Philosophy* 33, no. 5 (2014): 573–603.

Breakey, Hugh. 'What Human Rights Aren't For: Human Rights Function as Moral, Political and Legal Standards – but Not as Intervention-Conditions', *Research in Ethical Issues in Organizations* 13 (2015): 41–59.

Breakey, Hugh. 'Supply and Demand in the Development of Professional Ethics', in *Australian Association for Professional and Applied Ethics Annual Conference,* Auckland 2015.

Breakey, Hugh. 'Compromise Despite Conviction: Curbing Integrity's Moral Dangers', *Journal of Value Inquiry* (2016 forthcoming): 1–16.

Breakey, Hugh, Tim Cadman and Charles Sampford. 'Conceptualizing Personal and Institutional Integrity: The Comprehensive Integrity Framework', in *The Ethical Contribution of Organizations to Society*, edited by Michael Schwartz, Howard Harris and Debra Comer (Emerald Group Publishing, 2015): 1–40.

Brennan, Hon Sir Gerard. 'Commercial Law and Morality', *Melbourne University Law Review* 17 (1989): 100–106.

Brewer, E. Cobham. *Brewer's Dictionary of Phrase and Fable*. (London: Cassell, 1963 [1870]).

Brown, Rick. 'Patrick Waterfront Fight: Where It Finished [Who Won the Settlement and Who Didn't]', *News Weekly*, 25 July 1998: 6–7.

Browne, M. Neil, Carrie L. Williamson and Linda L. Barkacs. 'The Purported Rigidity of an Attorney's Personality: Can Legal Ethics Be Acquired?', *Journal of the Legal Profession* 55 (2006): 55–78.

Brownlie, I. and C.J. Apperley. 'Kosovo Crisis Inquiry: Memorandum on the International Law Aspects', *International and Comparative Law Quarterly* 49, no. 7 (2000): 878–905.

Bryant, Nick. 'Mal Brough Crashes Through', *The Monthly*, 2013.

Buffet, Warren E. 'Berkshire Hathaway Inc., 2002 Annual Report', www.berkshire hathaway.com/2002ar 2002ar.pdf.

Burke, Edmund. 'Thoughts on the Cause of the Present Discontents', in *Thoughts on the Cause of the Present Discontents and the Two Speeches on America*, edited by E.J. Payne. (Oxford: Clarendon, 1926).

Byrnes, Andrew and Hilary Charlesworth. 'The Illegality of the War against Iraq', *Dialogue* 22, no. 1 (2003): 4–9.

Cahn, N. 'Forward: Responsible Lawyers', *George Washington Law Review* 63 (1995): 921–930.

Campbell, Bill and Chris Moraitis. 'Memorandum of Advice to the Commonwealth Government on the Use of Force against Iraq', *Melbourne Journal of International Law* 4, no. 1 (2003): 178.

Castles, Margaret. 'Challenges to the Academy: Reflections on the Teaching of Legal Ethics in Australia', *Legal Education Review* 81, 84 (2001).

Cerutti, S.M. *Cicero's Accretive Style*. (Lanham: University Press of America, 1996).

Charlesworth, Hilary. 'Interview', *ABC 'Insiders' Program*, 9 March 2003.

Chesterman, M. and D. Weisbrot. 'Legal Scholarship in Australia', *Modern Law Review* 50 (1987): 709–724.

Chilcot, John. 'Letter to Prime Minister David Cameron Suggesting Date of Publication of Iraq War Inquiry Report', UK Government, 28 October 2015.

Chilcot Inquiry. *Transcript of Evidence to the Iraq Inquiry by Lord Goldsmith*, 27 January 2010.

Chow, W.W.S. and F. Tiba. 'Professional Legal Education Reviews: Too Many "What's", Too Few "How's" ', *European Journal of Law and Technology* 4, no. 1 (2013): 1–26.

Clarke, M.J.R. 'Report of the Inquiry into the Case of Dr. Mohamed Haneef', Canberra: Attorney-General's Dept., 2008.

Clarke, Thomas, ed. *Theories of Corporate Governance: The Philosophical Foundations of Corporate Governance*. (London, New York: Routledge, 2004).

Coady, C.A.J. *The Ethics of Armed Humanitarian Intervention*. (Washington: United States Institute of Peace, 2002).

Coke, Edwardo. *The First Part of the Institutes of the Laws of England: Commentary Upon Littleton*. Corrected ed. 2 vols. Vol. 1, (London: Clarke, Saunders, Bunning, Maxwell, Sweet, Butterworth, Stevens and Sons, Pheney and Richards, 1832).

Constitutional Affairs Committee. 'Constitutional Role of the Attorney General: Fifth Report', HC306. London: House of Commons, 19 July 2007.

Cooney, S. 'A Broader Role for the Commonwealth in Eradicating Foreign Sweatshops?', *Melbourne University Law Review* 28 (2004): 290–342.

Cooney, S. 'Improving Regulatory Strategies for Dealing with Endemic Labour Abuses', JSD thesis, Columbia University, 2005.

Cooper, G.S., R.L. Deutsch and R.E. Krever. *Income Taxation: Commentary and Materials*. (Sydney: Law Book Company, 1993).

Cornell, D. *The Philosophy of the Limit*. (London: Routledge, 1992).

Cosans, Christopher. 'Does Milton Friedman Support a Vigorous Business Ethics?', *Journal of Business Ethics* 87, no. 3 (2008): 391–399.

Costigan, F. 'How Dare Howard Applaud Patrick', *The Age*, 23 April 1998.

Cotterrell, Roger. 'Pandora's Box: Jurisprudence in Legal Education', *International Journal of the Legal Profession* 7, no. 3 (2000): 179–187.

Crawford, J. 'The Future of the Public Law Schools', *Journal of Professional Legal Education* 9, no. 1 (1991): 1–10.

Crime and Misconduct Commission. 'CMC Concludes No Official Misconduct by Newman in Assessment of Three BCC-Related Matters – 16.03.2012', www.ccc.qld.gov.au/news-and-media/cmc-media-releases statement-on-matters-concerning-brisbane-city-council (Accessed 16 March 2015).

Critchley, Simon. *The Ethics of Deconstruction: Derrida and Levinas*. (Oxford: Blackwell, 1992).

Crowe, Jonathan. 'Reasoning from the Ground Up: Some Strategies for Teaching Theory to Law Students', *Legal Education Review* 21, no. 1–2 (2011): 49–67.

Daicoff, Susan. 'Asking Leopards to Change Their Spots: Should Lawyers Change? A Critique of Solutions to Problems with Professionalism by Reference to Empirically-Derived Attorney Personality Attributes', *Georgetown Journal of Legal Ethics* 11 (1998): 547–595.

Dalton, J.F. 'Boardroom Ethics', in *Business Ethics in Australia and New Zealand: Essays and Cases*, edited by K. Woldring. (South Melbourne: Thomas Nelson, 1996): Chap. 173–182.

Davies (QC), S. 'Revenue Offences Generally: Can the Professional Adviser Be a Party or Conspirator', *Queensland Law Society Journal* 19, no. 3 (1989): 207.

Davis, Michael. 'Professionalism Means Putting Your Profession First', *Georgetown Journal of Legal Ethics* 2, no. 34 (1988): 340–357.

Davis, Michael. 'The Ethics Boom: What and Why', *The Centennial Review* 34, no. 2 (1990): 163–186.

Davis, Michael. 'Thinking Like an Engineer: The Place of a Code of Ethics in the Practice of a Profession', *Philosophy & Public Affairs* 20, no. 2 (1991): 150–167.

Dawkins, The Hon J. S., MP. *Higher Education: A Policy Statement*. (Canberra: Australian Government Publishing Service, 1988).

Derham, Sir David. 'An Overview of Legal Education in Australia', in *Legal Education in Australia: Proceedings of National Conference*. (Sydney, 1976): 7, 14.

Deva, S. 'Corporate Complicity in Internet Censorship in China: Who Cares for the Global Compact or the Global Online Freedom Act?', *George Washington International Law Review* 39 (2007): 255–319.

Dick, B., L. Godden, K. Healy and M.J. Le Brun, 'A Case Study of the Offices Project (Teacher-Less, Cooperative Learning Groups) at Griffith University: Implementing Educational Theory', *Legal Education Review* 4 (1993): 273–297.

Dinnen, S., R. May and A. Regan (eds). *Challenging the State: The Sandline Affair in Papua New Guinea*. (Canberra: ANU, 1997).

Dixon, Sir Owen. 'Remarks by Sir Owen Dixon on His Swearing in as Chief Justice of the High Court of Australia', in *The Role of Barristers* (Melbourne: Chancery Chambers, 1952).

Dolovich, Sharon. 'Ethical Lawyering and the Possibility of Integrity', in *Professional Ethics and Personal Integrity*, edited by Tim Dare and W. Bradley Wendel. (Newcastle upon Tyne: Cambridge Scholars Publishing, 2010): 125–185.

Donaldson, T. *The Ethics of International Business*. (New York: Oxford University Press, 1989).

Donaldson, T. 'Moral Minimums for Multinationals', in *Business Ethics: Readings and Cases in Corporate Morality*, edited by W.M. Hoffman and R.E. Fredrick. (New York: McGraw-Hill, 1995): Chap. 12.
Doneman, Paula and Lincoln Wright. 'Picture Puzzle', *The Sunday Mail*, 22 July 2007.
Dorney, S. *The Sandline Affair: Politics and Mercenaries and the Bougainville Crisis*. (Sydney: ABC Books for the Australian Broadcasting Corporation, 1998).
Douzinas, C. and R. Warrington. *Justice Miscarried: Ethics, Aesthetics and the Law*. (London: Harvester Wheatsheaf, 1994).
Douzinas, C. and R. Warrington. *Postmodern Jurisprudence: The Law of Texts in the Texts of Law*. (London: Routledge, 1991).
Dow, Steven. 'There's Madness in the Method: A Commentary on Law, Statistics, and the Nature of Legal Education', *Oklahoma Law Review* 57 (2004): 579–599.
Drawbaugh, Kevin. 'Senate Panel Slams Goldman in Scathing Crisis Report', www.reuters.com/article/2011/04/13/us-financial-regulation-report-idUSTRE73C8JR20110413, 2011 (Accessed 12 November 2015).
Duncan, W. 'It's Time for a Queensland Council for Legal Education', *Proctor*, November 1992: 21.
Dworkin, Ronald. 'No Right Answer?', in *Law, Morality and Society. Essays in Honour of H.L.A. Hart*, edited by P.M.S. Hacker and J. Raz. (Oxford: Oxford University Press, 1977): 58–84.
Dworkin, Ronald. *Law's Empire*. (Cambridge, Mass.: Harvard University Press, 1986).
Dworkin, Roland. 'Address on the Value of Integrity', in *17th World Congress of the International Association for Philosophy of Law and Social Philosophy (IVR)*. (Bologna, 1995).
Dyer, Clare. 'Attorney General Subject of Bar Complaint', *Guardian*, 2 May 2005.
Dyer, Clare. 'Attorney General Spared Trial by Bar', *Guardian*, 14 July 2005.
Eberle, E.J. 'Three Foundations of Legal Ethics: Autonomy, Community, and Morality', *Georgetown Journal of Legal Ethics* 7 (1993): 89–144.
Economides, Kim. 'Learning the Law of Lawyering', *Current Legal Problems* 52, no. 1 (1999): 392–418.
Economides, Kim and Majella O'Leary. 'The Moral of the Story: Toward an Understanding of Ethics in Organisations and Legal Practice', *Legal Ethics* 10, no. 1 (2007): 5–25.
Economides, Kim and Christine Parker. 'Roundtable on Legal Ethics in Legal Education: Should It Be a Required Course?', *Legal Ethics* 14, no. 1 (2011): 109–124.
Economides, Kim and Julian Webb. 'Do Law Schools Care About Law Students and Legal Values?', *Legal Ethics* 3, no. 1 (2000): 1–9.
Edgar, Andrew and Stephen Pattison. 'Integrity and the Moral Complexity of Professional Practice', *Nursing Philosophy* 12 (2011): 94–106.
Eisenhower, Dwight D. 'Remarks Upon Receiving an Honorary Degree of Doctor of Laws at Delhi University', (11 December 1959). www.presidency.ucsb.edu/ws/?pid=11617. (Accessed 12 February 2016).
Ellmann, S. 'Lawyers and Clients', *UCLA Law Review* 34 (1986): 717–179.
Faine, J. 'Lawyers to Spare', *Australian Lawyer* (1993): 24.
Felstiner, W. and A. Sarat. 'Enactments of Power: Negotiating Reality and Responsibility in Lawyer-Client Interactions', *Cornell Law Review* 77 (1992): 1447–1498.
Fidler, D. '"Geographical Morality" Revisited: International Relations, International Law, and the Controversy over Placebo-Controlled HIV Clinical Trials in Developing Countries', *Harvard International Law Journal* 42, no. 2 (2001): 299–354.
Finn, P. 'Commerce, the Common Law and Morality', *Melbourne University Law Review* 17 (1989): 87–99.

Finnis, John. *Natural Law and Natural Rights*. (Oxford: Clarendon, 1980).

Fiorelli, P.E. 'Guideline Amendments Dramatically Change the Structure of Organizational Fines', *Catholic Lawyer* 35 (1991): 181–197.

Fitzgerald, G.E. *Commission of Inquiry into Possible Illegal Activities and Associated Police Misconduct*. (Brisbane: Queensland Government Printer, 1989).

Freeman, M.D.A. *Lloyd's Introduction to Jurisprudence*. (London: Sweet & Maxwell, 1994).

Freeman, R. Edward. *Strategic Management: A Stakeholder Approach*. (Boston: Pitman, 1984).

Fried, C. 'The Lawyer as Friend: The Moral Foundations of the Lawyer–Client Relation', *Yale Law Journal* 85 (1976): 1060–1089.

Friedman, Lawrence. *Crime and Punishment in American History*. (New York: Basic Books, 1993).

Fukuyama, Francis. 'The End of History', *The National Interest*, Summer 1989.

Fuller, L.L. *The Morality of Law*. Revised edn. (New Haven: Yale University Press, 1969).

Gagliardi, J. 'Queensland Faces Jobless Lawyer Glut', *Courier Mail*, 5 February 1993.

Galbraith, John Kenneth. 'The Rush to Capitalism', *The New York Review of Books*, 25 October 1990.

Galligan, Brian and Charles Sampford. *Rethinking Human Rights*. (Annandale: Federation Press, 1997).

Gelineau, Kristen. 'Court Rejects Case against Australian Cigarette Logos Ban', *The Associated Press*, 18 December 2015.

Goldenberg, Suzanne. 'Abu Ghraib Leaked Report Reveals Full Extent of Abuse', *The Guardian*, 17 February 2006.

Goldring, John. 'The Place of Legal Theory in the Law School – a Comment', *Bulletin of the Australian Society of Legal Philosophy* 11, no. 3 (1987): 159–163.

Goldring, J. and G. Hawker. 'Lawyers in a Government Department: A Report and Suggestions for Further Research', *Australian Journal of Public Administration* 14, no. 3 (1985): 287–297.

Goldsmith QC, Lord. 'Memo: Lord Goldsmith to PM Blair (Iraq)'. (30 January 2003). www.iraqinquiry.org.uk/media 46496/Goldsmith-note-to-PM-30January2003.pdf.

Goldsmith QC, Lord. 'Government and the Rule of Law in the Modern Age', in *Clifford Chance Lecture series on Rule of Law*. (London: LSE Law Department, 22 February 2006).

Goldring, John, Charles Sampford and Ralph Simmonds. *New Foundations in Legal Education*. (Avalon, NSW: Cavendish Publishing, 1998): 117.

Gordon, Robert W. 'Corporate Law Practice as a Public Calling', *Maryland Law Review* 49 (1990): 255–292.

Gray, Darren. 'Faked Record Handed to Federal Police', *The Age*, 20 March 2002.

Greenwood, T. 'Ethics and Avoidance Advice', *Law Institute Journal* 65, no. 8 (1991): 724–726.

Greig, Don. 'War, Legality and Iraq', *Canberra Times*, 17 March 2003: 11.

Greig, Don. 'The Case for a Legal Attack', *The Australian*, 18 March 2003: 15.

Griffin, Gerard and Stuart Svensen. *Industrial Relations Implications of the Australian Waterside Dispute*. Working Paper No. 62. (Monash University: National Key Centre in Industrial Relations, 1998).

Griffith QC, Gavan. 'Notes on the Legal Justification for the Invasion of Iraq and Security Council Resolutions 678 and 1441', Fairfax Digital, 2003.

Gunningham, Neil, Robert A. Kagan and Dorothy Thornton. 'Social License and Environmental Protection: Why Businesses Go Beyond Compliance', *Law & Social Inquiry* 29, no. 2 (2004): 307–341.

Gutman, Amy. 'Can Virtue Be Taught?', *Stanford Law Review* 45 (1993): 1759–1771.

Gyles QC, R. 'Criminal Liability of Professional Advisers', *Taxation in Australia* 23, no. 7 (1989): 480.

Halpin, Andrew. 'Law, Theory and Practice: Conflicting Perspectives?', *International Journal of the Legal Profession* 7, no. 3 (2000): 205–223.

Hamilton, N. and V. Monson. 'The Positive Empirical Relationship of Professionalism to Effectiveness in the Practice of Law', *Geo. J. Legal Ethics* 24 (2011): 137–186.

Hamilton, N. and V. Monson. 'Legal Education's Ethical Challenge: Empirical Research on How Most Effectively to Foster Each Student's Professional Formation (Professionalism)', *University of St. Thomas Law Journal* 9, no. 2 (2012): 325–402.

Harding, Don. 'Some Comments on the Role of the Law School and the Goals of the Legal Education Offered', University of New South Wales, 1986.

Haskell, P.G. 'Teaching Moral Analysis in Law School', *Notre Dame Law Review* 66 (1991): 1025–1051.

Hazard, G.C. 'Ethical Opportunity in the Practice of Law', *San Diego Law Review* 27 (1990): 127–138.

Head, Michael. 'The Haneef Inquiry: Some Unanswered Questions', *Journal of the Australasian Law Teachers Association* 2 (2009): 99–112.

Heller, J. 'Legal Counselling in the Administrative State: How to Let the Client Decide', *Yale Law Journal* 103 (1994): 2503–2530.

Hicks, M. 'Bastard Feudalism, Overmighty Subjects and Idols of the Multitude During the War of the Roses', *History* 85, no. 279 (2000): 386–403.

Hierschbiel, Helen. 'Disclosing Client Confidences: When Doing the "Right" Thing May Be the Wrong Thing to Do', *Oregon State Bar Bulletin*, 2011.

Hobbes, Thomas. *Leviathan*. 1 ed. (Cambridge: Cambridge University Press, 1991 [1651]).

Hobbes, Thomas. *Hobbes, Thomas*. Translated by J.C.A. Gaskin. 6 ed. (Oxford: Oxford University Press, 1998).

Horwitz, M.J. 'Are Law Schools 50 Years out of Date?', *UMKC Law Review* 54 (1986): 385–398.

House of Commons. 'Debate on Kosovo', *Hansard* (23 March 1999): 162–175. www.publications.parliament.uk/pa/cm199899/cmhansrd/vo990323/debtext/90323-06.htm (Accessed 15 February 2016).

Howard, John. *Hansard*, House of Representatives, 6 March 2003.

Howard, M. *Clausewitz*. (Oxford: Oxford University Press, 1983).

Hunt, Alan 'Jurisprudence, Philosophy and Legal Education – Against Foundationalism', *Legal Studies* 6 (1986): 292–302.

ICC. 'Rome Statute of the International Criminal Court', Rome, 1 July 2002.

ICRC. *Convention (I) for the Amelioration of the Condition of the Wounded and Sick in Armed Forces in the Field*. (Geneva: International Committee of the Red Cross, 1949).

ICRC. *Convention (II) for the Amelioration of the Condition of the Wounded and Sick in Armed Forces in the Field*. (Geneva: International Committee of the Red Cross, 1949).

ICRC. *Convention (III) for the Amelioration of the Condition of the Wounded and Sick in Armed Forces in the Field*. (Geneva: International Committee of the Red Cross, 1949).

ICRC. *Convention (IV) Relative to the Protection of Civilian Persons in Time of War*. (Geneva: International Committee of the Red Cross, 1949).

ICRC. *Protocol Additional to the Geneva Conventions of 12 August 1949, and Relating to the Protection of Victims of International Armed Conflicts (Protocol I)*. (Geneva: International Committee of the Red Cross, 1977).

ICRC. *Protocol Additional to the Geneva Conventions of 12 August 1949, and Relating to the Protection of Victims of Non-International Armed Conflicts (Protocol II)*. (Geneva: International Committee of the Red Cross, 1977).

ICRC. *Protocol Additional to the Geneva Conventions of 12 August 1949, and Relating to the Adoption of an Additional Distinctive Emblem (Protocol III)*. (Geneva: International Committee of the Red Cross, 2005).

Iseda, Tetsuji. 'How Should We Foster the Professional Integrity of Engineers in Japan? A Pride-Based Approach', *Science and Engineering Ethics* 14 (2008): 165–176.

Itriago, D. 'Owning Development: Taxation to Fight Poverty', (2011). Published electronically September 2011. https://www.oxfam.org/sites/www.oxfam.org/files rr-owning-development-domestic-resources-tax-260911-en.pdf. (Accessed 10 October 2015).

Jakab, András. 'Dilemmas of Legal Education: A Comparative Overview', *Journal of Legal Education* 57, no. 2 (2007): 253–265.

James, Colin. 'Seeing Things as We Are: Emotional Intelligence and Clinical Legal Education', *International Journal Clinical Legal Education* 8 (2005): 123–149.

James, Nickolas John. 'Expertise as Privilege: Australian Legal Education and The Persistent Emphasis Upon Doctrine', *University of Western Sydney Law Review* 8, no. 1 (2004): 1–20.

Johnstone, Richard and Sumitra Vignaendra. 'Learning Outcomes and Curriculum Development in Law', in *A report commissioned by the Australian Universities Teaching Committee (AUTC)*. (Canberra: Higher Education Group Department of Education, Science and Training, January 2003).

Johnstone, Richard and Sumitra Vignaendra. 'Learning Outcomes and Curriculum Development in Law: A Report Commissioned by the Australian Universities Teaching Committee (AUTC)', (Online: Higher Education Group Department of Education, Science and Training, 2003).

Jones, C. 'Law Dean Warns of Graduate Glut', *The Australian*, 9 September 1992.

Joy, P. 'What We Talk About When We Talk About Professionalism: A Review of Lawyers' Ideals/Lawyers' Practices: Transformations in the American Legal Profession', *Georgetown Journal of Legal Ethics* 7 (1994): 987–1009.

Kann, Mark E. *Taming Passion for the Public Good: Policing Sex in the Early Republic*. (New York: NYU Press, 2013).

Kaye, B. 'The Real Issue in Business Ethics? Institutional Ethics and the Free Market', *Australian Journal of Management* 19, no. 1 (1994): 121–133.

Kelsen, Hans. *General Theory of Law and State*. Translated by A. Wedberg. (Cambridge. Mass.: Cambridge University Press, 1945).

Kennedy, Duncan. 'Legal Education as Training for Hierarchy', in *The Politics of Law*, edited by David Kairys. (London and New York: Pantheon Books, 1982): 54–76.

Keyes, Mary and Richard Johnstone. 'Changing Legal Education: Rhetoric, Reality, and Prospects for the Future', *Sydney Law Review* 26, no. 4 (2004): 537–564.

Keyes, Mary and Graeme Orr. 'Giving Theory a Life: First Year Student Conceptions of Legal Theory', *Legal Education Review* 7 (1996): 31–66.

Keyes, Mary and Michael J. Whincop. 'The Moot Reconceived: Some Theory and Evidence on Legal Skills', *Legal Education Review* 8 (1997): 1–42.

Kirby, Michael. *Through the World's Eye*, edited by Charles Sampford, Sophie Blencowe and Susan Condlln. (Sydney: Federation Press, 2000).

Kronman, A.T. 'Forward: Legal Scholarship and Moral Education', *Yale Law Journal* 90 (1981): 955–969.
Lagarde, Christine. 'Economic Inclusion and Financial Integrity—an Address to the Conference on Inclusive Capitalism', (27 May 2014). https://www.imf.org/external/np/speeches/2014/052714.htm.
Lake, P.F. 'Make Lawyers, Not Lethal Sheep', *Journal of Legal Education* 42 (1992): 271–277.
Langevoort, D.C. 'Where Were the Lawyers? A Behavioural Inquiry into Lawyers' Responsibility for Clients' Fraud', *Vanderbilt Law Review* 46 (1993): 75–119.
Laursen, A. 'Nato, the War over Kosovo, and the ICTY Investigation', *American University International Law Review* 17 (2002): 765–814.
Leach, Michael. '"Disturbing Practices": Dehumanizing Asylum Seekers in the Refugee "Crisis" in Australia 2001–2002', *Refuge* 21, no. 3 (2003): 25–33.
Le Brun, Marlene. 'Law at Griffith University: The First Year of Study', *Griffith Law Review* 1 (1992): 15–33.
Leicht, Kevin T. 'Market Fundamentalism, Cultural Fragmentation, Post-Modern Skepticism, and the Future of Professional Work', *Journal of Professions and Organization* (2015): 1–15.
Lemmings, P. *Gentlemen and Barristers: The Inns of Court and the English Bar 1680–1733*. (Oxford: Oxford University Press, 1990).
Leubsdorf, J. 'Essay: Pluralizing the Client–Lawyer Relationship', *Cornell Law Review* 77 (1992): 825–842.
Levin, C. and T Coburn. 'Wall Street and the Financial Crisis: Anatomy of a Financial Collapse. Majority and Minority Staff Report', Permanent Subcommittee on Investigations, United States Senate, 13 April 2011.
Levin, L.C. 'Testing the Radical Experiment: A Study of Lawyer Response to Clients Who Intend to Harm Others', *Rutgers Law Review* 47 (1994): 81–164.
Lewis, Steve. 'A Huge Feat to Fit Slipper in Fleet of Chauffeured Cars', *Daily Telegraph*, 16 April 2012.
Lewis, Steve. 'Slipper's Got Form on Travel Spending', *The Courier-Mail*, 16 April 2012.
Link, D.T. 'The Pervasive Method of Teaching Ethics', *Journal of Legal Education* 39 (1989): 485–489.
Lord Chancellor's Advisory Committee for Legal Education and Conduct (ACLEC). 'First Report on Legal Education and Training', (London: ACLEC, 1996).
Luban, David. 'Smith against the Ethicists', *Law and Philosophy* 9, no. 4 (1991): 417–433.
Luban, David. *Lawyers and Justice: An Ethical Study*. (Princeton, NJ: Princeton University Press, 1994).
Luban, David. 'Integrity: Its Causes and Cures', *Fordham Law Review* 72, no. 2 (2003): 279–310.
Luban, David. 'Introduction', in *Legal Ethics Stories*, edited by David Luban and Deborah L. Rhode. (New York: Foundation Press, 2006).
Lücke, H. 'Alec Committee Report on Core Subjects', Australian Law Education Council, 1982.
MacCormick, Neil and William Twining. 'Theory in the Law Curriculum', In *Theory of the Common Law*, edited by William Twining. (Oxford: Oxford University Press, 1986): 238–257.
Macdonald, Keith M. *The Sociology of the Professions*. (London: Sage, 1999 [1995]).
Mackie, K.J. *Lawyers in Business: And the Law Business*. (Hampshire: MacMillan, 1989).

Macmillan, Lord. 'The Ethics of Advocacy', in *The Law and Other Things*. (Cambridge: Cambridge University Press, 1937. Reprint, 2015): 191–200.

Maharg, Paul. *Transforming Legal Education: Learning and Teaching the Law in the Early Twenty-First Century*. (Burlington: Ashgate, 2007).

Maiden, Samantha. 'Dream Team Harmers Workplace Lawyers Swings Back into the Action', *Sunday Telegraph*, 22 April 2012.

Maley, William, Charles Sampford and Ramesh Thakur (eds). *From Civil Strife to Civil Society: Civil and Military Responsibilities in Disrupted States*. (Tokyo: UNU Press, 2003).

Margulies, P. 'Who Are You to Tell Me That? Attorney-Client Deliberation Regarding Non-Legal Issues and the Interests of Non-Clients', *North Carolina Law Review* 68 (1990): 213–252.

Mark, Steve. 'Views from an Australian Regulator', *Journal of the Professional Lawyer* 2009 (2009): 45–63.

Mark, Steve and Tahlia Gordon. 'Innovations in Regulation – Responding to a Changing Legal Services Market', *Georgetown Journal of Legal Ethics* 22 (2009): 501–533.

Marx, Karl. 'The Eighteenth Brumaire of Louis Bonaparte', *Die Revolution* 1 (1852).

Mason, Sir Anthony. 'The Independence of the Bench', *Australian Bar Review* 10 (1993): 1–10.

Mason, Sir Anthony. 'Preface: Universities and the Role of Law in Society', in *New Foundations in Legal Education*, edited by John Goldring, Charles Sampford and Ralph Simmonds. (Avalon, NSW: Cavendish, 1998): ix–xii.

Matasar, R.A. 'Teaching Ethics in Civil Procedure Courses', *Journal of Legal Education* 39 (1989): 587–607.

Matchett, S. 'Too Many Lawyers Spoiling the Tort?', *The Australian Higher Education Supplement*, 7 October 1992.

Mathews, M. Cash. *Strategic Intervention in Organizations: Resolving Ethical Dilemmas*. (Newbury Park: Sage Publications, 1988).

Mcconville, Chris. 'The Australian Waterfront Dispute 1998', *Politics & Society* 28, no. 3 (1 September 2000): 393–412.

McGarvie, Hon Mr Justice R.E. 'The Function of a Degree: Core Subjects', *Journal of Professional Legal Education* 9 (1991): 11–26.

McGraw, David K. 'A Social Contract Theory Critique of Professional Codes of Ethics', *Journal of Information, Communication and Ethics in Society* 2, no. 4 (2004): 235–243.

McHugh, J. 'Jeopardy of Lawyers and Accountants in Acting on Commercial Transactions', *Australian Bar Review* 5, no. 1 (1989): 1.

McIlwraith, Ian. 'How Fraser-Kirk Went from Victim to Villain', *Sydney Morning Herald*, 21 October 2010.

McInnis, C. and S. Marginson. *Australian Law Schools after the 1987 Pearce Report*. (Canberra: AGPS, 1994).

Menell, P.S. 'Legal Advising on Corporate Structure in the New Era of Environmental Liability', *Columbia Business Law Review* no. 1 (1990): 399–413.

Mill, John Stuart. *On Liberty*. Edited by Elizabeth Rapaport. (Cambridge: Hackett, 2003 [1859]).

Millar, T.J. 'The Attorney's Duty to Reveal a Client's Future Intended Criminal Conduct', *Duke Law Journal* 33, no. 3 (1984): 582–600.

Mitchell, W. *An Essay on the Early History of the Law Merchant*. (Cambridge: University Press, 1904).

Montgomery, John E. 'Incorporating Emotional Intelligence Concepts into Legal Education: Strengthening the Professionalism of Law Students', *University of Toledo Law Review* 39, no. Winter (2008): 323–352.

Morgan, D. 'Professional Military Firms under International Law', *Chicago Journal of International Law* 9 (2008): 213–245.

Morris, John K. 'Power and Responsibility among Lawyers and Clients: Comment on Ellmann's Lawyers and Clients', *UCLA Law Review* 34 (1987): 781–810.

Morris, Lord John. *Fifty Years of Politics and the Law*. (UK: University of Wales Press, 2011).

Morris, Richard. 'A Watershed on the Australian Waterfront? The 1998 Stevedoring Dispute', *Maritime Policy & Management* 27, no. 2 (1 April 2000): 107–120.

Murphy, Katharine, Mark Davis and Mark Skulley. 'The Docks of War: A $10m Plan to Break Unions', *The Australian Financial Review*, 4 December 1997.

Murphy, R. 'Defining and Practising Business Ethics', In *Business Ethics in Australia and New Zealand: Essays and Cases*, edited by K. Woldring. (Melbourne: Nelson, 1996).

Nelson, R. 'Symposium on the Law Firm as a Social Institution', *Stanford Law Review* 37 (1985): 503–551.

New York State Unified Court System. 'Rules of Professional Conduct: Part 1200', edited by Department of State. (New York: The New York State Bar Association, 2013).

Nicholson, Brendan, Cosima Marriner and Tom Allard. 'Local Suspects Linked to UK Plots', *The Age*, 4 July 2007.

Nickless, Rachel. 'Meet the Sexual Harassment Game Changer', *Australian Financial Review*, 30 July 2014.

Nicolson, Donald and Julian Webb. *Professional Legal Ethics: Critical Interrogations*. (Oxford: Oxford University Press, 1990).

Nozick, Robert. *Anarchy, State, and Utopia*. (Oxford: Basil Blackwell, 1974).

Nussbaum, Martha. 'The Use and Abuse of Philosophy in Legal Education', *Stanford Law Review* 45, no. 6 (1993): 1627–1645.

O'Keefe, R. 'Universal Jurisdiction: Clarifying the Basic Concept', *Journal of International Criminal Justice* 2, no. 3 (2004): 735–760.

Oliver, John. 'Last Week Tonight', *HBO*, 16 February 2015.

Olson, Mancur. *The Logic of Collective Action: Public Goods and the Theory of Groups*. (Cambridge, Mass.: Harvard University Press, 1965).

Page, Jeremy. 'Investigation Turns to Family Ties That Link Eight Suspects in Custody', *Times Online*, 5 July 2007.

Painter, R.W. 'The Moral Interdependence of Corporate Lawyers and Their Clients', *Southern California Law Review* 67 (1994): 507–574.

Palmer, Andrew and Charles Sampford. 'Judicial Retrospectivity', *Griffith Law Review* 4 (1995): 170–213.

Palmer, Andrew and Charles Sampford. 'Retrospective Legislation in Australia: Looking Back at the 1980s', *Federal Law Review* 22 (1993–1994): 217–277.

Parker, Christine. 'An Oversupply of Law Graduates? Putting the Statistics in Context', *Legal Education Review* 4 (1993): 255–267.

Pearce, Dennis Charles, Enid Mona Campbell and Don E. Harding. *Australian Law Schools: A Discipline Assessment for the Commonwealth Tertiary Education Commission (The Pearce Report)*. (Canberra: Australian Government Publishing Service, 1987).

Pepper, S.L. 'The Lawyer's Amoral Ethical Role: A Defence, a Problem, and Some Possibilities', *American Bar Foundation Research Journal* (1986): 613–635.

Peterson, Jonathan. 'Lockean Property and Literary Works', *Legal Theory* 14 (2008): 257–280.

Philipps, J.T. 'It's Not Easy Being Easy: Advising Tax Return Positions', *Washington and Lee Law Review* 50 (1993): 589–630.

Phillips, Robert. *Stakeholder Theory and Organizational Ethics*. (San Francisco Berrett-Koehler, 2003).

Phillipson, C. 'Andrea Alciati and His Predecessors', *Journal of the Society of Comparative Legislation New Series* 13, no. 2 (1913): 254–264.

Pincus, W. 'Future Employment of Lawyers', *Queensland Law Society Journal* 10 (1980): 45.

Pitt, H.L. and K.A. Groskaufmanis. 'When Bad Things Happen to Good Companies: A Crisis Management Primer', *Cardozo Law Review* 15 (1994): 951–969.

Popovski, Vesselin and Trudy Fraser (eds). *The Security Council as Global Legislator*. (Abingdon: Routledge, 2014).

Preston, Noel and Charles Sampford. 'Institutionalizing Ethics', *Encouraging Ethics and Challenging Corruption*, Charles Sampford, Noel Preston with Carmel Connors. (Annandale: Federation Press, 2002): 32–68.

Productivity Commission (PC). 'Trade and Assistance Review 2013–14', Australian Government, 2015.

Qureshi QC, Khawar. 'Constitutional Renewal or Re-Packaging?', *New Law Journal*, December 2008.

Ramsay, Ian. 'Ethical Perspectives on the Practice of Business Law', *Law Society Journal* 30, no. 5 (1992): 60–63.

Rasche, A. '"A Necessary Supplement" – What the United Nations Global Compact Is and Is Not', *Business & Society* 48, no. 4 (2009): 511–537.

Rawls, John. *Political Liberalism*. Expanded edn. (New York: Columbia University Press, 2005 [1993]).

Raz, J. *Ethics in the Public Domain: Essays in the Morality of Law and Politics*. (Oxford: Clarendon Press, 1994).

Rest, James. 'Background: Theory and Research', in *Moral Development in the Professions*, edited by James Rest and Darcia Narvez. (London: Taylor & Francis, 1994).

Rest, James. 'Morality', in *Handbook of Child Psychology*, edited by Paul Mussen. (New York: John Wiley & Sons, 1992): 556–629.

Rest, James R. 'A Psychologist Looks at the Teaching of Ethics', *The Hastings Center Report* 12, no. 1 (1982): 29–36.

Rhode, D.L. 'Ethics by the Pervasive Method', *Journal of Legal Education* 42 (1992): 31–56.

Rhodes, Rosamond. 'Two Concepts of Medical Ethics and Their Implications for Medical Ethics Education', *Journal of Medicine and Philosophy* 27, no. 4 (2002): 493–508.

Ridlon, D. 'Contractors or Illegal Combatants? The Status of Armed Contractors in Iraq', *The Air Force Law Review* 62 (2008): 199–253.

Rietti, Sophie. 'Emotional Intelligence and Moral Agency: Some Worries and a Suggestion', *Philosophical Psychology* 22, no. 2 (2009): 143–165.

Rizzo, P.L. 'Morals for Home, Morals for Office: The Double Ethical Life of a Civil Litigator', *Catholic Lawyer* 35 (1991): 79–96.

Rodgers, Emma. 'Ozcar Scandal: Controversy Explained', www.abc.net.au/news/2009-06-21ozcar-scandal-controversy-explained/1327966. (Accessed 12 February 2016).

Ross, S. *Ethics in Law: Lawyers' Responsibility and Accounting in Australia*. (Sydney: Butterworths, 1995).

Rubin, James. 'Countdown to a Very Personal War', *Financial Times*, 30 September 2000.

Ruggie, J. 'Protect, Respect and Remedy: A Framework for Business and Human Rights: Report of the Special Representative of the Secretary-General', United Nations, 2008.

Sampford, Charles. 'The Dimensions of Liberty and Their Protection by Courts', *Law in Context* 4 (1986): 29–52.
Sampford, Charles. 'The Dimensions of Rights and Their Protection by Statute', in *Law Rights and the Welfare State*, edited by Charles Sampford and D.J. Galligan. (Sydney: Croom Helm, 1986): 170–199.
Sampford, Charles. 'Recognize and Declare – an Australian Experiment in the Codification of Legal Conventions', *Oxford Journal of Legal Studies* 7 (1987): 369–421.
Sampford, Charles. 'The Senate and Supply: Some Awkward Questions', *Monash University Law Review* 13 (1987): 119–149.
Sampford, Charles. *The Disorder of Law*. (Oxford: Basil Blackwell, 1989).
Sampford, Charles. 'Rethinking the Core Curriculum', *Adelaide Law Review* 12 (1989): 38–63.
Sampford, Charles. 'Law, Institutions and the Public Private Divide (Keynote Address)', in *Australasian Law Teachers Association Conference, Brisbane*. Brisbane, 1990.
Sampford, Charles. 'Responsible Government and the Logic of Federalism', *Public Law* 90 (1990): 581–586.
Sampford, Charles. 'Coups D'état and Law', in *Shaping Revolution*, edited by E. Attwooll. (Aberdeen: Aberdeen University Press, 1991): 161–176.
Sampford, Charles. 'Dworkin's Claim to a Socialist Inheritance', *Bulletin of the Australian Society of Legal philosophy* 16, no. 56 (1991): 37–70.
Sampford, Charles. 'Law, Institutions and the Public Private Divide', *Federal Law Review* 20 (1991): 185–225.
Sampford, Charles. 'Editorial', *Griffith Law Review* 1, no. 1 (1992): v–xiv.
Sampford, Charles. 'The Future of Business Ethics: Legal Regulation, Ethical Standard-setting and Institutional Design', *Griffith Law Review* 1, no. 1 (1992): 56–74.
Sampford, Charles. 'The Griffith Curriculum', *Griffith Law Review* 1, no. 1 (1992): Appendix 1.
Sampford, Charles. 'Fundamental Legislative Principles: Their Meaning and Rationale', *Queensland Law Society Journal* 24 (1994): 531–544.
Sampford, Charles. 'Pearce Revisited', *Australian Universities Review* (August 1995): 70–74.
Sampford, Charles. 'Reflections of a Foundation Dean – the Griffith Experience', *Queensland Law Society Journal* 26 (1996): 227–242.
Sampford, Charles. 'Academy and Practice', in *Sir Zelman Cowen: A Life in the Law*, edited by Charles Sampford and Carol-Anne Bois. (Prospect Media: Melbourne, 1997): 150–157.
Sampford, Charles. 'Starting a Law School from Scratch: The Griffith Experience', in *New Foundations in Legal Education*, edited by John Goldring, Charles Sampford and Ralph Simmonds. (Avalon, NSW: Cavendish Publishing, 1998): 177–188.
Sampford, Charles. 'What's a Lawyer Doing in a Nice Place Like This? Lawyers and Ethical Life', *Legal Ethics* 1 (1998): 35–50.
Sampford, Charles. 'Challenges to the Concepts of "Sovereignty" and "Intervention" (Closing Keynote)', in *World Congress on Philosophy of Law and Social Philosophy*. (World Trade Centre: New York 1999).
Sampford, Charles. 'Educating Lawyers for Changing Process', in *Educating Lawyers for a Less Adversarial System*, edited by Charles Sampford, Sophie Blencowe and Suzanne Condlln. (Sydney: Federation Press, 1999): 173–233.
Sampford, Charles. 'Globalizing the Rule of Law', in *Legislative Council Chamber*. (Brisbane: Queensland Parliament, 2000).

Sampford, Charles. 'Challenges to the Concepts of "Sovereignty" and "Intervention" ', in *Human Rights in Philosophy and Practice*, edited by T. Campbell and B.M. Leiser. (Aldershot: Ashgate, 2001): 335–391.

Sampford, Charles. 'Get New Lawyers!', *Legal Ethics* 6, no. 1 (2003): 85–105.

Sampford, Charles. 'Reconceiving the Rule of Law for a Globalizing World', in *Globalization and the Rule of Law*, edited by Spencer Zifcak. (London: Routledge, 2004): 9–31.

Sampford, Charles. 'More and More Lawyers but Still No Judges', *Legal Ethics* 8, no. 1 (2005): 16–22.

Sampford, Charles. *Retrospectivity and the Rule of Law*. (Oxford: Oxford University Press, 2006).

Sampford, Charles. 'Adam Smith's Dinner', in *Future of Financial Regulation Conference, Glasgow, held to celebrate the 250th anniversary of the publication of Adam Smith's Theory of Moral Sentiments*, March 2009.

Sampford, Charles. 'Adam Smith's Dinner', in *The Future of Financial Regulation*, edited by Iain G MacNeil and Justin O'Brien. (Oxford: Hart, 2010): 23–40.

Sampford, Charles. 'Closing Keynote: Integrity in Finance and Accounting: A Key Role in Saving Capitalism from Itself 2.0', in *Australian CPA Conference*, 2011.

Sampford, Charles. 'Business and Human Rights: Reflections and Observations', in *Business and Human Rights*, edited by Wesley Cragg. (Cheltenham: Edward Elgar, 2012): 315–322.

Sampford, Charles. 'Legality and Legitimacy: A Dozen Years after Goldstone', in *Responsibility to Protect and Sovereignty*, edited by Charles Sampford and Ramesh Thakur. (Surrey: Ashgate, 2013): 143–170.

Sampford, Charles. 'Dreams and Nightmares of Alternative Powers' Futures', in *Shifting Global Powers and International Law*, edited by R. Maguire, B. Lewis and C. Sampford. (Abingdon, Oxon: Routledge, Taylor & Francis Group, 2013): 27–49.

Sampford, Charles. 'The Coming "Coke Moment" ', in *UN Security Council as Global Legislator*, edited by Vesselin Popovski. (London: Routledge, 2014): 34–50.

Sampford, Charles. 'Professions without Borders: Global Ethics and the International Rule of Law and Professional Ethics', in *International Rule of Law and Professional Ethics*, edited by Vesselin Popovski. (Aldershot: Ashgate, 2014): 129–147.

Sampford, Charles. ' "Thin Theories" of the Domestic and International Rule of Law', in *International Rule of Law and Professional Ethics*, edited by Vesselin Popovski. (Surrey: Ashgate, 2014): 49–76.

Sampford, Charles and V. Berry. 'Shareholder Values, Not Shareholder Value: The Role of "Ethical Funds" and "Ethical Entrepreneurs" in Connecting Shareholders' Values with Their Investments', *Griffith Law Review* 13, no. 1 (2004): 115–23.

Sampford, Charles and Virginia Berry. 'Ethical and Socially Responsible Investment: From Oxymoron to Tautology?', *GovNet eJournal* 1, no. 1 (Oct–Nov 2007): 1–9.

Sampford, Charles and Sophie Blencowe. 'Educating Lawyers to Be Ethical Advisers', in *The Ethical Challenge to Legal Education and Conduct*, edited by Kim Economides. (UK: Hart Publishing, 1998): 315–340.

Sampford, Charles and Sophie Blencowe. 'Raising the Standards: An Integrated Approach to Promoting Professional Standards and Avoiding Professional Criminality', in *Crime in the Professions*, edited by Russell Smith. (Aldershot: Ashgate, 2002): 251–267.

Sampford, Charles, Sophie Blencowe and Suzanne Condlln (eds). *Educating Lawyers for a Less Adversarial System*. (Sydney: Federation Press, 1999).

Sampford, Charles and T. Coady (eds). *Law, Ethics and Business*. (Sydney: Federation Press, 1993).
Sampford, Charles and R Lui. 'Australian Media Ethics Regime and Ethical Risk Management', *Journal of Mass Media Ethics* 19, no. 2 (2004): 86–107.
Sampford, Charles and Andrew Palmer. 'The Theory of Collective Response', *US Council on Foreign Relations* (1999). www.cfr.org/pdf/Dem_TF_International.pdf.
Sampford, Charles and Margaret Palmer. 'The Theory of Collective Response', in *Protecting Democracy: International Responses*, edited by Morton H. Halperin and Mirna Galic. (Lanham, MD: Lexington Books, 2005): Chapter 4.
Sampford, Charles and Margaret Palmer. 'The Constitutional Power to Make War: Domestic Legal Issues Raised by Australia's Action in Iraq', *Griffith Law Review: A Journal of Social and Critical Legal Studies* 18, no. 2 (2009): 350–384.
Sampford, Charles and Christine Parker. 'Quality Not Quantity – the Key Issue in Legal Education', *Law Institute Journal* 67 (1993): 798–802.
Sampford, Charles and Christine Parker. 'Legal Ethics: Legal Regulation, Ethical Standard-setting and Institutional Design', in *Legal Ethics and Legal Practice: Contemporary Issues*, edited by S. Parker and C. Sampford. (Oxford: Oxford University Press, 1995): 11–25.
Sampford, Charles and S. Parker (eds). *Legal Ethics and Legal Practice*. (Oxford: Oxford University Press, 1995).
Sampford, Charles and Kim Preston (eds). *Interpreting a Constitution: Theories, Principles and Roles*. (Sydney: Federation Press, 1996).
Sampford, Charles and William Ransome. *Just Ethical Business*. (London: Routledge 2016 (forthcoming)).
Sampford, Charles and David Wood. 'Codification of Conventions in Australia', *Public Law* Summer (1987): 231–245.
Sampford, Charles and David Wood. 'Legal Theory and the Law Curriculum', *Law Institute Journal* 61 (1987): 1–4.
Sampford, Charles and David Wood. 'Legal Theory in the Law School', *Bulletin of the Australian Society of Legal Philosophy* 11 (1987): 98–110.
Sampford, Charles and David Wood. 'Theoretical Dimensions of Legal Education – a Response to the Pearce Report', *Australian Law Journal* 62 (1988): 32–53.
Sampford, Charles and David Wood. 'Legal Theory and Legal Education – the Next Step', *Legal Education Review* 1, no. 1 (1989): 107–134.
Sampford, Charles and David Wood. 'The Future of Business Ethics', *Griffith Law Review* 1, no. 1 (1992): 56–72.
Sampford, Charles and David Wood (eds). *Business, Ethics and the Law*. (Sydney: Federation Press, 1993).
Sampford, Karen. 'Legislation Note', 1–9. Brisbane: Queensland Parliamentary Library, August 1998.
Schubert, Misha. 'Rudd, Swan Cleared over Ozcar Affair', *The Age*, 4 August 2009.
Schwabach, A. 'Nato's War in Kosovo and the Final Report to the Prosecutor of the International Criminal Tribunal for the Former Yugoslavia', *Tulane Journal of International and Comparative Law* 9 (2001): 167–186.
Schwarten, Evan. 'Haneef's Lawyer Cleared over Leak', *The Age*, 2 February 2008.
Senate Standing Committee on Finance and Public Administration. 'Media Articles Concerning Mr Peter Slipper, Member for Fisher: Alleged Misuse and Repayments of Entitlements', in *Supplementary Budget Estimates Hearing*, October 2010.
Shaffer, T.L. 'On Lying for Clients', *Notre Dame Law Review* 71, no. 2 (1996): 195–213.

Shakespeare, William. *Henry VI Part II*, Act IV, Scene II. Line 2379. George Mason University: www.opensourceshakespeare.org/views/plays/playmenu.php?WorkID=henry6p2, 1590. (Accessed 10 February 2016).

Sharp Sr., W.G. 'Revoking an Aggressor's License to Kill Military Forces Serving the United Nations: Making Deterrence Personal', *Maryland Journal of International Law and Trade* 22, no. 1 (1998): 1–79.

Sheldon, Kennon M. and Lawrence S. Krieger. 'Understanding the Negative Effects of Legal Education on Law Students: A Longitudinal Test of Self-Determination Theory', *Personality and Social Psychology Bulletin* 33, no. 6 (2007): 883–897.

Sherr, Avrom and David Sugarman. 'Theory in Legal Education', *International Journal of the Legal Profession* 7, no. 3 (2000): 165–177.

Shirvington, Virginia. 'Turning a Blind Eye: Professional Liability and Responsibility', *NSW Law Society*. Sydney, February 2001: 1–38.

Shumaker, H.D. 'The Economic Effects of the European Union Carbon Dioxide Emission Quota on the New Member States of the European Union: Can They Become Equal Economic Partners of the European Union While Complying with the 2008–2012 Quota?', *Pennsylvania State Environmental Law Review* 17 (2008): 99–117.

Silver, Marjorie A. 'Emotional Intelligence and Legal Education', *Psychology, Public Policy, and Law* 5, no. 4 (1999): 1173–1203.

Simon, William H. 'Ethical Discretion in Lawyering', *Harvard. Law Review* 101, no. 6 (1988): 1083–1145.

Singer, Peter. 'Famine, Affluence and Morality', *Philosophy and Public Affairs* 1 (1972): 229–243.

Singer, Peter. *Practical Ethics*. 2nd ed. (Cambridge: Cambridge University Press, 1993).

Singer, Peter. *How Are We to Live?* 2nd ed. (Oxford: Oxford University Press, 1997).

Singer, P.W. 'Corporate Warriors: The Rise of the Privatized Military Industry and Its Ramifications for International Security', *International Security* 26 (2001/02): 186–220.

Singer, P.W. *Corporate Warriors: The Rise of the Privatized Military Industry*. New York: Cornell University, 2003.

Smith, M.B.E. 'Should Lawyers Listen to Philosophers About Legal Ethics?', *Law and Philosophy* 9, no. 1 (1990): 67–93.

Solomon, R.C. *The New World of Business: Ethics and Free Enterprise in the Global 1990s*. (Maryland: Rowman and Littlefield, 1994).

Spruyt, Hendrik. *The Sovereign State and Its Competitors*. (Princeton, N.J.: Princeton University Press, 1996).

Stephen, Sir Ninian. 'Once and Future Law Schools', *Griffith Law Review* 1 (1992): 10–14.

Stinnett, D. 'Regulating the Privatization of War: How to Stop Private Military Firms from Committing Human Rights Abuses', *Boston College International and Comparative Law Review* 28 (2005): 213–223.

Stolker, C. *Rethinking the Law School: Education, Research, Outreach and Governance*. (Cambridge: Cambridge University Press, 2014).

Sullivan, E. Thomas. 'The Transformation of the Legal Profession and Legal Education', *Indiana Law Review* 46, no. 1 (2013):145–158.

Sunstein, Cass R. *Legal Reasoning and Political Conflict*. (New York: Oxford University Press, 1996).

Sutherland, John. 'Who Are America's Real Enemies?', *The Guardian*, 8 July 2002.

Swan, Jonathan and Michael Bachelard. 'PM Caught up in Expenses Row on Slipper Wedding', *Sydney Morning Herald*, 8 October 2013.

Tacha, Deanell Reece. 'Training the Whole Lawyer', *Iowa Law Review* 96 (2011): 1699–1706.

The Age Editorial. 'Mal Brough Is Setting a Terrible Standard over Peter Slipper Diaries Affair', *The Age*, 4 December 2015.
The Association of the Bar of the City of New York. 'Formal Opinion: Client Confidentiality and the Intention to Commit a Crime', (March 2002). www.nycbar.org/ethics/ethics-opinions-local/2002-opinions 831-client-confidentiality-and-the-intention-to-commit-a-crime. (Accessed 15 March 2015).
The International Military Tribunal. *Trial of the Major War Criminals before the International Military Tribunal (Blue Series) 14 November 1945–1 October 1946*. Vol. 2, Nuremberg: Hein, 1947. 1995. 1947.
The Iraq Inquiry. 'Declassified Documents', 2015. www.iraqinquiry.org.uk/transcripts/declassified-documents.aspx (Accessed 12 February 2016).
The Study Group of the International Law Association on the Practice and Procedure of International Courts and Tribunals. 'The Hague Principles on Ethical Standards for Counsel Appearing before International Courts and Tribunals', (2010). Published electronically 26 September 2010. www.ucl.ac.uk/laws/cict/docs Hague_Sept2010.pdf. (Accessed 12 February 2016).
Theobold, Robin. 'So What Really Is the Problem About Corruption?', *Third World Quarterly* 20 (1999): 503–513.
Thompson, G. 'Jobs Will Be Hard to Find in the Brave New Republic', *Australian Financial Review*, 5 May 1993.
Thomson, Judith. 'A Defense of Abortion', *Philosophy and Public Affairs* 1, no. 1 (1971): 47–66.
Thomson, Judith Jarvis. *The Realm of Rights*. (Cambridge, Mass.: Harvard University Press, 1990).
Transparency International (TI). 'What Is Corruption?', (2015). www.transparency.org/what-is-corruption/.(Accessed 12 February 2016).
Trevelyan, G. *England under the Stuarts* (New York: Methuen, 1980 [1904]).
Tur, Richard. 'An Introduction to Lawyers' Ethics', *Journal of Professional and Legal Education* 10, no. 2 (1992): 217–234.
Twining, William. *Blackstone's Tower: The English Law School*. (London: Sweet & Maxwell, 1994).
Unger, R.M. *Knowledge and Politics*. (New York: Free Press, 1975).
United Nations (UN). 'Charter of the United Nations', San Francisco, 1945.
United Nations (UN). 'Resolution 678 Adopted by the Security Council at Its 2963rd Meeting', S/RES/0678 29 November 1990.
United Nations (UN). 'Resolution 686 Adopted by the Security Council at Its 2978th Meeting', S/RES/0686 2 March 1991.
United Nations (UN). 'Resolution 687 Adopted by the Security Council at Its 2981th Meeting', S/RES/0687 8 April 1991.
United Nations (UN). 'United Nations Framework Convention on Climate Change', (1992).
United Nations (UN). 'Kyoto Protocol to the United Nations Framework Convention on Climate Change', (1998, 1992).
United Nations (UN). 'UN General Assembly Renews and Strengthens Global Compact Mandate', *Compact Quarterly*, 2007.
United Nations General Assembly. 'Universal Declaration of Human Rights (UDHR)'. 1948.
United Nations General Assembly. 'International Covenant on Civil and Political Rights (ICCPR)', New York: United Nations, 1966.
United Nations General Assembly. 'International Covenant on Economic, Social and Cultural Rights (ICESCR)', edited by UN General Assembly: United Nations, 1966.

United Nations General Assembly. 'International Convention against the Recruitment, Use, Financing and Training of Mercenaries (UN Mercenary Convention)', General Assembly, 1989.

United Nations General Assembly. 'Res. 60/1: World Summit Outcome Document'. 2005.

United Nations General Assembly. 'Towards Global Partnerships'. General Assembly, 2007.

United Nations Global Compact (UNGC). 'Annual Review 2006'. 2 (2007).

Victor, D.G. *The Collapse of the Kyoto Protocol and the Struggle to Slow Global Warming*. (New York: Princeton University Press, 2001).

Vignaendra, Sumitra and The Centre for Legal Education (CLE). *Australian Law Graduates Career Destinations*. (Canberra: Evaluations and Investigations Program Higher Education Division, 1998).

von Clausewitz, Carl. *On War [Vom Kriege]*. Translated by J.J. Graham. Revised ed. 3 vols. Vol. 1. (London: Kegan Paul, Trench, Trubner & C., 1918).

Wade, J. 'The Behaviour of Family Lawyers and the Implications for Legal Education', *Legal Education Review* 1 (1989): 165–182.

Warne, Stephen. 'White Industries V Flower & Hart: Unfounded Allegations of Fraud', In *The Australian Professional Liability Blog*, 2014.

Warren AC, Hon. Marilyn. 'Legal Ethics in the Era of Big Business, Globalization and Consumerism', *Joint Law Societies Ethics Forum*. Melbourne, 20 May 2010.

Wasserstrom, R.A. 'Lawyers as Professionals: Some Moral Issues', in *Ethical Issues in the Professions*, edited by Peter Y. Windt, Peter C. Appleby, Margaret Pabst Battin and Leslie Francis. (New Jersey: Prentice Hall, 1989).

Waters, Cara. 'Peter Slipper Case: Why Mark Mcinnes Is Grinning', *Crikey*, 13 December 2012.

Watt, Nicholas. 'Rupert Murdoch Pressured Tony Blair over Iraq, Says Alastair Campbell', *The Guardian (UK)*, 16 June 2012.

Weisbrot, David. *Australian Lawyers*. (Melbourne: Longman Cheshire, 1990).

Weisbrot, David. 'Recent Statistical Trends in Legal Education', *Legal Education Review* 2 (1991): 219–251.

Wendel, W. Bradley. 'Lawyers and Butlers: The Remains of Amoral Ethics', *Georgetown Journal of Legal Ethics* 9 (1995): 161–190.

Westfield Corporation. 'Annual Financial Report for Westfield Corporation'. (Sydney: AXS, 2008).

Whitaker, R. 'The Crawford Deal: Did Blair Sign up for War at Bush's Texas Ranch in April 2002?', *The Independent*, 27 February 2005.

White and Wintour. 'No Case for Attack Say Lawyers', *The Guardian*, 7 March 2003.

White, P.D. 'Teaching Philosophy of Law in Law Schools: Some Cautionary Remarks', *Journal of Legal Education* 36 (1986): 563–567.

Wilkins, D.B. 'Practical Wisdom for Practicing Lawyers: Separating Ideals from Ideology in Legal Ethics', *Harvard Law Review* 108 (1994): 458–476.

Wrong, Denis. *Power: Its Forms, Bases and Uses*. (Oxford: Basil Blackwell, 1979).

Wueste, Daniel E. 'Promoting Integrity Integritively: Avoiding the Scylla and Charybdis of Abdication and Zealotry', *Research in Ethical Issues in Organizations* 12 (2014): 5–27.

Zacharias, Fred C. 'The "Self-Regulation" Misnomer', in *Reaffirming Legal Ethics: Taking Stock and New Ideas*, edited by Kieran Tranter, Francesca Bartlett, Lillian Corbin, Reid Mortensen and Michael Robertson. (London: Routledge, 2010): 73–92.

Zerilli, John. 'Reflections on Legal Education and Philosophy: The Critical Role of Theory in Practice', *Legal Education Review* 6 (2007): 103–117.

Zifcak, Spencer, (ed.) *Globalization and The Rule of Law*. (London: Routledge, 2005).

Index

Page numbers in *italics* denote tables, those in **bold** denote figures.

For Product Safety Concerns and Information please contact our EU
representative GPSR@taylorandfrancis.com
Taylor & Francis Verlag GmbH, Kaufingerstraße 24, 80331 München, Germany

www.ingramcontent.com/pod-product-compliance
Ingram Content Group UK Ltd.
Pitfield, Milton Keynes, MK11 3LW, UK
UKHW020023200926
475702UK00014B/2024
* 9 7 8 1 1 3 8 5 9 7 7 7 8 *